*Dedicated
to
Our Parents*

Features of the Book

Example 16.2 First Servlet Program

```
L1    import javax.servlet.*;
L2    import javax.servlet.http.*;
L3    import java.io.*;
L4    public class FirstServlet extends HttpServlet
      {
L5    public void service(ServletRequest req, Servlet Response res) throws
      ServletException,IOException
      {
L6        res.setContentType("text/plain");
L7        PrintWriter pw = res.getWriter();
L8        pw.println("My First Servlet is running");
      }}
```

Explanation

L1–3 The packages `javax.servlet.*`, `javax.servlet.http.*`, and `java.io.*` have to be imported to create an `HttpServlet`.

L4 The class `FirstServlet` must be a public class and it must inherit `HttpServlet`, as http protocol is used for communication between client and server. So to handle http request from client and generate http response for client, we have to create an `HttpServlet`.

data to be sent to the client has to specified with the help of a method `res.setContentType ("text/plain")`. In other words, the MIME type (stands for multipurpose internet mail extension) has to set. Nowadays, web pages contain text, images, and multimedia. A servlet informs the browser about the type of data it will be sending to browser. The servlet in our example is transmitting plain text, so

16.5 INTRODUCTION TO JAVA SERVER PAGES

Java server pages(JSP), in contrast to servlets, is basically a page that contains embedded within html tags. Servlet is a Java program where html tags are embedded code or html responses are generated through Java. JSP files have an extension. js

16.6 JAVA BEANS

Java beans provides a standard format for writing Java classes. Java bean is a reusable component. Once it is designed and created, it can be used over and over again in many applications as per their requirements. Java Beans can be used by IDE and other Java

16.3 SERVLETS

Servlets are Java server-side programs that accept client's request (usually http request) them and generate (usually http response) responses. The requests originate from client browser and are routed to a servlet located inside an appropriate webserver. Servlet

16.8 REMOTE METHOD INVOCATION

Distributed computing allows parts of the system to be residing in separate machines different places. It allows business logic and data to be accessed from remote location anywhere by any one. RMI helps in accomplishing this by allowing objects running machine to be accessed by the clients running in different machines.

Note Higher priority threads will always preempt the lower priority threa[d]
how the priorities of threads set by the JVM are mapped to the
happen that a higher priority might not be considered higher by the
actually depends on the operating system and it varies from OS to

14.14 PRACTICAL PROBLEM: CITY MAP APPLET

CityMap applet shows map of a city (top view) with five buttons namely hospitals, shopping malls, police station, post office, and stadium. If a user presses the hospital button, all hospitals are shown on the map with a specific color and likewise for malls, police station, post office and stadium.

Example 14.18 CityMap.java

```
import java.applet.*;
import java.awt.*;
import java.awt.event.*;

/*<applet code = "CityMap2.class" width=650 height=600></applet>*/

public class CityMap2 extends Applet
{
   Button b1,b2,b3,b4,b5;
```


Programming Exercises

1. Write a program to connect to a database and retrieve all the data. The database type (Access or Oracle), driver name, database name, DSN, etc. have to be fed by the user.
2. Write a servlet program that fetches all the data from client and stores it in a database
4. Write a servlet that automatically redirects the client to another page.
5. Write a servlet that ensures authenticated users have access to important pages. The user name and password should be stored in a database and whenever a user tries to access the servlet,

Review Questions

1. What is the difference between Statement, PreparedStatement, and CallableStatement?
2. Explain the different types of JDBC drivers.
3. Explain the lifecycle of a Servlet.
4. Differentiate get and post requests.
5. Explain the role of registry services in RMI.
6. Explain the following:
   (a) Http Redirects
   (b) Cookie
   (c) Stubs and skeletons
   (d) ResultSet
   (e) ResultSet metadata
7. Explain all the steps used for establishing a

Objective Questions

1. Which packages contain the JDBC API?
   (a) java.jdbc   (b) java.sql
   (c) javax.jdbc   (d) javax.sql
2. Which class is used to establish a database connection?
   (a) Class   (b) DriverManager
   (c) Statement   (d) ResultSet
4. Which of the following is used for calling stored procedures?
   (a) Statement
   (b) PreparedStatement
   (c) CallableStatement
   (d) Connection
5. Which of the following methods return a Connec-

Preface to the Second Edition

Java is an easy-to-learn, versatile, robust, portable, and secure language with rich user interfaces. It has set up new benchmarks in the software development world ranging from desktop to web-based enterprise applications to mobile and embedded applications. Since its inception in 1995, it has come a long way by continuously evolving itself and in the process, changing the style of programming the world over. Java is not only found in laptops or data centres, it is also widely used in cell phones, SIM cards, smart cards, printers, routers and switches, set-top boxes, ATMs, and navigation systems, to name a few. According to Oracle, a staggering 1.1 billion desktops and 3 billion cell phones are based on Java.

This second edition of *Programming in Java* confirms to Java Standard Edition 7, the latest release since Oracle took over Sun Microsystems. It is significant in the sense that the last update was six years back and this major release comes bundled with plenty of enhancements which were overdue. To list a few noticeable enhancements, Java 7 includes support for strings in switch and try-with-resources statements, improved multi-catch, binary numeric literals, numeric literals with underscores, new APIs in NIO such as path and files, automatic resource management, and much more. All the new topics are appropriately explained with suitable examples.

New to the Second Edition

This revised edition has been updated thoroughly with greater topical coverage as well as more programming examples in every chapter, in addition to the confirmation to Java 7. Practically every chapter, with the exception of Chapter 11, has been revisited to refine the text as much as possible. The most noticeable changes are as follows:

- New practical programming examples to show how Java is used in practice.
- Enhanced coverage of servlets and JDBC along with an introduction to JSP, Java beans, Jar files and enterprise Java beans
- Enhanced coverage of swing components like JTree, JTable, layered pane, JDesktopPane, internal frames, JColorChooser, JFileChooser, and JEditorPane
- New classes of java.nio package and project coin language enhancements
- Enhanced coverage of utility classes
- Appendix B contains more interview questions to help students prepare for their interviews.
- The second edition is supplemented with a rich online resource centre that contains chapter-wise PPTs for teachers and additional practical programming examples for students.

Key Features

The most prominent feature of this book has been the line-by-line explanation section under each program. They facilitate in-depth understanding of the whole program. We have retained this feature in the second edition as it has been well appreciated by the users. Other noticeable features include the following:

- A recap of object-oriented programming concepts before introducing the concepts of Java
- Plenty of user-friendly programs and key notes at appropriate places to highlight important concepts
- A variety of end-chapter exercises that includes subjective as well as objective questions

Extended Chapter Material

The second edition includes the following changes:

Chapter 1, Introduction to OOP: Enhanced coverage of UML and its application in pictorial representation of OOP concepts.

Chapter 2, Getting Started with Java: New sections about the features of Java 7 and how to install JDK 1.7.

Chapter 3, Java Programming Constructs: Numeric literals with underscores, binary numeric literals, and how to use strings in switch statements.

Chapter 4, Classes and Objects: New topics such as inner classes, variable length arguments, arrays as return values from methods, and objects as arguments to and return type from methods. It contains a practical problem on complex numbers to demonstrate how OOP concepts can be put to practise.

Chapter 5, Inheritance: New section that highlights the differences between shadowing and overriding. At the end of the chapter, there is a practical programming example on circle and cylinder class.

Chapter 6, Interfaces, Packages, and Enumeration: Practical problem on banking concepts to demonstrate the usage of packages in creating applications.

Chapter 7, Exception, Assertions, and Logging: try-with-resources and catching multiple exceptions features which are new enhancements of Java 7.

Chapter 8, Multithreading in Java: Concrete practical example to show the use of threads in applications.

Chapter 9, Input/Output, Serialization, and Cloning: New classes included in java.nio package and how to perform cloning of objects.

Chapter 10, Generics, java.util and other API: Utility classes like Random class, Runtime class, Observer and Observable and reflection API.

Chapter 12, Applets: how to use threads and images in applets. The practical problem at the end of the chapter explains how to display a digital clock.

Chapter 13, Event Handling in Java: Practical programming example that explains how to create a cartoon on applet and performs its event handling. This is actually a series of examples with gradual and step-by-step revision in all of them in order to enhance their functionality and then eliminate their drawbacks.

Chapter 14, Abstract Window Toolkit: Mini project like programming example on CityMap Applet. The applet shows the map of a city from top angle with five buttons, namely, Hospitals, Shopping Malls, Police station, Post Office, and Stadium. If a user presses the Hospital button, all the hospitals are shown on the map with a specific color and likewise for Malls, Police station, Post office and Stadium.

Chapter 15, Swing: Explanation of new classes with examples and also includes a practical programming example to create a mini text editor.

Chapter 16, Introduction to Advanced Java: Introductory sections on JSP, Java Beans, Jar files and enterprise Java beans with lots of examples apart from enhanced coverage of servlets and JDBC. This chapter also encompasses a login application built using servlets and database to demonstrate how to create and use a web application.

Content and Structure

This book comprises 16 chapters and two appendices. A brief outline of each chapter is as follows.

Chapter 1 focuses on the object-oriented concepts and principles. It provides real life mapping of concepts and principles besides depicting them pictorially. In addition to this, the chapter also provides an introduction to Unified Modeling Language (UML), which is a modeling language to show classes, objects, and their relationship with other objects.

Chapter 2 introduces Java and its evolution from its inception to its current state. Besides introducing the features of Java, it also tells you about the structure of JDK (Java Development Kit) and the enhancements made to Java in its latest versions. It describes how to install and run the JDK that is in turn required for executing a Java program.

Chapter 3 describes the basic programming constructs used in Java such as variables, data types, identifiers, etc. Java reserved keywords are also depicted in this chapter. The operators (arithmetic, relational, boolean, etc.) that act on variables are also explained in this chapter. For each set of operators, we have provided sufficient examples along with their explanation and output. Apart from variables and operators, this chapter focuses on statements like if and other loops available in Java (for, while, do…while, and for...each).

Chapter 4 deals with classes and objects. A lot of practical problems and their solutions have been discussed in this chapter. It begins with how to define classes, objects, and method creation. Method overloading is also discussed. Later, it emphasizes on the differences between instance variables/methods and class variables and methods. Finally, a discussion about arrays, this keyword, and command-line arguments is also provided.

Chapter 5 focuses on inheritance and its uses. How it is realized in Java is discussed in this chapter. Apart from this, polymorphism concepts are visualized through method overriding and super keyword. How practical programming problems are solved through super keyword forms a major part of this chapter. Towards the end of the chapter, some related concepts like abstract classes are also discussed.

Chapter 6 covers interfaces, packages, and enumeration. It highlights the differences between abstract classes and interfaces and their practical usages with examples. The role of packages in Java and their creation and usage is also discussed. In-depth coverage of a predefined package *java.lang* is included in this chapter along with some of the famous classes such as String, StringBuffer, StringBuilder, and Wrapper classes.

Chapter 7 discusses exceptions in detail. Apart from explaining in detail the five keywords (try, catch, throw, throws, and finally) used in handling exceptions, it also discusses how a user can create his own exceptions and handle them. Concepts such as exception, encapsulation, and enrichment are also explained in this chapter. Besides these, the new facilities provided by Java like assertions and logging are also discussed.

Chapter 8 covers multithreading concepts, its states, priorities, etc. It also discusses in detail the inter-thread communication and synchronization concepts. Methods like wait(), notify(), and notifyAll() have also been discussed.

Chapter 9 emphasizes on the essentials of I/O concepts like how standard input can be taken and how output is delivered to the standard output. A few main classes of the java.io package are discussed with examples and their usages. Console class, used for taking user input, is also discussed. What is the use of making objects persistent and how will it be done is discussed towards the end of the chapter.

Chapter 10 discusses the java.util package in detail. The interfaces like Map, Set, and List etc have been discussed in detail as well as their subclasses like LinkedList, ArrayList, Vector, HashSet, HashMap, TreeMap, etc. Java 5 introduced a new feature named 'Generics' which forms the core of the *java.util* package. This concept along with its application has been covered in detail.

Chapter 11 explains how network programming can be done in Java. In-depth coverage of sockets is extended in this chapter. Client and server concept is illustrated by the programs created. TCP and UDP clients and server and their interactions are demonstrated. The concept of multithreading is merged with socket and illustrated to create server programs. Some main classes such as URL, URL connection, and network interface (new feature) are also discussed.

Chapter 12 focuses on applets, its lifecycle, methods, etc. and how they are different from applications. Besides providing an in-depth coverage of *java.applet* package, some of the classes of *java.awt* package are also discussed as they are very useful in creating applets such as Graphics class, Font class, Color class, and FontMetric class. All these classes are discussed and supported by an example for each of them.

Chapter 13 talks about event handling in Java. Basically for creating effective GUI applications, we need to handle events and this forms the basis of this chapter. The event handling model is not only discussed but applied throughout the chapter. All the approaches to event handling have been discussed such as Listener interfaces, Adapter classes, inner classes, and anonymous inner classes.

Chapter 14 focuses on GUI creation through *java.awt* package. It has an in-depth coverage of containers and components. Containers like Frame, Window, etc. and components like Label, Button, TextField, Choice, Checkbox, List, etc. are discussed in detail. How the components can be arranged in a container is also discussed, e.g. BorderLayout, GridBagLayout, and GridLayout.

Chapter 15 shows how to create more advanced and lightweight GUI applications in Java. More advanced layouts like SpringLayout have been discussed. Lightweight components like JButton, JLabel, JCheckBox, JToggleButton, JList, JScrollPane, JTabbedPane, etc. have been discussed. How to create Dialogs is also discussed. The pluggable look and feel of Java is explained in detail.

Chapter 16 focuses on advanced Java concepts such as servlets, JDBC, and RMI. An introduction to the advanced technologies has been discussed. This chapter is equipped with numerous figures showing how to install the necessary softwares required for executing an advanced Java program. The chapter also provides a step-by-step and simplified approach on how to learn advanced concepts.

Appendix A on practical lab problems will facilitate better understanding of the concepts explained in the book. *Appendix B* includes a list of interview questions along with their answers that provides an overview of the industry scenario and their requirements.

ACKNOWLEDGEMENTS

Several people have been instrumental throughout this tiring yet wonderful journey. First of all, we would like to express our sincere gratitude to our families without whose support, patience, and cooperation, this would not have been possible and we would not have been what we are today.

We are also thankful to our colleagues and friends for their endless support and suggestions during the entire process of writing this book. Lastly, we would also like to thank all our readers /students who have supported us, encouraged us, and provided feedback to us regularly which has helped us in shaping this edition.

Sachin Malhotra
Saurabh Choudhary

Preface to the First Edition

Java was primarily designed as a platform-independent language for usage in small consumer electronic devices. It was derived from C++ but with a lot of difference. Java's platform independence originally addressed the problem that applications for embedded devices must run on a wide variety of hardware. But since the Internet was emerging at the same time, Java soon got adopted as an Internet language because of its portable nature. Major Internet browsers such as Netscape Navigator and Microsoft Internet Explorer became Java-compatible, as it effectively addressed the concerns for security by providing a firewall between web applications and the computer. Eventually it became a standard programming language and is now being used for creating a variety of applications including standalone applications, web applications, enterprise-wide applications, and mobile games.

It can therefore be inferred that since its inception, Java has emerged as the most important programming language. As the domain of Java is quite vast and a bit more complex than other programming languages such as C, C++, and Visual Basic, it is observed that students and novice programmers strive hard to comprehend its core concepts. Hence, a need for a book in this area, which is both concise and simple, is a necessity.

About the Book

The book encapsulates the concepts of the latest version of Java, i.e. Java 6, encompassing a comprehensive coverage of curriculum and industry expectations. It is useful for the students of undergraduate and postgraduate courses of computer science and engineering and information technology disciplines as well as for the instructors at various levels.

The book provides a thorough understanding of the basic concepts of object-oriented programming principles and gradually moves on to the advanced concepts in Java. It includes numerous examples, line-by-line description of examples, figures, explanation of concepts, and key notes. Review questions and programming exercises are included as chapter-end exercises to assess the learning outcomes. Every topic in the book is supported by examples followed by an output and explanation. It also offers an appendix on general interview questions which provides students an insight into the current requirements of the industry and allows them to prepare accordingly.

The main features of this book include the following:

- an exhaustive coverage of Java features such as operators, classes, objects, inheritance, packages, and exception handling
- comprehensive discussion on the latest features of Java such as enumerations, generics, logging API, console class, StringBuilder class, NetworkInterface class, and assertions
- latest features combined with core concepts such as multithreading, applets, AWT, and swings
- an introduction to the advanced concepts in Java such as servlets, RMI, and JDBC

ACKNOWLEDGEMENTS

Several people have been instrumental throughout this tiring yet wonderful journey. First of all, we would like to express our sincere gratitude to our families without whose support, patience, and cooperation, this would not have been possible and we would not have been what we are today. We are very thankful to Dr R. K. Bharadwaj, Head of our institution, for his inspirational thoughts which inculcated urgency for writing this book. We are also thankful to our colleagues for their endless support and suggestions during the entire process of writing this book.

Sachin Malhotra
Saurabh Choudhary

Brief Contents

Detailed Contents

Introduction to OOP

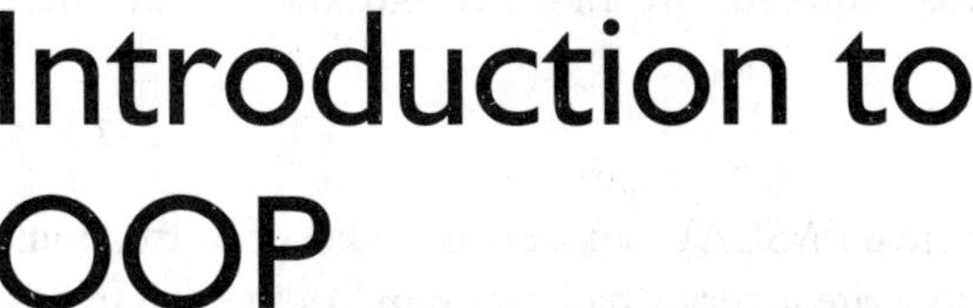

Beauty is our weapon against nature; by it we make objects, giving them limit, symmetry, proportion. Beauty halts and freezes the melting flux of nature.

Camille Paglia

After reading this chapter, the readers will be able to

- know what is object-oriented programming
- understand the principles of OOP
- understand how is OOP different from procedural languages
- comprehend the problems in procedural programming and how OOP overcomes them
- learn the applications of OOP
- use UML notations

1.1 INTRODUCTION

Object-oriented programming (OOP) is one of the most interesting and useful innovations in software development. OOP has strong historical roots in programming paradigms and practices. It addresses the problems commonly known as the *software crisis*. Software have become inherently complex which has led to many problems within the development of large software projects. Many software have failed in the past. The term 'software crisis' describes software failure in terms of

- Exceeding software budget
- Software not meeting clients' requirements
- Bugs in the software

OOP is a programming paradigm which deals with the concepts of object to build programs and software applications. It is modeled around the real world. The world we live in is full of objects. Every object has a well-defined *identity*, *attributes*, and *behavior*. Objects exhibit the same behavior in programming. The features of object-oriented programming also map closely to the real-world features like *inheritance*, *abstraction*, *encapsulation*, and *polymorphism*. We will discuss them later in the chapter.

1.2 NEED OF OBJECT-ORIENTED PROGRAMMING

There were certain limitations in earlier programming approaches and to overcome these limitations, a new programming approach was required. We first need to know what these limitations were.

1.2.1 Procedural Languages

In procedural languages, such as C, FORTRAN, and PASCAL, a program is a list of instructions. The programmer creates a list of instructions to write a very small program. As the length of a program increases, its complexity increases making it difficult to maintain a very large program. In the structured programming, this problem can be overcome by dividing a large program into different functions or modules, but this gives birth to other problems. Large programs can still become increasingly complex. There are two main problems in procedural language—(i) the functions have unrestricted access to global data and (ii) they provide poor mapping to the real world.

Here are some other problems in the procedural languages. Computer languages generally have built-in data types: integers, character, float, and so on. It is very difficult to create a new data type or a user-defined data type. For example, if we want to work with dates or complex numbers, then it becomes very difficult to work with built-in types. Creating our own data types is a feature called *extensibility*: we can extend the capabilities of a language. Procedural languages are not extensible. In the traditional languages, it is hard to write and maintain complex results.

1.2.2 Object-Oriented Modeling

In the physical world, we deal with objects like person, plane, or car. Such objects are not like data and functions. In the complex real-world situations, we have objects which have some attributes and behavior. We deal with similar objects in OOP. Objects are defined by their unique *identity*, *state*, and *behavior*. The state of an object is identified by the value of its attributes and behavior by methods.

Attributes

Attributes define the data for an object. Every object has some attributes. Different types of objects contain different attributes or characteristics. For example, the attributes of a student object are name, roll number, and subject; and the attributes for a car object would be color, engine power, number of seats, etc. These attributes will have specific values, such as Peter (for name) or 23 (for roll number).

Behavior

The response of an object when subjected to stimulation is called its *behavior*. Behavior defines what can be done with the objects and may manipulate the attributes of an object. For example, if a manager orders an employee to do some task, then he responds either by doing it or not doing it. The wings of a fan start moving only when the fan is switched ON. Behavior actually determines the way an object interacts with other objects. We can say that behavior is synonym to functions or methods: we call a function to perform some task. For example, an Employee class will have functions such as adding an employee, updating an employee details, etc.

Note If we try to represent the CPU of a computer in OOP terminology, then CPU is the object. The CPU is responsible for fetching the instructions and executing them. So fetching and executing are two possible functions (methods or behavior) of CPU. The place (attributes) where CPU stores the retrieved instructions, values and result of the execution (registers) will then be the attributes of the CPU.

1.3 PRINCIPLES OF OBJECT-ORIENTED LANGUAGES

OOP languages follow certain principles such as class, object, and abstraction. These principles map very closely to the real world.

1.3.1 Classes

A class is defined as the blueprint for an object. It serves as a plan or a template. The description of a number of similar objects is also called a *class*. An object is not created by just defining a class. It has to be created explicitly. Classes are logical in nature. For example, furniture does not have any existence but tables and chairs do exist. A class is also defined as a new data type, a user-defined type which contains two things: data members and methods.

1.3.2 Objects

Objects are defined as the instances of a class, e.g. table, chair are all instances of the class Furniture. Objects of a class will have same attributes and behavior which are defined in that class. The only difference between objects would be the value of attributes, which may vary. Objects (in real life as well as programming) can be physical, conceptual, or software. Objects have unique identity, state, and behavior. There may be several types of objects:

- *Creator objects*: Humans, Employees, Students, Animal
- *Physical objects*: Car, Bus, Plane
- *Objects in computer system*: Monitor, Keyboard, Mouse, CPU, Memory

1.3.3 Abstraction

Can you classify the following items?

- Elephant
- CD player
- Television
- Chair
- Table
- Tiger

How many classes do you identify here? The obvious answer anybody would give is three, i.e., Animal, Furniture, and Electronic items. But how do you come to this conclusion? Well, we grouped similar items like Elephant and Tiger and focused on the generic characteristics rather than specific characteristics. This is called *abstraction*. Everything in this world can be classified as living or non-living and that would be the highest level of abstraction.

Another well-known analogy for abstraction is a car. We drive cars without knowing the internal details about how the engine works and how the car stops on applying brakes. We are happy with the abstraction provided to us, e.g., brakes, steering, etc. and we interact with them. In real life, human beings manage complexity by abstracting details away. In programming, we manage complexity by concentrating only on the essential characteristics and suppressing implementation details.

1.3.4 Inheritance

Inheritance is the way to adopt the characteristics of one class into another class. Here we have two types of classes: *base class* and *subclass*. There exists a parent–child relationship among the classes. When a class inherits another class, it has all the properties of the base class and it adds some new properties of its own. We can categorize vehicles into car, bus, scooter, ships, planes, etc. The class of animals can be divided into mammals, amphibians, birds, and so on.

The principle of dividing a class into subclass is that each subclass shares common characteristics with the class from where they are inherited or derived. Cars, scooters, planes, and ships all have an engine and a speedometer. These are the characteristics of vehicles. Each subclass has its own characteristic feature, e.g., motorcycles have disk braking system, while planes have hydraulic braking system. A car can run only on the surface, while a plane can fly in air and a ship sails over water (see Fig. 1.1).

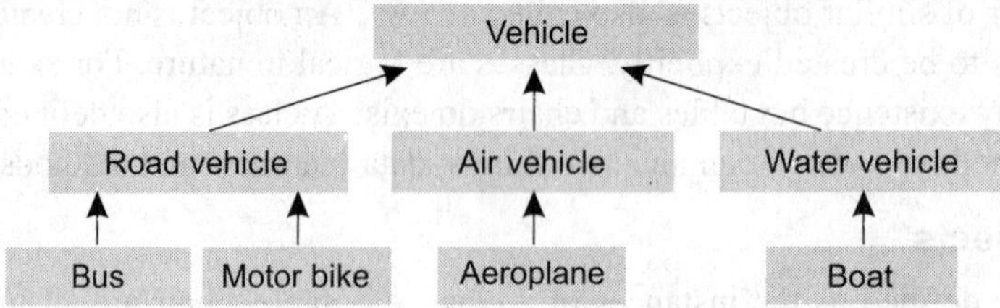

Fig. 1.1 Inheritance

Inheritance aids in *reusability*. When we create a class, it can be distributed to other programmers which they can use in their programs. This is called *reusability*. Suppose someone wants to make a program for a calculator, he can use a predefined class for arithmetic operations, and then he need not define all the methods for these operations. This is similar to using library functions in procedural language. In OOP, this can be done using the inheritance feature. A programmer can use a base class with or without modifying it. He can derive a child class from a parent class and then add some additional features to his class.

1.3.5 Encapsulation

Encapsulation is one of the features of object-oriented methodology. The process of binding the data procedures into objects to hide them from the outside world is called *encapsulation* (see Fig. 1.2). It provides us the power to restrict anyone from directly altering the data. Encapsulation is also known as *data hiding*. An access to the data has to be through the methods of the class. The data is hidden from the outside world and as a result, it is protected. The details that are not useful for other objects should be hidden from them. This is called *encapsulation*. For example, an object that does the calculation must provide an interface to obtain the result. However, the internal coding used to calculate need not be made available to the requesting object.

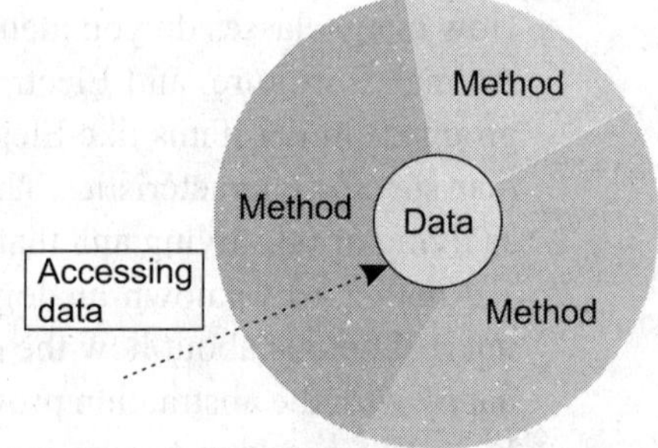

Fig. 1.2 Diagrammatic Illustration of a Class to Show Encapsulation

1.3.6 Polymorphism

Polymorphism simply means many forms. It can be defined as the same thing being used in different forms. For example, there are certain bacteria that exhibit in more than one morphological form. In programming, polymorphism is of two types: *compile-time* and *runtime polymorphism*. Runtime polymorphism, also known as *dynamic binding* or *late binding*, is used to determine which method to invoke at runtime. The binding of method call to its method is done at runtime and hence the term *late binding* is used. In case of compile-time polymorphism, the compiler determines which method (from all the overloaded methods) will be executed. The binding of method call to the method is done at compile time. So the decision is made early and hence the term *early binding*. Compile-time polymorphism in Java is implemented by *overloading* and runtime polymorphism by *overriding*. In overloading, a method has the same name with different signatures. (A *signature* is the list of formal argument that is passed to the method.) In overriding, a method is defined in subclass with the same name and same signature as that of parent class. This distinction between compile-time and runtime polymorphism is of *method invocation*. Compile-time polymorphism is also implemented by operator overloading which is a feature present in C++ but not in Java. Operator overloading allows the user to define new meanings for that operator so that it can be used in different ways. The operator (+) in Java is however an exception as it can be used for addition of two integers as well as concatenation of two strings or an integer with a string. This operator is overloaded by the language itself and the Java programmer cannot overload any operator.

1.4 PROCEDURAL LANGUAGE VS OOP

Table 1.1 highlights some of the major differences between procedural and object-oriented programming languages.

Table 1.1 Procedural Language vs OOP

Procedural Language	OOP
• Separate data from functions that operate on them.	• Encapsulate data and methods in a class.
• Not suitable for defining abstract types.	• Suitable for defining abstract types.
• Debugging is difficult.	• Debugging is easier.
• Difficult to implement change.	• Easier to manage and implement change.
• Not suitable for larger programs and applications.	• Suitable for larger programs and applications.
• Analysis and design not so easy.	• Analysis and design made easier.
• Faster.	• Slower.
• Less flexible.	• Highly flexible.
• Data and procedure based.	• Object oriented.
• Less reusable.	• More reusable.
• Only data and procedures are there.	• Inheritance, encapsulation, and polymorphism are the key features.
• Use top-down approach.	• Use bottom-up approach.
• Only a function call another.	• Object communication is there.
• Example: C, Basic, FORTRAN.	• Example: JAVA, C++, VB.NET, C#.NET.

1.5 OOAD USING UML

An object-oriented system comprises of objects. The behavior of a system results from its objects and their interactions. Interaction between objects involves sending messages to each other. Every object is capable of receiving messages, processing them, and sending to other objects.

Object-oriented Analysis and Design (OOAD)

It is an approach that models software as a group of interacting objects. A model is a description of the system that we intend to build. Each object is characterized by its class having its own state (attributes) and behavior. Object-oriented analysis (OOA) analyzes the functional requirements of a system and focuses on *what* the system should do. Object-oriented design (OOD) focuses on *how* the system does it. The most popular modeling language for OOAD is the *unified modeling language* (UML).

UML is a standard language for OOAD. It contains graphical notations for all entities (class, object, etc.) used in the object-oriented languages along with the relationship that exists among them. These notations are used to create models. UML helps in visualizing the system, thereby reducing complexity and improving software quality. The notations used for class and object are shown in Fig. 1.3. For example, consider an Employee class with attributes name, designation, salary, etc. and operations such as addEmployee, deleteEmployee, and searchEmployee. The notation for employee class and its object is as follows:

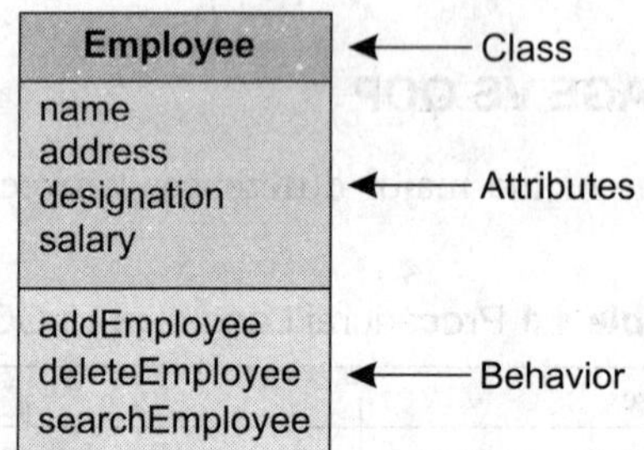

Fig. 1.3 UML Notation for Class

The notation for an object is very much similar to the class notation. The class name underlined and followed by a colon represents an object (Fig. 1.4).

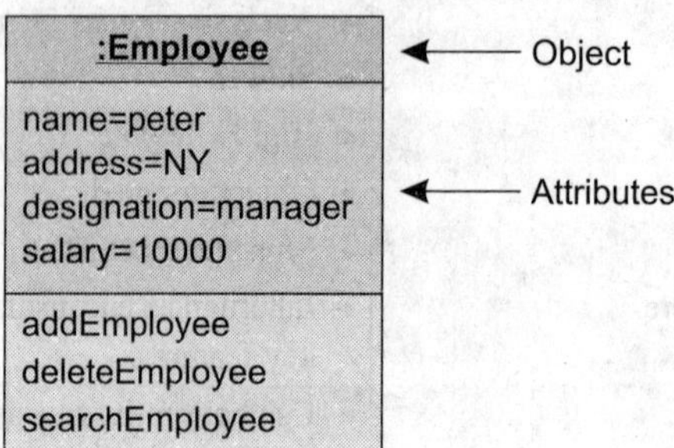

Fig. 1.4 UML Notation for Object

An instance of a class can be related to any number of instances of other class known as multiplicity of the relation. One-to-one, one-to-many, and many-to-many are different types of multiplicities that exist among objects. The multiplicities along with their examples and respective notations are shown below. Figure 1.5(a) illustrates the generic notation for representing multiplicity in object-oriented analysis and design. One-to-one mapping is shown as a straight line between the two classes. Figure 1.5(b) shows the UML notation for demonstrating the one-to-one mapping. The 1..1 multiplicity depicted on the straight line (both ends) indicates a single instance of a class is associated with single instance of other class. Figure 1.5 shows that each country has a president and a president is associated with a country.

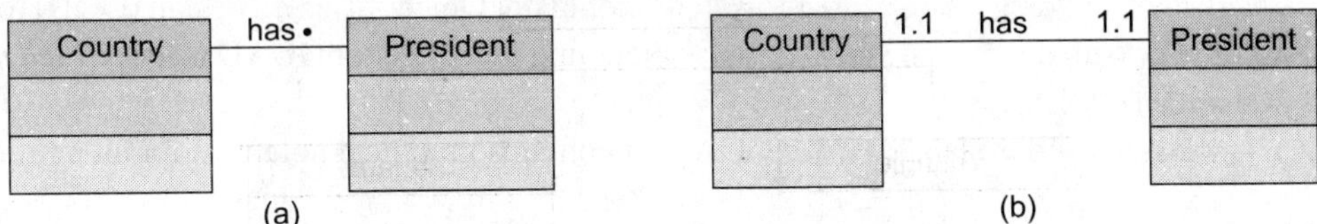

Fig. 1.5 One-to-one Relationship

A country has many states and many states belong to a country. So there exists a one-to-many relationship between the two. This relationship is shown in Fig. 1.6. Part (a) of this figure shows the generic notation where a solid dot is indicated on the many side and both classes are joined by a straight line. Figure 1.6(b) shows the UML notation where 1..* indicates the one to many relationship between country and states. On the country end, a 1..1 multiplicity is placed to indicate one country and on states end, a 1..* is placed to indicate many states.

Fig. 1.6 One-to-many Relationship

Let us take another example to explain many-to-many relationship. A teacher teaches many students and a student can be taught by many teachers. There exists a many-to-many relationship between them. Many-to-many relationship (Generic notation in OOAD) are represented by placing solid dots on both ends joined by a straight line as shown in Fig. 1.7(a). The respective notation in UML is shown in Fig. 1.7(b) where 1..* on both ends is used to signify many-to-many relationship.

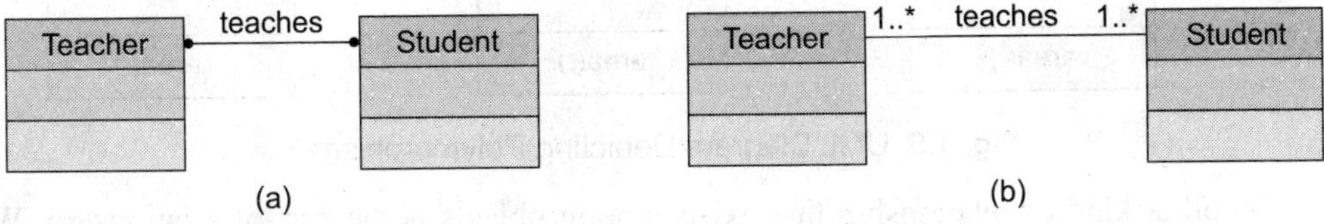

Fig. 1.7 Many-to-many Relationship

Besides multiplicity of relations, the relationships can be of various types: *inheritance, aggregation, composition*. These relationships can be denoted in UML with links and associations. The links represent the connection between the objects and associations represent groups of links between classes. If a class inherits another class, then there exists a parent-child relationship between them. This relationship is depicted in UML as shown in Fig. 1.8. For example, Shape is the superclass, and the subclasses of Shape can take any shape, e.g., Square, Triangle, etc.

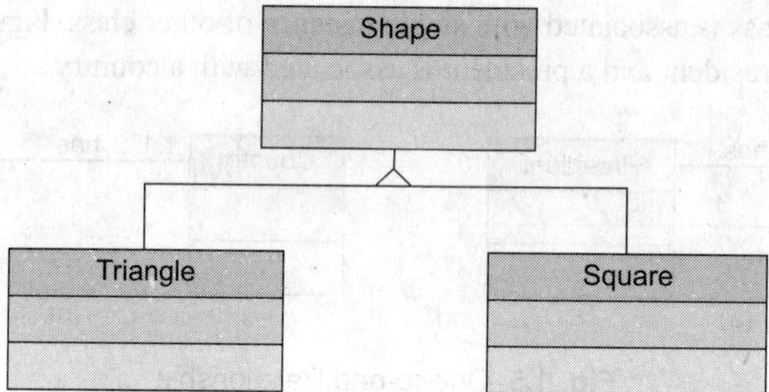

Fig. 1.8 UML Diagram Depicting Inheritance

The above diagram can be extended to depict the OOP principle of polymorphism. Every shape will have a method named area() which would calculate the area of that shape. The implementation of area() method would be different for different shapes. For example, the formula for calculating area of a triangle is different from a square. So the implementation is different but the name of the method is same. This is polymorphism (one name many implementations). In Fig 1.9 below, the area() method is overridden by Triangle and Square classes.

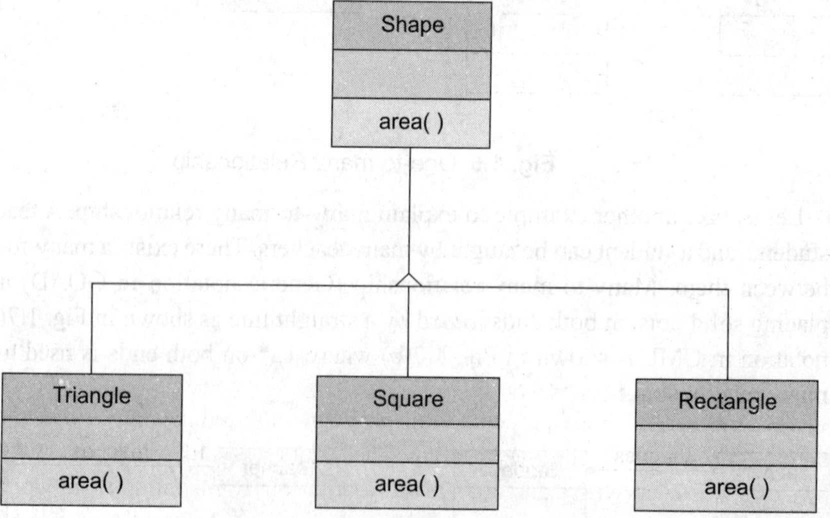

Fig. 1.9 UML Diagram Depicting Polymorphism

Another kind of relationship that exists among objects is the part-of-relationship. When a particular object is a part of another object then we say that it is *aggregation*. For example, car is an aggregation of many objects: engine, door, etc. and engine in turn is an aggregation of many objects, e.g., cylinder, piston, valves, etc. as shown in Fig. 1.10(a). A special kind of aggregation is composition where one object owns other objects. If the owner object does not exist, the owned objects also ceases to exist. For example, the human body is a very good example of composition. It is a composition of different organs. The hands, feet, and internal organs such as the lung and intestine are also parts of the body owned by the body.

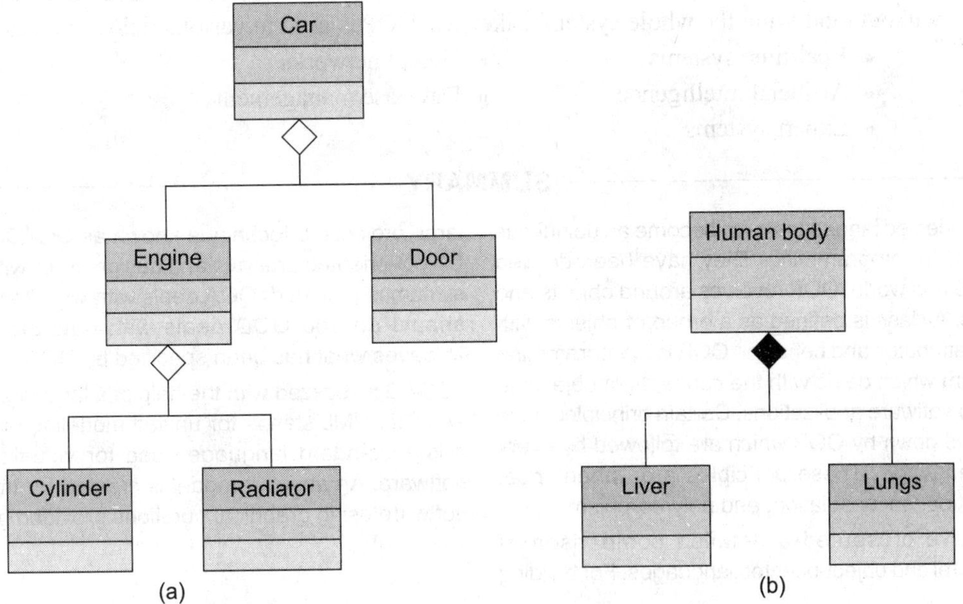

Fig. 1.10 (a) Aggregation and (b) Composition

1.6 APPLICATIONS OF OOP

The basic thought behind object-oriented language is to make an object by combining data and functions as a single unit and then operate on that data. In procedural approach, the focus is on business process and the data needed to support the process. For example, in the last decade, a problem bothered every programmer, popularly known as the Y2K problem. Everybody related to the computer industry was afraid of what will happen past midnight 31 December 1999. The problem arises due to the writing convention of the year attribute. In early programming days, a programmer wrote a year in two digits, so there was a problem to distinguish the year 1900 from 2000 because if we write only the last two digits of a year, the computer cannot differentiate between the two. Nobody perceived this problem and used the date and year code as and when required, thus aggravating the problem. The solution to this problem was to analyze multiple lines of codes everywhere and change the year to four digits rather than two. It seems simple to change the state variable of year but analyzing a code of several thousands of lines to find how many times you have used date in your code is not an easy task.

If object-oriented programming language had been used, we could have created a Date class with day, month, and year attributes in it. Wherever the date functionality would be required, a Date object would be created and used. At a later point of time, if a change is required, for example, the year of Date class needs to be changed to four digits, then this change would be incorporated in the class only and this change would automatically be reflected in all the objects of the Date class whenever they are created and used. So, the change would have to be done at one place only, i.e., the class and wherever the objects of the class are being used, the changes would be reflected automatically. There is no need to analyze the whole code and change it.

In OOP, we access data with the help of objects, so it is very easy to overcome a problem without modifying the whole system. Likewise, OOP is used in various fields, such as

- Real-time systems
- Artificial intelligence
- Expert systems
- Neural networks
- Database management

SUMMARY

Object-oriented languages have become an ubiquitous standard for programming. They have been derived from the real world. OOP revolves around objects and classes. A class is defined as a group of objects with similar attributes and behavior. OOP is a programming paradigm which deals with the concepts of objects to develop software applications. Certain principles have been laid down by OOP which are followed by every OOP language. These principles are: inheritance, abstraction, encapsulation, and polymorphism.

We have presented a detailed comparison of procedural and object-oriented languages. For building large projects, a technique known as OOAD is used. Object-oriented analysis and design deals with how a system is modeled. OOA deals with what the system should do and OOD deals with how the system achieves what has been specified by OOA.

OOAD is realized with the help of a language known as UML. UML stands for unified modeling language; it is a standard language used for visualizing the software. An abstract model is created for the entire software using graphical notations provided by UML.

EXERCISES

Objective Questions

1. In an object model, which one of the following is true?
   (a) Abstraction, encapsulation, and multitasking are the major principles
   (b) Hierarchy, concurrency, and typing are the major principles
   (c) Abstraction, encapsulation, and polymorphism are the major principles
   (d) Typing is the major principle

2. Which one of the following is not an object-oriented language?
   (a) Simula   (b) Java
   (c) C++   (d) C

3. The ability to hide many different implementations behind an interface is.
   (a) Abstraction   (b) Inheritance

   (c) Polymorphism   (d) None of the above

4. Which one of the following terms must relate to polymorphism?
   (a) Static allocation   (b) Static typing
   (c) Dynamic binding   (d) Dynamic allocation

5. Providing access to an object only through its member functions, while keeping the details private is called
   (a) Information hiding   (b) Encapsulation
   (c) Modularity   (d) Inheritance

6. The concept of derived classes is involved in
   (a) Inheritance
   (b) Encapsulation
   (c) Data hiding
   (d) Abstract data types

7. Inheritance is a way to
   (a) Organize data
   (b) Pass arguments to objects of classes
   (c) Add features to existing classes without rewriting them
   (d) Improve data-hiding and encapsulation
8. UML is used for
   (a) Creating models
   (b) Representing classes, objects and their relationships pictorially
   (c) Reducing complexity and improving software quality

   (d) All the above
9. Which of the following is true about class?
   (a) Class possesses data and methods
   (b) Classes are physical in nature
   (c) Collection of similar type of objects is a class
   (d) Both (a) and (c)
10. Which of the following is true about procedural languages?
   (a) Debugging is easier
   (b) analysis and design is easy
   (c) less reusable
   (d) difficult to implement changes

Review Questions

1. Explain the importance of object-oriented programming languages.
2. Explain the difference between class and object.
3. Differentiate between procedural languages and OOP languages.

4. Write short notes on: (a) inheritance, (b) polymorphism, (c) abstraction, (d) encapsulation.
5. Differentiate between runtime and compite-time polymorphism.

Programming Exercises

1. Identify the relevant classes along with their attributes for the following: A departmental store needs to maintain an inventory of cosmetic items which might be found there. You should include female as well as male cosmetic items. Keep information on all items such as item name, category, manufacturer, cost, date purchased, and serial number.
2. Identify the relevant classes along with their attributes from the following problem specification:

   A hospital wants to keep track of scheduled appointments of a patient with his doctor. When a patient is given an appointment, he should be given a confirmation that states the time and date of appointment along with the doctor's name. Meanwhile the doctor should also be informed about the patient details. Each doctor has one weekday as off-day and no patients should be assigned to a doctor on that day.

Answers to Objective Questions

1. (c)	**2.** (d)	**3.** (c)	**4.** (c)
5. (b)	**6.** (a)	**7.** (c)	**8.** (d)
9. (d)	**10.** (c) and (d)		

Getting Started with Java

The road of life can only reveal itself as it is traveled; each turn in the road reveals a surprise. Man's future is hidden.

Anon

After reading this chapter, the readers will be able to

- know the history of Java
- understand the features of Java and its runtime environment
- know the basic structure of a Java program
- know the details about JDK installation
- understand various constituents of JDK and its development environments

2.1 INTRODUCTION

Java is a popular and powerful language. Although it is a very simple language, there are a number of subtleties that can trip up less-experienced programmers. Java is an object-oriented programming language with a built-in application programming interface (API) that can handle graphical user interfaces (GUI) used to create applications or *applets*. Java provides a rich set of APIs apart from being platform-independent.

Much of the syntax in Java is similar to C and C++. One of the major differences between Java and other languages is that it does not have pointers. However, the biggest difference is that you are forced to write object-oriented code in Java. Procedural code is embedded in objects.

In Java, we distinguish between applications and applets, applications being programs that perform functions similar to those written in other programming languages and applets are programs that are meant to be embedded in a web page and downloaded over the Internet. When a program is compiled, a byte code is generated which can be executed on any platform, provided the runtime environment exists on the destination platform.

This chapter guides the readers to a step-by-step introduction to Java programming. An important thrust of this chapter is to cover the features of Java from an object-oriented perspective.

It also gives an insight about the installation of Java runtime environment and the various integrated development environments (IDEs) of Java.

This chapter also focusses on the different versions of Java (including the latest Java 7) and the Core API's (Java 7 is also known as Java 1.7).

2.2 HISTORY OF JAVA

It is often believed that the Java was developed specifically for the World Wide Web. Java as it was initially developed was intended for the Web. However, it was improved to be a standard programming language for the Internet application.

Bill Joy, the Vice President at Sun Micro systems, was thought to be the main person to conceive the idea of a programming language that later became Java. In late 1970s, Bill Joy wanted to design a language that could contain the best features of languages like MESA and C. He found that C++ was inefficient for rewriting Unix operating system. In 1991, it was this desire to invent a better programming tool that propelled Joy in the direction of Sun's mammoth project called as the 'Stealth Project.' This name was given by Scott McNealy, Sun's president. In January 1991, a formal team of persons like Bill Joy, James Gosling, Mike Sheradin, Patrick Naughton (formerly the project leader of Sun's Open Windows user environment), and several other individuals met in Aspen, Colorado for the first time to plan for the Stealth Project. Stealth Project was all about developing consumer electronic devices that could all be centrally controlled and programmed from a handheld remote control like device.

James Gosling was made responsible for suggesting a proper programming language for the project. Initially he thought of using C++, but soon after was convinced about the inadequacy of C++ for this particular project. He took the first step towards the development of an independent language that would fit the project objectives by extending and modifying C++.

The idea of naming the language as 'Oak' struck Gosling while staring at an oak tree outside his office window. Unfortunately, this name had already been patented by some other programming language. Owing to the fear of copyright violation, the name 'Oak' was dropped. The team struggled to find a proper name for the language for many days. After so many brainstorming sessions, one day finally a thought struck their mind during a trip to the local coffee shop as recalled by Gosling. The term 'Java' in USA is generally a slang used for coffee. Java is also the name of a coffee produced on the islands of Java in Indonesia. There are some other views also towards the naming convention used for naming the language as Java. One of it speculates that the name Java came from several individuals involved in the project: **James Gosling, Arthur Van Goff, Andy Bechtolsheim.**

2.3 JAVA'S JOURNEY: FROM EMBEDDED SYSTEMS TO MIDDLE-TIER APPLICATIONS

Java was designed to run standalone in small devices. The Java language was derived from C++ but with many differences. Java's platform-independence originally addressed the problem that applications for embedded devices must run on a wide variety of hardware. But later with the advent of Internet in 1995, Java was soon adopted, as it could run on heterogeneous operating systems. Netscape Navigator started using Java in its browser. Many applets (which run inside a browser) were built and Java achieved popularity and acceptance.

Microsoft developed its own virtual machine that it used in its Internet Explorer which differed from the specifications laid down. Therefore, Sun and Microsoft ran into a dispute, that was settled later. Sun saw a potential for Java beyond the browser (see Fig. 2.1).

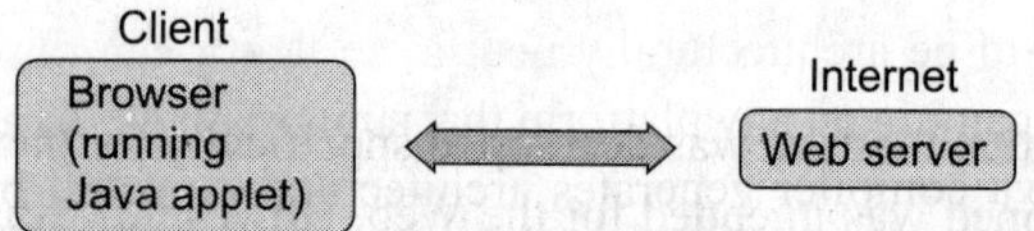

Fig. 2.1 Java Applets Running on the Client System

Still Java was not popular for the client-side because of the following reasons:

- **Less Impressive GUI** Java's early GUI (AWT) was primitive. The newer GUI (Swing) was not shipped until the late 90's (and Swing is still not supported by most modern browsers without plug-ins).

- **Microsoft's Strong Presence** Nearly 95% of the desktop world uses Microsoft.

- **Clients' Software Upgradation** Good alternative methods were found to update clients' software automatically (without having to download Java on-the-fly application code each time).

- **Success of DHTML** Browsers have their own dynamic capabilities and many developers found it easier to code in DHTML. In addition, DHTML pages tend to download and start faster than Java applets.

Figure 2.2 shows how Java could be used as middle-tier services between the database and a client browser. In 1997, Sun developed servlets, so that Java could be used to generate dynamic content based on clients' request. In 1999, Sun released its Java 2 Enterprise Edition (J2EE).

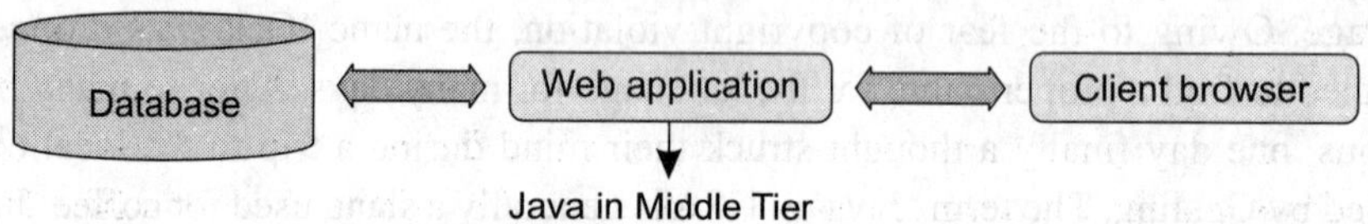

Fig. 2.2 Middle-tier Capabilities of Java to Run in Web/Application Server

Enterprise Java described how to build middle-tier components. Sun defined Enterprise Java Beans for developing business logic. The J2EE framework allows developers to concentrate on building applications rather than mulling over scalability, reliability, and security issues which are handled by the Web/application server vendors.

2.4 JAVA ESSENTIALS

Java is a platform-independent, object-oriented programming language. Java encompasses the following features:

- **A High-level Language** Java is a high-level language that looks very similar to C and C++ but offers many unique features of its own.

- **Java Bytecode** Bytecode in Java is an intermediate code generated by the compiler, such as Sun's `javac`, that is executed by the JVM.

- **Java Virtual Machine (JVM)** JVM acts as an interpreter for the bytecode, which takes bytecodes as input and executes it as if it was a physical process executing machine code.

Java is designed to be architecturally neutral so that it can run on multiple platforms. The same runtime code can run on any platform that supports Java. To achieve its cross-architecture capabilities, the Java compiler generates architecturally neutral bytecode instructions. These instructions are designed to be both easily interpreted on any machine and easily translated into native machine code on-the-fly, as shown in Fig. 2.3. Java Runtime Environment (JRE) includes JVM, class libraries, and other supporting files.

JRE = JVM + Core Java API libraries

JDK = JRE + development tools like compilers

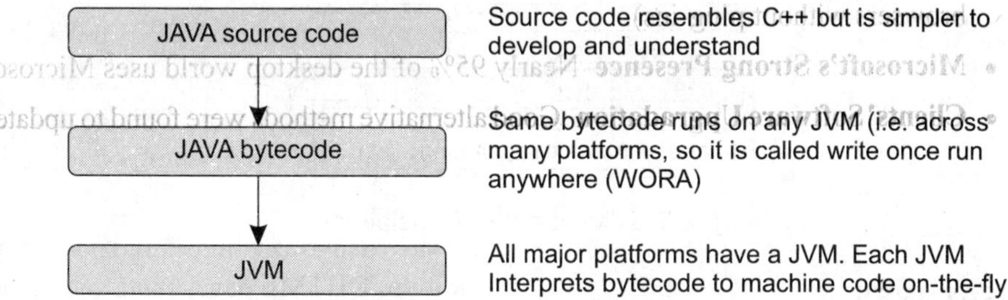

Fig. 2.3 Java Runtime Environment

Tools such as javac (compiler), java (interpreter), and others are provided in a bundle, popularly known as Java Development Kit (JDK). JDK comes in many versions (enhanced in each version) and is different for different platforms such as Windows and Linux. A runtime bundle is also provided as a part of JDK (popularly known as Java Runtime Environment).

2.5 JAVA VIRTUAL MACHINE

At the heart of the Java platform lies the JVM. Most programming languages compile the source code directly into machine code, suitable for execution on a particular microprocessor architecture. The difference with Java is that it uses bytecode, an intermediate code.

Java bytecode executes on a virtual machine. Actually, there wasn't a hardware implementation of this microprocessor available when Java was first released. Instead, the processor architecture is emulated by software known as the *virtual machine*. This virtual machine is an emulation of a real Java processor—a machine within a machine (Fig. 2.4). The virtual machine runs on top of the operating system, which is demonstrated in Fig. 2.5.

The JVM is responsible for interpreting Java bytecode, and translating this into actions or operating system calls. The JVM is responsible for catering to the differences between different platforms and architectures in a way that the developers need not be bothered about it.

The JVM forms a part of a large system, the JRE. JRE varies according to the underlying operating system and computer architecture. If JRE for a given environment is not available, it is impossible to run the Java software.

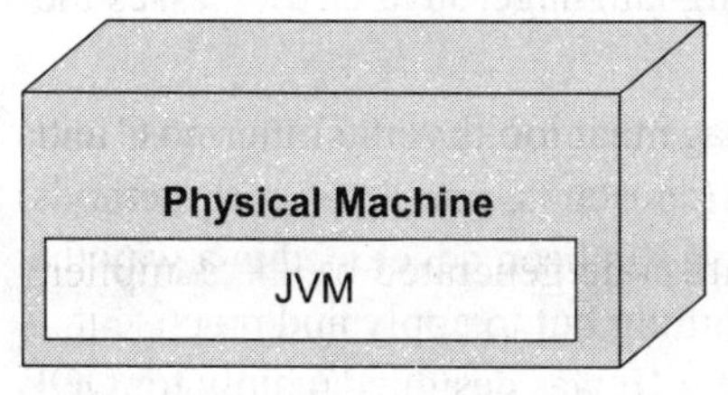

Fig. 2.4 JVM Emulation Run on a Physical CPU

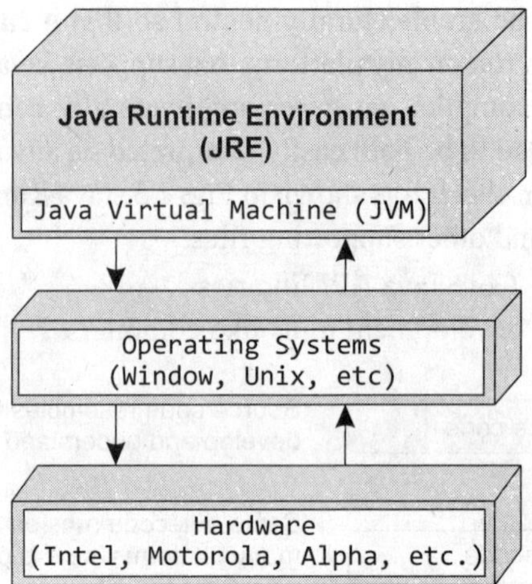

Fig. 2.5 JVM Handles Translations

2.6 JAVA FEATURES

Here we list the basic features that make Java a powerful, object-oriented, and popular programming language.

2.6.1 Platform Independence

Java was designed not only to be cross-platform in source form, like the previous languages (C, C++), but also in compiled binary form. To achieve this, Java is compiled to an intermediate form called the *bytecode* (see Figs 2.3 and 2.4). This *bytecode* is a platform-independent code that is read by a special native program called the Java interpreter that executes the corresponding native machine instructions. The Java compiler is also written in Java. The bytecodes are precisely defined to remain uniform on all platforms.

The second important part of making Java cross-platform is the uniform definition of architecture-dependent constructs. In contradiction to other languages, integers in Java are always four bytes long, and floating point variables follow the IEEE floating point arithmetic 754 standard. You don't have to worry about the meaning of any type, as it is not going to change when you transit between different architectures, e.g., Pentium to Sparc. In Java, everything is well defined. However, the virtual machine and some of its parts have to be written in native code, thus making it platform-dependent.

2.6.2 Object Oriented

It is conceived that Java is a *pure* object-oriented language, meaning that the outermost level of data structure in Java is the *object*. Everything in Java (constants, variables, and methods) are defined inside a class and accessed through objects. Java has been developed in a way that it allows the user to not only learn object-oriented programming but to apply and practise it.

But there are some constraints that violate the purity of Java. It was designed mainly for OOP, but with some procedural elements. For example, Java supports primitive data types that are not objects.

2.6.3 Both Compiled and Interpreted

Java incorporates the elements of both interpretation and compilation. Here is more information on these two approaches.

Interpretation

An interpreter reads one line of a program and executes it before going to the next line. The line is parsed to its smallest operations, the corresponding machine-level code is found, and then the instruction is executed (this could be done with something like the switch statement in C with every possible operation-case listed). Basic was one of the earliest interpreted languages where each text line was interpreted. Similarly, scripting languages like JavaScript, VBScript, and PHP are also interpreted.

In interpretation, there are no intermediate steps between writing/modifying the code and running it. The best part is: *debugging* is fast. Also, the programs are easily transportable to other platforms (if an interpreter is available). The drawback is its slow performance.

Compilation

The program text file is first converted to native machine code with a program called a *compiler*. A linker may also be required to connect together multiple code files together. The output of the compiler is an executable code. C and C++ are both compiled languages.

The biggest advantage of a compiled language is its fast performance, since the machine language code instructions load directly into the processor and get executed. In addition, the compiler can perform certain optimization operations because it looks at the program as a whole and not line by line. The disadvantages include slower debugging and reduced portability to other platforms. The source code must be recompiled on the destination platform.

Java Approach

Java incorporates both interpretation and compilation. The text program is compiled to the intermediate code, called *bytecode*, for the JVM. The JVM executes the bytecode instructions. In other words, JVM interprets the bytecode. The bytecode can run on any platform on which a JVM has been deployed. The program runs inside the JVM, so it does not bother which platform it is getting executed on.

Thus, Java offers the best of both worlds. The compilation step allows for code optimization and the JVM makes way for portability. Figure 2.4 will give you an idea about the two phases involved in the execution of a Java source program, i.e., *compile time* and *execution time* (*runtime*).

Once the source code is converted to bytecode or class file, it is loaded so that it can be processed by the execution engine of the JVM. Bytecode is loaded either through the bootstrap class loader (sometimes referred to as the *primordial class loader*) or through a user-defined class loader (sometimes referred to as the *custom class loader*). The bootstrap class loader (part of the JVM) is responsible for loading trusted classes (e.g., basic Java class library classes). User-defined class loaders (not part of JVM) are the subclasses of *java.util.Class Loader* class that are compiled and instantiated just like any other Java class. The *bytecode verifier* verifies the code and ensures that the code is fit to be executed by the JVM. Figure 2.6 shows the flow of data and control from Java source code through the Java compiler to the JVM. The code is not allowed to execute until it has passed the verifier's test.

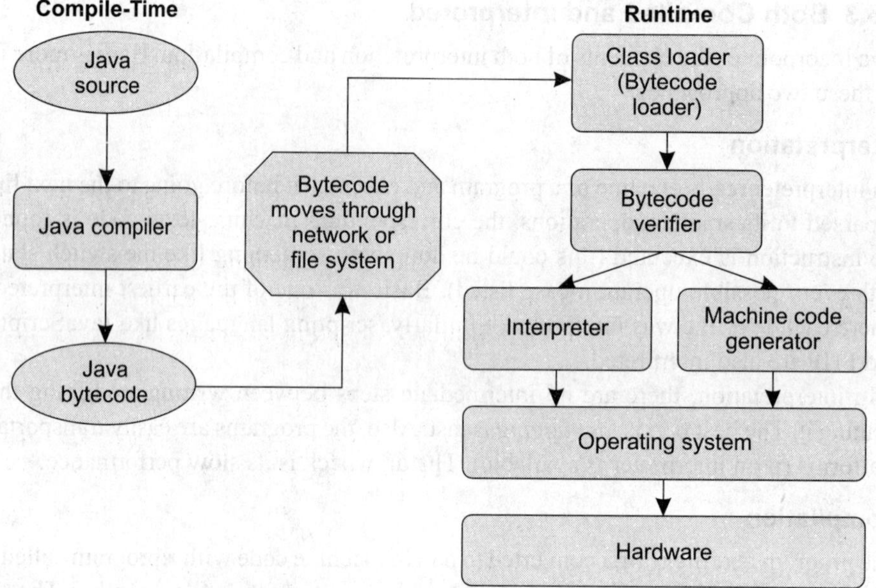

Fig. 2.6 Compilation and Interpretation in Java

But there remains the drawback of an extra compilation step after every correction during debugging. Also, the interpretation of bytecode is still slower in many cases than a program in local machine code. Advanced JVM can ameliorate this, and in many cases, reach speeds similar to programs compiled to local machine code.

2.6.4   Java is Robust

The type checking of Java is at least as strong as that of C++. The compile-time and runtime checks in Java catch many errors and make them crash-proof. The program cannot crash the system. To sum up, Java is one of the most robust languages to have ever evolved. Automatic garbage collection of allocated memory is the biggest contributor here.

2.6.5 JAVA Language Security Features

Java has several language features that protect the integrity of the security system and prevent several common attacks.

Security Through Definition Java is strict in its definition of the language:

- All primitive data types in the language have a specific size.

- All operations are defined to be performed in a specific order.

Security Through Lack of Pointer Arithmetic Java does not have pointer arithmetic, so Java programmers cannot forge a pointer to memory. All methods and instance variables are referred to with their symbolic names. Users cannot write a code that interprets system variables or accesses private information stored in a system.

Security Through Garbage Collection Garbage collection makes Java programs more secure and robust by automatically freeing memory, once it is no longer needed.

Security Through Strict Compile-Time Checking The Java compiler performs extensive, stringent compile-time checking so that as many errors as possible can be detected by the compiler. The Java language is strongly typed, that is:

- Objects cannot be cast to a subclass without an explicit runtime check.
- References to methods and variables of a class are checked to ensure that the objects are of the same class.
- Primitives and objects are not interconvertible.

Strict compilation checks make Java programs more robust and avoid runtime errors. The bytecode verifier runs the bytecode generated by the compiler when an applet is loaded and makes security checks. The compiler also ensures that a program does not access any uninitialized variables.

Java Security Model

Java's security model is focused on protecting users from hostile programs downloaded from untrusted sources across a network. Programs downloaded over the Internet are executed in a *sandbox*. It cannot take any action outside the boundaries specified by the sandbox.

The sandbox for untrusted Java applets, for example, prohibits many activities, including

- Reading or writing to the local disk
- Making a network connection to any host, except the host from which the applet came
- Creating a new process
- Loading a new dynamic library and directly calling a native method

By making it impossible for the downloaded code to perform certain actions, Java's security model protects the user from the threat of hostile codes.

Sandbox—Definition

Traditionally, you had to trust a software before you ran it. You achieved security by allowing a software from trusted sources only, and by regularly scanning for viruses. Once a software gets access to your system, it has full control and if it is malicious, it can damage your system because there are no restrictions placed on the software by the computer. So, in the first place, you prevent malicious code from ever gaining access to your system.

The sandbox security model makes it easier to work with the software that comes from untrusted sources by restricting codes from untrusted sources from taking any actions that could possibly harm your system. The advantage is—you don't need to figure out what code is trusted and what is not. In addition to that, you don't need to scan for viruses as well. The sandbox is made up of the following components operating together.

Class Loader It is the first link in the security chain. It fetches executable codes from the network and enforces the namespace hierarchy.

Bytecode Verifier The verifier checks that the applet conforms to the Java language guarantees and that there are no violations like stack overflows, namespace violations, illegal data type casts, etc.

Security Manager It enforces the boundary of the sandbox. Whenever an applet performs an action which is a potential violation, the security manager decides whether it is approved or not.

2.6.6 Java is Multithreaded

To explore this property, you must know the meaning of *multithreading*. It can be explained well with the help of an example. Consider a four-gas burner on which food is cooked. The cook, in order to save time, puts milk to boil on one gas burner, rice on the other, makes *chapattis* on the third, and vegetable on the fourth. The cook switches between all the items to be cooked so that neither of the items are red-heated to lose their taste. He may lower/brighten up the gas as and when required. Here the cook is the processor and the four items being cooked are threads. The processor (cook) switches from one thread to another.

A *thread* can be loosely defined as a separate stream of execution that takes place simultaneously and independent of everything else that might be happening. Threads are independent parts of a process that run concurrently. Using threads, a program cannot hold the CPU for a long duration intentionally (e.g. infinite loop). The beauty of multithreading is that the other tasks that are not stuck in the loop can continue processing without having to wait for the stuck task to finish. Threads in Java can place locks on shared resources so that while one thread is using it, no other thread is allowed to access it. This is achieved with the help of *synchronization*.

More about threads and its implementation will be taken up later in Chapter 8.

2.6.7 Other Features

Automatic Memory Management

Automatic garbage collection (memory management) is handled by the JVM. To create an instance of a class, the 'new' operator is used (refer to Chapter 4). However, Java automatically removes objects that are not being referenced. This is known as *garbage collection*. The advantages and disadvantages of garbage collection are listed below.

Advantages

- Reduces the possibility of memory leaks, since memory is freed as needed. A memory leak occurs when the memory allocated is not released, resulting in an unnecessary consumption of all the available memory.
- Memory corruption does not occur.

Disadvantage

- Garbage collection is considered one of the greatest bottlenecks in the speed of execution.

Dynamic Binding

The linking of data and methods to where they are located is done at runtime. New classes can be loaded at runtime. Linking is done on-the-fly, i.e., on-demand.

Good Performance

Interpretation of byte code slowed performance in early versions, but advanced virtual machines with adaptive optimization and just-in-time compilation (combined with other features) provide high speed code execution.

Built-in Networking

Java was designed with networking in mind and comes with many classes to develop sophisticated Internet communications. A detailed discussion on this topic is taken up later in Chapter 11.

No Pointers

Java uses *references* instead of pointers. A reference provides access to objects. The programmer is relieved from the overhead of pointer manipulation.

No Global Variables

In Java, the global namespace is the class hierarchy and so, one cannot create a variable outside the class. It is extremely difficult to ensure that a global variable is manipulated in a consistent manner. Java allows a modified type of the global variable called *static variable*.

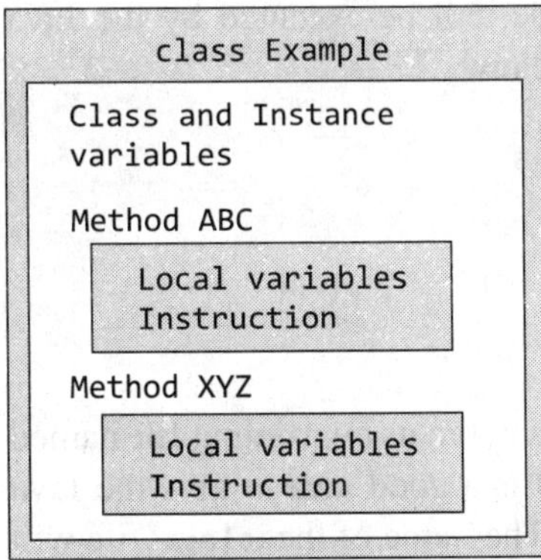

Fig. 2.7 Program Structure

2.7 PROGRAM STRUCTURE

A Java application consists of a collection of classes. A *class* is a template. An *object* is defined as an instance of the class. Each instance (object) contains the members (fields and methods) specified in the class. A *field* is one that holds a value. A *method* defines operations on the fields and values that are passed as arguments to the method (see Fig. 2.7).

Let us now create our first Java program. Example 2.1 below shows a very simple Java program which displays a string on the console. It has just one print statement (the program is explained in Section 2.7.3).

Example 2.1 **First Java Program**

```
L1      /* Call this file"Example.java".*/
L2      class Example {
L3      //your program starts execution with a call to main()
L4      public static void main (String args[ ]){
L5      System.out.println("This is a simple Java program");
L6      }
L7      }
```

2.7.1 How to Execute a Java Program?

There are three easy steps for successfully executing the Java program:

1. **Entering the Source Code** The above program (Example 2.1) can be written in any text editor (like Notepad) but make sure it is written exactly the same way it is shown.
2. **Saving the Source Code** Now that you've written the code in Notepad, this is how you'll save it

   - Select File | Save As from the notepad menu.
   - In the 'File name' field, type "Example.java" within double quotes.
   - In the 'Save as type' field select All Files (*.*).
   - Click enter to save the file.

3. **Compiling and Running the Source** Java programs are compiled using DOS. For opening OS, type *cmd* at the run prompt and move to the folder that contains the saved `Example.java` file. Now compile the program using `javac`, specifying the name of the source file on the command line as shown below. (Assuming the file was saved in a folder 'javaeg' in the C drive.)

```
C:\>cd javaeg // change to directory javaeg using cd command
C:\javaeg\>javac Example.java
```

The `javac` compiler creates a file called `Example.class` (in the same directory). This class contains the bytecode version of the program. This bytecode will be executed by the Java interpreter using `java` followed by the class name as shown below.

```
C:\javaeg\>java Example
```

Output

```
This is a simple Java program
```

2.7.2 Why Save as `Example.java`?

When the Java source code is compiled, each individual class is put in its own output file named after the class and using the `.class` extension. That is why it is a good idea to give the Java source files the same name as that of the class they contain. The name of the `.class` file will match exactly with the name of the source file.

In many programming languages, the name of the source code file can be arbitrary. This is not so with Java. In the above example, the name of the source file should be `Example.java`. In Java, a source file is a normal text file that contains one or more class definitions.

The extension for the source file must be `.java`. By convention, the name of the file and the name of class should be same (even the case should match) and that is why we named the above example as `Example.java`. Java is case-sensitive. So example and Example are two different class names.

> **Note** You can also provide a different name for naming a source file. For example, the above example can be saved as `First.java`. But in that case, when you compile the file, the `.class` that will be generated will have the name `Example.class`. So for executing the program, you have to mention `java Example` on the command line. This may lead to confusion, so it is advised that the name of the Java file should match with the name of the class defined in the file (case-wise also). Also note that in case the source file contains more than one classes defined within itself, the java file name should match exactly with the class name that contains the main method.

2.7.3 Explanation

L1 The program begins with the comment:

```
/* Call this file "Example.java".*/
```

The comments are ignored by the compiler. Comments are a good way to induce documentation in programming.

L2 The next line of code in the program is

```
class Example {
```

This line uses the keyword `class` to declare that a new class is being defined followed by the class name, i.e., **Example**. The entire class definition, including all its members, will be between the opening curly brace ({) and the closing curly brace (}).

L3 Another type of comment is used in this line.

```
// your program starts execution with a call to main()
```

This type of comment is called a single-line comment, and it begins with a double slash //.

L4 This line shows the main method for the class.

```
public static void main (String args []) {
```

This is the line from where the program will start its execution. All applications in Java start execution from `main()`. Every complete Java Application must contain a root class where the execution can begin. A root class must contain a main method defined with the header, as shown in this line. Let us take a brief look at the attributes of `main()`.

public It is an access specifier used to specify that the code can be called from anywhere. `main()` is declared public because it is called by codes outside the class it is a part of. It is called by the JVM.

static It is declared `static` because it allows `main()` to be called without having to instantiate the class. JVM need not create an instance of the class (i.e. object of the class) for calling the `main()` method.

void It does not return a value. The keyword `void` simply tells the compiler that `main()` does not return anything back to the caller, i.e., JVM.

String args[] It holds optional command line arguments passed to the class through the `java` command line. The curly bracket at the end marks the beginning of the main method and it ends in L6.

> **Note** The Java compiler will compile classes that do not contain a `main ()` method, but the Java interpreter has no way to run these classes.

L5 It shows a print statement. If you want to display anything on the standard output, this statement is used.

```
System.out.println ("This is a simple Java program");
```

This line prints the string `"This is a simple Java Program"` on the standard output. `System` is a predefined class. The string (mentioned in double quotes) passed to the `println` method is displayed as it is on the standard output. All statements in Java are terminated by a semicolon (;). Lines other than `println()` don't end with a semicolon because they are technically not statements.

L6 The closing curly bracket marks the closing of the `main` method.

L7 The closing curly bracket marks the closing of the class.

2.8 JAVA IMPROVEMENTS

Features of different versions of Java are discussed in the following sections.

2.8.1 Java 5.0 Features

We present a host of features in Java 5 and later discuss some of the improvements in Java 5.

Autoboxing and Unboxing

Chapter 3 explains that Java has primitive types like `int` for integers, and Chapter 4 explains classes and objects. The difference between the two types is very important. In Chapter 6, we examine the so-called *autoboxing* and *unboxing* features added to J2SE 5.0 that removes the need for explicit conversions in most cases and thus improves code readability and removes boilerplate codes and sources of errors.

Enhanced for Loop

Chapter 3 looks at several types of looping structures available in Java, one of which is the `for` loop (quite similar to the C/C++ `for` loop). Version 5.0 includes an enhanced `for` loop syntax that reduces code complexity and enhances readability. We introduce the enhanced `for` loop in Chapter 4 and describe the object types with which the enhanced `for` loop works.

Enumerated Types

Chapter 6 presents a feature of C/C++ that many programmers have missed in Java. An enumerated type has been added with the `enum` keyword. The new enumerated type includes all the features of C/C++ `enum` including type safety.

`StringBuilder` Class

We will be discussing this class in Chapter 6, along with the older `StringBuffer` class. It offers better performance than `StringBuffer` class.

Static Import

Release 5.0 includes a new technique for accessing Java static methods and constants in another class without the need to include the full package and class name every time they are used. (We will explain the terms `class`, `package`, `static`, `import`, etc. in Chapters 4 and 7). The 'static import' facility makes your code easier to write and less error-prone. We will discuss static import in more detail in Chapter 7 after discussing import in general.

Metadata

The metadata facility (*annotation*) is designed to reduce much of the boilerplate code that would be required in the earlier versions of Java. Annotations, though not a part of the program, provide information about the program to the compiler. This information can be used to detect errors and supply warnings. Annotations begin with '@'. The `javac` compiler processes some annotations and some require the annotation-processing tool, *apt*.

Formatted I/O and Varargs

In Chapter 9, we discuss how to format numerical output with Java. Version 5.0 adds the ability to produce formatted output easily in the form of a `printf()` method that behaves similar to the `printf()` function in C/C++. There is also a formatted input feature (`Scanner` class) that is described in Chapter 9. Both these features rely on '`varargs`,' which stands for *variable argument list* in which the number of parameters passed to a Java method is not known when the source is constructed (also known as *variable arity methods*) (see Chapter 4 for `varargs`).

Graphics System Improvements

Release 5.0 includes numerous bug fixes and minor tweaks to Java's graphics subsystems known as AWT and Swing, including reduced memory usage. The biggest improvement is that it is no longer necessary to call `getContentPane()` when adding Swing components.

New Concurrency Features

Chapter 8 discusses Java's multithreading support that has been present since Version 1.0. Release 5.0 enhances the multithreading features of Java. Some of these additions depend upon the generics concept, so we wait until Chapter 10 to introduce these important new capabilities.

Generics

In Chapter 10, we introduce the new generics feature, an important subject that we will cover in detail. Java is type-safe, which simply means that every variable has a well-defined type and that only compatible types can be assigned to each other. However, the use of generics adds a greater amount of compile-time safety to the Java language. The use of generics allows objects of only a specified type to be added to a collection, thereby enhancing the runtime safety and correctness of the program; otherwise a compile-time error occurs.

Other new features in J2SE 5.0 include core XML support, improvements to Unicode, improvements to Java's database connectivity package known as JDBC, and an improved, high-compression format for JAR files that can greatly reduce download times for applets and other networking applications.

Java 2 platform Standard Edition 5.0 (J2SE 5.0) dealt with improvements in the ease of development (EoD) category. The new EoD features were all about syntax shortcuts that greatly reduce the amount of code that must be entered, making coding faster and error-free. Some features enable improved compile-time type checking, thus producing fewer runtime errors. Apart from EoD category, new multithreading and concurrency features were added that provide capabilities previously unavailable. The designers of J2SE considered quality, stability, and compatibility to be the most important aspect of the new release. A lot of efforts were made to ensure compatibility with previous versions of Java. Faster JVM startup time and smaller memory footprint were important goals. These have been achieved through careful tuning of the software and the use of class data sharing. It is much easier to watch memory usage, detect and respond to a low-memory condition in Java 5.

2.8.2 Java 6 Features

Some of the major enhancements to Java 6 are given below.

Collections API

The motive was to provide bidirectional collection access. New interfaces have been added like `Deque`, `BlockingDeque`, etc. and existing classes like `Linked List`, `TreeSet`, and `TreeMap` have been modified to implement these new interfaces. A bunch of new classes have been added like `ArrayDeque`, `ConcurrentSkipListSet`, etc.

Input/Output

A new class named `Console` has been added to the `java.io` package. It contains methods to access character-based console. New methods have been added to `File` class.

Jar and Zip Enhancements

Two new compressed streams have been added.

- `java.util.zip.DeflaterInputStream`:for compressing data
- `java.util.zip.InflaterOutputStream`:for decompressing data

These classes are useful for transmitting compressed data over a network.

Enhancements Common to Java Web Start and Java Plug-in

All dialogs have been redesigned to be more user-friendly. Caching can be disabled via the Java control panel. A new support for SSL/TSL is added.

Enhanced Network Interface

It provides a number of new methods for accessing state and configuration information relating to a system's network adapters. This includes information such as MAC addresses and MTU size (discussed in Chapter 11).

Splash Screen

Applications can display the splash screen even before the virtual machine starts.

Java 6 also enhanced the monitoring and mangement API and made significant changes to JConsole.

2.8.3 Java 7 Features

A number of features have been added in Java 7 such as revised `switch...case` to accept strings, `multi-catch` statements in exception handling,`try-with-resource` statements, the new file input output API, the fork and join framework and a few others.

String in `switch...case` Statement

Java 7 added strings to be used in `switch...case` statements apart from primitives (`short`, `byte`, `int`, `char`), enumerated type and few wrapper classes (discussed in Chapter 3).

Unicode 6.0.0 Support

Java 7 supports Unicode 6.0.0. A new string representation is used to express unicode characters (discussed in Chapter 6).

Binary Literals and Numeric Literals (with Underscores)

Java 7 added binary literals and underscores to be used with numeric literals. This feature is particularly useful in increasing the readability of larger literals with a long sequence of numbers (discussed in Chapter 3).

Automatic Resource Management

A new try with resources statement is introduced so that resources specified with try are released/ nullified when try block exits. There is no need to manually free up the resources using finally block as was the case with earlier versions of Java (discussed in Chapter 7).

Improved Exception Handling

Java 7 introduced a multi-catch block where multiple exceptions can be caught using a single catch block (discussed in Chapter 7).

nio 2.0 (Non-blocking I/O)—New File System API

`java.nio.file` package was created in Java 7 to include classes and interfaces like `Path`,`Paths`, `File System`, `File Systems` and others. Simplified methods to efficiently copy, move, create links and receive file/directory change notifications were also incorporated (Chapter 9).

Fork and Join Fork and Join Framework is incorporated in Java 7 to have a more efficient kind of parallel processing. The task is divided (forked) into smaller task such that no thread is idle and whose results are combined (joined) to achieve the desired outputs. The classes for the Fork-Join mechanism are `ForkJoinPool` and `ForkJoinTask`.

Supporting Dynamism Java compiler performs the type checking of variables, methods, arguments etc. Java 7 incorporates a new feature `invokedynamic` to let JVM resolve type information at runtime like few other dynamic languages and incorporate non-java language requirements.

Diamond Operator The Generics declaration, prior to Java 7, required the types to be declared on both the sides of the declaration. Java 7 onwards the compiler can deduce the type on the right side, using the diamond operator (< >), by looking at the left-hand-side declaration.

Swing Enhancements Swings added a host of features like AWT and Swing components can be used together without any problems,`JLayer` class, Nimbus look and feel, HSV color selection tab in the `JColorChooser` class and more (see Chapter 15 for details).

Java FX 2.2.3 Java FX provides the new GUI toolkit for creating rich cross-platform user interfaces across different types of devices like TV, mobile, desktop etc. Java FX is bundled with JDK 7.

2.8.4 Brief Comparison of Different Releases

Table 2.1 presents a brief comparison of different releases of Java.

Table 2.1 Java JDK Major Releases and their Differences

Version	Name	New Features Introduced
1.0	Oak	Java released to public.
1.1	Sparkler	Added a totally new event model, using Listeners, anonymous classes, and inner classes.
1.2	Playground	Added `Array List` and other `Collections`, added swing. Added DSA code signing. Added buffered image.
1.3	Kestrel	`java.util.Timer`,`java.lang.StrictMath`,`java.awt.print.Page Attributes`, `java.media.sound` (MIDI) Hotspot introduced. RMI can now also use CORBA's IIOP protocol. Added RSA code signing.
1.4	Merlin	Added `regexes, assertions`, and `nio`.
1.5	Tiger	Added `StringBuilder`,`java.util.concurrent`, generics, enumerations and, annotations.
1.6	Mustang	Applet splash screens, table sorting, true double buffering, digitally signed XML files, `JavaCompilerTool`, JDBC 4.0, smart card API, `Console.readPassword`, improved drag and drop.
1.7	Dolphin	Automatic resource management, String in `switch…case`, Fork and join framework, dynamism support, Unicode 6 supported, Java Fx 2.2.3.
1.8	Not yet released	There is still on-going discussion on what should be included.

2.9 DIFFERENCES BETWEEN JAVA AND C++

Here is a technical overview of the differences between Java and C++. The following points list out the aspects that are present in Java and absent in C++.

Multiple Inheritance Not Allowed Multilevel inheritance is enforced, which makes the design clearer. Multiple inheritance among classes is not supported in Java. Interfaces are used for supporting multiple inheritance.

Common Parent All classes are *single-rooted*. The class `Object` is the parent of all the classes in Java.

Packages The concept of *packages* is used, i.e., a large, *hierarchical namespace* is provided. This prevents naming ambiguities in libraries.

In-source Documentation *In-source code documentation* comments are provided. Documentation keywords are provided, e.g. @author, @version, etc.

All Codes Inside Class Unlike C++, all parts of a Java program reside inside the class. Global data declaration outside the class is not allowed. However, `static` data within classes is supported.

Operator Overloading Operator overloading is not supported in Java but a few operators are already overloaded by Java, e.g. '+'. Programmers do not have the option of overloading operators.

Explicit boolean Type `boolean` is an explicit type, different from `int`. Only two `boolean` literals are provided, i.e. `true` and `false`. These cannot be compared with integers 0 and 1 as used in some other languages.

Array Length Accessible All array objects in Java have a `length` variable associated with them to determine the length of the array.

go to Instead of `goto`, `break` and `continue` are supported.

Pointers There are no pointers in Java.

Null Pointers Reasonably Caught Null pointers are caught by a `NullPointerException`.

Memory Management The use of *garbage collection* prevents memory leaks and referencing freed memory.

Automatic Variable Initialization All variables are automatically initialized, except local variables.

Runtime Checking of Container Bounds The bounds of containers (arrays, strings, etc.) are checked at runtime and an `IndexOutOfBoundsException` is thrown if necessary.

Platform Independence C++ is not a platform-independent language whereas Java is.

Sizes of the Integer Types Defined The sizes of the integer types `byte`, `short`, `int`, and `long` are defined to be 1, 2, 4, and 8 bytes.

Unicode Provided Unicode represents the characters in most of the languages, e.g. Japanese, Latin, etc.

String Class An explicit predefined `String` class is provided along with `StringBuffer` and new `StringBuilder` class.

Extended Utility Class Libraries: Package java.util Supported among others, `Enumeration` (an `Iterator` interface), `Hashtable`, `Vector`.

Default Access Specifier Added By default, all the variables, methods, and classes in Java have default privileges that are different from `private` access specifier. `Private` is the default access specifier in C++.

2.10 INSTALLATION OF JDK 1.7

Before writing a single line of code, the software application developer must first make sure that the best tool for the job are at his or her disposal. Java was designed to be a cross-platform, object-oriented programming language. Because of the huge amount of interest generated by the introduction of Java, new tools are being introduced every now and then that provide the developer with greater flexibility and ease of use.

2.10.1 Getting Started with the JDK

Sun (and now continued by Oracle) decided to give away a Java Developer's Kit (JDK) that would provide the basic tools needed for Java programming. The JDK provides the beginners with all the tools needed to write powerful Java applications or applets. It contains a compiler, an interpreter, a debugger, sample applications, applet viewer, and some other tools that you can use to test your code.

A quick visit to Oracle Java website will allow you to download the JDK to your local machine. Check for the latest version of JDK and download that from this site. The following operating systems are supported for JDK:

(a) Oracle Solaris   (b) Windows   (c) Linux   (d) Mac

Remember that the availability of JDK for these platforms simply means that Oracle has implemented the JVM and development tools for these platforms.

2.10.2 JDK Installation Notes

When the Java SE Development Kit is installed, the Java SE Runtime Environment is installed as well.

> **Note** For the installation of JDK 1.7 on Solaris platform (both 32-bit and 64-bit), you can refer to the installation documentation on Oracle official site:
>
> http://docs.oracle.com/javase/7/docs/webnotes/install/solaris/solaris-jdk.html
>
> Similarly, for installation of JDK 1.7 on Linux operating system (both 32 bit and 64 bit), visit:
>
> http://docs.oracle.com/javase/7/docs/webnotes/install/linux/linux-jdk.html
>
> For JDK installation on MAC OS visit:
>
> http://docs.oracle.com/javase/7/docs/webnotes/install/mac/mac-jdk.html
>
> The JDK for any OS can be downloaded from:
>
> www.oracle.com/technetwork/java/javase/downloads/jdk7u9-downloads-1859576.html.
>
> Refer to www.oracle.com/technetwork/java/javase/downloads/index.html for latest Java SE releases.

In this book, we intend to provide the details of installation of JDK 1.7 on Windows operating system only.

JDK has two versions numbers—an *external version number* 7 and an *internal version number*1.7.0_09, i.e., version 7 update 9.

The installation and configuration process can be broken down into the following steps:

1. Run the JDK installer.
2. Update the Path and Classpath variables.
3. Test the installation.

Step 1: Run the JDK Installer

If you have downloaded the JDK software file (JDK installer) instead of running the installer from the Java website, you should check to see that the complete file is downloaded:

```
jdk-7u9-windows-i586.exe
```

Note   The JDK documentation can be downloaded from the following URL: www.oracle.com/technetwork/java/javase/documentation/java-se-7-doc-download-435117.html.

Double-click on the icon of the JDK Installer.exe to run the installer and then follow the instructions. Figures 2.8(a)–(h) show some of the snapshots of the installation process. The first Welcome screen is displayed as soon as you double click on the installer.

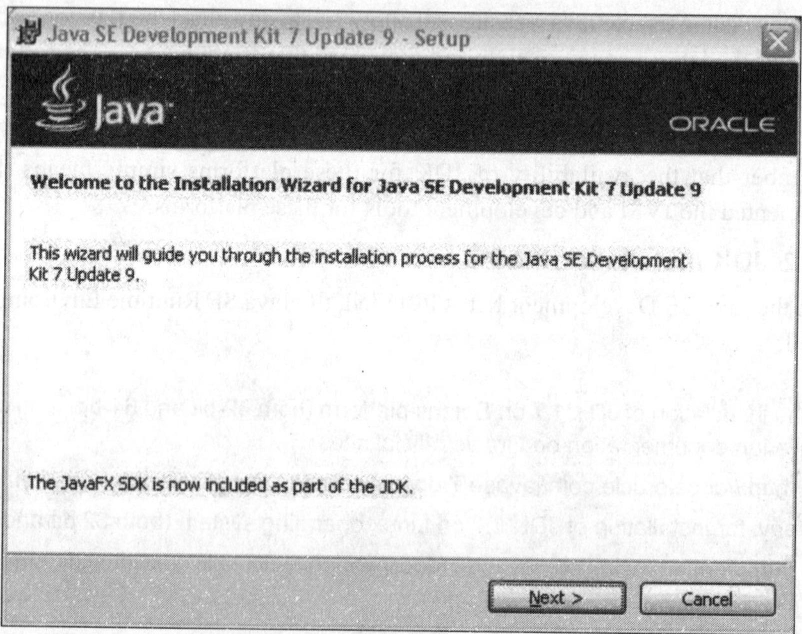

Fig. 2.8(a)

The welcome screen also tells you that Java FX SDK is now a part of Java 7. Click on Next>, the installer prompts you to select what all you want to install and where to install them in your system.

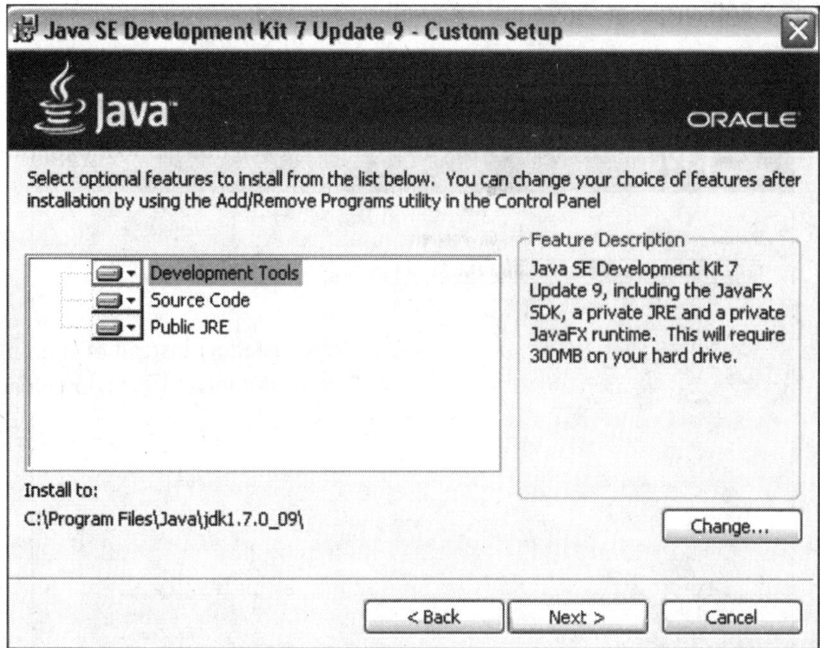

Fig. 2.8(b)

By default, the JDK will be installed at the path mentioned in `Install to`. You can change the default path by clicking the `Change…` button. As soon as you click on the `Next>` button, the installation starts.

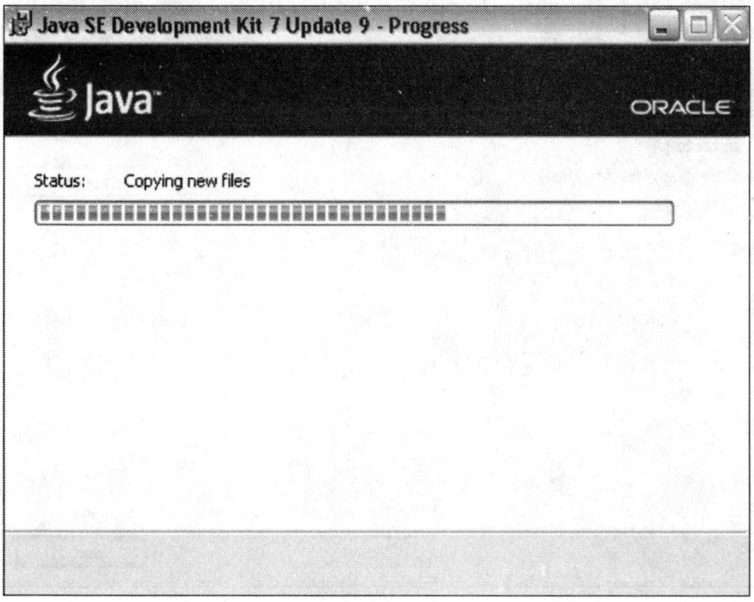

Fig. 2.8(c)

Figure 2.8(d) snapshot shows that JRE will be installed.

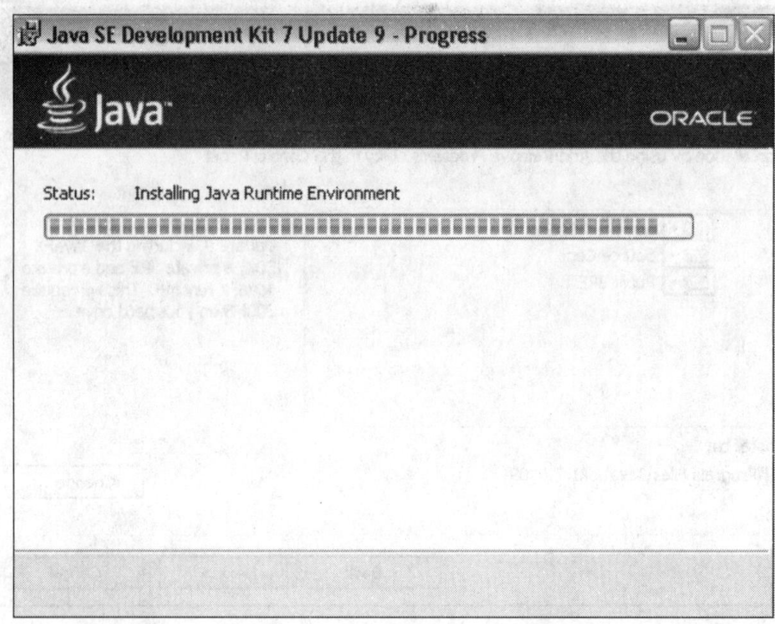

Fig. 2.8(d)

Figure 2.8(e) prompts you to make a selection for installing JRE. As soon as you click on Next>, the installation of JRE starts.

Fig. 2.8(e)

The following snapshot shows you that the JRE is getting registered.

Fig. 2.8(f)

Finally, Java is installed successfully as shown in the snapshot below.

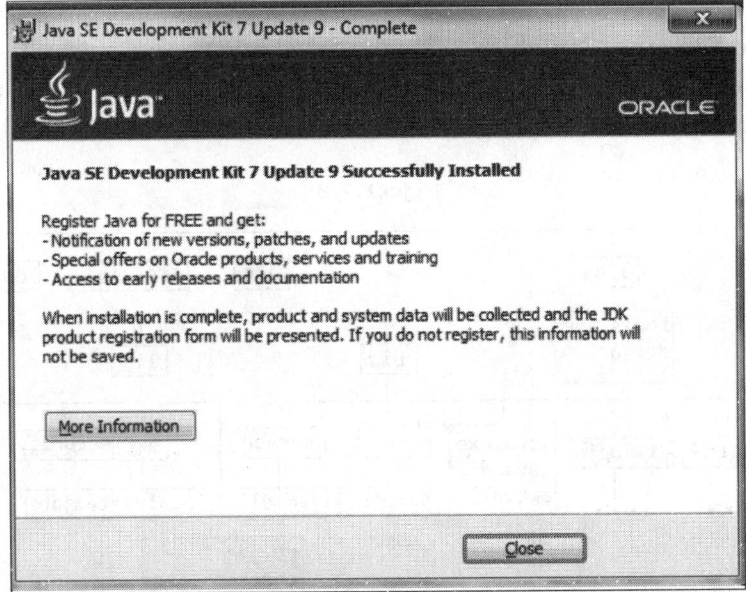

Fig. 2.8(g)

Once you are finished with installation of Java, you get a 'Thank You' message (Fig. 2.8(h)) from Oracle Corporation and asking you to register so that you can get alerts, notifications, special offers, and access to future releases and documentation.

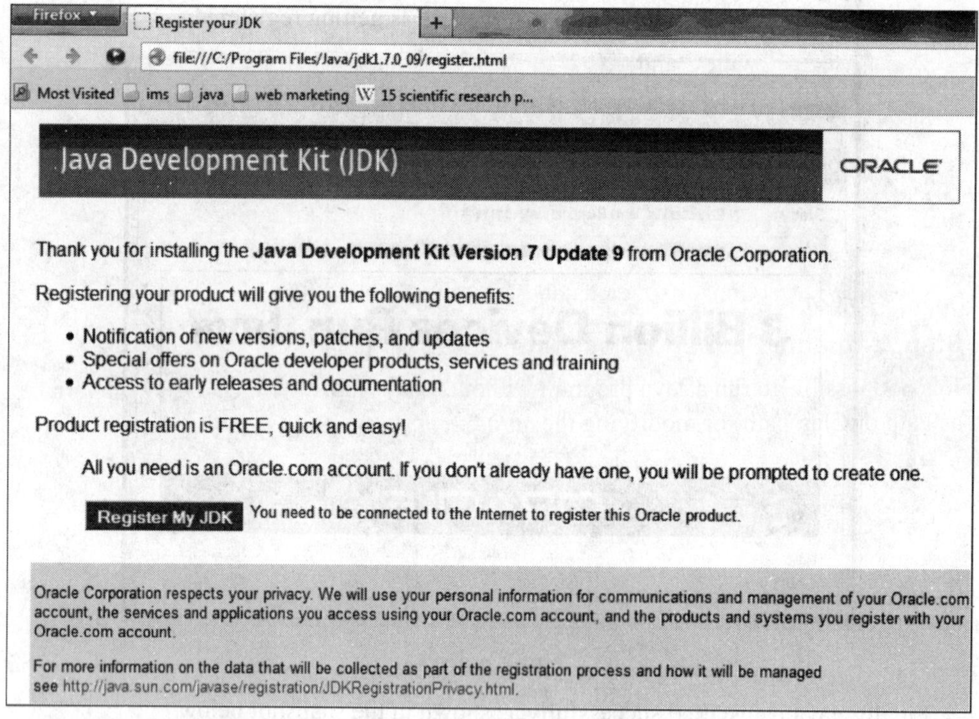

Fig. 2.8(h)

Installed Directory Structure

JDK 7 will be installed (by default) in `c:\program files\java\jdk1.7.0_09` and will have the following directory structure (Fig. 2.9):

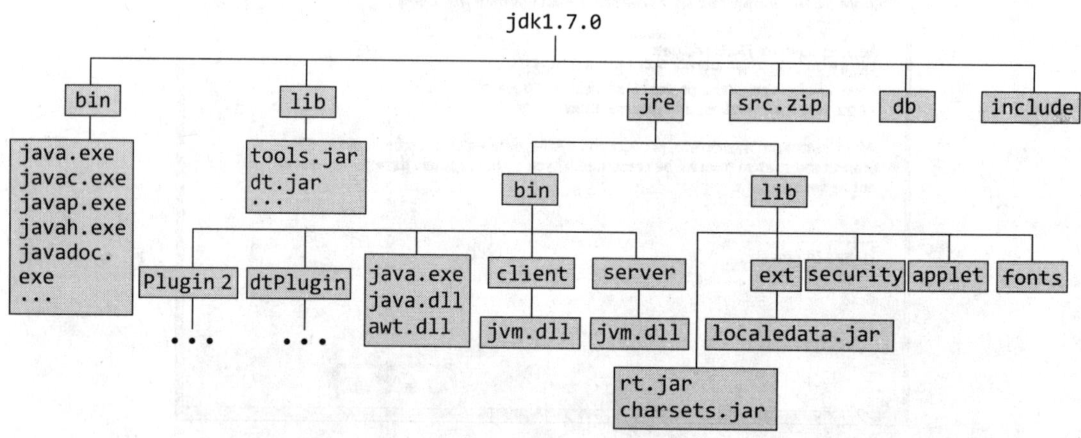

Fig. 2.9 Structure of JDK Software and Documentation Directories

Included in the directory structure is a file `src.zip`. Do not unzip the src.zip file as it contains all the core class binaries, and is used by JDK in this form.

- **include** The include directory contains a set of C and C++ header files for interacting with C and C++.
- **lib** This directory contains non-core classes like *dt.jar* and *tools.jar* used by tools and utilities in JDK.
- **bin** The bin directory contains the binary executables for Java. For example, Java Compiler (Java), Java Interpreter (Java) ,rmicompiler (rmic) etc.
- **jre** It is the root directory for the Java runtime environment.
- **db** Contains Java database.

Step 2: Update Path and Classpath Variables

It is not possible to run a Java program without modifying system environment variables (such as Path or Classpath) or modifying the *autoexec.bat.*

Why to Set Path Variable? The PATH environment variable needs to be set if you want to run the executables (javac.exe, java.exe, javadoc.exe, etc.) from any directory. If you want to find out the current value of your PATH, then type the following at the DOS prompt:

```
C:\>path
```

Windows NT/XP/Vista/7 It is preferable to make the following environment variable changes in the Control Panel instead of the autoexec.bat file. Start the Control Panel, select System, and then edit the environment variables. In case of other recent versions of Windows, right click on the My Computer icon, and select Properties, click on Environment. The System Properties window appears. Select Path from the list of system variables and append the following path to existing path: `C:\PROGRA~1\JAVA\JDK1.7\bin` (complete path of `\bin`).

Note Do not erase the existing paths in the path system variable; only append the new path separated by a semicolon.

Classpath—What it does? The Classpath tells the JVM and other Java applications where to find the class libraries and user-defined classes. You need to set the classpath for locating class libraries, user-defined classes, and packages.

Setting the Classpath

The same procedure (explained above) can be followed for setting the classpath environment variable with the exception that now you will not look for the path variable but for the classpath variable.

Step 3: Testing the Installation

Your computer system is now configured and ready to use the JDK. The Java tools do not have a GUI, as they are all run from the DOS command line. For testing the installation, type the following command at the command line:

```
C:\>javac and C:\>java
```

If the following screenshots are displayed on typing the command 'java' on the DOS prompt, it means that Java is properly installed and the path is set (Figs 2.10(a) and (b)).

```
C:\WINDOWS\system32\cmd.exe                                        _ | 5 | x

C:\>
C:\>
C:\>
C:\>javac -version
javac 1.7.0_09

C:\>javac
Usage: javac <options> <source files>
where possible options include:
  -g                         Generate all debugging info
  -g:none                    Generate no debugging info
  -g:{lines,vars,source}     Generate only some debugging info
  -nowarn                    Generate no warnings
  -verbose                   Output messages about what the compiler is doing
  -deprecation               Output source locations where deprecated APIs are u
sed
  -classpath <path>          Specify where to find user class files and annotati
on processors
  -cp <path>                 Specify where to find user class files and annotati
on processors
  -sourcepath <path>         Specify where to find input source files
  -bootclasspath <path>      Override location of bootstrap class files
  -extdirs <dirs>            Override location of installed extensions
  -endorseddirs <dirs>       Override location of endorsed standards path
  -proc:{none,only}          Control whether annotation processing and/or compil
ation is done.
  -processor <class1>[,<class2>,<class3>...] Names of the annotation processors
to run; bypasses default discovery process
  -processorpath <path>      Specify where to find annotation processors
  -d <directory>             Specify where to place generated class files
  -s <directory>             Specify where to place generated source files
  -implicit:{none,class}     Specify whether or not to generate class files for
implicitly referenced files
  -encoding <encoding>       Specify character encoding used by source files
  -source <release>          Provide source compatibility with specified release

  -target <release>          Generate class files for specific VM version
  -version                   Version information
  -help                      Print a synopsis of standard options
  -Akey[=value]              Options to pass to annotation processors
  -X                         Print a synopsis of nonstandard options
  -J<flag>                   Pass <flag> directly to the runtime system
  -Werror                    Terminate compilation if warnings occur
  @<filename>                Read options and filenames from file
```

Fig. 2.10(a)

```
C:\WINDOWS\system32\cmd.exe                                        _ | 5 | x

C:\>
C:\>java -version
java version "1.7.0_09"
Java(TM) SE Runtime Environment (build 1.7.0_09-b05)
Java HotSpot(TM) Client VM (build 23.5-b02, mixed mode, sharing)

C:\>java
Usage: java [-options] class [args...]
           (to execute a class)
   or  java [-options] -jar jarfile [args...]
           (to execute a jar file)
where options include:
    -d32          use a 32-bit data model if available
    -d64          use a 64-bit data model if available
    -client       to select the "client" VM
    -server       to select the "server" VM
    -hotspot      is a synonym for the "client" VM  [deprecated]
                  The default VM is client.

    -cp <class search path of directories and zip/jar files>
    -classpath <class search path of directories and zip/jar files>
                  A ; separated list of directories, JAR archives,
                  and ZIP archives to search for class files.
    -D<name>=<value>
                  set a system property
    -verbose[:class|gc|jni]
                  enable verbose output
    -version      print product version and exit
    -version:<value>
                  require the specified version to run
    -showversion  print product version and continue
    -jre-restrict-search | -no-jre-restrict-search
                  include/exclude user private JREs in the version search
    -? -help      print this help message
    -X            print help on non-standard options
    -ea[:<packagename>...|:<classname>]
    -enableassertions[:<packagename>...|:<classname>]
                  enable assertions with specified granularity
    -da[:<packagename>...|:<classname>]
    -disableassertions[:<packagename>...|:<classname>]
                  disable assertions with specified granularity
    -esa | -enablesystemassertions
                  enable system assertions
    -dsa | -disablesystemassertions
                  disable system assertions
    -agentlib:<libname>[=<options>]
                  load native agent library <libname>, e.g. -agentlib:hprof
                  see also, -agentlib:jdwp-help and -agentlib:hprof-help
    -agentpath:<pathname>[=<options>]
                  load native agent library by full pathname
    -javaagent:<jarpath>[=<options>]
                  load Java programming language agent, see java.lang.instrument

    -splash:<imagepath>
                  show splash screen with specified image
See http://www.oracle.com/technetwork/java/javase/documentation/index.html for m
ore details.
```

Fig. 2.10(b)

2.10.3 Exploring the JDK

It is important to know the complete structure of Java 7. The following diagrammatic representation (Fig. 2.11) can give you an idea about the various constructs Java 7 is made up of. It also shows the various components taken care by each construct.

It will be interesting to know, which part(s) of Java 7 will comprise the JDK, JRE, or Java API? The following representation answers the question in contention. It is worth noting that the Java API is a subset of JRE and the JRE is a subset of JDK.

The Java Standard Edition (Java^{TM}SE) Development Kit includes the JRE plus the command-line development tools such as compilers and debuggers that are necessary for *developing* applets and applications.

Tools and Tool APIs	java	javac	javadoc	jar	javap	JPDA	Java DB	jconsole	
	Security	Int'l	RM1	IDL	Deploy	Monito-ring	Trouble-shoot	Scripting	JVM T1	Web Services

Deployment Technologies	Web Start Java		Plug-in

User Inter-face Tookits	JavaFX					
	AWT		Swing		Java 2D	
	Accessibility	Drag and Drop	Input Methods	Image I/O	Print Service	Sound

Integration Libraries	IDL	JDBC	JNDI	RMI	RMI-IIOP	Scripting

Other Base Libraries	Beans	Int'l Support	I/O	JMX	JNI	Math
	Networking	Override Mechanism	Security	Serializ-ation	Extension Mechanism	XML JAXP

Lang and util Base Libraries	Lang & util	Collections	Concurrency Utilities	JAR	Logging	Management	
	Preferences API	Ref. Objects	Reflection	Regular Expressions	Versioning	Zip	Instrument

Java Virtual Machine

Fig. 2.11 Structure of Java 7

The JRE provides the JVM and other components necessary for you to *run* applets and applications written in the Java programming language (see Fig. 2.12).

Tools in JDK

The tools available in JDK are split into the following categories:

- Basic tools (javac, java, javadoc, apt, appletviewer, jar, jdb, javah, javap, extcheck)
- Security tools (keytool, jarsigner, policytool, kinit, klist, ktab)
- Internationalization tools (native2ascii)
- Remote Method Invocation (RMI) tools (rmic, rmiregistry, rmid, serialver)
- Java IDL and RMI-IIOP tools (tnameserv, idlj, orbd, servertool)

- Java deployment tools (pack200, unpack200)
- Java plug-in tools (html converter)
- Java Web Start tools (javaws)
- Java Monitoring and Management Console (jconsole)
- Java Web Services tools (schemagen, wsgen, wsimport, xjc)

Basic Tools

Figures 2.12 and 2.13 show the structure of Java and the basic tools available in JDK, respectively.

javac Java complier is named `javac`. The Java compiler takes input source code files (these files typically have the extension `.java`) and converts them into compiled bytecode files (these files have the extension `.class`).

java The Java interpreter, known eponymously as `java`, can be used to execute Java applications. The interpreter translates bytecodes directly into program actions.

javadoc As programmers, we have fought it in every way possible. Unfortunately, there is no longer any excuse for not documenting our source code. Using the `javadoc` utility provided with the JDK, you can easily generate documentation in the form of HTML files. To do this, you embed special comments and tags in your source code and then process your code through `javadoc`. All the online Java API documentation was created with `javadoc`.

apt It stands for Annotation Processing Tool, used for processing annotations.

```
         ┌─User Interface Toolkits
Java     │ ─Integration Libraries
API      │ ─Other Base Libraries
         └─Lang and util Base Libraries

         ┌─Deployment Technologies
JRE      │ ─Java API
         └─Java Virtual Machine

         ┌─Java Language Constructs
JDK      │ ─Tools and Tool APIs
         └─JRE
```

Fig. 2.12 Java Structure

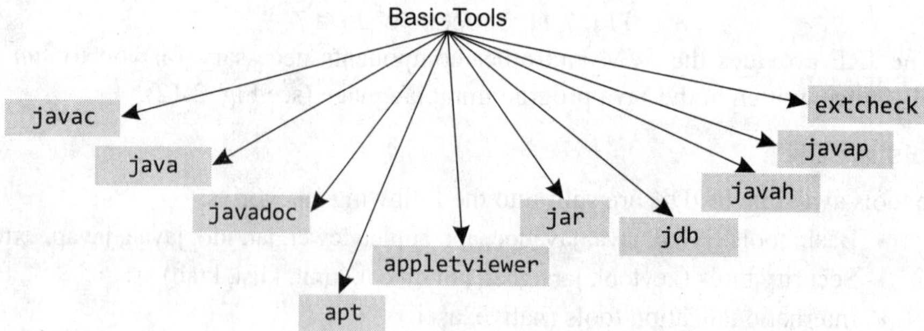

Fig. 2.13 Basic Tools Available in JDK

appletviewer This small program provides a real Java environment for testing applets. It loads the HTML file in which the applet has been embedded and displays the application in a browser-like window.

jar It is used for creating and managing jar (similar to WinZip file) files.

jdb The Java debugger, `jdb`, enables you to debug your Java classes. Unfortunately, the Java debugger is a throwback to the pre-GUI debugger dark ages of programming. The Java debugger is a command-line debugger. You can use the `jdb` to set breakpoints, inspect objects and variables, and monitor threads.

javah Because Java is a new language and must fit in a world dominated by C and C++, it includes the capability to use native C code within a Java class. One of the steps in doing this is by using the Java header file generator, `javah`.

javap One of the basic tenets of object-oriented programming is that programmers unfamiliar with a class need only concern themselves with the public interface of that class. If you want to use a class, you shouldn't be concerned with how this class has been written.

Because you should be interested only in the public interface of a class, the JDK includes a disassembler, `javap`, that can be used to display the public interface, both methods and variables, of a class. Additionally, the Java disassembler includes options to display private members or to display the actual bytecodes for the class's methods. This last option can be particularly useful if you want to achieve a greater understanding of the bytecodes used by the Java interpreter.

extcheck It is used for detecting Jar conflicts.

2.11 INTEGRATED DEVELOPMENT ENVIRONMENT

Integrated development environment (IDE) contains the tools specifically designed for writing Java codes. These tools offer a GUI environment to compile and debug your Java program easily from the editor environment as well as browse through your classes.

New Java IDEs are released every now and then, as Java is accepted as a viable programming language. Some of these IDEs are listed below.

Eclipse It is an open source extensible IDE. At present, it is a Java IDE and includes Java development tools. The requirement is that you should have the JRE installed on your machine. The IDE supports Windows XP, Windows 2000, Windows 7, Vista, Linux, and Solaris.

Gel It is an IDE for Java that features syntax highlighting (Java, JSP, HTML, XML, C, C++, Perl, Python, etc.), unlimited undo and redo, column selection mode, block indent and un-indent, highlighting of matching braces, spell-checking, automatic positioning of closing braces, auto indent, regular expression searches, find in files, code completion (Java and JSP), parameter hints, identifier hints, context-sensitive help linked to Javadoc, class browser, project management, integrated support for ANT and JUnit, differencing tool to compare files, etc. It works only on Windows.

DrJava It is an integrated development environment for Java, released under the GNU GPL that allows you to interactively evaluate Java expressions.

JCreator The light edition of this IDE for Java has support for project management, a syntax highlighting editor, wizards, class viewer, package viewer, tabbed documents, JDK profiles (which allows you to work with multiple JDK), a customizable user interface, etc. JCreator runs on Windows 95, 98, NT, and 2000.

NetBeans It is a cross-platform open source IDE for Java. It comes with a code editor that supports code completion, annotations, macros, auto-indentation, etc. It integrates with compilers, debuggers, JVMs, and other tools.

SUMMARY

Java is a programming language invented by James Gosling and others in 1994. Java was originally named Oak and was developed as a part of the Green Project at the Sun Company. Patrick Naughton, Mike Sheridan, and James Gosling were trying to figure out the next wave in computing and that wave came in 1995, when Java started to be visualized as a language for Internet applications.

It is conceived that Java is a pure object-oriented language, meaning that the outermost level of data structure in Java is the object. Java is designed to be platform independent, so it can run on multiple platforms. The same runtime code can be downloaded on any platform and be executed there, if that platform supports the Java runtime environment. For this, Java incorporates elements of both interpretation and compilation.

At the heart of Java Runtime Environment lies the Java Virtual Machine or JVM. Most programming languages compile source codes directly into machine codes, suitable for execution on a particular microprocessor architecture. But Java is somewhat different, as it uses bytecode—a special type of machine code. Java bytecode executes on a special type of microprocessor. As there was no hardware implementation of this microprocessor available when Java was first released, the complete processor architecture was emulated by a software known as the virtual machine.

Java is a robust language, as its two properties, type checking and interpretation makes Java programs crash-proof. Java has several other features that protect the integrity of the security system and prevent several common attacks. Java is inherently multithreaded, i.e., multiple threads developed in this language can be executed concurrently.

Other features of Java include automatic memory management, dynamic binding, optimal performance, built-in networking capabilities, etc. The garbage collector relieves the programmers from memory deallocation. Java uses references instead of pointers.

Every Java program consists of one or more classes. A class is nothing but a template for creating objects. In Java, codes reside inside a class. The name of the class must match with the name of the file.

EXERCISES

Objective Questions

1. What was the name of first version of Java?
   - (a) Oak
   - (b) Mustang
   - (c) Tiger
   - (d) Playground

2. What was the name of the team that developed Java?
   - (a) Green Team
   - (b) Star Seven
   - (c) Sun
   - (d) Java team

3. What is the name of the tool that is used for compiling a Java program?
   - (a) javap
   - (b) java
   - (c) javah
   - (d) javac

4. What is the name of the tool that is used for interpreting a Java program?
   - (a) javap
   - (b) java
   - (c) javah
   - (d) javac

5. What process automatically removes objects that are not being referenced?
   - (a) Multithreading
   - (b) Object Reclamation

(c) Garbage collection (d) Object collection

6. What is the name of the tool that is used for running Applets?
   (a) javap   (b) javac
   (c) java   (d) appletviewer

7. What is the extension of the source files in Java?
   (a) .jav   (b) .java
   (c) .bytecode   (d) .class

8. What is the extension of the bytecode files in Java?
   (a) .jav   (b) .java
   (c) .class   (d) .bytecode

9. Which all are correct for main method?
   (a) public static void main(String args[])
   (b) private static void main(String args[])
   (c) static void main(String args[])
   (d) public static void main(String a[])

10. Which of the following are added in Java 7?
    (a) String in switch case
    (b) meta data
    (c) annotations
    (d) automatic resource management

Review Questions

1. Why is Java known as a platform-independent language?
2. Explain the security model of Java that makes it more secured than other languages.
3. Why is Java known to be multithreading? How does it help Java in its performance?
4. C++ is an object-oriented language older than Java, then why did Java replace C++ in most of the application development?
5. Java had middle-tier capabilities. What does this statement mean?
6. Java was used in Internet applications. Cite reasons.
7. Explain the importance of JVM in JRE.
8. Explain the structure of a Java program.
9. Explain the steps for executing a Java program.
10. What is the importance of setting environment variables such as Path and Classpath?
11. Discuss the tools available in JDK. How do they help in application development?

Programming Exercise

1. Write a program to print 'Welcome' followed by your name and 'How are you?'

Answers to Objective Questions

1. (a)	**2.** (a)	**3.** (d)	**4.** (b)
5. (c)	**6.** (d)	**7.** (b)	**8.** (c)
9. (a) and (d)	**10.** (a) and (d)		

Java Programming Constructs

> *I often say . . . that when you can measure what you are speaking about, and express it in numbers, you know something about it; but when you cannot measure it, when you cannot express it in numbers, your knowledge is of a meager and unsatisfactory kind; it may be the beginning of knowledge, but you have scarcely, in your thoughts, advanced to the stage of science, whatever the matter may be.* **Lord Kelvin**

After reading this chapter, the readers will be able to

- understand how variables are used in
- know the basic data types
- learn expressions and conditional statements
- use all the available operations in Java
- know the basics of conversion and casting
- understand loops and branching statements

3.1 VARIABLES

Variable is a symbolic name refer to a memory location used to store values that can change during the execution of a program. Java declares its variables in the following manner:

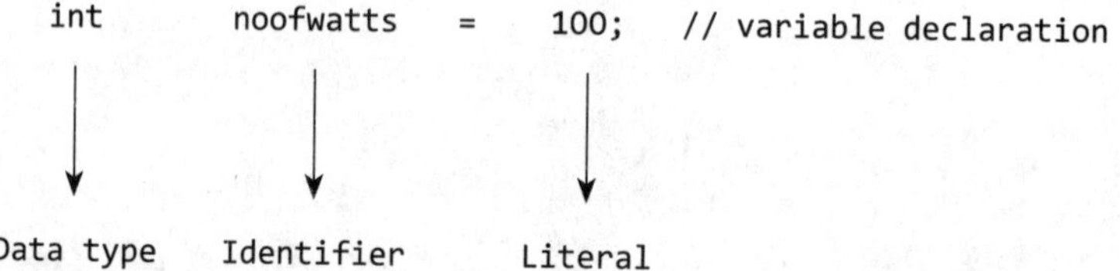

A variable declaration involves specifying the type (data type), name (identifier), and value (literal) according to the type of the variable. Let us have a look at the three components in detail.

3.2 PRIMITIVE DATA TYPES

Primitive data types are the basic building blocks of any programming language. A primitive data type can have only one value at a time and is the simplest built-in form of data within Java.

All variables in Java have to be declared before they can be used, that is why Java is termed as a *strongly typed language*. There are eight primitive data types in Java, as follows:

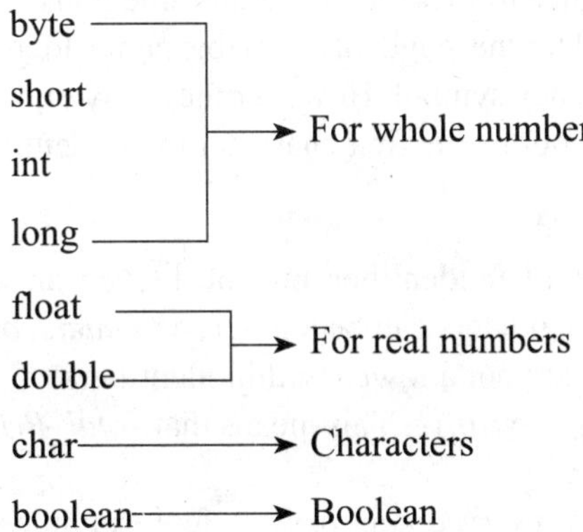

Java is portable across computer platforms. C and C++ leave the size of data types to the machine and the compiler, but Java specifies everything.

> **Note** All integer (byte, short, int, long) and floating-point types (float, double) are signed in Java.

byte It is a 1-byte (8-bit) signed 2's complement integer. It ranges from –128 to 127 (inclusive). The **byte** data type can be used where the memory savings actually matter.

short It is a 2-byte (16-bit) signed 2's complement integer. It ranges from –32,768 to 32,767 (inclusive). As with **byte**, you can use a **short** to save memory.

int It is a 4-byte (32-bit) signed 2's complement integer. It ranges from –2,147,483,648 to 2,147,483,647 (inclusive). For integral values, this data type is the default choice.

long It is an 8-byte (64-bit) signed 2's complement integer. It ranges from –9,223,372,036,854,775,808 to 9,223,372,036,854,775,807 (inclusive). This data type should be used only when you need a range of values wider than **int**.
Floating point conforms to the IEEE 754-1985 binary floating point standard.

float It is a single-precision 32-bit floating point. It ranges from 1.401298464324817e–45f to 3.402823476638528860e+38f.

double This data type is a double-precision 64-bit floating point. It ranges from 4.94065645841246544e–324 to 1.79769313486231570e (+) 308. For decimal numbers, this data type is the default choice.

boolean It has only two possible values: **true** and **false**. The size of this data type is not precisely defined.

char The unsigned **char** data type is a single 16-bit unicode character. It ranges from '\u0000' (or 0) to '\uffff' (or 65,535 inclusive).

> **Note** Unlike C/C++, where handling of character sequences is tedious, Java provides a class named "String" for handling character strings enclosed within double quotes. Although it is not a primitive data type, Java string solves much of the complexity with ease.

3.3 IDENTIFIER

Identifiers are names assigned to variables, constants, methods, classes, packages, and interfaces. No limit has been specified for the length of a variable name. Identifiers can have letters, numbers, underscores, and any currency symbol. However they may only begin with a letter, underscore, or a dollar sign. Digits cannot be the first character in an identifier.

3.3.1 Rules for Naming

1. The first character of an identifier must be a *letter*, an *underscore*, or a *dollar sign* ($).
2. The subsequent characters can be a *letter*, an *underscore*, *dollar sign*, or a *digit*. Note that *white spaces* are not allowed within identifiers.
3. Identifiers are *case-sensitive*. This means that *Total_Price* and *total_price* are different identifiers.

   Do not use Java's *reserved keywords*. A few examples of legal and illegal identifiers are shown below.

Legal Identifiers	Illegal Identifiers
MyClass	My Class
$amount	23amount
_totalPay	-totalpay
total_Commission	total@commission

3.3.2 Naming Convention

Names should be kept according to their usage, as it is meaningful and easy to remember as shown in Fig. 3.1.

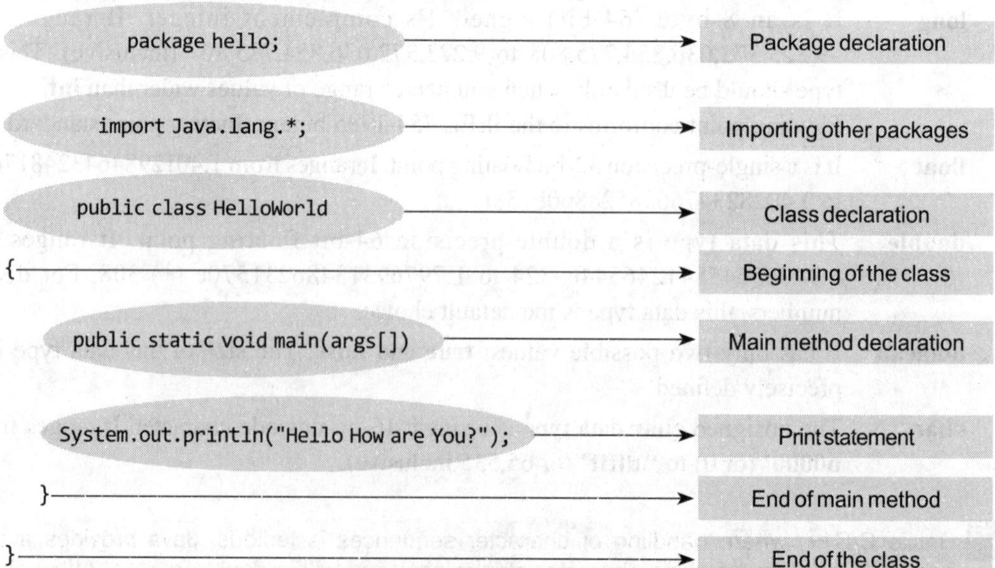

Fig. 3.1 Naming Convention Used in Java

Class or Interface Identifiers These begin with a capital letter. The first alphabet of every internal word is capitalized. All other letters are in lower case.

```
public class MyClass          // class identifier: MyClass
interface Calculator;         // interface identifier: Calculator
```

Variable or Method Identifiers These start with a lower-case letter. The first alphabet of every internal word is capitalized. All other letters are in lower case.

```
int totalPay;                                // variable identifier: totalPay
MyClass.showResult();
// MyClass is the Class Name and showResult() is a method of MyClass.
```

Constant Identifiers These are specified in upper case. Underscores are used to separate internal words.

```
final double TAX_RATE = 0.05;                // constant identifier: TAX_RATE
```

Package Identifiers These consist of all lower-case letters.

```
package mypackage.subpackage.subpackage;     //Package Declaration
```

3.3.3 Keywords

Keywords are predefined identifiers meant for a specific purpose and cannot be used for identifying used defined classes, variables, methods, packages, and interfaces. All keywords are in lower case. Table 3.1 lists the keywords in Java.

Table 3.1 Keywords in Java

abstract	assert	boolean	break	byte
case	catch	char	class	continue
default	do	double	else	enum
extends	final	finally	float	for
if	implements	import	instanceof	int
interface	long	native	new	package
private	protected	public	return	short
static	strictfp	super	switch	synchronized
this	throw	throws	transient	try
void	volatile	while	const*	goto*
*const and goto are reserved keywords.				

3.4 LITERALS

A literal is a value that can be passed to a variable or constant in a program. Literals can be numeric (for byte, short, int, long, float, double), boolean, character, string notations or null literals. **Numeric Literals** can be represented in binary, decimal, octal, or hexadecimal notations. These literals can be assigned to all numeric types in Java including char (based on their respective range and size).

Binary literals are a combination of 0's and 1's. Binary literals can be assigned to variables in Java 7. Binary literals must be prefixed with 0b or 0B (zerob or zeroB). For example,

```
char bin1 = 0b1010000;          // value in bin1 will be P
char bin2 = 0b1010001;          // value in bin2 will be Q
float bin3 = 0b1010000;         // value in bin3 will be 80.0
int bin4 = 0b1010001;           // value in bin4 will be 81
```

In case *octal literals* have to be specified, the value must be prefixed with a zero and only digits from 0 to 7 are allowed.

For example,

```
int x = 011;            //value in x is 9
char y=0150;            // value in y will be h
float z=0234;           // value in z will be 156.0
```

Hexadecimal literals are prefixed with *0x* or *0X*; the digits 0 through 9 and *a* through *f* (or *A* through *F*) are only allowed. For example,

```
int y = 0x0001;         //value in y is 1
char x=0x45;            // value in x will be E
float y=0xA3;           // value in y will be 163.0
```

All *integer literals* are of type **int**, by default. To define them as long, we can place a suffix of *L* or *l* after the number for instance:

```
long l = 2345678998L;
```

All *floating literals* are of type **double**, by default. To define them as float literals, we need to attach the suffix *F* or *f*. For double literals, *D* or *d* are suffixed at the end; however, it is optional. For instance,

```
float f = 23.6F;
double d = 23.6;
```

Java 7 onwards the readability of literals can be enhanced by using underscore with numeric literals. As the number of zeroes increase in a literal, counting the number of zeroes becomes tedious. In such big literals, underscores can be used as shown below:

```
int numlit=100_000_000;         // value in numlit will be 100000000
```

Underscores can be used not only with decimal literals but also with hexa, binary, and octal literals as shown below:

```
int numlit=0x100_000;                    // value in numlit1 will be 1048576
int bin=0B1_000_000_000_000_000_001;     // vale in bin will be 32769
float octlit=03_000;                     // value in octlit will be 1536.0
```


The following examples show some valid and invalid use of underscores.

```
int i =_23;                 // illegal, cannot start a literal with underscore
long f = 3_2_222_2_1;       // invalid use of underscore between value and suffix
long f = 3_2_222_21;        // legal
float e = 4_.2_3f;          // illegal use of underscore with a dot
```

```
float d = 4_2.2_3f;        // legal
float e = 4_2.2_3_f        // illegal
int i = 0_x_A_E;           // illegal use of underscore in prefix
int j = 0x_A_E;            // illegal use of prefix between prefix and literal
int k = 0xA_E;             // legal
```

For *char literals*, a single character is enclosed in single quotes. You can also use the prefix **\u** followed by four hexadecimal digits representing the 16-bit unicode character:

```
char c = '\u004E'; char sample = 'A'; char example = 'a';
```

A single quote, a backslash or a unprintable character (such as a horizontal tab) can be specified as a character literal with the help of an escape sequence. An *escape sequence* represents a character by using a special syntax that begins with a single backslash character. Unicode is a type of escape sequence (refer Table 3.2). Furthermore, the syntax of unicode escape sequence consists of **\uxxxx** (where each **x** represents a hexadecimal digit).

Table 3.2 Unicode Escape Sequences to Represent Printable and Unprintable Characters

'\u0041'	Capital letter A
'\u0030'	Digit 0
'\u0022'	Double quote "
'\u003b'	Punctuation ;
'\u0020'	Space
'\u0009'	Horizontal Tab

Table 3.3 Special Escape Sequences

\\	Backslash
\"	Double quote
\'	Single quote
\b	Backspace
\f	Form feed
\n	New line
\r	Carriage return
\t	Horizontal tab

For instance, `char c = '\t'; //` creates a character that represents horizontal tab (Refer Table 3.3).

Unicode characters can be assigned to strings in Java 7. Unicode 6, which has thousands of characters, cannot be accommodated in a 16-bit char data type. Increasing the size of char data type would lead to backward compatibility problems. To maintain compatibility with the application and standards, the string ("U+hex") is used to express unicode characters in Java.

A *boolean literal* is specified as either **true** or **false**. By default, it takes the value false (Refer Table 3.4). The following code fragment demonstrates a boolean literal:

```
boolean firstRoll = true;
```

String literals consist of zero or more characters within double quotes. For instance,

```
String s = "This is a String Literal";
```

Null literals are assigned to object reference variables (see Chapter 4 for object references).

```
s = null;
```

Table 3.4 shows a summary of the data types along with their respective default values, size, and range.

Table 3.4 Data Types: Size, Default Value, and Range

Data Type	Default Value	Size	Range
byte	0	8	–128 to 127 (inclusive)
short	0	16	–32,768 to 32,767 (inclusive)
int	0	32	–2,147,483,648 to 2,147,483,647 (inclusive)
long	0L	64	–9,223,372,036,854,775,808 to 9,223,372,036,854,775,807 (inclusive)
float	0.0F	32	1.401298464324817e–45f to 3.4028234766385288860e+38f
double	0.0D	64	4.94065645841246544e–324 to 1.79769313486231570e+308
char	'\u0000'	16	0 to 65535
boolean	false	Not defined	true or false

Table 3.5 lists the reserved literals in Java.

Table 3.5 Reserved Literals.

true	false	null

3.5 OPERATORS

An operator performs an action on one or more operands. An operator that performs an action on one operand is called a *unary operator* (+, –, ++, – –). An operator that performs an action on two operands is called a *binary operator* (+, –, / , * , and more). An operator that performs an action on three operands is called a *ternary operator* (? :). Java provides all the three operators. Let us begin the discussion with binary operators.

3.5.1 Binary Operators

Java provides *arithmetic, assignment, relational, shift, conditional, bitwise,* and *member access* operators.

Assignment Operators

It sets the value of a variable (or expression) to some new value. The simple '=' operator sets the left-hand operand to the value of the right-hand operand. The assignment operator has right to left associativity (discussed in Section 3.7); so the statement a = b = 0; would assign 0 to b then b to a. Java supports the following list of *shortcut* or *compound* assignment operators:

```
+= –= *= /= %= &= |= ^= <<=>>= >>>=
```

These operators allow you to combine two operations into one: one fixed as assignment plus another one. These operators will be explained shortly according to their counterparts.

Arithmetic Operators

Arithmetic operators are used for adding (+), subtracting (–), multiplying (*), dividing (/), and finding the remainder (%).

Java does not support operator overloading. There are certain languages like C++ that allow programmers to change the meaning of operators enabling them to act in more than one way depending upon the operands. But there are certain operators which are overloaded by Java itself like + operator which behaves differently when applied to different operands. For example, if + operator is used and one of the operands is a string, then the other operand is converted to a `String` automatically and concatenated. It is evident in the following examples in the `System.out.println` statement when the `String` in the quotes is concatenated with the values of the result or individual primitives. In addition to these operators, arithmetic compound assignment operators are also provided by Java: +=, – =, /=, *=, %=. For example,

```
a += b;              // evaluated as a = a + b;
a -= b;              // evaluated as a = a - b;
a *= b;              // evaluated as a = a * b;
a /= b;              // evaluated as a = a / b;
a % = b;             // evaluated as a = a % b
```

Let us take an example to demonstrate the use of these operators in Java. A close look at the program will show us that the + operator can be used for two purposes: concatenation and addition in the print statements.

Example 3.1 **Demonstration of Arithmetic Operators**

```
class ArithmeticDemo{
  public static void main(String args[]){

      int a = 25, b = 10;
      System.out.println("Sum "+ a +" +" + b +" = " + (a + b));
      //adding two variables a and b

      System.out.println("Subtraction "+ a +" - " + b +" = " + (a - b));

      //multiplying a with b
      System.out.println("Multiplication "+ a +" * " + b +" = " + (a * b));

      // Division
      System.out.println("Division "+ a +" / " + b +" = " + (a / b));

      // Remainder Operator
      System.out.println("Remainder "+ a +" % " + b +" = " + (a % b));

      // a and b can be added and the result can be placed in a
      // Let us see how?
      a += b;
      System.out.println("Added b to a and stored the result in a" + a);
  }
}
```

Output

```
C:\Javaprg\>Java ArithmeticDemo
Sum 25 + 10 = 35
Subtraction 25 - 10 = 15
Multiplication 25 * 10 = 250
Division 25 / 10 = 2
Remainder 25 % 10 = 5
Added b to a and stored the result in a 35
```

Figure 3.2 shows how the '+' operator concatenates and adds the operands.

```
System.out.println("Sum "+ a +" and " + b +" = " + (a + b));
```

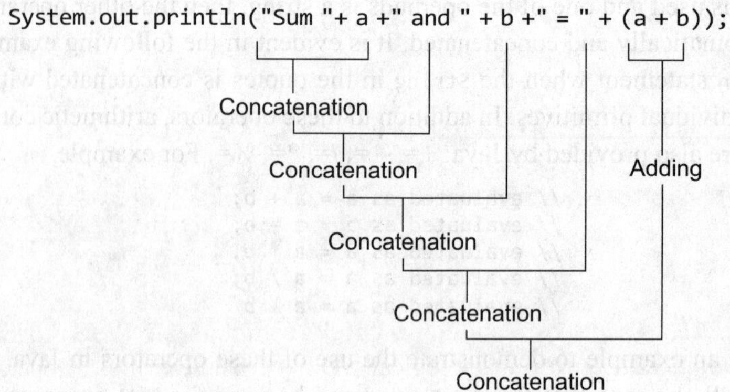

Fig. 3.2 The Operation of '+' Operator

Relational Operators

Relational operators in Java return either *true* or *false* as a boolean type. Table 3.6 shows a list of all the relational operators in Java.

Relational operators in C++ returns an integer where the integer value of zero may be interpreted as false and any non-zero value may be interpreted as true.

Table 3.6 Relational Operators

equal to	==
Not equal to	!=
less than	<
greater than	>
less than or equal to	<=
greater than or equal to	>=

Example 3.2 **Demonstration of Relational Operators**

```
class RelationalOperatorDemo
{
    public static void main(String args[])
    {

    int a = 10,b = 20;
    System.out.println("Equality Operator: a == b : \t\t\t" +(a == b));
    System.out.println("Not Equal To Operator: a != b : \t\t" +(a != b));
    System.out.println("Less Than Operator: a == b : \t\t\t" +(a < b));
    System.out.println("Greater Than Operator: a == b : \t\t" +(a > b));
    System.out.println("Less than or equal to Operator: a == b : \t" +(a <= b));
    System.out.println("Greater than or equal to Operator: a == b : \t" +(a >= b));
    }

}
```

Output

```
C:\Javaprg\>Java RelationalOperatorDemo
Equality Operator: a == b :                 false
Not Equal To Operator: a != b :             true
Less Than Operator: a == b :                true
Greater Than Operator: a == b :             false
Less than or equal to Operator: a == b :    true
Greater than or equal to Operator: a == b : false
```

Boolean Logical Operators

Boolean logical operators are: conditional OR (||), conditional AND (&&), logical OR (|), logical AND (&), logical XOR (^), unary logical NOT (!). Boolean logical operators are applied to boolean operands or expressions (Section 3.6) and return a boolean value. The bitwise logical AND (&), logical OR (|), logical XOR (^) and logical NOT (~) operators are applied to integers to perform bitwise logical operations discussed later.

Logical OR results in true if one of the operands is true. **Logical AND** results in false if one of the operands is false. **Logical XOR** works like OR with an exception, that is, in case if both the operands of an XOR operator are true then the answer is false. **Logical NOT** is just the compliment of the boolean operand.

Conditional OR (||) and AND (&&) operators also known as *short-circuit operators* conditionally evaluate the second operand or expression. In case of OR, if the first operand is true, no matter what the second operand is, the answer is true. In case of AND, if the first operand is false, no matter what the second operand is, the answer is false. So there is no need to evaluate the second operand.

In addition to these operators, boolean compound assignment operators are also provided by Java: &=, |=, ^=. For example,

```
a &= b;     // evaluated as a = a & b;
a |= b;     // evaluated as a = a | b;
a ^= b;     // evaluated as a = a ^ b;
```

Example 3.3 **Demonstration of Boolean Operators**

```java
class BooleanLogicalOperatorDemo
{
    public static void main(String args[])
    {
    boolean a = true,b = false;
    System.out.println("Logical OR: "+ a +" | "+b+": " +(a|b));
    System.out.println("Logical XOR: "+ a +" ^ "+b+": "+(a^b));
    System.out.println("Logical AND: "+ a +" & "+b+": "+(a&b));
    System.out.println("Logical NOT: !a : "+(!a));
    System.out.println("Conditional OR: "+ a +" || "+b+": "+(a||b));
    System.out.println("Conditional AND: "+ a +" && "+b+": "+(a&&b));
    // shortcut operator
    a |= b;
    System.out.println("Shortcut OR: "+ a +" | "+b+" = "+(a));
    }
}
```

Output

```
Logical OR: true | false: true
Logical XOR: true ^ false: true
Logical AND: true & false: false
Logical NOT: !a : false
Conditional OR: true || false: true
Conditional AND: true && false: false
Shortcut OR: true | false = true
```

Bitwise Operators

Bitwise operators include *and, or, xor, not, right shift, left shift,* and *unsigned right shift*. In Java, *bitwise* operators operate on `int` and `long` values. If any of the operand is shorter than an `int`, it is automatically promoted to `int` before the operations are performed (see Section 3.8). Table 3.7 lists the bitwise operators and how they function.

> **Note** It is important to understand how integers are represented in binary. For example, the decimal number 4 is represented as 100 in binary and 5 is represented as 101. Negative integers are always represented in 2's complement form. For example, −4 is 1111 1111 1111 1111 1111 1111 1111 1100.

Bitwise shortcut operators are used in the same way as boolean operators. Bitwise shortcut operators include the following:

```
AND: &=
OR: |=
XOR: ^=
Shift Operator: >>=,<<=,>>>=
```

Table 3.7 Bitwise Operators

a & b	1 if both bits are 1
a | b	1 if either of the bits is 1
a ^ b	1 if both bits are different
~a	Complement the bits.
a << b	Shift the bits left by b positions. Zero bits are added from the LSB side. Bits are discarded from the MSB side.
a >> b	Shift the bits right by b positions. Sign bits are copied from the MSB side. Bits discarded from the LSB side.
a >>> b	Shift the bits right by b positions. Zero bits are added from the MSB side. Bits are discarded from the LSB side.

Example 3.4 Demonstration of Bitwise Operators

```java
class BitwiseOperatorDemo
{
    public static void main(String args[])
    {
        int x = 2,y = 3;
        System.out.println("Bitwise AND: " +x+ "&" +y+ " = " +(x&y));
```

```java
        System.out.println("Bitwise OR :" +x+ "|" +y+ " = " +(x|y));
        System.out.println("Bitwise XOR:" +x+ "^" +y+ " = " +(x^y));
        System.out.println("Bitwise NOT: ~" +x+ "=" +(~x));
    }
}
```

Output

```
Bitwise AND: 2&3 = 2
Bitwise OR : 2|3 = 3
Bitwise XOR: 2^3 = 1
Bitwise NOT: ~2=-3
```

Shift operators shift the bits depending upon the type of operator. The left shift operator shifts the numbers of bits specified towards the left. Bits are discarded from the left and added from the right with the value of bits being zero. The right shift operator shifts the numbers of bits specified towards right. Bits are discarded from the right and added from the left side with the value of bits being that of the sign bit. The unsigned right shift shifts the numbers of bits specified towards right. Bits are discarded from the right and added from the left side with the value of bits being zero. For example, let us assume $x = 4$ and this x is to be shifted by the shift distance of 1.

```java
int y = x >> 1;
//y has the value 2, value is halved in each successive right shift
      = 00000000 00000000 00000000 00000100 >> 1
      = 00000000 00000000 00000000 00000010 (which is 2)
int y = x << 1;
// y has the value 8, value is doubled in each successive left shift

int y = x >> 1;        // same as right shift for positive numbers.
```

If we provide a negative number to be left or right shifted, then the negative numbers are represented in 2's compliment arithmetic and then shifted. If we provide an `int` negative shift distance as shown in the following example, first the negative shift distance is ANDed with the mask 11111 (i.e., 31) and the result is the new shift distance. If we provide a `long` negative shift distance as shown in the following example, first the negative shift distance is ANDed with the mask 111111 (i.e., 63), and the result is the new shift distance.

Example 3.5 Shift Operators

```java
class ShiftOperatorDemo
{
    public static void main(String args[])
    {
        int x = 5,y = 1;
        System.out.println("Left shift: "+x+"<<"+y+"="+(x<<y));
        System.out.println("Right shift: "+x+" >> "+y+"="+(x >> y));
        System.out.println("Unsigned Right Shift: "+x+" >>> "+y+"="+(x >>> y));

        //negative numbers
```

```
System.out.println("Right Shift: -"+x+" >> "+y+"="+(-x >> y));
System.out.println("Unsigned Right Shift: -"+x+" >>> "+y+"="+(-x >>> y));
System.out.println("Left shift: -"+x+" << "+y+"="+(-x << y));

//negative shift distance of -31 actually means shifting 1 bit
System.out.println("Left shift:"+x+"<<-31 ="+(x << -31));
    }
}
```

Output

```
Left shift: 5 << 1 = 10
Right shift: 5 >> 1 = 2
Unsigned Right Shift: 5 >>> 1 = 2
Right Shift: -5 >> 1 = -3
Unsigned Right Shift: -5 >>> 1 = 2147483645
Left shift: -5 << 1 = -10
Left shift: 5 << -31 = 10
```

Bitwise operators are particularly used where bit-level or low-level programming is required such as writing device drivers, working with embedded systems, compression of data, encryption and decryption of data, setting mask and flags, and creating networking protocols for communication.

3.5.2 Unary Operators

Unary operators, as the name suggest, are applied to only one operand. They are as follows: ++, - -, !, and ~. The unary boolean logical not (!) and bitwise logical not (~) have already been discussed.

Increment and Decrement Operators

Increment and decrement operators can be applied to all integers and floating-point types. They can be used either in prefix (- -x, ++x) or postfix (x- -, x++) mode.

Prefix Increment/Decrement Operation

```
int x = 2;
int y = ++x; // x = 3, y = 3
int z = --x; // x = 1, z = 1
```

Postfix Increment/Decrement Operation

```
int x = 2;
int y = x++; // x == 3, y == 2
int z = x--; // x = 1, z = 2
```

We will discuss these operators in Example 3.6.

3.5.3 Ternary Operators

Ternary operators are applied to three operands. This conditional operator (? :) decides, on the basis of the first expression, which of the two expressions to be evaluated.

```
operand1 ? operand2 : operand3
```

`operand1` must be of boolean type or an expression producing a boolean result. If `operand1` is true, then `operand2` is returned. If `operand1` is false, then `operand3` is returned. This operator is similar to an `if` conditional statement. For example,

```
String greater = x < y ? "Y is greater" : " X is greater";
```

If the value of x is less than y, "Y is greater" string is retuned and stored in the variable: greater, else "X is greater" is retuned and stored in the variable: greater.

3.6 EXPRESSIONS

An *expression* is a combination of operators and/or operands. Java expressions are used to create objects, arrays, pass values to methods and call them, assigning values to variables, and so on. Expressions may contain identifiers, types, literals, variables, separators, and operators (we have already discussed all these topics). For example,

```
int m = 2,n = 3,o = 4;
int y = m * n * o;
```

`m=2` is an expression which assigns the value 2 to variable `m`. Similarly, `n=3` and `o=4` are expressions where `n` and `o` are being assigned values 3 and 4. `m * n * o` is also an expression wherein the values of `m`, `n`, and `o` are multiplied and the result is stored in the variable `y`.

3.7 PRECEDENCE RULES AND ASSOCIATIVITY

Precedence rules are used to determine the order of evaluation priority in case there are two operators with different precedence. Associativity rules are used to determine the order of evaluation if the precedence of operators is same. Associativity is of two types: Left and Right. *Left associativity* means operators are evaluated from left to right and vice versa for right associativity. Precedence and associativity can be overridden with the help of parentheses.

Table 3.8 Precedence Rule and Associativity

Operators	Associativity
`., [], (args), i++, i--`	L R
`++i, --i, +i, -i, ~, !`	R L
`new, (type)`	R L
`*, /, %`	L R
`+, -`	L R
`<<, >>, >>>`	L R
`<, >, <=, >=, instanceof`	Non Associative
`= =, ! =`	L R
`&`	L R
`^`	L R
`|`	L R
`&&`	L R
`||`	L R
`? :`	R L
`=, +=, -=, *=, /=, %=, <<=, >>=, >>>=, &=, ^=, |=`	R L

Table 3.8 lists the operators in Java according to their precedence (from highest to lowest) and their respective associativity's. Operators in a row have same precedence.

Here L → R indicates associativity from left to right and R → L indicates associativity from right to left.

Example 3.6 Precedence Rules

```
class AssociativityAndPrecedenceTest
{
public static void main(String[] args)
{
//precedence of * is more than that of +
```

L1
```
        System.out.println(" 2 + 3 * 2 = \t " + (2 + 3 * 2));
```

```
        //Associativity applies in case of operators with equal
        //Precedence. below is a case of Left Associativity
```
L2
```
        System.out.println(" 2 * 5 / 3 = \t " + (2 * 5 / 3 ));
```

```
        // Precedence overridden with help of parentheses
```
L3
```
        System.out.println("(2 + 3) * 2 = \t " + ((2 + 3) * 2));
        int x;
        int y = 3;
        int z = 1;
        //Assignment associates from right to left
```

L4
```
        x = y = z;
```
L5
```
        System.out.println(" x = y = z: \t" + x);
```

```
        //+ and - have left associativity
```
L6
```
        System.out.println(" 3 - 2  + 1 = \t " + (3 - 2 + 1));
```

```
        //evaluating long expressions to check Precedence and Associativity
        int i = 10;
        int j = 0;
        int result = 0;
```

L7
```
        result = i-- + i / 2 - ++i + j++ + ++j;
        System.out.println("i: " +i+ " j " +j+ " result: "+result );
```

```
        // + operator has a left to right associativity
```
L8
```
        System.out.println("Hello "+1+2);
```

```
        // First two numbers are added and the added result is concatenated with
        // String "Hello"
```

L9
```
        System.out.println(1+2+" Hello");

    }
}
```

Output

```
C:\Javabook\programs\chap3>Java AssociativityAndPrecedenceTest
2 + 3 * 2 = 8
```

```
2 * 5 / 3 = 3
(2 + 3) * 2 = 10
x = y = z: 1
3 - 2 + 1 = 2
i: 10 j 2 result: 6
Hello 12
3 Hello
```

Explanation

L1 Shows the precedence of * is more than +, that is why 3 is first multiplied with 2 and the result (6) is added with 2 and then printed.

L2 Shows two operators with equal precedence, * and /. In this case, associativity plays a role instead of precedence. As is evident from Table 3.9, * and / have left associativity, so the operators will be evaluated from the left side. That is why 2 is multiplied with 5 first and then the result (10) is divided by 3 to give the integer quotient 3, which is then printed.

L3 Shows the precedence of (nudge) is more than * and + (or any other operator, refer Table 3.9). In this case, operation within parentheses is performed first, that is, 2 is added to 3 and then the result (5) is multiplied with 2 to give 10 which is then printed. Also note that when no parentheses were used in L1, the answer was 8.

L4 Shows the assignment operator which is right associative, so first the value of z is assigned to y and then the value of y is assigned to x.

L6 Portrays the case of same precedence, so associativity is used for expression evaluation. Table 3.9 shows + and − have left associativity, so 2 is subtracted from 3 first and then the result (1) is added to 1 to output 2, which is then printed on the screen.

L7 In this expression, i-- + i / 2 - ++i + j++ + ++j, the decremented value of i will be reflected while evaluating the sub-expression i/2, i.e., i--+i/2 will be evaluated as 10 + 9/2 (result of sub-expression is 14). At this point i will have the value 9. While evaluating ++i, the value of i is incremented first and then added, so the value of i becomes 10 again (result of expression at this point is 14 − 10 = 4). The value of j (i.e. 0) is added to the expression first and then incremented in the sub-expression j++. Now j has the value 1 (result of expression at this point i-- + i/2 - ++i + j++is 4). In the last sub-expression ++j, the value of j (which is 1 now) is incremented first and then added to the expression (value of j is now 2 which is added to 4 to produce 6 as the result).

L8 & 9 Show the usage of + operator between different operands. The important point to note is that associativity and not precedence will be used for evaluating expression. The associativity of + operator is from left to right, so the String "Hello" is concatenated to 1 first and then String "Hello 1" is concatenated to the second number 2. In L9, the numbers are added first and then the sum is concatenated with the String.

3.8 PRIMITIVE TYPE CONVERSION AND CASTING

In Java, type conversions are performed automatically when the type of the expression on the right-hand-side of an assignment operation can be safely promoted to the type of the variable on the left-hand-side of the assignment.

$$\text{char} \searrow$$
$$\text{byte} \rightarrow \text{short} \rightarrow \text{int} \rightarrow \text{long} \rightarrow \text{float} \rightarrow \text{double} \quad \text{Widening conversion}$$

Conversions that are implicit in nature are termed as *widening conversions*. In an assignment statement, the types of the left-hand-side and right-hand-side must be compatible. If the right-hand-side can fit inside the left-hand-side, the assignment is completed. For example, a smaller box can be placed in a bigger box and so on. A byte value can be placed in short, short in an `int` , int in `long` , and so on (see widening conversion). Any value can be assigned to a double. Any value except a double can be assigned to a float. Any whole number value can be assigned to a long; and int, short, byte, and char can all fit inside `int`. For example,

```
byte b = 10;          // byte variable
int i = b;            // implicit widening byte to int
```

Type conversion or promotion also takes place while evaluating the expressions involving arithmetic operators. For example,

```
int i = 10;           //int variable
double d = 20;        //int literal assigned to a double variable
d = i + d;            //automatic conversion int to double
```

In the previous statement, the `int` value *i* is promoted to double and then the two double values (i & d) are added to produce a double result. The basic rule is that if either of the variables in a binary operation (involving arithmetic, relational, equality) is `double`, then Java treats both values as `double`. If neither value is a `double` but one is a `float`, then Java treats both values as `float`. If neither is a `float` or a `double` but one is a `long`, then Java treats both values as `long`. Finally, if there are no `double`, `float`, or `long`, then Java treats both values as an `int`, even if there are no `int` in the expression. Therefore, the result will be a `double`, `float`, `long` or `int` depending on the types of the operands. For example, consider the following declarations:

```
byte b = 10;
short s = 30;
```

The following statement is invalid because while evaluating the expression, `byte` and `short` are automatically promoted to `int`, so the result is an `int` and `short` is used to store the result which is smaller than `int`.

```
short z = b*s;        //invalid
int i = b*s;          //valid
```

In case of bitwise `and`, `or`, `xor`, if one of the operand is broader than `int`, then both operands are converted to `long`; else both are converted to `int`. If bitwise `not` operator is applied to an operand shorter than `int`, it is promoted to `int` automatically. In case of shift operators, if a single operand has a type narrower than `int` then it is also promoted to `int`, otherwise not.

Let us take an interesting case

```
float f=3;            // legal; int literal assigned to a float variable
```

The last declaration of a float variable shows that suffix `f` of `F` was not used while assigning value and yet it was considered a legal statement. The reason is because 3 is an `int` and an `int` value can be directly assigned to a `float`. But if the declaration would have been

```
float f = 3.0;        // illegal;
```

Note Java treats all real numbers as `double` so 3.0 is treated as `double`, which cannot be assigned directly to a `float`, as `float` is smaller than `double`. There are two possible solutions which can be applied to the above statement: (a) suffix F or f with the literal i.e. 3.0f (b) cast it.

```
float f = 3.0f;        // legal;
```

Casting is also known as *narrowing conversion* (reverse of *widening conversion*).

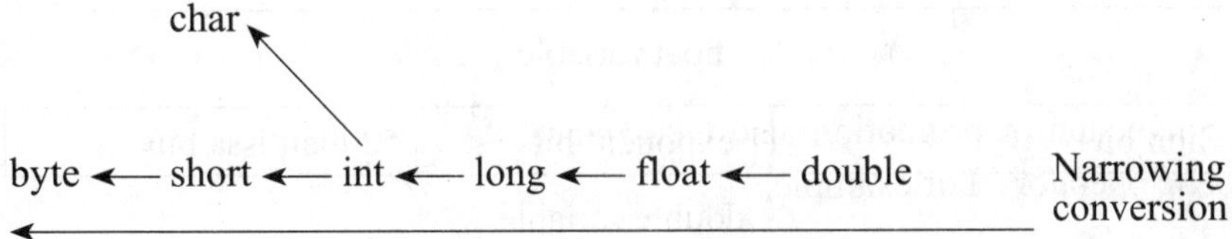

If you want to assign `long` values to `int` variables or `double` values to `float` variables, then the compiler will not allow you to do so unless you explicitly tell it that you really want to do so with the help of a cast. When it is necessary to put a bigger value into a particular smaller type, use a cast. For example, consider the reverse of the box example. A bigger box has to be placed in a small box. Then the bigger box has to be chopped so that the bigger box (which has now become smaller) can be placed in the small box. Casting is not implicit in nature. It has to be explicitly mentioned by preceding it with the destination type specified in the parentheses. For instance,

```
int i = (int)(8.0/3.0);
```

A cast lets the compiler know that you are serious about the conversion you plan to make. When a value is cast before assignment, the right hand side is chopped down to fit into the left hand side. For casting a floating-point number to an `int` or a `long`, the fractional part is truncated resulting in an integer. If the resulting integer is small enough to fit in the left hand side, the assignment is completed. But if the number is too large, then the integer is set to the largest possible value of its left-hand-side type. If the real number is too small, the integer is set to the smallest possible value of its left-hand-side type. For byte and short, if the value is small enough to fit in the byte and short destination, the assignment is completed. The dark side of casting is that it may result in the loss of sign, magnitude, and precision.

One more point worth mentioning is that if you try to put a `long` value into `float` variable, Java treats this as a legal statement. For example,

```
long x = 321;
float y = x;          // legal statement
```

The point worth pondering is that how can a long value, which is of 64 bits, be assigned to a float variable which is of 32 bits? To understand why this is a legal statement we need to know how floating point numbers are represented. A `float` or `double` value is represented using IEEE 754 binary floating point standard. A floating point number is represented in four components—sign, mantissa, radix, and exponent. A sign bit is used to denote a positive number or a negative number. A value of zero in sign bit indicates positive number and 1 in sign bit indicates a negative number. Mantissa holds the significant digits of the floating point number and exponent is used for indicating the power (positive or negative) of the radix. The first bit of the exponent indicates its sign. The format of a floating point number is shown below:

```
sign bit * mantissa * 2^exponent
```

Java uses a radix of 2. A float variable has 23 bits for mantissa and 8 bits for exponent. A `double` variable uses 52 bits for mantissa and 11 bits for exponent. The bit representation of these variables is shown below:

Sign bit	8 exponent bits	23 mantissa bits

float variable

Sign bit	11 exponent bits	52 mantissa bits

double variable

So you can easily imagine that a `float` variable can accommodate a lot more values that what a long variable can because of its representation and format. For a more detailed discussion on floating point standard refer to IEEE 754 floating point standard.)

Let us take an example to understand the concepts.

Example 3.7 Conversion and Casting

```
class CastingAndConversionExample
{
    public static void main(String args[])
    {

        //casting
L1      int i = (int)(8.0/3.0);
        // j will have the largest value of its type as 2147483648.0f is too large
L2      int j = (int)2147483648.0f;
        System.out.println("i = " +i+ " j =" +j);

        //casting: answer will contain 8 low order bits of the int value of 257
L3      byte b = (byte)257;
        //casting: answer will contain 16 low order bits of the int value of 65537
L4      short s = (short)65537;
        System.out.println("b =" +b+ " s ="+s);

        //casting int to char
L5      System.out.println("Converting int to char " +(char)75);

        //conversion: int * byte * short * double is double
L6      double d = i * b * s * 2.0;
        System.out.println("Conversion to double result is : "+d);

        //implicit conversion to int in case of shift operator
L7      i = b << 2;
        System.out.println("i = "+i);
        // compound operator automatically perform casting
        byte c = 0;
```

```
L8          //c = c + b;     does not compile
L9          c += b;          // complies
            System.out.println("Result: "+c);
        }
    }
```

Output

```
i = 2 j = 2147483647
b = 1 s = 1
Converting int to char K
Conversion to double result is : 4.0
i = 4
Result: 1
```

Explanation

L1 It shows the casting of a double expression into an int. The result of dividing a double value by a double value is a double, which is then casted into an int.

L2 It shows the casting of a float literal into an int, which is larger than the maximum value an int variable can hold. So j is set to the maximum value an int can hold.

L3 It shows the casting of an int literal into a byte. It is again larger than the maximum a byte can hold. In this case, byte variable will contain the value which is present in the 8 low order bit of the int literal 257. The int literal 257 has the binary value 00000000 00000000 00000001 00000001. After casting, byte will have the low order 8 bits (00000001), which is the decimal value 1.

L4 It shows the casting of an int literal into a short, which is larger than the maximum a short can hold. In this case, the short variable will contain the value that is present in the 16 low order bits of the int literal 65537. int literal 65537 has the binary value 00000000 00000001 0000000 00000001. After casting, short will have the low order 16 bits (00000000 00000001) which is the decimal value 1.

L5 It shows the casting of an integer into a char. Characters are represented by integral ASCII values, which can be casted back to character. An integer variable can hold a character, e.g. int x ='K'. This is a case of automatic promotion; here x will have the value 75 which is the ASCII value of 'K'.

L6 It shows the multiplication automatic promotion. The expression involves multiplication that is left associative. First, byte variable b is automatically promoted to int and multiplied with i giving an int result (i.e., 2*1 = 2). Then short is automatically promoted to an int and multiplied with the previous int result to give a new int result (i.e., 2*1 = 2). Now this int result is automatically promoted to double because it has to be multiplied to a double literal (i.e., 2.0) giving a double result of 4.0.

L7 It shows the left shifting of bits in the expression b << 2. Before shifting, there is an automatic promotion of byte variable b to an int and then the 32 bits are shifted towards left by two places.

L8 It is commented, as it will not compile. During evaluation of this expression c and b are automatically promoted to int and added to produce an int result. This result cannot be stored directly in a byte variable.

L9 It complies because the operator used in this case is a compound operator that automatically casts the result into the destination type.

3.9 FLOW OF CONTROL

Control flow statements help programmers make decisions about which statements to execute and to change the flow of execution in a program. The four categories of control flow statements available in Java are *conditional statement, loops, exception,* and *branch.*

3.9.1 Conditional Statements

Java programs accomplish their tasks by manipulating the program data using operators and making decisions by testing the state of program data. When a program makes a decision, it determines, based on the state of the program data whether certain lines of code should be executed. For example, a program may examine a variable called *flag* to determine if it should execute a block of code that saves data into a file on to the disk. If flag is true, the data is saved; else the data is not saved. The two conditional statements provided by Java are: `if … else` and `switch-case`.

if…else

The syntax of `if` statement is as follows:

```
if (x = = 0)
    {// Lines of code}
else if(x = = 1)
    {// Lines of code}
    ………
else
    {// Lines of code}
```

The arguments to a conditional statement like `if` must be a boolean value, which is something that evaluates to true or false. You can have *n* number of `else if ()[]` statements in your program, as per your requirement. The `if...else` condition can also be nested as shown.

```
if (condition)
{
    if (condition)
            {//do something based on the condition}
}
```

The following example shows how `if...else` conditional statements can be used in Java.

Example 3.8 `if...else`

```
class IFElseExample
{
    public static void main(String args[])
    {
        int x=20,y=18,z=22;
L1      if (x < y)                      // x comes before y
L2      {
L3      if (z < x)                      // z comes first
L4      System.out.println( z + " " + x + " " + y);
L5      else if (z > y)                 // z comes last
L6      System.out.println(x + " " + y + " " + z);
L7      else                            // z is in the middle
L8        System.out.println(x + " " + z + " " + y);
L9      }
L10     else
```

```
L11        {                              // y comes before x
L12        if (z < y)                     // z comes first
L13        System.out.println(z + " " + y + " " + x);
L14        else if ( z > x)               // z comes last
L15        System.out.println(y + " " + x + " " + z);
L16        else                           // z is in the middle
L17        System.out.println(y + " " + z + " " + x);
           }
        }
    }
```

Output

```
C:\>Java IFElseExample
18 20 22
```

Explanation

L1   It shows `if` statement comparing x with y. If x is less than y, then control passes into the enclosing curly brackets starting from L2. But in our example, x is greater than y, so the control passes to the `else` statement in L10.

L3   It uses the nested `if` statement. This `if` clause is within the `if` statement on L1. If condition in L1 returns true, then the condition on this line is checked. The condition checks whether z is less than x, which is already less than y from L1. If (z < x) is true, then z is the smallest of the three, y is the largest, and x lies in between.

L4   It prints the facts of L3.

L5   If condition on L3 returns false, the control passes on to L5, which means z is not less than x and in L5, z is compared with y. If z is greater than y, it means z is the largest, x is smallest, and y lies in between. (We already know the fact from L1 that x is less than y).

L6   It prints the facts of L5.

L7   If condition on L5 returns false, then the control passes on to the `else` on L7, which means that x is less than y (L1) and z is not less than x (L3) and is not greater than y (L5). So x is the smallest, y is the largest, and z lies in between.

L8   It prints the facts of L7.

L10   The `else` of `if` on L1. The control passes on to this `else` if L1 returns false, which means x is not less than y.

L11   The starting curly bracket of `else`.

L12   It checks if z is less than y. If true, z comes first, then y, and x is the largest.

L13   It prints the facts of L12.

L14   It checks if z is greater than x. If true, y comes first, then x, and z is the largest. In our example, this case is executed as the value of x is 20, y is 18, and z is 22.

L15   It prints the facts of L14.

L16   If z is not less than y (L12) and z is not greater than x, i.e., z is in the middle, y is the smallest, and x is the largest.

L17   It prints the facts of L16.

Switch-case

Java has a shorthand for multiple `if` statement—the `switch-case` statement. Here is how we can write the above program using a `switch-case`:

```
switch (x) {

case 0:
    // Lines of code
```

```
            doSomething0();
            break;

        case 1:
            // Lines of code
            doSomething1();
            break;
            . . .
        case n:
            // Lines of code
            doSomethingN();
            break;

        default:
            doSomethingElse();
        }
```

switch-case works with byte, short, char, and int primitive type. It can also be an enum type (see Chapter 6) or one of the four special wrapper classes (see Chapter 6) namely: Byte for byte, Short for short, Character for char, Integer for int. We can use strings also with the switch-case from Java 7 onwards. It means that x must be one of these int, byte, short, char, enum type, String or (one of the four) wrapper classes. It can also be an expression that returns an int, byte, short, char or String. The value in x is compared with the value of each case statement until one matches. If no matching case is found, the default case is executed.

Once a case is matched, all subsequent statements are executed till the end of the switch block or you break out of the block. Therefore, it is common to include the break statement at the end of each case block, unless you explicitly want all subsequent statements to be executed. The following example shows how switch-case can be used in Java. A switch-case is more efficient than an if-then-else statement, as it produces a much efficient byte code.

Example 3.9 switch-case

```
class SwitchCaseDemo
{
    public static void main(String args[])
    {
L1      char c='B';
L2      switch(c)
L3      {
L4      case 'A':
L5          System.out.println("You entered Sunday");
L6          break;
L7      case 'B':
            System.out.println("You entered Monday");
            break;
L8      case 'C':
            System.out.println("You entered Tuesday");
            break;
L9      case 'D':
```

```
              System.out.println("You entered Wednesday");
              break;
L10      case 'E':
              System.out.println("You entered Thursday");
              break;
L11      case 'F':
              System.out.println("You entered Friday");
              break;
L12      case 'G':
              System.out.println("You entered Saturday");
              break;
L13      default:
L14              System.out.println("Wrong choice");
L15      }
L16    }
     }
```

Output

```
You entered Monday
```

Explanation

L1 It declares a character variable c with the value 'B'. \

L2 It switches the control the case where a match was found. In our case, the control passes to L7.

L3 It is the start of switch statement.

L4–6 These show the first case, that is, case 'A'. If the value in the character variable is 'A', then this case is executed, and the output will be You entered Sunday. L6 shows the break statement, to break out of the switch-case statement. If the break statement is not included in the code, then subsequent cases will also be executed.

L7 It shows the second case similar to L4. In our example, the value of the char variable is 'B', so L2 switches control to this line and the output will be You entered Monday. After printing the output, the control moves out of the switch-case because a break statement is included in the case.

L8–12 These are similar to L7 but will only be executed in case the value of the char variable is 'C' (L8), 'D' (L9), 'E' (L10), 'F' (L11), and 'G' (L12), respectively.

L13 It shows the default case. It is executed in case the char variable takes a value other than A to G.

Note The value of character 'c' is fixed as 'B' in our example. This value should be set based on the user's input. But taking user's input is not yet discussed; so we have fixed the value of character 'c'. We will discuss it in Chapter 9.

3.9.2 Loops

The purpose of loop statements is to execute Java statements many times. There are three types of loops in Java—for, while, and do-while.

for Loop

The for loop groups the following three common parts together into one statement:

(a) Initialization
(b) Condition
(c) Increment or decrement

To execute a code for a known number of times, `for` loop is the right choice. The syntax of `for` loop is

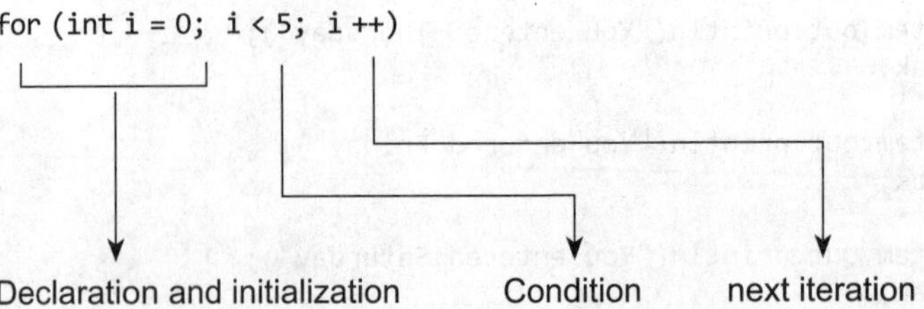

Example 3.10   for loop

```
class ForDemo
{
   public static void main(String args[])
   {
L1     for(int i = 1;i <= 5;i++)
L2     System.out.println("Square of "+i+" is "+ (i*i));
   }
}
```

Output

```
Square of 1 is 1
Square of 2 is 4
Square of 3 is 9
Square of 4 is 16
Square of 5 is 25
```

Explanation

L1 It shows the `for` loop with its three parts: initialization (`i` is initialized to 1), condition (`i` is less than or equal to 5) and the third is increment (i++). The loop will be executed five times. This loop has only one statement. Initially the value of `i` will be 1, for which the print statement in L2 will be executed and likewise for i = 2, 3, 4, and 5.

L2 It prints the square of `i` (i.e., i*i). This line will be executed five times, once for each value of `i`.

while Loop

The `while` loop is used to repeatedly execute a block of statements based on a condition. The condition will be evaluated before the iteration starts. A `for` loop is useful when you know the exact number of iterations. If you want to execute some statements for an indefinite number of times (i.e., number of iterations is unknown), a `while` loop may be the better choice. For example, if you execute a query to fetch data from a database, you will not know the exact numbers of records (rows or columns) returned by the query. A `for` loop cannot be used to iterate the returned records in this case.

The `while` statement has the following syntax:

```
while (condition)
{
        Statements to execute while the condition is true
}
```

The program in Example 3.10 can also be written using a `while` loop.

Example 3.11 `while` Loop

```
class WhileDemo
{
    public static void main(String args[])
    {
L1      int i = 1;
L2      while(i <= 5)
L3      {
L4      System.out.println("Square of " +i+ "is" +(i*i));
L5      i++;
L6      }
    }
}
```

Output

```
Square of 1 is 1
Square of 2 is 4
Square of 3 is 9
Square of 4 is 16
Square of 5 is 25
```

Explanation

L1 It initializes an `int` variable i to 1.
L2 It demonstrates the `while` loop. In this loop, the value of i is checked to be less than or equal to 5, which in the first iteration is 1 (less than 5), so the control passes into the loop. After executing the statements within the enclosing curly brackets of the `while` loop, again the condition of the `while` loop is checked. It goes on until the condition in the `while` returns false (i.e., when value of i becomes 6), in which case the control comes out of the loop.
L3 Curly bracket to denote the start of `while` loop.
L4 It prints the square of i.
L5 It increments the value of i.
L6 Curly bracket denoting the end of `while` loop.

do-while Loop

A `do-while` loop is also used to repeatedly execute (iterate) a block of statements. But, in a `do-while` loop the condition is evaluated at the end of the iteration. So the `do-while` loop (unlike the `while` loop) will execute at least once and after that depending upon the condition.

The general form of a `do-while` loop is

```
do
{
        Statements to execute once and thereafter while the condition is true
        } while (test);
        Next-statement;
```

Example 3.12 `do-while` Loop

```
class DoWhileDemo
{
      public static void main(String args[])
L1        { int i = 1;
L2        do
L3        {
L4        System.out.println("Square of" +i+ "is" + (i*i));
L5        i++;
L6        }while(i <= 5);
      }

   }
```

Output

```
Square of 1 is 1
Square of 2 is 4
Square of 3 is 9
Square of 4 is 16
Square of 5 is 25
```

Explanation

L1 It initializes an `int` variable i to 1.
L2 It shows the starting do statement of the do-while loop.
L4 to 6 The statement on L4 and L5 will be executed at least once and later it depends on the condition specified in the `while` loop on L6. In this case, the statements on L4 and L5 will be executed not only once, but five times (value of i loops from 1 to 5 inclusive).

for-each Loop

Java 5 introduced what is sometimes called a `for-each` statement that accesses each successive element of an array, list, or set without being associated with iterators or indexing. This new `for` statement is called the `enhanced for` or `for-each`. This loop is used to access each value successively in a collection of values (like array). It is commonly used to iterate over an array or a collections class (e.g., `ArrayList`). Like `for` loops, these loops perform a fixed number of iterations. But unlike them, the `for-each` loop determines its number of steps from the size of the collection.

The general form of `for-each` loop is

```
for (type var : arr)
{
    // Statements to repeat
}
```

We will return to `for-each` loop when we discuss arrays and collections in Java.

3.9.3 Branching Mechanism

Java does not offer a `go to` type of statement as in some older languages, because it leads to unreadable code. However, Java supports other ways to jump from one statement to another. Two types of branching statements are available in Java—*break* and *continue*.

break Statement

break statement is used in case the user needs to jump out of a loop, while the continue statement is used where the user wants to go back to the top of the loop. A break statement is used to jump out of a loop when a particular condition occurs, as shown below:

```java
while (i < 5) {
      //do Something;
      if(i < 0) break; // jump out of the loop
}
```

The break will result in the program flow moving out of the loop to the next statement following the loop statement. The following example is a program statement to choose prime numbers within a given range.

Example 3.13 **Usage of break**

```java
class PrimeDemo{
public static void main(String[] args){
      int j,k;
      System.out.print("Prime numbers between 1 to 30 : ");
L1    for (j = 1; j < 30; j++){
L2    for (k = 2; k < j; k++){
L3      if(j % k == 0) break;
        }
L4              if(j == k) {
L5              System.out.print(j+ " ");
        }
    }
  }}
```

Output

```
C:\Javabook\programs\chap3>Java PrimeDemo
Prime numbers between 1 to 30 : 2 3 5 7 11 13 17 19 23 29
```

Explanation

L1 It creates a for loop which ranges from 1 to 30 (as we need to find primes between 1 and 30).
L2 It creates an inner for loop which starts from 2 (as 1 is not a prime number) to j.
L3–5 Condition to check whether j is divisible by any number in the range 2 to j-1. If it is divisible by any number in this range (i.e., remainder is 0), break out of the inner for loop and check (in L4) whether the numerator (j) and denominator (k) are same. (Prime numbers are divisible by 1 and itself). If both are same, it is a prime number.

If, instead, you want the flow to jump out of both the loops, use the labeled break as shown in the next example.

Example 3.14 **Labeled break**

```java
class LabeledBreakDemo{
public static void main(String args[])
```

```
      {
L1      Outer : for(int i = 0; i < 4; i++){
L2          for(int j = 1; j < 4; j++){
L3              System.out.println("i:" + i + " j:" + j);
L4              if(i == 2) break Outer;
      }}}}
```

Output

```
C:\Javabook\programs\chap3>Java LabeledBreakDemo
i:0 j:1
i:0 j:2
i:0 j:3
i:1 j:1
i:1 j:2
i:1 j:3
i:2 j:1
```

Explanation

L1   A label named `Outer` is placed on the outer `for` loop with a colon after the label name.
L2   An inner `for` loop is created.

L3   Prints the value of `i` and `j`.
L4   If the value of `i` is equal to 2, the control comes out of both the loops and the program terminates.

Continue Statement

Situations can occur where you do not want to jump out of a loop, but simply stop the current iteration and go back to the top and continue with the next iteration, as shown in the following code.

Example 3.15   Code Snippet for `continue`

```
L1      while (i < 5){
L2      //doSomething1;
L3      if(i < 4) continue;
L4      //doSomething2;
        }
```

Explanation

L1   Beginning of `while` loop.
L2   Inside the loop, there are some statements shown in comments (`//do something1`).
L3   If `i` is less than 4, `continue` to the top of the loop for next iteration.
L4   The `doSomething2` statement will not execute until `i` equals 4 because the `continue` statement keeps sending the program flow back to the next iteration of the loop.

Sometimes you may want to jump out of not only the inner loop but the outer loop as well. In that case, you can put a label (similar to label in break) on the outer loop and jump to it and continue its next iteration, as in the following example.

Example 3.16   Code Snippet for Labeled `continue`

```
L1      jmp0: while (i < 5){
L2      for (int i = 0; i < 4; i++){
L3      if(i = = 2) continue jmp0; //do something;
        }

        }
```

Explanation

L1 Labelled continue (i.e., jmp0) on the beginning of while loop.
L2 Inner for loop.

L3 The if statement inside the inner for loop states to jump to the outer while loop if i is equal to 2, else execute the statements (do something).

SUMMARY

Java is an object-oriented programming language that can be used to solve problems. All the Java keywords have a fixed meaning and form the building block for program statements.

Variables hold data at memory locations allocated to them. There are eight basic data types in Java, namely byte, short, int, long, float, double, boolean, and char. Java is portable across computer platforms. Java does not leave the size of data types to the machine and the compiler, but specifies everything. All integer (byte, short, int, long) and floating-point types (float, double) are signed in Java. Java 7 introduced binary literals to be assigned to numeric variables and underscores to be used with literals. Apart from this, Java 7 added strings to be used with switch case statements.

There are several operators in Java that can be classified as arithmetic, relational, logical, assignment, increment and decrement, conditional, bit-wise, and special. Expressions are formed with variables and operators. Operators in Java have certain precedence and associativity rules that are followed while evaluating expressions. Automatic-type conversion takes place according to a set of rules in expressions with mixed types. Explicit type conversion (casting) is also possible in Java.

EXERCISES

Objective Questions

1. In the following class definition, which is the first line (if any) that causes a compilation error? Select the correct answer.

```java
public class CastTest {
 public static void main(String args[]){
   char a;
   int j;
   a = 'A';        //1
   j = a;          //2
   a = j + 1;      //3
   a++;            //4
 }
}
```

   (a) The line labelled 1.
   (b) The line labelled 2.
   (c) The line labelled 3.
   (d) The line labelled 4.

2. Which of these assignments are valid?
   (a) short s = 48;   (b) float f = 4.3;
   (c) double d = 4.3;   (d) int I = '1';

3. What is the output when the following program is compiled and run?

```java
class test {
 public static void main(String args[]){
   int i,j,k,l=0;
   k = l++;
   j = ++k;
   i = j++;
   System.out.println(i);
 } }
```

   (a) 0   (b) 1   (c) 2   (d) 3

4. What gets printed on the standard output when the following class is compiled and executed? Select the correct answer.

```java
public class SCkt {
 public static void main(String args[]) {
   int i = 0;
   boolean t = true;
   boolean f = false, b;
   b = (t && ((i++) == 0));
```

```
    b = (f && ((i+=2) > 0));
    System.out.println(i);
    }
  }
```

(a) 0   (b) 1   (c) 2   (d) 3

5. Which operator is used to perform bitwise inversion in Java?

(a) . ~   (b) !   (c) &   (d) |

6. Which of the following statement(s) are correct?

(a) Java provides two operators to do left shift – << and <<<.

(b) >> is the zero fill right shift operator.

(c) >>> is the signed right shift operator.

(d) For positive numbers, results of operators >> and >>> are same.

7. What is the result of compiling and running the following program?

```
public class test {
 public static void main(String args[]){
        int i = -1;
        i = i >> 1;
        System.out.println(i);
    }

}
```

(a) 63   (b) –1   (c) 0   (d) 1

8. What is the output when the following class gets compiled and run?

```
public class example{
 public static void main(String args[]){
   int x = 0;
   if(x > 0) x = 1;
   switch(x){
   case 1:
          System.out.println(1);
   case 0:
          System.out.println(0);
   case 2:
```

```
          System.out.println(2);
          break;
   case 3:
          System.out.println(3);
   default:
          System.out.println(4);
          break;
}}}
```

(a) 0   (b) 1   (c) 2   (d) 3

9. Select the lines that form a part of the output when the following code is compiled and run.

```
public class test{
 public static void main(String args[]){
   for(int i = 0; i < 3; i++)
   {
       for(int j = 3; j >= 0; j--)
       {
       if(i == j) continue;
       System.out.println(i + " " + j);
       }
   }
}}
```

(a) 0 0   (b) 0 1   (c) 0 2   (d) 0 3

10. Select the lines that form a part of the output when the following code is compiled and run.

```
public class test {
 public static void main(String args[]){
   for(int i = 0; i < 3; i++)
   {
       for(int j = 3; j >= 0; j--)
       {
           if(i == j) break;
           System.out.println(i + " " + j);
       }
   }
}}
```

(a) 0 0   (b) 0 1   (c) 0 2   (d) 0 3

Review Questions

1. What are the rules for naming an identifier in Java?

2. Explain conversion. How is it different from casting?

3. What are shift operators? How many types of shift operators are available in Java?

4. What are the differences between for, while and do...while loops?

5. What is the difference between right shift and unsigned right shift operator?

6. What is precedence? Explain how precedence and associativity are useful in evaluating expressions.

7. Explain the following:
   (a) variable
   (b) literal
   (c) keywords in Java
   (d) data types in Java

   (e) break
   (f) continue

8. What are binary literals and how are they used in Java?

9. Explain how underscores are used with literals along with their purpose.

10. Explain why long having 64 bits gets automatically converted to a float, which is only 32 bits in size, when we try to assign a long value to a float variable.

Programming Exercises

1. Write a program `Pattern.Java` that takes an integer, N and prints out a two-dimensional N-by-N pattern with alternating spaces and asterisks, like the following 4-by-4 pattern.

   ```
   * * * *

     * * * *

   * * * *

     * * * *
   ```

2. Write a program that does binary-to-decimal and decimal-to-binary conversions. (Do not use the predefined methods.)

3. Write a program that takes a price and prints out the appropriate tax along with the total purchase price assuming the sales tax in your city is 12.35%.

4. Write a program that takes the number of hours worked by an employee and the basic hourly pay, and outputs the total pay due.

5. Write a program that takes an integer n and calculates n!.

6. Write a program that converts inches to centimetres.

7. Write a program that converts acres to hectares and vice versa.

8. Write a program that accepts resistances and outputs the equivalent resistance when they are connected in series. (Assuming the Resistance R1=12, R2=14, R3=15).

9. Write a program that calculates the equivalent resistance arranged in parallel. The formula for calculating the equivalent resistance arranged in parallel is

$$\mathrm{Re\,quiv} = \frac{1}{\dfrac{1}{R1} + \dfrac{1}{R2}}$$

10. Write a program that calculates how much a $10,000 investment would be worth if it increased in value by 20% during the first year, lost $500 in value in the second year, and increased 16% in the third year.

Answers to Objective Questions

1. (c), integer cannot be assigned to a character without a cast.
2. (a), (c), (d), the value 4.3 is of type double, so it cannot be assigned to a float without a cast.
3. (b)
4. (b), in the second assignment to variable b, the expression (i += 2) does not get evaluated.
5. (a)   6. (d)   7. (b)   8. (a), (c)
9. (b), (c), (d)   10. (b), (c), (d)

Classes and Objects

Space is big. You just won't believe how vastly, hugely, mind-bogglingly big it is. I mean, you may think it's a long way down the road to the chemist's, but that's just peanuts to space.

Douglas Adams

After reading this chapter, the readers will be able to

- know how classes and objects are created and applied in Java
- know how methods are created and used
- understand the concepts of polymorphism and overloading
- understand what is a constructor
- establish familiarity with static keyword
- know about arrays and command-line arguments
- understand inner classes
- understand and use arrays

4.1 CLASSES

Java is an object-oriented language. In the first chapter, we have learnt the concepts of object-oriented programming (OOP). Before applying these concepts in Java, we must understand the basic building blocks of OOP, i.e., *classes* and *objects*.

In the real physical world, everyday we come across various objects of the same kind. One of the many things we come across are motorbikes. In terms of object-oriented language, we can say that the bike object is one instance of a class of objects known as 'motorbikes.' Bikes have gears, brakes, wheels, etc. They also follow certain behaviors, when functions are applied on them, e.g., bikes slow down when brakes are applied, they accelerate when geared up and acceleration is applied, and so on.

Manufacturers produce many bikes from the same blueprint by taking advantage of the fact that bikes share similar characteristics. It would be very inefficient to produce a new blueprint for every individual bike they manufactured.

In the object-oriented software, there are many objects of the same kind, i.e., belonging to the same classes that share certain characteristics. Like the bike manufacturer, we can take advantage of the fact that objects of the same kind are similar and a blueprint for those objects can be created. Software 'blueprints' for objects are called *classes*.

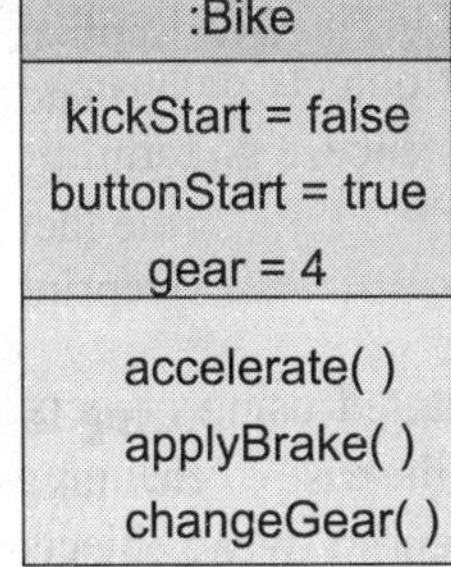

<table>
<tr><td align="center">Bike</td></tr>
<tr><td>boolean kickStart
boolean buttonStart
int gears</td></tr>
<tr><td align="center">accelerate( )
applyBrake( )
changeGear( )</td></tr>
</table>

Fig. 4.1 Bike Class

Let us come back to our bike class, which would also declare and provide implementations for the instance methods or functions that allow the rider to change gears, apply brakes, and accelerate. Figure. 4.1 shows the bike class.

> **Note** A class is a blueprint or prototype that defines the variables and methods common to all objects of a certain kind. In other words, a class can be thought of as a user-defined data type and an object as a variable of that data type that can contain data and methods, i.e., functions working on that data.

4.2 OBJECTS

The object-oriented technology revolves around objects. We see many objects around us such as table, chair, dog, fan, computer, pen, and car. These objects need not be tangible ones only, but can be intangible also, e.g., bank accounts, marks, fees, etc. All these real-world objects have different *states* and *behaviors*. The state of an object is defined by the values of the attributes at any instant. Bikes have attributes (speed, engine capacity, number of wheels, number of gears, brakes), behaviors (braking, accelerating, slowing down, and changing gears) and on application of this behavior on attributes, the state of the object will change. Bike object can be in various states, it can be stationary, moving etc. For example, when we apply brakes, the speed will reduce and when we accelerate speed increases. A state will change over time and at any instant a state would be somewhat like current speed = 60 km/hr and current gear = 4th. Similarly, the state of a fan would be either off or on.

We can conceptualize these real-time objects as software objects. They are similar natured in the sense they too have states and behaviors. The state in software objects is maintained in variables and the behavior can be implemented using methods. It is interesting to know that these real-world objects can be represented using software objects.

> **Note** An object is a software bundle that encapsulates variables and methods operating on those variables.

<table>
<tr><td align="center">:Bike</td></tr>
<tr><td align="center">kickStart = false
buttonStart = true
gear = 4</td></tr>
<tr><td align="center">accelerate( )
applyBrake( )
changeGear( )</td></tr>
</table>

Fig. 4.2 Bike Object

You might want to represent a real-world bike as a software object in a gaming application. Abstract objects representing abstract concepts can also be modeled using software objects. For example, a *bank account* is a common object used in banking solutions to represent the details of bank accounts of various customers of a bank.

Figure. 4.2 shows a common visual representation of a software object.

It would be correct to say that everything the software object knows (state) and can do (behavior) is expressed by the variables and methods within that object. A software object that models the real-world bike would have variables that indicate the bike's current state: its speed is 10 mph, its acceleration in terms of revolutions per minute is 5000 rpm, and its current gear is 4th. These variables are known as *instance variables*.

The object *bike* would also have methods to brake, accelerate, and change gears. These are known as *instance methods*. Only relevant fields and behaviors are added into a class. For example, a bike does not have a surname, and it cannot speak or sleep. A bike class can be created that declares several instance variables to contain the gears, the brakes, and so on, for each bike object and every bike will have its own brakes, gears, etc.

It is worth noting here that all object instances have their own copies of instance variables. This means that if there are five object instances of a bike class, there are five copies of each instance variable defined in that class. Each object has its own copy of instance variables which is different from other objects created out of the same class.

The values of the instance variables are provided by each instance of the class. So, after you have created the bike class, you must *instantiate* it (create an object of it) before you can use it. When an instance of a class is created, an object of that type is created and memory is allocated by the system for the instance variables declared by the class. Then the object's instance methods can be invoked to perform operations.

> **Note** Instances of the same class share the instance method implementations (method implementations are not duplicated on a per object basis).

In addition to instance variables and methods, classes can define their own *class variables* and *methods*. Every object will have its own *instance variables* but *class variables* will be shared by all the objects of the class. You can access *class variables* and *methods* using an instance of the class or using the class name. You need not instantiate a class to use its *class variables* and *methods*. Class methods can only access the class variables directly. They don't have direct access to instance variables or methods. A single copy of all *class variables* is created and all instances of that class share it. For example, suppose all cars had the same number of gears. In such a situation, a class variable can be created that defines the number of gears. All instances of the class will share this variable. If any object manipulates the class variable, then it changes for all objects of that class.

4.2.1 Difference Between Objects and Classes

Both objects and classes look the same. Yes, it is a fact that the difference between classes and objects is often the source of some confusion. In the real world, it is obvious that classes are not themselves the objects that they describe—a blueprint of a bike is not a bike. However, it is difficult to differentiate between classes and objects in programming. This is partially because objects in programming are merely the electronic models of real-world objects or abstract concepts. Classes have logical existence, whereas objects have physical existence, e.g., furniture itself does not have any physical existence, but chairs, tables, etc. do have.

4.2.2 Why Should we Use Objects and Classes?

Modularity, information hiding, i.e., *data encapsulation*, can be incorporated using objects. Classes, being blueprints, also provide the benefit of reusability along with the ease of changing and debugging code. For example, bike manufacturers reuse the same blueprint over and over again to build lots of bikes. Programmers use the same class repeatedly to create many objects.

4.3 CLASS DECLARATION IN JAVA

Declaring a class is simple. A class can be declared using the keyword `class` followed by the name of the class that you want to define. Giving a name to a class is something which is totally in the hands of the programmer. But while doing so, he must take care of the relevance of the class name, the legality of Java identifiers used as the class name, and the naming convention used in Java. Thus, the simplest class declaration looks as follows:

```
class Bike
{
    //Variables declaration
    //Methods declaration
}
```

Example 4.1 **Class Declaration**

```
class GoodbyeWorld
{
public static void main (String args[])
    {
    System.out.println("Goodbye World!");
    }
}
```

Here the name of the class is `GoodbyeWorld`. The class just contains the `main()` method, which is responsible for displaying `GoodbyeWorld` on the screen.

To sum up, all the action in a Java program takes place inside the class. Methods and variables are defined inside the classes. The class is the fundamental unit of programming in Java. The class declaration can specify more about the class, like you can:

- declare the superclass of a class
- list the interfaces implemented by the class
- declare whether the class is `public`, `abstract`, or `final`

For each of the cases above, the class declaration will differ accordingly. We will talk about that as and when we cover the related concepts. Taking all the possibilities of class declaration in Java, we can summarize the class declaration syntax as

```
[modifiers] class ClassName [extends SuperClassName] [implements InterfaceNames]
{ . . . }
```

The items enclosed inside [ ] are optional. A class declaration defines the following aspects of the class:

- `modifiers` declare whether the class is `public`, `protected`, `default`, `abstract` or `final`
- `ClassName` sets the name of the class you are declaring
- `SuperClassName` is the name of the `ClassName`'s superclass
- `InterfaceNames` is a comma-delimited list of the interfaces implemented by `ClassName`

Only the `class` keyword and the class name are mandatory. Other parameters are optional.

Certain terms in the above syntax such as `modifiers`, `extending superclasses`, and `implementing interfaces`, which are presently unfamiliar, will be discussed in the later chapters.

4.3.1 Class Body

The class contains two different sections: variable declarations and method declarations. The variables of a class describe its state, and methods describe its behavior. All the member variables and methods are declared within the class. There are three types of variables in Java: *local variables*, *instance variables*, and *class variables*. Local variables are defined inside a method. Instance variable is defined inside the class but outside the methods, and class variables are declared with the static modifier inside the class and outside the methods. For now, we will concentrate on instance variables.

Instance Variables

It is important to understand that a class can have many instances (i.e., objects) and each instance will have its own set of instance variables. Any change made in a variable of one particular instance will not have any effect on the variables of another instance. For more details on class variables, local variables, and instance variables, see Section 4.7.

Normally, you declare the member variables first followed by the method declarations and implementations.

```
classDeclaration
{
    memberVariableDeclarations
    methodDeclarations
}
```

Let us see how you can declare instance variables in a class. Example 4.2 shows a sample class declaration with two instance variables. We will return to the discussion of instance variables later in the chapter. Please note that if you try to run this example it won't show any output because it is not fully functional and there are certain statements/methods that we need to add so that this program can display any output, which will follow later in the chapter.

Example 4.2 **Class Declaration**

```
L1      class SalesTaxCalculator {
L2          float amount = 100.0f;    // instance variable
L3          float taxRate = 10.2f;    // instance variable
L4      }
```

Explanation

L1 Class declared with the keyword `class` followed by the name of the class `SalesTaxCalculator`.

L2 A instance variable *amount* is declared to denote the amount on which sales tax has to be calculated.

L3 Declares another float instance variable `taxRate` to denote the rate of tax on the sale amount.

L4 End of the class.

The above example shows a class with two instance variables. Instance variables are part of the instance of the class (object). These instance variables will be created when the instance is created. In order to be able to access/manipulate these instance variables, we need to create objects of this class. We have already seen what objects are. Let us see how objects are created and used in Java.

4.4 CREATING OBJECTS

In Java, you create an object by creating an instance of a class or, in other words, instantiating a class. A Java object is defined as an instance of a class. The type of the object is the class itself. Often, you will see a Java object created with a statement like

```
SalesTaxCalculator obj1 = new SalesTaxCalculator();
```

This statement creates a new `SalesTaxCalculator` object. This single statement declares, instantiates, and initializes the object. `SalesTaxCalculator obj1` is a reference variable declaration which simply declares to the compiler that the variable `obj1` will be used to refer to an object whose type is `SalesTaxCalculator`. The new operator instantiates the `SalesTaxCalculator` class (thereby allocating memory and creating a new `SalesTaxCalculator` object), and `SalesTaxCalculator()` initializes the object.

4.4.1 Declaring an Object

Object declarations are same as variable declarations. For example,

```
SalesTaxCalculator obj1;
```

Generally, the declaration is as follows:

```
type name
```

where `type` is the type of the object (i.e., class name) and `name` is the name of the *reference variable* used to refer the object. Classes are like new data types. So `type` can be any class such as the `SalesTaxCalculator` class or the name of an *interface.*

Note A variable holds a single type of literal, i.e., 1, bat, 345, etc. An object is defined as an instance of a class with a set of instance variables and methods that perform certain tasks depending on what methods have been defined for. A reference variable is used to refer/access an object. A reference variable is of a specific type name of the class is its type. Unlike normal variable, reference variables can be static, instance or local variables as well as they can be passed to or returned from the method.

The above declaration won't create an object. It will create a variable with a name and specify its type. For example, `SalesTaxCalculator` is the type and `obj1` is the reference variable.

4.4.2 Instantiating an Object

After declaring a variable to refer to an object, an actual, physical copy of the object must be acquired and assigned to that variable. This can be achieved by the new operator. The new operator instantiates a class by dynamically allocating (i.e., at runtime) memory for an object of the class type and returns a reference to it. This reference is nothing but the address in the memory of the object allocated by new. This reference or memory address is then stored in the variable declared. The new operator requires a single argument, i.e., a constructor call. The new operator creates the object or instantiates an object and the constructor initializes it.

```
SalesTaxCalculator obj1 = new SalesTaxCalculator()
```

The above statement just creates an instance of a class, SalesTaxCalculator. In other words, the new operator creates an object obj1 by allocating memory for its member variables, i.e., amount and taxRate (Example 4.2) and few other items.

4.4.3 Initializing an Object

By initializing an object, we mean the instance variables are assigned initial values. The instance variables of a particular object will have different values during the lifetime of an object. But to start with, initial values are required. If no value is specified for the instance variables, then the default values will be assigned to those variables based on their respective types. Initial values can be provided by *instance variable initializers* and *constructors*.

Instance variable initializers are values directly assigned to the instance variable outside any method/constructor but within the class. [As shown in L2 and L3 of Example 4.2(a)].

The best and convenient approach is to create your own constructor. Constructors should be provided within classes to initialize objects. Constructors have the same name as that of the class. Constructors are invoked as soon as the object is created. In case you do not create a constructor for your class, Java compiler provides a default constructor for your class automatically. The default constructor is a zero argument constructor with an empty body. The implicitly created default constructor is invoked as soon as the object is instantiated with new keyword as shown below.

```
new SalesTaxCalculator()
```

We will come back to the concepts of constructors along with the examples explaining them in Section 4.6.

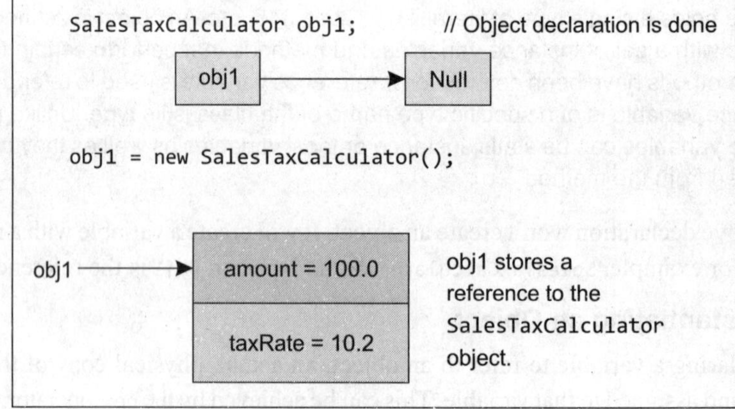

Fig. 4.3 Steps in Object Creation

To sum up, the final object creation can be said as complete, when the objects are initialized, either with an implicit constructor or an explicit constructor. This object creation can be used in a programming code in two ways:

```
SalesTaxCalculator obj1 = new SalesTaxCalculator();
```

Here all the three operations, object declaration, object instantiation, and object initialization are done by a single statement. The above process takes place in the following way:

Now that we know how to create a class and objects for that class, we can rewrite Example 4.2 where we can do these things in one program only. The following program displays a class SalesTaxCalculator, with two instance variable (initialized to some values) and two objects of the class SalesTaxCalculator, obj1 and obj2 (created inside the main method). Instance variable initializers are used in this example to initialize objects: obj1 and obj2 (Fig. 4.3).

Example 4.2 (a) **Object and Classes**

```
L1      class SalesTaxCalculator {
        // instance variable initializer
L2      float amount = 100.0f;
        // instance variable initializer
L3      float taxRate = 10.2f; //instance variable
        // instance method
L4      public static void main (String args[ ])
        {
L5          SalesTaxCalculator obj1 = new SalesTaxCalculator();
L6          SalesTaxCalculator obj2 = new SalesTaxCalculator();
L7          System.out.println("Amount in Object 1: "+ obj1.amount);
L8          System.out.println("Tax Rate in Object 1: "+ obj1.taxRate);
L9          System.out.println("Amount in Object 2: "+ obj2.amount);
L10         System.out.println("Tax Rate in Object 2: "+ obj2.taxRate);
        }}
```

Output

```
D:\javabook\programs\chap4\java SalesTaxCalculator
Amount in Object 1: 100.0
Tax Rate in Object 1: 10.2
Amount in Object 2: 100.0
Tax Rate in Object 2: 10.2
```

Explanation

L1 Class declaration.
L2 & L3 Instance variable have been declared with their initializer.
L4 Main method declared.
L5 & L6 Two objects of this class are created in these lines. As already discussed, the new keyword allocates memory to these objects according to the size of instance variables (plus a few more bits for some more items). Note that no constructor has been created in this class, so the Java compiler will automatically provide a default constructor for this class which is being invoked while creating object in these

statements. The default constructor is empty, so it is the responsibility of the Java compiler to ensure that the instance variable are initialized to their respective values (`amount = 100.0f` and `taxRate = 10.2f`) according to their initializer (mentioned in L2 and L3) by the JVM at runtime. (How does it ensure this? We will discuss it later in the chapter). For instance, we will consider that the instance variable initializers are used by the Java compiler to initialize these instance variables.

L7 Is a print statement that prints the value of the instance variable present in `obj1`. The variable can be accessed through the object followed by the dot operator from main method or outside the class (depends on access and scope of the object).`obj1.amount` will return the value of amount stored in the instance `obj1`. The value of the variable can be changed by using the following syntax:

```
obj1.amount=200.0f;
```

L8, 9 & 10 Similar to L7.

Note Setter methods can also be used for assigning or modifying values of instance variables (i.e., `set X()` or `set Y()` where x and y are the names of the instance variables) They are declared inside a class, as shown in Examples 4.3 and 4.5 (methods will be discussed in the next section).

The above program has a limitation that all objects created will have the same value for `amount` and `taxRate`. Later on it can be changed using object references. But it would be wiser to let all objects have their own different amount and tax rates as soon as they are created. This problem will be solved using constructors (Section 4.6).

4.5 METHODS

The word *method* is commonly used in object-oriented programming. It is similar to a function in any other programming language. Many programmers use different terms, especially *function*, but we will stick to the term *methods*. None of the methods can be declared outside the class. All methods have a name that starts with a lowercase character.

4.5.1 Why Use Methods?

- **To Make the Code Reusable** If you need to do the same thing or almost the same thing, many times, write a method to do it and then call the method each time you have to do that task.

- **To Parameterize the Code** You will often use parameters to change the way the method behaves.

- **For Top-down Programming** You can easily solve a bigger problem or a complex one (the 'top') by breaking it into smaller parts. For the same purpose, we write methods. The entire complex problem (functionality) can be broken down into methods.

- **To Simplify the Code** Because the complex code inside a method is hidden from other parts of the program, it prevents accidental errors or confusion.

4.5.2 Method Type

There are two types of methods in Java: *instance methods* and *class methods*. Instance methods are used to access/manipulate the instance variables but can also access class variables. Class methods can access/manipulate class variables but cannot access the instance variables unless and until they use an object for that purpose.

4.5.3 Method Declaration

The combined name and parameter list for each method in a class must be unique. The uniqueness of a parameter is decided based on the number of parameters as well as the order of the parameters. So,

```
int methodOne (int x, String y)
```

is unique from

```
int methodOne (String y, int x).
```

Let us take a look at the general syntax of a method declaration:

```
[modifiers] return_typemethod_name (parameter_list)
   [throws_clause] {
      [statement_list]
   }
```

The parameters enclosed within square brackets [ ] are optional. The square brackets are not a part of the code; they are included here to indicate optional items. We will discuss only those parts that are required at the moment and leave the rest for the later chapters. The method declaration includes

- **Modifiers** If you see the syntax of the method declaration carefully, there is an optional part of it, *modifiers*. There are a number of *modifiers* (optional) that can be used with a method declaration. They are listed in Table 4.1.

Table 4.1 Optional Modifiers used While Declaring Methods

Modifier	Description
`public, protected, default or private`	Can be one of these values. Defines the scope—what class can invoke which method?
`static`	Used for declaring class methods and variables. The method can be invoked on the class without creating an instance of the class.
`abstract`	The class must be extended and the abstract method must be overridden in the subclass.
`final`	The method cannot be overridden in a subclass.
`native`	The method is implemented in another language (out of the scope of this book).
`synchronized`	The method requires that a monitor (lock) be obtained by calling the code before the method is executed.
`throws`	A list of exceptions is thrown from this method.

- **Return Type** It can be either `void` (if no value is returned) or if a value is returned, it can be either a primitive type or a class. If the method declares a return type, then before it exits, it must have a `return` statement.
- **Method Name** The method name must be a valid Java identifier. We have already discussed Java identifiers in Section 3.3.
- **Parameter List** Zero or more type/identifier pairs make up a parameter list. Each parameter in the parameter list is separated by a comma.
- **Curly Braces** The method body is contained in a set of curly braces. Methods contain a sequence of statements that are executed sequentially. The method body can also be empty.

In Example 4.2(a), we have stored data: *amount* and *taxRate* but we have not calculated the tax amount based on the rate. We need to calculate the tax amount. This operation would require some calculation (operations) to be performed on the data variables. These operations will be performed inside a method so we need to add a method to that class and revise the class. The method added is `calculateTax()` (L4) which calculates the taxed amount. This method is invoked in L10 and 11 by the two objects using the dot operator. Note that the answer in both cases is the same because the data in both cases is same, i.e., amount and tax rate are same for both objects so the taxed amount is same.

Example 4.2 (b) Added Instance Method

```
L1      class SalesTaxCalculator {
        // instance variable initializer
L2      float amount = 100.0f;
        // instance variable initializer
L3      float taxRate = 10.2f;                  //instance variable
        // instance method
L4      void calculateTax() {
L5          float taxAmt = amount*taxRate/100;
L6      System.out.println("The Taxed Amount is: "+taxAmt);
        }
L7      public static void main (String args[ ])
        {
L8          SalesTaxCalculator obj1 = new SalesTaxCalculator();
L9          SalesTaxCalculator obj2 = new SalesTaxCalculator();
L10         obj1.calculateTax();
L11         obj2.calculateTax();
        }}
```

Output

```
The Taxed Amount is: 10.2
The Taxed Amount is: 10.2
```

Let us take a different example to explain the concepts in more detail. The following example has a couple of *instance* methods, `setRadius()` and `calculateArea()`, declared inside the class, `Circle`. The word *instance* has been particularly used to distinguish between instance and class methods. The modifier `static` has not been used while declaring methods so the methods become instance methods.

Example 4.3 Instance Method Declaration

```
L1      class Circle
L2      {
L3          float pi = 3.14f;
L4          float radius;
            //setter method to change the instance variable: radius
L5          void setRadius(float rad)
L6          {
L7          radius = rad;}
L8          float calculateArea()
L9          {
L10            float area = pi * radius * radius;
L11            return (area);
L12     }   }
```

Explanation

L1 Class declaration.

L3 & 4 Instance variable declaration.

L5 Declares an instance method popularly known as setter or mutator methods (note that `static` modifier is not used in this declaration). They are known as setter or mutator methods because they set or change (mutate) the values of instance variables. The data type `void` indicates that this method will not return any value. The name of the instance method is `setRadius()`and it accepts a `float` parameter `rad`. This method is used to assign a value to the instance `variableradius`. The method argument `rad` is assigned to the instance variable `radius` in this method on L7. It also shows that instance methods can access instance variables directly. Instance methods are invoked using objects, so data residing in objects can be easily accessed (set or get) by instance methods.

L6 The body of the method starts with the left brace, "{".

L7 `rad` is assigned to an instance variable `radius` of type `float`. The right brace "}" signifies the end of the method.

L8 Declares another instance method. The instance method `calculateArea()` has been declared to return a value of type `float`.

L9 "{" signifies the start of the method body.

L10 Instance variables `pi` and `radius` are multiplied to calculate the area of the circle. As shown, instance variables can be used by instance methods directly to produce result. An important point to note is that different `Circle` objects will have different values of `radius` and obviously the calculated area will be different but the instance methods remains the same. In other words, instance methods are not implemented on a per object basis as is the case with instance variables. The area of the circle is stored in the local variable, `area`, declared as `float`.

L11 The value stored in the variable area is returned by the `return` statement.

L12 The first right brace "}" signifies the end of method, `calculateArea()`, and the second brace "}" signifies the end of class, `Circle`.

Note The responsibility of providing initial values is that of constructors, and constructors are called only once, i.e., during object creation. If the value of instance variables has to be changed, setter methods should be used and that too can be invoked any number of times.

4.5.4 Instance Method Invocation

If you run Examples 4.2, 4.2(a), and even Example 4.3, you won't see any output for a very simple reason that we have created methods but we have not invoked (called) them. Methods (instance or class methods) cannot run on their own, they need to be invoked. Instance methods will be invoked by the objects of the class they are a part of. Class methods invocation will be discussed later in this chapter.

When an object calls a method, it can pass on certain values to the methods (if methods accept them) and the methods can also return values from themselves if they wish to. Data that are passed to a method are known as *arguments* or *parameters*; the required arguments for a method are defined by a method's parameter list (method signature). Let us take an example and see how invoking is done.

Example 4.4 **Instance Method Invocation**

```
L1      class CallMethod
L2      {
L3      public static void main (String args[])
L4      {
L5          float area1;
L6          Circle circleobj = new Circle();
L7          circleobj.setRadius(3.0f);
L8          area1 = circleobj.calculateArea();
L9          System.out.println("Area of Circle = " + area1);
L10     }}
```

Output

```
Area of Circle = 28.26
```

Explanation

L6 Creates an object of `Circle` class. `setRadius()` and `calculateArea()` are instance methods of the class, `Circle`. So an instance is required to invoke these instance methods and that instance must be of the class the methods are a part of, i.e., `Circle` (Example 4.3). That's why an object of the `Circle` class named `circleobj` is created.

L7 & 8 Using the instance created in L6, we call the methods `setData()` and `calculateArea()` with the help of a `dot` operator. A value `3.0f` (f to indicate float value) is passed as an argument in the `setRadius()` method invocation. This value `3.0f` is assigned to the local float variable `rad`, which is actually an argument in the method declaration (see Example 4.3, L5). The `calculateArea()` method calculates the area and returns the value which is captured in a float variable `area1`.

The following definitions are useful in the above context.

Formal Parameter The identifier used in a method to stand for the value that is passed into the method by a caller. For example, the parameter defined for `setRadius()`, i.e., `rad` in L5 of Example 4.3 is a formal parameter, as it will be bound to the actual value sent by the caller method. These formal parameters come in the category of local variables which can be used in their respective methods only.

Actual Parameter The actual value that is passed into the method by a caller. For example, in L7 of Example 4.4, `3.0f`, passed to `setRadius()`, is the actual parameter.

Note The number and type of the actual and formal parameters should be same for a method. Also note that the class having the `main()` method is to be executed first by the *Java interpreter*.

In Example 4.3, we have created a class (`Circle`) and two methods in that class. Example 4.4 shows how the methods of `Circle` class (Example 4.3) are called from another class, i.e., `CallMethod`. The methods can also be called from within the class, as shown in Example 4.5.

Example 4.5 Adding Instance Variable(s) and Instance Method(s)

```
L1      class Circle
L2      {    float pi=3.14f;
L3           float radius;
L4      void setRadius(float rad){
L5           radius = rad;
L6      }
L7      float calculateArea(){
L8      float area = pi* radius*radius;
L9      return (area);
L10     }
L11     public static void main (String args[]) {
L12         Circle circleobj = new Circle();
L13         circleobj.setRadius(3.0f);
L14         System.out.println("Area of Circle = " + circleobj.calculateArea());
            // The above two lines can be compressed to one, i.e.
            // System.out.println(circleobj.setRadius(3.0f).calculateArea());
L15     }}
```

Explanation

The example is entirely same as that of Example 4.3 up to L10. (The output is entirely same as that of the previous program.)

L11 The execution begins at `main()`. Because `main()` is defined in this class, it can execute on its own and there is no need of a separate class like `CallMethod` (Example 4.4) for invoking the methods of the `Circle` class. The main method from that class has been squeezed out and inserted in the class `Circle` as shown in the lines 11–15.

L12 An object of the `Circle` class, named `circleobj`, is created using the `new` operator.

L13 `setRadius()` is called with the help of an object of the `Circle` class and a float argument is passed to it.

L14 `calculateArea()` is called using the object created in L12.

Note In Java, all values are passed by value. This is unlike some other programming languages that allow pointers to memory addresses to be passed into methods. When a primitive type value is passed to a method, the value is copied. The copied value, if changed inside the method, does not affect the original value. When an object is passed, only the reference is copied. There is just one object that has two references now on it. The changes made to the object through one reference will be reflected when the object is accessed through other references.

4.5.5 Method Overloading

Method overloading is one way of achieving polymorphism in Java. Each method in a class is uniquely identified by its name and parameter list. What it means is that you can have two or more methods with the same name, but each with a different parameter list. This is a powerful feature of the Java language called *method overloading*. Overloading allows you to perform the same action on different types of inputs. In Java whenever a method is being called, first the name of the method is matched and then, the number and type of arguments passed to that method are matched.

In method overloading, two methods can have the same name but different signatures, i.e., different number or type of parameters. The concept is advantageous where similar activities are to be performed but with different input parameters. Example 4.6 shows an example of overloading a method `max()` in order to calculate the maximum value for different combinations of inputs.

Example 4.6 **Method Overloading**

```
class OverloadDemo
        {
L1      void max(float a, float b)
L2      {
L3        System.out.println("max method with float argument invoked");
L4        if(a > b)
L5            System.out.println(a + " is greater");
L6
          else
L7            System.out.println(b + " is greater");
        }
L8      void max(double a, double b)
        {
        System.out.println("max method with double argument invoked");
        if(a>b)
                System.out.println(a + " is greater");
        else
                System.out.println(b + " is greater");
L9      }
L10     void max(long a, long b)
        {
        System.out.println("max method with long argument invoked");
        if(a>b)
                System.out.println(a + " is greater");
        else
                System.out.println(b + " is greater");
L11     }
L12     public static void main(String args[])
L13     {
L14             OverloadDemo o = new OverloadDemo();
L15             o.max(23L,12L);
L16             o.max(2,3);
L17             o.max(54.0,35f);
L18             o.max(43f,35f);
        }}
```

Output

```
C:\javabook\programs\chap4>java OverloadDemo
max method with long argument invoked
23 is greater
max method with long argument invoked
3 is greater
max method with double argument invoked
54.0 is greater
max method with float argument invoked
43.0 is greater
```

Explanation

L1 Method `max` is defined inside class `OverloadDemo` with two arguments of type float.

L2 Marks the beginning of the method.

L3 Shows a print statement describing the method that has been invoked.

L4 `if` statement is used to check whether the float argument a is greater than b. If a is greater, then L5 prints a is greater, else L7 prints b is greater.

L8 & 9 Overloaded method `max` is defined in these lines. This overloaded version of the method accepts two arguments of type `double`. This is different from the `max` method defined in L1. The processing inside this method is entirely similar to the previous method with the exception that now the maximum will be chosen from two double values instead of float values.

L10 & 11 Another version of overloaded method `max` is defined in these lines. This overloaded version of the method accepts two arguments of type long. This is different from the max method defined in lines L1 and L8. The processing inside this method is entirely similar to the previous method with the exception that now the maximum will be chosen from two double values instead of float values.

L12 `main` method has been defined. Execution starts from `main` method.

L13 Marks the beginning of the `main` method.

L14 An object of the class is created to invoke the instance methods.

L15 Shows the invocation of the method, `max`, and two arguments that are passed to it. The question arises, which version of the `max` method will be invoked? (**Remember:** The invocation will be based upon the number and type of arguments). In our case, we have only two arguments in all the overloaded methods. So the decision is taken according to the type of arguments. In this particular statement, two `long` arguments are passed. First of all, Java tries to find an exact match, i.e., a method named `max` in class `OverloadDemo` which accepts two `long` arguments. Java finds the method in L10. The method is called. If an exact match could not be found (say for example, the method `max` with long arguments is not present in the `OverloadDemo` class), then Java looks for a method named `max` which has the arguments to accommodate these `long` values (**Remember:** `long` values can be accommodated implicitly only in `float` and `double`). This example has `max` methods with both `float` and `double` arguments. So which method will be called? The `max` method with `float` arguments will be called (`long` values are promoted to float and passed). And in case the `max` with `float` arguments is also not available, then the method with `double` arguments will be called (`long` values are promoted to `double` and passed).

L16 `max` method is called with two `int` arguments passed to it. In `OverloadDemo` class, Java does not find a method which accepts two `int` arguments, but it finds a method `max` that accepts two `long` arguments. These two `int` arguments are automatically promoted to `long` and passed to the method with the name `max` accepting two `long` arguments (automatic type promotion has taken place here).

L17 Shows the invocation of `max` method with a double argument and a `float` argument. In this case, Java does not find an exact match, as there is no such method named `max` that accepts a `double` argument and a `float` argument. So, automatic promotion takes place in this case also. The question arises that which overloaded method will be called? The `max` method with both `float` arguments cannot be called, as the first argument that is being passed is a `double`. Similarly, the `max` method with both `long` arguments cannot be called, as both the arguments are bigger than `long`. So, the `max` method with both `double` arguments will be called, as the first argument is a perfect match and the second will be automatically promoted to `double` (see output).

L18 The `max` method with both `float` arguments will be called in this case.

Note As a general rule, automatic type promotion takes place while passing parameter values to methods. In overloading, the decision of choosing which method to invoke is resolved by the Java compiler at compile time (early-binding) rather than delaying it till runtime because

(a) Java is a strongly typed language.
(b) Resolving all these issues at compile time will avoid unnecessary exceptions at runtime.
(c) Enhanced performance.

4.6 CONSTRUCTORS

Whenever an object is created for a class, the instance variables of the class needs to be initialized, i.e., they need to be given initial values. It can be done through instance variable initializers (as shown in L2 and L3 [Examples 4.2 and 4.2(a)], L3 (Example 4.3) and L2 (Example 4.5)) and instance initialization blocks. An instance initialization block is a block of statement enclosed in parenthesis with initialization placed in it as shown below:

```
class Rectangle
{
// Instance initialization blocks
{
        length=10;
        width=10;
}
}
```

But Java has a simple and concise method of doing it. It has a mechanism for automatically initializing the values for an object, as soon as the object is created. The mechanism is to use *constructors*.

Constructors have the same name as the class they reside in and they are syntactically similar to a method. Constructors are automatically called immediately after the object for the class is created by a `new` operator. Constructors have no return type, not even `void`, as the implicit return type of a constructor is the class type itself.

In Section 4.4.3, we discussed a little about constructors, promising that we would come back to this topic. Now it is time to recall that section on object creation. An implicit or default constructor is used as a parameter to the `new` operator, just as shown below.

```
SalesTaxCalculator r1 = new SalesTaxCalculator ();
```

Here, the `new` operator is calling the `SalesTaxCalculator()` constructor. If the constructor is explicitly defined within the class just as shown in Example 4.7, it is known as *explicit constructor*, otherwise Java automatically creates a default constructor as soon as the object is instantiated by the `new` operator. They are known as *implicit* or *default* or *no-argument constructors*. In earlier examples, no constructor was explicitly provided, so Java provided them with a default constructor. But in case you define your own constructor within the class (Example 4.7), the default constructor will not be provided by Java. In that case, the constructor defined within the class will be called.

The default constructor, provided by Java compiler, is a no-argument constructor with empty body. The only question that would arise now is that if the default constructor is an empty constructor, then how are the variables initialized to the user specific values or default values and who does it? For example in case of Examples 4.2, 4.2(a), and 4.2(b), when instance variable initializers are used and no constructors has been defined in the `SalesTaxCalculator` class, how are the objects `obj1` and `obj2` initialized with the values specified in instance variable initializers as the default constructor is an empty constructor. What happens in the background is that Java compiler creates a special method known as `<init>` method for each of the constructors specified in the class. The code explicitly written in the constructors is placed within the `<init>` method after some operations like calling the superclass constructor, instance variable initializers and instance initialization blocks in the order in which they appear in the source code. When no constructors have been specified, the Java compiler creates a default constructor and an `<init>` method for the default constructor. This method will also include a call to superclass constructor as well as the instance variable initializers and instance initialization block (if any mentioned in the class and in the order mentioned in the source code). When no constructors and no instance variable initializer or block have been specified, the Java compiler creates a default constructor and `<init>` method for the default constructor, which initializes the instance variables with their respective default values.

> **Note** `<init>` is a special method, meant for the JVM (to initialize objects) and not the programmer. So you cannot create a method by this name in your program. Also note that the arguments of this method would be same as that of the constructors and the return type would be void. This `init` mechanism was created in Java to ensure that memory allocated is initialized properly and any bugs should not arise due to garbage values in memory as in the case of other languages like C and C++.

Table 4.2 provides a summary on constructors versus methods.

Table 4.2 Constructors vs Methods

Constructor	Methods
Do not have any return type not even `void`	Will have a return type
Will have the same name as that of class	Can have any name even the name of class (although should not be used)
Invoked as soon as the object is created and not thereafter	Invoked after the object is created (instance methods) and can be called any number of times thereafter
Constructors cannot be inherited	Methods can be inherited
Constructors can be overloaded	Methods can also be overloaded
Constructors can be private, protected, default or public	Methods can also be private, protected, default or public
Role of constructor is to initialize object	Role of method is to perform operations
Constructors cannot be abstract, final, static or synchronized	Methods can be abstract, final, static or synchronized

Let us take an example to illustrate the usage of constructor. L3 of Example 4.7 defines an explicit default constructor that does not accept any argument but initializes the instance variables to the specified values.

Example 4.7 Constructor

```
L1      class Room{
L2          double length, breadth, height, volume;
            No Argument Constructor
L3          Room(){
L1              length = 14;
L5              breadth = 12;
L6              height = 10;
L7          }

L8          // Computation of volume of the room
L9          double volComp(){
L10         volume = length * breadth * height;
L11         return volume;
L12         }
L13         public static void main (String args[ ]){
L14         Room r1 = new Room();
L15         Room r2 = new Room();
L16         System.out.println("The volume of the room is " +r1.volComp());
L17         System.out.println("The volume of the room is " +r2.volComp());
L18         }
L19     }
```

Output

```
D:\javabook\programs\chap 4>java Room
The volume of the room is 1680.0
The volume of the room is 1680.0
```

Explanation

L3 A constructor with the name of the class, `Room`, is defined. It should be noted that the constructor declaration is very much like a method declaration but does not have a return type.

L4 & 6 Various instance variables are initialized with certain values.

L9 & 12 Instance method `volComp()`is defined and implemented for calculating and returning the volume of the room to the caller. The return type of the method is specified as `double`. Return values are expected from methods when you would like to perform more operations on the returned values or want to pass them further. Here volume is returned specifically to denote how values are returned from methods. The volume calculated is stored in the instance variable `volume`, which is returned at the end of the method with the help of `return` keyword. Please note that if a method specifies a return type then it must return a value of that type using a `return` keyword.

L14 & 15 Two objects, `r1` and `r2`, are created or instantiated using `new` operator. As soon as this is done, the constructor `Room()`on L3 is called automatically, which in turn initializes all the variables that it is defined for. The default constructor will not be provided by Java because we have defined a constructor for our class. So when we create object our defined constructors will be invoked which would initialize the objects. Obviously, in the background this task will be achieved using `<init>` method.

L16 & 17 The volume of both the objects of the `room` class is printed. Note that, `volComp()`is called by their respective objects, in order to return the value of volume. Here, the volume for both the instances will be same, because both the objects call the method `volComp()`, which uses the same set of dimensions for the volume calculation. It is so because both the objects are initialized with the same set of values, while being instantiated by the new operator.

Note Instance method, `volComp()`, directly uses the instance variable: `length`, `breadth`, `height`, and `volume`. A very common mistake that many novice OOP programmers make, is to pass arguments to methods, multiply them and return the result. Although this might produce correct result but would not be correct OOPs approach as you are working with local variable rather than instance variables. Suppose if you create the `volComp()` method as shown below:

```
double volComp (double length, double breadth, double height){
        volume = length * breadth * height;
        return volume;
    }
```

In this case, you are using local variables for calculating volume. The purpose is to calculate the volume of the room whose dimensions are already encapsulated in the Room object. So for that we need to access the instance variables as shown in Example 4.7 and not local variables. The usage of local variables defeats our purpose.

4.6.1 Parameterized Constructors

Just like methods, arguments can be passed to the constructors, in order to initialize the instance variables of an object. The above example had a limitation. Each Room has its own `length`, `breadth`, and `height` and it is very unlikely that each room is of the same size. In the previous example, all objects of Room class will have the same `volume` because the values for `length`, `breadth` and `height` are fixed for all objects. You can explicitly change them using an object instance, e.g.,

```
r1.length = 30
```

and then invoke the method `volComp` for calculating volume of the Room. But there should be a mechanism for specifying different values of instance variables for different objects of a class, as soon as the object is created. For example, if different dimensions can be specified for a Room then each Room will have its own volume. For this, the instance variables should be assigned a different set of values for different objects of the class. Hence we need to create a parameterized constructor that accepts arguments to initialize the instance variables with the arguments. Let us take an example to see how parameterized constructors can be used.

Example 4.8 **Parameterized Constructor**

```
L1      class Room2 {
L2      double length, breadth, height, volume;
L3      Room2(double l, double b, double h) {
L4          length = l;
L5          breadth = b;
L6          height = h;
L7      }
L8      // Computation of volume of the room
L9      double volComp(){
```

```
L10        volume = length * breadth * height;
L11        return volume;
L12    }
L13    public static void main (String args[ ]) {
L14        Room2 r1 = new Room2(14, 12, 10);
L15        Room2 r2 = new Room2(16, 15, 11);
L16        System.out.println("The volume of the room is " +r1.volComp());
L17        System.out.println("The volume of the room is " +r2.volComp());
L18    }
L19 }
```

Output

```
The volume of the room is 1680.0
The volume of the room is 2640.0
```

Explanation

Here we will explain only the relevant lines of the above example.

L3–7 The constructor Room2 is defined, which has three arguments: l, b, and h, of type double. These are assigned to instance variables, length, breadth and height, respectively.

L13 Instance r1 of class Room2 is created. The values for the parameters are passed to the constructor in L3, with the invocation of the explicit constructor.

L14 Second instance r2 of class Room2 is created. Another set of values for the parameters is passed to the constructor in L3, with the invocation of the explicit constructor.

L15 & 16 The volumes for both the instances of Room are printed. You can see in the output that both the volumes are different, because different sets of parameters are used to calculate the volumes.

Note In the above program, we have created a parameterized constructor. If we create an object as shown below:

```
Room2 r3 = new Room2();
```

Instead of

```
Room2 r1 = new Room2(14, 12, 10);
```

The compiler will not compile this program. The obvious reason is that we have created a parameterized constructor in this class and we are trying to call the default constructor. Java states that if you provide a constructor for your class, the (automatically created) default constructor will not be provided to your class. And here we are invoking a no argument constructor which is neither explicitly created in our class nor will it be implicitly provided by Java.

4.6.2 Constructor Overloading

Just like methods, constructors can also be overloaded. Constructors are declared just as we declare methods, except that the constructors don't have any return type. Constructors for a class have the same name as that of the class, but they can have different signatures, i.e., different types of arguments or different number of arguments.

Such constructors can be termed as *overloaded constructors*. Constructors are differentiated on the basis of arguments passed to them.

In the example below, we have used two overloaded constructors, each having a different number of arguments, so that the JVM can differentiate between the various constructors.

Here we have two different classes, `Rectangle` and `ConstOverloading`. The `Rectangle` class has two constructors, both with the same name but different signatures. Each constructor is used for the initialization of instance variables.

Example 4.9 Rectangle Class Depicting Constructor Overloading

```
L1      Class Rectangle{
L2      int l, b;
L3      Rectangle(){
L4          l = 10;
L5          b = 20;
L6      }
L7      Rectangle(int x, int y){
L8          l = x;
L9          b = y;
L10     }
L11     int area()
L12     {
L13         return l * b;
L14     }
L15     }
```

Explanation

L3–5 Explicit default constructor is defined for the `Rectangle` class. This constructor initializes the instance variables with integer values.

L7–10 An overloaded constructor is defined for the `Rectangle` class, which accepts two integer values for initializing two instance variables.

L11–14 An instance method `area()` is defined to return the area of the rectangel.

Example 4.10 shows the second class `ConstOverloading,` which has the `main()` method inside it. While creating different instances of the `Rectangle` class, different overloaded constructors of the class are invoked with different number of parameters passed through the constructors. The values passed through the various constructors are used to initialize different instances of the `Rectangle` class.

Example 4.10 Testing the Overloaded Constructors

```
L1      class ConstOverloading {
L2      public static void main(String args[]) {
L3      Rectangle rectangle1 = new Rectangle();
L4    System.out.println("Area using first constructor:" +rectangle1.area());
L5    Rectangle rectangle2 = new Rectangle(4,5);
L6    System.out.println("Area using second constructor:" +rectangle2.area());
        }}
```

Output

```
Area using first constructor: 200
Area using second constructor: 20
```

Explanation

L3 The `Rectangle` object is created and the default constructor (i.e., no argument constructor, explicitly provided) is called.

L5 Another `Rectangle` object is created and the parameterized constructor is invoked. If there are a number of parameterized constructors in the class, then which constructor will be invoked will depend upon the exact matching of the number of argument and the type of arguments in order. In our case, two integer arguments are passed, so a constructor is searched which accepts two integer arguments which is already defined in L7, Example 4.9.

The above example shows a case of overloaded constructors with differing number of arguments. Another case would be where different type of arguments can also be passed into the overloaded constructors.

4.7 CLEANING UP UNUSED OBJECTS

Many other object-oriented languages require that you keep a track of all the objects you create and that you destroy them when they are no longer needed. Objects are allocated memory from the heap memory and when they are not needed their allocated memory should be reclaimed. The clean-up code is tedious and often error-prone. Java allows programmer to create as many objects as they want, but frees them from worrying about destroying (deallocating memory) objects. The Java runtime environment deletes objects when it determines that they are no longer required. It has its own set of algorithms for deciding when the memory allocated to an object must be reclaimed. This automated process is known as *garbage collection*.

An object is eligible for garbage collection when no references exist on that object. References can be either implicitly dropped when it goes out of scope or explicitly dropped by assigning `null` to an object reference.

4.7.1 Garbage Collector

The Java runtime environment has a garbage collector that periodically frees the memory used by objects that are no longer needed. Two basic approaches used by garbage collectors are *Reference counting* and *tracing*. Reference counting maintains a reference count for every object. A newly created object will have count as 1. Throughout its lifetime, the object will be referred to by many other object thus incrementing the reference count and as the referencing object move to other objects, the reference count for that particular object is decremented. When reference count for a particular object is 0, the object can be garbage collected.

Tracing technique traces the entire set of objects (starting from root) and all objects having reference on them are marked in some way. Tracing garbage collector algorithm popularly known as is *mark and sweep* garbage collector scans Java's dynamic memory areas for objects, marking those objects that are referenced. After all the objects are investigated, the objects that are not marked (not referenced) are assumed to be garbage and their memory is reclaimed. Mark and sweep collectors further use the techniques of `Compaction` and `Copying` for fragmentation problems (refer to memory management in operating system for details) that may arise once you sweep the unreferenced objects. Compaction moves all the live objects towards one end making the other end a large free space and copying techniques copies all live objects besides each other into a new space and the old space is considered free now.

The garbage collector runs either synchronously or asynchronously in a low priority daemon thread. The garbage collector executes *synchronously* when the system runs out of memory or *asynchronously* when the system is idle. The garbage collector can be invoked to run at any time by calling `System.gc()` or `Runtime.gc()`. But asking the garbage collector to run does not guarantee that your objects will be garbage collected.

4.7.2 Finalization

Before an object gets garbage collected, the garbage collector gives the object an opportunity to clean up itself through a call to the object's `finalize()` method. This process is known as *finalization*.

All occupied resources (sockets, files, etc.) can be freed in this method. The `finalize()` method is a member function of the predefined `java.lang.Object` class. A class must override the `finalize()`method to perform any clean up if required by the object.

4.7.3 Advantages and Disadvantages

There are many advantages of using garbage collection apart from freeing the programmer from worrying about deallocation of memory. It also helps in ensuring integrity of programs. There is no way by which Java programmers can knowingly or unknowingly free memory incorrectly.

The disadvantage of garbage collection is the overhead to keep track of which objects are being referenced by the executing program and which are not being referenced. The overhead is also incurred on finalization and freeing memory of the unreferenced objects. These activities will incur more CPU time than would have been incurred if the programmers would have explicitly deallocated memory.

4.8 CLASS VARIABLES AND METHODS—`static` KEYWORD

When we create an object, a primitive type variable, or call a method, some amount of memory is set aside for the said object, variable, or method. Different objects, variables, and methods will occupy different areas of memory when created/called. Sometimes we would like to have multiple objects, shared variables, or methods. The `static` keyword effectively does this for us. It is possible to have *static methods* and *variables*.

Before going further, we must discuss the kind of variables Java supports. These include: *local variables*, *instance variables*, and *class/static variables*.

Local Variables Local variables are declared inside a method, constructor, or a block of code. When a method is entered, its contents (values of local variables) are pushed onto the call stack. When the method exits, its contents are popped off the stack and the memory in stack is now available for the next method. Parameters passed to the method are also local variables which are initialized from the actual parameters. The scope of local variables is limited to the method in which they have been defined. They have to be declared and initialized before they are used. Access specifiers like `private`, `public`, and `protected` cannot be used with local variables.

Instance Variables Instance variables are declared inside a class, but outside a method. They are also called *data member*, *field*, or *attributes*. An object is allotted memory for all its instance variables on the heap memory. As objects instance variables remain live as long as the object is active. They are accessible directly in all the instance methods and constructors of the class in which they have been defined. By default, they are initialized to their default values according to their respective types.

Class/static Variables Class/static variables declaration is preceded with the keyword `static`. They are also declared inside a class, but outside a method. The most important point about static variables is that there exists only a single copy of static variables per class. All objects of the class share this variable. Static variables are normally used for constants. By default, static variables are initialized to their default values according to their respective types.

4.8.1 Static Variables

Java does not allow global variables. The closest thing we can get to a global variable in Java is to make the instance variable in the class `static`. The effect of doing this is that when we create multiple objects of that class, every object shares the static variable, i.e. there is only one copy of the variable declared as `static`. To make an instance variable static we simply precede the declaration with the keyword `static`.

```
static int var = 0;
```

In effect, what we are really doing is that this instance variable, `var`, no matter how many objects are created, should always reside in the same memory location, regardless of the object. This then simulates like a 'global variable.' We usually declare a variable as final and static as well, since it makes sense to have only one instance of a constant. It is worthwhile to note that people refer to static instance variables as 'class variables.' Before proceeding further, let us take an example to depict how static variables are declared.

Note **Instance Variables vs Class Variables**
Class variables can be declared with the 'static' keyword. For example,

```
static int y = 0;
```

All instances of the class share the static variables of the class. A class variable can be accessed directly with the class name, without the need to create an instance.
Without the 'static' keyword, it is called an 'instance variable' and each instance of the class has its own copy of the variable.

Example 4.11 **Instance and Class Variables**

In the following code, the class `Test1` has two variables, `x` and `y`.

```
L1    class Test1 {
L2    int x = 0;            // instance variable
L3    static int y = 0;     // class variable

      //setter methods
L4    void setX (int n) {x = n;}
L5    void setY (int n) {y = n;}

      //getter methods
L6    int getX() { return x;}
L7    int getY() { return y;}
      }
```

We could have another class `Test2` having the `main()` function where the use of static variable declared in the class `Test1` can be shown:

Example 4.12 **A Class Showing the Use of Class (Static) Variables**

```
L1   class Test2 {
L2   public static void main(String[] arg){
L3       Test1 t1 = new Test1();
L4       Test1 t2 = new Test1();
L5       t1.setX(9);
L6       t2.setX(10); // object t1 and t2 have separate copies of x
L7   System.out.println("Instance variable of object t1 : " +t1.getX());
L8   System.out.println("Instance variable of object t2 : " +t2.getX());
     // class variable can be accessed directly through Class Name
     // (if changed to Test2.x, it won't compile)
L9       System.out.println("Value of y accessed through class Name: " +Test1.y);
L10      Test1.y = 7;
L11      System.out.println("Changed value of y accessed through class Name: " +Test1.y);
     // class variable can be manipulated thru methods as usual
L12      t1.setY(Test1.y+1);
     // class variable can be accessed through objects also
L13      System.out.println("Value of y accessed through object t2:" +t2.getY());
L14      }
L15  }
```

Output

```
Instance variable of object t1 : 9
Instance variable of object t2 : 10
Value of y accessed through class Name: 0
Changed value of y accessed through class Name: 7
Value of y accessed through object t2: 8
```

Explanation

L7 Output printed is 9, i.e., the instance variable is printed with the help of the object.

L8 Output printed is 10, i.e., another instance variable is printed with the help of the object.

L9 Output printed is 0. It is important to note that here, we need not have an object for class Test 1 to access the static variable of Test 1 (refer to L3 of class Test 1).

L10 Static variable is assigned a value 7 using the class name itself.

L11 Output printed is 7.

L12 Instance method setY() is invoked using the object t1, where the value of static variable, y (i.e., 7), accessed through class name Test1 is incremented by 1 and passed as argument.

L13 Output printed is 8, as t2.getY() returns the value set by t1.setY() in L12. This is done to show that the value of y is being shared by all the objects of the class, as it is a static variable.

4.8.2 Static Methods

Like static variables, we do not need to create an object to call our static method. Simply using the class name will suffice. Static methods however can only access static variables directly. Variables that have not been declared static cannot be accessed by the static method directly, i.e., the reason why we create an object of the class within the main (which is static) method to access instance variables and call instance methods. To make a method static, we simply precede the method declaration with the keyword static.

```
static void a Method(int param1) { ..... ..... }
```

> **Note**   **Instance Method vs Class Method**
>
> `static` methods can be accessed through the class name itself. Methods declared without the `static` keyword (instance methods) can be accessed using the object/instance of the residing class. `static` methods are also known as class methods.
>
> `static` methods can call other static methods directly. If a static method to be invoked is within the same class, then only the `static` method name can be mentioned to invoke it. Else if the `static` method is outside the class, then the class name has to be prefixed with the `static` method name to invoke it. But invoking `non-static` methods (instance methods) from static methods requires an instance of the class. Also note that methods declared as `static` cannot access the variables declared without the `static` keyword. It is quite evident in the following example where it gives a compilation error, un less x is also static.
>
> ```java
> class Test {
> int x = 3;
> static int returnX(){
>     return x;
> }
> public static void main(String args[])
> {
> System.out.println(returnX()); // static method invoked directly
> }}
> ```

Let us take an example to show the use of static methods.

Example 4.13   A Class Having Static Members

```java
L1          class Area {
L2          static int area; // class variable
L3          static int computeArea (int width, int height){
L4              area = width * height;
L5              return area;
L6              }
L7          }
```

The above class `Area` has a class variable declared in L2 and a static method, `computeArea()` with two arguments in L3.

Example 4.14   Calling Static Method from Another Class

```java
L1      class CallArea{
L2      public static void main(String args[]){
L3          System.out.println(Area.computeArea(4,3));
L4          }
L5      }
```

Output

```
12
```

Explanation

L3 The method `computeArea()` of class `Area` is being called without referencing it through any object/instance. Instead, it can be invoked using that class name only, which it belongs to. It is so because this method has been declared as static in L3 of class `Area`. The return value of the method is printed using `System.out.println()`.

4.8.3 Static Initialization Block

A block of statements can be enclosed in parenthesis with `static` keyword applied to it. This block of statement is used for initializing static or class variables. If the initialization logic is simple, the class variables can be assigned values directly but in case some logic is used for assigning values to the variables, static blocks can be used. The syntax for static block is as follows:

```
static
{
    ...
}
```

The `static` executes as soon as the class loads even before the JVM executes the main method. There can be any number of `static` blocks within the class and they will be executed in the order in which they have appeared in the source code.

Note In case the `static` keyword is dropped from this block, it becomes an instance initialization block and all code placed inside this block is placed inside the constructors before the source code written in the constructor by the Java compiler. Actually the code of instance initialization block is placed in the <init> method, which is created for every constructor by the compiler, before the source code mentioned by programmer in the constructor.

Let us take an example to see how `static` block, instance initialization block, instance variable initializes and constructor executes. The program clearly shows that static block executes even before main method. This program also includes an instance variable instance initialization blocks with a constructor. Both the instance block and the constructor code gets invoked as soon as the object of the class is created. How? As already stated, the code of initializer instance initialization block is placed within the constructor, before the constructors own code, by Java compiler. This is evident by seeing the output, the print statement in the instance initialization block executes before statement mentioned in the constructor. The static block also shows declaration of a variable which is local to the block.

Example 4.15   **Static Initialization Block, Instance Initialization Block and Constructor**

```
class StaticBlockDemo
{
```

```java
int x=10;    // instance variable initializer
/* static initialization block */
static
{

        int z=10; // local variable
        System.out.println("In static block");
}
// Instance initialization block
{
        System.out.println("In Instance Initialization block");
        System.out.println("Printing Instance variable Initializer
        value through Block: " +x);
}
// Constructor
StaticBlockDemo(int y)
{
        System.out.println("Within Constructor");
        System.out.println("Instance variable printed using constructor: "+x);
        x=y;
        System.out.println("Instance variable initialized using constructor: "+x);
}

        /* To see whether the code of instance variable initializer
        and block is copied within every constructor we create another
        constructor and see the output. The following constructor when
        invoked also prints the contents of instance variable intializer
        and block.  So the contents of instance variable initializer and
        block are copied in every constructor by the compiler. In other
        word, they are copied in every <init> method created for every
        constructor before the constructors own code.*/

StaticBlockDemo()
{
        System.out.println("Within Constructor");
        System.out.println("Instance variable printed using constructor: "+x);
}
public static void main(String[] args)
{
        System.out.println("In main");
        StaticBlockDemo st = new StaticBlockDemo(100);
        System.out.println("-------------------------------------------");
        StaticBlockDemo st1 = new StaticBlockDemo();
    }
}
```

Output

```
D:\javaprg>java StaticBlockDemo
In static block
In main
In Instance Initialization block
Printing Instance variable Initializer value through Block: 10
Within Constructor
Instance variable printed using constructor: 10
Instance variable initialized using constructor: 100
-------------------------------------------
In Instance Initialization block
Printing Instance variable Initializer value through Block: 10
Within Constructor
Instance variable printed using constructor: 10
```

4.9 this KEYWORD

The keyword this is used in an instance method to refer to the object that contains the method, i.e., it refers to the current object. Whenever and wherever a reference to an object of the current class type is required, this can be used.

It can also differentiate between instance variables and local variables. Let us revisit the code segment of Example 4.8. Here the use of this will make you understand its use.

```
L3      Room2(double l, double b, double h){
L4        this.length = l;
L5        this.breadth = b;
L6        this.height = h;
L7      }
```

Here, the use of this does not do anything differently than the earlier code in Example 4.8. It is perfectly legitimate to use it in the way it has been done. Inside Room2, this will always refer to the current object, of Room2. The obvious question that would arise is when and why should we use this in an application?

The exact purpose of this is to remove ambiguity between local and instance variables. In Example 4.8, we had three instance variables declared in L2. Look carefully. The formal (local variables) parameters of Room() in L3 have different names, (l, b, and h) from the instance variables (length, breadth, and height). The values of these formal parameters are passed to the instance variables. If a like names are provided for both the parameters (formal and instance variables) then the instance variables will be hidden (or shadowed) by the local variables. Suppose the formal parameters had been named as length, breadth, and height, which are also the names of the instance variables used in the class, then it is difficult to distinguish between local variable and instance variable as shown below:

```
Room2 (double length, double breadth, double height){
       length = length;
       breadth = breadth;
       height = height;
       }
```

It is an ambiguous situation for the JVM as it does not understand what has to be done; whether instance variables have to be initialized with formal parameters or vice versa. The problem arises because JVM cannot clearly distinguish which is a local variable and which is an instance variable. In this case the local variables shadow or hide the instance variables. If you try to access or print the `length` variables in the constructor `Room2`, the local variable `length` will be printed and not the instance variable: `length`, this allows you to solve the problem of a variable's scope, because it lets you refer to the object directly. `this` keyword makes a clear cut distinction between local and instance variable. `this.length` refers to the `length` instance variable of the current object. The above block of code can be re-written as follows.

```
Room2 (double length, double breadth, double height){
      this.length = length;
      this.breadth = breadth;
      this.height = height;
      }
```

In the above code it is clearly evident local variable `length` value should be assigned to the instance variable `length` of the current object and soon for other variables.

Hence, the names of instance variables and the formal parameters can be kept similar because `this` has made it possible for the JVM to differentiate between instance and local variables. Still, one can argue that a programmer can very well use different variable names for instance and local variables.

Constructor Chaining It means a constructor can be called from another constructor. Let us revisit Example 4.8.

```
/* First Constructor */
   Room2( )
   {


          // constructor chained
          this(14,12,10);
   }
/* Second Constructor */
   Room2 (double l, double b, double h)
   {
   length = l;
         breadth = b;
         height = h;
   }
```

In the above code, two constructors have been created: one without arguments and another with three arguments. In the first constructor, we have used `this` keyword to call the second constructor and passed the required arguments in the call to second constructor.

Whenever we create an object of the class `Room2` as,

```
Room2 r1 = new Room2();
```

the first constructor will be invoked which is chained to the second constructor.

4.10 ARRAYS

Till now, we have discussed how to declare variables of a particular data type, which can store a single value of that data type. The allocation of memory space, when a variable is declared, cannot further be sub-divided to store more than one value. There are situations where we might wish to store a group of similar type of values in a variable. It can be achieved by a special kind of data structure known as *arrays*.

An *array* is a memory space allocated that can store multiple values of same data type in contiguous locations. This memory space, which can be perceived to have many logical contiguous locations, can be accessed with a common name. For example, we can define an array as 'marks' to represent a set of marks of a group of students. Now the next question is how to access a particular value from a particular location? A specific element in an array is accessed by the use of a subscript or an index used inside the brackets, along with the name of the array. For example, `marks[5]` would store the marks of the fifth student. While the complete set of values is called an array, the individual values are known as *elements*. Arrays can be two types:

- one dimensional array
- multi-dimensional array

4.10.1 One-dimensional Arrays

In a one-dimensional array, a single subscript or index is used, where each index value refers to an individual array element. The indexation will start from 0 and will go up to $n-1$, i.e., the first value of the array will have an index of 0 and the last value will have an index of $n-1$, where n is the number of elements in the array. So, if an array named marks has been declared to store the marks of five students, the computer reserves five contiguous locations in the memory, as shown in Fig. 4.4.

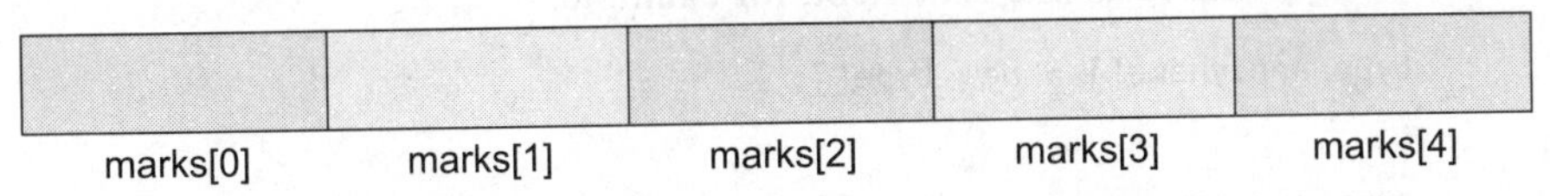

Fig. 4.4 Marks Array

Suppose, the five marks to be assigned to each array element are 60, 58, 50, 78, and 89. It will be done as follows:

```
Marks[0] = 60;
Marks[1] = 58;
Marks[2] = 50;
Marks[3] = 78;
Marks[4] = 89;
```

Figure 4.5 shows the marks array with data elements.

60	58	50	78	89
marks[0]	marks[1]	marks[2]	marks[3]	marks[4]

Fig. 4.5 Marks Array Having Data Elements

Creation of Array

Creating an array, similar to an object creation, can inherently involve three steps:

- Declaring an array
- Creating memory locations
- Initializing/assigning values to an array

Declaring an Array Declaring an array is same as declaring a normal variable except that you must use a set of square brackets with the variable type. There can be two ways in which an array can be declared.

- `type arrayname[];`
- `type[] arrayname;`

So the above `marks` array having elements of integer type can be declared either as

```
int marks[];
```

or

```
int[] marks;
```

Creating Memory Locations An array is more complex than a normal variable, so we have to assign memory to the array when we declare it. You assign memory to an array by specifying its size. Interestingly, our same old `new` operator helps in doing the job, just as shown below:

```
Arrayname = new type [size];
```

So, allocating space and size for the array named as `marks` can be done as,

```
marks = new int[5];
```

Both (declaration of array and creation of memory location), help in the creation of an array. These can be combined as one statement, for example,

```
type arrayname[] = new type[];
```

or

```
type[] arrayname = new type[];
```

It is interesting to know what the JVM actually does while executing the above syntax. During the declaration phase, `int marks[];`

marks ⟶ `Null`

Figure 4.6 shows the marks array after memory is allocated to the array on execution of the following statement:

```
marks = new int[5];
```

Here is an example to show how to create an array that has 5 marks of integer type.

```
class Array{
public static void main(String[]
args){
    int[] marks = new int[5];
    }
}
```

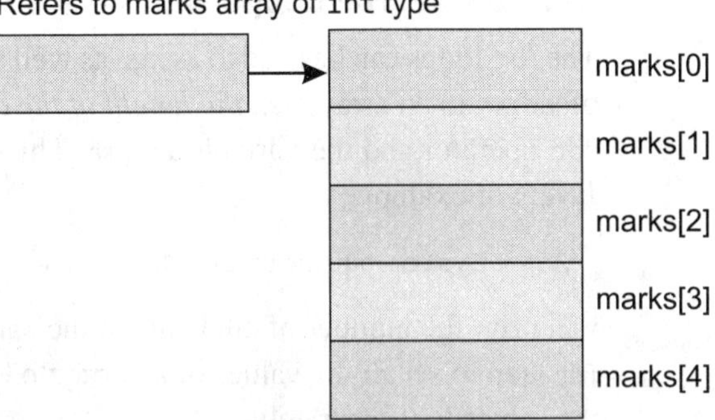

Fig. 4.6 Creation of Arrays

Initializing/assigning Values to an Array Assignment of values to an array, which can also be termed as initialization of array, can be done as follows:

```
Arrayname[index] = value;
```

We have just discussed how to create a list of parameters to be assigned in an array. Example 4.16 shows how to set the values for an array of 5 marks (Fig. 4.6).

Example 4.16 **Setting Values in an Array**

```
L1    class Array {
L2    public static void main(String[] args){
L3       int[] marks = new int[5];
L4       marks[0] = 60;
L5       marks[1] = 58;
L6       marks[2] = 50;
L7       marks[3] = 78;
L8       marks[4] = 89;
L9       }
L10   }
```

Arrays can alternately be assigned values or initialized in the same way as the variables, i.e., at the time of declaration itself. The syntax for the same can be,

```
type arrayname[] = {list of values};
```

For example, `int marks[] = {60, 58, 50, 78, 89}`

Here, the `marks` array is initialized at the time of creation of array itself. The above statement does the same thing as the code between L3 to 8 of Example 4.16. An example of array creation and initialization is given below.

Example 4.17 **Creation and Initialization of an Array**

```
class Array
{
public static void main(String[] args){
   int[] marks = {60, 58, 50, 78, 89};
}
}
```

How to Use for Loops with Arrays?

The for loops can be used to assign as well as access values from an array. To obtain the number of values in an array, i.e., *the length of the array,* we use the name of the array followed by the dot operator and the variable length. This length property is associated with all the arrays in Java. For example,

```
System.out.println("There are " + marks.length + "in the array");
```

will print the number of elements in the marks array, i.e., 5. Example 4.18 shows how to use a for loop to set all the values of an array to 0 which, you will see, is much easier than setting all the values to 0 separately.

Example 4.18 Setting Values in an Array Using for Loop

```
L1    class Array {
L2    public static void main(String[] args){
L3      int[] marks = new int[5];
L4      for (int i = 0; i<marks.length; i++)
L5      marks[i] = 0;
L6      }
L7    }
```

Explanation

L3 Creates an array marks, having five locations to store five elements.

L4 i signifies the subscript of the array, which is always an integer type. The for loop starts with the first location of the array, it stands at the 0th subscript and iterates by 1 up to the last location of the array, which is returned by marks.length.

Various operations can also be performed on the values of an array, which can again be assigned to the array. For example, the following code increments all the marks in the class by 5.

Example 4.19 Incrementing the Values of Data Elements in an Array

```
for (inti = 0; i<grades.length; i++){
    grades[i] = marks[i] + 5;
}
```

To access a particular value in the array, we use the name of the array, followed by an open bracket, followed by an expression that gives the index, followed by a close bracket. For example, here is a simple code to print all the marks in the array of marks declared above.

Example 4.20 Printing the Values of Data Elements of an Array

```
for (inti = 0; i<marks.length; i++){
    System.out.println(marks[i]);
}
```

Sorting an Array Let us take an example where we apply all the concepts of array that we have learnt until now. If we have been given a set of marks and we have to sort the marks in ascending order.

Example 4.21 | **Sorting an Array**

```java
class SortArray{
public static void main(String[] args)
{
    int[] marks = {3, 5, 1, 2, 4};
    int temp, n;
    n = marks.length;
    System.out.print("The list of marks is: ");
    for(int i =  0; i< n; i++){
    System.out.print(marks[i]+ " ");
}

    for (int i = 0; i< n; i++){
    for (int j = i+1; j < n; j++){
    if (marks[i] < marks[j])
    {
        temp = marks[i];
        marks[i] = marks[j];
        marks[j] = temp;
    }
    }
    }
System.out.print("\nList of marks sorted in descending order is: ");
    for (int i = 0; i< n; i++)
    {
        System.out.print(marks[i]+" ");
    }
    }
    }
```

Output

```
c:\javabook\programs\chap4>java SortArray
The list of marks is: 3 5 1 2 4
List of marks sorted in descending order is: 5 4 3 2 1
```

Explanation

L1 Class `SortArray` declared.

L2 `main()` declared and its body starts with left {.

L3 Array named `marks` created with initialized values.

L4 Instance variables, `temp` and `n` declared to be integer type.

L5 Length of the array is stored in n.

L7–9 for loop is used to print the values of the original list, i.e., `marks`.

L10 Defines for loop which iterates from 0 to length of the array −1.

L11 A nested for loop is declared which iterates from i + 1 to n −1. L12–16 are part of the inner for loop, and these statements are executed for each value of i from 0 to n –1 and j from 1 to n–1 as shown in Fig. 4.7 below.

L12–16 In the first iteration, value of i is 0 and j is 1. The marks at the 0th index are compared with the marks at the first index. If marks at 0th index are less than marks at the 1st index they are swapped. For swapping, a temporary variable named temp is created (L13). Marks at ith index (first iteration value of i is 0) are assigned to temp (L14). The marks at jth (first iteration value of j is 1) index are assigned to marks at marks at ith index (L15) and marks in temporary variable are assigned to marks at the jth position. Thus the value of jth position is swapped with the value at ith position. Figure 4.7 illustrates how the outer and inner loops execute for each value of i and j. It also shows when the values of the array are swapped.

L20–22 Display the sorted array. The array has been sorted in descending order.

When i = 0		
j = 1	marks[0] < marks[1] (3)　　　(5)	Yes, so they are swapped New Array is 5, 3, 1, 2, 4
j = 2	marks[0] < marks[2] (5)　　　(1)	No, not swapped New Array is 5, 3, 1, 2, 4
j = 3	marks[0] < marks[3] (5)　　　(2)	No, not swapped New Array is 5, 3, 1, 2, 4
j = 4	marks[0] < marks[4] (5)　　　(4)	No, not swapped New Array is 5, 3, 1, 2, 4
When i = 1		
j = 2	marks[1] < marks[2] (3)　　　(1)	No, not swapped New Array is 5, 3, 1, 2, 4
j = 3	marks[1] < marks[3] (3)　　　(2)	No, not swapped New Array is 5, 3, 1, 2, 4
j = 4	marks[1] < marks[4] (3)　<　(4)	Yes, swapped New Array is 5, 4, 1, 2, 3
When i = 2		
j = 3	marks[2] < marks[3] (1)　<　(2)	Yes, swapped New Array is 5, 4, 2, 1, 3
j = 4	marks[2] < marks[4] (2)　<　(3)	Yes, swapped New Array is 5, 4, 3, 1, 2
When i = 3		
j = 4	marks[3] < marks[4] (1)　<　(2)	Yes, swapped New Array is 5, 4, 3, 2, 1
When i = 4		
j = 5	Inner for loop does not execute.	
When i = 5, Outer for loop exits		

Fig. 4.7 Execution of Loops in SortArray Example

4.10.2 Two-dimensional Arrays

Sometimes values can be conceptualized in the form of a table that is in the form of rows and columns. Suppose we want to store the marks of different subjects. We can store it in a one-dimensional array.

Now if we want to add a second dimension in the form of roll no of the student. This is possible only if we follow a tabular approach of storing data, as shown in Table 4.4.

You can easily notice that Table 4.3 can store only subject names and the marks obtained by one student, while Table 4.4 can store the details of multiple students. There can be enumerable such situations where we can use a two-dimensional structure. Java provides a solution for the storage of such a structure in the form of two-dimensional arrays.

If you want a multidimensional array, the additional index has to be specified using another set of square brackets. The following statements create a two-dimensional array, named as marks, which would have 4 rows and 5 columns, as shown in Table 4.4.

Table 4.3 One-dimensional Marks Array

Subjects	Marks
Physics	60
Chemistry	58
Mathematics	50
English	78
Biology	89

Table 4.4 Two-dimensional Marks Array

Subject Roll No.	Physics	Chemistry	Mathematics	English	Biology
01	60	67	47	74	78
02	54	47	67	70	67
03	74	87	76	69	88
04	39	45	56	55	67

```
int marks[][]           //declaration of a two-dimensional array
marks = new int[4][5];  //reference to the array allocated, stored in marks
                        variable
```

This is done in the same way as it has already been explained while discussing one-dimensional arrays. The two statements, used for array creation, can be merged into one as,

```
int marks[][] = new int[4][5];
```

Another way of representing the above statement can be,

```
int[][] marks = new[4][5];
```

This statement just allocates a 4×5 array and assigns the reference to the array variable marks. The first subscript inside the square bracket signifies the number of rows in the table or matrix and the second subscript stands for the number of columns. This 4×5 table can store 20 values altogether. Its values might be stored in contiguous locations in the memory, but logically, the stored values would be treated as if they are stored in a 4×5 matrix. Table 4.5 shows how the marks array is conceptually placed in the memory by the above statement.

Table 4.5 4 × 5 Marks Array

60 (marks[0][0])	67 (marks[0][1])	47 (marks[0][2])	74 (marks[0][3])	77 (marks[0][4])
54 (marks[1][0])	47 (marks[1][1])	67 (marks[1][2])	70 (marks[1][3])	67 (marks[1][4])
74 (marks[2][0])	87 (marks[2][1])	76 (marks[2][2])	69 (marks[2][3])	88 (marks[2][4])
39 (marks[3][0])	45 (marks[3][1])	56 (marks[3][2])	55 (marks[3][3])	67 (marks[3][4])

Like a one-dimensional array, two-dimensional arrays may be initialized with values at the time of their creation. For example,

```
int marks[2][4] = {2, 3, 6, 0, 9, 3, 3, 2};
```

This declaration shows that the first two rows of a 2 × 4 matrix have been initialized by the values shown in the list above. It can also be written as,

```
int marks[][] = {(2, 3, 6, 0), (9, 3, 3, 2)};
```

In the above declaration, subscripts need not be shown, as it is evident from the manner in which the list of values have been presented. Here, the list of values has two different sets of values, separated by a comma, each standing for a row.

It is important to understand how Java treats 2-D arrays. 2-D arrays are treated as 1-D array. For example, the above declaration of 2 × 4 array will create three 1-D array. One for storing the number of row arrays (i.e. 2) and the other two arrays will be used for storing the contents of the rows. The size of these two arrays will be 4. As shown in Fig. 4.7, the size of row array is the number of rows and each field in the row array points to a 1-D array that contains the column values for the rows. So marks[0][0]will have the value 2, marks [0][1] will have 3, marks[1] [0] with 9, and so on.

Assigning and accessing the values in a two-dimensional array is done in the same way, as was done in a one-dimensional array. The only difference is that, here you have to take care of the positional values of the array using two subscripts (shown in square brackets), while in a one-dimensional array, only one subscript was used for the purpose. Table 4.5 shows the positional values of a two-dimensional array.

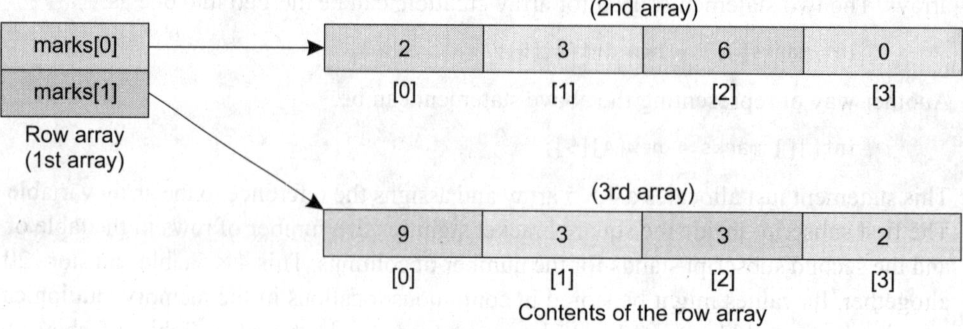

Fig. 4.8 2-D Array

All that you need to do to create and use a 2-D array is to use two square brackets instead of one.

Example 4.22   **Setting Values in a Two-dimensional Array**

```
L1    class DemoArray1 {
L2    public static void main(String[] args) {
L3    int a[][]  = new int [2][];
L4    /* int a1[][]  = new int [][2]; */
L5    int m[][] = {{2,3,6,0},{9, 3, 3, 2}};
L6    for(int i=0;i<m.length;i++)
         {
L7           for(int j=0;j<m[i].length;j++)
L8           System.out.print(m[i][j] +" ");
L9       System.out.println();
         }
    }}
```

Output

```
C:\javabook\programs\chap4>java DemoArray1
2 3 6 0
9 3 3 2
```

Explanation

L3–4   Shows the declaration of a 2-D integer array having two rows. The number of columns is not specified but the reverse declaration is illegal as shown in L4.

L5   Shows a declaration of a 2-D array with values assigned to it. No number has been specified in the row and column square brackets of array m. The rows and columns are decided on the basis of how the values are passed to the array. m is having 2 rows and 4 columns. The number of inner curly bracket (opening and closing) determines the number of rows (row array) and the number of individual values in a particular curly bracket (opening and closing) will determine the columns in a row (separate 1D array will be created for each row). Each index in a row array will point to a column array.

L6   A `for` loop is created. This `for` loop is used for iterating through the row array and that is why it iterates from 0 to the length of the array m.

L7   An inner `for` loop is created for iterating the columns in a row array. The inner `for` loop iterates from 0 to the length of the 1D array pointed by the individual fields in the row array. That is why the loop iterates up to `m[i].length`.

L8   Prints the individual items of the array at all row and column combinations.

Let us take a more complex but useful example of matrix multiplication. Two matrices are to be multiplied, so two arrays capable of holding the same number of rows and columns as matrices are required.

Example 4.23　Matrix Multiplication

```
L1   class MatrixMul {
L2   public static void main(String args[]) {
L3       int array[][] = {{3,7},{6,9}};
L4       int array1[][] = {{5,4},{3,6}};
L5       int array2[][] = new int[2][2];
L6       int x = array.length;
L7       System.out.println("Matrix 1: ");
L8       for (int i=0; i<array.length; i++) {
L9       for (int j=0; j<array[i].length; j++) {
L10          System.out.print(" "+array[i][j]);
L11      }
L12      System.out.println();
L13      }
L14      int y = array1.length;
L15      System.out.println("Matrix 2: ");
L16      for (int i=0; i<array1.length; i++) {
L17      for (int j=0; j<array1[i].length; j++)
         {
L18          System.out.print(" "+array1[i][j]);
L19      }
L20      System.out.println();
L21      }
L22      for (int i=0; i<x; i++) {
L23      for (int j=0; j<y; j++) {
L24      for(int k=0; k<y; k++) {
L25              array2[i][j] += array[i][k]*array1[k][j];
L26              }
L27          }
L28      }
L29      System.out.println("Multiplication of both matrices: ");
L30      for (int i=0; i<x; i++) {
L31      for (int j=0; j<y; j++) {
L32                  System.out.print(" "+array2[i][j]);
L33          }
L34              System.out.println();
L35      }
L36      }
L37 }
```

Output

```
Matrix 1:
 3 7
 6 9
Matrix 2:
 5 4
 3 6
Multiplication of both matrices:
 36 54
 57 78
```

Like 2-D arrays, we can define any multidimensional array having *n* dimensions. While declaring an *n*-dimensional array, *n* number of square brackets will be used. All the operations in any type of multidimensional array will be similar to that of a one-dimensional or two-dimensional array.

4.10.3 Using `for-each` with Arrays

The enhanced `for` loop, i.e., `for-each` was introduced in Java 5 to provide a simpler way to iterate through all the elements of an array or a collection. The format of `for-each` is as follows:

```java
for (type var : arr){
    // Body of loop
}
```

For example, we can use `for-each` loop to calculate the sum of elements of an array as follows:

```java
int[] arr = {2,3,4,5,6};
int sum = 0;
for(int a : arr) // a gets successively each value in arr
{
    sum += a;
}
```

The disadvantage of `for-each` approach is that it is possible to iterate in forward direction only by single steps.

4.10.4 Passing Arrays to Methods

Arrays can be passed to methods as well. The following example shows a two-dimensional array being passed to a method. The static method displays the contents of that array.

Example 4.24 **Arrays as Arguments to Methods**

```java
L1   class PassingArray
L2   {
L3     static void show(int[][] a)
L4     {
L5       for(int i=0;i<a.length;i++)
L6       {
L7          for(int j=0;j<2;j++)
L8          {
L9              System.out.print(" " +a[i][j]);
L10         }
L11     System.out.println();
L12     }
L13    }
L14    public static void main(String args[])
L15    {
L16       int a[][]={{1,2},{2,3}};
L17       show(a);
L18    }
L19  }
```

Output

```
D:\javabook\programs\chap4\PassingArray
1 2
2 3
```

Explanation

L1 Class declaration.
L3 Declares a static method 'show' that accepts an argument i.e., a two-dimensional array.
L5 Shows a for loop that would loop from 0 to the length of array. This for loop is basically used to refer to the first dimension of the 2D array.
L6 Marks the beginning of for loop defined in L5.
L7 Shows another for loop that would represent the second dimension. Our 2D array has only two elements as each array item. So the index for referencing any individual element would be a[0][0] or a[0][1] for the first row of the Array. Subsequently The next row items can be referenced as a [1][0] and a [1][1] and so on (a [2][0], a [2][1] etc.). As is evident, the second index does not go beyond 1, so we have declared a for loop, in this statement, that iterates for less than 2 times.

L9 Prints the individual elements of the array based on the values of indexes set by the values of i and j.
L10 Marks the closure of the inner for loop.
L11 Is a simple print statement used for formatting the output. This will move the cursor to new line. Basically it is used to show the individual elements of the array on a new line.
L12 Marks the closure of the outer for loop.
L13 Ends the method show.
L14 Main method declaration.
L16 An int array is defined and initialized with values.
L17 Static method show is invoked and array is passed as an argument to it. As show is a static method it can be invoked directly.
L18 & 19 Ends the main method and the class.

4.10.5 Returning Arrays from Methods

Arrays can not only be passed to methods but we can use arrays as return value from methods. If you are faced with a situation where you want to return multiple values from a method, all the values can be encapsulated in an array and returned. The following example shows a two dimensional array being returned from a method. The main method displays the contents of that array.

Example 4.25 **Returing Multiple Values**

```java
class ReturningAnArray
{
    // static method declared to return a 2D Array
    static int[][] show(){
    int a[][]={{1,2},{2,3}};
    return a;
}
public static void main(String args[])
{
    int a[][]=show();    // return value is captured in a 2D Array
    for(int i=0;i<a.length;i++)
    {
        for(int j=0;j<2;j++)
        {
            System.out.print(" " +a[i][j]);
```

```
            }
            System.out.println();
            }
        }
    }
```

Output

```
D:\javabook\programs\chap4\ReturningAnArray
1 2
2 3
```

Explanation

This program is almost the same as that of previous program. The difference is that the show method now returns a two-dimensional array. The logical steps to iterate the two-dimensional array is same as that of previous program with a change i.e., now they belong to main method instead of show method.

4.10.6 Variable Arguments

Variable arguments can be used when the number of arguments that you want to pass to a method are not fixed. The method can accept different number of arguments of same type whenever they are called. The generic syntax for this notation is:

```
returntype methodName(datatype...arrayname)
```

Let us take an example to show how it can be implemented.

Example 4.26   **Variable Arguments**

```
class VarArgs
{
    // integer variable argument used in add method
    static void add(int...a)
    {
        int sum=0;
        for(int i=0;i<a.length;i++)
        sum=sum+a[i];
        System.out.println("SUM = "+sum);
    }

    // variable arguments syntax used in main method
    public static void main(String...args)
    {

    // four arguments are passed to the add method
        add(2,3,4,5);
        // Three arguments are passed to the same add method
        add(2,3,4);
    }
}
```

Output

```
D:\javabook\programs\chap 4\java VarArgs
SUM = 14
SUM = 9
```

4.11 COMMAND-LINE ARGUMENTS

You must be aware of the basic DOS commands. Have you ever used the command to move a file from one location to another, say `abc.txt` from C:\ to D:\, `Move C:\abc.txt D:\`

Here, `Move` is the program or application responsible for moving the file, while `C:\abc.txt` and `D:\` can be termed as command-line arguments, which are passed to the `Move` program at the time of invocation of the program. As the application is invoked from the command line and the arguments are also passed to the application at the command line itself, these are called *command-line arguments*. Just like C++, programs can be written in Java to accept command-line arguments.

```
public static void main (String args[]){
      . . . . . .
} // end of the main() method
```

In this case, each of the elements in the array named `args` (including the elements at position zero) is a reference to one of the command-line arguments, each of which is a string object.

Suppose, you have a Java application, called `sort`, that sorts the lines in a file named `Sort. text`. You would invoke the Sort application as, `java Sort Example.txt`.

When the application is invoked, the runtime system passes the command-line arguments to the application's `main()` method via an array of strings. In the statement above, the command-line argument passed to the Sort application contains a single string, i.e., `Example.txt`. This String array is passed to the `main()` method and it is copied in *args*.

You must be wondering how many arguments you can supply through a command line. As we have discussed in Section 4.10, the number of elements in an array can be obtained from the `length` property of the array. Therefore, in the signature of `main()`, it is not necessary in Java to pass a parameter specifying the number of arguments. Example 4.27 explains the use of command-line arguments.

Example 4.27 **Echo Application**

```
L1   class Echo {
L2   public static void main(String args[]){
L3      int x = args.length;
L4      for (int i = 0; i< x; i++)
L5      System.out.println(args[i]);
L6      }
L7    }
```

After compiling the program, when it is executed, you can pass the command-line arguments as follows:

```
C>java Echo A B C
```

Output

```
A
B
C
```

Note that there is one space between each of the three arguments passed to the `Echo` application through the command line. If you have to pass a string of characters as an argument, then you must use quotes (" ") to mark that string. For example,

```
C>java Echo "A is first alphabet" "B is second" "C is third"
```

Output

```
A is first alphabet
B is second
C is third
```

<table>
<tr><td colspan="2" align="center">Explanation</td></tr>
<tr><td>L2 <code>main()</code>is declared, with an array variable, <code>args</code>, referring to an array of strings, passed as command line arguments to the program.
L3 An integer-type variable, <code>x</code> is declared to hold</td><td>the length of the array.
L4–5 <code>for</code> loop is iterated from 0 to the length of the array and the value obtained from each iteration is printed in a separate line.</td></tr>
</table>

4.12 NESTED CLASSES

Nested class is a class within a class. Nested classes are of the following types:

- Non-static inner classes
- Static nested classes
- Local classes
- Anonymous classes

4.12.1 Inner Class

A *non-static inner class* is a member of the outer class declared outside the functions within a class. The non-static inner class is bound to the instance of the enclosing class and has access to all the members of the enclosing class even the parent's `this` reference and `private` members. An inner class can be defined as `private`, `default`, `protected`, `public`, `final` and even `abstract`. Each instance of an inner class has a reference to an enclosing outer instance. A reference to the outer class instance can be explicitly obtained through `OuterClassName.this`. You cannot have static variables or methods in an inner class except for compile-time constant variables, i.e., static constant. Inner class's objects can be created within instance methods, constructors of the outer class or through an instance of outer class as they must have a reference to the instance of the outer class. This would be evident from the following example as well. Let us take an example to show how non-static inner classes can be created and used.

Example 4.28 **Inner Classes**

```
L1    class InnerClassTest
      {
```

```
L2    int y=20;              // instance variable of outer class
L3    static int a=30;       // class variable of outer class
L4    class InnerClass       // inner class begins
      {
L5      int x=10;
        // cannot have static variable but only static constants
L6      final static int z=50;
L7      void show()
        {
L8          System.out.println("Within Non static Inner Class");
L9          System.out.println("Can Access Inner class variable "+x);
L10         System.out.println("Can Access Outer class variables "+y);
L11         System.out.println("Can Access Outer class static variables "+a);
L12         System.out.println("Inner class instance accessed using this:"+this);
L13         System.out.println("Outer class referred from inner class using
            InnerClassTest.this: "+ InnerClassTest.this);
L14         outerInstanceMethod();
L15     // or InnerClassTest.this.outerClassMethod can also be used
L16         outerClassMethod();
        }

L17     //static void staticInner(){}
      }
L18   void outerInstanceMethod()
      {
        System.out.println("Outerclass Instance method called from Inner class");
      }
L19   static void outerClassMethod()
      {
        System.out.println("Outerclass static method Called from Inner class");
      }
L20   void createInnerObject()
      {
L21     new InnerClass().show();
      }
L22   public static void main(String args[])
      {
L23     InnerClassTest object = new InnerClassTest();
L24     object.createInnerObject();
        //Another way of invoking the show method of inner class
L25     //object.newInnerClass().show();
      }
    }
```

Output

Compilation

```
D:\javabook\programs\chap 4>javac InnerClassTest.java
D:\javabook\programs\chap 4>dir
InnerClassTest.java
InnerClassTest$InnerClass.class
InnerClassTest.class
```

Execution

```
D:\javabook\programs\chap 4>java InnerClassTest
Within Non static Inner Class
Can Access Inner class variable 10
Can Access Outer class variables 20
Can Access Outer class static variables 30
Inner class instance accessed using this: InnerClassTest$InnerClass@f72617
Outer class referred from inner class using InnerClassTest.this:
InnerClassTest@1e5e2c3
Outerclass Instance method Called from Inner class
Outerclass static method Called from Inner class
```

Explanation

L1 Class declaration (outer).

L2 Declares an instance variable of the outer class.

L3 Declares a static (class) variable of the outer class.

L4 Shows the declaration of inner class.

L5 An instance variable of the inner class is defined here.

L6 Shows the declaration of class constants. Constant in Java can be created by applying final keyword to the variable declaration. Non-static inner classes can have static constants but not static variables because inner classes operate within the context of its enclosing (outer class) instance therefore allowing static variables or methods will be contradictory as static members apply to class (or all objects of class) rather than be constrained within a single object.

L7 Declares the instance method named show of the inner class.

L8 Print statement which gets executed as and when the instance method show of the inner class is called.

L9 Prints the value of the instance variable of the inner class. Since show is an instance method of the inner class, it can directly access the instance variables of the inner class

L10 Prints the value of the instance variable of the outer class. A non-static inner class instance is closely associated with an instance of the outer class that is reason why inner class methods can directly access any of the members (fields or methods) of its enclosing outer class. It is a part of the outer class and therefore it has access to other parts of the outer class. But this being a special part, the outer class members (e.g., methods) cannot directly access the inner class members. For example, the show method can access the variable y of the outer class directly.

L11 Similar to the previous statement. The inner class can access any members of the outer enclosing class. This line shows a print statement which prints the static variables of the outer class.

L12 Shows the use of this keyword within inner class to refer to an instance of inner class. It can also be verified from the output. this keyword is used as an argument to the println method of System.out object. The result printed on screen shows the class of the instance (object) @ followed by a number, i.e., InnerClassTest$InnerClass@ f72617. Java internally uses the following notation for referring to inner classes instance i.e., OuterclassName$InnerclassName as is evident from the output. As soon as the Java file (i.e., InnerClassTest.java in our case) is compiled, the Java compiler generates two class file; one for the outer class (InnerClassTest.class) and one for the inner class (InnerClassTest$InnerClass.class) using the above notation. This number is an unsigned hexadecimal representation of the hash code of the object. The hash code returns the internal memory address of the object in hexadecimal.

L13 Outer class instance can be accessed from within inner class using this keyword as outerclassname. this. Please note that notation should be used from the method of an inner class.

L14 Shows outer class instance methods (on L18) can be called from within inner class.

L15 This, if used, in show method of inner class would refer to an instance of inner class. `InnerClassTest.this` refers to an instance of outer class. So L14 shows another way of invoking outer class methods. This line is commented deliberately as it shows another way of achieving the same output as in L13.

L16 Shows outer class static methods can be called (on L19) from within inner class.

L17 Inner classes cannot have static methods similar to static variables. The reasons are same as that of static variables that inner class instances operate within the context of a particular outer class instance. So creating static methods does not make any sense which applies to all instances of the class.

L18 Instance method of outer class has been defined.

L19 Class method of outer class has been defined.

L20 Another instance method named `createInnerObject` of the outer class is created.

L21 Object of inner class is created within this instance method (L20) and `show` method of the inner class is invoked. Note that an object of inner class can be created only from within the instance method (L20) of the outer class or through an instance of the outer class as shown in L24. Because, as already explained, every instance of a non-static inner class exists (or is encapsulated) within the outer class instance. Also note that, a single outer class instance can have many inner class instances associated with it.

L22 `main` method declaration.

L23 An object of outer class `InnerClassTest` is created.

L24 Using the outer class instance, method `createInnerObject` (L20) of outer class is called.

L25 Shows another way of creating an instance of inner class using `new` keyword on the outer class instance and invoking the method of inner class simultaneously.

4.12.2 Static Nested Class

A *static nested class* is a static member of a class just like normal static members of any class. They have access to all static methods of the enclosing parent class. The static nested classes cannot directly refer to instance variables and method of the outer class, similar to static parts of any class. They can only do it through an object of the outer class. Unlike the inner classes, the static nested classes can have static members.

Example 4.29 Static Nested Classes

```
L1    class StaticNestedClassTest
      {
L2    int y; // instance variable
L3    static int z=100;  // class variable
      // static inner class begins here
L4    static class StaticNestedClass
      {
L5       int x;
L6       static int staticinner=200;
L7       void nestedClassNonStaticMethod()
         {
L8           // y cannot be referenced here
L9           System.out.println("Accessing static variable of outer class within Static
             Inner Class "+z);
L10          //outerClassInstanceMethod();
L11          outerClassStaticMethod();
```

```
       }
L12    static void nestedClassStaticMethod()
       {
L13    System.out.println("Within Static method of Inner Class ");

L14        //outerClassInstanceMethod();
L15        outerClassStaticMethod();
       }
       } // static nested class ends here

L16    static void outerClassStaticMethod()
       {
L17       System.out.println("Outer Class Static method");
       }
L18    void outerClassInstanceMethod()
       {
L19       System.out.println("Outer Class Instance method");
       }
L20    public static void main(String args[])
       {
L21    StaticNestedClassTest.StaticNestedClass object = new
       StaticNestedClassTest.StaticNestedClass();
L22    object.nestedClassNonStaticMethod();
L23    object.nestedClassStaticMethod();
       }
       }
```

Output

Compilation

```
D:\javabook\programs\chap 4>javac StaticNestedClassTest.java
D:\javabook\programs\chap 4>dir
StaticNestedClassTest.java
StaticNestedClassTest.class
StaticNestedClassTest$StaticNestedClass.class
```

Execution

```
D:\javabook\programs\chap 4>java StaticNestedClassTest
Accessing static variable of outer class within Static Inner Class 100
Outer Class Static method
Within Static method of Inner Class
Outer Class Static method
```

Explanation

L1 Outer class declaration.

L2 Defines the instance variable y of the outer class.

L3 Defines the class variable z of the outer class.

L4 Shows the declaration of the static nested class named `StaticNestedClass`.

L5 Declares an instance variable of the static nested class.

L6 Shows the declaration of static variable within the static nested class. Static variables, unlike inner classes, can be created in static nested classes.

L7   Declares non-static method of the nested class.

L8   Comment that states instance variables of the enclosing class cannot be accessed inside the static nested class directly. However, it can be accessed by creating an object of the outer class.

L9   Prints the static variables of the outer class. Static nested classes can directly access the static members of its enclosing class.

L10   Commented because instance methods cannot be directly invoked from a static nested class.

L11   Invokes the static method on L16 of outer class directly.

L12–15   Shows the declaration of a static method in the static nested class. L14 is commented because instance methods of outer class cannot be called from within the static nested class. L15 executes because static method of the outer class (on L16) can be invoked from within the static nested class.

L16–17   Shows the declaration of static method of the outer class with a print statement within itself.

L18–19   Shows the declaration of instance method of the outer class with a print statement within itself.

L20   `Main` method begins.

L21   The object of static nested is created as shown below:

```
StaticNestedClassTest.StaticNestedClass
object = new
StaticNestedClassTest.StaticNested-
Class();
```

The generic notation for creating object is

```
<OuterClass.StaticNestedClassName>
<reference variable name> = new
 <OuterClass.StaticNestedClassName>();
```

L22–23   Invokes the different methods of static nested class using object created in previous line, L21.

Note   Unlike inner classes, an instance of outer class is not needed for creating an object of static nested class. Moreover, creating an instance of outer class does not create an instance of static nested class. Also note that a static nested class can be private, default, protected, public, final and even abstract. (We will discuss these keywords in detail in the chapters to follow)

Local inner classes are declared within a block of code and are visible only within that block, just as any other method variable. These classes are declared within a function. They can use only final (constant) local variables and parameters of the function

An *anonymous inner* class is a local class that has no name.

4.12.3 Why do we Create Nested Classes?

Nested classes let you turn logic into their own classes which normally you would not turn into thus allowing even more object orientation into your programming as nested classes lets you encapsulate logic into classes. Inner classes provide a structured hierarchy.

Inner member classes and anonymous classes allow callbacks to be defined conveniently. Callback allows an object to call back the originating object at a later point in time. Nested classes are very effective in implementing event handling in Java.

Another advantage of nested classes would be to group classes that would be required at one place only. If you are certain that a class will be useful to only one class then it is better to embed a class into another.

The obvious advantages would be ease of readability and ease of maintaining the code.

4.13 PRACTICAL PROBLEM: COMPLEX NUMBER PROGRAM

We will take a practical problem to summarize most of the concepts that we have learnt in this chapter by creating a Complex Number program. But let us first understand, what is a complex number? A complex number is a number that can be represented in the form $a + bi$, where a and b are real numbers and i is the imaginary part. In the expression $a + bi$, a is the real part and b is the imaginary part of the complex number. Complex numbers are used in situations where some part is predictable (real) and some part is unpredictable (imaginary – to be assumed). Complex numbers are used in a variety of areas like electrical analysis, stress analysis of bridges and buildings, electronics etc. We will create a program to add and subtract two complex numbers. The further task of multiplying two complex numbers is left as an assignment to you.

Example 4.30 **Complex Number Program**

```
L1    class Complex
      {
      // instance variables
L2        int real,imaginary;
      // No argument Constructor
L3        Complex()
          {
L4          real=0;
L5          imaginary=0;
          }
      // Overloaded Constructor
L6        Complex(int real,int imaginary)
          {
L7          this.real= real;
L8          this.imaginary= imaginary;
          }
L9    // setter method for real part of complex number
L10       void setReal(int real)
          {
L11         this.real=real;
          }
L12   // getter methods for real part of complex number
L13       int getReal()
L14         {
L15         return real;
          }
L16   // setter method for imaginary part of complex number
L17       void setImaginary(int imaginary)
          {
L18         this.imaginary=imaginary;
          }
      // getter method for imaginary part of complex number
L19       int getImaginary()
          {
L20         return imaginary;
          }
L21       void add(Complex c1,Complex c2)
          {
L22             real=c1.real+c2.real;
```

```
L23            imaginary=c1.imaginary+c2.imaginary;
           }
L24    void subtract(Complex c1,Complex c2)
           {
L25    real=c1.real-c2.real;
L26            imaginary=c1.imaginary-c2.imaginary;
           }

       /* A better way of displaying complex number object is to override toString() */
L27    void display()
           {
L28                if(imaginary>0)
L29        System.out.println(real+"+"+imaginary+"i");
L30                else
L31          System.out.println(real+""+imaginary+"i");
       }
L32    public static void main(String args[])
          {
L34            // command line arguments for First Complex Number
L35            int n1=Integer.parseInt(args[0]);
L36            int n2=Integer.parseInt(args[1]);
L37            // command line arguments for Second Complex Number
L38            int n3=Integer.parseInt(args[2]);
L39            int n4=Integer.parseInt(args[3]);
L40            Complex c1=new Complex(n1,n2);
L41            Complex c2=new Complex(n3,n4);
L42            Complex d=new Complex();
L43            System.out.print("First complex number is = ");
L44            c1.display();
L45            System.out.print("Second complex number is = ");
L46            c2.display();
L47            d.add(c1,c2);
L48            System.out.print("Addition of two complex numbers = ");
L49            d.display();
L50            d.subtract(c1,c2);
L51            System.out.print("Subtraction of two complex numbers = ");
L52            d.display();
L53        }
L54    }
```

Output

```
D:\javabook\programs\chap 4>java Complex 1 2 3 4
First complex number is = 1+2i
Second complex number is = 3+4i
Addition of two complex numbers = 4+6i
Subtraction of two complex numbers = -2-2i
```

Explanation

L1   Class declaration.

L2   Shows two integer instance variables have been defined A complex number comprises of two parts: real and imaginary. So a complex number object should have two instance variables.

L3   A no-argument constructor is created to initializes these variables. This can be termed as an explicit default constructor.

L4 & 5   Instance variables are initialled to zero.

L6   The constructor is overloaded to accept different values for real and imaginary part of a complex number. If the previous constructor is used while creating objects, then real and imaginary part will have a value of 0. If this constructor is used during object creation, then objects can pass on different values as argument to the constructors which can be assigned to instance variables. So every complex number can have different real and imaginary values.

L7   `this` keyword is used to differentiate between instance variable and local variable as both variables bear the same name and clearly specify that value of the argument (local variable) has to be assigned to instance variable.

L8   Same as previous statement.

L9–11   Defines the setter method for the instance variable: `real`. As the name suggest, these methods are used to set the value of the instance variable: `real` and hence the name `setReal`. The purpose of setter method is to set the values. So the setter methods accept an argument which is assigned to the instance variable. Basically setter methods (or getter methods) are created for depicting clean structured programming and these are basic fundamental used in Java Beans or component architecture. These methods are also very useful while working with IDE.

L12–15   Defines the getter method for the instance variable: `real`. As the name suggests, these method are used to return the value of the instance variable: `real` and hence the name `getReal`.

L16–18   Setter method for imaginary part has been defined.

L19–20   Getter method for imaginary part has been defined.

L21   We need to add two complex numbers. Instance method, `add` is created which accepts two complex number objects. Not only variables, object references can also be passed as arguments to methods. For adding two complex numbers, we need to add the real parts of these two numbers separately and imaginary parts separately and encapsulate the resultant real and imaginary parts in a complex number object because the result of addition of two complex numbers will also be a complex number. The two complex numbers to be added are passed as arguments to the `add` method. The `add` method is invoked using a third complex number object (L47), which will store the resultant real and imaginary part after addition.

L22   Real part of both the complex numbers objects are accessed, added and stored in real part of the object which invoked the `add` method. The complex number object that invoked `add` method will also have real and imaginary instance variables.

L23   Imaginary part of both the complex numbers objects are accessed, added and stored in imaginary part of the object which invoked the `add` method.

L24–26   We need to subtract two complex numbers. Instance method `subtract` is created which accepts two complex number objects. The two complex numbers to be subtracted are passed as arguments to the `subtract` method. The `subtract` method is invoked using a third complex number object (L50), which will store the resultant real and imaginary part after subtraction.

L27–31   `Display` method is created to display the complex numbers in the format `a+bi`.

L32   `Main` method declaration.

L35–39   Command line arguments are used to capture integer real and imaginary parts of two complex numbers. These numbers will be captured in the String array argument of the main method. The numbers entered through command line will become strings. These numbers have to be added/subtracted so they have to be converted to integers and hence we use the predefined static method of `Integer` class as shown:

```
Integer.parseInt(args[0])
```

L40–42   Three complex number objects (`c1`, `c2`, and `d`) are created. We need to add/subtract two complex numbers so two objects (`c1` and `c2`) of `Complex` class are created so that add and subtract operations can be applied on them. The third object is used to invoke the instance method `add` and `subtract` and store the result within itself.

L44 The `display` method is called through `c1` to display the first complex number. Complex numbers have to be displayed in their format: `a+bi`. As the `display` method is invoked through `c1`, the display method can access the instance variable of `c1` directly and display the real and imaginary parts of `c1`.

L46 The `display` method is called to display the second complex number.

L47 The `add` method is invoked through the third object `d` and `c1` and `c2` are passed to this method.

L48–49 Statements display the object `d`.

L50–52 The `subtract` method is invoked similar to the `add` method and later on the result is displayed.

Note A common mistake that is committed by many students is that they pass two real and two imaginary integer values to the `add` method, add the real and imaginary values differently and print them.

```java
void add(int real1, int imaginary1, int real2, int imaginary2)
{
    int real=real1+real2;
    int imaginary=imaginary1+imaginary2;
    System.out.println(real+"i"+imaginary);
}
```

The answer may be correct but the approach is wrong. We have to add two complex numbers and not two integers. So for adding two complex numbers, complex number objects have to be passed to the add method.

SUMMARY

In this chapter, we have discussed many fundamental principles of the object-oriented model, used while implementing Java constructs. We discussed how classes and their objects can be created in Java. We have also seen how these objects are used in a Java program and what these are actually made of.

A class provides a sort of template or blueprint for an object. An object is a software bundle that encapsulates variables and methods operating on those variables. A Java object is defined as an *instance of a class*. A class can have many instances of objects, each having its own copy of variables and methods. The variables declared inside a class (but outside a method) are termed as instance variables. Attributes of a class are defined by instance variables, while its behavior is defined by methods.

We have discussed the use of methods in depth. These methods declared as part of one object can be invoked or called from another object. The methods or variables belonging to a particular class can be accessed by specifying the name of the object to which they belong to.

A special type of variable whose value remains the same across all the objects of a class is known as class or static variable. Likewise, a method can also be declared as static, which sticks to a particular location in the memory no matter how many times it is called from multiple objects. Both static variables and static methods can be called directly from anywhere inside a class, without or with specifying any object name.

In Java, the objects are automatically freed after their use. The garbage collector periodically frees the memory used by objects that are no longer needed. All resources held by the object can be also be freed explicitly through the `finalize()` method. A class must override the `finalize()` method in order to perform any clean up required by the object.

Methods in Java, just like C++, can be overloaded, where different methods can have the same name but different signatures. This concept of method overloading will come into play , when there is a need to perform same kind of functions on different input parameters. In Java, when a value is passed into a method invocation as an argument, it is passed by value. A special type of method having the same name as the class is used to initialize object values. These are known as constructors. Like ordinary methods, these constructors too can be overloaded.

A variable can hold only a single value of a particular data type. An important data structure known as arrays is used to store a set of values of the same data type. Command line arguments were also discussed and practical examples were undertaken to show how user input can be passed to the program.

A very interesting concept of Nested classes along with different types has been discussed in this chapter. Nested classes are classes within classes.

EXERCISES

Objective Questions

1. Given a one-dimensional array arr, what is the correct way of getting its number of elements?

    (a) `arr.length` (b) `arr.length - 1`
    (c) `arr.size` (d) `arr.size - 1`

2. Which of these statements are legal?

    (a) `intarr[][] = new int[5][5];`
    (b) `int []arr[] = new int[5][5];`
    (c) `int[][] arr = new int[5][5];`
    (d) `int[] arr = new int[5][];`

3. Which of the following statements are legal declarations and definitions of a method?

    (a) `void method() {}`
    (b) `void method(void) {};`
    (c) `method() {};`
    (d) `method(void) {};`

4. What is the outcome of compiling and running the following class?

    ```
    class Demo {
    public static void  main(){
      System.out.println("Demo");
      }
    }
    ```

    (a) The program does not compile as there is no main method defined
    (b) The program compiles and runs generating an output of "test"
    (c) The program compiles and runs but does not generate any output
    (d) The program compiles but does not run

5. What happens when the following program is compiled and executed with the command

    `-java Demo.`

    ```
    class Demo{
    public static void main(String
    args[]){
     if(args.length> 0)
        System.out.println(args.
        length);
     }

    }
    ```

    (a) The program compiles and runs but does not print anything
    (b) The program compiles and runs and prints 0
    (c) The program compiles and runs and prints 1
    (d) The program compiles and runs and prints 2

6. What is the output when you try to compile and run the following?

    ```
    class Demo
    {
      void Demo()
      {
        System.out.println("In Demo");
      }
      public static void main(String
      args[])
      {
        Demo d=new Demo();
      }
    }
    ```

    (a) Compile time error: Illegal Constuctor declaration
    (b) Run Time error
    (c) Compiles and prints " In Demo"
    (d) None of the above

7. What is the output when you try to compile and run the following?

    ```
    class Demo
    {
    ```

```
int x = 20;
Demo()
{
    x = 40;
}
public static void main
(String args[])
{
        Demo d = new Demo();
        System.out.println(d.x);
}
}
```

(a) Compile time error
(b) Run Time error
(c) Compiles and prints " 20"
(d) Compiles and prints " 40"

8. Which statement is true about a static nested class?
    (a) An instance of the enclosing class is required to instantiate it.
    (b) It does not have access to non-static members of the enclosing class.
    (c) It must have static variables and methods only.
    (d) None of the above

9. What will be the output of the program?
```
public class A
{
```

```
public static void
main (String [] args)
{
    class B
    {
        public String name;
        public B(String s)
        {
            name = s;
        }
    }
    B obj = new B("Yupee");
    System.out.println(obj.name);
}
}
```

(a) An exception occurs at runtime at line 10.
(b) It prints "Yupee".
(c) Compilation fails because of an error on line 7.
(d) Compilation fails because of an error on line 13.

10. Which of the following statements are true?
    (a) Constructors cannot be inherited
    (b) There is an <init> method created implicitly for each constructors
    (c) Default constructors will not be provided if a class declares a constructor for itself.
    (d) All the above

Review Questions

1. What are classes and objects?
2. What is method overloading? Explain with the help of a program.
3. What are constructors used for? Can constructors be overloaded? Write a program in support of your answer.
4. Explain the difference between instance variables and class variables.
5. Explain the keyword `this` with the help of a program.
6. What are command-line arguments and how are they used?
7. What are inner classes? What is the need for creating an inner class?
8. Explain static keyword with all its usages.
9. What are the possible ways in which multiple values can be returned from a method?
10. Explain static nested classes with help of a program.

Programming Exercises

1. Modify Example 4.2(a) to accept instance variable values using a constructor with no arguments and execute it.
2. Overload the constructor in the previous example and then try to execute it.

3. Make use of `this` keyword in the previous example to show its usages.

4. Write a program to implement `Money` class. This class should have fields for initializing a rupee and paisa value. The paisa value will be in the range from 0–99 with the paisa being the same sign as that of rupees. The class should have all reasonable constructors, addition and subtraction methods, and a `main()` method that provides a thorough test of all the methods in the class.

5. Modify the complex number practical problem to multiply two complex numbers, and return the result.

6. Create a class `Rectangle`. The class has two attributes, length and width, each of which defaults to 0. It has methods that calculate the perimeter and area of the rectangle. It has set and get methods for both length and width. The set method should verify that length and width are floating-point numbers larger than 0.0 and less than 20.0.

7. Modify the `Circle` class in Example 4.5 to calculate:
   (a) `circleCircumference()`—compute the circumference of a circle
   (b) `arcLength()`—compute the length of the arc for a given angle

Within the `main()` method of the class named Circle, create an object of the class Circle. Compute Circle's circumference when the radius is 10 and arc length when the angle is 45.

Answers to Objective Questions

1. (a)	**2.** (a), (b), (c)	**3.** (a)	**4.** (d)
5. (a)	**6.** (c) void Demo is treated as a method not as a constructor		
7. (d)	**8.** (b)	**9.** (b)	**10.** (d)

Inheritance

After reading this chapter, the readers will be able to

- know the difference between inheritance and aggregation
- understand how inheritance is done in Java
- learn polymorphism through method overriding
- learn the keywords: super and final
- understand the basics of abstract class
- understand the difference between shadowing and overriding

5.1 INHERITANCE VS AGGREGATION

Inheritance, in real life, is the ability to derive something specific from something generic. For example, Fiat Palio parked next to a shopping mall is a specific instance of the generic category, car.

Inheritance aids in the reuse of code, i.e., a class can inherit the features of another class and add its own modification. The parent class is known as the *superclass* and the newly created child class is known as the *subclass*. A subclass inherits all the properties and methods of the super class, and can have additional attributes and methods as shown in Fig. 5.1.

On the other hand, the term aggregation is used when we make up objects out of other objects. The behavior of the bigger object is defined by the behavior of its component objects separately and in conjunction with each other. For example, cars contain an engine which in turn

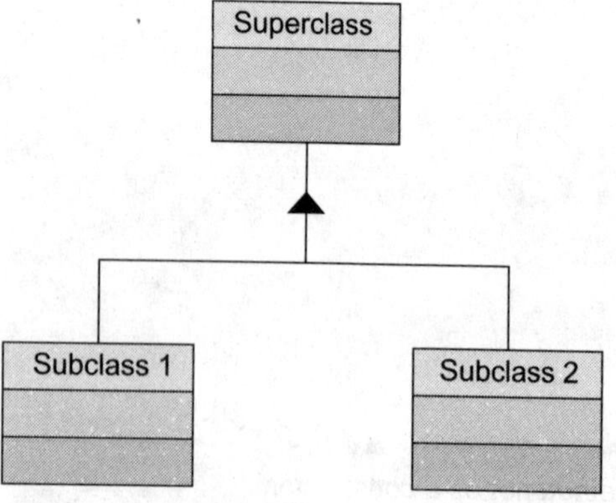

Fig. 5.1 Inheritance

contains an ignition system and starter motor (Fig. 5.2). Basically it is different from inheritance in the sense that there exists a whole-part relationship in aggregation, car being the whole and engine being its part.

> **Note** The test for inheritance is that there exists an 'is-a-kind-of-relationship' among classes. For example, Manager is a kind of Employee. The test for aggregation is that there exists an 'is-a-part-of' relationship among classes.

5.1.1 Types of Inheritance

There are five different types of inheritance:

- Single inheritance
- Multilevel inheritance
- Multiple inheritance
- Hierarchical inheritance
- Hybrid inheritance

Single Inheritance In single inheritance, classes have only one base class. Consider the relationship shown in Fig. 5.3.

Multilevel Inheritance As shown in Fig. 5.4, C not only inherits from its immediate superclass, i.e., B, but also from B's superclass, A. Thus, class C will have all the attributes and behavior that A and B possesses in addition to its own. There is no limit to this chain of inheritance (known as multilevel inheritance) but getting down deeper to four or five levels makes the code excessively complex.

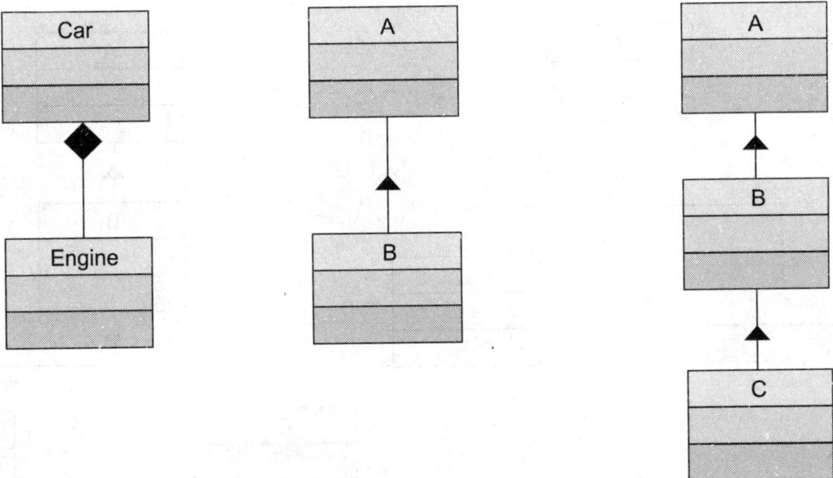

Fig. 5.2 Aggregation   **Fig. 5.3** Single Inheritance   **Fig. 5.4** Multilevel Inheritance

Multiple Inheritance In multiple inheritance, a class can inherit from more than one unrelated class, as shown in Fig. 5.5. Class C inherits from both A and B.

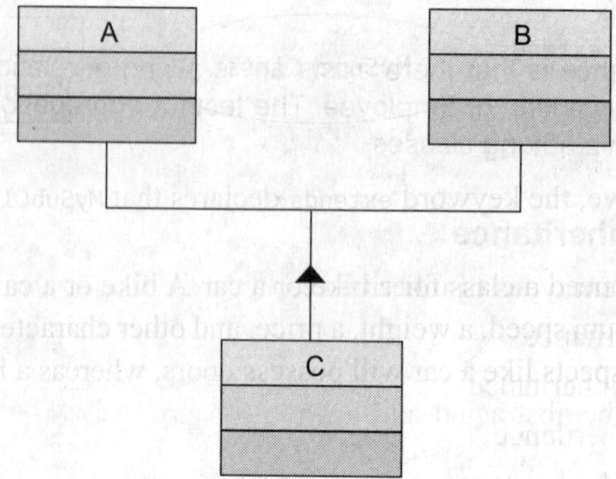

Fig. 5.5 Multiple Inheritance

Note Java does not support multiple inheritance amongst classes. It can still be achieved with the help of Interfaces.

Hierarchical Inheritance In hierarchical inheritance, more than one class can inherit from a single class, as shown in Fig. 5.6. Class C inherits from both A and B.

Hybrid Inheritance Hybrid inheritance is any combination of the above defined inheritances as shown in Fig. 5.7.

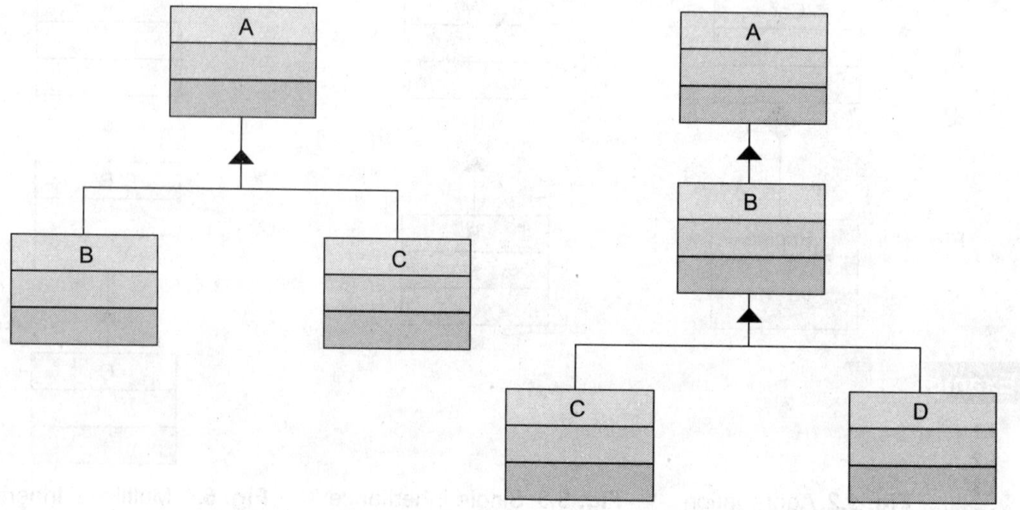

Fig. 5.6 Hierarchical Inheritance

Fig. 5.7 Hybrid Inheritance

5.1.2 Deriving Classes Using extends Keyword

In Java, classes are inherited from other class by declaring them as a part of its definition, as shown below.

```
class MySubClass extends
{
...
}
```

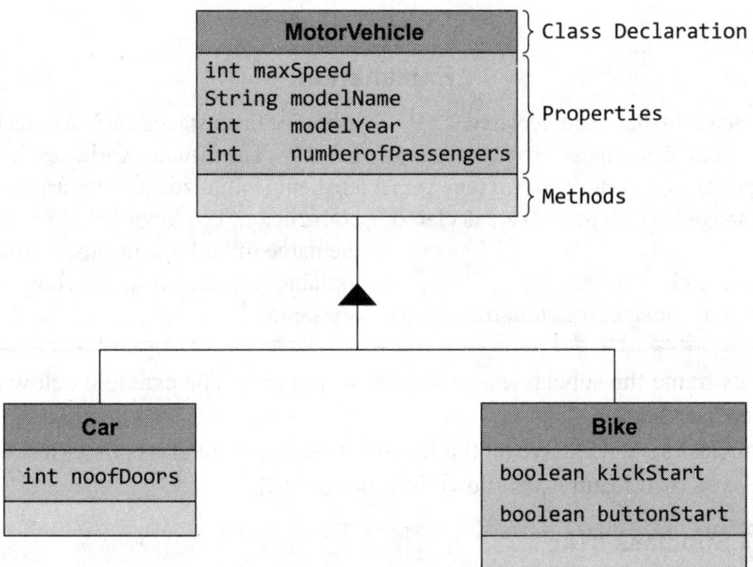

In the definition above, the keyword `extends` declares that `MySubClass` inherits the parent class `MySuperClass`.

Now suppose you need a class for a bike or a car. A bike or a car will have a model name, a model year, a maximum speed, a weight, a price, and other characteristic features, but these two will differ in some aspects like a car will possess doors, whereas a bike will not. The properties that are similar can be abstracted and put in a generic class having common behavior. This generic class will be the parent class for both these classes, as shown in Fig. 5.8.

Fig. 5.8 UML Notation for `Car` and `Bike` Class Along with their Parent Class `MotorVehicle`

Now let us frame classes for the above diagram and see how inheritance is actually done in Java. First of all, let us frame the parent class `MotorVehicle`, shown in Example 5.1.

Example 5.1 **Parent Class `MotorVehicle`**

```
L1    class MotorVehicle{
L2    int maxSpeed;            // miles per hour
L3    String modelName;        // e.g. "Fiat"
L4    int modelYear;           // e.g. 2006,2007,2008
L5    int numberOfPassengers;  // 2, 4, 6

      // we can add some more properties, as above, like the
      // engineCapacity etc. but we would leave it as an
```

```
        // exercise for you.
        // constructor
L6   MotorVehicle()
        {
            maxSpeed = 200;
            modelName = "";
            modelYear=1997;
            numberOfPassengers=2;
        }

L7   MotorVehicle(int maxSpeed, String modelName, int modelYear, int numberOfPassengers)
        {
L8       this.maxSpeed = maxSpeed;
L9       this.modelName = modelName;
L10      this.modelYear = modelYear;
L11      this.numberOfPassengers = numberOfPassengers;
        }
    }
```

Explanation

L1 Class `MotorVehicle` has been declared.

L2–5 Instance variable `maxSpeed` (of type `int`), `modelName` (of type `String`), `modelYear` (of type `int`) and `numberOfPassangers` (of type `int`) are declared in these lines.

L6 Default constructor.

L7 Parameterized constructor declaration to

initialize the instance variables declared in L2 to L5.

L8–11 The instance variables declared in L2 to L5 are being initialized with the arguments passed in the constructor. The keyword `this` has been used, as the name of both the instance variable and the local variable (arguments in the constructor declaration) are same.

Now let us frame the subclasses, as shown in Fig. 5.8. The example below shows one of the subclasses, i.e., `Bike`.

The subclass `Bike` will have all the features that its parent class possesses. In addition to that, it can have its own features, as shown in Example 5.2.

Example 5.2 Subclass Bike

```
L1   class Bike extends MotorVehicle {
L2   boolean kickStart;
L3   boolean buttonStart;
        /* A kick start bike may or may not be a button start bike but a button start bike
        will always have an option of kick starting */
        // constructor
L4   Bike()
        {
            kickStart = true;
            buttonStart = false;
        }

L5   Bike(boolean ks, boolean bs)
        {
            kickStart = ks;
            buttonStart = bs;
```

```
      }
L6   public static void main(String args[]) {
L7   Bike b = new Bike ();
      }}
```

Explanation

L1 Usage of extends keyword to show inheritance.
L2 and 3 Declaration of two boolean variables: `kickStart` and `buttonStart`.
L4 Default constructor.
L5 Overloaded constructor.

L6 `main()` method.
L7 `Bike` object is created and the default constructor of the parent class is called first of all and after that, the subclass constructor is called because the parent needs to be initialized before the child.

5.2 OVERRIDING METHOD

When a method in a subclass has the same name and type signature as a method in its super-class, then the method in the subclass is said to *override* the method in the superclass. Like overloading, it is a feature that supports polymorphism.

When an overridden method is called from within a subclass, it will always refer to the version of the method defined by the subclass. The superclass version of the method is hidden.

In the code below, we see that subclass B overrides the method doOverride() in class A.

Example 5.3 **Method of Overriding**

```
L1    class A {
L2    int i = 0;
L3    void doOverride (int k) {
L4    i = k;
      } }


      // Subclass definition starts here
L5    class B extends A {              // Method Overriding
L6    void doOverride(int k){
L7       i = 2 * k;
L8       System.out.println("The value of i is: " +i);
         }
L9    public static void main (String args[])
      {
L10      B b = new B();               // Create an instance of class B
L11      b.doOverride(12);            // class B method doOverride() will be called
      }}
```

Output

```
The value of i is: 24
```

Explanation

L1   Class declaration.
L2   Instance variable declaration.
L3   Method declaration with an integer argument passed to it.
L4   Instance variable being assigned with the value of the arguments.
L5   Subclass declaration.
L6   Method is overridden, as the name and signature of the method match.
L7   The variable i is being initialized with a value twice to that of the argument passed in the method doOverride. Also note that we have not declared the variable i in the subclass B, it is the parent class variable i that is being referred to in the subclass.

This is actually what inheritance is all about. Objects of the subclass need not define their own definition of data and methods which are generic in nature. The generic behavior is left for the super classes.
L8   Print statement.
L9   main()method.
L10   Object of the subclass B is created.
L11   When we create an instance of class B, an invocation of the method doOverride() will result in a call to the doOverride() code in class B rather than A because it is actually the instance that matters when we call any instance method and the instance in this case is B.

A superclass reference variable can be assigned a subclass object. This is illustrated by the following code:

```
A a1 = new B ();
/* Create an instance of class B but uses reference of type A . */


a1.doOverride();
/* Though the A type reference is used, the doOverride() method of
class B will be called. */
```

Note   Remember when you write two or more classes in a single file, the file will be named upon the name of the class that contains the main method. For example, if you write the complete Example 5.3 in a notepad editor file, the file will be named as B.java.

Here we see that even though the superclass type variable a1 references the subclass object, the subclass's overridden method will be executed rather than the superclass's instance method.

This is very useful when, for example, an array of the superclass type contains references to various subclasses. The overridden method in the subclass will be called rather than the method of the superclass.

Code Snippet 5.1 Superclass and Subclass Object

```
L1   A a[] = new A[2];        // Parent Class A type array of two objects
L2   a[0] = new B();          // A type reference is assigned an instance of B.
L3   a[1] = new C();          // A type reference is assigned an instance of C.
L4   for (int i = 0; i<a.length; i++)
L5   a[i].doOverride();
```

Explanation

Considering A as the superclass of class B and C.

L1 An array of superclass A is defined with a size of two elements.

L2 The first element of the array is assigned an object of class B. An array of int contains integers; an array of characters contains characters in its various elements, and so on. An array of superclass A will either contain objects of type A or its subclasses because *a superclass variable can refer to a subclass object*. So basically, it is an array of objects.

L3 The second element of the array contains the object of class C.

L4 for loop is used to iterate through various array elements. Value of i will vary from 0 to a.length which is 2.

L5 In the first iteration, the value of i is 0, so a[0] refers to B class object, so B's doOverride() method will be executed even though the array is of the superclass A, the code used for the doOverride()method will be that of the actual object that is referenced, not of the method in the base class A. The same applies for the second iteration. The only difference with the second iteration is that the object will be of class C. The reason why subclass methods are being invoked is because these methods are overridden and overridden methods are dynamically binded. Dynamic Binding occurs at runtime and methods are called based on the object from which they have been invoked.

Note Binding is the process of connecting a method call to its body. When binding is performed before a program is executed, it is called *early binding*. When multiple methods with the same name exist within a class (i.e., case of method overloading) which method will be executed depends upon the argument (number, type or order of arguments) passed to the method. So, this binding can be resolved by the compiler (at compile time) and hence overloaded methods are early binded.

When a method with the same name and signature exists in superclass as well as subclass (i.e., a case of Method overriding) which method will be executed (superclass version or subclass version) will be determined by the type of object from which it has been called (Example 5.3) and so it cannot be done by compiler. Objects exist at runtime, and hence *late binding* is done by the JVM at runtime for resolving which overridden method will be executed. It is also known as *dynamic binding* or *runtime binding*.

A superclass reference variable can refer to a subclass object but vice versa is not possible because a superclass can have many subclasses and all of these subclasses can have their additional (different) members (fields and methods) not present in the superclass and its peer classes. Hence a variable of type subclass can expose more details and can perform more operations than a variable of type superclass. So every superclass can refer to its subclass object but every subclass cannot refer to its superclass object. Consider the case of Furniture class and its subclasses Table and Chair. We can say that every table or chair is furniture but we cannot ascertain that all furniture is table or chair, etc. Consider another example of animal and its subclasses like elephant, tiger, dog, cat, etc. Tiger is an animal, elephant is an animal but we cannot say that animal is a tiger or elephant because it is not true in all cases. Let us take an example to see how fields are accessed when we refer to subclass objects using a reference variable of superclass.

Example 5.4 Superclass Can Refer to a Subclass Object

```
L1      class SuperClass
        {
L2              int instanceVariable = 10;
L3              static int classVariable = 20;
        }

L4      class SubClass extends SuperClass
        {
L5        int instanceVariable = 12;
L6        static int classVariable = 25;
L7        public static void main(String args[])
          {
L8          SuperClass s=new SubClass();
L9          System.out.println("Superclass Instance variable: "+s.instanceVariable);
L10         System.out.println("Superclass static variable: "+s.classVariable);
L11         SubClass st=new SubClass();
L12         System.out.println("Subclass Instance variable: "+st.instanceVariable);
L13         System.out.println("Subclass static variable: "+st.classVariable);
          }
        }
```

Output

```
D:\javabook\programs\chap 4>java SubClass
Superclass Instance variable: 10
Superclass static variable: 20
Subclass Instance variable: 12
Subclass static variable: 25
```

Explanation

L1 Class declaration.

L2 Instance variable defined.

L3 Class variable defined.

L4 Subclass declaration.

L5 Instance variable of the subclass has been declared with the same name as that of superclass (shadowing).

L6 Class variable of the subclass has been declared the with same name as that of superclass (shadowing).

L7 Main method declaration.

L8 A reference variable s of superclass is declared to hold an object of subclass.

L9 The instance variable is printed using s (created in L8). The value that is printed (see output) will be of superclass as the reference is of superclass.

This binding is made by the compiler at the compile time which checks whether the instance variable belongs to class Superclass through which it is being accessed and if yes the binding is made, no matter which object the reference refers to.

L10 Same as L9. The only difference is it is for class variables.

L11 A reference variable st of subclass is declared to hold an object of subclass.

L12 The instance variable is printed using st (created in L11). The value that is printed (see output) will be of subclass as the reference is of subclass. As already stated, this binding is made by the compiler at the compile time which checks whether the instance variable belongs to class Subclass through which it is being accessed and if yes, the binding is made, no matter which object the reference refers to.

L13 Same as L12. The only difference is it is for class variables.

In the following topics, we will revisit *method overriding* combined with some new topics.

5.3 super KEYWORD

The super keyword refers to the parent class of the class in which the keyword is used. It is used for the following three purposes:

1. For calling the methods of the superclass.
2. For accessing the member variables of the superclass.
3. For invoking the constructors of the superclass.

Case 1: Calling the Methods of the Superclass

super.<methodName>() represents a call to a method of the superclass. This call is particularly necessary while calling a method of the superclass through the subclass object that is overridden in the subclass.

Example 5.5(a) **Simple Example Showing Method Overriding**

```
L1    class A {
L2    void show()
        {
L3          System.out.println("Superclass show method");
      }}

L4    class B extends A { // Method Overriding
L5    void show()
        {
L6          System.out.println("Subclass show method");
        }
L7    public static void main (String args[]){
L8    A s1 = new A();    // call to show method of Superclass A.
L9    s1.show();
L10   B s2 = new B();
L11   s2.show();          // call to show method of Subclass B
        }}
```

Output

```
Superclass show method
Subclass show method
```

Explanation

As discussed earlier in Example 5.3, methods will be called on the basis of the objects from which they are called.

L8 Shows the creation of an object of class A.

L9 Shows calling the methods of class A through the object created in L8.

L10 and 11 The object being used is that of class B.

Problem and Solution In Example 5.5, two methods (`show()` and overridden `show()`) are being called by two different objects (`A` and `B`), instead the job can be done by one object only, i.e., by using the keyword `super`. Example 5.5 can be reshaped as shown below:

Example 5.5 (b) Usage of super Keyword for Calling Parent Class Methods

```
L1    class ANew {
L2    void show()
        {
L3        System.out.println("Superclass show method");
        }
      }
L4    class BNew extends ANew { // Method Overriding
L5    void show()
      {
L6        super.show();         //call to show method of the super class A
L7        System.out.println("Subclass show method");
      }
L8    public static void main (String args[]) {
L9        BNew s2 = new BNew();
L10       s2.show();            // call to show method of Subclass B
      }}
```

Output

```
Superclass show method
Subclass show method
```

Explanation

L5 Method `show()` is defined.

L6 Shows how `super` is used for calling the parent class method which has been overridden in the subclass. If this line is omitted, only the subclass method will be called; we have used `super` in this line so that both the version (parent and subclass) of methods can be called by one object only.

L9 `BNew` object is created.

L10 The method `show()` of class `BNew` is called using the object created in L9. The control passes to `show()` in L5 and the statements within the method are executed. L6 gets executed which is `super.show()` and the control passes to `ANew.show` method. Lines of `show()` in `Anew` class are executed and the control passes back to L7, which is a print statement. After executing the print statement (L7), the control passes back to the main method which has no more statements to execute, so the program automatically terminates.

Case 2: Accessing the Instance Member Variables of the Superclass

Example 5.6 demonstrates how the keyword `super` can be used to access the instance variables of the superclass. The keyword is particularly useful when the variable of the superclass is shadowed by the subclass variable. The concept of *shadowing* occurs when variables in super class and subclass have same name. The superclass variables in this case will be hidden in the subclass and only subclass variables will be accessible within the subclass. To access the shadowed variable of superclass `super` keyword is used as shown below.

Example 5.6   Usage of super Keyword for Accessing Parent Class Variables

```
L1      class Super_Variable {
L2      int b = 30;     //instance Variable
        }
L3      class SubClass extends Super_Variable {
L4      int b = 12;     // shadows the superclass variable
L5      void show()
        {
L6        System.out.println("subclass class variable:" + b);
L7        System.out.println("superclass instance variable:" + super.b);
        }
L8      public static void main (String args[]) {
L9        SubClass s = new SubClass();
L10       s.show();     // call to show method of Subclass B
        }}
```

Output

```
subclass class variable: 12
superclass instance variable: 30
```

Explanation

L1 Superclass declaration `Super_Variable`.
L2 Instance variable declaration band it is assigned the value 30.
L3 Subclass declaration `SubClass`.
L4 Instance variable b (same name as that of superclass instance variable) within the subclass defined and assigned the value 12.
L5 `Show ()` method defined within the subclass.
L6 and 7 In the above example, specifically we have kept the names of two instance variables in the super and subclass same, i.e., b. In L6 when we print the value of b by simply writing b, the value of subclass variable b is printed. In L7, with the help of super keyword, we have accessed the value of the superclass instance variable b and in this case, it prints the value of the superclass variable. If the variable b in L4 is not defined, then both print statements would have printed the same value, i.e., value of the superclass variable b. In our case, both the super and the subclass contain the variable with the same name, so to differentiate between the two and to access the value of the superclass variable from the subclass, we use the keyword super.

Case 3: Invoking the Constructors of the Superclass

super as a standalone statement (i.e., `super()`) represents a call to a constructor of the superclass. This call can be made only from the constructor of the subclass and that too it should be the first statement of the constructors. The default constructors implicitly include a call to the super class constructor using the super keyword.

Example 5.7   Constructor Calling Mechanism

```
L1      class Constructor_A {
L2      Constructor_A()
        {
L3        System.out.println("Constructor A");
```

```
     }}
L4   class Constructor_B extends Constructor_A {
L5   Constructor_B() {
L6     System.out.println("Constructor B");
     }}

L7   class Constructor_C extends Constructor_B {
L8   Constructor_C() {
L9     System.out.println("Constructor C");
     }

L10  public static void main (String args[]) {
L11    Constructor_C a = new Constructor_C();
     }}
```

Output

```
Constructor A
Constructor B
Constructor C
```

Explanation

L1 Parent class declaration `Constructor_A`.

L2 Default constructor of class `Constructor_A`.

L4 Subclass declaration `Constructor_B` of the class defined in L1.

L5 Default constructor of class `Constructor_B`.

L7 Subclass declaration `Constructor_C` of class defined in L4.

L8 Default constructor of class `Constructor_C` is declared explicitly.

L10 `main` method declaration.

L11 An object of class `Constructor_C` is created here. If the class does not provide any constructor, the default constructor (no argument constructor) provided by Java is implicitly called when an object of the class is created. All three classes define their respective no argument constructors. Object creation of `Constructor_C` class results in the explicit default constructor of this class being called on L8. An `<init>` method is created for every constructor for the class and this `<init>` includes a call to the super-class default (no argument) constructor, any instance variable initializer provided in the class followed by the code written in the constructor. So when an object of class `Constructor_C` is invoked, the superclass constructor is invoked automatically. Also its parent, i.e., `Constructor_B` needs to be initialized before the child class can be initialized and instantiated. The same case applies for `Constructor_B` which in itself is inherited from `Constructor_A`. Therefore, first of all, the constructor of class `Constructor_A` gets executed, then `Constructor_B` and lastly, `Constructor_C`.

Example 5.7 (a) Usage of super Keyword for Calling Parent Class Constructor

```
L1   class Constructor_A_Revised {
L2   Constructor_A_Revised()
     {
L3     System.out.println("Constructor A Revised");
     }}
L4   class Constructor_B_Revised extends Constructor_A_Revised {
       // this constructor is commented
       /* Constructor_B_Revised() {
       System.out.println("Constructor B");
```

```
     }
     */
L5   Constructor_B_Revised(int a)
         {
         a++;
L6       System.out.println("Constructor B Revised " +a);
         }}
L7   class Constructor_C_Revised extends Constructor_B_Revised {
L8   Constructor_C_Revised()
         {
L9       super(11);      // if omitted compile time error results
L10      System.out.println("Constructor C Revised");
         }
L11  public static void main (String args[]){
L12  Constructor_C_Revised a = new Constructor_C_Revised();
     }}
```

Output

```
Constructor A Revised
Constructor B Revised 12
Constructor C Revised
```

Explanation

(Only the changes are being explained)

L5   The parameterized constructor of class `Constructor_B_Revised` is defined with an integer argument.

L6   The integer argument is being post incremented.

L9   `super` keyword for calling constructor, followed by the argument to be passed to the parent class constructor.

L12   An object of `Constructor_C_Revised` is created due to which the default constructor of this class will be invoked. But as already explained, it is inherited, so its parent's (i.e.,`Constructor_B_Revised`) default constructor will be called automatically. But instead of the default constructor in `Constructor_B_Revised`, a parameterized constructor is provided. If a class does not provide any constructor (default or parameterized), it will be provided with an implicit default constructor automatically by Java. In case the class does provide a constructor, Java will not provide it with a default constructor. An implicit call to the parent class default constructor of `Constructor_C_Revised` results in an error, because the default (no argument) constructor is neither provided nor it will be implicitly available through Java, as a parameterized constructor is provided in the class `Constructor_B_Revised`.

The solution for this is either to explicitly provide a default (no argument) constructor in `Constructor_B_Revised` (shown in comments) or use `super` in the constructor of the subclass `Constructor_C_Revised` (as shown in L9) for making an explicit call to the parameterized constructor in its immediate super-class and in this case, the compiler will not show you an error. The constructor of class `Constructor_A_Revised` is normally called as the default constructor is provided in the class.

Note   It is mandatory for a `super` statement in a constructor to be the first statement within the constructor. As the parent must be initialized before its child, an explicit call to the parent must be done before any initialization within the child constructor begins.

5.4 final KEYWORD

The keyword final is used for the following purposes:

1. To declare constants (used with variable and argument declaration)
2. To disallow method overriding (used with method declaration)
3. To disallow inheritance (used with class declaration)

Basically, it is used to prevent inheritance and create constants. Let us take an example.

Example 5.8 **Final Keyword**

```
L1    class Final_Demo {
L2    final int MAX = 100;    //constant declaration
      // final mOethod declaration with final arguments
L3    final void show(final int x) {
L4    // MAX++; illegal statement as MAX is final
L5    // x++; illegal statement as x argument is final
L6    System.out.println("Superclass show method:" +x);
      }}
L7    class Final_Demo_1 extends Final_Demo {
      // cannot override show method as it is final in
      // parent class,that is why we have commented it

L8    /* void show(){
          System.out.println("Subclass show method");
      }*/

L9    public static void main (String args[]){
L10   Final_Demo_1 f2 = new Final_Demo_1();
      //show of the parent class will be called
L11   f2.show(12);
      }}
```

Output

```
C:\examples\> java Final_Demo_1
Superclass show method: 12
```

Explanation

L1 Class declaration Final_Demo.

L2 Integer constant declaration MAX with value 100.

L3 The final method show()is defined with final arguments. This method cannot be overridden in its subclasses as is shown in the comments in L8. The final argument's value cannot change, as it has become a constant now (shown in L5).

L7 Subclass declaration. If the parent class would have been a final class, then this class could not have been subclassed. The final class can be declared as follows:

```
final class Final_Demo
```

5.5 ABSTRACT CLASS

The literary meaning of *abstract* is — "a concept or idea that is not associated with any specific instance." Abstract classes adopt this very concept. Abstract classes are classes with a generic concept, not related to a specific class. They define the partial behavior and leave the rest for the subclasses to provide.

Abstract classes contain one or more abstract methods. It does not make any sense to create an abstract class without abstract methods, but if done, the Java compiler does not complain about it. An abstract method is a method that is declared, but contains no implementation, i.e., no body.

Abstract classes cannot be instantiated, and they require subclasses to provide implementation for their abstract methods by overriding them and then the subclasses can be instantiated. If the subclasses do not implement the methods of the abstract class, then it is mandatory for the subclasses to tag itself as *abstract*, making way for its own subclasses to override the abstract methods.

Why do We Create Abstract Methods?

We use abstract methods, when we want to force the same *name and signature pattern* in all the subclasses and do not want to give them the opportunity to use their own naming patterns, but at the same time give them the flexibility to code these methods with their own specific requirements. Example 5.9(a) shows an abstract `Animal` class. This class has been specifically created as an abstract class due to the presence of abstract methods in it. There are certain features that are common to all the animals but certain other features are specific to a category of animal. We may also argue that the common features are performed in a variety of ways by different animals. For example, every animal in this world produce a particular kind of sound, unique to their own species.

Example 5.9 (a) Abstract Class with Abstract Method

```
L1    abstract class Animal
      {
L2      String name;
L3      String species;
      // constructor of the abstract class
L4      Animal(String n, String s)
        {
L5      name = n;
L6      species = s;
        }
L7    void eat(String fooditem)
        {
L8      System.out.println(species + " " + name + " likes to have " + fooditem);
        }
L9    abstract void sound();
      }
```

Explanation

L1 Abstract class declared with the keyword abstract used before the class declaration.

L2 and 3 Two string variables declared, named name and species.

L4 Parameterized constructor to initialize the instance variable.

L5 and 6 Instance variables, name and species,

are initialized with the arguments passed to the constructors in L4.

L7 A non-abstract method has been defined, just like other normal methods.

L8 Print statement.

L9 Abstract method declared. Note that this method does not have any body.

The abstract keyword is used for defining both abstract methods and abstract classes. Any animal that wants to be instantiated must override the sound()method, otherwise it is impossible to create an instance of that class. Let us take a look at the Lion subclass that inherits the Animal class.

Example 5.9 (b)   Class Implementing Abstract Methods

```
L1    class Lion extends Animal
      {
L2    Lion() {
L3      super("Lion","Asiatic Lion");
      }
L4    void sound() {
L5      System.out.println ("Lions Roar! Roar!");
      }
L6    public static void main(String args[])
      {
L7      Lion l = new Lion();
L8      l.eat("flesh");
L9      l.sound();
      }}
```

Output

```
Asiatic Lion likes to have flesh
Lions Roar! Roar!
```

Explanation

L1 Subclass declaration of the abstract class Animal.

L2 Default constructor created for Lion class.

L3 The keyword super used to set up an explicit call to the parent class constructor.

L4 It is mandatory for the subclass Lion to override the sound() method because the sound()method has been declared abstract by the parent class.

L7 The object of Lion class is created.

L8 The eat()method (Example 5.9(a)) of the parent class will be called with the help of the object created in L7.

L9 The sound() method is called which has been declared in L4.

Some key features of an abstract class are as follows:

1. They cannot be instantiated, but they can have a reference variable.
2. A class can inherit only one abstract class, as multiple inheritance is not allowed amongst classes.
3. They can have abstract methods as well as non-abstract methods.
4. It is mandatory for a subclass to override the abstract methods of the abstract class, otherwise the subclass also need to declare itself as abstract. Overriding other methods (non-abstract) is up to the requirement of the subclass.
5. Abstract classes can have constructors and variables, just like other normal classes.

5.6 SHADOWING VS OVERRIDING

Shadowing of fields occurs when variable names are same. It may occur when local variables and instance variable names collide within a class or variable names in superclass and subclass are same. In case of methods, instance methods are overridden whereas static methods are shadowed. The difference between the two is important because shadowed methods are bound early whereas instance methods are dynamically (late) bound. The difference is illustrated in the following example.

Example 5.10 **Shadowing vs Overriding**

```
L1    class Shadowing
      {
L2      static void display()
        {
L3          System.out.println("In Static Method of Superclass");
        }
L4      void instanceMethod()
        {
L5          System.out.println("In instance Method of Super Class");
        }
      }

L6      class ShadowingTest extends Shadowing
        {
            // Static Methods are not Overridden but Shadowed
L7          static void display()
            {
L8          System.out.println("In Static Method of Sub Class");
            }
        // instance methods are Overridden not shadowed
L9          void instanceMethod()
            {
L10            System.out.println("The Overridden instance Method in Sub Class");
            }
L11     public static void main(String args[])
```

```
        {
L12         Shadowing s=new ShadowingTest();
            // invokes the Superclass display as they are
            // early binded at Compile time.
L13         s.display();

            // invokes the overridden version as they are
            // dynamically binded at runtime
L14         s.instanceMethod();

L15         ShadowingTest st=new ShadowingTest();
            // invokes the Sub class display as they are
            // early binded at Compile time
L16         st.display();
            // invokes the overridden version as they are
            // dynamically binded at runtime
L17         st.instanceMethod();
        }
    }
```

Output

```
D:\javabook\program\java ShadowingTest
In Static Method of Superclass
The Overridden instance Method in Subclass
In Static Method of Subclass
The Overridden instance Method in Subclass
```

Explanation

L1   Class declaration

L2–3   Declares a static method with a print statement within itself.

L4–5   Declares a instance method with a print statement within itself.

L6   Subclass (ShadowingTest) of the class, declared in L1, is declared.

L7–8   Declares a static method within the subclass with the same name and signature as the static method of superclass with a print statement within the method.

L9–10   The instance method of the superclass is overridden with a print statement within it.

L11   main() method.

L12   A reference variable of super (shadowing) class is declared to hold an object of subclass (ShadowingTest).

L13   The static method is invoked using this object created in L12. But as static methods are not overridden, they are early binded. The compiler creates this binding at compile time based on the type of reference through which method has been invoked. As the reference is of superclass, the superclass static method is invoked.

L14   The instance method is invoked using this object created in L12. But as instance methods are overridden, they are dynamically (late) binded. The compiler delays this binding till runtime and JVM invokes the methods based on the type of object through which method has been invoked. As the object is of subclass, the subclass instance method is invoked.

L15   An object of subclass is created. (A reference variable of subclass (ShadowingTest) class is declared to hold an object of subclass (ShadowingTest)).

L16   Same as L13 (refer output).

L17   Same as L14 (refer output).

5.7 PRACTICAL PROBLEM: `circle` AND `cylinder` CLASS

Let us take a practical example to show the power of inheritance and usage of `super` keyword. We will create a `Circle` class and then inherit the `Circle` class in a `Cylinder` class to calculate its area.

Example 5.11 (a) **Class Implementing Abstract Methods**

```
L1    class Circle {
      //declaring the instance variable
L2      float radius;
L3      final float PI = 3.141f;  //value of pi is fixed
L4      Circle()
        {
L5      radius = 1.0f;
        }
        // parameterized constructor
L6    Circle(float radius) {
L7          this.radius = radius;
        }
        // returns the area of the circle, i.e. πr²
L8    float getArea() {
L9          return PI * radius * radius;
        }}
```

Explanation

L1 `Circle` class has been defined.

L2 The `float` instance variable `radius` has been defined.

L3 The final float instance variable `PI` has been defined (similar to π, i.e., `PI` of mathematics) and initialized with the value 3.141`f` (`f` for float). Why we have created it as `final` will become clear in the next topic.

L4 Default constructor of class `Circle`.

L5 Instance variable `radius` has been initialized.

L6 The overloaded constructor has been declared with an argument of type `float`, to initialize the instance variable `radius`.

L7 The instance variable is differentiated from the local variable with the help of `this` keyword and initialized with the value passed as an argument to the constructor.

L8 Instance method declaration `getArea()` with a return type `float`.

L9 The keyword `return` is used to return the area of the circle back to the caller.

The next step is to create a subclass `Cylinder` of the `Circle` class. The `Cylinder` class will override the `getArea()` method of the `Circle` class which will return the surface area of a cylinder. The `Cylinder` class is defined in Example 5.11(b).

Example 5.11 (b) **Inheritance**

```
L1    class Cylinder extends Circle {

      // instance variable to denote height of the cylinder
L2    float height;
L3    Cylinder(float radius, float height){
      // explicit call to superclass constructor
L4      super(radius);
```

```
L5        this.height = height;
          }
          // overridden method returns the cylinder surface area
          // Surface Area = (2πr²) + (2πr.height)
          // where (2 π r²) is the surface area of the "ends" and
          //(2πr.height) is the area of the "side"
          // superclass method being invoked using super keyword
L6        float getArea() {
L7          return 2 * super.getArea() + 2 * PI * radius * height;
          }

L8        public static void main(String args[]) {
L9          Circle c = new Circle(1.5f);
L10         System.out.println("The Area of Circle is: " + c.getArea());
L11         Cylinder cy = new Cylinder(1.5f,3.5f);
L12         System.out.println("The Surface Area of Cylinder is: " + cy.getArea());
          }}
```

Output

```
C:\examples\chap 5>java Cylinder
The Area of Circle is: 7.0672503
The Surface Area of Cylinder is: 47.114998
```

Explanation

L1 Cylinder class inherits Circle class.

L2 Instance variable height has been defined by the subclass Cylinder.

L3 Parameterized constructor to initialize radius and height.

L4 The keyword super is used to pass the radius accepted as an argument in the subclass constructor (L3) to the Circle class, i.e., the parent constructor. It shows the reuse of code, as radius is defined only once and being used by the subclass.

L5 The instance variable height is initialized with the local variable height(argument).

L6 getArea()of Circle class has been overridden, because the Cylinder class wanted the name of the method to be same as that of the superclass, i.e., getArea() but perform a different function, i.e., return the surface area of the cylinder.

L7 getArea() of the superclass has been called with the help of super, i.e., super.getArea()because if you look at the formula for calculating the surface area of the cylinder, it says:

Surface area $= (2 \pi r^2) + (2 \pi r \text{ height})$

where $(2\pi r^2)$ is the surface area of the "ends" and $(2\pi r.\text{ height})$ is the area of the "side", and πr^2 is the area of the circle, and we already have created a method for calculating the area of the circle in the parent class. For this reason, we have called the super class getArea method (reuse of code).radius has already been passed in L4 using the super keyword. The return value from the parent class getArea() method is multiplied by 2 and added to the area of the sides $(2 \pi rh)$.

L8 main() method.

L9 The object of Circle class is created with a radius of 1.5f.

L10 Calling the method getArea()with the help of Circle class object. The return value is concatenated with the string present in the println method and printed on the screen as can be seen in the output.

L11 Creation of an object of Cylinder class with a radius of 1.5f and height of 3.5f.

L12 The getArea()method is invoked with the help of Cylinder class object.

SUMMARY

The concept of inheritance is derived from real life, wherein children inherit the good/bad qualities from their parents and add to that their own identity and behavior. This has been absorbed by object-oriented programming, wherein the properties and methods of a parent class are inherited by the children or subclasses. The subclasses can implement the inherited methods in a different way using method overriding, keeping the method names and signatures same as that of the parent class.

The super keyword can be used to access the overridden methods, variables, and even the constructors of the superclass. Abstract classes are used to force the subclasses to override abstract methods and provide body and code for them. The difference between overriding and shadowing is also discussed with examples. Shadowed methods are binded early by the compiler whereas overridden methods are dynamically binded by JVM.

The `final` keyword is used to create constants and disallow inheritance. The keywords `abstract` and `final` cannot coexist because `final` is used to prevent inheritance and `abstract` is used to allow subclasses to inherit it and override methods.

EXERCISES

Objective Questions

1. What will happen when you attempt to compile and run the following class?

```
class Demo{
Demo(inti){
    System.out.println("Demo");
}}
class Inner extends Demo{
public static void main(String
args[]){
    Inner s = new Inner();
}
void Inner(){
    System.out.println("Inner");
}}
```

(a) Compilation and output of the string "Inner" at runtime
(b) Compile-time error
(c) Compilation and no output at runtime
(d) Compilation and output of the string "Demo".

2. Which of the following statements are true?
(a) If a class has abstract methods, it must be declared as abstract.
(b) If the abstract methods are not overridden, the subclass need not be declared as abstract.
(c) A final class cannot be subclassed.
(d) All methods in an abstract class must be declared as abstract.

3. Which is the keyword used for deriving classes?
(a) implements   (b) extends
(c) throws   (d) inherits

4. What will happen when you attempt to compile and run the following class?

```
class Base{
void Base()
{
    System.out.println("In Base");
}
Base(inti)
{
    System.out.println("In Base: "+i);
}}
```

(a) Compile time error
(b) Compiles but gives runtime error
(c) Compiles and executes successfully but does not show any output
(d) Compiles and prints "In Base"

5. What will happen when you attempt to compile and run the following class?

```
abstract class Demo
{
    abstract void show();
}
class Demo_1 extends Demo
{
```

```
Demo_1()
{ System.out.println("In Demo"); }
public static void main(String
args[])
{ Demo_1 d = new Demo_1(); }
}
```

(a) Compile-time error
(b) Compiles but gives runtime error
(c) Compiles and executes successfully but does not show any output
(d) Compiles and prints "In Demo"

6. What will happen when you attempt to compile and run the following class?

```
class Test
{
   Test (int a)
   {
       System.out.println ("Test" +);
   }
}
Class Test_1 extends Test
{
   Test_1 (int a)
   {
       System.out.println ("Test_1")';
   }
   public static void main (string
   args [])
   {
       Test t = new Test_1(10);
   }
}
```

(a) Compile-time error
(b) Compiles but gives runtime error
(c) Compiles and prints Test 10 followed by Test_1
(d) Compiles and prints "Test_1"

7. How can the above program be rectified to give the output as stated in option (c)?

(a) use super for a method call in subclass constructor
(b) use super for constructor call in subclass constructor
(c) make the superclass as abstract
(d) provide default constructor in Test.

8. Which keyword is used to prevent inheritance?
(a) final   (b) super
(c) this   (d) Final

9. What will happen if the following line is present in a program?

```
abstract final class Demo {
    // Lines of code
}
```

(a) does not compile, as no class can be abstract
(b) runtime error
(c) does not compile, as no class can be final
(d) does not compile, as no class can be abstract and final.

10. What will be the output when you try to compile and run the program?

```
class Demo
{
    int a;
    Demo(int a)
    {
        a = a+10;
        System.out.println(a);
    }
    public static void main(String
    args[])
    {
        Demo d = new Demo(4);
        System.out.println(d.a);
    }
}
```

(a) 14 and 0   (b) 0 and 14
(c) 14 and 14   (d) Compile time error

Review Questions

1. What is inheritance? How is it different from aggregation?

2. What is method overriding? Explain with an example.

3. Explain `super` keyword with all its usages. Support explanation with a program.

4. Explain final keyword with all its usages. Support explanation with a program.

5. What is an abstract class? Can an abstract class have constructors? Explain.

6. What is shadowing of instance variables?

7. What is the difference between shadowing and overriding?

8. Overloaded methods are early bound whereas Overridden methods are late bound. Comment.?

Programming Exercises

1. Define a class `MotorVehicle` as described below:

   Data members:
   - (a) `modelName`
   - (b) `modelNumber`
   - (c) `modelPrice`

   Methods:
   - (a) `display()` method to display the name, price, and model number.

   Define another class named `Car` that inherits the class `MotorVehicle` and has the following:

   Data members:
   - (a) `discountRate`

   Methods:
   - (a) `display()` method to display the Car name, Car model number, Car price, and the discount rate.
   - (b) `discount()` method to compute the discount Create the classes `MotorVehicle` and `Car` with suitable constructors and test it.

2. Create an abstract class `Accounts` with the following details:

   Data members:
   - (a) `balance`
   - (b) `accountNumber`
   - (c) `accountHoldersName`
   - (d) `address`

   Methods:
   - (a) `withdrawl()` – abstract
   - (b) `deposit()` – abstract
   - (c) `display()` to show the balance of the account number

   Create a subclass of this class `SavingsAccount` and add the following details:

   Data members:
   - (a) `rateOfInterest`

   Methods:
   - (a) `calculateAmount()`

9. Why subclass reference variables cannot refer to a superclass object?

   - (b) `display()` to display rate of interest with new balance and full account holder details

   Create another subclass of the `Accounts` class, i.e. `CurrentAccount` with the following:

   Data members:
   - (a) `overdraftLimit`

   Method:
   - (a) `display()` to show overdraft limit along with the full account holder details

   Create objects of these two classes and call their methods. Use appropriate constructors.

3. Create a class named `Employee` with the following details:

   Data members:
   - (a) `name`
   - (b) `address`
   - (c) `age`
   - (d) `gender`

   Method:
   - (a) `display()` to show the employee details

   Create another class `FullTimeEmployee` that inherits the `Employee` class:

   Data members:
   - (a) `salary`
   - (b) `designation`

   Method:
   - (a) `display()` to show the salary and designation along with other employee details

   Create another class `PartTimeEmployee` that inherits the `Employee` class:

   Data members:
   - (a) `workingHours`
   - (b) `ratePerHour`

   Methods:
   - (a) `calculatePay()` to calculate the amount payable
   - (b) `display()` to show the amount payable along with other employee details

   Create objects of these classes and call their methods. Use appropriate constructors.

Answers to Objective Questions

1. (a)   2. (a), (c)   3. (b)   4. (b)

5. (a), either abstract is to be used with `Demo_1` or override show in `Demo_1`   6. (a)

7. (b) and (d), use super for constructor call in `Test _1` or provide default constructor in `Test`

8. (a)   9. (a)

10. (a), Local variable shadows instance variable in the constructors

Interfaces, Packages, and Enumeration

The greater our knowledge increases, the more our ignorance unfolds.

John F. Kennedy

After reading this chapter, the readers will be able to

- ◆ understand what interfaces are and how they are different from abstract classes
- ◆ understand the concept behind packages and how they are used
- ◆ know about the `java.lang` package
- ◆ understand object class and wrapper class
- ◆ know how strings are created, manipulated, and split in Java
- ◆ understand enumerations

6.1 INTERFACES

Interfaces in Java are like a contract or a protocol which the classes have to abide with. Interfaces are basically a collection of methods which are public and abstract by default. These methods do not have any body. The implementing objects have to override all the methods of the interface and provide implementation for all these methods. There is no code at all associated with any method of the interface. The best part of an interface is that a class can inherit any number of interfaces, thus allowing *multiple inheritance* in Java, provided the class now has to override all the methods of all the interfaces it inherits. Java does not support multiple inheritance among classes, but interfaces allow Java to support this feature.

Interfaces are declared with the help of a keyword `interface`. Note that none of the methods have a body. It is the responsibility of the implementing class to override the methods and provide the implementation for these methods.

```
interface interfacename
{
      returntype methodname(argumentlist);
      ...
}
class classname implements interfacename{}
```

Example 6.1(a) shows a very simple calculator program. There are a few basic operations that do not change for any calculator: be it a normal, scientific, or a programmable calculator. The basic operations (add, subtract, divide, and multiply) can be squeezed out of various implementing classes and put into an interface. Now all the implementing objects will have to keep the name and signature of the methods exactly same as has been defined in the interface, that is why we have created an interface and this is what we actually wanted for all the subclasses to follow. We do not want the classes to follow their own set of rules like their own created method names and their signatures. We wanted the classes to follow the rules set up by the interfaces and it will be a binding upon them, but these rules will be implementation independent. That is, the objects have to code according to their own requirement within the overridden methods. For simplicity, we have created an interface named `Calculator` and four methods have been defined in it to denote four basic operations of a calculator and these methods perform operations only on integers. You can later on extend this program to accept different kinds of arguments such as `double`, `float`, and `byte`.

Classes, while inheriting other classes, use the keyword `extends`; whereas while inheriting an interface, they use the keyword `implements`, as shown in Example 6.1(b).

Example 6.1 (a)   `Calculator.java`: **Interface Definition**

```
L1        interface Calculator
          {
L2          int add(int a,int b);
L3          int subtract(int a,int b);
L4          int multiply(int a,int b);
L5          int divide(int a,int b);
          }
```

Explanation

L1 The keyword `interface` has been used to declare an interface followed by the name of the interface and opening curly brackets to denote the starting of interface.

L2 A method named `add` has been declared with the return type `int` that accepts two arguments of type `int`.

L3 A method named `subtract` has been declared with the return type `int` that accepts two arguments of type `int`.

L4 A method named `multiply` has been declared with the return type `int` that accepts two arguments of type `int`.

L5 A method named `divide` has been declared with the return type `int` that accepts two arguments of type `int`, followed by the closing curly bracket of the interface.

Example 6.1 (b)   `Normal_Calculator.java`: **Class Implementing Calculator Interface**

```
L1      class Normal_Calculator implements Calculator
          {
L2        public int add(int a,int b){
L3          return a + b; }
L4        public int subtract(int a,int b) {
L5          return a - b; }
L6        public int multiply(int a,int b) {
L7          return a * b; }
L8        public int divide(int a,int b)
```

```
       {
L9       return a / b;
       }
L10    public static void main(String args[]) {
L11    Normal_Calculator c = new Normal_Calculator();
L12    System.out.println("Value after addition = "+c.add(5,2));
L13    System.out.println("Value after Subtraction = " +c.subtract(5,2));
L14    System.out.println("Value after Multiplication = " +c.multiply(5,2));
L15    System.out.println("Value after division = " +c.divide(5,2));
       }}
```

Output

```
C:\javabook>java Normal_Calculator
Value after addition = 7
Value after Subtraction = 3
Value after Multiplication= 10
Value after division = 2
```

Explanation

L1 Class `Normal_Calculator` has been declared and it inherits the interface `Calculator` with the help of *implements* keyword.

L2 Method `add` has been overridden and the body of the method has been provided.

L3 The keyword `return` is used to return the result (to the caller) of addition of two arguments passed into the add method followed by the closing curly bracket.

L4–9 The methods `substract`, `multiply`, and `divide` are overridden and the results are returned.

L11 An object of the class `Normal_Calculator` is created.

L12–15 Print statements to print the result of addition/subtraction/multiplication/division. Respective methods have been called in these lines with the object created in L11 like `c.sum(5,2)`. These method calls return the result and the result is concatenated with the strings passed as an argument to the `println` method and displayed on the screen (see output).

Note It is mandatory to add the access specifier `public` to the method declaration, otherwise the compiler will not compile the program. As already discussed, all the methods in the interface are public, so when the implementing classes override the methods defined in the interface, they have to tag it as public.

Not making it public or leaving the access specifier blank (default) will reduce the privileges from public to default, which is not allowed in overriding. Either you have to increase the privileges or keep it intact. Widening conversion in case of overriding takes place automatically, i.e., from default to public (lesser privileges to more privileges), but narrowing conversion is not allowed.

It is recommended to create two java files in a directory: (a) `Calculator.java` for defining the interface and (b) `Normal_Calculator.java` for declaring the class implementing the `Calculator.java` interface. The compiler upon compilation of `Normal_Calculator.java` will create two class files automatically: `Calculator.class` and `Normal_Calculator.class`.

6.1.1 Variables in Interface

Just like methods in an interface (by default `public` and `abstract`; no need to tag them), variables defined in an interface also carry a default behavior. They are implicitly `public`, `final`, and `static` and there is no need to explicitly declare them as *public*, *static*, and *final*. As they are `final`, they need to be assigned a value compulsorily. Being `static`, they can be accessed directly with the help of an interface name and as they are `public`, we can access them from anywhere. Example 6.2 shows the usage of variables in an interface.

Example 6.2 **Variables in an Interface**

```
L1    interface Limit_Test {
L2       int LOWERLIMIT = 0;
L3       int UPPERLIMIT = 100;
         }
L4    class Variable_Test implements Limit_Test {
L5    void findNumberWithinLimits(int a) {
L6    if(a > LOWERLIMIT && < < UPPERLIMIT)
L7       System.out.println(a+ " lie in between" + Variable_Test.LOWERLIMIT + " and " +
         Variable_Test.UPPERLIMIT);
L8    else
L9       System.out.println(a+ " does not lie in between " + Variable_Test.LOWERLIMIT +
         " and " +Variable_Test.UPPERLIMIT);
         }
L10   public static void main(String args[]) {
L11      Variable_Test vt = new Variable_Test();
L12      //LOWERLIMIT++; illegal statement
L13      //UPPERLIMIT++;
L14      vt.findNumberWithinLimits(23);
L15      vt.findNumberWithinLimits(233);
         }}
```

Output

```
C:\javabook\>java Variable_Test
23 lie in between 0 and 100
233 does not lie in between 0 and 100
```

Explanation

L1 We have created an interface `Limit_Test`, wherein we will set the upper and lower limits.

L2 and 3 The upper and lower limits are being set with the help of two variables in the interface, i.e., `UPPERLIMIT` and `LOWERLIMIT`. They have to be assigned a value, as they are implicitly final.

L4 Class `Variable_Test` inheriting the interface `Limit_Test`.

L5 Method `findNumberWithinLimits` is declared with an argument. This argument will be checked by the method whether it is within the limit or not.

L6 A simple `if` condition to check whether the argument passed in the function (L5) is greater than the `LOWERLIMIT` and lesser than the `UPPERLIMIT`. If the condition satisfies, L7 is executed, else L9.

L7 print statement to print that the argument lies in between the limits defined by the interface. Note that the static variable's `LOWERLIMIT` and `UPPERLIMIT` have been accessed with the help of the interface `Variable_Test`.

L9 print statement to print that the argument does not lie in between the limits defined by the interface (same as in L7).

L11 An object of the class `Variable_Test` is created.

L12 and 13 Commented statements to modify the variables: `LOWERLIMIT` and `UPPERLIMIT`. If uncommented, these statements will result in a compile-time error because the variables defined in an interface are final, and final variable values cannot be modified.

L14 `findNumberWitihinLimits()` is called through the object of `Variable_Test`, and an argument of 23 is passed. This argument is checked by the method to be within the lower limit and the upper limit and if yes, the value is printed on screen.

L15 `findNumberWitihinLimits()` is called through

the object of `Variable_Test`, and an argument of 233 is passed. This argument is checked by the method to be within the lower limit and the upper limit and if it is not, print on screen.

6.1.2 Extending Interfaces

Just like normal classes, interfaces can also be extended. An interface can inherit another interface using the same keyword extends, and not the keyword `implements`. Example 6.3 shows how interfaces are extended.

Example 6.3 **Extending Interfaces**

```
L1    interface A {
L2       void showA();
         }
L3    interface B extends A{
L4       void showB();
         }
L5    class InDemo implements B {
L6    public void showA()
             {
             System.out.println("Overriden method of Interface A");
             }
L7    public void showB()
             {
             System.out.println("Overriden method of Interface B");
             }
      public static void main (String args[])
         {
         InDemo d = new InDemo();
         d.showA();
         d.showB();
         }}
```

Output

```
C:\javabook\>java InDemo
Overriden method of Interface A
Overriden method of Interface B
```

Explanation

L1 An interface named A has been declared.

L2 Method `showA()` has been defined in interface A.

L3 Interface B is defined and we have used extends in its declaration to indicate that the parent interface of B is A. Any class that inherits B will have to override all the methods of interface A as well as B.

L4 Method `showB()` has been defined in interface B.

L5 Class declaration shows that it inherits the interface B.

L6 Shows the overridden method `showA()`. Note that while overriding, `public` access specifier is added.

L7 Shows the overridden method `showB()`.

6.1.3 Interface vs Abstract Class

Table 6.1 lists the differences between interface and abstract class.

Table 6.1 Interface vs Abstract Class

Interface	Abstract Class
Multiple inheritance possible; a class can inherit any number of interfaces.	Multiple inheritance not possible; a class can inherit only one class.
implements keyword is used to inherit an interface.	**extends** keyword is used to inherit a class.
By default, all methods in an interface are **public** and **abstract**; no need to tag it as **public** and **abstract**.	Methods have to be tagged as **public** or **abstract** or both, if required.
Interfaces have no implementation at all.	Abstract classes can have partial implementation.
All methods of an interface need to be overridden.	Only abstract methods need to be overridden.
All variables declared in an interface are by default **public**, **static**, or **final**.	Variables, if required, have to be declared as **public**, **static**, or **final**.
Interfaces do not have any constructors.	Abstract classes can have constructors.
Methods in an interface cannot be static.	Non-abstract methods can be static.

It is not that interfaces and abstract classes are entirely dissimilar, they have some similarities also.

1. Both cannot be instantiated, i.e., objects cannot be created for both of them.
2. Both can have reference variables referring to their implementing classes objects. For example, if X is an interface and its implementing class name is Y, then we cannot code:

```
         X x1 = new X();        // illegal code
```
But we can code,   `X x1 = new Y();        // legal code`

3. Interfaces can be extended, i.e., one interface can inherit another interface, similar to that of abstract classes (using `extends` keyword).
4. `static/final` methods can neither be created in an interface nor can they be used with abstract methods.

6.2 PACKAGES

You must have encountered situations wherein you try to organize too many files in folders/directories and subdirectories. Similarly, if you have too many classes at your disposal, some sort of grouping is required. Java package is one such mechanism for organizing Java classes into groups. In fact, a package is indeed a directory for holding Java files. Java has many such predefined packages which can be used in programs. Some of the predefined packages in Java are `applet`, `awt`, `lang`, `util`, `event`, `io`, `swing`, etc. Programmers are also permitted to develop their own packages in order to organize classes belonging to the same category or providing similar functionality.

Note A package can be defined as a collection used for grouping a variety of classes and interfaces based on their functionality.

It is also possible to house these Java packages, as these can be stored in compressed files called JAR files (a JAR file or Java ARchive is used for aggregating many files into one) allowing classes to download faster as a group rather than one at a time.

A package declaration resides at the top of a Java source file. All source files to be placed in a package have a common package name.

- A package provides a unique namespace for the classes it contains.
- A package can contain the following:
  - Classes
  - Interfaces
  - Enumerated types
  - Annotations (metadata facility for elements introduced in Java 5)
- Two classes in two different packages can have the same name, which is not possible without using the package mechanism.
- Packages provide a mechanism to hide its classes from being used by programs or packages belonging to other classes.

6.2.1 Creating Packages

Until now, we have studied what packages are and why they are used. The packages in Java can be of two kinds, predefined Java API packages and user-defined packages. Java 6 API has a large number of classes and interfaces, housed according to their functionality into different packages. Some of these are listed in Table 6.2.

Table 6.2 Commonly Used Predefined Packages

Package	Functionality
java.lang	Basic language fundamentals
java.util	Utility classes and collection data structure classes
java.io	File handling operations
java.math	Arbitrary precision arithmetic
java.net	Network programming
java.sql	Java Database Connectivity (JDBC) to access databases
java.awt	Abstract window toolkit for native GUI components
javax.swing	Lightweight programming for platform-independent rich GUI components

The above-mentioned packages are pre-designed to be a part of Java API. Now the question arises—how can the users create their own packages?

The name of the package should be followed by the keyword `package`, declared at the top of the program. Anything else, say class declaration and so, may only be followed by the package declaration. Thus, we can define a class belonging to a package as follows:

```
package packexample;              //package declaration
public class ClassinPackage
{
  //class definition inside package
  //Body of class
}
```

Saving, Compiling, and Executing Packages

Here, the package name is `packexample` and the class `ClassinPackage` has been made a part of this package. There are two ways of saving, compiling, and executing Java files stored in a package.

1. Remember the file must be saved with the name of the class, i.e., `ClassinPackage` and placed in the directory named exactly the same as the package, i.e., `packexample`. The file is compiled from within the package and the class file generated after compilation is stored in the same directory (package). For executing the file, move up the current directory and execute the file by mentioning the name of the `package()` followed by the class name. For example, suppose the package `packexample` is within the directory *pack*. The sequence of statements would be:

```
// compiling the class
C:\pack\packexample\> javac ClassinPackage.java
```
L1

```
// executing the class
C:\pack\> java packexample.ClassinPackage
```
L2

```
// This will not execute as c does not have packexample directory.
C:\> java packexample.ClassinPackage
```
L3

> **Note** Classes that reside inside a package cannot be referred by their own name alone. The package name has to precede the name of the class of which it is a part of. All classes are a part of some or the other package. If the keyword package is not used in any class for mentioning the name of the package, then it becomes a part of the default/unnamed package. In that case, we execute the classes as shown earlier.

2. This Java source file could be saved in any directory. During compilation time, you need to specify an option of the Java compiler *–d* which specifies the destination where you want to place your generated compiled files. After successful compilation, you would see that your package has been already created in your specified path and the `.class file` has been placed in that package. For executing the class, same steps need to be followed as explained above. Let us consider, the `ClassinPackage.java` file is stored in the `javaeg` directory.

```
//-d option used with javac for specifying destination c:\pack
// syntax: javac –d destination directory followed by java source file
C:\javaeg\>javac –d c:\pack ClassinPackage.java
```
L1

```
// executing the class /
C:\pack\> java packexample.ClassinPackage
```
L2

```
// This will not execute
C:\> java packexample.ClassinPackage
```
L3

> **Note** In both the cases, the execution takes place from the parent directory of the package where the class files are placed as shown in L2. If we want to execute the package from any of the directories, the `classpath` should be set.

Setting the Classpath

`Classpath` is used for storing the path of the third-party and user-defined classes. Whenever we execute/compile any class file, jdk tools `javac` and `java`, search the package/class file in the user classpath which is the current directory by default. If the classes are not in the current directory, then we need to set the `classpath`.

The classpath can be set in two ways:

1. It is an environment variable which can be set using the *System* utility in the control panel or at the DOS prompt as shown.

```
Set CLASSPATH = %CLASSPATH%;c:\pack;
```

%Classpath% is used to keep the existing path intact and append our new path to it. Now L3 of both the above cases will execute.

> **Note** Setting classpath at the DOS prompt will have to be done each time you open the DOS prompt, as closing the prompt resets the classpath to its original value. To make the changes permanent, edit the environment variable in the control panel.
>
> Do not delete the existing classpath; edit the variable to append your classpath to the environment variable.

2. Use classpath option –classpath or –cp of javac/java tools to override the user-defined classpath and find the user-defined specific package/classes used in the Java source files.

```
//syntax: javac –cp path of the directory/package used in java source file
followed by name of the java source file
C:\pack\packexample> javac –cp c:\javaeg DemoClass.java
```

–cp specifies that the user-defined package/classes used in DemoClass.java will be found at c:\javaeg.

Subpackages

Subpackages can be designed in hierarchy, i.e., one package can be a part of another package. This can be achieved by specifying multiple names of the packages at various levels of hierarchy, separated by dots. For example,

```
package rootpackage.subpackage1;
```

As related classes can be collected in a package, related packages can also be collected in a larger package. In the above statement, subpackage1 is designed to be a part of rootpackage. Of course the hierarchical packages have to be stored in a hierarchical structure of directories and subdirectories. For example, the above package subpackage1 (which is a part of rootpackage) will be stored within the directory rootpackage.

> **Note** The names of the packages and the directories have to be same, and the names being used should be carefully selected.

6.2.2 Using Packages

In Java, the names of classes that are defined inside various packages can always be referenced by specifying the names of the corresponding packages to which these classes belong to. For example, the Rectangle class belonging to the package java.awt can be referred to

```
java.awt.Rectangle, i.e.
```

```
java.awt.Rectangle box = new java.awt.Rectangle (5, 10, 20, 30);
```

But Java provides an import mechanism which can be used and classes can be used without prefixing the names of packages they belong to.

The point worth noting here is that the class `Rectangle` is referred to by preceding it with the name of the package `java.awt`. Certainly, this is a tedious process. The statement given below is a convenient form of the above statement.

```
Rectangle box = new Rectangle (5, 10, 20, 30);
```

This statement will do fine only if you *import* the class beforehand, i.e., at the start of the program itself.

Now the question is how to import the classes belonging to the various packages. Classes in a package like `java.lang` are automatically imported. For all other classes, you must supply an `import` statement to either import a specific class

```
import java.awt.Rectangle;
```

or to import all the classes in a package, using the *wildcard* notation.

```
import java.awt.*;
```

Let us try and implement the things we have discussed till now. In the following example, we have created two packages `packexample` and `packexample1`. The `packexample` has a class `ImportExmaple` which will be used in the class `UseImportExmaple` of another package `packexample1`.

Example 6.4 Recursive Program to Calculate Factorial in a Package

```
L1      package packexample;
L2      public class ImportExample{
L3      public int fact(int a){
L4        if(a == 1)
L5           return 1;
L6        else
L7           return a*fact(a-1);
        }}
```

Explanation

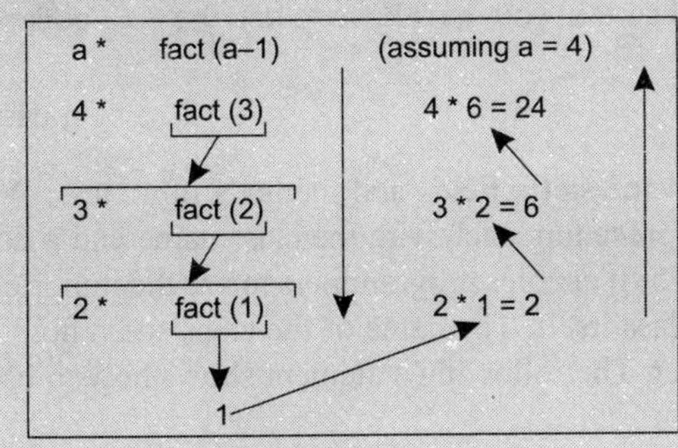

Fig. 6.1 Recursion

L1 Package named `packexample` has been declared.

L2 Public class named `ImportExample` within the package `packexample` has been declared.

L3 Public method `fact` has been defined.

L4 and 5 If the value of a is 1, return 1.

L6 and 7 Else return a * call to `fact` method with the argument a – 1. A function is being called from within, i.e., recursion. Fig. 6.1 shows the sequence of execution of this recursive function.

Example 6.5 Using a Package in Another Package and Calling the Recursive Factorial Method

```
L1    package packexample1;
L2    import packexample.*;
L3    class UseImportExample{
L4    public static void main(String args[]){
L5      int a = 4;
L6      ImportExample i = new ImportExample();
L7    System.out.println("factorial of " +a+ " is " +i.fact(a)); }}
```

Output

```
factorial of 4 is 24
```

Explanation

L1 Package `packexample1` is defined.
L2 We wanted to access the class `ImportExample` in our class, so we need to import the package of the class `ImportExample`, i.e., `packexample`. If we do not use the import statement, the compiler would complain about using `ImportExample` in L6.

Following are the steps to compile and execute this program:

```
C:\javabook\programs\packexample1>javac -cp c:\javabook\programs
    UseImportExample. java
C:\javabook\programs\packexample1>java -cp c:\javabook\programs;. packexample1.
    UseImportExample
factorial of 4 is 24
```

The-cp option specifies the path of package(directory) from where to access classes used in `UseImportExample.java`. The dot at the end in the classpath has been added to allow the UseImportExample in packexample1 locate itself. The dot represents the current directory. The `programs` directory is the common parent directory of both `packexample` and `packexample1`, so the package `packexample` can be easily imported as the `classpath` is specified using –cp option (i.e., `c:\javabook\programs`). There is no problem in locating `packexample` in `packexample1`. `UseImportExample` as classpath for both package is same which has already been given in the commmand.

> **Note** You can also set the `classpath` using the set command at the DOS prompt or set it permanently in the environment variables in the control panel so that you don't have to use the – cp option again and again with the JDK tools.

Static Import

In Section 4.7, we have already discussed about the static fields and methods of a class. We invoked the static fields and methods of a class preceding each with the class name and a dot (.). Static import a feature was introduced in Java 5. It enables programmers to use the imported static members as if they were declared in the class itself. The name of the class and a dot (.) are not required to use an imported static member. The following statement shows how to use static import:

```
import static pkgName.[subPkgName].ClassName.staticMemberName;
```

- `pkgName` is the name of the package containing the class whose static members need to be imported.
- `subpkgName` is the name of the subpackage to which the class belongs. The square brackets indicate that it is optional.
- `ClassName` is the name of the class whose static members need to imported.
- `staticMemberName` is the name of the static field or method. But the above statement would import only the mentioned static member of the class.

If you want to import all the static members of the class, then use the following:

```
import static pkgName.ClassName.*;
```

Note Static import imports only static members of the class. Normal import statements should be used to import the classes used in a program.

Example 6.6 demonstrates the use of static import.

Example 6.6 **Usage of Static Import**

```
L1    import static java.lang.Math.*;
L2    public class ExampleStaticImport {
L3    public static void main(String args[]) {
L4      System.out.println("power of 2 raise to 2 is: " +pow(2,2));
L5      System.out.println("ceil(-10.2)is: " + ceil(-10.2));
L6      System.out.println("floor(-10.2)is: " +floor(-10.2));
L7      System.out.println("ceil(10.2)is: " + ceil(10.2));
L8      System.out.println("floor(10.2)is: " +floor(10.2));
L9      System.out.println("maximum of 23 and 24 is: " +max(23,24));
L10     System.out.println("minimum of 23 and 24 is: " +min(23,24));
L11     System.out.println("value of PI is: " +PI);
L12     System.out.println("Value of E is: " +E);
    }}
```

Output

```
C:\javabook>java ExampleStaticImport
power of 2 raise to 2 is: 4.0
ceil(-10.2)is: -10.0
floor(-10.2)is : -11.0
ceil(10.2)is: 11.0
floor(10.2)is: 10.0
maximum of 23 and 24 is: 24
minimum of 23 and 24 is: 23
value of PI is: 3.141592653589793
Value of E is: 2.718281828459045
```

Explanation

L1 It is a static import declaration that imports all static fields and methods of the class `Math` from the package `java.lang`.

L4–12 Show a few static methods (`pow`, `floor`, `ceil`, `min`, and `max`) and fields PI and E being accessed without preceding the field name or method names with the class name `Math` and a dot as we had used `import static` at the top. If we use normal import instead of static import, then each function and field has to precede with the class name.

6.2.3 Access Protection

Access protection defines how much an element (class, method, variable) is exposed to other classes and packages. There are four types of access specifiers available in Java (shown in the decreasing order of access).

- `public` — applied to variables, constructors, methods, and classes
- `protected` — applied to variables, constructors, methods, and inner classes (not top-level classes)
- `default` — applied to variables, constructors, methods, and classes
- `private` — can be applied to variables, constructor, methods and inner classes (not top-level classes)

`public` and `private` are easy to define. The former means accessibility for all and the latter means accessibility from within the class only. The discussion settles down to two access specifiers: `protected` and `default`. `default` (blank) access specifiers are accessible only from within the package and protected access is beyond the package also but only to the subclasses outside the package. Let us take an example to understand the access specifiers. Assuming

```
x & y    are packages
A        is a public class within package x
B        is another class within package x
C        is subclass of A in package x
D        is subclass of A within package y
E        is class within package y
abc()    is a method with default access in class A
xyz()    is a method with protected access specifier in class A
pqr()    is a method with public privileges in class A
```

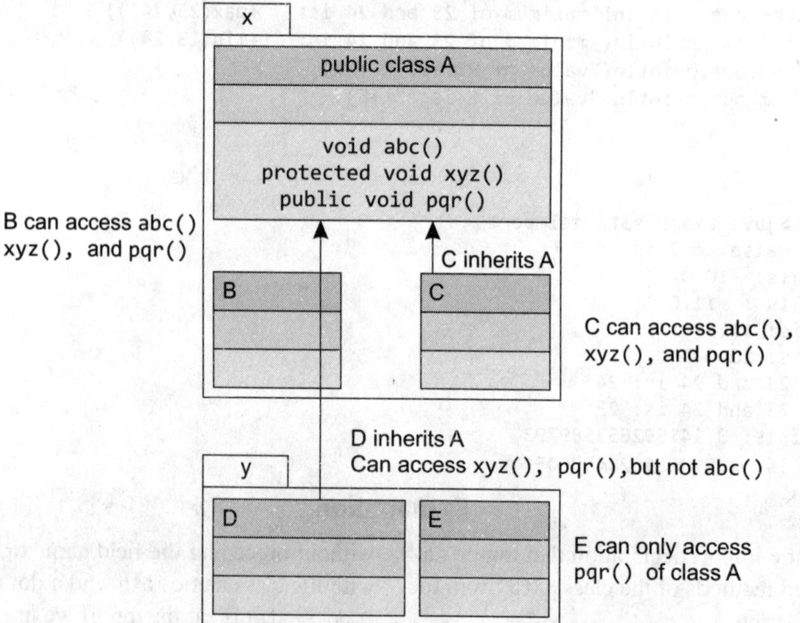

Fig. 6.2 UML Representation of Package and Classes to Show Access Protection

This method abc() is accessible from A, B, and C, but neither from D nor E. protected methods are also accessible outside the package, but only to the subclasses outside the package. For example, the method xyz() is accessible from classes A, B, C, D, but not from E. This is pictorially shown in Fig. 6.2. The method pqr() is accessible from all the classes, as it is a public method in a public class.

Note Access of any element, such as variable and method, is also governed by its container. For example, suppose a default access level class has a public method. This method is available to all the classes within the package, but not outside it, as the class in which the method has been defined is not accessible outside the package.

6.3 java.lang PACKAGE

java.lang is a special package, as it is imported by default in all the classes that we create. There is no need to explicitly import the lang package. It contains the classes that form the basic building blocks of Java.

Note Remember we have been using String and the System class from the first example in this book, but we have not imported any package for using these classes, as both these classes lie in the lang package. There are various classes in the lang package and it is not possible to discuss all the classes, but we will discuss some of the very important ones.

6.3.1 java.lang.Object Class

Object class is the parent of all the classes (predefined and user-defined) in Java. For all the classes that we have created so far or will be creating further, Object class is the parent by default and there is no need to explicitly inherit the Object class. The methods of Object class can be used by all the objects and arrays. The method toString() and equals() have been overridden by many of the predefined classes already. We have already seen what happens when we try to print an object. The toString() method is implicitly invoked when an object of any class is printed. If class does not provide a toString() method, the toString() of the superclass is invoked. If any of the class in the hierarchy does not provide implementation for the toString method, the Object class method is called. If toString() method of the Object class is called, classname@hexadeciaml representation of hash code of the object is printed. In case you wish to provide your own definitions for the objects which should be returned once you try to print your objects, then you must override the toString() method and return your own defined strings for the objects (Table 6.3).

Table 6.3 Methods of the java.lang.Object Class

Method	Description
Object clone()	A copy of the object is created and returned
boolean equals(object o)	Checks whether an object is equal to another or not. If both references refer to the same object, they are equal, else not.
void finalize()	Used by classes to dispose of their occupied resources

(Contd)

(Table 6.3 Contd)

Method	Description
`final Class getClass()`	Returns the class of the object
`int hashCode()`	Return the hash code of the object
`final void notify()`	Used by threads, to wake up a thread that is in waiting state
`final void notifyAll()`	Used by threads, to wake up all the threads in waiting state
`String toString()`	A string definition of the object is returned
`final void wait()`	Puts the current thread in waiting state
`final void wait(long time)`	Puts the current thread in waiting state for the specified time
`final void wait(long time, int n)`	Puts the current thread in waiting state for the specified amount of real time

Example 6.7 `toString()` Method of Object Class

```
L1    class Demo {
L2    public String toString()
      {
L3      return "My Demo Object created";
      }
L4      public static void main(String args[])
      {
L5      System.out.println(new Demo());
      }}
```

Output

```
C:\javabook\chap 6>java Demo
My Demo Object created
```

Explanation

L2 `toString()` method of the `Object` class has been overridden with the return type as `String`. This method is basically used for returning a `String` that identifies an object. This method is automatically invoked when we try to print an object. It can also be explicitly invoked with the help of an object.

L3 Returns a string `"My Demo Object created"`.

L5 Within the print statement, an object of class `Demo` is created and whenever an attempt to print an object occurs, the `toString()` method is called automatically.

Note You may now rewrite the complex number program to add the `toString()` method to it instead of `display` method of that class.

6.3.2 Java Wrapper Classes

Java primitive types are not objects, i.e., we cannot term Java as a pure object-oriented language. The language designers decided that the higher processing speed and memory efficiency of simple, non-class structures for such heavily used data types simply overweighed the elegance of a pure object-only language.

For each primitive type, there is a corresponding `wrapper` class designed. As the name suggests, the `wrapper` class is a wrapper around a primitive data type. These classes represent primitive data types, e.g., a `boolean` data type can be represented as a `Boolean` class instance.

As we have said earlier, an instance of a wrapper contains or *wraps* a primitive value of the corresponding type. Wrappers allow for situations where primitives cannot be used but their corresponding objects are required. For example, a very useful tool is the `ArrayList` class (see Chapter 10), which is a list that can grow or shrink, unlike an array. So if one wants to use an `ArrayList` to hold a list of numbers, the numbers must be wrapped in an integer instance. Mostly you will use wrapper class methods to convert a numeric value to a string or vice versa.

Table 6.4 Wrapper for Primitive Types

Primitive	Wrapper
boolean	java.lang.Boolean
byte	java.lang.Byte
char	java.lang.Character
double	java.lang.Double
float	java.lang.Float
int	java.lang.Integer
long	java.lang.Long
short	java.lang.Short
void	java.lang.Void

Table 6.4 lists the primitive data types and their corresponding wrapper classes.

You can easily make out that except for integer; the wrappers come with the same name as the corresponding primitive type except that the first letter is capitalized. Wrappers are normal classes that extend the `Object` as a superclass like all Java classes. The wrapper constructors create class objects from the primitive types. For example, for a double floating point number "d":

```
double a = 4.3; Double wrp = new Double(a);
```

Here a `Double` wrapper object is created by passing the double value in the `Double` constructor argument. In turn, each wrapper provides a method to return the primitive value.

```
double r = wrp.doubleValue();
```

Each wrapper has a similar method to access the primitive value: `intValue()` for integer, `booleanValue()` for boolean, and so on.

Features of Wrapper Classes Some of the sound features maintained by the wrapper classes are as under:

- All the wrapper classes except `Character` and `Float` have two constructors—one that takes the primitive value and another that takes the String representation of the value. `Character` has one constructor and `float` has three.
- Just like strings, wrapper objects are also immutable, i.e., once a value is assigned it cannot be changed.

Wrapper Classes: Constructors and Methods

The wrapper classes have a number of static methods for handling and manipulating primitive data types and objects. The methods along with their usage are listed below:

Constructors Converting primitive types to wrapper objects.

```
Integer ValueOfInt = new Integer(v)    // primitive integer to integer object
Float ValueOfFloat = new Float(x)      // primitive float to float object
Double ValueOfDouble = new Double(y)   // primitive double to double object
Long ValueOfLong = new Long(z)         // primitive long to long object
```

Here v, x, y, and z are `int`, `float`, `double`, and `long` values, respectively. There is one more way of converting a primitive value to a wrapper, the `valueOf()` method, which we will discuss later.

Ordinary Methods

Converting Wrapper Objects to Primitives All the numeric wrapper classes have six non-static methods, which can be used to convert a numeric wrapper to their respective primitive numeric type. These methods are `byteValue()`, `doubleValue()`, `floatValue()`, `intValue()`, `longValue()`, and `shortValue()`. Some of them are used as follows:

```
int v = ValueOfInt.intValue();          // Converting wrapper object to primitive integer
float x = ValueOfFloat.floatValue();     // Converting wrapper object to primitive float
long y = ValueOfLong.longValue();        // Converting wrapper object to primitive long
double z = ValueOfDouble.doubleValue();  // Converting wrapper object to primitive double
```

Converting Primitives to String Object The method `toString()` is used to convert primitive number data types to `String`, as shown below:

```
String xyz = Integer.toString()          // Converting primitive integer to String
String xyz = Float.toString()            // Converting primitive float to String
String xyz = Double.toString()           // Converting primitive double to String
String xyz = Long.toString()             // Converting primitive long to String
```

Parser Methods

Converting Back from String Object to Primitives The six parser methods are `parseInt`, `parseDouble`, `parseFloat`, `parseLong`, `parseByte`, and `parseShort`. They take a string as the argument and convert it to the corresponding primitive. They throw a `NumberFormatException` if the value of the String does not represent a proper number. Parser methods can be used as shown below:

```
int v = Integer.parseInt(xyz)
```
// For converting String containing int values like "10" to primitive integer

```
long y = Long.parseLong(xyz)
```
// For converting String containing long values like "123456" to primitive integer

Converting Primitive Value Represented by String Object to Wrapper Object All wrapper classes define a static method called `valueOf()`, which returns the wrapper object corresponding to the primitive value represented by the string argument as shown below. `valueOf()` is overloaded: one version accepts integer values and another accepts a String. String argument method generates a `NumberFormatException` in case the value in a String does not contain a number.

```
Double ValueOfDouble = Double.valueOf(xyz);
```
// For converting String containing `double` values to wrapper objects

```
Float ValueOfFloat = Float.valueOf(xyz);
```
// For converting String containing `float` values to wrapper objects

```
Integer ValueOfInteger = Integer.valueOf(xyz);
```
// For converting String containing `int` values to wrapper objects

```
Long ValueOfLong = Long.valueOf(xyz);
// For converting String containing long values to wrapper objects

Double ValueOfDouble = Double.valueOf(xyz);
// For converting primitive value double to wrapper objects

Float ValueOfFloat = Float.valueOf(xyz);
// For converting primitive values float to wrapper objects

Integer ValueOfInteger = Integer.valueOf(xyz);
// For converting int to wrapper objects

Long ValueOfLong = Long.valueOf(xyz);
// For converting long to wrapper objects
```

Binary and Hexadecimal Conversion The following method converts an integer to its binary/ hexadecimal equivalent and returns it as a String object.

```
System.out.println(Integer.toBinaryString(8));
System.out.println(Integer.toHexString(32));
```

The integer value 8 is converted to its binary equivalent using toBinaryString(), i.e., 1000, and 32 is converted to its hexadecimal equivalent, i.e. 20.

Autoboxing and Unboxing of Wrappers

Java 5.0 introduced a new feature for converting back and forth between a wrapper and its corresponding primitive. The conversion from primitives to wrappers is known as *boxing*, while the reverse is known as *unboxing*.

In the previous section, we have already seen boxing and unboxing being enforced by the use of a certain amount of clumsy code. Before J2SE 1.5, Java had primitive data types with wrappers around them, so programmers had to convert from one type to another programmatically.

```
public void manualConversion()
{
  int a = 12;
  Integer b = Integer.valueOf(a);
  int c = b.intValue();
}
```

If you are dealing with a lot of instances of wrappers and conversions, you will need to deal with a lot of method invocations. The to and fro conversion between primitives and wrappers is simplified by the use of *autoboxing* and *unboxing*. Behind the scenes, the compiler creates codes to implicitly create objects for you.

```
public void autoBoxing()
{
  int a = 12;
  Integer b = a; // wrapping
  int c = b;
}
```

Here, the wrapping is done automatically. There is no need to explicitly call the integer constructor. Autoboxing means a primitive value is automatically converted into the wrapper object. The reverse process, i.e., automatic conversion back from wrapper object to primitive value, is known as *unboxing*.

To sum up the complete essence of autoboxing and unboxing, we take the following piece of code:

```
Integer wrap_int = 5;          //primitive 5 autoboxed into an Integer object
int prim_int = wrap_int;       //automatic unboxing of Integer into int
```

There is one thing that you must remember: boxing and unboxing too many values can put undue pressure on the garbage collector.

6.3.3 String Class

Strings are basically immutable objects in Java. Immutable means once created, the strings cannot be changed. In fact there is a class named `String` in the `java.lang` package for creating strings. Whenever we create strings, it is this class that is instantiated. In Java, strings can be instantiated in two ways:

```
L1      String x = "String Literal Object";
L2      String y = new String ("String object is created here");
```

L1 Shows a string literal being assigned to a string reference: x.
L2 Shows the creation of a string object with the help of `new` keyword and the string literal is passed as an argument to the constructor. Does it mean that in L1, no object is created? Well actually an object of class `String` is created in both the lines, the only difference is that in L1, it is created implicitly and the memory is allocated from a memory pool which is created specifically for string literals. In L2, the object is created explicitly using the `new` keyword, so the memory required for the object is allocated out of the memory pool.

Before creating objects for string literals (L1), JVM checks the memory pool for the existence of string literals in the pool and if found, a reference to the existing String object is passed, else a new string instance in the pool is created and it is returned. In other words, string objects in the pool are shared and because it is a sharable thing, it is made immutable so that strings may not become inconsistent and corrupt. The concept of memory pool for string literals was created to save time (speed up working) and memory because strings are very often used by programmers. Let us take an example to clearly understand the concept.

Example 6.8 String Creation and Test for Equality

```
     class StringTest
     {
     public static void main(String args[]){
L1     String a = "Hello";
L2     String b = "Hello";
L3     String c = new String("Hello");
L4     String d = new String("Hello");
L5     String e = new String("Hello, how are you?");
L6     if(a == b)
```

```
L7        System.out.println("object is same and is being shared by a & b");
      else
L8       System.out.println("Different objects");
L9        if(a == c)
L10           System.out.println("object is same and is being shared by a & c");
else
L11           System.out.println("Different objects");
L12   if(c == d)
L13           System.out.println("same object");
      else
L14           System.out.println("Different objects");
L15           String f = e.intern();
L16   if(f == a)
L17           System.out.println("Interned object f refer to the already created object a
              in the pool");
      else
L18           System.out.println("Interned object does not refer to the already created
              objects, as literal was not present in the pool. It is a new object which has
              been created in the pool");
      }}
```

Output

```
C:\examples\chap 6>java StringTest
object is same and is being shared by a & b
Different objects
Different objects
Interned object does not refer to the already created objects, as literal was not present
in the pool. It is a new object which has been created in the pool.
```

Explanation

References

Objects

a

b

Hello

(a) Objects in the memory pool

c

Hello

d

Hello

e

Hello, how are you?

(b) Explicit memory allocation

f

Hello, how are you?

(c) Interned object in the memory pool

Fig. 6.3 String Objects

L1 An implicit string object has been created for a string literal `Hello` in the memory pool and the reference to the newly created object in the pool is return to a.

L2 As explained earlier, string literal is same as that of L1, i.e., `Hello`. JVM does not create a new object but passes the reference of the previously created object (L1) to **b**, which means **a** and **b** now point to the same object. See the following Fig. 6.3.

L3 Although the same string literal `Hello` is being used, but the object created is not a part of the memory pool, as the keyword `new` is used for object creation. Whenever `new` is used to create an object, it is allocated explicit memory and that memory is apart from the memory pool of strings.

L4 A new object is created which is different from a, b, and c as well.

L5 A new string object is created with a different literal this time "Hello, how are you?". This object is also different from all the objects that we have created till this point in our example.

L6 Equality operator (= =) is used in the if statement to check whether both references a and b are pointing to the same location or not. Equality operator is not used for matching the contents of the strings, i.e., literals. The two references that are being matched are a and b and as both point to the same location, L7 is executed. If a and b do not point to the same location, L8 would be executed.

L7 Print statement to show that references point to the same object.

L8 Print statement to show that references point to different objects.

L15 As already discussed, Strings created with the help of new are not allocated memory from the pool, but are interned. The method java.lang.String. intern() is used for this purpose. The intern() method creates a string object in the pool with the same String literal as that of the invoking String object and returns a reference of the newly created object in the pool. In this Line, f points to the newly created object in the pool because the string literal object Hello, how are you? does not exist in the pool. The intern method is called from the string object which needs to be interned, i.e., the previous String object will be garbage collected as it is no longer in use.

L16 Checks whether f and e point to the same object in the pool or not. They actually point to different locations and that is why L18 gets executed.

String Manipulation

Strings in Java are immutable (read only) in nature. That is, once the Strings are defined, they cannot be altered. Let us have a look at the following lines of code:

```
L1      String x = "Hello";          // ok
L2      String x = x +"World";       // ok, but how?
```

Java does not support operator overloading, but the '+' operator is already overloaded to accept different operands and it acts accordingly. If at least one of the operand is a string, it concatenates. The question that arises is that if strings are immutable, then how L2 gets executed? Actually L2 gets converted into the following statement:

```
String x = new StringBuffer().append(x).append("World").toString();
```

A new StringBuffer object is created which is used for the mutable set of characters. Mutable characters can change their values. The append (add at the end) method of the StringBuffer object is used to append the string Hello contained in x into the newly created StringBuffer object. Again the append method is used to append the string World to existing Hello in the new object. The method toString() converts StringBuffer object back to String and x points to this newly created String object. No references exist for the existing object Hello; it will be garbage collected.

String Methods

The String class provides a lot of methods. Table 6.5 lists a few common methods of the String class.

Table 6.5 Few Methods of `string` Class

Method Name with Signature	Method Details
`int length()`	To find the length of the string.
`boolean equals(String str)`	Used to check the equality of String objects. In contrast to == operator, the check is performed character by character. If all the characters in both the Strings are same, it returns true, else false.
`int compareTo(String s)`	Used to find whether the invoking String (Fig. 6.2) is Greater than, less than or equal to the String argument. It returns an integer value. If the integer value is (a) less than zero – invoking string is less than String argument (b) greater than zero – invoking String is greater than String argument (c) equal to zero – invoking String and String argument are equal
`boolean regionMatches (int startingIndx, String str, int strStartingIndx, int numChars)`	Matches a specific region of the String with a specific region of the invoking String. The argument details: **startingIndx**—specifies the region from the invoking String to be matched. **str**—is the second string to be matched. **strStartingIndx**—specifes the region from the string to be matched with the invoking String. **numChars**—specifies the number of characters to be matched in both strings from their respective starting indexes.
`int indexOf(char c)`	To find the index of a character in the invoking `String` object.
`int indexOf(String s)`	Overloaded method to find the starting index of a String argument in the invoking `String` object.
`int lastIndexOf(char c)`	To find the last occurrence of a character in the invoking String.
`int lastIndexOf(String s)`	Overloaded method to find the last occurrence of the String argument in the invoking `String` object.
`String substring(int s Index)`	To extract the `String` from the invoking `String` object starting with Index till the End of the `String`.
`String substring(int startingIndex, int endingIndex)`	Overloaded method to extract the String starting with starting Index till the ending Index from the invoking String object string.
`int charAt(int pos)`	To find the character at a particular position (pos).
`String toUpperCase()`	To change the case of an entire string to capital letters.
`String toLowerCase()`	To change the case of an entire string to small letters.
`boolean startsWith(String ss)`	To find whether an invoking string starts with a string argument.
`boolean endsWith(String es)`	To find whether an invoking string ends with a string argument.
`Static String valueOf(int is)`	Converts primitive type `int` value to string.
`Static String valueOf(float f)`	Overloaded static method to convert primitive type float value to string.
`Static String valueOf(long l)`	Overloaded static method to convert primitive type long value to string.
`Static String valueOf(double d)`	Overloaded static method to convert primitive type double value to string.

Example 6.9 String Class Methods

```java
class StringDemo {
public static void main(String args[]){
// String Declaration
String x = "This is a Demo String";
String y = "This is a Demo String 2";


// int declaration
int i = 20;
// finding the length of String
System.out.println("Length of String = " +x.length());
/* equals method of Object class has been overridden by the String class for per-
forming different function i.e., equating two string objects by matching strings
character by character */
System.out.println("x and y are equal = " +(x.equals(y)));
// comparison of Strings
if((x.compareTo(y)) < 0)
    System.out.println("x is less than y");
else if((x.compareTo(y)) > 0)
    System.out.println("x is greater than y");
else
    System.out.println("x is equal to y");
    // Region Matching within Strings
    System.out.println("x region matches with y:" + ((x.regionMatches(0,y,0,11))));
    // finding index of Characters
    System.out.println("index of \" i\" in String x is: " +x.indexOf("i"));
    // finding index of particular String
    System.out.println("index of \"is\" in String x is: " +x.indexOf("is"));

    // finding the last occurrence of a particular character
    System.out.println("Last index of \"i\" in String x is: " +x.lastIndexOf("i"));
    // finding the last occurrence of a particular character
    System.out.println("Last index of \"is\" in String x is: " +x.lastIndexOf("is"));
    // sub string
    System.out.println("Substring of String x from character 4 is: " +x.substring(4));
    System.out.println("Substring of String x from character 4 to 15 is:
    " +x.substring(4,15));

    // finding character at particular position
    System.out.println("character at position 6 is:" +x.charAt(6));

    // upper case and lower case
    System.out.println("UpperCase: " +x.toUpperCase());
    System.out.println("LowerCase: " +x.toLowerCase());

    // finding whether strings start and end with a particular string
    System.out.println("x starts with \"Th\":" +x.startsWith("Th"));
```

The lines above are labelled L1 (Length), L2 (equals), L3–L8 (compareTo), L9 (regionMatches), L10–L11 (indexOf), L12–L13 (lastIndexOf), L14–L15 (substring), L16 (charAt), L17–L18 (toUpperCase/toLowerCase), L19 (startsWith).

```
L20    System.out.println("x ends with \" Th\": " +x.endsWith("Th"));
L21    System.out.println("Converts int to String: " +String.valueOf(i));
       }}
```

Output

```
C:\javabook\ chap 6>java StringDemo
Length of String = 21
x and y are equal = false
x is less than y
x region matches with y : true
index of "i" in String x is: 2
index of "is" in String x is: 2
Last index of "i" in String x is: 18
Last index of "is" in String x is: 5
Substring of String x from character 4 is: is a Demo String
Substring of String x from character 4 to 15 is: is a Demo
character at position 6 is: s
UpperCase: THIS IS A DEMO STRING
LowerCase: this is a demo string
x starts with "Th" : true
x ends with "Th" : false
converts int to String: 20
```

Explanation

As discussed earlier, all instance methods of the String class are invoked with the help of String objects and class methods through the String class name. Table 6.4 describes these functions in brief. Figure 6.4 pictorially depicts how are the methods of String class invoked.

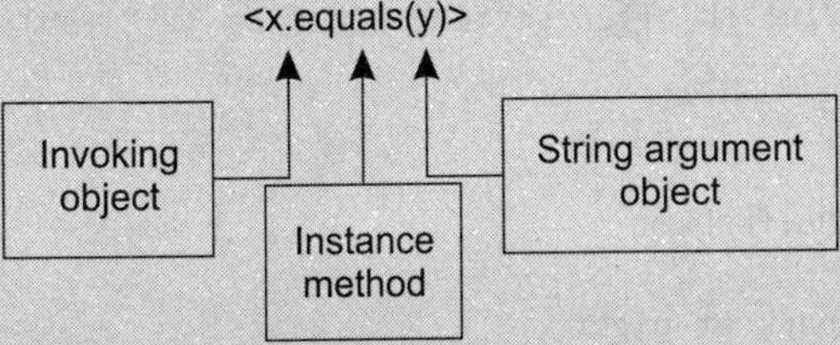

Fig. 6.4 Invoking the Methods of String Class

6.3.4 StringBuffer Class

The StringBuffer class is used for representing changing strings. As already discussed, StringBuffer offers more performance enhancement whenever we change strings, because it is this class that is used behind the curtain. So it is advisable to use StringBuffer rather than String in such a situation. If String class is used, it would result in wastage of memory and time, as temporary string objects would be needed while changing strings. StringBuffer contains a sequence of characters which can be altered through the methods of this class. Just like any other buffer, StringBuffer also has a capacity and if the capacity is exceeded, then it is automatically made larger. The initial capacity of StringBuffer can be known by using a method capacity(). A few common methods of the StringBuffer class are shown in Table 6.6.

Table 6.6 Methods of `StringBuffer` Class

Method name with signature	Method details
`int capacity()`	Returns the current capacity of the storage available for characters in the buffer. When the capacity is approached, the capacity is automatically increased.
`StringBuffer append(String str)`	Appends String argument to the buffer
`StringBuffer replace (int sindx,int eIndx,String str)`	The characters from start to end are removed and the string is inserted at that position
`StringBuffer reverse()`	Reverses the buffer character by character
`Char charAt(int index)`	Returns the character at the specified index
`Void setCharAt(int indx,char c)`	Sets the specified character at the specified index

Example 6.9 shows how the `StringBuffer` class is used in a program.

Example 6.10 `StringBuffer` **Object**

```
      class StringBufferDemo {
      public static void main(String args[]){
L1      StringBuffer sb = new StringBuffer();
L2      System.out.println("Initial Capacity : " +sb.capacity());
L3      System.out.println("String appended : " +sb.append ("Dogs bark at night"));
L4      System.out.println("String replaced: " +sb.replace  (10,12,"during"));
L5      System.out.println("String reversed : " +sb.reverse());
L6      System.out.println("Current Capacity : " +sb.capacity());
L7      System.out.println("character at position 3 is: " + sb.charAt(3));
L8      sb.setCharAt(3,'a');
L9      System.out.println("sb after setting \"a\" at 3: " +sb);
      }}
```

Output

```
C:\javabook>java StringBufferDemo
Initial Capacity : 16
String appended : Dogs bark at night
String replaced : Dogs bark during night
String reversed : thgin gnirud krab sgoD
Current Capacity : 34
character at position 3 is: i
sb after setting "a" at 3: thgan gnirud krab sgoD
```

Explanation

The description of the methods used in the program is available in Table 6.6.

6.3.5 StringBuilder Class

Java 5 introduced a substitute of `StringBuffer`: the `StringBuilder` class. This class is faster than `StringBuffer`, as it is not synchronized. The methods of both the classes are same with the exception that the methods (`append()`, `insert()`, `delete()`, `deleteCharAt()`, `replace()`, and reverse()) return `StringBuilder` objects rather than `StringBuffer` objects. The line below shows the creation of a `StringBuilder` object.

```
StringBuilder s=new StringBuilder();
/* construct a StringBuilder object with an initial capacity of 16 characters.
Similar to that of StringBuffer.*/
```

6.3.6 Splitting Strings

`StringTokenizer` is a utility class provided by the `java.util` package. Now a legacy code, this class used to be of utmost importance when we want to divide the entire string into parts (tokens) on the basis of delimiters. The delimiters can be any of the `whitespace`, `tab space`, `semicolon`, `comma`, etc. J2SE 1.4 added `split()` method to the `string` class for simplifying the task of splitting a string and also added `Pattern` and `Matcher` classes in the `java.util.regex` package. We will discuss the `split()` method and `Pattern` in our next example and also the `StringTokenizer` class for backward compatibility.

Example 6.11 Splitting Strings

```
L1    import java.util.*;
L2    import java.util.regex.*;
L3    class StringTokenizerDemo {
L4    public static void main(String args[]) {
L5    int i = 1;
L6    String str = "Never look down on anybody unless you're helping him up";
      System.out.println("Splitting String Using StringTokenizer class");
L7    StringTokenizer tr = new StringTokenizer(str, " ");
L8    while(tr.hasMoreTokens()) {
L9          System.out.print(" Token " +i+ " : ");
L10         System.out.println(tr.nextToken());
L11         ++i;
      }
      // Another way of splitting String

L12   System.out.println("Splitting String Using split() method");
L13   String[] tk = str.split(" ");
L14   for(String tokens: tk)
L15   System.out.println(tokens);
      // Using Pattern class
      System.out.println(" Splitting String Using Pattern class");
L16   Pattern p = Pattern.compile(" ");
L17   tk= p.split(str,3);
L18   for(String tokens: tk)
L19   System.out.println(tokens);
      }}
```

Output

```
C:\javabook>java StringTokenizerDemo
Splitting String Using StringTokenizer class
Token 1 :Never
Token 2 :look
Token 3 :down
```

```
Token 4 :on
Token 5 :anybody
Token 6 :unless
Token 7 :you're
Token 8 :helping
Token 9 :him
Token 10 :up
Splitting String Using split() method
Never
look
down
on
anybody
unless
you're
helping
him
up
Splitting String Using Pattern class
Never
look
down on anybody unless you're helping him up
```

Explanation

L1   Importing the package `java.util.*` is mandatory because `StringTokenizer` is a part of this package.

L2   Importing the subpackage `java.util.regex.*` is mandatory because the class `Pattern` is a part of this subpackage `regex`. An important point to note here is that importing any package does not mean that the sub-packages are also implicitly imported. The sub-packages need to be imported explicitly.

L5   Integer `i` declared and initialized to 1.

L6   `String` to be split has been declared, `str`.

L7   An object of `StringTokenizer` class is created. The constructor accepts two arguments: (a) `str` and (b) the delimiter, i.e., whitespace in our example. The string `str` is cut into tokens wherever the specified delimiter, i.e., the white space is encountered and the tokens are stored in the `StringTokenizer` object `tr`. This `tr` object is iterated for retrieving the tokens one by one.

L8   The condition in the `while` loop checks whether the `StringTokenizer` object has more tokens or not with the help of `hasMoreTokens()`. which returns a boolean value to indicate whether `tr` has more tokens or not.

L9   Statement to print "Token" followed by the value of i, i.e., Token 1 (for the first iteration, see the output).

L10   This statement prints the first Token. In the first iteration, the method `nextToken()` points to the first token which is printed on the screen and the cursor moves to the new line afterwards.

L11   The value of `i` is incremented. In the next iteration, the value of `i` will be 2, and so on.

L12–15   Show another way of splitting the string using the `split()`method.

L13   `split()` method of the String class is used for splitting the string, `str`. It accepts one arguments, i.e., `regex`.

The regular expression, `regex`, can be a character, a group of characters, or a word which is to be searched in a string. Here we want to split the string on the basis of `regex` which is a whitespace. So wherever a whitespace is encountered in the `str`, it is split and stored in the String array `tk` as the next array item.

L14–15   In each iteration, the String *tokens* are assigned successively a value from 'tk' and printed.

L16–19   Show another way of splitting the string using the `Pattern` class.

L16   Shows how the `Pattern` class of the `regex` sub-package is used for splitting a string. The `Pattern` class provides a static method named `compile()` to compile the regular expression to a pattern. The

regular expression is passed as an argument to the method, i.e., a whitespace in our example. This pattern will be searched in the string.
L17 Another method of the `Pattern` class: `split()` is used to split the string. This method takes two arguments:

(a) `str`– String to be split.
(b) `limit`– Sets the number of times the pattern will be searched in the `str`. If the limit is n, the pattern will be searched n–1 times. In our example, the limit is 3, so the pattern, i.e., whitespaces will be searched twice and the string will be stored in an array.

6.4 Enum TYPE

An enumerated type (`enum` type) is a kind of class definition, wherein we define the type along with the possible set of `enum` values which are listed in the curly braces, separated by commas. All `enum` types are the subclasses of the `java.lang.Enum` class. Each value in an `enum` is an identifier. For example, the following statement declares a type, named `Games`, with the values `CRICKET`, `FOOTBALL`, `TENNIS`, and `BASKETBALL`. Remember, here we are talking about an ordered list. By convention, all names must be in upper case. An enumeration is like a class, so the naming convention of classes also applies to enumerations. Moreover, values are constants, so they should be named as regular constants.

```
enum Games { CRICKET, FOOTBALL, TENNIS, BASKETBALL };
```

Once a type is defined, you can declare a variable of that type:

```
Games G;
```

The variable `G` can hold one of the values defined in the enumerated type `Games` or null, but nothing else. An attempt to assign a value other than the enumerated values mentioned in the enumeration or null will result in a compilation error. The enumerated values can be accessed using the following syntax:

```
enumeratedTypeName.valueName
```

For example, the following statement assigns the enumerated value `TENNIS` to the variable `G`:

```
G = Games.TENNIS;
```

An enumerated type is treated as a special class. An enumerated type variable is similar to a reference variable. Like all other classes in Java, an enumerated type is a grandchild of the `Object` class. In addition to this, it inherits `Comparable` interfaces. It is an implicit `final` subclass of the `Enum` class in the `java.lang` package. All the methods of the `Object` class and the `compareTo()` method of the `Comparable` interface can be used by an enumeration. Additionally, you can use the following methods on an enumerated object:

- `public String name();`

It returns the name of the value for the object.

- `public int ordinal();`

It returns the ordinal value associated with the enumerated value. The first value has an ordinal value of 0, the second has an ordinal value of 1, and so on. Example 6.11 demonstrates the use of enumerated types. Example 6.12 shows an alternative way of using enumerated types.

Example 6.12 Use of Enumerated Type

```
L1    public class EnumDemo {
L2    static enum Games {CRICKET, FOOTBALL, CHESS, BASKETBALL, TENNIS, BADMINTON};
L3    public static void main (String[] args) {
L4      Games G1 = Games.CHESS;
L5      Games G2 = Games.TENNIS;
L6      System.out.println("First game is " +G1.name());
L7      System.out.println("Second game is " +G2.name());
L8      System.out.println("First game's ordinal is " +G1.ordinal());
L9      System.out.println("Second game's ordinal is " +G2.ordinal());
L10     System.out.println("G1.equals(G2) returns " +G1.equals(G2));
L11     System.out.println("G1.toString() returns " +G1.toString());
L12     System.out.println("G1.compareTo(G2) returns " +G1.compareTo(G2));
}}
```

Output

```
First game is CHESS
Second game is TENNIS
First game's ordinal is 2
second game's ordinal is 4
G1.equals(G2) returns false
G1.toString() returns Chess
G1.compareTo(G2) returns -2
```

Explanation

L2 An enumerated type is defined, having the ordered list of games.

L4 and 5 Variables G1 and G2 are declared as the Games type and assigned enumerated values.

L8 Since G1's value is Chess, its ordinal value is 2.

L9 Since G2's value is Tennis, its ordinal value is 4.

L10–12 An enumerated type is a subclass of the Object class and the Comparable interface, so you can invoke the methods equals, toString, and compareTo from an enumerated object reference variable. G1.equals(G2) returns true if G1 and G2 have the same ordinal value. G1.compareTo(G2) returns the difference between G1's ordinal value to G2's. The enum type has a toString() method defined that returns the string values. So it is easy to print these values without any special conversion effort. For example, System.out.println(G1) will print CHESS.

Example 6.13 Alternative Way of Using Enumerated Type

```
L1    public class EnumExample{
L2    public static void main(String[] args){
L3      Games G1 = Games.Chess;
L4      Games G2 = Games.Tennis;
L5      System.out.println("G1's name is " + G1.name());
L6      System.out.println("G2's name is " + G2.name());
L7      System.out.println("G1's ordinal is " + G1.ordinal());
L8      System.out.println("G2's ordinal is " + G2.ordinal());
L9      System.out.println(" G1.equals(G2) returns " +G1.equals(G2));
L10     System.out.println (" G1.toString() returns " +G1.toString());
L11     System.out.println (" G1.compareTo(G2) returns " +G1.compareTo(G2));
L12   }}
L13   enum Games {Cricket, Football, Chess, Basketball, Tennis, Badminton};
```

Output

```
C:\javabook\PROGRA~1>java EnumExample
G1's name is Chess
G2's name is Tennis
G1's ordinal is 2
G2"s ordinal is 4
G1.equals(G2) returns false
G1.toString() returns Chess
G1.compareTo(G2) returns -2
```

An enumerated type defined inside a class behaves as an inner class, as shown in the L2 of Example 6.11, or standalone as shown in the L13 of Example 6.12. When an enumerated type is declared inside a class, it is a member of the class and cannot be declared inside a method. The enumerated type is always `static`. So, the `static` keyword in L2 of Example 6.11 may be omitted. After Example 6.11 is compiled, a class named `EnumDemo$Games.class` is created. After Example 6.12 is compiled, a class named `Games.class` is created.

6.4.1 Using Conditional Statements with an Enumerated Variable

An enumerated type holds a set of values. If you need to perform a specific action depending on the value, then you can use `if` or `switch-case` for the same. For example, if the value is `Games.CRICKET`, book ticket; if the value is `Games.FOOTBALL`, bunk the class; and so on. You can use an `if` statement or a `switch` statement to test the value in the variable, as shown below.

If statement

```
if (G1.equals(Games.CRICKET)) {
// action to be performed}
} else if (G1.equals(Games.FOOTBALL)) {
// action to be performed}
else ....
```

Switch statement

```
switch (Games){
case CRICKET:          // case CRICKET and not Games.CRICKET
// action to be performed;

case FOOTBALL:
// action to be performed;
...
}
```

6.4.2 Using for Loop for Accessing Values

Each enumerated type has a static method `values()` associated with them that returns all enumerated values for the type in an array. For example,

```
Games[] G = Games.values();
```

You can use a for loop to process all the values in the array.

```
for (int i = 0; i < G.length; i++)
    System.out.println(G[i]);
```

6.4.3 Attributes and Methods within Enumeration

You can also define an enumerated type with attributes and methods similar to a class, as shown in Example 6.13(a). Example 6.14(b) shows a test program to use the enumerated type created in Example 6.14(a).

Example 6.14 (a) Defining an Enumerated Type with Attributes and Methods

```
L1    public enum Desc {
L2    CRICKET ("Sachin Tendulkar"), CHESS("Vishwanathan Anand"), TENNIS ("Sania Mirza");
L3    private String description;
      // Constructor
L4    private Desc(String description){
L5       this.description = description;
L6    }
L7    public String getDesc(){
L8       System.out.print("Indian Delight: ");
L9       return description;
L10   }}
```

Explanation

L1 An enumeration named `Desc` is declared.
L2 The enumerated values are listed with their description (mentioned in double quotes). This declaration must be the first statement in the class, otherwise a compile-time errors results.
L3 A datafield named `description` is declared to denote an enumerated description.

L4–6 The constructor `Desc` is declared. This constructor is invoked whenever an enumerated value is accessed. The value (`description`) is passed to the constructor, which is then assigned to `description`.
L7–9 `getDesc()` has been declared with the return type `String` to return the description.

Example 6.14 (b) Enumerated Type with Attributes and Methods

```
L1    public class UseDesc{
L2    public static void main(String[] args)
      {
L3       Desc player = Desc.TENNIS;
L4       System.out.println(player.getDesc());
L5    }
L6    }
```

Output

```
C:\javabook\PROGRA~1>java UseDesc
Indian Delight: Sania Mirza
```

Explanation

L3 An enumerated value `Desc.TENNIS` is assigned to the variable `player` (L3). Accessing `Desc.TENNIS` causes the JVM to invoke the constructor with the argument `SaniaMirza`.

L4 The methods in enumerated type are invoked in the same way as the methods in a class. `player.getDesc()` returns the description for the enumerated value.

6.5 PRACTICAL PROBLEM: BANKING EXAMPLE

We will be creating a banking example to revise the concepts learned so far. Banks contain customers who hold accounts within the bank. An account can be of two types—Saving Account or Current Account. Customers can perform deposit or withdrawal operation on their respective accounts. Banks provide interest to the saving account holders which it can change any time. Banks provide a upper limit to the current account holders. In case the balance in their account is less than what needs to be withdrawn, banks provide the shortfall amount to the customers upto the credit limit but on a returnable basis. So whenever the current account holder deposits the amount in the bank, the bank first reclaims its money and then its left over amount is added to the balance. (We have assumed that banks are not charging any interest on the amount provided by the bank to the current account holder. Normally banks would charge an interest on that. You can take that part as an exercise.)

A customer will have a name, an id, and will be holding an account (either saving or current). Every account will have an id and balance. Saving accounts will have an interest rate apart from id and balance. Current accounts will have an overdraft limit apart from id and balance.

So we have created five classes: `Customer` class, `Account` class with its two subclasses (`SavingAccount` and `CurrentAccount`) and a `Bank` class to hold `Customers`. All these classes have been packaged into an package named `banking`. Let us see all these classes. Let us first see the `Account` class.

Example 6.15 (a) `Account.java`

```java
/*package declaration. The class belongs to the banking package*/
package banking;
/*abstract class declared with default previliges. it can only be accessed from
within the package. This class has two abstract methods:
debit and credit. The subclasses will have to override the abstract methods.*/
abstract class Account
{
    /*balance within the account*/
    float balance;

    /*Account No*/
    private String accountNo;

    /*constructor to initialize balance and account no*/
    Account(float b, String acc)
    {
        balance = b;
        accountNo = acc;
    }
    /*getter method to access balance*/
    float getBalance()
    {
        return balance;
```

```
        }

        /*setter method to modify balance*/
        void setBalance(float b)
        {
            balance = b;
        }

        /*The methods are declared abstract so that the subclasses can code them according
        to their respective needs keeping their names in tact*/

        abstract void debit(float amount);
        abstract void credit(float amount);

        /*getter method to access account no*/
        String getAccountNo()
        {
            return accountNo;
        }

        /*setter method to modify balance*/
        void setAccountNo(String acc)
        {
            accountNo = acc;
        }
        /* Print Account No and balance details*/
        void display()
        {
            System.out.println("Account Number: "+accountNo);
            System.out.println("Account balance: "+balance);
        }
}
```

Now let us create its subclasses—SavingAccount and CurrentAccount.


```
/*This class is also part of the same package and hence the package
declaration */

package banking;

/*SavingAccount is a type of Account. So this class inherits the Account class*/

class SavingAccount extends Account
{
/* Interest rate is common for all Saving Accounts. So this field is
declared as static.*/
static float interest = 4;

/* Constructor declared to initailize both the account number and
balance by calling the Account (super class) constructor using super
keyword */

SavingAccount(float b, String acno)
```

```
        {
                super(b,acno);
        }
/*explicit default constructor*/
        SavingAccount()
        {
                super(0,"");
        }
```

/* Static method is created to change the interest rate. If the bank
wishes to change the interest rate, it can do so without creating an
instance of SavingAccount class*/

```
        static void setInterest(float i)
        {
                interest = i;
        }
```

/*display method to print account no, balance and interest rate. The super class
display method already prints the account no and balance so it is invoked using the
super keyword.*/

```
        public void display()
        {
                super.display();
                System.out.println("Interest rate: "+interest);
        }
```

/*Account is credit with amount. The balance increases by the amount
passed in this method*/

```
        public void credit(float amount)
        {
                System.out.println("Amount to be credited: "+amount);
                System.out.println("Old balance: "+balance);
                balance = balance+amount;
                System.out.println("New balance: "+balance);
        }
```

/*Account is debited with amount.*/
```
        public void debit(float amount)
        {
                System.out.println("Amount to be debited: "+amount);
                System.out.println("Old balance: "+balance);
```

/*if the amount to be withdrawn is less than the balance, it is de-
creased by the amount otherwise the request is denied*/

```
        if(amount < balance)
        {
                balance = balance-amount;
                System.out.println("New balance: "+balance);
        }
        else
                System.out.println("Request Denied");
        }
```

```java
/*SavingAccount earn interest on the balance.This method when invoked
will calculate the interest on the balance and add it to the balance*/

        public void creditInterest()
        {
                float temp = balance*interest/100;
                System.out.println("Interest paid: "+temp);
                balance = balance+temp;
                System.out.println("New Balance: "+balance);
        }

/*toString method has been overridden to return a String representa-
tion of the SavingAccount object */

        public String toString()
        {
return "Saving Account No: "+getAccountNo()+ " Balance : "+balance;
        }
}
```

Example 6.15 (c) `CurrentAccount.java`

```java
/*This class is also part of the same package and hence the package declaration states
the package as banking */

package banking;
class CurrentAccount extends Account
        {
        /* borrowed amount, cannot be greater than the limit */
        float overdraftborrowed;
        /* Maximum credit limit */
        float overdraftlimit;
        /*Constructor to initialize the current account. every current account holder
        will have a different overdraft limit. so while creating current account object
        we have to pass the limit as well*/
        CurrentAccount(float b,String acno, float od)
        {
                super(b,acno);
                overdraftlimit = od;
        }
        /*limits may change over time so an option is provided to change the limit*/
        void setOverdraft(float o)
        {
                overdraftlimit = o;
        }
        /*credit method is used to deposit the amount in the current account. if the
        customer has borrowed some amount from the bank, then first the borrowed
        amount is returned to the bank and the rest  is added to the balance. */
        public void credit(float amount)
        {
                System.out.println("Amount to be credited: "+amount);
                System.out.println("Old Balance: "+balance);
                System.out.println("Overdraft Borrowed: " + overdraftborrowed);
        /*checks whether amount to be deposited is greater than overdraftborrowed,
        deducts it by overdraftborrowed thus making the overdraftbor-
```

```java
rowed nil and add the rest amount in balance. otherwise the overdraft-
borrowed is reduced by the amount making no changes to the balance */
        if(amount > overdraftborrowed)
        {
                amount = amount - overdraftborrowed;
                overdraftborrowed = 0;
                balance = balance + amount;
        }
        else if(amount<overdraftborrowed)
        {
                overdraftborrowed = overdraftborrowed-amount;
        }
        System.out.println("New Overdraft Borrowed: " + overdraftborrowed);
        System.out.println("New Balance: "+balance);
}
/* deducts the amount from the balance. If amount to be deducted is less than
balance; the amount is deducted from balance. But, if amount is greater than
balance but less than the limit, then the shortfall will be fulfilled by the
bank by setting the overdraftborrowed for the customer. Hence overdraftbor-
rowed is set to shortfall (amount-balance) and balance will be nil. If amount
is greater than balance as well as the ODlimit then the
request is denied */
public void debit(float amount)
{
        System.out.println("Amount to be debited: "+amount);
        System.out.println("Old Balance: "+balance);
        if(amount <= balance)
                balance = balance - amount;
        else if((amount > balance) &&  (amount < (balance + overdraftlimit)))
        {
                overdraftborrowed = amount - balance;
                balance = 0;
                System.out.println("Overdraft Borrowed: " + overdraftborrowed);

        }
        else
                System.out.println("Request Denied");
                System.out.println("New Balance: "+balance);
                System.out.println("Overdraft Borrowed: "+overdraftborrowed);
}
public void display()
{
        super.display();
        System.out.println("Overdraft limit: "+overdraftlimit);

}
public String toString()
{
        return "Current Account No: "+getAccountNo()+ " Balance :"+balance+"
        Overdraft limit: "+overdraftlimit;
}
}
```

Now let us create a `Customer` class that will own any one of these accounts.

Example 6.15 (d) `Customer.java`

```java
package banking;
class Customer
{
        // customer name
        String custName;

        // customer id
        String custId;
```

/* every customer of the bank is assigned an Account which is its private attribute. So an instance variable of type Account is defined here. A customer can either have a saving account or a current account. That is why we have added an attribute of type Account in this class and not SavingAccount or CurrentAccount. Account reference variable can refer to objects of both its subclasses: SavingAccount and CurrentAccount. So whatever account the customer wishes to open, its object can be saved into this instance variable of type Account */

```java
        private Account account;

        /*constructor to initialize the customer attributes*/
        Customer(String custName,String custId,        Account account)
        {
                this.custName = custName;
                this.custId = custId;
                this.account = account;
        }
```

/* deposit method declared to add amount to the balance. Here we have to call the appropriate method according to the type of the account. So first e check what is the type of account held by the customer using the instanceof keyword and based on that we call the credit method of the respective classes.*/

```java
        public void deposit(float amt)
        {
                if(account instanceof SavingAccount)
```

/* credit method belongs to the SavingAccount class or the CurrentAccount class and not the Account class. So if the method is invoked as account.credit(amt), the compiler will not compile the program. The reason is that the compiler looks for credit method in the Account class (as the type of account reference variable is Account) which is not there. The account variable is casted into SavingAccount or CurrentAccount and then the credit method is invoked. The cast is possible as the classes are subclasses of the Account class. The account refernce variable will actually hold objects of either SavingAccount or CurrentAccount class*/

```java
                        ((SavingAccount)account).credit(amt);

                else if(account instanceof CurrentAccount)

                        ((CurrentAccount)account).credit(amt);
        }
```

/*Only Saving Account to be credited with interest on balances*/

```java
        void depositInterest()
```

```java
    {
        System.out.println("Depositing Interest in : "+custId);

        if(account instanceof SavingAccount)
                ((SavingAccount)account).creditInterest();
    }
```

/* withdrawal method declared to deduct amount from the balance. Here we have to
call the appropriate method according to the type of the account. So first we check
what is the type of account held by the customer using the instanceof keyword and
based on that we call the debit method of the respective classes.*/

```java
    public void withdrawl(float amt)
    {
    if(account instanceof SavingAccount)
            ((SavingAccount)account).debit(amt);
    else if(account instanceof CurrentAccount)
            ((CurrentAccount)account).debit(amt);
    }
    /*display the customer details along with the account held by the customer*/

    public void display()
    {
            System.out.println("Customer Name: "+custName);
            System.out.println("Customer Id: "+custId);
            account.display();
            System.out.println(account);
    }
}
```

Let us now create a `Bank` class to test all the classes that we have created. First of all we will create a `Bank` class in which we will be creating `Customers`. These customers will be holding accounts on which we will be performing deposit, withdrawal, and display operations.

Example 6.15 (e) `Bank.java`

```java
/*This class is also part of banking package */

package banking;

/*class declared with default privileges so it can only be used within
the package*/
public class Bank
{
  /* customers are part of the bank and their details should not accessible to oth-
  ers. So Customer array is declared to be private. We have considered only three
  customers. Each element of the Customer array will hold an object of type Custom-
  er. */

  private Customer c[]=new Customer[3];

  /* constructor for the Bank class is declared */
  public Bank()
```

```java
{
/* Customer objects created and put in the individual array elements.
Constructor of the Customer class accepts three arguments: Customer name, Customer
id and an object of type Account.*/

    c[0]=new Customer("Rahul","C001",new SavingAccount(12000,"A001"));
    c[1]=new Customer("Ram","C002",new SavingAccount(12000,"A002"));
    c[2]=new Customer("Shyam","C003",new CurrentAccount (12000, "A003", 10000));
    }

/* Banks can change its interest rate for all Saving Account holders by invoking
this method*/

void changeInterestRate(float i)
{
/*SavingAccout class contains the attribute for interest rate. A setter method is
created for setting the interest rate. This interest rate is applicable for all sav-
ing bank account holders. The static method 'setInterest" of the SavingAccount class
is used to change the interest rate.*/

SavingAccount.setInterest(i);
    }

    /*main method declaration*/
    public static void main(String[] args)
    {
    /*An object of Bank class is created which invokes the constructor of the Bank
    class. */
        Bank b = new Bank();

        /*Banks change its interest rate*/
        b.changeInterestRate(6);

        /*Invokes its demo method- which deposits and makes withdrawals from the cus-
        tomer accounts*/
        b.demo();

        /* bank deposits interest into its customer accounts*/
        b.c[0].depositInterest();

        /* bank deposits interest into another customer accounts*/
        b.c[1].depositInterest();
    }

    public void demo()
    {
        /*display method of the Customer object is called*/
        c[0].display();

        /*customer deposits 1000 Rupees into his account*/
        c[0].deposit(1000);

        /*customer withdraws 500 Rupees into his account*/
        c[0].withdrawl(15000);

        /*display method of the another Customer object is called*/
```

```
        c[1].display();

        /*customer deposits 2000 Rupees into his account*/
        c[1].deposit(2000);

        /*customer withdraws 8000 Rupees into his account*/
        c[1].withdrawl(8000);

        /*display method of the Customer object is called*/
        c[2].display();

        /*Customer deposits 1000 rupees into his account*/
        c[2].deposit(1000);

        /*Customer withdraws 15000 rupees into his account*/
        c[2].withdrawl(5000);

        /*Customer again deposits 3000 rupees into his account*/
        c[2].deposit(3000);
    }
}
```

Compilation

During compilation of these programs, make sure the classpath is set or you can use the
-cp option of javac as well,for e.g. if the banking package is part of d:\javabook\
chap 6, then you can invoke the compilation as

```
        javac -cp d:\javabook\chap 6 savingAccount.java
```

Output

To run the example you have to set the `classpath` with the path up to the directory that contains
the banking package. For example, if banking package (directory) is within "chap 6" then the
command to edit the `classpath` would be

```
        set classpath = %classpath%;d:\javabook\chap 6;
```

```
D:\javabook\chap 6>java banking.Bank
Customer Name: Rahul
Customer Id: C001
Account Number: A001
Account balance: 12000.0
Interest rate: 6.0
Saving Account No: A001 Balance : 12000.0
Amount to be credited: 1000.0
Old balance: 12000.0
New balance: 13000.0
Amount to be debited: 15000.0
Old balance: 13000.0
Request Denied
Customer Name: Ram
Customer Id: C002
Account Number: A002
Account balance: 12000.0
Interest rate: 6.0
Saving Account No: A002 Balance : 12000.0
```

```
Amount to be credited: 2000.0
Old balance: 12000.0
New balance: 14000.0
Amount to be debited: 8000.0
Old balance: 14000.0
New balance: 6000.0
Customer Name: Shyam
Customer Id: C003
Account Number: A003
Account balance: 12000.0
Overdraft limit: 10000.0
Current Account No: A003 Balance :12000.0 Overdraft limit: 10000.0
Amount to be credited: 1000.0
Old Balance: 12000.0
Overdraft Borrowed: 0.0
New Overdraft Borrowed: 0.0
New Balance: 13000.0
Amount to be debited: 5000.0
Old Balance: 13000.0
New Balance: 8000.0
Overdraft Borrowed: 0.0
Amount to be credited: 3000.0
Old Balance: 8000.0
Overdraft Borrowed: 0.0
New Overdraft Borrowed: 0.0
New Balance: 11000.0
Depositing Interest in : C001
Interest paid: 780.0
New Balance: 13780.0
Depositing Interest in : C002
Interest paid: 360.0
New Balance: 6360.0
```

SUMMARY

Java does not support multiple inheritance among classes. The only exception to this is interfaces. Multiple inheritance can be done using interfaces. A class can inherit any number of interfaces. The only fact mandatory for a class to follow is that it has to override and provide implementation for all the methods of all the interfaces it inherits. Such classes can be grouped together to form a package. Package is a collection of Java files similar to a directory. As subdirectories exist within a directory, subpackages can exist within a package.

There are a number of predefined packages in Java—one of them is discussed in this chapter: java.lang package. This is a fundamental package. For all the primitive data types, wrapper classes have been defined in this package. These wrappers encapsulate the functionality of the primitive data types. A few other classes like Object, String, StringBuffer, and StringBuilder class have been discussed, as these classes are frequently used in programming. All classes, whether predefined or user-defined, inherit ultimately from the Object class implicitly. So String, StringBuffer, and StringBuilder also have objects as their parents.

Strings in Java are immutable, i.e., one cannot change a string once it is defined. StringBuffer and StringBuilder are both used for mutable set of characters. StringBuilder (added in Java 5) is much more efficient in terms of performance as compared to StringBuffer because the former is not synchronized and the latter class is. At the end of the chapter, we have discussed enumerations. Enum type is a kind of class and is basically useful when we know the type along with the possible set of values in that type.

EXERCISES

Objective Questions

1. What will happen if the following line is present in a program?

   ```
   interface x extends interface y {}
   ```

   (a) run time error
   (b) compile time error
   (c) will compile but not execute
   (d) will compile and execute

2. What will happen when you try to compile the following code?

   ```
   interface x {void show();}
   class y implements x{
   void show(){
      System.out.println("in show");
      }
   }
   ```

   (a) runtime error
   (b) compile time error
   (c) will compile but not execute
   (d) will compile and execute

3. What will be the output if the following declarations are there in a given sequence? If it is not correct, what is the correct sequence?

   ```
   class x{}
   package y;
   import a.b;
   ```

   (a) runtime error
   (b) compile time error
   (c) will compile but not execute
   (d) will compile and execute

4. Which keyword is used for accessing the features of a package?
   (a) export (b) import
   (c) package (d) extends

5. What will happen when you try to compile the following code?

   ```
   protected class example{
   public static void main(String
   args[]) {
      String s = "abc";
      s = s + "def";
      System.out.println(s);
   ```

   ```
      }
   }
   ```

   (a) will compile and print abcdef
   (b) will compile but will not print anything
   (c) will not compile as top level class is protected
   (d) will compile and print def

6. Name the modifier of a method that makes the method available to all classes in the same package and to all the subclasses of this class.
   (a) private (b) default
   (c) protected (d) public

7. All enumerations declared inside a class are by default
   (a) static (b) non static
   (c) default (d) protected

8. What will happen when you try to compile the following code?

   ```
   interface test{int CHECK;}
   ```

   (a) runtime error
   (b) compile time error
   (c) will compile but not execute
   (d) will compile and execute

9. What will happen when you try to compile the following code?

   ```
   interface test {static void show();}
   ```

   (a) runtime error
   (b) compile time error
   (c) will compile but not execute
   (d) will compile and execute

10. What will happen when you try to compile and execute the following code?

    ```
    class Test{
    public static void main(String args[]){
      char c;
      String t1 = " The World ";
      String t2 = new String(" The World ");
      if(t1.equals(t2))
        System.out.println("String
        Concatenated : " + t1.concat
        ("is beautiful"));
      else
        System.out.println("String
    ```

```
        Concatenated:" +t1.concat("is not
        beautiful"));
}}
```

(a) run time error
(b) compile time error
(c) will compile but not execute
(d) will compile and Print "The World is beautiful"

Review Questions

1. What is an interface? How is it different from an abstract class?
2. What are packages? How are they created and used?
3. What are wrapper classes?
4. What is enum type? Explain with the help of a program.

5. Explain the following:
   (a) public   (b) private
   (c) default   (d) protected
   (e) import   (f) static import
6. Explain the difference between `String` and `StringBuffer`.

Programming Exercises

1. Design an interface named `Stack` with the following methods:
   (a) Push and pop elements from the stack.
   (b) Check whether the stack is empty or not. Implement the stack with the help of arrays and if the size of the array becomes too small to hold the elements, create a new one. Test this interface by inheriting it in its subclass `StackTest.java`.
2. Design an interface named `Queue` with the following methods:
   (a) To add and remove elements from the queue.
   (b) Check whether queue is empty or not Implement the queue with the help of arrays and if the size of the array becomes too small to hold the elements, create a new one. Test this interface by inheriting it in its subclass `QueueTest.java`
3. Create a class within this package "AmountIn-Words" to convert the amount into words. (Consider the amount to be not more than 100000.)

4. Write a program to count the number of words and characters in a string.
5. Design an enumeration for weekdays and print their corresponding description according to the traditional rules:

Description	Weekdays
Sun	Sunday
Moon	Monday
Mars	Tuesday
Mercury	Wednesday
Jupiter	Thursday
Venus	Friday
Saturn	Saturday

6. Design an interface with a method reversal. This method takes a string as its input and returns the reversed string. Create a class `StringReversal` and implement the method [Do not use predefined methods].

Answers to Objective Questions

1. (d)
2. (b), it will not compile as public is not applied to the overridden `show` method in class y.
3. (b), the correct sequence is `package y: import a.b: class{}`   4. (b)
5. (c), the class does not compile because the top-level class cannot be protected.
6. (c)   7. (a)
8. (b), compile time error as value is not given for this variable
9. (b), it will not compile, as static cannot be applied to method defined in an interface   10. (d)

Exception, Assertions, and Logging

7

When the imagination and willpower are in conflict, are antagonistic, it is always the imagination which wins, without any exception.

Emile Coue

After reading this chapter, the readers will be able to
- understand the concepts and applications of exception handling
- understand all the keywords used for exception handling
- create user-defined exceptions
- know what assertions are and how to use them
- know the basics of logging

7.1 INTRODUCTION

Exceptions in real life are rare and are usually used to denote something unusual that does not conform to the standard rules. For example, Abraham Lincoln was an exception who, despite all hurdles in his life, rose to become the sixteenth president of the USA. In computer programming, exceptions are events that arise due to the occurrence of unexpected behavior in certain statements, disrupting the normal execution of a program.

Exceptions can arise due to a number of situations. For example,

- Trying to access the 11th element of an array when the array contains only 10 elements (`ArrayIndexOutOfBoundsException`)
- Division by zero (`ArithmeticException`)
- Accessing a file which is not present (`FileNotFoundException`)
- Failure of I/O operations (`IOException`)
- Illegal usage of null (`NullPointerException`)

There are predefined classes (mentioned in the parenthesis above) for all exception types representing each such situation. The topmost class in the hierarchy is `java.lang.Throwable`. This class has two siblings: `Error` and `Exception`. All the classes representing exceptional conditions are subclasses of the `Exception` class. Whenever an exception occurs in a method, the runtime environment identifies the type of `Exception` and throws the object of it. If the method does not employ any exception handling mechanism (discussed later in the chapter), then the exception is passed to the caller method, and so on. If no exception handling mechanism is employed in any of the call stack (also known as runtime stack, i.e., the sequence of method calls from the current method to the main method) methods, the runtime environment passes the exception object to the default exception handler available with itself. The default handler prints the name of the exception along with an explanatory message followed by the stack trace at the time the exception was thrown and the program is terminated.

> **Note**　Stack trace is a record of the active stack frames generated by the execution of a program. It is used for debugging.

Example 7.1　Exception

```
L1    class ExDemo
L2    {
L3    public static void main(String args[])
L4    {
L5        method1();
L6    }
L7    static void method1()
L8    {
L9        System.out.println("IN Method 1, Calling Method 2");
L10       method2();
L11       System.out.println("Returned from method 2");
L12   }
L13   static void method2()
L14   {
L15       System.out.println("IN Method 2, Calling Method 3");
L16       method3();
L17       System.out.println("Returned from method 3");
L18   }
L19   static void method3()
L20   {
L21       System.out.println("IN Method 3");
L22       int a = 20,b = 0;
L23       int c = a/b;
L24       System.out.println("Method 3 exits");
      }}
```

Output

```
C:\javabook\programs\chap 7>java ExDemo
IN Method 1, Calling Method 2
IN Method 2, Calling Method 3
IN Method 3
Exception in thread "main" java.lang.ArithmeticException: / by zero
  at ExDemo.method3(ExDemo.java:23)
```

```
at ExDemo.method2(ExDemo.java:16)
at ExDemo.method1(ExDemo.java:10)
at ExDemo.main(ExDemo.java:5)
```

Explanation

L1 Class declaration.

L3 `main` method declaration.

L5 Call to `method1()`. Control passes to `method1()`. Call stack populated by pushing `method1()` call to top of the stack.

L7 `method1()` declaration.

L9 Prints `IN Method 1, Calling Method 2` (as shown in the output).

L10 Call to `method2()`. Control passes to `method2()`. Call stack again populated by pushing `method2()` call to the top of the stack above `method1()` call.

L11 Prints `Returned from method 2` if successfully returns from method 2.

L13 `method2()` declaration.

L15 Prints `IN Method 2, Calling Method 3` (as shown in the output).

L16 Call to `method3()`. Control passes to `method3()`. The call stack is again populated by pushing `method3()` call to the top of the stack above `method2()` call.

L17 Prints `Returned from method 3` if successfully returns from `method3()`.

L19 `method3()` declaration.

L21 Prints `IN Method 3`.

L22 Two integer variables initialized with a value of 20 for a and 0 for b.

L23 An integer variable is being divided by zero. We have intentionally written this statement to show you what happens when an exception occurs. Normally, in practice, nobody would attempt such a thing. You cannot divide a number by zero. It results in an `ArithmeticException` in Java. The execution halts at this point. The JVM throws an object of class `ArithmeticException` for an exception handler to catch it. No exception handler is provided with `method3()`. So the caller methods are looked upon to see if they can handle this particular exception. None of the caller methods, `method2()`, `method1()`, and `main()` employ any exception handling technique, so the JVM passes the exception to the default exception handler which in turn prints `Exception in thread "main"` followed by the name of the exception along with an explanatory message. In the next line, it prints the stack trace to help programmers debug the program and finally terminates the program. Take a look at the stack trace shown in Fig. 7.1.

`method3` was called by `method2` (line 16) and `method2` by `method1` (L10). `method1()` was called by `main` (L5). As you can see in the output, the call stack is printed as it is from top to bottom. Also note the line numbers are printed in the output.

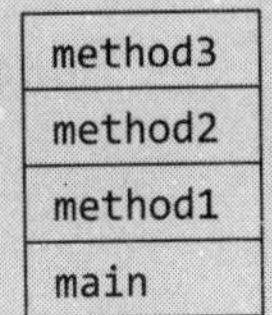

Fig. 7.1 Call Stack

7.1.1 Exception Types

Exceptions are broadly classified into two categories: *checked* and *unchecked exceptions*. (The Java specification treats Error as the third type of exception). Checked exceptions are those for which the compiler checks to see whether they have been handled in your program or not. Unchecked or runtime exceptions are not checked by the compiler. Table 7.1 shows a few checked and unchecked classes.

Table 7.1 Checked and Unchecked Exception Classes

Checked Exceptions	Unchecked Exceptions
ClassNotFoundException	ArithmeticException
NoSuchFieldException	ArrayIndexOutOfBoundsException
NoSuchMethodException	NullPointerException
InterruptedException	ClassCastException
IOException	BufferOverflowException
IllegalAccessException	BufferUnderflowException

Figure 7.2 shows the exception hierarchy in Java. Not all the Exception and Error subclasses have been depicted in the figure. The dots in the diagram are an indicator that there are other classes also within the immediate superclass. Example 7.1 can be modified to handle the exception generated in method3.

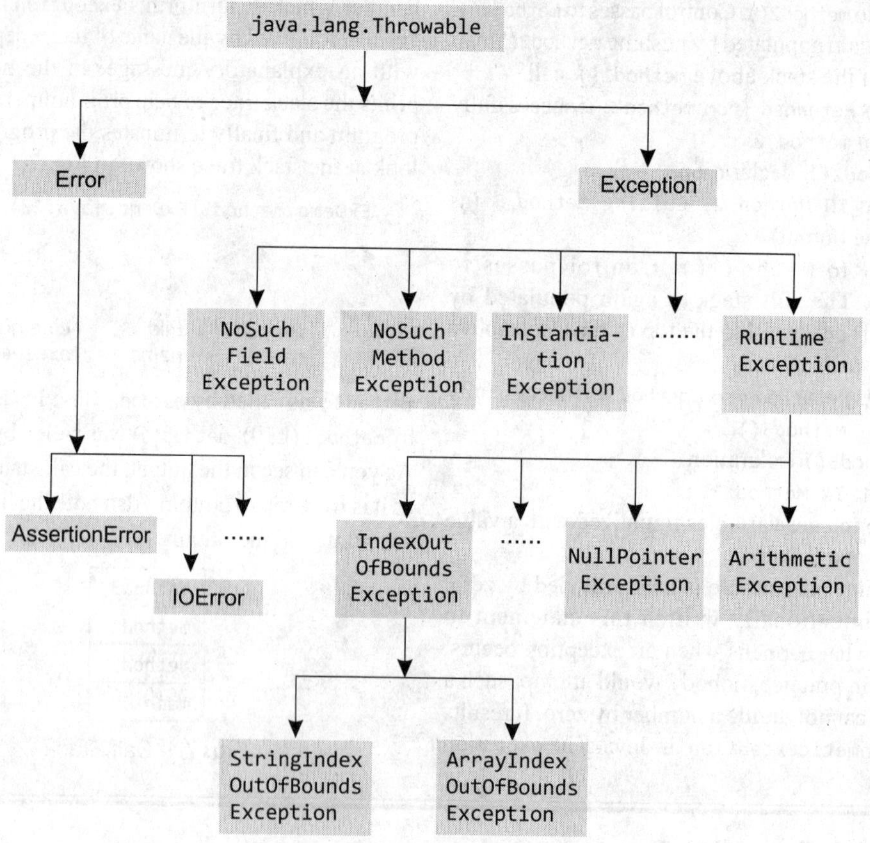

Fig. 7.2 Exception Hierarchy

7.2 EXCEPTION HANDLING TECHNIQUES

Java provides five keywords for exception handling: try, catch, throw, throws, and finally. Let us take a look at all these one by one.

7.2.1 try...catch

The `try/catch` block can be placed within any method that you feel can throw exceptions. All the statements to be tried for exceptions are put in a `try` block and immediately following the `try` is the `catch` block. `catch` block is used to catch any exception raised from the `try` block. If exception occurs in any statement in the `try` block, the following statements are not executed and control immediately passes to the corresponding `catch` block.

Example 7.2 **try...catch**

```
L1    class ExDemo1
L2    {
L3    public static void main(String args[])
L4    {
L5        method1();
L6    }
L7    static void method1()
L8    {
L9        System.out.println("IN Method 1, Calling Method 2");
L10       method2();
L11       System.out.println("Returned from method 2");
L12   }
L13   static void method2()
L14   {
L15   System.out.println("IN Method 2, Calling Method 3");
L16   try{
L17       method3(); }
L18   catch(Exception e)
L19   {
L20       System.out.println("Exception Handled");
L21   }
L22   System.out.println("Returned from method 3");
L23   }
L24   static void method3()
L25   {
L26       System.out.println("IN Method 3");
L27       int a = 20,b = 0;
L28       int c = a/b;
L29       System.out.println("Method 3 exits");
      }}
```

Output

```
C:\javabook\programs\chap 7>java ExDemo1
IN Method 1, Calling Method 2
IN Method 2, Calling Method 3
IN Method 3
Exception Handled
Returned from method 3
Returned from method 2
```

Explanation

L28 Exception occurred. No handling mechanism in method3(), so the control passes to the try...catch block in method2().

L29 It is not executed, as the statements following the occurrence of an exception are not executed.

L16 try block declared. The statements to be monitored for exceptions should be placed in the try block within a method.

L17 A call to method3() is placed within the try block.

L18 catch clause defined with an argument of type Exception (parent class) so that the exception objects thrown from the try block can be caught here. *A superclass reference variable can refer to a subclass object.* The try block is immediately followed by a catch block. As soon as an exception is encountered in the try block, statements following the statement on which the exception occurred are not executed. The runtime environment creates an object of class representing the exception and throws it. Control passes to the appropriate catch block (first appropriate catch in case multiple catch clauses are present) where the thrown object is caught and assigned to e, i.e., the Exception reference variable.

L20 Prints ExceptionHandled.

L22 Prints Returned from method3(). After the exception has been caught (try...catch mechanism implemented), execution resumes as normal. This was not possible in Example 7.1. After this, the control passes back to method1() from where method2() was called and L11 gets executed (see output).

A single try can have multiple catch clauses, for catching specific exceptions. As soon as an exception is thrown, the first appropriate catch clause responsible for handling that exception is located and the exception is passed to it. By first appropriate catch, we mean, if ArrayIndexOutOfBoundsException is generated, then the control passes to the first catch that either specifies the ArrayIndexOutOfBoundsException or the IndexOutOfBoundsException superclass of the ArrayIndexOutOfBoundsException or Exception. All exceptions can be caught by the Exception class. Example 7.3 shows how multiple catch clauses are incorporated in a program.

Example 7.3 Multiple Catch Clauses

```
L1    class Multiple_Catch
L2    {
L3    public static void main(String args[])
L4    {
L5       method1();
L6    }
L7    static void method1()
L8    {
L9      System.out.println("IN Method 1, Calling Method 2");
L10     method2();
L11     System.out.println("Returned from method 2");
L12   }
L13     static void method2()
L14     {
L15          System.out.println("IN Method 2, Calling Method 3");
L16     try {
L17     method3(); }
L18     catch(ArithmeticException ae)
```

```
L19    {
L20        System.out.println ("Arithmetic Exception Handled: " +ae);
L21    }
L22    catch(Exception e)
L23    {
L24        System.out.println("Exception Handled");
L25    }

L26        System.out.println("Returned from method 3");
L27    }
L28    static void method3()
L29    {
L30        System.out.println("IN Method 3");
L31        int a = 20, b = 0;
L32        int c = a/b;
L33        System.out.println("Method 3 exits");
    }}
```

Output

```
C:\javabook\programs\chap 7>java Multiple_Catch
IN Method 1, Calling Method 2
IN Method 2, Calling Method 3
IN Method 3
Arithmetic Exception Handled: java.lang.ArithmeticException: / by zero
Returned from method 3
Returned from method 2
```

Explanation

L16 try block defined.

L17 Call to `method3()`.

L18 The first `catch` clause defined with an argument of type `ArithmeticException` class.

L20 Prints Exceptionhandled concatenated with the output of ae.`toString()`. Remember `toString()` is called automatically when you try to print any object. `toString()` method is overridden in the `ArithmeticException` class to print its own `string` rather than that of the `Object` class.

L22 The second `catch` clause defined with an argument of type `Exception` class. This has been specified intentionally because if any other exception is thrown apart from `ArithmeticException`, then that exception will be caught in this particular `catch` clause.

Note While specifying multiple catch clauses for exception handling, the `catch` clause having the `Exception` type as its argument should be the last catch block in your program. This is because if the `catch` having the reference variable of type `Exception` class is placed as the top catch clause, then all the exceptions thrown from the try block will be caught in the first catch and the control will never pass onto the lower catch blocks, leading to an unreachable code.

An unreachable code in Java is easily recognized by the Java compiler and it complains about it during compilation. For example, if the `catch` clauses in Example 7.3 are reversed, as shown, the program will not compile.

```
catch(Exception e){}
catch(ArithmeticExceptionae) {}
```

7.2.2 throw Keyword

The `throw` keyword is used to explicitly throw an exception. In the earlier examples, this job was being done implicitly. Whether implicit or explicit, objects of exception need to be created before they are thrown. Execution of the program is suspended as in previous cases and the runtime environment looks for the appropriate catch to handle the exception. `throw` is more useful when we want to throw a user-defined exception. The syntax for `throw` is as follows:

```
throw new NullPointerException(); // throw new ThrowableInstance
```

Let us rework Example 7.3 to throw an exception explicitly.

Example 7.4 **throw Keyword**

```
L1    class ThrowDemo
L2    {
L3        public static void main(String args[])
L4        {
L5            method1();
L6        }
L7        static void method1()
L8        {
L9            System.out.println("IN Method 1, Calling Method 2");
L10           method2();
L11           System.out.println("Returned from method 2");
L12       }
L13       static void method2()
L14       {
L15           System.out.println("IN Method 2, Calling Method 3");
L16           try {
L17           method3(); }
L18           catch(Exception e)
L19           {
L20                   System.out.println("Exception Handled:" + e);
L21           }
L22           System.out.println("Returned from method 3");
L23       }
L24       static void method3()
L25       {
L26           System.out.println("IN Method 3");
L28           throw new ArithmeticException("Testing Throw");
      // This line is intentionally commented. If not, it results
      // in compile time error as it leads to unreachable code.
L29       // System.out.println("Method 3 exits");
      }}
```

Output

```
C:\javabook\programs\chap 7>java ThrowDemo
IN Method 1, Calling Method 2
IN Method 2, Calling Method 3
```

```
IN Method 3
Exception Handled: java.lang.ArithmeticException: Testing throw
Returned from method 3
Returned from method 2
```

Explanation

L28 Instead of an expression which leads to the runtime environment throwing an exception, we have used `throw` keyword to throw the exceptions ourselves. Just like the runtime environment, we also need to create an object for throwing it. So the `ArithmeticException` object is created with the help of `new` keyword and an argument is passed to its constructor. This argument is printed onto the console via the `toString()` method of the `ArithmeticException` class, when we catch this exception and print the exception object (see output).

This argument can also be separately printed using the `getMessage()` method of the `ArithmeticException` class.

L29 It is commented. If it is not commented, the compiler will give an error stating Unreachable Code. Particularly, in this program, the control will always move out after the throws clause, searching for a handler, so this line will never be executed. The Java compiler is intelligent enough to understand this and raises an error.

This exception is caught and printed in the catch present in L18–21. Rest of the logic is similar to the previous example.

7.2.3 throws

The `throws` is added to the method signature to let the caller know about what exceptions the called method can throw. It is the responsibility of the caller to either handle the exception (using `try...catch` mechanism) or it can also pass the exception (by specifying `throws` clause in its method declaration). If all the methods in a program pass the exception to their callers (including `main()`), then ultimately the exception passes to the default exception handler. A method should use either of the two techniques—`try/catch` or `throws`. Usually (for checked exceptions specifically), it is the `catch` or `specify` mechanism that is used. A method can throw more than one exception; the exception list is specified as separated by commas. The syntax for the `throws` keyword is shown below:

```
public void divide(int a, int b) throws ArithmeticException, IllegalArgumentException
```

Let us take a look at the following example.

Example 7.5 **throws Keyword**

```
L1    class ThrowsDemo
L2    {
L3       public static void main(String args[])
L4       {
L5            method1();
L6       }
L7       static void method1()
L8       {
L9            System.out.println("IN Method 1, Calling Method 2");
L10           method2();
L11           System.out.println("Returned from method 2");
```

```
L12        }
L13        static void method2()
L14        {
L15        System.out.println("IN Method 2, Calling Method 3");
L16        try{
L17            method3(4,0); }
L18        catch(Exception e)
L19            {
L20                    System.out.println("Exception Handled: " + e);
L21            }
L22            System.out.println("Returned from method 3");
L23        }
L24        static void method3(int a, int b) throws Exception
L25        {
L26        System.out.println("IN Method 3");
L27        if(b == 0)
L28            throw new ArithmeticException("Testing throw");
L29        else
                System.out.println("Result: "+a/b);
           }}
```

Output

When a = 4 and b = 2

```
C:\javabook\programs\chap 7>java ThrowsDemo
IN Method 1, Calling Method 2
IN Method 2, Calling Method 3
IN Method 3
Result: 2
Returned from method 3
Returned from method 2
```

When a = 4 and b = 0

```
C:\javabook\programs\chap 7>java ThrowsDemo
IN Method 1, Calling Method 2
IN Method 2, Calling Method 3
IN Method 3
Exception Handled: java.lang.ArithmeticException: Testing throw
Returned from method 3
Returned from method 2
```

Explanation

L24 method3() has been declared with throws clause specifying that it may throw an exception. The parent class (Exception) has been specified in the throws clause, so there is no need to explicitly mention the subclass name (ArithmeticException). If throws is omitted in this line, the program works as usual. If the try/catch in method2() (L16, L18–21 and L23) is omitted and throws in method3() declaration is kept intact, the compiler will not compile the program as now, it is mandatory for the calling method to either pass or catch the exception.

L26 Print statement.

L27 if statement checks the value of b. If it is zero, L28 is executed, else L29.

L28 An object of ArithmeticException is created and thrown.

L29 else prints the result of division of a by b.

7.2.4 finally Block

The finally block is always executed in try-catch-finally statements irrespective of whether an exception is thrown from within the try/catch block or not. Statements following the exception in a try block are not executed. Some statements are mandatory to execute such as the statements related to the release of resources. All these statements can be put in a finally block. The syntax of the finally keyword is as follows:

```
try {...} catch(Throwable e){...} finally {....}
```

Let us take an example to understand it better.

Example 7.6 **finally Keyword**

```
L1     class FinallyDemo
L2     {
L3       public static void main(String args[])
L4       {
L5           method1();
L6           System.out.println("Result : "+method2 (24,0)); }
L7           static void method1()
L8           {
L9           try {
L10              System.out.println("IN Method 1");
L11              throw new NullPointerException(); }
L12          catch(Exception e)
L13          {
L14              System.out.println("Exception Handled: " + e);
L15          }
L16          finally {
L17          System.out.println("In method 1 finally"); } }
L18          static int method2(int a, int b)
L19          {
L20          try{
L21              System.out.println("IN Method 2");
L22              return a/b; }
L23          finally {
                 System.out.println("In method 2 finally");
             }
          }
       }
```

Output

When a = 24 and b = 4

```
C:\javabook\programs\chap 7>java FinallyDemo
IN Method 1
Exception Handled: java.lang.NullPointerException
In method 1 finally
IN Method 2
In method 2 finally
Result : 6
```

When a = 24 and b = 0

```
C:\javabook\programs\chap 7>java FinallyDemo
IN Method 1
Exception Handled: java.lang.NullPointerException
In method 1 finally
IN Method 2
In method 2 finally
Exception in thread "main" java.lang.ArithmeticException: / by zero
at FinallyDemo.method2(FinallyDemo.java:24)
at FinallyDemo.main(FinallyDemo.java:6)
```

Explanation

L5 Call to `method1()`. Control passes to L7.

L6 Call to `method2()` and if any, return is printed on the screen.

L7 `method1()` declaration.

L9 `try` block defined.

L11 `NullPointerException` is thrown. Control passes to catch in L12.

L12 `catch` block corresponding to try in L9.

L14 Prints the exception object e. (`e.toString()` is called by default).

L16 Shows the `finally` block. The exception thrown in L11 is caught at L12. The `finally` block following catch gets executed after that (see output).

L17 The statement within `finally` gets executed.

L18 `method2()` declared expecting two integer arguments. Value passes are 24 and 0.

L20 `try` block within `method2()`.

L22 As already discussed, the value of b being zero, an attempt to divide any number by zero results in an `ArithmeticException` being thrown.

L23 Just to show that the `finally` block executes in all cases, we have intentionally not given the catch in `method2()`. A `try` can either have a corresponding `catch` with `finally` or it can also have a `finally` following it. In the earlier examples, we have seen that as soon as an exception is encountered, its appropriate handler is looked upon and nothing gets executed until and unless the exception is handled. The only exception to this fact is the `finally` block. In our example, the exception is thrown in L22. `method2()` does not have its own catch to handle exceptions, so its caller is to be looked upon but before control passed to the caller, i.e., main method, the `finally` in `method2()` is executed. And then the control passes to `main()` where no handler is present, so the runtime environment handles the exception as already discussed (see output).

7.2.5 try-with-resources Statement

Java 7 added a new enhancement to the exception handling mechanism, i.e., automatic resource management with a `try-with-resources` statement. The applications uses many resources during their lifetime by creating their objects, e.g., creating a data base connection for accessing/updating databases, or creating file objects for working with files, or creating sockets for transmission/receiving of data, etc. A common mistake committed by programmers is that they often do not close/release the resources occupied by the programs, after their task is complete. This leads to many orphaned instances, inefficient memory allocation, and garbage collection. Hence the need for automatic resource management arises.

To address this problem `AutoCloseable`, a new interface has been created in the `java.lang` package. The resources that want to be closed must implement this interface. This interface has just one method,

```
public void close() throws Exception
```

This close method will be overridden by the class that implements the interface and all resources releasing code can be put in this method. The close method of the `AutoCloseable` object is called automatically when it is used with a `try-with-resources` statement as soon as the `try-with-resources` block has finished execution regardless of whether an exception is thrown or not. The syntax of a `try-with-resources` statement is as follows:

```
try (resources to be used and automatically released)

{
     // statements within the block
}
```

For example

```
try (abc a=new abc(); pqr p=new pqr())

{
     // statements within the block
 }
```

More than one `AutoCloseable` resources can be used in try-with-resources statement separated by semicolon. Hence it is mandatory for `abc` and `pqr` objects to implement the `AutoCloseable` interface as shown below in the example. The resources created in the `try-with-resources` statement are closed in the reverse order of creation. We will elaborate these concepts in Example 7.7.

Example 7.7 **`AutoCloseable` Resources and `try-with-resource` Statement**

```
L1    class abc implements AutoCloseable
      {
L2      public void close()
        {
        System.out.println("Within close method of abc");
        }
      }
L3    class pqr implements AutoCloseable
      {
L4      public void close()
        {
            System.out.println("Within close method of pqr");
        }
      }
L5    class TestTryWithResources
      {
L6    public static void main(String args[])
      {
L7    try (abc a=new abc(); pqr p=new pqr())
        {
        System.out.println("Within try with resources block");
L8      throw new Exception();
        }
```

```
L9        catch(Exception e)
          {
          System.out.println("Within catch block");
          }
      }
  }
```

Output

```
D:\javabook\programs\chap 7\java TestTryWithResources
Within try with resources block
Within close method of pqr
Within close method of abc
Within catch block
```

Explanation

L1–4 All resources that need to be closed automatically after their use must implement the Auto-Closeable interface and override the close method.
L5 Another class is created to test the AutoCloseable resources created above.
L6 main method declaration.
L7 try-with-resources statement is used to create two resources which will be automatically closed once the block exits by calling their respective close methods in reverse order of creation. The close method of pqr is called first and then the close method of abc (see output). Note that these two objects have already inherited the AutoCloseable interface otherwise a compile time error will be raised by the compiler.
L8 An explicit Exception is raised to show that the close methods are called irrespective of whether an exception occurs or not. In case an Exception is raised, the close methods are called prior to handling the Exception (see output).
L9 catch block is declared to handle the exception raised from the try-with-resource block.

Note It is not mandatory for a try-with-resource block to have a catch or finally block unlike the previous version of JDK. They are optional in Java 7 with a try-with-resource block.

7.2.6 Multi catch

Java 7 introduced the multi catch statement to catch multiple exception types using a single catch block. Example 7.3 showed the older ways of catching multiple exceptions using separate catch blocks. Assuming that Exception1, Exception2, and Exception3 are belonging to different hierarchies and may be thrown from try block, they can be handled in a single catch block using the newer syntax for catching multiple exceptions as follows:

```
try

{
    // statements
}
catch (Exception1 | Exception2 | Exception3 e)
{
    // statements
}
```

So you might get the feeling that the `catch` block in Example 7.3 can be rearticulated as:

```java
catch (ArithmeticException | Exception e)
{
    // statements
}
```

But the problem with the `catch` block above is that both `ArithmeticException` and `Exception` belong to the same hierarchy. (Actually every exception has branched out of `Exception`.) If the `catch` block is rearticulated as shown below, it compiles because now both exceptions belong to different inheritance hierarchy.

```java
catch (ArithmeticException | NullPointerException | NumberFormatException e)
{
    // Statements
}
```

The benefit of using `multi catch` is that it results in more efficient byte code as you have just one `catch` block (instead of more as in the above case). Moreover same treatment can be applied to exceptions of different hierarchies. A way of applying different treatment while using `multi catch` syntax is by using `instanceof` operator as shown below. `instanceof` operator checks whether an instance is of a particular class and return true or false.

```java
catch(ArithmeticException | ArrayIndexOutOfBoundsException | NumberFormatException e)
{
    if(e instanceof ArithmeticException)
            System.out.println("Arithmetic Exception Handled: " +e);
    else if(e instanceof NumberFormatException)
            System.out.println("Exception Handled: " +e);
    else
        System.out.println(e);
}
```

> **Note** In case the `multi catch` syntax is used, the parameter e is implicitly final.

7.2.7 Improved Exception Handling in Java 7

Prior to Java 7, a method can specify only those exceptions in the `throws` clause that have been specified in the `catch` clause while re-throwing exceptions from within `catch` block. But Java 7 onwards the `throws` can specify more refined exceptions to be rethrown. Suppose there are two user defined exceptions `Exception1` and `Exception2` which can be rethrown from within the catch block of a method. Prior to Java 7 only the exceptions specified in the `catch` block can be mentioned as argument to the `throws` keyword. Let us take an example to show this.

Example 7.8(a) **Re-throwing an Exception**

```java
class Exception1 extends Exception { }
class Exception2 extends Exception { }
class DemoException{
  void throwException(int a, int b) throws Exception {
   try {
```

```
        if (a<b)
L2          throw new Exception1();
     else
L3          throw new Exception2();
L4   } catch (Exception e) {
L5       throw e;
     }
   }
   public static void main(String args[]) throws Exception
   {
     new DemoException().throwException(4,0);
   }
 }
```

The above method `throwException` could throw either `Exception1` (L2) or `Exception2` (L3) based on the value of a or b. Prior to Java 7, it was not possible to specify these exception types in the `throws` clause of the `throwException` method declaration (L1). The exception e is re-thrown from the `catch` block (L5) and as e is of type `Exception` so only `Exception` can be specified in the `throws` clause of method declaration on L1.

Java 7 onwards you can specify `Exception1` and `Exception2` in the `throws` clause of the `throwException` method declaration. The compiler deduces that the exceptions thrown by `throw` e (L5) must have come from the `try` block, and the exceptions thrown by the `try` block can be `Exception1` or `Exception2`. Although e is defined of type `Exception` (L4), the compiler can determine that e would be an instance of either `Exception1` or `Exception2`. Let us rephrase the method in the program.

Example 7.8(b)   Re-throwing an Exception

```
 class DemoException{
L1   void throwException(int a, int b) throws Exception1, Exception2 {
     try {
         if (a<b)
L2          throw new Exception1();
     else
L3          throw new Exception2();
L4   } catch (Exception e) {
L5       throw e;
     }
   }
   public static void main(String args[]) throws Exception1,Exception2
   {
     new DemoException().throwException(4,0);
   }
 }
```

In other words, Java 7 onwards you can rethrow (L5) an exception that is a supertype (in our case it is `Exception`) of any of the types declared in the `throws` (i.e., `Exception1` and `Exception2`).

7.3 USER-DEFINED EXCEPTION

Java provides you with the opportunity to create your own exceptions, i.e., user-defined exceptions. The mandatory requirement is that the class should be a subclass of the Exception class. We will create a sample exception and use it in a different class and throw this particular exception on some particular condition.

Example 7.9 **User-defined Exception**

```
L1    class ExcepDemo extends Exception
      {
L2      ExcepDemo(String msg)
        {
L3          super(msg);
        }
L4      public String toString()
        {
L5          return "Exception in thread \"main\" ExcepDemo Exception:" +getMessage();
        }
      }
L6    class TestException
      {
L7      static void testException() throws ExcepDemo
        {
L8          throw new ExcepDemo("Testing User Defined Exception");
        }
L9      public static void main(String args[])
        {
L10         try
            {
L11         testException();
            }
L12         catch(ExcepDemo e)
            {
L13         System.out.println(e);
            }
      }}
```

Output

```
C:\javabook\programs\chap 7>java TestException
Exception in thread "main" ExcepDemo Exception: Testing User Defined Exception
```

Explanation

L1 To create your own exception, your class has to extend the Exception class as shown.

L2 Constructor for the exception subclass has been defined accepting a String argument.

L3 The String argument is passed to the superclass constructor using super. This argument can be retrieved using a method of the superclass, i.e., getMessage().

L4 toString method has been overridden. This is automatically called when you print the object of the exception subclass.

L5 String is being returned concatenated with the output of the getMessage() function. It returns the string passed to the constructor of the superclass.

The user-defined class is ready and now we need a sample class to test it, so we created the `TestException` class.

L6 `TestException` class defined.

L7 `static` method declaring that it can throw `ExcepDemo` exception.

L8 Exception thrown using the keyword `throw`.

L9 `main` method declaration.

L10 `try` block defined.

L11 `testException()` method called.

L12 `catch` corresponding to `try` (L10).

L13 Prints the exception. `toString()` is called automatically, which returns the string `Exceptionin-thread "main" ExcepDemoException:` concatenated with the argument passed in the constructor of the `ExcepDemo` class in L8 (see output). This `String` is returned through the method `getMessage()`, defined in the `Throwable` class.

7.4 EXCEPTION ENCAPSULATION AND ENRICHMENT

Java 1.4 introduced *exception encapsulation* (chaining), which is the process of wrapping a caught exception in a different exception and throwing the wrapped exception. The `Throwable` class (parent class) has added a cause parameter in its constructors for wrapped exceptions and a `getCause()` method to return the wrapped exception. If you pass all your exception, your top level method might have to deal with a lot of exceptions; and declaring or handling exceptions in all the previous methods is a tedious task. The solution is to wrap exceptions and throw it. Wrapping is also used to abstract the details of implementation. You might not want your working details (including the exception that are thrown) to be known to others. Let us see how wrapping is done.

```
try{
    throw new InstantiationException();
}
catch(InstantiationException t)
  {
      // wrapping InstantiationException in ExcepDemo
      throw new ExcepDemo("Wrapped Instantiation Exception",t);
  }
```

Wrapping has some disadvantages also. It leads to long stack traces; one for each exception in the wrapping hierarchy. Secondly, due to wrapping, it becomes difficult to figure out the problem that led to exceptions.

The possible solution is *exception enrichment*. In exception enrichment, you do not wrap exceptions but add information to the already thrown exception and rethrow it, which leads to a single stack trace. Let us take an example to see exception enrichment.

Example 7.10 **Exception Enrichment**

```
L1    class ExcepDemo extends Exception{
      String message;
L2    ExcepDemo(String msg){
L3        message = msg;}
L4    public String toString(){
L5    return "Exception in thread \"main\" ExcepDemo Exception:" +message;
      }
L6    public void addInformation(String msg) {
L7        message += msg;
      }}
```

```
L8    class ExceptionEnrichmentDemo{
L9    static void testException() throws ExcepDemo
L10   {
      try
          {
L11           throw new ExcepDemo("Testing User Defined Exception");
          }
L12   catch(ExcepDemo e)
      {
L13           e.addInformation("\nexception was successfully enriched and
              re-thrown from catch");
L14           throw e;
      }
      }
L15   public static void main(String args[]) {
L16   try
      {
L17           testException();
      }
L18   catch(ExcepDemo e){
L19           System.out.println(e);
      }
      }}
```

Output

```
C:\javabook\programs\chap 7>java ExceptionEnrichmentDemo
Exception in thread "main" ExcepDemo Exception: Testing User Defined
Exception exception was successfully enriched and re-thrown from catch
```

Explanation

L6 `addInformation` method has been added in the user-defined exception class: `ExcepDemo`. This method accepts an argument of type `String`, so that additional information about the exception can be added to the exception object.

L7 The string is concatenated to the instance variable message.

L8 To test this, a new class has been created: `ExceptionEnrichmentDemo`

L9 Method named `testException` has been defined stating that it can throw `ExcepDemo` exception.

L11 Exception `ExcepDemo` is thrown.

L12 The exception thrown in L11 is caught at the catch defined in this line.

L13 Additional information regarding the exception is appended by calling the `addInfomation()` method of the `ExcepDemo` object.

L14 The exception object is re-thrown. When an exception is re-thrown from the `catch` block, then the control passes directly to the caller's `catch` (if any). In our case, it is present on L18.

L18 It shows the `catch` in the `main` method. This catch is responsible for handling.

(a) Exceptions occurring in its own `try` (L16).

(b) Exceptions occurring in the methods that are called from the `try` block (L16) corresponding to this `catch`.

(c) Exceptions re-thrown from the `catch` of the other method that are called from your `try` (L14).

L19 The exception object is printed.

7.5 ASSERTIONS

Assertions were added in Java 1.4 to create reliable programs that are correct and robust. Assertions are boolean expressions that are used to test/validate the code. They are basically used during testing and development phases. Assertions are used by the programmers to be doubly sure about a particular condition, which they feel to be true. Conditions such as a number is positive or negative, array/reference is null or not can be checked by asserting them. Assertions in Java are declared with the help of `assert` keyword as shown below:

```
        assert expression1;                    // assert x > 0;
or
        assert expression1: expression2        // assert x < 0:" Value Ok ";
```

where `expression1` is the condition to be evaluated. In case, the condition is evaluated as false, an `AssertionError` is thrown. `expression2` is a string which is passed to the constructor of the `AssertionError` object.

Assertions have to be enabled explicitly; they are disabled by default. Using the –ea and –da options of Java, we can enable or disable assertions (see output).

```
        -ea enable assertions
        -da disable assertions
```

Example 7.11   Assertion

```
L1    class AssertDemo {
L2    static void check(int i)
        {
L3          assert i> 0: "Value must be positive";
L4          System.out.println("value fine "+i);
        }
L5    public static void main(String args[])
        {
L6    check(Integer.parseInt(args[0]));
        }}
```

Output

When i = 1

```
C:\javabook\programs\chap 7>java -ea AssertDemo 1
value fine 1
```

When i = –1

```
C:\javabook\programs\chap 7>java -ea AssertDemo -1
Exception in thread "main" java.lang.AssertionError: Value must be positive
at AssertDemo.check(AssertDemo.java:4)
at AssertDemo.main(AssertDemo.java:9)
```

Without Enabling Assertions

```
C:\javabook\programs\chap 7>java AssertDemo -1
value fine -1
```

Explanation

L2   The `static` method has been declared with an integer argument.

L3   `assert` keyword is used to check if the value of `i` is greater than 0 or not. If the value of `i` is less than 0, an `AssertionError` is thrown and the string `Valuemustbepositive` is passed to the constructor of the `AssertionError` object (see output). This has been handled in the same way exceptions were handled (refer Example 7.1).

L4   Prints `valuefine` followed by the value of `i`.

L6 The method `check` is called. The first command-line argument is converted to `int` using the `Integer.parseInt()` function and passed to the `check` method.

As you can see in the output, if assertions are not enabled, problems can arise. We never expected –1 to be a fine value in our program but in the (without enabling assertion) output, you can see it for yourself.

7.6 LOGGING

The logging feature was added in the `java.util.logging` package of Java 1.4 for debugging purpose. Logs are basically used to report messages regarding the functioning of the application to the programmer. These logs are supposed to be saved and reviewed later by the programmer. Logs are created with the help of a `Logger` class in the `util.logging` package. These messages are passed to handler objects which pass these messages to console, log files, etc. Loggings have nine levels in Java (illustrated in Table 7.2) to indicate the severity of logged messages. These levels are `final` and `static` fields of `Level` class (`util.logging` package).

Table 7.2 Logging Levels

Level	Description
SEVERE	Indicates severe problem, requiring attention (highest)
WARNING	Indicates potential problem
INFO	Informational messages; written on the console
CONFIG	Message regarding configuration information
FINE	Less detailed messages
FINER	More detailed messages
FINEST	Least of all three: FINE, FINER, FINEST. Used for most detailed output (lowest)
OFF	Turns off logging
ALL	Logs all messages

By default, the level is set to INFO. All messages above and including level INFO are sent to the console. You can set and get these levels using the methods of the `Logger` class. In addition to setting the level for the `Logger`, one has to set the level for the handler also.

```
public void setLevel(Level l)
public Level getLevel()
```

The `Logger` class provides methods similar to the names of the levels for logging messages. All these methods take a String argument as shown:

```
public void severe(String msg)   – for logging messages of SEVERE level.
public void warning(String msg)  – for logging messages of WARNING level.
public void config(String msg)   – for logging messages of CONFIG level.
public void info(String msg)     – for logging messages of INFO level.
public void finest(String msg)   – for logging messages of FINEST level.
public void finer(String msg)    – for logging messages of finer level.
public void fine(String msg)     – for logging messages of finer level.
```

In addition to these, it also provides a method that sets the level as well as prints the message on the console.

```
public void log(Level l,String msg)
```

Let us take an example to better understand the concept behind logging.

Example 7.12 Logging

```
L1    import java.util.logging.*;
L2    class LoggingDemo {
L3      static Logger l = Logger.getLogger ("LoggingDemo");
L4      void demo() {
L5      l.log(Level.SEVERE,"Shows Severe level of the Logger ");
        }
L6    public static void main(String[] args)
      {
L7      LoggingDemo d = new LoggingDemo();
L8      d.demo();
      }}
```

Output

```
C:\javabook\programs\chap 7>java LoggingDemo
22 Feb, 2009 11:18:49 AM LoggingDemo demo
SEVERE: Shows Severe level of the Logger
```

Explanation

L1 Package `java.util.logging` has been imported, as the class `Logger` is a part of this package.
L3 Normally, we use one `Logger` per class. That is the reason why we have created the `Logger` object as static.
L4 The method `demo()` has been declared.
L5 The `log` method of the `Logger` object has been called to log the message to the console. The first argument sets the level of the logger and the second argument is a String message that is the output on the console. The details of the output are shown below:
L7 An object of the class `LoggingDemo` has been declared.
L8 The method `demo` has been called using the `LoggingDemo` object.

Output Details			
22 Feb,	**2009 11:18:49AM**	**LoggingDemo**	**demo**
Date	Time of execution	ClassName	methodName where error occurred
SEVERE:	Shows Severe level of the Logger		
Level	**Message passed to constructor of Assertion Error**		

SUMMARY

This chapter focused on how to handle unusual conditions/situations in Java. Exception handling is the key. Two types of exceptions have been defined: checked and unchecked. All exceptions, whether checked or unchecked, inherit from the parent class `Throwable`. There are five keywords in exception handling, namely try, `catch`, `throw`, `throws`, and `finally`.

Apart from using the predefined exception, you can code your own exceptions according to your own requirements. Exception chaining (introduced in JDK 1.4) wraps a particular exception into another.

Assertions (introduced in JDK 1.4) are helpful in assuring the programmer about a particular condition using the assert keyword. They help in increasing the reliability of a Java program. Logging features (part of `java.util.logging` package introduced in JDK 1.4) help the user to debug his program.

Java 7 introduced the automatic resource management with the help of a new `try` block, i.e., `try-with-resource` block. This chapter also highlights the new syntax for compressing multiple catch blocks used in Java 7.

EXERCISES

Objective Questions

1. What are the two types of exceptions available in Java?
   - (a) Checked and compiled
   - (b) Unchecked and compiled
   - (c) Checked and unchecked
   - (d) Compiled and non-compiled

2. The parent class of all the exceptions in Java is
   - (a) Throwable
   - (b) Throw
   - (c) Exception
   - (d) Throws

3. What is the result of attempting to compile and execute the program?

```java
class Demo
{
    void show() throws ClassNotFound
    Exception{}
}
class Demo2 extends Demo {
    void show() throws IllegalAccess
    Exception,
    ClassNotFoundException, Arithmetic
    Exception
    {
        System.out.println("In Demo1
        Show");
    }
public static void main(String ar[]) {
    try{
        Demo2 d = new Demo2();
        d.show();
    }
    catch(Exception e){}
    } }
```

   - (a) Does not compile
   - (b) Compiles successfully
   - (c) Compiles successfully and prints "In Demo1 show"
   - (d) Complies but does not execute

4. If the assert statement returns false, what is thrown?

   - (a) Exception
   - (b) Assert
   - (c) Assertion
   - (d) Assertion Error

5. What is the result of attempting to compile and execute the program?

```java
class Demo
{
    void show() throws ArithmeticEx
    ception{}
}
class Demo1 extends Demo {
    void show()
    {
        System.out.println("In Demo1
        Show");
    }
public static void main(String ar[])
    {
        Demo1 d = new Demo1();
        d.show();
    }
}
```

   - (a) Does not compile
   - (b) Compiles successfully
   - (c) Executes successfully and prints "In Demo1 show"
   - (d) Complies but does not execute

6. What is the result of attempting to compile and execute the program?

```java
class Test
{
    static void test() throws Runtime-
    Exception
    {
        throw new ArithmeticException();
    }
public static void main(String args[])
    {
        try{
        test();
```

```
        }
        catch(RuntimeException re)
        {
            System.out.println("Exception
        Handled");
        }
    } }
```

(a) Checked exception is generated

(b) Does not compile

(c) Prints "Exception Handled", as `RuntimeEx-`
    `ception` is superclass of the `ArithmeticEx-`
    `ception` class

(d) Class compiles but nothing is printed on the
    console

7. The two subclasses of `Throwable` are
   (a) Error and AssertionError
   (b) Error and Exception
   (c) Checked and Unchecked Exception
   (d) Error and RuntimeException

8. Messages above what level will only be logged
   to the console by default?
   (a) INFO   (b) SEVERE
   (c) WARNING   (d) FINE

9. What is the purpose of creating a `Logger` object
   as `static`?
   (a) Applies to all objects of the class

(b) Each for individual objects of the class

(c) Applies only to static objects

(d) Applies only to non-static objects

10. What is the result of attempting to compile and
    execute the program?

```
class Demo
{
    void show(){}
}
class Demo2 extends Demo {
    void show() throws IllegalAccess
    Exception, ArithmeticException
    {
        System.out.println("In Demo1
        Show");
    }
    public static void main(String ar[]) {
    try{
        Demo2 d = new Demo2();
        d.show();
    }
        catch(Exception e){}
} }
```

(a) Compiles successfully but throws Runtime
    Exception

(b) Compiles and prints nothing

(c) Compiles and prints In Demo1 Show

(d) Does not compile

Review Questions

1. What are exceptions? How are they handled in
   Java?

2. Explain logging in Java with all its levels.

3. Explain exception changing and environment.
   Write a program in support of your answer.

4. What is the difference between checked and
   unchecked exception?

5. Explain the need for automatic resource
   management.

6. What is a `try-with-resources` block and how
   is it used?

7. Explain the Java 7 enhancement regarding
   multiple catch clauses.

8. Explain in detail the Java 7 enhancements
   regarding re-throwing an exception.

Programming Exercises

1. Create a user-defined exception named `Check-`
   `Argument` to check the number of arguments
   passed through command line. If the number of
   arguments is less than five, throw the `CheckAr-`
   `gumentexception`, else print the addition of all
   the five numbers.

2. Consider a Student examination database
   system that prints the marksheet of students.
   Input the following from the command line:

(a) Students' name

(b) Marks in six subjects

These marks should be between 0 and 50. If the marks are not in the specified range, raise a `RangeException`, else find the total marks and print the percentage of the students.

3. Use Assertions in the above program to ensure that the total marks of a student will always be greater than or equal to 0.

4. Use Logging in Question 2 to log the print status of the students' marksheet along with the name, total marks, and percentage. Keep the log level at INFO.

Multithreading in Java

A person who learns to juggle six balls will be more skilled than the person who never tries to juggle more than three.
Marilyn vos Savant

After reading this chapter, the readers will be able to
- know what are threads and how they can be implemented in Java
- understand how multiple threads can be created within a Java program
- understand different states of a thread in Java
- appreciate the `Thread` class of `java.lang` package
- understand how runnable interface is helpful in creating threads

8.1 INTRODUCTION

Until now, whatever programs we have discussed were sequential ones, i.e., each of them has a beginning, an execution sequence, and an end. While the program is being executed, at any point of time, there is a single line of execution. One thing that you must note that a thread in itself is not a program, as it cannot run on its own. However, it can be embedded with any other program.

> **Note** A thread is a single sequential flow of control within a program.

The concept of single thread is quite simple to understand. Things become somewhat complex when there are multiple threads running simultaneously, each performing different tasks, within a single program. This can be enabled by multithreading, where you can write programs containing multiple paths of execution, running concurrently, within a single program. In other words, we can say that a single program having multiple threads, executing concurrently, can be termed as multithreaded program.

Let us go to the basics of multithreading, which is actually a form of multitasking. Multitasking can either be *process-based* or *thread-based*. If we assume programs as processes, then process-based multitasking is nothing but execution of more than one program concurrently. On the other hand, thread-based multitasking is executing a program having more than one thread, performing different tasks simultaneously. Processes are heavyweight tasks, while threads are lightweight tasks. In process-based multitasking, different processes are different programs, thus they share different address spaces. The context switching of CPU from one process to another requires more overhead as different address spaces are involved in the same. On the contrary, in thread-based multitasking, different threads are part of the same program, thus they share the same address space and context switching of CPU occurs within the program, i.e., within the same address space. Obviously, this will require less overhead.

The objective of all forms of multitasking including multithreading is to utilize the idle time of the CPU. Ideally a CPU should always be processing something. The idle time of CPU can be minimized using multitasking.

Have you ever paid attention to one thing? When you prepare a document using a word processor program, the spelling can also be checked simultaneously. This is one such example of thread-based multitasking. While you type in the document, the CPU sits idle and waits for you to enter characters but because of thread-based multitasking, the word processor minimizes the CPU idle time somewhat by simultaneously involving the CPU in checking the spelling of the text. From now onwards, we will call thread-based multitasking as *multithreading*.

> **Note** Multithreading enables programs to have more than one execution paths (separate) which execute concurrently. Each such path of execution is a thread. Through multithreading, efficient utilization of system resources can be achieved, such as maximum utilization of CPU cycles and minimizing idle time of CPU.

8.2 MULTITHREADING IN JAVA

Every program that we have been writing has at least one thread, i.e., the `main` thread. Whenever a program starts executing, the JVM is responsible for creating the main thread and calling the `main()` method, from within that thread. Alongside, many other invisible daemon threads responsible for supporting other activities of Java runtime such as finalization and garbage collection are also created.

Threads are executed by the processor according to the scheduling done by the Java Runtime System by assigning priority to every thread. It simply means, threads having higher priority are given preference for getting executed over the threads having lower priority.

When a Java program is executed, the JVM creates at least a single non-daemon thread (which calls the `main()` method of the corresponding class). A thread can either die naturally or be forced to die. The execution of the thread will go on until one of the following conditions occur:

- A thread dies naturally when it exits the `run()` method normally. The normal exit from `run()` means, the instructions of the `run()` has been processed completely.
- A thread can always be killed or interrupted by calling `interrupt()` method.

8.3 `java.lang.`THREAD

Creation of threads in Java is not as complex as the concept itself. There is a class named as `Thread` class, which belongs to the `java.lang` package, declared as,

```
public class Thread extends Object implements Runnable
```

This class encapsulates any thread of execution. Threads are created as the instance of this class, which contains `run()` methods in it. In fact the functionality of the thread can only be achieved by overriding this `run()` method. A typical `run()` would have the following structure:

```
        public void run()
        {
            ......
            // statement for implementing thread
            ......
        }
```

Table 8.1 Methods of thread Class

Methods	Description
`static Thread currentThread()`	Returns a reference to the currently executing thread.
`static intactiveCount()`	Returns the current number of active threads.
`long getID()`	Returns the identification of thread.
`final String getName()`	Returns the thread's name.
`final void join()`	Waits for a thread to terminate.
`void join (long m)`	Waits at the most for 'm' milliseconds for the thread to die.
`void join (long m, int n)`	Waits at the most for 'm' milliseconds and 'n' nanoseconds for the thread to die.
`void run()`	Entry point for the thread.
`final void setDaemon(boolean how)`	If how is true, the invoking thread is set to daemon status.
`boolean isInterrupted()`	Returns true if the thread on which it is called has been interrupted.
`final boolean isDaemon()`	Returns true if the invoking thread is a daemon thread.
`final boolean isAlive()`	Returns boolean value stating whether a thread is still running.
`void interrupt()`	Interrupts a thread.
`static boolean holdsLock(Object anyObj)`	Returns true if the invoking thread holds the lock on anyObj.
`Thread.State getState()`	Returns the current state of the thread.
`final int getPriority()`	Returns the priority of the thread.
`static boolean interrupted()`	Returns true if the invoking thread has been interrupted.
`final void setName(String thrdName)`	Sets a thread's name to `thrdName`.
`final void setPriority(int newPriority)`	Sets a thread's priority to `newPriority`.
`static void sleep(long milliseconds)`	Suspends a thread for a specified period of milliseconds.
`void start()`	Starts a thread by calling its `run()` method.
`void destroy()`	Destroys the thread, without any clean up.
`static int enumerate (Thread[] thrdArray)`	Copies into the specified array, every active thread of thread's group and sub group.
`static void yield()`	Cause the current executing thread to pause and allow the other threads to execute.

This method is automatically invoked when a thread object is created and initiated using the start() method. Some of the methods belonging to the Thread class, which help in manipulating thread instances, are shown in Table 8.1.

Apart from these, some constructors are also defined in the Thread class. These constructors can be classified in two different categories. We will discuss one category here and the other in the next section when we will discuss about Runnable interface. The constructors responsible for creating threads are

1. Thread()
2. Thread(String threadName)
3. Thread(ThreadGroup threadGroup, String threadName)

In the first constructor, you can see that there are no arguments, which simply means it uses the default name and the thread group. In the second constructor, the name of the constructor can be specified as String. While in the third, you can specify the thread group and thread name.

8.4 MAIN THREAD

Even if a thread is not created by a programmer, every Java program has a thread, the main thread. When a normal Java program starts executing, the JVM creates the main thread and calls the program's main()method from within that thread. Apart from this, the JVM also creates some invisible threads, which are important for its housekeeping tasks such as, threads taking care of garbage collection and threads responsible for object finalization. The main thread spawns the other threads. These spawned threads are called *child threads*. This main thread is always the last to finish executing because it is responsible for releasing the resources used during the program execution, such as network connections.

As a programmer, you can always take control of the main (or any other) thread. For this, a static method, currentThread(), is used to return a reference to the current thread. The main thread can be controlled by this reference only.

Now let us put these into practicality by creating a reference to the main thread. We could also change the name of the main thread from main to any new name. The following piece of code serves the purpose for you.

Example 8.1   **Renaming a Thread**

```
L1    class MainThreadDemo {
L2      public static void main (String args[] ) {
L3      Thread threadObj = Thread.currentThread();
L4      System.out.println("Current thread: " +threadObj);
L5      threadObj.setName("New Thread");
L6      System.out.println("Renamed Thread: " +threadObj);
L7    } }
```

Output

```
Current thread: Thread[main, 5, main]
Renamed Thread: Thread[New Thread, 5, main]
```

Explanation

L1 Class `MainThreadDemo` declared.

L2 `main` method declared.

L3 A reference to the current `Thread` is returned and is stored in the `threadObj`. Here the current thread is the `main` thread itself. The reference is declared by specifying the name of the class, i.e., `Thread` class in this case followed by the name for the reference, which is done as in the following line of code:

```
Thread threadObj
```

We acquire a reference to the main thread by calling the static method `currentThread()` of the `Thread` class using the following method call:

```
Thread.currentThread()
```

The reference to the current thread object (i.e., `main`) is returned by the `currentThread()` method and stored in the reference previously declared.

L4 The thread object (i.e., `main`) is passed to the `println` method. The `toString()` method of the `Thread` class is called by default, which displays the first line of the output.

L5 The `setName()` method of `Thread` class is used to change the name of the `Thread`. This example uses the `setName()` method to change the main thread's name from `main` to `New Thread`.

If we see the output now, the information within the square brackets is the signature of the thread. The first element in the bracket is the name of the thread. The second element signifies the thread priority (explained later in the Chapter under the topic *thread priority*). The range for setting the priority can be between 1 and 10; 1 for lowest priority 10 for highest priority and 5 for normal priority. The last element in the bracket is the group name for threads to which the thread belongs. The state of collection of threads can be controlled by a data structure, known as *thread group*. The thread group is automatically handled by the Java runtime system.

8.5 CREATION OF NEW THREADS

Once we have mentioned some of the methods and constructors of the `Thread` class, we can concentrate on different ways to create a new thread:

- By inheriting the `Thread` class
- By implementing the `Runnable` interface

8.5.1 By Inheriting the `Thread` Class

Threads can be created by inheriting the `java.lang.Thread` class. All the thread methods belonging to the `Thread` class can be used in the program because of the extension (inheritance).

Steps to be followed for thread creation:

- Declare your own class as extending the `Thread` class.
- Override the `run()` method, which constitutes the body of the thread.
- Create the thread object and use the `start()` method to initiate the thread execution.

Let us elaborate these steps in detail.

Declaring a Class Any new class can be declared to extend the `Thread` class, thus inheriting all the functionalities of the `Thread` class.

```
classNewThread extends Thread
{
    ......
    ......
    ......
}
```

Here, we have a new type of thread, named as 'NewThread'.

Overriding the `run()` Method The `run()` method has to be overridden by writing codes required for the thread. The thread behaves as per this code segment. A typical `run()` method would look like

```
public void run( )
{
    ......
    //code segment providing the functionality of thread
    .....
}
```

Starting New Thread The third part talks about the `start()` method, which is required to create and initiate an instance of our `Thread` class. The following piece of code is responsible for the same:

```
newThread thread1 = new newThread();
thread1.start();
```

The first line creates an instance of the class `NewThread`, where the object is just created. The thread is in *newborn state*. Second line, which calls the `start()` method, moves the thread to *runnable state*, where the Java Runtime will schedule the thread to run by invoking the `run()` method. Now the thread is said to be in *running state*.

| Example 8.2 | **Creating a Thread Using the Thread Class** |

```
L1    class ThreadOne extends Thread {
L2    public void run(){
L3    try {
L4      for(int i = 1; i<= 5; i++) {
L5      System.out.println("\tFrom child thread 1 : i =" +i);
L6      Thread.sleep(600);
L7    }
L8    } catch(InterruptedException e){
L9    System.out.println("child thread1 interrupted");
L10   }
L11   System.out.println("Exit from child thread 1");
L12   }
L13   }
L14   class ThreadTwo extends Thread{
L15   public void run(){
L16   try {
L17     for(int j = 1; j <= 5; j++){
L18     System.out.println("\t From child thread 2 : j =" +j);
```

```
L19      Thread.sleep(400);
L20    }
L21    } catch(InterruptedException e){
L22    System.out.println("child thread 2 interrupted");
L23    }
L24    System.out.println("Exit from child thread 2");
L25    }
L26  }
L27  class ThreadThree extends Thread {
L27  public void run(){
L28  try {
L29     for(int k = 1; k <= 5; k++) {
L30     System.out.println("\tFrom child thread 3 : k =" +k);
L31     Thread.sleep(800);
L32  }
L33  } catch(InterruptedException e){
L34  System.out.println("child thread 3 interrupted");
L35  }
L36  System.out.println("Exit from child thread 3");
L37  }
L38  }
L39  class ThreadDemo {
L40     public static void main(String arg[]) {
L41     ThreadOne a = new ThreadOne();
L42     a.start();
L43     ThreadTwo b = new ThreadTwo();
L44     b.start();
L45     ThreadThree c = new ThreadThree();
L46     c.start();
L47     try {
L48     for(int m=1; m<=5; m++){
L49     System.out.println("\t From Main Thread : m =" +m);
L50     Thread.sleep(1200);
L51     }
L52  } catch (InterruptedException e) {
L53  System.out.println("Main interrupted");}
L54  System.out.println("Exit form main thread");
L55  }
L56  }
```

Output

```
From child thread 1 :i =1
From Main Thread : m =1
From child thread 2 : j =1
From child thread 3 : k =1
From child thread 2 : j =2
From child thread 1 :i =2
From child thread 3 : k =2
From child thread 2 : j =3
From Main Thread : m =2
From child thread 1 :i =3
```

```
  From child thread 2 : j =4
  From child thread 3 : k =3
  From child thread 2 : j =5
  From child thread 1 :i =4
Exit from child thread 2
  From Main Thread : m =3
  From child thread 1 :i =5
  From child thread 3 : k =4
Exit from child thread 1
  From child thread 3 : k =5
  From Main Thread : m =4
Exit from child thread 3
  From Main Thread : m =5
Exit from main thread
```

Explanation

L1 Class ThreadOne extends the Thread class, thus inheriting all the functions and members of the Thread class.

L2–7 run() method, returning void is overridden. The for loop incrementing the counter variable, i, is looped 5 times (L3). Each value of i is displayed on the screen (L4) and before moving to the next value of i, the thread sleeps for 0.6 seconds (L6). Thread.sleep() method throws an exception, InterruptedException, so it should be within a try…catch block.

L14 Just like the class ThreadOne, a new class ThreadTwo, extending the Thread class is declared.

L15–20 run() method responsible for providing the functionality of the thread of this class is overridden. The code of this method is similar to that of the run(), explained in the previous paragraph.

L27 Third class, ThreadThree, extending the Thread class is declared.

L28–36 run() method for the third class' thread is implemented, similar to the previously explained run() methods.

L39 Class ThreadDemo encapsulating the main() method is declared. This class, which acts as the main thread, is responsible for spawning the other three child threads.

L40 main() method declared.

L41 Reference for ThreadOne class is created and stored in a.

L42 The start() method is invoked on the thread object a. This method puts the thread in a ready-to-execute state. As soon as the CPU is allocated to the thread by the thread scheduler, the run() method for the thread is called automatically. As you can see in the example also, the run()method is not called explicitly.

L43–46 Just like creating the object for ThreadOne, we create the reference objects for ThreadTwo and ThreadThree and store them in b and c, respectively. L44 is responsible for starting the second thread pertaining to ThreadTwo class and L46 is responsible for starting the third thread pertaining to ThreadThree class, thus resulting in invocation of the corresponding run() methods.

L47–55 Certain functionalities, similar to the functionalities of the above child threads, are provided inside the main thread also. It has been made to sleep for 1.2 seconds (L50), which has been kept more than the three child threads, so that the main thread completes its execution at last, otherwise there is always a possibility for the system to get hung.

8.5.2 Implementing the Runnable Interface

We have already mentioned that there can be two ways for implementing threads. First method has already been discussed in the previous section. Now let us talk about the second way, i.e., by implementing the Runnable interface. Before taking on the second method of implementing Runnable interface, we must know the ins and outs of this interface. It is actually implemented by class Thread in the package java.lang. This interface is declared public as,

```
public interface Runnable
```

The interface needs to be implemented by any class whose instance is to be executed by a thread. The implementing class must also override a method named as run(), defined as the only method in the Runnable interface as,

```
public void run( )
{
    ......
    ......
}
```

The object's run() method is called automatically whenever the thread is scheduled for execution by the thread scheduler. The functionality of the thread depends on the code written within this run() method. One thing worth noting is that other methods can be called from within run(). Not only this, use of other classes and declaration of variables, just like the main thread, are also possible inside run(). The thread will stop as soon as the run() exits.

The question that arises here is, when and how shall we resort to the second method? The approach to be undertaken is dependent on the requirement of the class. If the class requires inheriting any other class, then obviously the Thread class cannot be inherited, as multiple inheritance is not allowed in Java. So the obvious solution in this case is to use the interface, i.e., Runnable. [Remember: any numbers of interfaces can be inherited by a class.]

Some other constructors belonging to the Thread class are worth mentioning here, as these can be used while creating thread using Runnable interface.

- Thread(Runnable threadObj)
- Thread(Runnable threadObj, String threadName)
- Thread(ThreadGroup threadGroup, Runnable threadObj)
- Thread(ThreadGroup threadGroup, Runnable threadObj, String threadName)

The above threadObj is a reference to an instance of a class that implements the Runnable interface and overrides the run() method. This defines where the execution will begin. As mentioned earlier, the object's run() method's code is responsible for giving the functionality to the new thread. threadName is the name of the thread. In case no name is passed externally to the constructors, the JVM is automatically going to name it. The third argument, threadGroup is the group name to which the thread belongs. If no thread group is externally specified, the group is determined by the security managing component or the group is set to the same group, which the invoking thread is a part of.

Once a class that implements the Runnable interface is created, an object of the Thread class must be instantiated from within that class. In Example 8.3, we are going to use the second constructor described in the previous paragraph, i.e.,

```
Thread (Runnable threadObj, String threadName)
```

Even if a thread is created, it will not start executing unless the start() method of the Thread class is called.

Example 8.3 Creating a Thread Using Runnable Interface

```
L1    class ThreadChild implements Runnable {
L2    ThreadChild() {
L3    Thread t = new Thread (this, "Example Thread");
L4    System.out.println("Detail of child thread :" +t);
L5    t.start();
L6    }
L7    public void run(){
L8    try {
L9       for(int i = 1; i<= 5; i++) {
L10      System.out.println("\tFrom child thread 1 : i =" +i);
L11      Thread.sleep(500);
L12   }
L13   } catch(InterruptedException e) {
L14   System.out.println("child Thread 1 interrupted");
L15   }
L16   System.out.println("Exit from child Thread 1");
L17   }
L18   }
L19   class ThreadDemo2 {
L20      public static void main(String args[]) {
L21      new ThreadChild();
L22      try{
L23      for(int m=1; m<=5; m++) {
L24      System.out.println("\tFrom Main Thread : m =" +m);
L25      Thread.sleep(1000);
L26   }
L27   } catch(InterruptedException e){
L28   System.out.println("Main interrupted");
L29   }
L30   System.out.println("Exit from main thread");
L31   }
L32   }
```

Output

```
Detail of child thread :Thread[Example Thread,5,main]
From Main Thread : m = 1
From child thread 1 :i = 1
From child thread 1 :i = 2
From child thread 1 :i = 3
From Main Thread : m = 2
From child thread 1 :i = 4
From Main Thread : m = 3
From child thread 1 :i = 5
Exit from child Thread 1
From Main Thread : m = 4
From Main Thread : m = 5
Exit from main thread
```

Explanation

L1 A class, `ThreadChild`, implementing the `Runnable` interface is declared. This class is responsible for the creation of the child thread, spawning out of the main thread.

L2 A constructor, `ThreadChild()`, is declared.

L3 Inside `ThreadChild()` constructor, a thread object `t` is created. Passing `this` as the first argument shows that the current class has inherited the `Runnable` interface. It is this class' object that will tell what the thread is going to perform because it has overridden the `run()` method.

L5 The `start()` method is called, which starts the execution of the thread by invoking the `run()`.

L7–15 `run()` is declared (L7) . It will be called automatically whenever this thread is scheduled by the thread scheduler. [Remember: explicit call to `run()`will invoke it from the caller thread rather than its own thread]. A `for` loop is declared to loop five times to display the numbers from 1 to 5. After displaying each number on the screen, the thread sleeps for half a second. You can see the `try...catch` block, which is placed to catch the `InterruptedException` thrown by the `sleep()` method.

L16 We intend to display the exit of the child thread created inside the `ThreadChild` class.

L19 Class `ThreadDemo2` containing the `main` thread is declared (L31).

L20–26 The `main` method is declared (L20). The constructor `ThreadChild()` is instantiated (L21). This instantiation invokes the constructor declared between L2–6. The `try...catch` block between L22–26 constitutes the body of the `main` thread. A `for` loop is declared to loop five times and it displays the number from 1 to 5. After displaying each number on the screen, it sleeps for one second.

8.6 `Thread.State` IN JAVA

In the process-based multitasking, the operating system manages the context switching between programs based on the time slice provided for each program segment, but in case of multithreading, Java Runtime manages threads. Here, execution of one thread stops while the other continues, as the switching takes place within the same program amongst different threads. Before Java 5.0, Java had thread states similar to the thread states of an operating system. Java 5.0 came up with a static nested class named as `State`, which is made a part of the `Thread` class. This `Thread` class is made to inherit the abstract class `Enum`. This class `Enum` is a common base class of all Java language enumeration types. In other words, `Thread.State` is actually an enumeration type declared as follows:

```
public static enum Thread.State extends Enum
```

The enumeration `Thread.State` has the possible states of a Java thread in the underlying JVM. At any time, a thread is said to be in one of the states mentioned below. Figure 8.1 shows the various states in which a Java thread exists during its life. Some of the methods responsible for the transition from one state to another are also shown. Obviously, the diagram is not exhaustive, as it does not mention all such responsible methods. It is just an overview of a thread's life.

New In this state, a new thread is created but not started. The following line of code is responsible for the same (assuming `ThreadDemo` class has inherited the `Thread` class or `Runnable` interface):

```
Thread threadObj = new ThreadDemo();
```

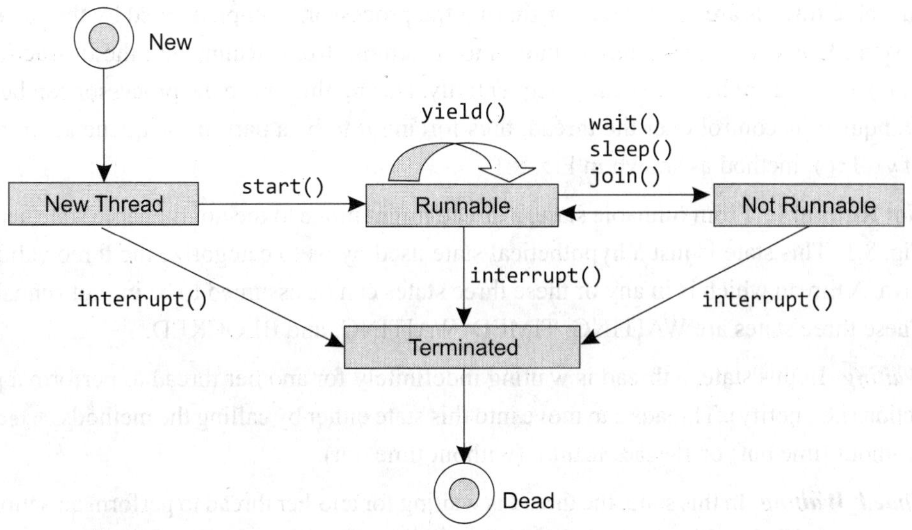

Fig. 8.1 Thread States

The above statement is responsible for creating a new `Thread` object. In 'New' state, no system resource (such as CPU) is allotted to the newly born `Thread` object. From this state, the thread can either be started (by using `start()` of `Thread` class) or stopped (by using `interrupt()` of `Thread` class), thus moving to 'Runnable' or 'Terminated' state, respectively. No other method apart from `start()` and `interrupt()` can be called from this state and if tried to do so, it would cause an exception, `IllegalThreadStateException`.

Runnable In this state, a thread is ready for execution by the JVM. It represents the running state of the thread, as well. Ready state of a thread can be defined as it is ready for execution but it might be in the queue, waiting for the operating system to provide it the required resource, like processor. Once a thread is actually being executed by the processor then it is termed as "Running". From 'New' state the thread might move to the 'Runnable' state on execution of the following statements:

```
Thread threadObj = new ThreadDemo();
threadObj.start();
```

As soon as `start()` is called, the thread is allotted the system resource as per the scheduling done by the Java Runtime Environment. Now the thread has entered into the runnable state. In Fig. 8.1, no differentiation is made between a running thread and a runnable thread. Even the running threads are made a part of the runnable state. But there is a difference between the two. A running thread is the one which is being executed by the processor. Such a thread can be called as the *current thread*. Runnable threads are those which are not actually running, but are scheduled in queue to get the processor. The scheduling scheme, under which all the runnable threads are prioritized for sharing the processor, is implemented by the Java Runtime system. However, when a thread moves to 'Running' from 'Runnable', the instructions of the `run()` method are being executed sequentially. During this phase the processor can be forced to relinquish its control over the thread, thus forcing it to be a part of the queue again by the use of `yield()` method as shown in Fig. 8.1.

Not Runnable   From runnable state, a thread might move to the not runnable state, as shown in Fig. 8.1. This state is just a hypothetical state used by us to categorize the three valid states of Java. A thread which is in any of these three states can be assumed to be in 'not runnable' state. These three states are WAITING, TIMED_WAITING, and BLOCKED.

Waiting   In this state, a thread is waiting indefinitely for another thread to perform a particular action (i.e., notify). Threads can move into this state either by calling the methods `Object.wait()` (without time out) or `Thread.join()` (without time out).

Timed_Waiting   In this state, the thread is waiting for another thread to perform an action (notify) up to a specified waiting time. A thread can get into this state by calling either of these methods: `Thread.sleep()`, `Object.wait()`, and `Thread.join()` (all these methods should be called with time out specified).

Blocked   In this state, a resource cannot be accessed because it is being used by another thread. A thread can get into this state by calling `Object.wait()` method.

Before proceeding further, we must discuss the concept of monitors in Java. This is taken up in greater detail in Section 8.8. Monitor is an object that is a mutually exclusive lock on the resource to be accessed. A monitor can be owned by only one thread at a time. When a thread calls `Object.wait()` method, it releases all the acquired monitors and is put into WAITING state, until some other thread enters the same monitor and calls `notify()/notifyAll()`. When `notify()` is called, it wakes up a thread that called `wait()` on the same object. The method `notifyAll()` will wake up all the threads that called `wait()` on the same object. The difference between two methods is that, if `notify()` is used, then only one thread (selected by the JVM scheduler) is granted the monitor and all other threads are put into BLOCKED state, whereas if you use `notifyAll()`, it wakes up all the threads and puts them into ready state. The threads that can execute, start executing, and the rest move into the waiting state. The three methods mentioned above are `final` methods of the `ObjectClass`, so all classes have them.

```
final void wait() throws InterruptedException;
final void notify()
final void notifyAll()
```

Additional form of `wait()` where time can be specified for the thread to wait for that period, is also available. It puts the thread in TIMED_WAITING state. We can easily figure out that a WAITING state thread will always be dependent on an action performed by some other thread, whereas a thread in TIMED_WAITING is not completely dependent on an action performed by some other thread, as in this case, the wait ends automatically after the completion of the time out period. Similarly, if a thread has put itself into WAITING state by calling `Thread.join()` method, then it will keep waiting until the specified thread terminates or the specified time elapses. There seems to be no difference between `sleep()` and `wait()` as both of them do the same job of making a thread wait for a specified time. The differences between the start methods have been specified in Table 8.2.

Table 8.2 Difference between `wait()` and `sleep()`

`Object.wait()`	`Thread.sleep()`
`wait()` belongs to `Object` class	`sleep()` belongs to `Thread` class.
It can only be used from within the synchronized method or statements.	It can be used from outside the synchronized methods and statements.
Wait state can be terminated by calling `Object.notify()` method.	The sleep state can be terminated by invoking `interrupt()` method of the thread instance.
`Object.wait()` is used in concurrent thread access codes only.	`Thread.sleep(int ms)` is used wherever and whenever required method.
It stops the current thread execution and releases the lock of the object. Now other threads can use this released object.	`Thread.sleep(int ms)` causes the current thread to suspend execution for a specified number of milliseconds. This can let other threads to use the resources being held by the previous thread

Terminated

This state is reached when the thread has finished its execution. A thread can move to 'Terminated' state, from any of the above mentioned states. In this state, the thread is dead. The death of a thread can either be natural or forceful. A thread dies naturally when it exits `run()` normally. The normal exit from `run()` means the instructions of the `run()` has been processed completely. For example, the `for` loop in the following method is a finite loop which would iterate 5 times (i.e., from 1 to 5) and then exit.

```java
public void run(){
for(int i = 1; i<= 5; i++)
{
    System.out.println("i =" +i);
    Thread.sleep(500);
}
}
```

A thread with the above `run()` method will die naturally after the last statement of `run()` completes. A thread can always be interrupted by using `interrupt()`. The following block of code does the job of killing a thread by calling `interrupt()` method.

We can know the state of a particular thread by using `getState()` method. The following program shows the usage of `getState()` and `interrupt()` methods.

Example 8.4 Using `interrupt()` and `getState()`

```
L1    class ThreadInterrupt extends Thread {
L2    boolean interrupt = false;
L3    String name;
L4    ThreadInterrupt(String n){
L5    super(n);
L6    name = n;
      }
L7    public void run(){
L8    while (!interrupt){
L9    System.out.println("Thread running: " +name+ " state: " +getState());
L10   try{
L11   Thread.sleep(1000);
L12   } catch(InterruptedException e){
L13   System.out.println("Thread Interrupted:" +name + "state:" +getState());
      }
      }
L14   System.out.println("Thread exiting under request: "+name + "state: "+getState());
      }
L15   public static void main(String args[]) throws Exception {
L16   ThreadInterrupt thread = new ThreadInterrupt("InterruptExample");
L17   System.out.println("Starting Thread: " +thread.name + "state: " +thread.getState());
L18   thread.start();
L19   Thread.sleep(3000);
L20   System.out.println("Stopping Thread: " +thread.name + "state: " +thread.getState());
L21   thread.interrupt = true;
L22   thread.interrupt();
L23   System.out.println(thread.name +" state: "+thread.getState());
L24   Thread.sleep(3000);
L25   System.out.println("Exiting application state: " +thread.getState());
L26   System.exit(0);
      }}
```

Output

```
C:\javabook\programs\chap 8>java ThreadInterrupt
Starting Thread: InterruptExample state: NEW
Thread running: InterruptExample state: RUNNABLE
Thread running: InterruptExample state: RUNNABLE
Thread running: InterruptExample state: RUNNABLE
Stopping Thread: InterruptExample state: TIMED_WAITING
InterruptExample state: TIMED_WAITING
Thread Interrupted: InterruptExample state: RUNNABLE
Thread exiting under request: InterruptExamplestate : RUNNABLE
Exiting application state: TERMINATED
```

Explanation

L1 A thread class is created.

L2 A Boolean variable `interrupt` (similar to a flag) has been defined to check the thread interrupted status.

L3 A string instance variable `name` has been defined to assign a name to the thread.

L4–6 Constructor for the class has been defined. This constructor sets the name of the thread by using the `super` constructor call and assigns the argument value to the string variable `name`.

L7 The `run()` method which states what the thread has to perform is overridden.

L8 It checks the status of the `interrupt` flag and if it is false, the `while` loop keeps on executing.

L9 It is a print statement that displays the name of the thread along with its state. The current state of the thread is obtained using the method `getState()`. The state of a thread if enquired from a run method will always be RUNNABLE as the run method is only executed when a thread is executing. (See output)

L10–13 A `try...catch` block has been defined because the thread is made to sleep for a second using `Thread.sleep(1000)` method and the `sleep` method may throw `InterruptedException`, if interrupted. So it has to be caught. The `throws` keyword cannot be used with the `run` method as the method is overridden and the parent interface (`Runnable`) does not mention any `throws` clause with the definition of the `run` method. So during overriding, the definition of the method cannot be changed. If an exception is generated, it is caught by the catch defined in L12 and L13 is executed, which displays `Thread Interrupted:` followed by the name of the thread and its state (i.e. RUNNABLE).

L14 It is the final print statement in the `run` method that displays the thread exiting under request followed by the name of the thread and its state, i.e., RUNNABLE. This line will be executed after the while loop exits.

L15 It defines the starting point for the execution of the program, i.e., the `main` method.

L16 A new thread is created and the name for the thread is passed as an argument in the constructor of the thread.

L17 Shows a print statement that displays `Starting Thread` followed by the name of the thread and its state. The thread has just been created, so its state will be NEW.

L18 Starts the thread by using the `start()` method on the newly created thread instance in L16. The `run` method for this thread will be called automatically as the thread is scheduled for execution (L7). As the interrupt flag is initially false, the while loop in the run method will execute and L9 will keep on executing.

L19 The `main` thread is made to sleep for 3 seconds. So the other thread `InterruptedExample` will keep on executing and sleeping (1 second only).

L20 Shows a print statement that displays the `Stopping Thread:` followed by the name of the thread and its state. If you see the output, the state of the thread displayed is TIMED_WAITING because the `InterruptedExample` thread is sleeping for 1 second and the main thread is executing at this moment.

L21–22 The `interrupt` boolean variable is set to `true` and the `InterruptedExample` thread is interrupted using `interrupt()`. Note that the `InterruptedThread` is sleeping and if a thread is interrupted while it is sleeping, an `InterruptedException` is generated. This exception will be caught at the `catch` defined in L12 and this block will execute as soon as the thread regains CPU, in other words is scheduled by the scheduler.

L23 Shows a print statement that displays the name of the thread and its state. If you see the output, the state of the thread is still TIMED_WAITING because the `InterruptedExample` thread is still not allowed to execute as the `main` thread is executing.

L24 The `main` thread is deliberately made to sleep to allow the other thread to execute. At this stage, the control passes to `catch` in L12. L13 executes followed by L14 and then the `run` method exits.

L25 Shows a print statement that displays Exiting Application followed by the state of the child thread (created from main) i.e., `InterruptedExample`. The `run` method for the thread `InterruptedExample` has exited, so the state is now TERMINTAED (see output).

L26 The application is terminated using the `exit` method of the `System` class.

There was one more method, stop(), which has now been deprecated, used to terminate a thread. The reason for this deprecation is that it throws a ThreadDeath object at the thread to kill it. Apart from this, calling stop() method results in sudden termination of thread's run() method, which might lead to the results achieved by the thread program in inconsistent or undesirable state.

8.7 THREAD PRIORITY

Each thread has a set priority, which helps the scheduler to decide the order of sequence of thread execution, i.e., when should which thread run? By default the threads created, carry the same priority, due to which the Java scheduler schedules them for the processor on first-come-first-serve basis. It is to be noted that Java follows preemptive scheduling policy, just like an operating system. When a high priority thread becomes ready for execution, the currently executing low priority will be stopped. On the contrary, a low priority thread cannot preempt a currently running high priority thread. It has to wait until the high priority thread is dead or blocked because of some reason or the other. The reasons for this can be any of the following:

- Thread stops as soon as it exits run()
- It sleeps (by using sleep())
- It waits (by using wait() or join())

Once it resumes from the blocked state, it will again preempt the low priority thread to which it had relinquished its control earlier, thus forcing the low priority to move to the runnable state from the running state.

Note Higher priority threads will always preempt the lower priority threads. Actually it depends on how the priorities of threads set by the JVM are mapped to the operating system. It might happen that a higher priority might not be considered higher by the operating system. So this actually depends on the operating system and it varies from OS to another.

As shown in Table 8.3, the Thread class has a method setPriority(), responsible for setting the priority of the thread by programmer. The signature of the method is

```
final void setPriority(int x)
```

where x specifies the value used to signify the thread's priority. Thread class defines several predefined priority constants (as static final variables) as shown in Table 8.3.

Table 8.3 Priority Constants and their Corresponding Value for Threads

Constant	Value	Meaning
MIN_PRIORITY	1	Max priority a thread can have
NORM_PRIORITY	5	Default priority a thread can have
MAX_PRIORITY	10	Min priority a thread can have

From the above table, it is clear that priority can be set in the form of values between 1 and 10. If this priority is not externally assigned, by default it is set to NORM_PRIORITY, i.e., 5.

A thread's current priority can be obtained by the getPriority() of the thread class, which returns an integer value.

```
finalintgetPriority()
```

Here is an example that shows the use of priority constants and `getPriority()` method.

Example 8.5   Setting and Getting Priorities of Threads

```
L1   class ThreadOne extends Thread {
L2   public void run(){
L3   try {
L4     for(int i = 1; i<= 5; i++){
L5         System.out.println("\tFrom child thread 1 : i =" +i);
L6         Thread.sleep(500);
L7       }
L8   } catch(InterruptedException e){
L9     System.out.println("child Thraed 1 interrupted");
L10  }
L11  System.out.println("Exit from child Thread 1");
L12  }
L13  }
L14  class ThreadTwo extends Thread {
L15  public void run() {
L16  try {
L17    for(int j = 1; j <= 5; j++) {
L18        System.out.println("\tFrom child thread 2 : j =" +j);
L19        Thread.sleep(500);
L20      }
L21  } catch (InterruptedException e) {
L22    System.out.println("child thread 2 interrupted");
L23  }
L24  System.out.println("Exit from child thraed 2");
L25  }
L26  }
L27  class ThreadThree extends Thread {
L28  public void run() {
L29  try{
L30    for(int k = 1; k <= 5; k++) {
L31        System.out.println("\tFrom child thread 3 : k =" +k);
L32        Thread.sleep(500);
L33      }
L34  } catch (InterruptedException e) {
L35    System.out.println("child thread 3 interrupted");
L36  }
L37  System.out.println("Exit from child thread 3");
L38  }
L39  }
L40  class ThreadPriority {
L41  public static void main(String args[]) {
L42    ThreadOne a = new ThreadOne();
L43    ThreadTwo b = new ThreadTwo();
L44    ThreadThree c = new ThreadThree();
L45    System.out.println("Default Priority for thread 1:" +a.getPriority());
L46    System.out.println("Default Priority for thread 2:" +b.getPriority());
```

```
L47      System.out.println("Default Priority for thread 3:" +c.getPriority());
L48      System.out.println(" ");
L49      a.setPriority(Thread.MIN_PRIORITY);
L50      b.setPriority(Thread.NORM_PRIORITY);
L51      c.setPriority(Thread.MAX_PRIORITY);
L52      System.out.println("Priority set for thread 1 :" +a.getPriority());
L53      System.out.println("Priority set for thread 2 :" +b.getPriority());
L54      System.out.println("Priority set for thread 3 :" +c.getPriority());
L55      System.out.println(" ");
L56      System.out.println("All the Three threads start from here");
L57      a.start();
L58      b.start();
L59      c.start();
L60   }
L61   }
```

Output

```
Default Priority for thread 1 :5
Default Priority for thread 2 :5
Default Priority for thread 3 :5
New Priority set for thread 1 :1
New Priority set for thread 2 :5
New Priority set for thread 3 :10
All the Three threads start
  from here From child thread
  3 : k = 1 From child thread
  2 : j = 1 From child thread
  1 : i = 1 From child thread
  3 : k = 2 From child thread
  2 : j = 2 From child thread
  1 : i = 2 From child thread
  3 : k = 3 From child thread
  2 : j = 3 From child thread
  1 : i = 3 From child thread
  3 : k = 4 From child thread
  2 : j = 4 From child thread
  1 : i = 4 From child thread
  3 : k = 5 From child thread
  2 : j = 5 From child thread
  1 : i = 5
Exit from child thread 3
Exit from child thread 2
Exit from child thread 1
```

Explanation

L1–39   These lines have the details about declaring three different classes, ThreadOne, ThreadTwo, and ThreadThree, each extending the Thread class. Each of these child thread classes have already been explained in Example 8.2.

L40   Main thread class threadPriority is declared.

L41   The main() method is declared.

L42–45   Reference objects for the three child thread classes are created and stored in a, b, and c.

L45 Default priority for child thread one is displayed. You can see the use of `getPriority()` method, which has been called using the object of `ThreadOne` class. This method returns the current priority of the thread pertaining to `ThreadOne` class.

L46–47 Just like child thread one, the current priority of child thread two and child thread three is displayed.

L49 Object a of child thread class, `ThreadOne` invokes its `setPriority()` method to set the priority for the execution of threads, so as to schedule the threads externally. You can see that the priority for thread one is set to minimum priority, i.e., 1, by passing it as argument to `setPriority()`.

L50 Similar to thread one, the object of child thread two invokes its `setPriority()` method to set the priority of the thread to normal priority, i.e., 5.

L51 The object of child thread three is used to call its `setPriority()` method to set the priority of the thread to highest priority, i.e., 10.

L52–54 New priorities of the three children threads are displayed. Once more, `getPriority()` method can prove to be instrumental for the purpose of obtaining the newly set priorities of the threads.

L57–59 From within the main thread, all the three threads started using the `start()`methods corresponding the thread objects. The respective `run` () methods of the thread objects will be executed as and when the threads are scheduled for execution.

8.8 MULTITHREADING—USING `isAlive()` AND `join()`

The main thread should always be the last thread to end, i.e., all the child threads spawned out of the main thread should end executing before the main itself. The execution of main thread can be prolonged using `Thread.sleep()` method. The time for which the main should be made to sleep cannot be estimated exactly, as the time taken by child thread is difficult to estimate. If we fall short on our estimation, then the child thread will terminate after the termination of main thread, which is not something we want. This is the lacuna associated with sleep technique.

Two other methods which generally work in tandem can be used to resolve the above mentioned crisis: `isAlive()` and `join()`. Both the methods as mentioned in Table 8.1 are part of the `Thread` class. `isAlive()` method returns a boolean value. It returns 'true' if the thread is active, i.e., it has started and not stopped. If it returns 'false', the thread can either be a new thread or a dead thread. In other words, if `isAlive()` returns 'true', the thread can be comprehended to be either in 'Runnable' or 'Not Runnable' state, otherwise it is in 'Dead' state. The `isAlive()` method can be used to check whether the child thread is running or not. The method as defined in the `Thread` class is as follows:

```
final boolean isAlive()
```

As far as the `join()` method is concerned, it waits until the thread on which it is called terminates. It waits for the child thread to terminate and then *joins* the main thread. Apart from this, `join()` method can also be used to specify the amount of time you want the child thread to wait before terminating. Example 8.6 shows the use of these two methods.

Example 8.6 **Use of `join()` in Forcing a Thread to Wait for Other's Termination**

```
L1    class ThreadJoin implements Runnable {
L2    String thread;
L3    Thread thrd;
```

```
L4      ThreadJoin (String threadName) {
L5      thread = threadName;
L6      thrd = new Thread (this, thread);
L7      thrd.start();
L8      }
L9      public void run() {
L10     try {
L11     Thread.sleep(2000);
L12     for(int i = 1; i<= 3; i++) {
L13     System.out.println("\t From child thread " + thread + " : i = "+i);
L14     }
L15     } catch(InterruptedException e ) {
L16     System.out.println("Exception: Thread "+ thread + " interrupted");
L17     }
L18     System.out.println("Terminating thread: " + thread );
L19     }
L20     }
L21     class JoinDemo {
L22     public static void main (String args []) {
L23     ThreadJoin threadA = new ThreadJoin ("A");
L24     ThreadJoin threadB = new ThreadJoin ("B");
L25     ThreadJoin threadC = new ThreadJoin ("C");
L26     ThreadJoin threadD = new ThreadJoin ("D");
L27     System.out.println("Thread Status: Alive");
L28     System.out.println("Thread A: " +threadA.thrd.isAlive());
L30     System.out.println("Thread B: " +threadB.thrd.isAlive());
L31     System.out.println("Thread C: " +threadC.thrd.isAlive());
L32     System.out.println("Thread D: " +threadD.thrd.isAlive());
L33     try {
L34     System.out.println("Threads Joining......");
L35     threadA.thrd.join();
L36     threadB.thrd.join();
L37     threadC.thrd.join();
L38     threadD.thrd.join();
L39     } catch (InterruptedException e){
L40     System.out.println("Exception: Thread main interrupted.");
L41     }
L42     System.out.println("Thread Status: Alive");
L43     System.out.println("Thread A: " + threadA.thrd.isAlive());
L44     System.out.println("Thread B: " + threadB.thrd.isAlive());
L45     System.out.println("Thread C: " + threadC.thrd.isAlive());
L46     System.out.println("Thread D: " + threadD.thrd.isAlive());
L47     System.out.println("Terminating thread: main thread.");
L48     }
L49     }
```

Output

```
Thread Status: Alive
Thread A: true
Thread B: true
Thread C: true
```

```
Thread D: true
Threads Joining......
    From child thread A :i = 1
    From child thread A :i = 2
    From child thread A :i = 3
Terminating thread: A
    From child thread B :i = 1
    From child thread B :i = 2
    From child thread B :i = 3
Terminating thread: B
    From child thread C :i = 1
    From child thread C :i = 2
    From child thread C :i = 3
Terminating thread: C
    From child thread D :i = 1
    From child thread D :i = 2
    From child thread D :i = 3
Terminating thread: D
  Thread Status: Alive
  Thread A: false
  Thread B: false
  Thread C: false
  Thread D: false
  Terminating thread: main thread.
```

Explanation

(*Only those lines relevant to the topic are explained.*)

L28–32 After the threads are declared using the constructor of the `MyThread` class, the `isAlive()` method is called for each thread. The value returned by the `isAlive()` method is then displayed on the screen.

L35–38 The `join()` method is called for each thread. The `join()` method causes the main thread to wait for all child threads to complete execution before the main thread terminates.

L43–46 Again the `isAlive()` method is used with each thread's object to check whether the child threads are alive or dead and the boolean values are displayed on the screen.

8.9 SYNCHRONIZATION

There can be instances when two or more threads access a common resource, say a common data or file. In order to maintain consistency, it becomes imperative that the resource is made available to only one thread at a time. For example, there are two threads, one responsible for writing to a file (here, a resource) and other for reading from the same file. If both the threads start concurrently, both would try to access the file at the same time. Obviously, if the first thread has not written the values completely, the values read by the second thread would be inconsistent. Java has such inbuilt mechanism, which lets only one thread use a resource at a time, known as *synchronization*. Usually, operating systems do provide for such mechanism, but Java has a unique language level support for it.

How does it work? Many of you, having the knowledge of operating systems, would know what *semaphores* are. Likewise, we have the concept of *monitor*s here. *Monitor* is an object that is used as a mutually exclusive lock on the resource to be accessed. A monitor can be owned by only one thread at a time. A thread enters the *monitor* as soon as it acquires the lock. All the other threads cannot enter the locked *monitor*, unless it is unlocked or the first thread exits the monitor. During this period, other threads are waiting for the lock on the *monitor*. If a thread exits the *monitor*, it can again enter the same *monitor* at some later stage.

This synchronizing mechanism mentioned above can be achieved in Java in two ways:

(a) By using the synchronized keyword with the method definition (synchronized methods)

(b) By using the synchronized keyword with any block of code (synchronized statements)

8.9.1 Synchronized Methods

We can make a particular method synchronized by declaring it so, as under,

```
class Xyz {
  synchronized anyMethod()
  {
  ......
  //method body
  }
}
```

You can see the use of 'synchronized' prefixing the method declaration. Now, if 'n' number of threads want to use the method, anyMethod(), the system will not allow them to do so. The highest priority thread will lock the monitor for the method, making it inaccessible to other threads. Once the thread locking for the monitor finishes its job, it releases the monitor for the use of other waiting threads.

8.9.2 Synchronized Statements

We can synchronize a block of code by using the keyword synchronized. Just like synchronizing a method, here the word synchronized is used before the block of code to be synchronized. This synchronized statement must specify the object that provides the monitor lock. An example for such a block is given below,

```
public void anyBlock()
{
synchronized (this)
{
......
//statement for the body of block
......
}
}
```

8.10 SUSPENDING AND RESUMING THREADS

There are two methods, suspend() and resume(), used for suspending an executing thread temporarily and resuming the suspension, respectively. But since Java 1.2, these methods have been deprecated. Then, how will you deal with the requirements that used to be fulfilled by these methods? These objectives can be achieved by defining your own suspend and resume methods, as shown in the following example:

Example 8.7 Suspending and Resuming a Thread

```
L1    class SusResThread implements Runnable {
L2    String n;
L3    Thread thrd;
L4    boolean suspended;
L5    SusResThread() {
L6      thrd = new Thread(this, "Suspend-Resume Thread");
L7      suspended = false ;
L8      thrd.start();
L9      }
L10   public void run() {
L11     try {
L12         for (int i = 0; i< 10; i++){
L13         System.out.println("Thread: " + i );
L14         Thread.sleep(200);
L15         synchronized (this) {
L16         while (suspended) {
L17               wait();
L18         }
L19     }
L20   }
L21   } catch (InterruptedException e) {
L22   System.out.println("thread interrupted.");
L23   }
L24   System.out.println("Exit from thread.");
L25   }
L26   void susThread() {
L27   suspended = true;
L28   }
L29   synchronized void resThread(){
L30   suspended = false;
L31   notify();
L32   }
L33   }

L34   class SuspendResume {
L35   public static void main (String args []) {
L36     SusResThread thrd1 = new SusResThread ();
L37     try{
L38         Thread.sleep(1000);
L39         thrd1.susThread();
L40         System.out.println("Thread has been Suspended");
L41         Thread.sleep(1000);
L42         thrd1.resThread();
L43         System.out.println("Thread has been Resumed");
L44     }catch (InterruptedException e) {
L45   }
L46   try {
L47   thrd1.thrd.join();
L48   } catch (InterruptedException e){
```

```
L49   System.out.println ("Main Thread: interrupted");
L50   }
L51   }
L52   }
```

You can easily see in the output shown below that the thread displays the value of the variable used in the loop, i.e., i, until the thread is suspended. It resumes its work of displaying the values from the point where it was suspended.

Output

```
Thread: 0
Thread: 1
Thread: 2
Thread: 3
Thread: 4
Thread: Suspended
Thread: Resume
Thread: 5
Thread: 6
Thread: 7
Thread: 8
Thread: 9
Exit from thread.
```

Explanation

L1 Defines a SusResThread class that implements the Runnable interface. This class houses three methods, run(), susThread(), and resThread().

L4 An instance variable, suspended, is declared, whose value is used to indicate whether or not the thread is suspended.

L10–19 run() is declared, which contains a for loop that displays the value of the counter variable, i. Each time the counter variable is displayed, the thread pauses briefly due to the method sleep(1000). In L15, it then enters a synchronized statement to determine whether the value of the suspended instance variable is 'true'. If so, wait() is called, which causes the thread to be suspended until notify() is called.

L26–28 susThread() is declared, which is used for assigning 'true' to the instance variable, suspended.

L29–32 resThread() is declared, which is used for assigning 'false' to the instance variable, suspended. In L31, notify() is called to resume the processing of the suspended thread.

L35–51 The main() method of the SuspendResume class is declared, where an instance of SusResThread class is created, as shown in L36. The execution then pauses for about a second because of sleep(1000) at L38, before calling susThread() and displaying a message about the suspension of the thread on the screen (L39). Similarly, it pauses for another second because of another sleep (1000) at L41, before calling resThread() (L42) and again displaying a message about the resumption of the thread on the screen, as shown in L43.

8.11 COMMUNICATION BETWEEN THREADS

As we have said, threads are parts of a program which execute simultaneously. But at times, these threads need to coordinate amongst themselves. This communication between the threads, while their simultaneous execution is on, can be termed as *inter-thread communication*.

We have already discussed about the methods, `wait()`, `notify()`, and `notifyAll()`. These are the methods, which help the threads in communicating with each other. One important thing is the use of synchronization in communication between threads, as the above three methods are called from `synchronized` methods and `synchronized` statements.

The following example shows you how to use the above methods in an application. This example defines four classes: the `Carrier` class, the `Giver` class, the `Taker` class, and the `Comm Thread` class. The objective of the program is to have the `Giver` class give a value to the `Taker` class through the use of a `Carrier` class. The `Giver` class places a value on the `Carrier` and then waits until the `Taker` class retrieves the value before the `Giver` class places another value on the queue.

Example 8.8 Communication Between Threads

```
L1    class Carrier {
L2    int CommunicatedValue;
L3    boolean busy = false;
L4    synchronized void putValue (int CommunicatedValue){
L5    if (busy)
L6    try {
L7    wait();
L8    } catch(InterruptedException e) {
L9    System.out.println("Put Value: InterruptedException");
L10   }
L11   this.CommunicatedValue = CommunicatedValue;
L12   busy = true;
L13   System.out.println("Put: " + CommunicatedValue);
L14   notify();
L15   }
L16   synchronized int getValue() {
L17   if (!busy)
L18   try {
L19   wait();
L20   } catch (InterruptedException e) {
L21   System.out.println("Get Value: InterruptedException");
L22   } busy = false;
L23   System.out.println("Get: " + CommunicatedValue);
L24   notify();
L25   return CommunicatedValue;
L26   }
L27   }
L28   class Giver implements Runnable {
L29   Carrier c;
L30   Giver(Carrier c){
L31   this.c = c;
L32   new Thread (this, "Value Giver").start();
L33   }
L34   public void run(){
L35     for (int i = 0; i< 5; i++){
L36     c.putValue(i);
```

```
L37        }
L38     }
L39     }
L40     class Taker implements Runnable {
L41       Carrier c;
L42       Taker (Carrier c){
L43         this.c = c;
L44         new Thread (this, "Taker thread").start();
L45     }
L46     public void run(){
L47        for (int i = 0; i< 5; i++){
L48        c.getValue();
L49        }
L50     }
L51     }
L52     class CommThread {
L53     public static void main(String args []){
L54     Carrier c = new Carrier ();
L55     new Giver (c);
L56     new Taker (c);
L57     }
L58     }
```

One thing worth noting is that the value placed on the `Carrier` by the `Giver` is retrieved by the `Taker`. The `Giver` places the next value only when the previous value is retrieved by the `Taker`.

Output

```
Put: 0
Get: 0
Put: 1
Get: 1
Put: 2
Get: 2
Put: 3
Get: 3
Put: 4
Get: 4
```

Explanation

L1 The `Carrier` class is defined.

L2 Instance variable, `communicatedValue`, is used to store the value placed on the `Carrier` by the `Giver`.

L3 A flag variable of boolean type, `busy`, is declared, which is used to check whether a value has been placed on the `Carrier`. It is set to 'false' by default, which enables the `Giver` to place a value onto the `Carrier`.

L4–15 `putValue()` is declared and defined (L4). The purpose is to place a value on the `Carrier` (i.e., to assign a value to the communicated Value variables

(L11)). Once the value is assigned, `putValue()` changes the value of the flag from 'false' to 'true' (L12), indicating there is a value on the `Carrier`.

L5–15 The value of the flag is used within the two methods to make the thread that calls the method wait until either there is a value on the `Carrier` or there is no value on the `Carrier`, depending on which method is being called.

L16–27 `getValue()` is defined (L16). This method is used to retrieve the value contained on the `Carrier` (i.e., to return the value of `communicatedValue` (L23)).

L28–38 The thread class `Giver` is declared, which implements `Runnable` (L28). This class declares an instance of the `Carrier` class (L29) and then calls `putValue()` to place five integers on the `Carrier` (L36). Although the `putValue()` method is called within a `for` loop, each integer is placed on the `Carrier` and then, there is a pause until the integer is retrieved by the `Taker` class. The `Taker` class is very similar in design to the `Giver` class, except the `Taker` class calls `getValue()` five times from within a `for` loop. Each call to `getValue()` is paused until the `Giver` class places an integer in the `Carrier`. **L52–58** The `main()` method of the `CommThread` class creates instances of the `Carrier` class (L45). Notice that a reference to the instance of the `Carrier` class is passed to both the constructors of the `Giver` class and the `Taker` class. They use the instance of the `Carrier` class for inter-thread communication.

8.12 PRACTICAL PROBLEM: TIME CLOCK EXAMPLE

Let us take a concrete example to illustrate the utility of threads in applications. We will create a time thread which would display the current date and time on the console with every tick of the second similar to a clock (as is evident from the output). The GUI cannot be implemented in this example so we will be printing the time at the DOS prompt. We have not dealt with graphics in Java as yet so we will defer that part till Applets and GUI. We will rework this example in Applets to show how `Threads` can be used in Applets along with GUI. This example creates a thread apart from the main thread when an object of the class is created.

Example 8.9 **Time Clock**

```
L1     import java.util.*;
L2     class TimeThreadDemo
       {
L3       Thread t;
L4       TimeThreadDemo(String name)
L5       {
L6            t = new Thread(new Task(),name);
L7            t.start();
       }
L8       public static void main(String args[])
         {
L9            TimeThreadDemo d=new TimeThreadDemo("Digital clock");
         }
       }
L10    class Task implements Runnable
       {
L11         Calendar c;
L12         Date d;
L13         public void run()
            {
L14                 for(;;)
                    {
L15                 try {
L16                 c = Calendar.getInstance();
L17                 d = c.getTime();
```

```
L18                     System.out.println(d);
L19                     Thread.sleep(1000);
                        }
L20                     catch(Exception e){}
                    }
                }
            }
```

Output

```
Command Prompt - java TimeThreadDemo

D:\javabook\chapter of java book\First Edition\programs>java TimeThreadDemo
Sat Jan 05 18:20:18 IST 2013
Sat Jan 05 18:20:19 IST 2013
Sat Jan 05 18:20:20 IST 2013
Sat Jan 05 18:20:21 IST 2013
Sat Jan 05 18:20:22 IST 2013
Sat Jan 05 18:20:23 IST 2013
Sat Jan 05 18:20:24 IST 2013
Sat Jan 05 18:20:25 IST 2013
Sat Jan 05 18:20:26 IST 2013
Sat Jan 05 18:20:27 IST 2013
Sat Jan 05 18:20:28 IST 2013
Sat Jan 05 18:20:29 IST 2013
Sat Jan 05 18:20:30 IST 2013
Sat Jan 05 18:20:31 IST 2013
Sat Jan 05 18:20:32 IST 2013
Sat Jan 05 18:20:33 IST 2013
Sat Jan 05 18:20:34 IST 2013
Sat Jan 05 18:20:35 IST 2013
```

Explanation

L1 The `java.util` package is imported because we will be using `Calendar` and `Date` classes in this class which are part of the `java.util` package.

L2 Class `TimeThreadDemo` is declared

L3 Instance variable of type `Thread` class is created within the class.

L4 Constructor for the class has been defined to accept a `String` argument which will be used to name the thread created within the constructor.

L6–7 A thread is created by instantiating the `Thread` class and assigning it to the instance variable created in L3. The name of the thread (`string` argument in L4) is passed within the constructor of the `Thread` class along with the object responsible for telling what the thread is going to perform. The object of `Task` class has been passed within the constructor of the `Thread` class to indicate that the object will override the run method and will provide

implementation for the thread. What the thread is going to perform will be implemented by the object of `Task` class. In our earlier examples, we have used this keyword while creating threads because the current object was providing the implementation for `run()` in those cases and setting the task for the threads. `start()` method is invoked on the thread to put it in a ready state where it can be scheduled by the thread scheduler. Please note that this thread is a separate thread now apart from the main thread.

L8–9 `main` method is defined and the object of the `TimeThreadDemo` class is created within this method. This results in calling the constructor of the class which instantiates the `Thread` object and implicitly instantiation of the `task` class also occurs.

L10 Class `Task` is defined to implement `Runnable` interface. The `Runnable` interface is inherited because we want this class to override `run()` and tell the thread what is expected of it. We want this thread to perform a predefined set of task every second, i.e., print the date and time which keeps on ticking like a clock. These steps are implemented within `run()`.

L11–12 Instance variables of `Calendar` class and `Date` classes are defined to get the current date and time.

L13 `run()` is overridden. As soon as the thread created in L6 is scheduled by the scheduler, this method is invoked automatically.

L14 An infinite loop is created to print the time indefinitely second on second.

L15 `try` block is created within the infinite `for` loop.

L16 As `Calendar` is an abstract class, it cannot be instantiated directly. The `Calendar` class provides a static method `getInstance()` which return an instance of `Calendar` class initialized to the current date and time.

L17 Using the instance created in previous line, `getTime()` is invoked to return the date and time encapsulated as a `Date` object. This date object is referenced by instance variable created in L12.

L18 Prints the `Date` object.

L19 We deliberately provide a delay of one second using the `Thread.sleep(1000)` method to give it a feeling of a normal clock. The Thread sleeps for one second and return to its work of printing the date object.

L20 `catch` block has been defined to catch the `InterruptedException` that the `sleep` method might throw.

Note Please note that as the thread works in an infinite loop, the program will not terminate on its own. It has to be terminated by pressing Ctrl+C at the DOS prompt.

SUMMARY

Java has the capability to support multithreading. Thread is a single sequential flow of execution. It is not a program in itself, but it can just be a part of a program. Multithreading enables to write such programs which can have more than one thread, each executing simultaneously. Multithreading ensures running different parts of the same program (different threads) concurrently. It simply helps in increasing the efficiency of CPU, thus reducing its idle time.

Every program written in Java has at least one thread running inside it, i.e., the main thread. At the start of the program, JVM starts executing the main thread which simply calls the `main()` method. The main class supporting multithreading in Java is the `Thread` class, which is a part of `java.lang` package. Threads are created as the instances of this class, which contains the `run()` method. Actually the functionality of the thread can only be achieved by overriding this `run()` method in the class extending the `Thread` class. This `Thread` class is made to inherit the abstract class `Enum`. The `Enum` class is a common base class of all Java language enumeration types. There are two ways of creating a new thread: (i) by extending the `thread` class or (ii) by implementing the runnable interface which is actually implemented by `thread` class. `Thread.State` is an enumeration type, which has five possible states. At any time, a thread is said to be in one of these five states. These states are: new, runnable, waiting, timed_waiting, and terminated.

Threads in Java run on the concept of preemptive scheduling, done by the Java runtime system by assigning priority to every thread. It simply means, threads having higher priority are given preference for getting executed over the threads having lower priority. Thus, we can say that the lower priority thread is preempted by higher priority thread. There is a facility in Java, to synchronize threads so as to avoid unwarranted interleaving between them.

A thread can either die naturally or be forced to die. A thread dies naturally when it exits the `run()` method normally. The normal exit from `run()` means, the instructions of the `run()` have been processed completely. A thread can always be killed or interrupted by calling `interrupt()` method.

EXERCISES

Objective Questions

1. Which type of exception does a `sleep()` method throw?
   - (a) Arithmetic exception
   - (b) Nullpointer exception
   - (c) Arrayindex out of bounds exception
   - (d) Interrupted exception

2. Which state is entered once a thread is created?
   - (a) Ready
   - (b) Running
   - (c) New
   - (d) Terminated

3. Which method is used to know the current state of a thread?
   - (a) `geThreadState()`
   - (b) `getState()`
   - (c) `get()`
   - (d) `getThreadCurrentState()`

4. Which package contains `Thread` classes and interfaces?
   - (a) `java.lang`
   - (b) `java.io`
   - (c) `java.util`
   - (d) `java.thread`

5. Which of the following are termed as not runnable states?
   - (a) READY
   - (b) WAITING
   - (c) TIMED_WAITING
   - (d) BLOCKED

6. Which type of exception does a `join()` method throw?
   - (a) Arithmetic exception
   - (b) Null pointer exception
   - (c) Array index out of bounds exception
   - (d) Interrupted exception

7. Which interface is used to create a Thread?
   - (a) Thread
   - (b) Runnable
   - (c) Cloneable
   - (d) Serializable

8. Which class is used to create a Thread?
   - (a) Thread
   - (b) Runnable
   - (c) ThreadGroup
   - (d) Synchronization

9. Which type of exception does an `interrupt()` method throw?
   - (a) Arithmetic exception
   - (b) Null pointer exception
   - (c) Array index out of bounds exception
   - (d) Interrupted exception

10. What is the priority assigned to all Java threads by default?
    - (a) 1
    - (b) 5
    - (c) 10
    - (d) unassigned

Review Questions

1. Define each of the following terms:
   - (a) Thread
   - (b) Multithreading
   - (c) Waiting state and Timed_waiting state
   - (d) Running state
   - (e) Preemptive scheduling
   - (f) Runnable interface
   - (g) Monitor
   - (h) Notify method
   - (i) `Join()` method
   - (j) Thread class

2. What is a thread? How do threads behave in Java?

3. Distinguish between preemptive scheduling and non-preemptive scheduling. Which one does Java use?

4. What is the purpose of calling the `yield()` method?

5. What is multitasking? Is multithreading a form of multitasking?

6. What is thread priority? How can it be set for a thread?

7. What is synchronization and why is it important?

8. What is runnable interface? How can you use this interface in creating threads?

9. When should you extend the Thread class for creating a thread?

10. If you create two threads in your program, how many threads actually run? Explain the complete flow of execution of threads inside a program.

11. Which method is responsible for creating the body or giving the functionality to a thread in your program? Explain with an example program.

12. Distinguish among each of the following means of pausing threads:
    - `wait()`
    - `sleep()`
    - `yield()`

Programming Exercises

1. Create and run a threaded class using `Runnable` interface.

2. Write a Java program to demonstrate the execution of a high-priority thread and how it delays the execution of all lower-priority threads.

3. Write a Java program that demonstrates how a high-priority thread using sleep makes way for the lower-priority threads to execute.

4. Write a Java program showing the actions from three threads. Use runnable interface to create the threads. Make sure that the main thread always executes last (Hint: use `join()`).

5. Write a program that uses thread synchronization to guarantee data integrity in a multithreaded application.

Input/Output, Serialization, and Cloning

Unless each man produces more than he receives, increases his output, there will be less for him than all the others.

Bernard Baruch

After reading this chapter, the readers will be able to

- understand the basics of file handling
- understand how input/output operation is done in Java
- understand how input is taken from the user
- understand the concept behind serialization and how it is done
- know about the new classes and interfaces in the new IO packages
- perform shallow copy and deep copy

9.1 INTRODUCTION

The two most important parts of a computer are *input* and *output*. It is the input that is processed to generate output. Input/output classes form the core of any programming language. As of Java 1.4, there are two predefined packages named *io* (input/output) and *nio* (new I/O or non-blocking i/o) which contain classes to perform I/O operations. `java.io` package deals with operations such as reading/writing to console and reading/writing to files. The `java.nio` package contains classes that support the classes in the `java.io` package and perform advanced operations such as buffering, memory mapping, character encoding and decoding, pattern matching, and locking a file.

The `java.io` package provides separate classes for reading and writing data (byte and character data). The Java I/O facility is based on *streams*. Stream is a continuous flow of data. In Java, streams for both types of data have been defined: *byte stream classes* and *character stream classes*. Byte stream classes deal with reading and writing of bytes to files, socket, etc. Character stream classes deal with reading and writing of characters to files, socket, etc.

The `java.io` package contains two top level byte stream abstract classes: `java.io.InputStream` (for reading bytes) and `java.io.OutputStream` (for writing bytes). It also contains two other top level character stream abstract classes: `java.io.Reader` (for reading characters) and `java.io.Writer` (for writing characters). The subclasses of these classes are actually used for reading and writing data. We will discuss some of the subclasses in detail.

9.1.1 `java.io.InputStream` and `java.io.OutputStream`

`InputStream` and `OutputStream` are abstract classes which specify certain methods that are applicable to all its subclasses. A list of the methods of `InputStream` and `OutputStream` classes is given in Tables 9.1 and 9.2.

Table 9.1 Methods of `InputStream` Class

Methods	Description
`int available() throws IOException`	Returns the number of available bytes that can be read from an input stream.
`void close() throws IOException`	Closes the input stream.
`void mark(int readlimit)`	Makes a mark at the current position in the input stream. `readlimit` defines after reading how many bytes this mark is nullified.
`boolean markSupported()`	`mark()` method works if this method returns true.
`abstract int read()`	Reads the next byte from the input stream. Subclasses provide implementation for this method. It returns the byte read and –1 if EOF encountered.
`int read(byte[] b)`	Reads bytes and stores them in the byte array b. It returns the number of bytes read into the array and –1 if EOF encountered.
`int read(byte[] b, int off, int len)`	Reads bytes and stores them in byte array b upto length (len) starting from offset (off) in b.
`void reset()`	Resets the current pointer to the mark set by the `mark()` method only if `readlimit` has not expired.
`long skip(long n)`	Skips the specified number of bytes (n) and returns the number of bytes actually skipped.

Table 9.2 Methods of `OutputStream` Class

Methods	Description
`void close()`	Closes the output stream.
`void flush()`	Flushes the output stream.
`void write(byte b[])`	Writes the contents of the byte array to output stream.
`void write(byte b[], int off, int len)`	Writes the specified number of bytes (len) to the output stream starting at offset (off) in b.
`abstract void write(int b)`	Abstract method to write byte to the output stream. Subclasses to provide implementation.

Figures 9.1 and 9.2 show the hierarchy of classes (beneath input stream/output stream and reader/writer) as well as the interfaces in `java.io` package that they inherit. These figures do not show all the classes in `java.io` package. For all classes, refer JDK 6 documentation.

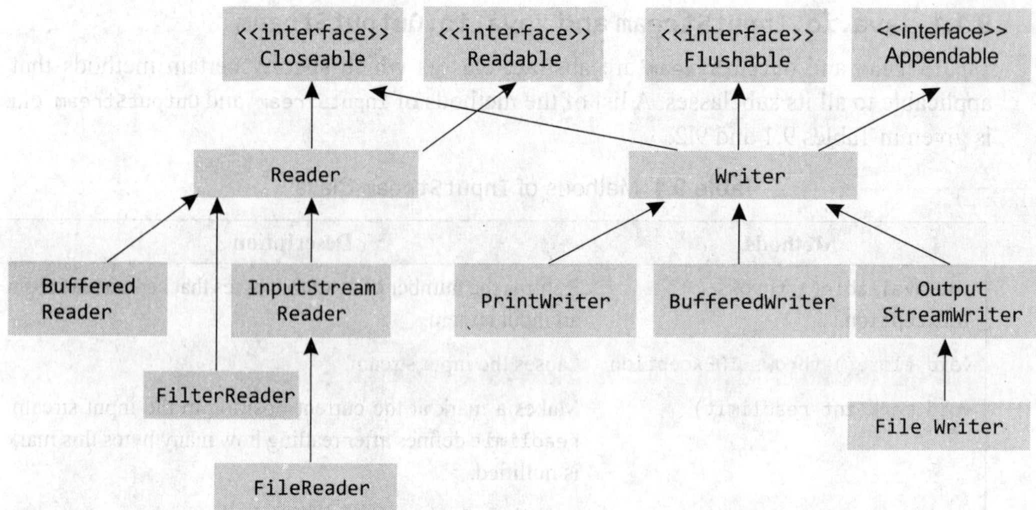

Fig. 9.1 Few Classes Shown Under Reader and Writer

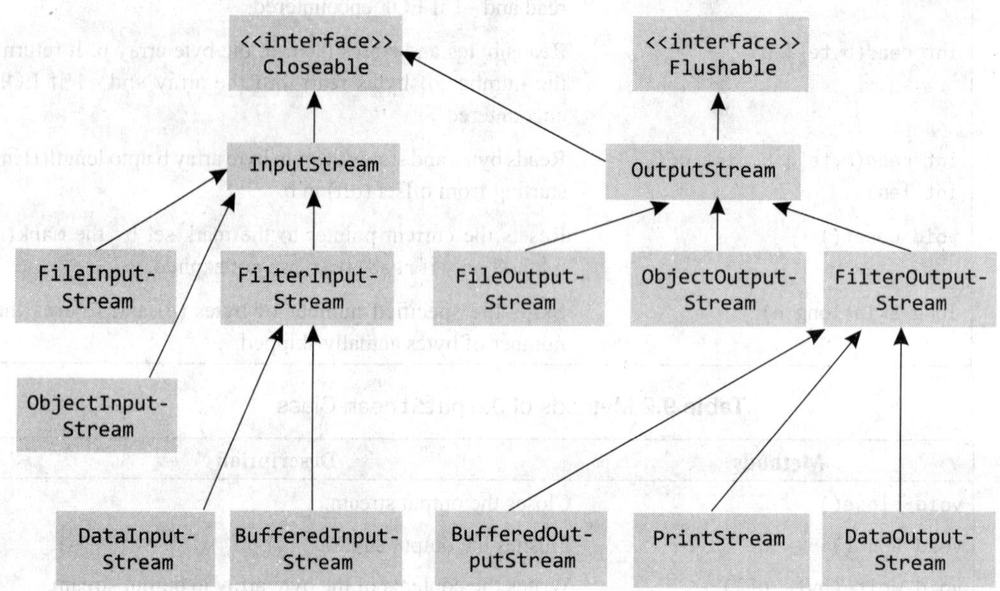

Fig. 9.2 Few Classes Shown under InputStream and OutputStream

9.2 java.io.FILE CLASS

The java.io.File class is worth mentioning, as it neither belongs to the byte stream nor the character stream used for reading or writing a file. This class is used to know the properties of a file-like path of the file, whether the file exists or not, whether the file is a file or a directory, and length of the file. Let us take a look at the example of File class.

Example 9.1 File Class

```java
import java.io.*;
class FileDemo {
public static void main(String args[]) {
File f = new File(args[0]);
  System.out.println("File exists: "+f.exists());
  System.out.println("File can be read:"+f.canRead());
  System.out.println("File can be written: "+f.canWrite());
  System.out.println("File can be executed:"+f.canExecute());
  System.out.println("File name: "+f.getName());
  System.out.println("parent of File:"+f.getParent());
  System.out.println("path of the File:"+f.getPath());
  System.out.println("Hidden File: "+f.isHidden());
  System.out.println("length of the file: "+f.length());
  System.out.println("last modified time: "+f.lastModified());
  System.out.println("it is a File: "+f.isFile());
  if(f.isDirectory()) {
      System.out.println(f.getPath()+ "is a irectory");
      String l[] = f.list();
      System.out.println("\nDirectory Listing for "+f.getPath() + "is:");
      for(String a:l) {
      File f1 = new File(f.getPath() + "/" +a);
      if(f1.isDirectory()) {
          System.out.println(a+ "is a directory");
          f1 = null;
        }
  else
          { System.out.println(a+ "is a File");
          f1 = null;
          }
        }
}}}
```

Output

For 'Sample.txt' file

```
C:\javabook\programs\chap09>java FileDemo sample.txt
File exists: true File can be read: true
File can be written: true
File can be executed: true
File name: sample.txt
parent of File: null
path of the File: sample.txt
Hidden File: false
length of the file: 105
last modified time: 1236860698637
it is a File: true
```

For 'programs' directory

```
C:\javabook\programs\chap09>java FileDemo
c:\javabook\programs
File exists: true
```

```
File can be read: true
File can be written: true
File can be executed: true
File name: programs
parent of File: c:\javabook
path of the File: c:\javabook\programs
Hidden File: false
length of the file: 12288
last modified time: 1237062320960
it is a File: false
c:\javabook\programs is a Directory
Directory Listing for c:\javabook\programs is:
A.class is a File
B.class is a File
chap 6 is a directory
chap 7 is a directory
chap09 is a directory
chap3 is a directory
```

Explanation

L1 To use `File` class, we need to import the package `java.io`.

L4 `File` object is created and the file name/directory name is passed to it through command line argument. Some of the methods of the `File` class are used to know the properties of a file. All the methods have been called from the `println` method so that their return values can be printed.

L5 `exists()` returns boolean value to indicate whether file/directory exists or not.

L6 `canRead()` returns boolean value to indicate whether file/directory can be read or not.

L7 `canWrite()` returns boolean value to indicate whether file/directory can be written or not.

L8 `canExecute()` returns boolean value to indicate whether file/directory can be executed or not.

L9 `getName()` returns the name of the file/directory.

L10 `getParent()` returns the name of the directory of which the file/directory is a part of.

L11 `getPath()` returns the complete path of file/directory (see output).

L12 `isHidden()` returns boolean value to indicate whether file is hidden or not.

L13 `length()` returns long value to indicate length of file in bytes.

L14 `lastModifiedTime()` returns the time the file was last modified. The time was calculated in milliseconds since 1 January 1970, GMT 00:00:00.

L15 `isFile()` returns true if argument to `File` object is a file.

L16 `isDirectory()` returns true if argument to `File` object is a directory. If it is, then the following lines will be executed.

L18 `list()` method is used to list all the directory and files within a directory and it returns them as a string array.

L20 `for-each` loop is used to iterate through the contents of the array one by one. L21–27 are executed for all the elements of the array.

In the following lines, we find whether an element of the array is a file or directory and print it accordingly.

L21 `File` object is created for each and every element in the string array.

L22 `isDirectory()` method of the file object is used to find whether the element is a Directory or not.

L23 Prints "it is a directory".

L24 As we are creating a new `File` object in every iteration, assigning null to the file object makes it eligible for garbage collection.

L25–27 `else` prints, "it is a File" and null is assigned to the `File` object.

9.3 READING AND WRITING DATA

The data can be read/written to files, console, sockets, etc. using both the streams. The classes under these streams are used for reading/writing data. In the following subheadings, we will see how to read and write data using the subclasses of `InputStream`, `OutputStream`, `Reader`, and `Writer`.

9.3.1 Reading/Writing Files Using Byte Stream

`FileInputStream` (inherits `InputStream`) class is used for reading a file and `FileOutputStream` (inherits `OutputStream`) is used for writing to a file. A complete list of all methods of `FileInputStream` and `FileOutputStream` is shown in Tables 9.3 and 9.4, respectively. Let us take an example to see how files can be read and written using these classes.

Table 9.3 Methods of `FileInputStream` Class

Methods	Description
`int available()`	Returns the number of remaining bytes that can be read from this input stream.
`void close()`	Closes this file input stream and releases all system resources.
`void finalize()`	Ensures that the close method of this file input stream is called when there are no more references to it.
`FileChannel getChannel()`	Returns the unique `FileChannel` object associated with this file input stream.
`final FileDescriptor getFD()`	Returns the `FileDescriptor` object that represents the connection to the actual file in the file system being used by this `FileInputStream`.
`int read()`	Reads a byte of data from this input stream.
`int read(byte[] b)`	Reads up to b.length bytes of data from this input stream into the byte array b.
`int read(byte[] b, int off, int len)`	Reads up to len bytes of data from this input stream into an array of bytes starting at offset off in byte array b.
`long skip(long n)`	Skips over and discards n bytes of data from the input stream.

Table 9.4 Methods of `FileOutputStream` Class

Methods	Description
`void close()`	Closes this file output stream and releases all system resources.
`protected void finalize()`	Cleans up the connection to the file.
`FileChannel getChannel()`	Returns the unique `FileChannel` object associated with this stream.
`FileDescriptor getFD()`	Returns the file descriptor associated with this output stream.
`void write (byte [] b)`	Writes bytes from the specified byte array to this file output stream.
`void write (byte [] b, int off, int len)`	Writes len bytes from the specified byte array starting at offset off (in the byte array) to this file output stream.
`void write(int b)`	Writes the specified byte to this file output stream.

Example 9.2 Reading and Writing Files

```
L1    import java.io.*;
L2    class ReadWriteDemo{
L3    public static void main(String args[]) throws IOException
      {
L4      if(args.length!= 2){
L5      System.out.println("Usage: java ReadWriteDemoSample.txt Demo.txt");
L6      System.exit(0); // terminate the program
      }
L7      File f = new File(args[0]);
L8      byte[] b = {};

      //Reading a file
L9      if(f.exists()){
L10         FileInputStream f1 = new FileInputStream(f);
L11         int num = f1.available();
L12         b = new byte[num];
L13         int n = f1.read(b);
L14         String s = new String(b);
L15         System.out.println("Contents of "+args[0]+ ":"+ s);
L16         f1.close();
L17         f = null; }
L18     else {
L19         System.out.println("File does not exist");
L20         System.exit(0); }

      //writing to file
L21     f = new File(args[1]);
L22     if(!f.exists())
L23         System.out.println(args[1] + "is a New File");
L24     else
L25         System.out.println(args[1] + "File exists, will be overwritten");
L26         System.out.println("Opening File: "+ args[1]);
L27         FileOutputStream fs = new FileOutputStream(args[1]);
L28         System.out.println("File Opened, now writing contents");
L29         fs.write(b);
L30         fs.flush();
L31         System.out.println("contents written");
L32         System.out.println("Closing File");
L33         fs.close();
      }}
```

Output

```
C:\javabook\programs\CHAP09~1>java ReadWriteDemo Sample.txt Demo.txt
Contents of Sample.txt: This is my sample file
Demo.txt is a New File
Opening File: Demo.txt
File Opened, now writing contents
contents written
Closing File
```

```
C:\javabook\programs\CHAP09~1>java ReadWriteDemo Sample.txt Demo.txt
Contents of Sample.txt: This is my sample file
Demo.txt File exists, will be overwritten
Opening File: Demo.txt
File Opened, now writing contents
Contents written
Closing File
```

Explanation

Reading a File

L4–6 `if` statement checks whether the number of command-line arguments is equal to 2. If the condition is evaluated as true, it prints how to run the program and terminates the program.

L7 `File` class object is created and the first command line argument (`args[0]`, i.e., `Sample.txt`) is passed as an argument to the constructor. We have mentioned only the name of the file, as the file exists in the current working directory. If you wish to refer to a file stored in some other directory, specify the full path of the file.

L8 An empty byte array is created. As we are using byte stream classes, files will be read and written in the form of bytes. The contents of the file will be read into this byte array and later, the contents of the byte array will be written on to a different file.

L9 A check is made using `exists()` of the `File` object to check whether the file (denoted by `args[0]`, exists or not. If file exists, L10–17 are executed, otherwise L19–20 are executed.

L10 `FileInputStream` object is created to read the contents of the file and the `File` class object (`f`) created in L7 is passed to the constructor of this object.

L11 The `available()` method of the `f1` object is used to find the number of bytes that can be read from the file. The return value is stored in `num`.

L12 Now when we know the number of bytes in a file (`num`), we create a byte array of that size so that the bytes from the file can be read into this byte array.

L13 `read()` is an overloaded method. It reads the entire contents of the file into the byte array. It returns the number of bytes actually read into the byte array.

This number should be equal to `num`.

L14 Directly displaying the bytes on to the standard output would lead to confusion, as the contents of the file are in the form of bytes. We want to read the file as it was (readable string format). So we look up in the `String` class for a constructor that accepts byte array and converts it into a readable format. The one we found is shown.

L15 Prints the contents of the file.

L16 Closes the `FileInputStream` object.

L17 `File` object is assigned null.

L18 `Else` part of `if` in L9.

L19 Prints `File does not exist`.

L20 Terminates the program.

Writing to a File

L21 Similar to L7. The only difference lies in the argument.

L22 Similar to L9.

L23 Gets printed if L22 returns the statement `file does not exist`, else L25 is printed.

L27 `FileOutputStream` object is created to write bytes to a file and filename (string argument, i.e., `args[1]`) is passed to the constructor of the `FileOutputStream` object. We could have passed the file object also created in L21 (as done in the creation of `FileInputStream` object created in L11), but we wanted to show you that the constructor in these classes are overloaded to accept different kinds of argument.

L28 Shows statement to print "`File Opened, now writing contents`".

L29 `write` method is used to write the entire byte array to the file.

L30 Flushes the contents to the file if any in the output stream using the `flush()` method.

L33 Closes the `FileOutputStream`.

9.3.2 Reading/Writing Console (User Input)

Prior to JDK 6, JDK 5 introduced the `Scanner` class (`java.util` package) which can be used for getting input from user (both lines of text as well as primitives) apart from breaking the input string into tokens separated by a delimiter which is by default a white space. A snapshot of the `Scanner` class is shown below.

Example 9.3	Scanner Class

```
L1    import java.util.*;
L2    class ScannerDemo {
L3    public static void main(String args[]){
L4       Scanner sc = new Scanner(System.in);
L5       System.out.print("Enter your name: ");
L6       String name = sc.nextLine();
L7       System.out.print("Enter your age: ");
L8       int age = sc.nextInt();
L9       System.out.println("you entered "+name+ " as your name");
L10      System.out.println("you entered "+age+" as your age");
      }}
```

Output

```
C:\javabook\programs\chap 09>java ScannerDemo
Enter your name: Tom
Enter your age: 31
you entered Tom as your name
you entered 31 as your age
```

Explanation

L1 The `java.util` package is imported as `Scanner` class belongs to it.

L4 An object of the `Scanner` class is created and `System.in` is passed to the constructor of the object.

L6 Reads the input from the user using `nextLine()` method of `Scanner` class and returns the string. `nextLine()` keeps on taking the user input until the user presses enter.

L7 Print statement asking the user to enter his age.

L8 Using the `Scanner` class, we can directly read a primitive value from the user. This line shows `nextInt()` that reads directly `int` from the user. Similarly if required, `nextByte()`, `nextDouble`, `nextFloat()`, `nextBoolean()`, etc. can be used. A list of methods of `scanner` class is shown in Table 9.5.

Note `System` is a class in the `java.lang` package. This class has three predefined variables: `in`, `out`, and `err`. `System.in` refers to standard input stream, more specifically keyboard input. Together they give an object of type `InputStream`. `System.out` refers to standard output stream, more specifically display device. Together they give an object of type `PrintStream` which contains `println()` method. We have been using this method from our first example (`System.out.println()`). `System.err` refers to standard error output stream, more specifically display device. Together they give an object of type `PrintStream`.

Table 9.5 Methods of Scanner Class

Methods	Description
`void close()`	Closes this scanner.
`boolean hasNext()`	Returns true if this scanner has another token else false.
`boolean hasNext(Pattern p)`	Returns true if the next token matches the specified pattern (p).
`boolean hasNext(String p)`	Returns true if the next token matches the pattern in the specified string (p).
`boolean hasNextBoolean()`	Returns true if the next token in this input can be interpreted as a boolean value.
`boolean hasNextByte()`	Returns true if the next token in this input can be interpreted as a byte value.
`boolean hasNextDouble()`	Returns true if the next token in this input can be interpreted as a double value.
`boolean hasNextFloat()`	Returns true if the next token in this input can be interpreted as a float.
`boolean hasNextInt()`	Returns true if the next token in this input can be interpreted as an int.
`boolean hasNextLine()`	Returns true if there is another line in the input.
`boolean hasNextLong()`	Returns true if the next token in this scanner's input can be interpreted as a long.
`boolean hasNextShort()`	Returns true if the next token in this scanner's input can be interpreted as a short.
`String next()`	Returns the next complete token from this scanner.
`String next(Pattern pattern)`	Returns the next token if it matches the specified pattern.
`boolean nextBoolean()`	Scans the next token of the input into a boolean value and returns that value.
`byte nextByte()`	Returns the next token of the input as a byte.
`double nextdouble()`	Returns the next token of the input as a double.
`float nextFlot()`	Returns the next token of the input as a float.
`short nextInt()`	Returns the next token of the input as an int (L8, Example 9.3).
`short nextLine()`	Advances this scanner past the current line and returns the input as a string (L6, Example 9.3).
`short nextLong()`	Returns the next token of the input as a long.
`short nextShort()`	Returns the next token of the input as a short.
`Scanner useDelimiter (String pattern)`	Sets the delimiting pattern for scan to pattern constructed from the specified string.

In Example 9.3, `nextLine()` has been used before `nextInt( )`. If `nextInt()` is used before `nextLine()`, then the output is not what you would expect it to be. Let us take another example to show what happens when `nextLine` is used after any of the `nextInt` or `nextFloat` methods.

Example 9.4 Scanner Class

```
import java.util.*;
class ScannerInput
{
    public static void main(String args[])
    {
        Scanner in=new Scanner(System.in);
        // nextInt reads the next integer till the delimiter (whitespace by default)
```

```
L1          System.out.println("Enter First Integer");
L2          int number = in.nextInt();
L3          System.out.println("Enter a String:");
L4          String string = in.nextLine();
L5          System.out.println("Enter next Float: ");
L6          float real = in.nextFloat();
L7          System.out.println("Enter next String:");
L8          String string2 = in.nextLine();
L9          System.out.println(number+" "+string+" "+real+" "+string2);
         }
      }
```

Output

```
C:\Windows\system32\cmd.exe

D:\javabook\chapter of java book\First Edition\programs\chap 9>java ScannerInput

Enter First Integer
12
Enter a String:
Enter next Float:
13
Enter next String:
12     13.0

D:\javabook\chapter of java book\First Edition\programs\chap 9>java ScannerInput

Enter First Integer
12 13
Enter a String:
Enter next Float:
14 15
Enter next String:
12     13   14.0    15
```

Explanation

We run this example with two sets of input to clarify the differences.

L2 `nextInt()` returns the integers value typed till the delimiter which is a whitespace by default.

L4 The `nextLine()` method continues reading the input till carriage return and returns it as a string. The carriage return is consumed and not appended to the string. So when a `nextLine()` is used after a number is read using `nextInt` or `nextFloat()` or `nextLong()` etc., the number is returned by the respective methods and methods return. The empty string with the carriage return is consumed by the `nextLine()` and returned. So it does not prompt for an input on L4 as the carriage return typed while reading integer input for L2 is consumed by `nextLine()`.

| Note | The first output of the program shows 12 is returned as an integer by `nextInt()` and user is not prompted for value as carriage return is consumed by `nextLine()` and it returns. Similarly, 13 is returned as a `float` by `nextFloat()` and user is not prompted for any value for the same reason explained above. The second output of the program clears the concept where 12 is returned as an integer by `nextInt()` and 13 as a string by `nextLine()`. Similarly, 14 is returned as a float by `nextFloat()` and 15 as a string by `nextLine()`. |

Prior to JDK 5, `BufferedReader` was used to read inputs from the user. The following statements show how to get the input from the user using the `BufferedReader` class.

```
      try
      {
      . . .

L1    BufferedReader br = new BufferedReader(new InputStreamReader (System.in));
L2    String x = br.readLine();
      . . .

      }
      catch(IOException e)
      {. . .}
```

Explanation

L1 `BufferedReader` object is created to get input from the user. The constructor of `BufferedReader` accepts an object of type `InputStreamReader`, which in turn accepts an argument of type `InputStream` (`System.in`). `InputStream` is a byte stream class and `InputStreamReader` is a character stream class. So actually the byte stream is getting converted to character stream and then the concept of buffering is used to enhance performance.

L2 `readLine()` of the `BufferedReader` class is used to read the input. It can throw an `IOException`, so either place `readLine()` call in a `try/catch` block or specify `throws` in the method declaration using `readLine()`.

Java 6 introduced the `Console` class in the `java.io` package for gathering user input from the user and output it to the standard output. A list of methods of the `console` class is shown in Table 9.6. Let us take an example to see the `Console` class.

Table 9.6 Methods of Console Class

Methods	Description
`void flush()`	Flushes the console and writes the buffered output immediately.
`Console format(String fmt, Object ... args)`	Writes a formatted string to the console's output stream using the specified format string and arguments.
`Console printf(String format, Object ... args)`	Writes a formatted string to the console's output stream using the specified format string and arguments (L10, Example 9.5).
`Reader reader()`	Returns the unique `Reader` object associated with this console.
`String readLine()`	Reads a single line of text from the console.
`String readLine (String fmt, Object ... args)`	Provides a formatted prompt, then reads a single line of text from the console (Lines 5, 7, and 9; Example 9.5).
`char[] readPassword()`	Reads a password from the console with echoing disabled (L13, Example 9.5).
`char[] readPassword(String fmt, Object ... args)`	Provides a formatted prompt, then reads a password from the console with echoing disabled.
`PrintWriter writer()`	Returns the unique `PrintWriter` object associated with this console.

Example 9.5   Console Input

```
L1    import java.io.*;
L2    class ConsoleDemo {
L3    public static void main(String args[]) throws IOException {
L4      Console c = System.console();
L5      String user =c.readLine("Enter your username: ");
L6      c.printf("Welcome %1$s. Hope You had a Nice Day. ",user);
L7      String pno = c.readLine("\nEnter your Phone No.: ");
L8      c.printf("You entered %1$s as your phone Number ",pno);
L9      String age = c.readLine("\nEnter your Age: ");
L10     c.printf("name: %3$s, Age: %2$s Phone No.: %1$s",pno,age,user);
        // another way of writing to the Console
L11     PrintWriter out = c.Writer();
L12     out.println("\nEnter your password");
L13     char[] pass = c.readPassword();
L14     c.printf("The password you entered is %1$s ", new String(pass));
      }}
```

Output

```
Enter your username: Tom
Welcome Tom. Hope You had a Nice Day.
Enter your Phone No.: 34343434
You entered 34343434 as your phone Number
Enter your Age: 31
Name: Tom, Age: 31, Phone No: 34343434
Enter your password

The password you entered is $T123
```

Explanation

L4 System class has a static method `console()` to return the `Console` object.

L5 `readLine()` is an overloaded method in the `Console` class, used to read input from the user. The string argument is displayed on the console and then program blocks for user input. The value entered by the `user` method is returned as a string.

L6 Print statement, similar to C language, has been added in this class, i.e., `printf ("","")`. The first argument in the method (`"Welcome %1$s. Hope you had a Nice Day"`) is the format string to be displayed on the standard output. The value for `%1$s` is picked up from the arguments referred by the format string which starts from the second argument of the method. We have only two arguments in this method, but if required, you can have more.

- % sign is for specifying literals.
- n$ specifies the argument index in the argument list. 1$ is the index of the first argument. 2$ is used to refer to the second argument, and so on.

- s specifies strings.

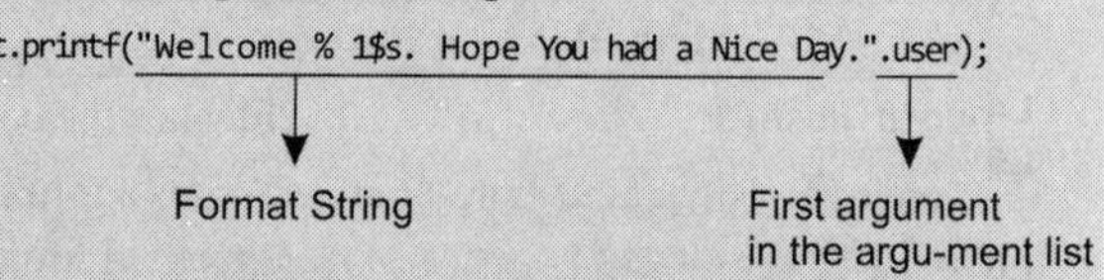

So in place of %1$s, the value in the string user (i.e., Tom) is placed while displaying on the console (see output).

L7 Similar to L5. The '\n' is placed in the beginning of the string to print it on a new line.

L10 We have specifically added this line and changed the order of the arguments in the argument list so that you can better understand it.

```
c.printf("name: %3$s, Age: %2$s
        Phone No: %1$s",pno,age,user);
```

First of all `"name:"` is printed followed by the third argument (`%3$s`), i.e., `user` (Tom), then `"Age:"` followed by the second argument (`%2$s`), i.e., age (31) and lastly `"Phone No.:"` followed by the first argument (`%1$s`), i.e., pno (34343434).

L11 Another way of writing to the console is shown in this line. You can get the `PrintWriter` object using the `writer()` method of the `Console` class.

L12 `println()` of `PrintWriter` is used to write to the console, prompting the user to enter password.

L13 `Console` class provides a unique method `readPassword()`, used for reading the passwords from the user without echoing it on to the screen. It returns the password in a character array.

L14 Similar to the previous print statements. But here, we have a character array that is to be displayed on the screen. To display the character array, we have passed the character array to String class constructor and then it is displayed.

> **Note** The `readLine()` method returns a string. Suppose we want numeric input, in that case, the string returned can be converted to its respective numeric values using certain static methods of the wrapper classes in the `java.lang` package.
>
> ```
> int using Integer.parseInt()
> float using Float.parseFloat()
> double using Double.parseDouble()
> long using Long.parseLong()
> byte using Byte.parseByte()
> short using Short.parseShort()
> ```

9.3.3 Reading/Writing Files Using Character Stream

Files can be read and written using character stream classes also. `FileReader` class is used to read the contents of a file. `FileWriter` class is used to write the contents to a file. Remember reading and writing will be in the form of characters. Reading can be done character by character (as shown in the Example 9.6) or line by line.

Example 9.6   Reading and Writing Files

```
L1    import java.io.*;
L2    class ReadWriteDemo1{
L3    public static void main(String args[]) throws IOException
          {
L4    File f = new File(args[0]);
L5    int n;
          //Reading a File
L6    if(f.exists())
L7    { FileReader fr = new FileReader(f);
      System.out.println("Reading" +args[0]);
L8    while((n = fr.read())!= -1)
L9    System.out.print((char)n);
L10       }else
L11   System.out.println(args[0]+ "does not exist");
      //writing to a file
      System.out.println("\nWriting " +args[1]);
L12   FileWriter fw = new FileWriter(args[1]);
L13   String s = "This is my sample File";
L14   fw.write(s);
L15   fw.close(); }}
```

Output

```
C:\javabook\programs\CHAP09~1>java ReadWriteDemo1 Sample1.txt Demo1.txt
Reading Sample1.txt
This is my sample File
Writing Demo1.txt
```

Explanation

Reading a file

L4 File object is created and file name is passed as a command line argument.

L5 Integer variable `n` is declared for reading characters.

L6 Checks whether the file exists or not. If it exists, L7–9 are executed, else L11 is executed.

L7 `FileReader` object is created and `File` object created in L4 is passed to it. If the file referenced by the `FileReader` object does not exist, a `FileNotFoundException` results.

L8 A `while` loop that reads the file character by character using `read()` of the `FileReader` object. This method returns the character read as an integer or −1 if EOF is reached. The value read is put in variable *n* and checked for equality to −1. `read()` is overloaded to read the file character by character or place the entire file into a character array. This method throws an `IOException` in case of problem.

L9 Integer variable `n` is cast to character and printed.

L10 `else` clause of `if` statement defined in L6.

Writing to a file

L12 `FileWriter` object is created and the second command line argument is passed to the constructor of the object. If the file exists, it is overwritten and if does not, a new file is created.

L13 A sample string is declared.

L14 The string is written to the file using `write()` of the `Writer` class. The `write()` method is overloaded to accept character array, integer, and string.

L15 Closes the `FileWriter` object.

9.3.4 Reading/Writing using Buffered Byte Stream Classes

`BufferedInputStream` class is used for buffering the input and it supports operation to re-read the files. `BufferedOutputStream` class is used to buffer the output and enhance the performance. A list of methods of `BufferedInputStream` and `BufferedOutputStream` are shown in Tables 9.7 and 9.8, respectively. Let us take an example to show these two classes.

Table 9.7 Methods of `BufferedInputStream` Class

Methods	Description
`int available ()`	Returns the number of bytes that can be read from this input stream without blocking.
`void close ()`	Closes this input stream and releases all the resources.
`void mark (int readlimit)`	Similar to mark the methods of `InputStream`.
`boolean markSupported ()`	Tests if this input stream supports the mark and reset methods.
`int read ()`	Similar to read of `InputStream` class.
`int read (byte [] b, int off, int len)`	Reads bytes from the `inputStream` into the byte array starting at offset off and returns the number of bytes read. Len specifies the maximum number of bytes to read.
`void reset ()`	Similar to reset method of `InputStream` class.
`long skip(long n)`	Similar to skip method of `InputStream` class.

Table 9.8 Methods of `BufferedOutputStream` Class

Methods	Description
`void flush ()`	Flushes the output stream.
`void write(byte[] b,int off, int len)`	Writes the specified number of bytes (len) to the output stream starting from the offset (off).
`void write(int b)`	Write the specified byte to the output stream.

Example 9.7 Buffered Input/Output

```
L1      import java.io.*;
L2      class BufferedInOutStreamDemo {
L3      public static void main(String args[]) throws IOException
        {
L4      FileInputStream fis = new FileInputStream(args[0]);
L5      BufferedInputStream bis = new BufferedInputStream(fis);
L6      int n = fis.available();
L7      bis.mark(n);
L8      System.out.println ("Marked the stream");
L9      byte b[] = new byte[n];
L10     byte b1[] = new byte[n];
L11     bis.read(b);
L12     System.out.println("Contents of "+args[0]+ ":"+new String(b));
L13     System.out.println("Resetting the stream");
L14     bis.reset();
L15     System.out.println("Reading the stream again from the marked point");
L16     bis.read(b1);
L17     System.out.println(new String(b1));
L18     bis.close();
L19     fis.close();
L20     System.out.println ("Writing contents to : "+args[1]);
L21     FileOutputStream fos = new FileOutputStream(args[1]);
L22     BufferedOutputStream out = new BufferedOutputStream(fos);
L23     out.write(b);
L24     System.out.println ("Contents written");
L25     out.close(); fos.close();
        }}
```

Output

```
C:\javabook\programs\chap09>java BufferedInOutStreamDemo sample.txt Demo.txt
Marked the stream
Contents of sample.txt: This is my sample file
Resetting the stream
Reading the stream again from the marked point
This is my sample file
Writing contents to : Demo.txt
Contents written
```

Explanation

L4 and 5 `BufferedInputStream` object is created and the `FileInputStream` object created (L4) is passed to the constructor of `BufferedInputStream` object. The input is buffered and operations like `mark` and `reset` are supported. `mark()` and `reset()` are the methods of `BufferedInputStream` class. But why are we using `BufferedInputStream` class? Since, it is not possible to re-read the file with an object of `FileInputStream`, we use `mark` and `reset` operations to read the file again.

L7 The stream is marked. The reset method sets the pointer to the marked point. The read operation will begin from the marked point after resetting the stream. The `n` passed as an argument is the limit which is the maximum number of bytes that can be read before the mark expires. A reset in that case raises an `IOException`.

L9 and 10 Two byte arrays have been created. One for reading the content before the stream is reset and the second one for reading the stream after it is reset.

L11 `read` method reads the entire file into the byte array.

L12 byte array is converted to string and displayed on the standard output.

L14 reset method is used to reset the stream to the marked point. In our case, it is the beginning of file.

L16 read method again reads the entire file into the second byte array. If the mark and reset methods are not used, then it is not possible to read the file again using FileInputStream class and its methods.

L21 FileOutputStream object is created and filename is passed as argument.

L22 BufferedOutputStream object is created and OutputStream object (created in L21) is passed to it.

L23 write method is used to write contents of byte array to file.

L25 Closes the output streams.

9.3.5 Reading/Writing Using Buffered Character Stream Classes

BufferedReader class is used for buffering the input and it supports operation to re-read the files (just like BufferedInputStream). BufferedWriter class is used to buffer the output and enhance the performance (just like BufferedOutputStream). Let us take an example to show these two classes.

Example 9.8 **Buffered Character Stream**

```
L1    import java.io.*;
L2    class BufferedReadWriteDemo {
L3    public static void main(String args[]) throws IOException
         {
L4       int n;
L5       FileReader fr = new FileReader(args[0]);
L6       System.out.println("File opened: "+args[0]);
L7       BufferedReader br = new BufferedReader(fr);
L8       PrintWriter out = new PrintWriter(System.out,true);
L9       String str;
L10      FileWriter fw = new FileWriter(args[1]);
L11      BufferedWriter bw = new BufferedWriter(fw);
L12      while((str = br.readLine()) != null)
         {
L13         out.println(str);
L14         bw.write(str+"\n");
         }
L15   System.out.println("Contents copied to: "+args[1]);
L16   br.close();
L17   bw.close();
L18   fr.close();
L19   fw.close();
      }}
```

Output

```
C:\javabook\programs\CHAP09~1>java BufferedReadWriteDemo Sample1.txt Demo2.txt
 File opened: Sample1.txt
This is my sample file
Contents copied to: Demo2.txt
```

Explanation

L5 `FileReader` object is created and file name passed as an argument to the constructor of this class. **L7** `BufferedReader` object is created and `FileReader` object is passed to it. The `BufferedReader` object buffers the characters for efficiency purpose and it also supports the `mark` and `reset` methods. **L8** `PrintWriter` object is created to write contents to the standard output (`system.out`). The true specified as the constructor is for auto-flushing the output buffer.

L10 and 11 `BufferedWriter` object is created and `FileWriter` object is passed into the constructor of the `BufferedWriter` object. **L12 to 14** `readLine()` method of `BufferedReader` is used to read the String from the file whose name has been specified while creating the `FileReader` object. The return value is placed in the `str` and is checked for equality to null. The loop continues until `str` is null (EOF). The `while` loop prints the file line by line (L13) and then writes it to another File using `BufferedWriter` object (L14).

9.4 RANDOMLY ACCESSING A FILE

`RandomAccessFile` gives an opportunity to read or write files from a specific location. This class has a method named `seek (long pos)` that sets the file pointer at the specified position (`pos`). Now any read/write operation on the file will start from this marked position. A complete list of methods of `RandomAccessFile` class is shown in Table 9.9. In the following example, we have used `seek()` to set the file pointer to end of file (EOF) and then write the contents to the file. In other words, we are appending the file.

Table 9.9 Methods of `RandomAccessFile` Class

Methods	Description
`void close ()`	Closes this random access file stream.
`final FileChannel getChannel()`	Returns the unique `FileChannel` object associated with this file.
`long getFilePointer()`	Returns the current offset in this file.
`long length ()`	Returns the length of the file.
`int read ()`	Reads a byte of data from this file.
`int read (byte [] b)`	Reads up to b.length bytes of data from this file into an array of bytes.
`int read(byte[] b, int off, int len)`	Reads up to len bytes of data from this file into an array of bytes starting at offset off in the byte array.
`final boolean readBoolean()`	Reads a boolean from this file.
`byte readByte()`	Reads a signed eight-bit value from this file.
`final char ceadChar()`	Reads a character from this file.
`final double readDouble()`	Reads a double from this file.
`final float readFloat()`	Reads a float from this file.
`final int readlnt ()`	Reads a signed 32-bit integer from this file.
`final String readLine()`	Reads the next line of the text from this file.
`final long readLong()`	Reads a signed 64-bit integer from this file.
`final short readShort()`	Reads a signed 16-bit number from this file.

(Contd)

(Table 9.9 Contd)

Methods	Description
`void seek(long pos)`	Sets the file-pointer, measured from the beginning of this file, at which the next read or write operation occurs.
`void setLength (long newLength)`	Sets the length of this file.
`int skipBytes(int n)`	Skips n bytes of input discarding skipped bytes.
`final void write (byte [] b)`	Writes b.length bytes from the specified byte array to this file, starting at the current file pointer.
`final void write (byte [] b, int off, int len)`	Writes len bytes from the specified byte array starting at offset off to this file.
`final void write(int b)`	Writes the specified byte to this file.
`final void writeBoolean(boolean v)`	Writes a boolean to the file as a one-byte value.
`final void writeByte(int v)`	Writes a byte to the file as a one-byte value.
`final void writeBytes(String s)`	Writes the string to the file as a sequence of bytes.
`final void writeChar(int v)`	Writes char to the file as a two-byte value, high byte first.
`final void writeChars(String s)`	Writes string to the file as a sequence of characters.
`final void writeDouble(double v)`	Converts the double argument to a long using the `doubleToLongBits` method in class `Double`, and then writes that long value to the file as an eight-byte quantity, high byte first.
`final void writeFloat (float v)`	Converts the float argument to an int using the `floatToIntBits` method in class `Float`, and then writes that int value to the file as a four-byte quantity, high byte first.
`final void writeInt(int v)`	Writes an int to the file as four bytes, high byte first.
`final void writeLong(long v)`	Writes a long to the file as eight bytes, high byte first.
`final void writeShort(int v)`	Writes a short to the file as two bytes, high byte first.

Note Java 5 added an interface `java.lang.Appendable` which is implemented by the writer class. This interface has three methods to append characters and string to the writer object. The methods have the following forms:

```
public Writer append(char c)
public Writer append(CharSequence c)
public Writer append(CharSequence c, int start, int end)
```

`java.lang.CharSequence` is another interface for denoting sequence of character values. Its implementing classes are `String`, `StringBuffer`, `StringBuilder`, etc.

Example 9.9 Random Access File

```
L1    import java.io.*;
L2    class RandomAccessFileDemo {
L3    public static void main(String args[]) throws IOException
        {
L4        System.out.println("Opening the file in read write mode");
L5        RandomAccessFile raf = new RandomAccessFile ("Sample.txt","rw");
L6        raf.seek(raf.length());
```

```
L7      String str = "\nContents appended using RandomAccessFile";
L8      System.out.println("Appending contents to file");
L9      raf.write(str.getBytes());
L10     System.out.println("Contents appended");
L11     System.out.println("Reading the contents of the file....");
L12     raf.seek(0);
L13     while((str = raf.readLine())!= null)
L14     System.out.println(str);
L15     raf.close();
        }}
```

Output

```
C:\javabook\programs\CHAP09~1>java RandomAccessFileDemo
Opening the file in read write mode
Appending contents to file
Contents appended
Reading the contents of the file....
This is my sample File
Contents appended using RandomAccessFile
```

Explanation

L5 An object of `RandomAccessFile` is created. The filename is passed as the first argument and the second argument is the mode in which to open the file. There are four modes that can be applied as a string. If the file denoted by the first argument does not exist, a `FileNotFoundException` results. The various modes are shown in Table 9.10.

L6 seek (`long pos`) method is used to set the file pointer at a particular position (pos) in the file. read/write begins from this point. We are setting the pointer to the end of file, as we have passed the entire length of the file as an agreement to seek method.

L7 Shows the contents to be written to file.

L9 `write()`method of `RandomAccessFile` is used to write bytes to file. Writing of bytes starts from the position set by seek method in the file. This method can throw an `IOException`.

L12 `seek(0)`sets the file pointer to the beginning of the file.

L13–14 `readLine()` reads an entire line of text from file and puts it in `str`. This `str` is printed until `str` is null.

L15 `RandomAccessFile` object is closed.

Table 9.10 Modes of RandomAccessFile

Mode	Description
r	File will be opened in read-only mode.
rw	File will be opened in read–write mode. If a file does not exist, it will be created.
rws	File is opened in read–write mode and every update in file contents and its metadata will be synchronously written to the storage device.
rwd	Similar to "rws" with the exception that any update in metadata is not synchronously written to the storage device, thereby reducing the number of interactions with the storage device.

9.5 READING AND WRITING FILES USING NEW I/O PACKAGE

The `java.nio` package is used to perform advanced I/O operations like memory mapping of files, file locking, buffer classes have been provided for all primitive types, channels representing connections to files. Memory mapping is a concept used in virtual memory. The entire file or region of a file (for large files) is mapped byte to byte between the file and the virtual memory. The mapped file is treated as it is actually present in the primary memory, thereby increasing the performance of I/O.

> **Note** *nio* stands for non-blocking io. A non-blocking i/o or asynchronous i/o operation is one in which the program is not blocked waiting for the i/o operations to complete. Instead the other parts of the program that do not require i/o can proceed further. The parts requiring input or outputs would still be blocked or waiting for the i/o to finish.

nio package provides extensive support for buffer management that is used in our example below. So let us first understand what is a buffer? A buffer is a container which can be used to store the contents of the file or primitive data types like `byte`, `short`, `char`, `int`, `long`, `float` and `double`. `Buffer` is an abstract superclass of `ByteBuffer`, `ShortBuffer`, `CharBuffer`, `IntBuffer`, `LongBuffer`, `FloatBuffer`, and `DoubleBuffer` in `java.nio` package. We also use the `MappedByteBuffer` class which is a subclass of `ByteBuffer` class and which represents a memory mapped region of a file. A mapped buffer is obtained using the `map` method of the `FileChannel` object as shown in the example below.

Example 9.10 **New I/O**

```
L1    import java.io.*;
L2    import java.nio.*;
L3    import java.nio.channels.*;
L4    public class ReadWriteUsingNIO {
L5      public static void main(String args[]) {
L6        try {
      //Use a mapped file to read a text file
L7        FileInputStream fis = new FileInputStream ("Sample.txt");
L8        FileChannel fc = fis.getChannel();
L9        long fs = fc.size();
L10       MappedByteBuffer mBuf = fc.map(FileChannel.MapMode.READ_ONLY, 0, fs);
L11       for (int i = 0; i < fs; i++)
L12       System.out.print((char) mBuf.get());
L13       fc.close();
L14       fis.close();
      // write to a file using nio
L15       String str = "welcome, writing to a file using nio package";
L16       FileOutputStream fos = new FileOutputStream ("samplenio.txt");
L17       FileChannel fc1 = fos.getChannel();
L18       ByteBuffer buffer = ByteBuffer.allocate(str.length());
L19       byte[] b = str.getBytes();
L20       buffer.put(b);
L21       buffer.flip();
L22       fc1.write(buffer);
```

```
L23     fc1.close();
L24     fos.close();
    }catch (Exception e){
    System.out.println(e); }}}
```

Output

```
C:\javabook\programs\chap09>java ReadWriteUsingNIO
This is my sample File
C:\javabook\programs\chap09>edit samplenio.txt
welcome, writing to a file using nio package
```

Explanation

L1–3 Show the importing of packages. The `java.io`, `java.nio` and `java.nio.channels` packages are imported. `ByteBuffer` and `MappedByteBuffer` classes are part of `java.nio` package and `FileChannel` class is a part of `java.nio.channels` package.

L7 and 8 Using the `getChannel()` method of `FileInputStream` object, a `FileChannel` object is obtained. Now this channel actually represents a connection to the file (Sample.txt). A `FileChannel` object apart from reading and writing a file can

(a) map the file to memory
(b) lock the file
(c) read and write files at specified positions
(d) you can force the file changes to be written to the storage device.

L9 `size()` method returns the size of the file.

L10 Static method map of `FileChannel` class is used to get a `MappedByteBuffer` object. `MappedByteBuffer` object is a byte buffer whose content defines the memory mapped file. The `map` method takes three arguments:

1. **Mode** Three modes for mapping are available.
   (a) **Read** read only mapping (`FileChannel.MapMode.READ_ONLY`)
   (b) **Read-write** (`FileChannel.MapMode.READ_WRITE`). If the contents of the buffer are manipulated, then they are written to the mapped file.
   (c) **Private** Buffer manipulations will not be written to file.

   `MapMode` is a static inner class in `FileChannel` class. `READ_ONLY`, `READ_WRITE`, `PRIVATE` are static fields within the class.

2. **Position** Point at which mapping in a file starts. This value cannot be negative.
3. **Size** Size of the mapping. This value cannot be negative.

L11 and 12 for loop to extract the characters from the mapped buffer through get method. Get method returns the byte read and then advances the positions. The byte value read is cast to character and printed.

L13 and 14 closes the `FileChannel` and `FileInputStream` objects.

Writing a String to a file

L15 String declared.

L16 and 17 Same as L7 and 8. The difference is that here, `FileOutputStream` object is used to obtain the `FileChannel` object.

L18 `java.nio` package contains a class `ByteBuffer` used for storing bytes. The `ByteBuffer` class has a static method `allocate` used for creating a `ByteBuffer`. This method accepts an argument that sets the size of the buffer in bytes.

L19 The string is converted to byte array using the `getBytes()` method of the `String` class.

L20 `put` method is used to transfer the bytes from byte array to `ByteBuffer`.

L21 `flip` method is used to set the position to the beginning of the buffer. After the put operation, this method prepares the buffer for write operations.

L22 The `ByteBuffer` is written to the `FileChannel` connected to the `FileOutputStream`.

L23 and 24 Closes the `FileChannel` object and the `FileOutputStream` object.

9.6 JAVA 7 nio ENHANCEMENTS

java.nio.file package has been added to the java.nio package in Java 7 to enhance the nio functionality and motivate the programmers to use the new classes like Files and interfaces like Path instead of the legacy class like java.io.File. A new interface SeekableByteChannel was also added in java.nio.channels package which provides functionality similar to the java.io.RandomAccessFile, etc. java.nio.file.Files class provides a number of static methods that operate on files and directories like move a file, copy a file, creating a new file, and deleting it.   The Path object is used to locate a file on the system. Let us take an example to illustrate how these classes and interfaces can be used. The program below shows the various methods of these interfaces and classes to check whether a file/directory exists, read a file, rename a file, copy a file, traverse a directory, whether two files are same and much more.

Example 9.11 `java.nio.file`

```
L1    // To use IOException and File class
      import java.io.*;

L2    // To Use classes like Paths, Files and Interface like Path,
      // DirectoryStream and Enum like StandardCopyOption
      import java.nio.file.*;

L3    // To use classes like StandardCharsets
      import java.nio.charset.*;

L4    class NewFileIO
      {
L5    public static void main (String args[]) throws IOException
      {
      // static method Paths.get(String first, String... more) returns
      // a Path object. Converts a path string to a Path.
L6    Path file = Paths.get("D:/javabook/chapter of java book/Second Edition/programs/
      chap9/DemoThis.java");

      // Returns the number of name elements in the path
L7    System.out.println("Name Count: "+file.getNameCount());

      // Returns the file system (FileSystem object) that created
      // this object
L8    System.out.println("File System: "+file.getFileSystem());

      // Returns the name of the file or directory denoted by this
      // path as a Path object
L9    System.out.println("File Name: "+file.getFileName());

      // Returns the parent of path as a Path object or null if this path // does not have a parent.
L10   System.out.println("Parent: " +file.getParent());

      // checks whether the path starts with the specified string.
L11   System.out.println ("Name starts with a DemoThis.java: "+file.startsWith("Demothis.java"));
L12   System.out.println("Hidden File: " +   Files.isHidden(file.getFileName()));

L13   System.out.println("Directory: "+Files.isDirectory(file.getFileName()));

L14   System.out.println("Regular File: " +  Files.isRegularFile(file.getFileName()));
```

```
L15   System.out.println("Executable:"+Files.isExecutable(file.getFileName()));

L16   System.out.println("Readable:"+Files.isReadable(file.getFileName()));

L17   System.out.println("Writable:"+Files.isWritable(file.getFileName()));

L18   System.out.println("Exists: "+Files.exists(file.getFileName()));

L19   System.out.println("Last Modified Time: "+Files.getLastModifiedTime(file.getFileName()));

L20   System.out.println("Size: "+Files.size(file.getFileName()) +" bytes");

L21   Path anotherFile=Paths.get("D:/javabook/chapter of java book/Second Edition/
      programs/chap 9/ScannerInput.java");

      // checks whether path starts with d:/javabook not D or
      //DemoThis or chap 9
L22   System.out.println("Name starts with d:/javabook : "+ anotherFile.startsWith("d:/ja
      vabook"));

L23   System.out.println("Another File exits : "+ Files.exists(anotherFile));

      // checks whether two files in two paths are same
L24   System.out.println(file.getFileName() +" is same as "+ anotherFile.getFileName() + ":
      "+Files.isSameFile(file.getFileName(),anotherFile.getFileName()));

      // make a copy of the file
L25   Path copy = Paths.get("D:/javabook/chapter of java book/Second Edition/programs/chap
      9/CopyOfDemoThis.java");

      // static Path Files.copy(Path source, Path target, CopyOption... options)
      // Copy a file to a target file.
      // Apart from REPLACE_EXISTING - Replace an existing file if it exists.
      // ATOMIC_MOVE - Move the file as an atomic file system operation.
      // COPY_ATTRIBUTES - Copy attributes to the new file.

L26     System.out.println ("File Copied: "+ Files.copy (file.getFileName(),
        copy.getFileName(),StandardCopyOption.REPLACE_EXISTING));

      // read the contents of the copied file and prints it on the screen
L27   System.out.println(Files.readAllLines(copy.getFileName(),StandardCharsets.US_ASCII));

      // rename a file in the same directory
L28   System.out.println (Files.move(copy.getFileName(),copy.getFileName().
      resolveSibling("Renamed"+copy.getFileName()), StandardCopyOption.REPLACE_EXISTING));

      // beacause file has been renamed so copy does not exists and thus only deleted
      // method raises exception so we used deleteIfExists()
      // delete a file
L29     System.out.println("Copy File deleted if existed "+Files.deleteIfExists(copy));

      // check for deletion of file
L30     System.out.println(copy.getFileName() +" Exists: "+Files.exists(copy.getFile
        Name()));

      // traversing a directory

L31     try(DirectoryStream<Path>
        ds=Files.newDirectoryStream(Paths.get("d:/javabook/chapter of java book/Second
        Edition/programs/chap 9")))
```

```java
        {
          System.out.println("--------------------------------------");
L32       System.out.println("Directory Listing: "+ds);
L33       for(Path iterate:ds)
          {
L34         if(Files.isDirectory(iterate))
L35         System.out.println("Directory: "+iterate.getFileName());
L36         else
L37           System.out.println(iterate.getFileName());
          }
        }
L38     File f = file.toFile();
L39     System.out.println ("File object : "+f);
        }
        }
```

Output

```
D:\javabook\chapter of java book\Second Edition\programs\chap 9>java NewFileIO
Name Count: 6
File System: sun.nio.fs.WindowsFileSystem@16fa474
File Name: DemoThis.java
Parent: D:\javabook\chapter of java book\Second Edition\programs\chap 9
Name starts with a DemoThis.java: false
Hidden File: false
Directory: false
Regular File: true
Executable:true
Readable:true
Writable:true
Exists: true
Last Modified Time: 2012-08-28T15:03:12.972079Z
Size: 116 bytes
Name starts with d:/javabook : true
Another File exits : true
DemoThis.java is same as ScannerInput.java : false
File Copied: CopyOfDemoThis.java
[class DemoThis, {,        int a,b;,        DemoThis(),      {,                  this();,
},         DemoThis(int a, int b),              {,                 a=10;,
b=10;,    }, }]
RenamedCopyOfDemoThis.java
Copy File deleted if existed false
CopyOfDemoThis.java Exists: false
--------------------------------------
Directory Listing: sun.nio.fs.WindowsDirectoryStream@165f738
Database.class
Database.java
DemoThis.java
GameVr3.java
GameVr4.java
NewFileIO.class
NewFileIO.java
RenamedCopyOfDemoThis.java
RenamedCopyOfGameVr4.java
ScannerInput.class
ScannerInput.java
File object : D:\javabook\chapter of java book\Second Edition\programs\chap 9\De
moThis.java
```

Explanation

L1–3 Imports the relevant packages so that the new classes and interfaces in `java.io` and `java.nio` packages can be used.

L6 get method of the `Paths` class is used specify the path of the file whose attributes need to be accessed and create a `Path` object. A few basic methods can be used on this `Path` object as well as this can be passed to some other methods as we will see.

L7–11 Shows the usage of various methods of `Path` object to extract information about the path like

`getNameCount`—is used to extract the names present in the path.

`getFileSystem()`—to know the files system on which the files was created,

`getFileName()`—to know the name of the file

`getParent()`– to know the parent of the path object (file).

`startsWith()`—returns a boolean value to indicate whether the path start with the string argument passed to the method. The path starts with `DemoThis.java` and not D or De (see Output).

L12–20 Shows the usage of static methods of `Files` class to extract information about the file like.

- `Files.isHidden()`—returns a boolean value to indicate whether the file is hidden or not.

- `Files.isDirectory()`— returns a boolean value to indicate whether the path refers to a directory or not.

- `Files.isRegularFile()`—returns a boolean value to indicate whether the file is a regular file or not.

- `Files.isExecutable()`—returns a boolean value to indicate whether the file is executable or not.

- `Files.isReadable()`—returns a boolean value to indicate whether the file is readable or not.

- `Files.isWriteable()`—returns a boolean value to indicate whether the file is editable or not.

- `Files.exists()`—returns a boolean value to indicate whether the file exists or not.

- `Files.getLastModifiedTime()`—returns a `FileTime` object to indicate the files last modified time.

- `Files.size()`—returns a long value indicating the size of the file in bytes.

All the above methods accept an argument, i.e., the file name or path as a `Path` object.

L21 Creates another `Path` object.

L22 Same as L11.

L23 Checks for the existence of the file as already discussed.

L24 Checks whether two files are same using the static method `isSameFile()` of `Files` class. The two files are passed as `Path` arguments to the method.

L25–26 Shows how to create a copy of a file. The `Files.copy` static method is used copy the contents of a file into another. The general notation for the copy method is as follows:

```
Files.copy(Path source, Path target,
CopyOption... options)
```

The first two arguments are source and destination files as `Path` objects and last is the `CopyOption` object. The `CopyOption` interface is inherited by an `Enum`, `StandardCopyOption` which has three `Enum` constants. These can be specified as the last argument. These constants are:

`REPLACE_EXISTING`—Replace an existing file

`ATOMIC_MOVE`—Move the file as an atomic file system operation.

`COPY_ATTRIBUTES`—Copy attributes to the new file.

L27 `readAllLines` method of the `Files` class is used to read all line of the `Path` object.

L28 Shows how to rename a file. The method requires three arguments source, destination, and copy options. Source and destination are `Path` objects. If you want to rename a file and keep it in the same directory then you can use the method as shown in the program above. The destination `Path` object (file name can be specified in it) can be specified by using the `resolveSibling` method on the source `Path` object. In case you want to move a file to a new directory (newdir as `Path` object) then the destination `Path` object can be obtained by using the `resolve` method on the new directory `Path` object as shown below keeping the file name same.

```
Files.move(source, newdir.resolve(source.
getFileName()), REPLACE_EXISTING);
```

Or any name can be specified.

```
Files.move(source, newdir.resolve(" "),
   REPLACE_EXISTING);
```

L29 Shows how to delete a file.

L31–37 Shows how to traverse a directory, i.e., it prints all the files within the directory. L31 demonstrates the usage of try with resources statement. The newDirectoryStream method of the Files class is used to access a Path object. The Path object will refer to a directory that needs to be traversed. The newDirectoryStream method returns a collection DirectoryStream object that will hold only Path objects, i.e., files and directories within the Path object passed to the newDirectoryStream method. Please refer to the syntax used:

```
DirectoryStream<Path> ds
```

(We will discuss more on this syntax in Chapter 10.) A for-each loop is used to iterate the contents of the collection one by one.

L38–39 Shows how to convert a Path object to legacy File object.

Some of the other methods of the Files class are shown in Table 9.11.

Table 9.11 Few methods of Files Class

Methods	Description
long copy(InputStream in, Path target, CopyOption... options)	Copies all bytes from an input stream to a file.
Path copy(Path source, Path target, Copy Option... options)	Copy a file to a target file.
Path createDirectory(Path dir, File Attribute<?>... attrs)	Creates a new directory.
Path createFile(Path path, File Attribute<?>... attrs)	Creates a new and empty file, failing if the file already exists.
Path createLink(Path link, Path existing)	Creates a new link for an existing file.
Path createSymbolicLink(Path link, Path target, FileAttribute<?>... attrs)	Creates a symbolic link to a target.
Path createTempDirectory(Path dir, String prefix, FileAttribute<?>... attrs)	Creates a new directory in the specified directory, using the given prefix.
Path createTempDirectory(String prefix, File Attribute<?>... attrs)	Creates a new directory in the default temporary-file directory, using the given prefix.
void delete(Path path)	Deletes a file.
boolean deleteIfExists(Path path)	Deletes a file if it exists.
boolean exists(Path path, LinkOption... options)	Tests whether a file exists.
Path write(Path path, byte[] bytes, Open Option... options)	Writes bytes to a file.
Path setAttribute(Path path, String attribute, Object value, LinkOption... options)	Sets the value of a file attribute.
Object getAttribute(Path path, String attribute, LinkOption... options)	Reads the value of a file attribute.
Path walkFileTree(Path start, FileVisitor<? super Path> visitor)	Walks a file tree.

(Contd)

(Table 9.11 Contd)

Methods	Description
`InputStream newInputStream(Path path, OpenOption... options)`	Opens a file, returning an input stream to read from the file.
`OutputStream newOutputStream(Path path, OpenOption... options)`	Opens or creates a file, returning an output stream that may be used to write bytes to the file.
`SeekableByteChannel newByteChannel (Path path, OpenOption... options)`	Opens or creates a file, returning a seekable byte channel to access the file.

9.7 SERIALIZATION

Serialization is the process of converting an object to bytes so that its state can be made persistent. The state is made persistent by writing the bytes to a file. *De-serialization* is the reverse of serialization. It is the process of converting bytes back to object.

The question arises: Why should an object be made persistent? The state of object is defined by its properties (value of the instance variables). Normally we create objects, work with them, and when the job is done, they are garbage collected automatically. But suppose, we need the value of the instance variables at a later point of time, then the values will not be available. So in this case, serialization is helpful. A class that wants its objects to be serialized has to implement the `Serializable` interface. This interface is empty. It does not contain any method. This interface is implemented by the class to inform that the objects of that class can be serialized. The attributes that we do not want to serialize are made transient, e.g. temperature. By default, static variables of a class are also not serialized.

Example 9.12   **Serialization and De-serialization**

```
L1    import java.io.*;
L2    import java.util.*;
L3    class DayTimeTemp implements Serializable {
L4    Calendar d;
L5    transient float temperature;
L6    public DayTimeTemp(Calendar d,float f){
L7    this.d = d;
L8    this.temperature = f; }}
         // class to test serialization
L9    class TestSerialization {
L10   public static void main(String args[]) throws Exception
         {
L11   Calendar c = Calendar.getInstance();
L12   DayTimeTemp t = new DayTimeTemp(c,94.3f);
L13   FileOutputStream fos = new FileOutputStream("Serialize");
L14   ObjectOutputStream oos = new ObjectOutputStream (fos);
L15   System.out.println("Serializing Object......");
L16   System.out.println("Values to be serialized......");
L17   System.out.println("Time:" +c.getTime());
L18   oos.writeObject(t);
L19   System.out.println("Object Serialized......");
L20   oos.close();
```

```
L21    fos.close();
L22    FileInputStream fis = new FileInputStream("Serialize");
L23    ObjectInputStream ois = new ObjectInputStream(fis);
L24    System.out.println("Deserializing Object......");
L25    DayTimeTemp c1 = (DayTimeTemp)ois.readObject();
L26    System.out.println("Temperature: " +c1.temperature);
L27    System.out.println("Day, Date & Time: " +c1.d.getTime());
L28    ois.close();
L29    fis.close();
       }}
```

Output

```
C:\javabook\programs\CHAP09~1>java TestSerialization
Serializing Object......
Values to be serialized......
Time: Thu Mar 12 20:46:12 IST 2009
Object Serialized......
Deserializing Object......
Temperature: 0.0
Day, Date & Time: Thu Mar 12 20:46:12 IST 2009
```

Explanation

L1 io package is imported.

L2 util package is imported as Calendar class is part of it.

L3 Class inherits the serializable interface.

L4 Reference variable of Calendar class is created.

L5 float transient variable is declared. The values in transient fields are not written during serialization.

L6 Constructor of the class has been defined and it accepts two arguments: the Calendar object and the float value for temperature.

L7 and L8 Instance variables are initialized with the values passed in the constructor.

L9 Test class is created to serialize the DayTimeTemp class created in previous lines.

L11 As Calendar is an abstract class, it cannot be instantiated directly. So getInstance() static method of Calendar class is used to get Calendar instance.

L12 An object of DayTimeTemp class is created and Calendar instance is passed to it along with a float value as temperature. This object t will be serialized.

L13 For serialization, we need to write bytes to a file. So we need a byte stream class which can write to a file. FileOutputStream has been chosen and it is used to open the file 'serialize'. If the file already exists, it will be overwritten and if does not exist, a new file will be created.

L14 Now we need a class which can write object to OutputStream. So the ObjectOutputStream object is created and the FileOutputStream object (L13) is passed to the constructor of ObjectOutputStream object.

L15 Prints "Serializing Object......".

L16 Prints "Values to be serialized......".

L17 getTime() method of the Calendar class is used to return the Date object. This Date object when printed results in a call to the toString() method of the Date class automatically. The toString method of Date class returns a String containing current day (Sun), month (March), day of the month (15), time (HH:MM:SS format), time zone (IST), and year (2009) (see output).

L18 writeObject(t) method is used to write the DayTimeTemp object t to the FileOutputStream connected to it.

L19 Prints "Object Serialized......".

L20 and 21 Closes the ObjectOutputStream and FileOutputStream.

L22 We have to convert the bytes stored in the file (serialize) back to the object. So for this purpose, we need to first open the file for reading the bytes. That is why, FileOutputStream object is created and the filename is passed to the constructor of this object.

L23 `ObjectInputStream` is used for de-serialization of objects. Its object is created and `FileInputStream` object (L23) is passed to it.
L24 Prints `"Deserializing Object......"`.
L25 `readObject()` method is used to read the object from the `ObjectInputStream`. This method returns an object of type 'Object' which is casted to type of your defined class, i.e., `DayTimeTemp`. If it is not casted, an attempt to access the variables of `DayTimeTemp` will result in a compile time error, as these variables are not a part of the Object class.
L27 Prints the temperature in the retrieved object, i.e., 0.0, as it was a transient field (see output).
L28: Same as L17 but in this line, the object used is the de-serialized object.
L28 and 29 Closes the `InputStream`.

9.8 CLONING

Cloning is basically making copy of an existing object. There are two types of cloning: *shallow copy* and *deep copy*. Shallow copy creates a new instance of the same class and copies all the fields to the new instance and returns it. In case a class contains references to other classes as instance variables, shallow copy does not create new object (for instance variables defined in the class) when cloned, instead the objects (defined as instance variables in the class) are shared in the original and cloned object. In deep copying the object references contained within the original object are copied recursively and the important point is that they are different objects.

Note Serialization could also be used as an alternative to deep copying because serialization includes deep copying implicitly.

Java offers two more ways to create objects, i.e., `clone()` and `newInstance()` apart from the new operator. The `newInstance()` is a method of `java.lang.Class` class, it is commonly used by class loaders and dynamic program extension. The `clone()` method is a member of `Object` class and is used for creating copies of objects. Let us discuss the `clone()` method in detail.

The `clone` method is available to all the classes of Java as it is a part of the `Object` class. If you wish to create a copy of an existing object then you can invoke the `clone` method on that object provided the object inherits the `Cloneable` interface. The `Cloneable` interface is an empty interface. A class that wants its objects to be cloned must implement the `Cloneable` interface. If a class does not implement the `Cloneable` interface and clone method is invoked on its object, then a `CloneNotSupportedException` is thrown. Otherwise it returns an exact copy of the object as an `Object` reference. Let us take an example to show how cloning is done. The example below illustrates shallow copying.

Example 9.13 **Shallow Copy**

```
L1    class CloneDemo implements Cloneable
      {
        // instance variable
L2      private int value;
        // Constructor
L3      CloneDemo(int v)
        {
           value=v;
        }
L4      public Object clone()
```

```java
     {
L5      try {
L6         return super.clone();
        }
L7      catch(CloneNotSupportedException e)
        {
L8          System.out.println(e);
L9          return null;
        }
     }
L10  public int increment()
     {
L11     return ++value;
     }
L12  public int getValue()
     {
L13     return value;
     }
L14  public void setValue(int v)
     {
L15     value=v;
     }
}// CloneDemo class ends here

L16  class TestClone
     {
L17  public static void main(String args[])
     {
L18    CloneDemo d=new CloneDemo(23);

L19    System.out.println("Value in original object: "+d.getValue());

L20    CloneDemo cd=(CloneDemo)d.clone();

L21    System.out.println("Original object d: "+d);

L22    System.out.println("Cloned object cd: "+cd);

L23    System.out.println("Value in Cloned object: "+cd.getValue());

L24    cd.increment();

L25    System.out.println("Value after increment in Cloned object: "+cd.getValue());

L26    System.out.println("Value in original object: "+d.getValue());
     }
     }
```

Output

```
D:\javabook\Second Edition\programs>java TestClone
Value in original object: 23
Original object d: CloneDemo@18a992f
Cloned object cd: CloneDemo@4f1dOd
Value in Cloned object: 23
Value after increment in Cloned object: 24
Value in original object: 23
```

Explanation

L1 Class implements the `Cloneable` interface to signify that the objects of this class can be cloned.

L2 Declares an instance variable

L3 Declares a constructor which initializes the instance variable.

L4 Overrides the clone method of the `Object` class.

L5–6 Declares a `try` block with a call to the superclass `clone()` method from within itself (`super.clone()`). The clone method creates a copy of the object from which it has been invoked with similar values for its instance members. The `clone()` method might throw `CloneNotSupportedException` if the class did not implement the `Cloneable` interface. This clone method creates a copy of the object on which this method has been invoked. This copy is a new object which is a replica of that object.

L7–9 Declares a `catch` block corresponding to the `try` block to catch `CloneNotSupportedException`. Lastly a null is returned in case an exception is generated by the `clone` method.

L10–11 `increment` method is declared to increment the value of the instance variable.

L12–13 `getValue` method is defined to return the value of the instance variable.

L14–15 `setValue` method is defined to set the value of the instance variable.

L16 `TestClone` class is defined to test cloning of `CloneDemo` objects.

L17 `main` method is declared.

L18 An object of `CloneDemo` is created (see Fig. 9.3).

L19 The value in the object created is obtained using the `getValue` method and printed (see output).

L20 A clone of the original object (created in L18) is created using the clone method. The return type of the clone method is `Object` so it returns the copy of the cloned object as an `Object` which has to be casted back to the `CloneDemo` to access the method and variables of that class (see Fig. 9.3).

L21–22 Prints both the objects: the original and the cloned one to show that they are different objects. It is evident from the output printed on the screen. The hexadecimal representation of the internal addresses of the objects is not same. It clearly states that they are two different objects not referring to the same memory location (see output and Fig. 9.3).

L23 Prints the value of the instance variable of the cloned object, i.e., 23.

L24 Increments the value of the instance variable of the cloned object.

L25 Prints the value of the instance variable of the cloned object. Now the value is 24 (see output).

L26 Prints the value of the instance variable of the original object, i.e., 23. The increment on the cloned object does not have any effect on the instance variable of the original object.

Note The clone method is a protected method in the `object` class. Thus, only subclasses and classes within a package are able to access it. In case you wish to make it accessible to any class in any package, then you need to override it and declare it as a public method.

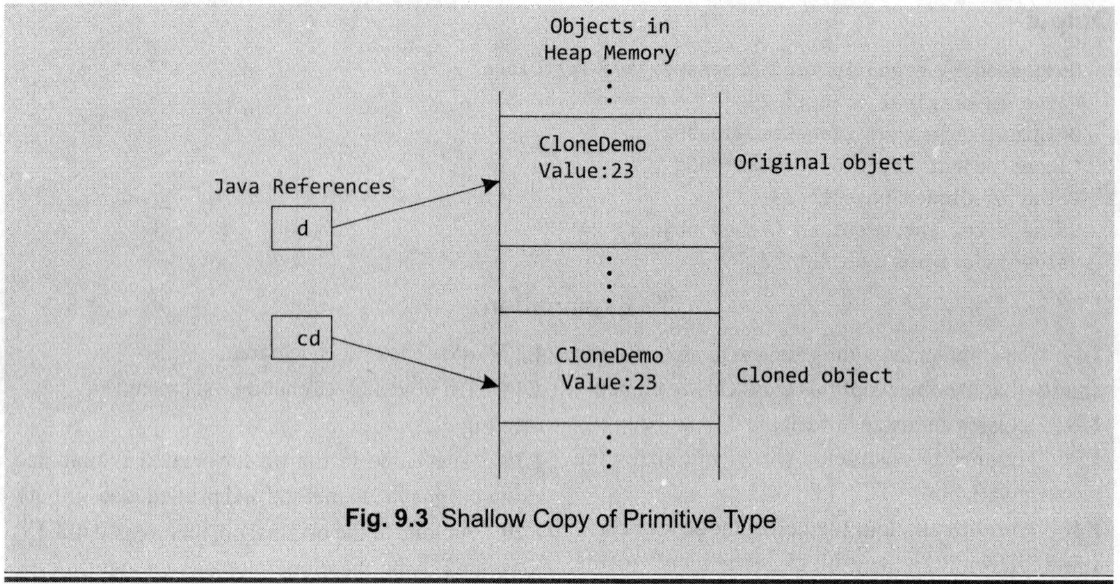

Fig. 9.3 Shallow Copy of Primitive Type

The above class contains a primitive type value and when cloned the object contains its own copy of the primitive type. Let us see what happens when the same class contains a reference type.

Example 9.14   Shallow Copy of a Class Containing References to Other Classes

```
     /* class whose reference will be used as instance variable in another class */
L1   class CloneReferenceTest
     {
L2     int value;
L3     CloneReferenceTest(int v)
       {
L4       this.value=v;
       }
     }
L5   class CloneDemo implements Cloneable
     {
     // object reference created
L6   CloneReferenceTest br;
L7   CloneDemo()
     {
L8     br = new CloneReferenceTest(12);
     }
     // clone method overridden
L9   public Object clone()
     {
L10    try {
L11      return super.clone();
       }
L12    catch(CloneNotSupportedException e)
       {
```

```
L13            System.out.println(e);
L14            return null;
            }
          }
        }
    // class declared for Testing Cloning
L15    class TestClone
       {
L16    public static void main(String args[])
       {
L17       CloneDemo d = new CloneDemo();
L18       CloneDemo cd =(CloneDemo)d.clone();
L19       System.out.println("Original object d: " +d);
L20       System.out.println("Original object inner reference: " +d.br);
L21       d.br.value--;
L22       System.out.println("Original object inner reference instance variable: "+d.
          br.value);

L23       System.out.println("Cloned object cd: "+cd);
L24       System.out.println("Cloned object inner reference: "+cd.br);
L25       System.out.println("Cloned object inner reference instance variable: "+cd.
          br.value);
       }
     }
```

Output

```
D:\javabook\Second Edition\programs>java TestClone
Original object d: CloneDemo@c3c749
Original object inner reference: CloneReferenceTest@150bd4d
Original object inner reference instance variable: 11
Cloned object cd: CloneDemo@1bc4459
Cloned object inner reference: CloneReferenceTest@150bd4d
Cloned object inner reference instance variable: 11
```

Explanation

L1–4 Declares a class, i.e., `CloneReferenceTest` which will be used within the class `CloneDemo`. Earlier we used a primitive as an instance variable. In this example we will be using a reference variable of class `CloneReferenceTest` as an instance variable of class `CloneDemo`. This reference variable is instantiated within the constructor of class `CloneReferenceTest`.

L5 Class `CloneDemo` is defined. This class inherits the `Cloneable` interface as we want to create clone of this class.

L6 Instance variable for the class if defined. It is basically a reference variable of type `CloneReferenceTest`.

L7–8 Constructor for `CloneDemo` is declared. This constructor initializes the instance variable of the class. So basically the reference variable (L6) is initialized by creating an object of `CloneReferenceTest` and assigning it to the reference variable.

L9–14 The clone method is overridden and implemented as in the previous example.

L15 For testing and cloning the object we have created a class `TestClone` as in the previous example.

L16 Main method declaration.

L17–18 An object of class `CloneDemo` and its clone is created. An object of class `CloneDemo` results in creation of an object of `CloneReferenceTest` automatically from within the constructor of `CloneDemo` class. The `CloneReferenceTest` constructor initializes its value instance field to 12. The return type of the clone method is Object so it returns the copy of the cloned object as an `Object` which has to be casted back to the `CloneDemo` to access the method and variables of that class.

L19–20   Prints the original object and the object reference it is using (as its instance variable).

L21   Instance variable in the original object is decremented. This variable is contained within the class `CloneReferenceTest`. So to access the variable we use `d.br.value` where br being an instance member of d can be accessed using dot operator and similarly for `value` instance variable of br.

L22   Prints the decremented value of the instance variable: `value`.

L23–24   Prints the cloned object and the object reference it is using (as its instance variable). The hexadecimal representation of the internal addresses of the original and the cloned objects is not the same. It clearly states that they are two different objects. But the hex representation of the internal addresses of the object references that both these objects are using (their respective instance variables) is same. It means both original and cloned objects instance variable object references are pointing to the same memory location. A change in instance variable (`value`) of `CloneReferenceTest` through original object (d) will be reflected when the instance variable will be accessed using cloned object (cd) (see Fig. 9.4).

L25   Prints the instance variables value using cloned object. This value is similar to the value printed using original object for the reason explained above.

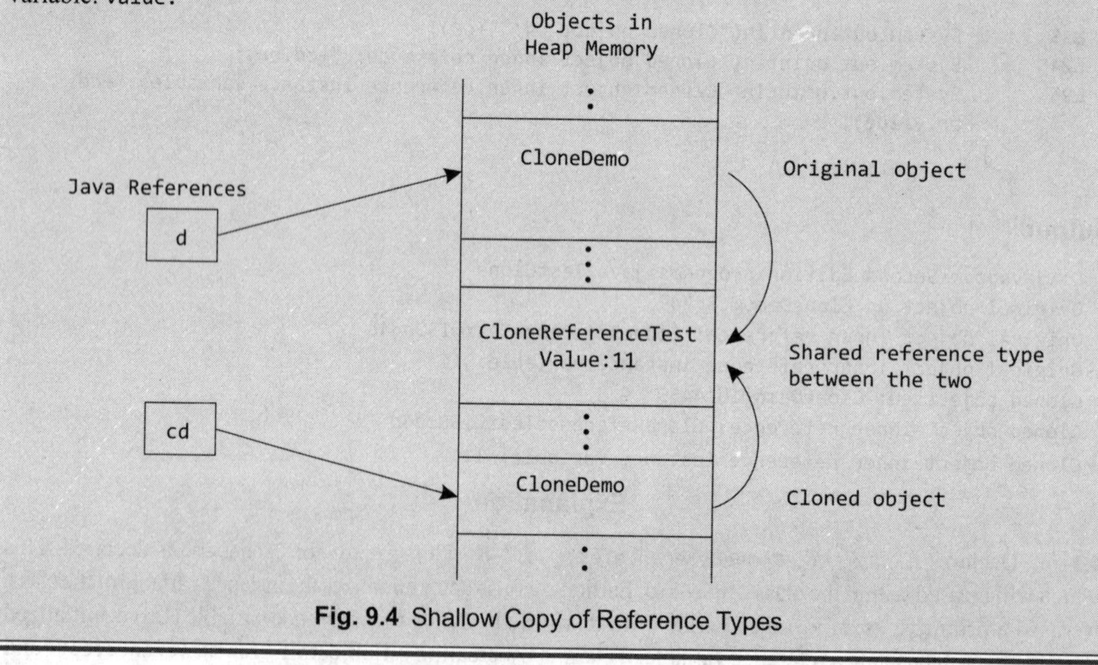

Fig. 9.4 Shallow Copy of Reference Types

As we have seen from Example 9.13 that the object references contained within an object are not copied during cloning instead they are shared. In case we want to clone object with all the object references contained within the object, we should deep copy the object. For deep copying, the object references (used within the class) should also implement the `Cloneable` interface and override the clone method in their respective classes.

Example 9.15   Deep Copy

```
L1    class CloneReferenceTest implements Cloneable
      {
L2      int value;
```

```
L3      CloneReferenceTest(int v)
        {
L4        value = v;
        }
L5      public Object clone()
        {
L7        try {
L8          return super.clone();
          }
L9        catch(CloneNotSupportedException e)
          {
L10         System.out.println(e);
L11         return null;
          }
        }
      }
L12  class CloneDeepDemo implements Cloneable
     {
       // reference of another class declared here
L14    CloneReferenceTest br;
L15    CloneDeepDemo()
       {
L16        br = new CloneReferenceTest(12);
       }
       // clone method
L17    public Object clone()
       {
L18        CloneDeepDemo cdd = null;
L19        try {
L20            cdd =(CloneDeepDemo) super.clone();
       }
L21        catch(CloneNotSupportedException e)
          {
L22            System.out.println(e); //return null;
          }
L23        cdd.br =(CloneReferenceTest)br.clone();
L24        return cdd;
       }
     }
L25  class TestDeepClone
     {
L26    public static void main(String args[])
       {
L27        CloneDeepDemo d = new CloneDeepDemo();
L28        CloneDeepDemo cd = (CloneDeepDemo)d.clone();
L29        System.out.println("Original object d: "+d);
L30        System.out.println("Original object inner reference: "+d.br);
L31        d.br.value--;
L32        System.out.println("Original object inner reference    instance variable:
           "+d.br.value);
L33        System.out.println("Cloned object cd: "+cd);
L34        System.out.println("Cloned object inner reference: "+cd.br);
L35        System.out.println("Cloned object inner reference Instance variable:
           "+cd.br.value);
       }
     }
```

Output

```
D:\javabook\Second Edition\programs>java TestDeepClone
Original object d: CloneDeepDemo@c3c749
Original object inner reference: CloneReferenceTest@150bd4d
Original object inner reference instance variable: 11
Cloned object cd: CloneDeepDemo@1bc4459
Cloned object inner reference: CloneReferenceTest@12b6651
Cloned object inner reference instance variable: 12
```

Explanation

L1–11 Class `CloneReferenceTest` is defined as in Example 9.14. The difference is that now it inherits `Cloneable` interface and overrides the `clone()` method. It clearly signifies that this class objects can also be cloned. The implementation of the clone method is similar to that of previous programs.

L12 Declares `CloneDeepDemo` class similar to `CloneDemo` of the previous program. The only difference lies in the implementation of the clone method.

L17–24 We have to deep copy the object. So, an empty reference variable of class `CloneDeepDemo` is created and the clone method is invoked through the existing `CloneDeepDemo` object i.e., d. This gives us a clone of `CloneDeepDemo` object (i.e., d). In order to deep copy, all the references types within `CloneDeepDemo` should also be cloned so on L24 we invoke the clone method on br (i.e., of `CloneReferenceTest` class) object to create a clone of this object. It returns an object of type Object which is casted into `CloneReferenceTest` and stored in the br instance variable of the cd object. Note that we have not enclosed L24 in the try catch block because the clone method of `CloneReferenceTest` class includes a try-catch and catches all exceptions thrown from clone method (Fig. 9.5).

L25–35 `TestDeepClone` class is declared. (Same as `TestClone` of the previous program).

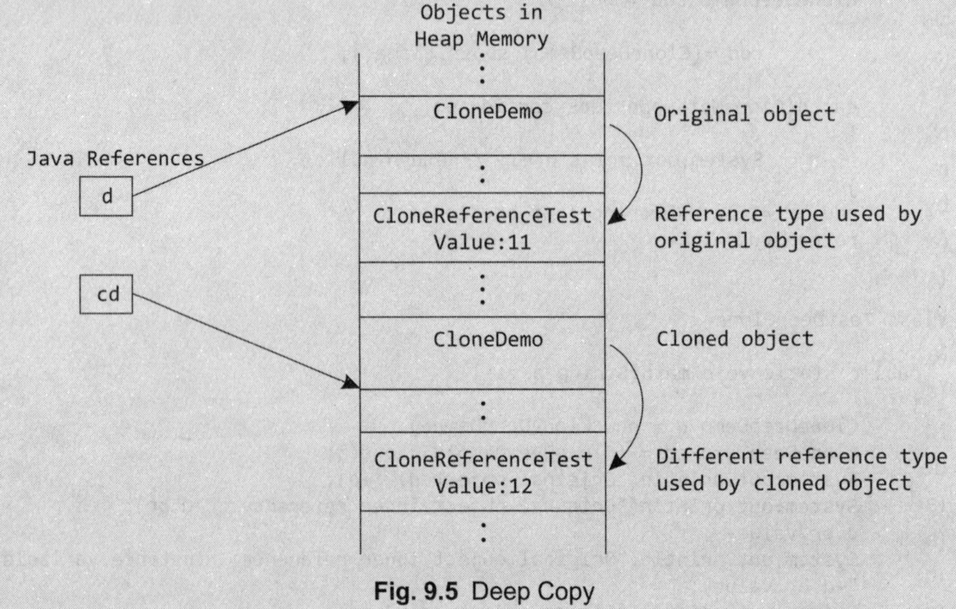

Fig. 9.5 Deep Copy

Note Clone method should be applied only to mutable objects which are referenced by instance variables of the cloned object. Objects whose state can change are mutable and whose state cannot are immutable like String and wrapper classes.

SUMMARY

JDK 1.4 introduced `java.nio` package in addition to the `java.io` package. The I/O in Java is based on streams: byte and character. A few classes in both categories have been discussed in the chapter. These files show how to read and write data (both byte and character) to files. `RandomAccessFile` class is used for reading and writing a file randomly by setting the file pointer at a particular position in the specified file. Java 6 introduced `Console` class for user input and output to the user. `java.nio` has a few subpackages also like `java.nio.channels` (used for creating channels to files). The `FileChannel` is used for establishing connection to file so that they can be read, written, mapped, and locked. `MappedByteBuffer` class provided in `java.nio` package is used for mapping files. Serialization is used to convert object to bytes and de-serialization does the reverse. Java 7 introduced `java.nio.file` package and added new classes like files and interfaces like `Path` to replace the legacy class like `java.io.File`. A new interface `SeekableByteChannel` was also added in `java.nio.channels` package which provides functionality similar to the `java.io.RandomAccessFile`, etc. This chapter also discusses in detail about cloning—shallow and deep.

EXERCISES

Objective Questions

1. Which abstract class is the superclass of all classes used for reading characters?
   - (a) `Reader`
   - (b) `FileReader`
   - (c) `ByteReader`
   - (d) `InputStream`

2. Which abstract class is the superclass of all classes used for writing bytes?
   - (a) `Writer`
   - (b) `FileWriter`
   - (c) `CharWriter`
   - (d) `OutputStream`

3. Name the class that allows reading of binary representations of Java primitives from an input byte stream.
   - (a) `DataWriter`
   - (b) `FileWriter`
   - (c) `DataInputStream`
   - (d) `DataOutputStream`

4. Which of these classes are abstract?
   - (a) `FilterWriter`
   - (b) `Reader`
   - (c) `InputStream`
   - (d) All the above

5. Name the exception thrown by the read method defined in the `InputStream` class.
   - (a) `ArithmeticException`
   - (b) `NullPointerException`
   - (c) `IOException`
   - (d) `IllegalAccessException`

6. What will happen when you try to compile and run the following code and pass the following at the user prompt–"MyValue"?

```java
import java.io.*;
class Demo6{
  public static void main(String
  args[]){
    Console c = System.console();
    String x = c.readLine("Enter ur value");
    int a = Integer.parseInt(x)+10;
    c.printf("the value is %1$d",a);
}}
```
   - (a) `ArithmeticException`
   - (b) `NullPointerException`
   - (c) `IOException`
   - (d) `NumberFormatException`

7. What will happen when you try to compile and run the following code?

   (Assuming `abc.txt` exists in the current directory)

```java
import java.io.*;
class Demo6{
  public static void main(String
  args[]){
    FileInputStream f = new
    FileInputStream("abc.txt");
    System.out.println("size:"
    +f.available());
}}
```
   - (a) does not compile
   - (b) compiles successfully but generates an exception at run time.

(c) executes successfully

(d) generates an IOException while reading the available byes in file

8. What will happen when you try to compile and run the following code and the file `abc.txt` does not exist?

```java
import java.io.*;
class Demo6{
    public static void main(String args[])
    throws Exception{
        FileInputStream f = new
        FileInputStream("abc.txt");
        System.out.println("size:"
        +f.available());
}}
```

(a) `ArithmeticException` is thrown

(b) `NullPointerException` is thrown

(c) `IOException` is thrown

(d) `FileNotFoundException` is thrown

9. Which of the following was introduced in Java 7 to replace `RandomAccessFile` class?

(a) `java.nio.SeekableByteChannel`

(b) `java.nio.channels.ByteChannel`

(c) `java.nio.channels.SeekableByteChannel`

(d) `java.nio.files.SeekableByteChannel`

10. Which of the following was introduced in Java 7 to replace `java.io.File` class?

(a) Files class and Path interface

(b) `ava.nio.Files` class

(c) `java.nio.file.File` class

(d) none of the above

Review Questions

1. Explain the utility of `RandomAccessFile` class with all its modes.

2. Explain in detail all the possible ways of taking inputs from the user.

3. Explain the difference between `FileInputStream` and `BufferedInputStream`. Show an example in support of your answer.

4. Explain the following terms:
   (a) Memory mapping   (b) Virtual memory
   (c) File channel

5. What is serialization and de-serialization? Why is it required? Name the interface used for serialization.

6. Explain Java 7 new io enhancements.

7. Explain shallow copy and deep copying.

Programming Exercises

1. Write a program that lists all the files in a directory including the files present in all its subdirectories as well. Get name/path of the directory from the user through standard input. [Hint: Use recursion]

2. Using classes under the `Appendable` interface, append string data to a file. Get the name of the file from the user.

3. Write a program to read the contents of a file byte by byte and copy it into another file. Get names of the files from the user through standard input.

4. Write a program to read the contents of a file into a character array and write it into another file. Get names of the files from the user through standard input.

5. Write a program that writes primitives (byte, short, int, long) followed by the string "Starting File Now...." to the beginning of a file.
   [**Hint:** Use `RandomAccessFile`]

6. Write a program that appends data to the file using `FileWriter` class.
   [**Hint:** Use a different constructor of `FileWriter` class]

7. Write a program that maps a file. Use this mapping to write contents to the file.
   [Use `java.nio` package]

8. Create a class that has a static field x, a non-static field y, and a transient field z. Initialize them through a constructor. Serialize the class and then deserialize it.

9. Write a program to create a sequential file that could store details about the employees of an organization. Details include empId, empName, empAge, empDept, and empSal. These are provided through keyboard.

10. How many lines, words, and characters does a file have? Write a program for the same.

PROJECT WORK

Simulate an Employee database using files in Java. This database contains name, address, phone number, designation, and salary. The provision of adding new record, deleting an existing record, searching a record, and updating a record should be provided. An employee id should be automatically generated whenever a new record is added. This employee id will be similar to the primary key in databases. For searching, deleting, and updating a record, the user should be prompted to enter the Employee ID. Before deletion and updating, the user must be prompted for a confirmation, e.g.

"Are you sure you want to delete the record? yes/no".

Answers to Objective Questions

1. (a) **2.** (d) **3.** (c) **4.** (d)

5. (c) **6.** (d) **7.** (a) Compile time error as in two statements, two exceptions may be thrown, so a try/catch or throws clause should be used

8. (d) **9.** (c) **10.** (a)

Generics, java.util, and other API

In the absence of willpower, the most complete collection of virtues and talents is wholly worthless.
Aleister Crowley

After reading this chapter, the readers will be able to

- understand collections
- understand and use generics
- understand how basic data structures are embedded in `util`
- know the basic concept of `LinkedList`, `ArrayList`, and `Vector`
- understand the basic concept behind `Set`, `HashSet`, and `TreeSet` as also `Map`, `HashMap`, and `TreeMap`
- use collections class, enumeration, and iterator
- understand the usage of random class
- implement observer pattern using observer class and observable interface
- understand runtime class
- learn about reflection API

10.1 INTRODUCTION

Utility means usefulness. Utility classes are those that help in creation of other classes. The `java.util` package contains utility classes such as Date, Calendar, Stack, LinkedList, and StringTokenizer, etc. The classes in `java.util` package use collections, i.e., a group of objects. Collection classes work on objects, i.e., they store/retrieve objects.

Note Primitives cannot be directly stored and retrieved in collections. Wrapper classes representing primitives were created in `java.lang` package to work with collections.

The `java.util` package has an interface called *collection*. A collection supports a group of objects. A collection may be ordered/unordered as well as some collections may possess duplicates while others may not. This collection interface has sub-interfaces such as set, list, and queue. Figure 10.1 shows the inheritance hierarchy of collection interface. These interfaces have concrete subclasses

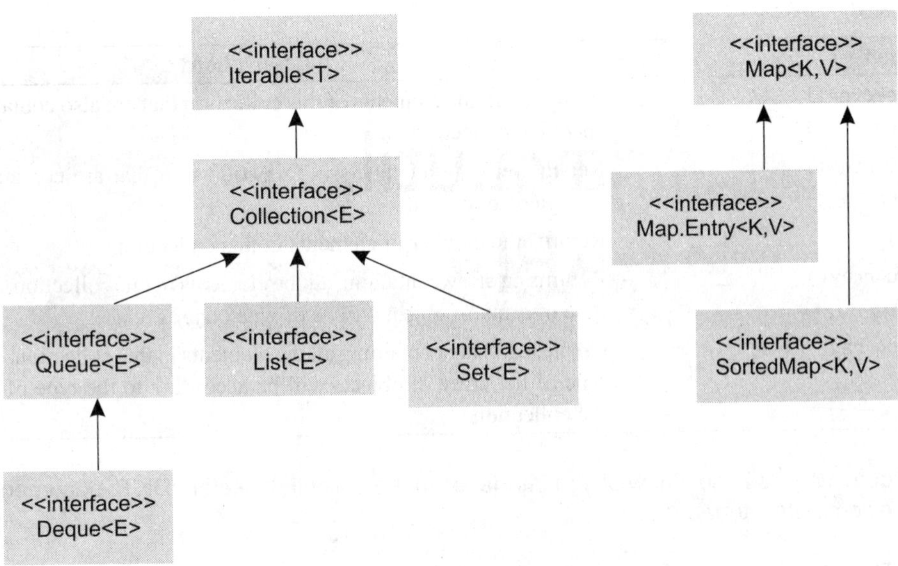

Fig. 10.1 Collection Inheritance Hierarchy

such as `LinkedList`, `Stack`, and `Vector`. Besides collection, we have shown another interface `Map` which work on pairs—key/value pairs. This interface has a nested interface named entry. We will discuss the details later in the chapter. Table 10.1 lists the methods of `collection` interface.

Table 10.1 Methods of `collection` Interface

Method	Description
`boolean add(E e)`	Adds the specified element to the collection and returns true. It returns false only in case the collection does not accept duplicates (like Set).
`boolean addAll (Collection<? extends E> c)`	Adds all the elements in the specified collection to this collection and returns true if collection changed.
`void clear()`	Clears the collection by removing all the elements from this collection.
`boolean contains(Object o)`	Returns true if this collection contains the specified object.
`boolean containsAll (Collection<?> c)`	Returns true if this collection contains all the elements in the specified collection.
`boolean equals(Object o)`	Compares the specified object with this collection for equality and returns true if equal.
`int hashCode()`	Returns the hash code value for the collection.
`boolean isEmpty()`	Returns true if this collection is empty.
`Iterator<E> iterator()`	Returns an iterator to iterate the elements in this collection.
`boolean remove(Object o)`	Removes a single instance of the specified element from this collection, if it is present.

(Contd)

(*Table 10.1 Contd*)

Method	Description
`boolean removeAll (Collection<?> c)`	Removes all the elements of this collection that are also contained in the specified collection.
`boolean retainAll (Collection<?> c)`	Retains only the elements in this collection that are contained in the specified collection.
`int size()`	Returns the number of elements in this collection.
`Object[]toArray()`	Returns an array containing all the elements in this collection. The return type of array of object will be of type `Object` class.
`<T> T[] toArray(T[] a)`	Creates an array containing all the elements in this collection. The return type of the array of objects will be according to the type of objects in the collection.

Note Figure 10.1 does not show all the interfaces in the collection. Refer JDK 6 documentation for the complete interface list.

The `java.lang.Iterable` interface was added by JDK 1.5 and collection interface was made to inherit it so that the objects can be iterated using a `for-each` loop. This interface provides a method named `iterator()` that returns an iterator object to iterate all the objects in the collection. The collection interface is implemented by an abstract class `AbstractCollection`, which is the parent of all the collection classes and it implements almost all the methods of the collection interface.

`List` interface refers to an ordered but duplicate collection of objects. We refer to a list as ordered because the user has full control over the order in which an object is inserted into the list. The top level class for `list` interface is an abstract class `AbstractList` (which is a subclass of `AbstractCollection`). `AbstractList` implements almost all the methods of `list` interface (as given in Table 10.2) and has three subclasses `AbstractSequentialList`, `ArrayList`, and `Vector`. `LinkedList` class is subclass of `AbstractSequentialList` and its definition has been modified in JDK 1.6 to implement the `Queue` interface. Methods of `Queue` interface are listed in Table 10.3. `Stack` is a subclass of the `vector` class. We will discuss these classes later in the chapter.

Table 10.2 Methods of `list` Interface

Method	Description
`boolean addE(E e)`	Appends the specified element to the list.
`void add (int index, E element)`	Inserts the specified element at the specified position in this list.
`boolean addAll(Collection<? extends E> c)`	Appends all the elements in the specified collection to the end of this list, in the order that they are returned by the specified collection's iterator.
`boolean addAll(Collection<? extends E> c)`	Appends all the elements in the specified collection to the end of this list, in the order that they are returned by the specified collection's iterator.
`boolean addAll(int index, Collection<? extends E> c)`	Inserts all of the elements in the specified collection into this list at the specified position.
`void clear()`	Clear by removing all the elements from this list.
`boolean contains(Object o)`	Returns true if this list contains the specified element.

(Table 10.2 Contd)

Method	Description
`boolean containsAll (Collection<?> c)`	Returns true if this list contains all the elements of the specified collection.
`boolean equals(Object o)`	Compares the specified object with this list for equality.
`E get(int index)`	Returns the element at the specified position in this list.
`int hashCode()`	Returns the hash code value for this list.
`int indexOf(Object o)`	Returns the index of the first occurrence of the specified element in this list, or −1 if this list does not contain the element.
`boolean isEmpty()`	Returns true if this list contains no elements.
`Iterator<E> iterator()`	Returns an iterator over the elements in this list in proper sequence.
`int lastIndexOf (Object o)`	Returns the index of the last occurrence of the specified element in this list, or −1 if this list does not contain the element.
`ListIterator<E> listIterator()`	Returns a list iterator over the elements in this list.
`ListIterator<E> list Iterator(int index)`	Returns a list iterator of the elements in this list, starting at the specified position in this list.
`E removeint(int index)`	Removes the element at the specified position in this list.
`boolean removejava.lang. Object(Object o)`	Removes the first occurrence of the specified element from this list, if it is present.
`boolean removeAll (Collection<?> c)`	Removes from this list all of its elements that are contained in the specified collection.
`boolean retainAll (Collection<?> c)`	Retains only the elements in this list that are contained in the specified collection.
`E set(int index, E element)`	Replaces the element at the specified position in this list with the specified element and returns the elements previously stored at the specified position.
`int size()`	Returns the number of elements in this list.
`List<E>subList(intfrom Index, int toIndex)`	Returns a sub list containing elements between the specified from `Index`, inclusive, and to `Index`.
`Object[]toArray()`	Returns an array containing all of the elements in this collection. The return type of array of object will be of type `Object` class.
`<T> T[] toArray(T[] a)`	Creates an array containing all of the elements in this collection. The return type of the array of objects will be according to the type of objects in the collection.

Table 10.3 Methods of queue Interface

Method	Description
`boolean addE(E e)`	Inserts the specified element into this queue and returns true and throws an `IllegalStat-eException` if no space is currently available.
`E element()`	Retrieves, but does not remove, the head of this queue.
`boolean offer(E e)`	Preferred over `add(E e)` when using a capacity based queue, as it returns a boolean value if unsuccessful rather than an exception.
`E peek()`	Retrieves, but does not remove, the head of this queue, or returns null if this queue is empty.
`E poll()`	Retrieves and removes the head of this queue, or returns null if this queue is empty.
`E remove()`	Retrieves and removes the head of this queue.

Queue interface was added in JDK 1.5 to support the data structure. Queue operates in FIFO (first in first out fashion). Elements inserted into the collection first are removed from the collection first. It provides methods to examine elements at the head of the queue. This interface is inherited by the Queue interface to support double-ended queue. These queues support operations to add/remove/examine elements at both ends (head and tail) of the queue. Table 10.3 shows the methods of Queue interface.

Set is a collection that does not contain duplicate objects. This interface is implemented by an abstract class AbstractSet which implements some of the methods of Set interface. The concrete classes, HashSet, EnumSet, etc., are subclasses of AbstractSet. This interface is inherited by SortedSet interface to access the element in a sorted order (ascending). The class TreeSet inherits the SortedSet interface and the AbstractSet class. Table 10.4 shows the methods of Set interface.

Map interface provides mapping of key/value pairs. These key/value pairs are unique. A static inner interface named Entry is declared inside the Map interface for referring to each key/value pair. This Map is inherited by an interface SortedMap to access the elements stored in Map in a sorted order. AbstractMap class inherits the Map interface and provides implementation for most of the

Table 10.4 Methods of Set Interface

Methods	Description
boolean add(E e)	Adds the specified element to this set if it is not already present and returns true, else false.
boolean addAll(Collection<? extends E> c)	Adds all the elements in the specified collection to this set if they are not already present, and returns true if set is changed, else false.
void clear()	Clears the set by removing all the elements from this set.
boolean contains(Object o)	Returns true if this set contains the specified object.
boolean containsAll(Collection<?> c)	Returns true if this set contains all the elements of the specified collection.
boolean equals(Object o)	Compares the specified object with this set for equality.
int hashCode()	Returns the hash code value for this set.
boolean isEmpty()	Returns true if this set is empty.
Iterator<E> iterator()	Returns an iterator over the elements in this set.
boolean remove(Object o)	Removes the specified element from this set if it is present.
boolean removeAll(Collection<?> c)	Removes from this set all its elements that are contained in the specified collection.
boolean retainAll(Collection<?> c)	Retains only the elements in this set that are contained in the specified collection.
int size()	Returns the number of elements in the set.
Object[]toArray()	Returns an array containing all the elements in this set. The return type of array of objects will be of type Object class.
<T> T[]toArray(T[] a)	Creates an array containing all the elements in this set. The return type of the array of objects will be according to the type of objects in the collection.

methods in the interface. This class is inherited by concrete classes such as `HashMap`, `EnumMap`, etc. `TreeMap` also inherits this class as well as the interface `SortedMap`.

Most of the interfaces and classes in the `java.util` package use generics. This is evident from the syntax (e.g.,<E>, <?>, <? extends E>) used in most of the interface and class declaration as well as some of the methods. So first let us discuss the concepts behind generics.

10.2 GENERICS

This feature was added in Java 5 with an aim to provide strict-type checking at compile time. Generic feature also allows same class to be used by many different collections of objects such as string, integer, etc. Consider the following example, where we have created three classes named `A`, `B`, and `GenericTest`. The class `GenericTest` has a collection of `ArrayList` class to hold objects. The objects of A and B are placed in it and later we try to retrieve them. When we try to compile the program, two notes appear at the DOS prompt asking the user to recompile the program specifying the `-Xlint:unchecked` option of `javac`. This option is used to show all lint warning, specifically the unchecked warnings (as shown in the section 'what happens while compiling the program?' below). These warnings are appearing as the code does not use the newer generic syntax. These warnings can be suppressed if we compile the program using the `-source` option and specify the JDK version prior to 1.5 (i.e., `javac -source 1.4 GenericTest.java`).

Example 10.1(a)   Use of Generics

```
L1    import java.util.*;
L2    class A
      {
L3      public String toString(){return "Class A Object";}
      }
L4    class B
L5    {
      public String toString(){return "Class B object";}
      }
L6    class GenericTest {
L7      public static void main(String args[])
        {
L8      List v = new ArrayList();
L9      v.add(new A());
L10     v.add(new A());
L11     v.add(new B());
L12     Iterator en = v.iterator();
L13     while(en.hasNext())
          {
L14       A o = (A)en.next();
L15       System.out.println(o);
          }
      }}
```

What happens while compiling the program?

```
C:\javabook\programs\chap 10>javac GenericTest.java
Note: GenericTest.java uses unchecked or unsafe operations.
Note: Recompile with -Xlint:unchecked for details.
```

```
C:\javabook\programs\chap 10>javac -Xlint:unchecked GenericTest.java
GenericTest.java:14: warning: [unchecked] unchecked call to add(E) as a member of the raw
type List v.add(new A());
            ^
  where E is a type-variable:
  E extends Object declared in interface List
GenericTest.java:15: warning: [unchecked] unchecked call to add(E) as a member of the raw
type List v.add(new A());
            ^
  where E is a type-variable:
  E extends Object declared in interface List
GenericTest.java:16: warning: [unchecked] unchecked call to add(E) as a member of the raw
type List v.add(new B());
            ^
  where E is a type-variable:
  E extends Object declared in interface List
3 warnings
```

Output

```
C:\javabook\programs\chap 10>java GenericTest
Class A Object
Class A Object
Exception in thread "main" java.lang.ClassCastException: B cannot be cast to A
at GenericTest.main(GenericTest.java:21)
```

Explanation

L1 Import java.util package.

L2–5 Two classes named A and B are defined with their own toString() methods.

L6 Class GenericTest defined.

L7 main method is defined within it.

L8 An object of ArrayList class is created. This object will act as a container for other objects. ArrayList supports the functionality of dynamic array. Array have a limitation that they cannot grow/shrink in size but ArrayList objects can grow and shrink in size as and when required.

L9–11 Using the add method, objects are added to the ArrayList. Two objects of class A are added and one object of B is added to collection.

L12 An Iterator object is obtained using iterator() method to iterate the collection one by one.

L13–15 A while loop to iterate the collection one by one. The hasNext() method tells whether the collection has more elements or not. The loop continues till the time collection has more elements to iterate. The next()method returns the next object in the collection. The return type of next() method is an object of type Object (Parent class). This object is cast to A and then printed. When you try to run the program for the first two iterations, the cast is legal as the object retrieved is of type A. But in the third iteration the object retrieved is of type B, so the cast is illegal. That is why a ClassCastException results as shown in the output. (It is for this very reason that we have received unchecked warnings on compilation of the program).

Note The problem occurred because there was no restriction on the type of objects that can be put into a collection. In the earlier example we had put objects of A as well as B into the collection and we are casting all objects into A which raised an alarm at runtime. It would be much better to check at compile-time what goes into a collection so that no exception occurs at run time.

If we could ensure only objects of A should go into the collection then the problem can be solved and that is where generics help. Most of the interfaces, classes as well as some of the methods have been modified to use generic syntax. The generic declaration of list is as follows:

```
List<E> v = new ArrayList<E>();
//This E has been replaced by A as shown. Normally single Capital
//character are used to denote generic Formal parameterized types
//refer JDK6 docs for details
List<A> v = new ArrayList<A>();
// a List of objects of A (actual parameter)
```

The name placed in the angle brackets (commonly known as specifying *parameterized type*) is class name whose objects we want to put into a collection. Now this collection will not contain objects of class other than the class-name mentioned in the angle brackets. For example, if we try to insert an object of type B into collection 'v' (after using parameterized types), a compile time error results.

Note that the list now contains only objects of type 'A' and the compiler assures us of this. So is the cast on L14 really required? Well logically it should not be required but if you remove the cast on L14, the compiler complains about it. Why? The reason is we did parameterize the list but we did not parameterize the iterator which continued to return an object of type object on invocation of the next method. Similar to list, iterator also uses the generic parameterized types. So if we change L12 as shown, the problem gets solved and the cast can now be removed safely.

```
Iterator<A> en = v.iterator();
   while(en.hasNext())
   {
      A o = en.next();
      System.out.println(o);
   }
```

Also note that if you rewrite the program that uses the generics parameterized types the warnings are all gone.

Example 10.1(b) Generics Parameterized Types

```
class GenericTest {
  public static void main(String args[])
  {
  // Collection that will hold only object of A
    List<A> v = new ArrayList<A>();
    v.add(new A());
    v.add(new A());
  // to show that the Iterator will also hold objects of A
    Iterator<A> en = v.iterator();
    while(en.hasNext())
    {
        A o = en.next();                 // the cast in this line is gone
        System.out.println(o);
    }
  }
  }}
```

Output

```
Class A object
Class A object
```

10.2.1 Using Generics in Arguments and Return Types

Generics are applicable for passing parameters to a method as well as returning parameters from a method. Let us take a look at how parameterized type is used in passing arguments and how to return parameterized types. The following example creates a list that holds only string objects.

Example 10.2 **Parameterized Type as Argument and Return Types**

```
L1    import java.util.*;
L2    class ParamArgsGeneric
      {
      // method returning parameterized types
L3    List<String>getList()
      {
L4        List<String> l = new ArrayList<String>();
L5        l.add("Hello");
L6        l.add("Generics");
L7        return l;
      }

      // method accepting parameterized types
L8    void print(List<String> c)
      {
L9        Iterator<String> i = c.iterator();
L10       while(i.hasNext())
L11       System.out.println(i.next());
      }

      public static void main(String args[])
      {
L12       ParamArgsGeneric pag = new ParamArgsGeneric();
L13       List<String> l = pag.getList();
L14       pag.print(l);
      }}
```

Output

```
C:\javabook\programs\chap 10>java ParamArgsGeneric
Hello
Generics
```

Explanation

L3 The method `getList()` returns a `List` object that holds only string objects.

L8 Shows a method `print()` accepting a `List` that should hold only string objects.

10.2.2 Wildcards

In Example 10.2, if we change L13 as follows:

```
List<Object> l = pag.getList();
```

Anybody would consider it legal arguing `Object` is the superclass of `String` so the assignment should be legal, but that is not the case. A List of Object is not a List of String. Why?

Consider the case if a List of String is a List of Object that means the above modified L13 is supposedly working. Then we could also insert lines in the program to add objects of type Object to the List. Now when we retrieve them and try to store in a List of String it gives a cast exception because we are trying to store an Object into a String. So a List of Object is not a List of String and vice versa.

If you want to be flexible in using the classes as they were used earlier (i.e., without parameterized types), then either you will have to suppress the warnings or you will have to be rigid in using the collection of a particular type. Well, there is a midway wherein we can use the collection to hold different types of object not just a particular type using generic syntax. This is possible with the help of wildcards, i.e.,'**?**'. Let us take a look at how wildcards can be used.

Example 10.3 **Usage of Generics Wildcards**

```
L1    import java.util.*;
L2    class ParamArgsGeneric {
L3    List<?>getList()
         {
L4         List<String> l = new ArrayList<String>();
L5         l.add("Hello");
L6         l.add("Generics");
L7         return l;
         }
      // accepts any Collection
L8    void print(Collection<?> c)
         {
L9    Iterator<?> i = c.iterator();
L10        while(i.hasNext())
L11        System.out.println(i.next());
         }
         public static void main(String args[])
         {
L12        ParamArgsGeneric pag = new ParamArgsGeneric();
L13        List<?> l = pag.getList();
L14        pag.print(l);
         // another List created and passed to print()
L15        List<Integer> li = new ArrayList<Integer>();
L16        li.add(new Integer(1));
L17        li.add(new Integer(2));
L18        li.add(new Integer(3));
L19        pag.print(li);
      }}
```

Output

```
C:\javabook\programs\chap 10>java ParamArgsGeneric
Hello
Generics
1
2
3
```

Explanation

L3 The getList method returns a list of unknowns, i.e., List<?>. Just to show you that list of unknown can be returned from a method we have used this syntax here.

L4 An ArrayList of string is created.

L8 Method print has been defined to accept a collection that can hold any type of object. You would probably think that a collection holding any type of object would also be rewritten as Collection<Object> but that is not the case as explained earlier. This method (as shown in the example) prints a list of strings as well as integers.

L9 The iterator object obtained, can hold any type of objects to be iterated as the wildcard has been specified. Iterator<?> i=c.iterator(); In Example 10.2 we had created an iterator of string objects specifically so it could iterate only on a collection of string. Iterator<String> i=c. iterator();

L10–11 Loops through the iterator and prints any type of collection.

L13 The getList method is called to return a collection in the form of a list of any type of objects. The return list is captured in a list of unknowns, i.e., List<?>.

Note Can we re-write L4 as:

```
List<?> l = new ArrayList<String>();
```

This is illegal because a list of unknowns need not necessarily be a list of strings. So wildcards can be used in passing parameterized types as arguments or return types as well as capturing the return values from the methods.

10.2.3 Bounded Wildcards

In the previous section, we have discussed wildcards (?) which means unknown types. There is no restriction on the type of object that can be contained in the collection. Bounded wildcards place certain restriction on the type of objects that a collection can hold. For example,? extends X.

Note ? specifies unknown type, but this unknown type will be a subclass of X. So in this case we know that this unknown type is either X or one of its subclasses.

In the following example we have created three classes A, B, and C. Class B inherits from A. C is an independent class. Now let us see how bounded wildcards place a restriction on collection of objects.

Example 10.4 **Bounded Generic Wildcards**

```
        import java.util.*;
        class A
L1          { public String toString(){return "class A";}}
L2      class B extends A
L3          { public String toString(){return "class B";}}

L4      class C {}

L5      class BoundedWildcard {              // shows Bounded wildcard
L6      void print(List<? extends A> c)
L7      {
L8          Iterator<?> i = c.iterator();
L9          while(i.hasNext())
```

```
L10         System.out.println(i.next());
        }
L11     public static void main(String args[]){
L12     BoundedWildcard pag = new BoundedWildcard();
L13     List<B> li = new ArrayList<B>();
L14     li.add(new B());
L15     li.add(new B());
L16     pag.print(li);
L17     List<A> la = new ArrayList<A>();
L18     la.add(new A());
L19     la.add(new A());
L20     pag.print(la);
L21     List<C> lc = new ArrayList<C>();
L22     lc.add(new C());
L23     lc.add(new C());

        /*illegal to pass List holding objects of class C to print method as it will
        accept only those list that have either objects of A or the objects of its sub-
        classes*/
L24     //pag.print(lc);
        }}
```

Output

```
C:\javabook\programs\chap 10>java BoundedWildcard
class B
class B
class A
class A
```

Explanation

L6 Shows a method `print` that accepts any unknown type (?) of objects with the restriction that it must either be an object of A or an object of subclass of A.

L13–16 A list collection is created to hold objects of class B only. The object of B are added using add method and the list is passed to the print method. The print method accepts the list as B is a subclass of A.

L17–20 Another `List collection` is created to hold objects of class A only. The object of A are added using add method and the list is passed to the print method. The print method accepts the list as objects are of type A.

L21–24 A third `List collection` is created to hold objects of class C only. The object of C are added using add method and the `List` is not passed to the print method as it will not accept this `List` because C is not a subclass of A. we have specifically commented L24 because it is illegal.

Now if you revisit Tables 10.1 to 10.4, you will realize most of the methods defined in the interface return and accept generic types.

10.2.4 Defining Your Own Generic Classes

You can create your own classes that use generic syntax. For using a generic syntax in your classes, a normal naming convention should be followed for specifying parameterized types. The naming convention is a single capital letter used for specifying parameterized types. For example,

T is for specifying any type. The letter E has been used in the Java collection API extensively to denote collection elements. In Map, the alphabet K is for keys and V is for values. Let us take an example to see how to use generics in user defined classes. In the following example we will create a class that will hold objects of a particular type and we can get and set (change) the object.

Example 10.5 **User Defined Generic Class**

```
L1    class A<T> {
L2    private T var;
L3    public A()
      {
L4      var = null;
      }
L5    public A(T a)
      {
L6        var = a;
      }
L7    public T getVar()
      {
L8        return var;
      }
L9    public void setVar(T a)
      {
L10       var = a;
      }}
      class TestGeneric{
      public static void main(String args[]){
        System.out.println("The User Defined Generic class holds Integer Object");
L11     A<Integer> v = new A<Integer>(new Integer(1));
L12     System.out.println("Value: " +v.getVar());
L13     v.setVar(new Integer(3));
L14     System.out.println("New Value: " +v.getVar());
        System.out.println("The User Defined Generic class holds String Object");
L15     A<String> a = new A<String>("User Defined Generics");
L16     System.out.println("Value: " +a.getVar());
        }}
```

Output

```
C:\javabook\programs\chap 10>java TestGeneric
The User Defined Generic class holds Integer Object
Value: 1
New Value: 3
The User Defined Generic class holds String Object
Value: User Defined Generics
```

Explanation

L1   We have created a class named A that accepts a parameterized type T. This class will hold objects of only a particular type 'T'.

L2   An instance variable var has been defined in this class and the type of this var will be determined by the parameterized type.

L3 and 4   Default constructor for the class has been defined which assigns null to the var.

L5 and 6   Parameterized constructor is defined that takes an argument of type `T` and assigns it to var.

L7 and 8   getVar() method is defined to return the var instance variable. The return type of the method has to be `T` as the type of var is still unknown.

L9 and 10   setVar(T a) method has been defined to set and mutate the value of var. The method accepts an argument of type T.

L11   We create an object of A and specify the type of object that A will hold as integer. (T is now automatically an integer). The type of var is now integer. The return type of getVar() is integer and the `setVar(Integer a)` method now accepts an argument of type integer.

L12   getVar() is used to return the value of var.

L13   An integer object is passed in the setVar(T a) method.

L14   getVar() is used to return the new value of var.

L15   We create another object of A and specify the type of object that A will hold as string now. (T now automatically becomes a string). The type of var is now string. The return type of getVar() is string and the setVar (String a) method now accepts an argument of type String.

L16   getVar() is used to return the value of var initialized by passing string in the parameterized constructor.

10.3 LINKED LIST

Linked list is a fundamental data structure that contains records. A record contains data as well as a reference to the next record. A record can be inserted or removed at any point in the `Linked List`. In comparison to normal arrays which allow random access, linked lists allow sequential access. To support this data structure, Java has a class named `LinkedList`. `LinkedList` is a collection class that can act as a stack, queue as well as a double-ended queue. `LinkedList` permits null to be added to the list. Let us take an example to see how `LinkedList` can act as a list, stack, queue as well as a double-ended queue.

Example 10.6   **Demonstration of `LinkedList` Class**

```
     import java.util.*;
     class LinkedListDemo {
     public static void main(String args[])
     {
L1       LinkedList<String> lis = new LinkedList<String>();
L2       lis.add("Hello");
L3       lis.add("Linked List");
L4       lis.add("Demo");
L5       lis.add(null);
L6       for(String s:lis)
         System.out.println(s);

     // as a Stack (LIFO order)
L7       LinkedList<Integer> st = new LinkedList<Integer>();
L8       st.push(new Integer(1));
L9       st.push(new Integer(2));
L10      st.push(new Integer(3));
L11      st.add(new Integer(4));
L12      System.out.println("Object popped: " +st.pop());
```

```
L13        System.out.println("Object popped: " +st.pop());
L14        System.out.println("Object popped: " +st.pop());
L15        System.out.println("Object popped: " +st.pop());
L16        LinkedList<Long> l = new LinkedList<Long>();
      // as queue (FIFO order)
L17        l.add(new Long(1));
L18        l.add(new Long(2));
L19        l.add(new Long(3));
L20        l.add(new Long(4));
L21        System.out.println("Queue : "+l);
L22        System.out.println("head of queue: "+l.peek());
L23        System.out.println("head of queue removed and returned: " +l.poll());
L24        System.out.println("Queue : " +l);
      //as a double ended queue
      // insertion and deleltion at both ends
L25        l.addFirst(new Long(0));
L26        System.out.println("Double ended Queue : "+l);
L27        l.addLast(new Long(5));
L28        System.out.println("Double ended Queue : "+l);
L29        System.out.println("head of queue removed and returned:" +l.removeFirst());
L30        System.out.println("tail of Queue removed and returned:" +l.removeLast());
L31        System.out.println("Double ended Queue : " +l);
           }}
```

Output

```
C:\javabook\programs\chap 10>java LinkedListDemo
Hello
Linked List
Demo
null
Object popped: 3
Object popped: 2
Object popped: 1
Object popped: 4
Queue : [1, 2, 3, 4]
head of queue: 1
head of queue removed and returned: 1
Queue : [2, 3, 4]
Double ended Queue : [0, 2, 3, 4]
Double ended Queue : [0, 2, 3, 4, 5]
head of queue removed and returned: 0
tail of Queue removed and returned: 5
Double ended Queue : [2, 3, 4]
```

Explanation

L1 A linked list of String is created.

L2–5 Objects of type String are added to the linked list using add() method. This method adds elements to the end of the list and returns a boolean to indicate the element has been added to the list.

L6 for-each loop is used to iterate through each element of the linked list. The next element of linked list is assigned to s in every iteration and then it is printed.

L7–15 Show how linked list acts as a stack.

L7 A new linked list is created which holds Integer objects.

L8–10 The push method is used to add elements at the head of the list. (push method is used to push contents to the top of the stack). Top of the stack is now 3 and bottom is 1.

L11 add method is used to add contents to the end of the list. So the new bottom of the stack now is 4.

L12–15 pop operation of the stack is used to remove the top of the stack. The first pop operation removes 3, the second one 2, third 1, and last pop results in 4 (see output).

L16–31 Shows how linked list can be used as a queue and a double-ended queue.

L16 A new linked list is created which holds Long objects.

L17–20 Elements are added to the end of the list using the add method.

L21 Prints the list.

L22 The first element of the list is returned (but the element is not removed from the list) by the peek method.

L23 poll method is used to return and remove the first element of the list.

L24 Prints the list (see output).

L25–31 Show that a LinkedList can be used as a double ended queue. A double ended queue is one that supports addition and deletion from both ends.

L25 addFirst() method adds the element at the head of the list.

L26 Prints the list (see output).

L27 addLast method is used to add element at the end of the list.

L28 Prints the list (see output).

L29 removeFirst() method removes the element at the head of the list.

L30 removeLast() method removes the element at the end of the list.

L31 Prints the list (see output).

10.4 SET

Set is a collection that does not contain duplicates. Set collection in java.util models the mathematical concept set. The concepts of union, intersection, and the difference of a set are available in the Set interface and supported by its subclasses. We will discuss two classes under this interface, i.e., HashSet and TreeSet. TreeSet is a sorted collection as it inherits the SortedSet interface (sub-interface of Set), whereas HashSet is not a sorted collection. HashSet uses the concept of hashing.

Note Hashing is a technique to quickly find, add, and remove elements from a collection. This technique is useful in situations like we have a directory of words and we need to find a particular word. A directory would contain thousands and thousands of words. If we want to search a word; matching each and every word with the word we wanted to search would consume a lot of time.

Hashing stores the data in such a way that retrieval of data is fast. It uses a function (hash function) to create an index (hash code) and this index is used to narrow down the search. These indexes are maintained in a hash table, as shown in Fig. 10.2.

The hash table is an array of linked list. To find a place in the bucket array, the index is divided by the total number of buckets in the array. The remainder that we get is the position of the element in the array. If no element is present at that position in the bucket then it is added else a collision occurs. If bucket is full, then also a collision occurs and the table has to be rehashed. Actually the load factor (i.e., n/m where n is the number of items to be stored and m is the size of the bucket) determines when a table needs to be rehashed. The default value for load factor is 0.75; it means when the table is 75% full, it will be rehashed and the bucket size will be doubled.

Note

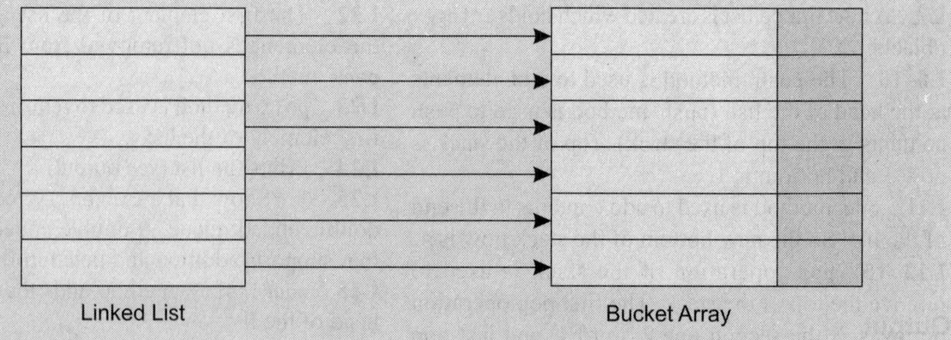

Fig. 10.2 Hash Table

The size of the bucket is always specified in power of 2. Even if you provide a value that is not a power of 2, it is automatically rounded to the next power of 2.

10.4.1 HashSet Class

This class can be used for effectively storing and retrieving the elements but the order is not guaranteed by this class. In case you need to retrieve the elements in a sorted order use TreeSet class. HashSet permits null to be added to the collection. Let us take an example to demonstrate HashSet class

Example 10.7 Demonstration of HashSet

```
import java.util.*;
class HashSetDemo{
    public static void main(String args[])
    {
L1      HashSet<String> hs = new HashSet<String>();
L2      hs.add("D");
L3      hs.add("B");
L4      hs.add("A");
L5      hs.add("C");
L6      hs.add(null);
L7      hs.add("E");
L8      System.out.println("Hash Set: " +hs);
L9      System.out.println("Re-adding C to set:" +hs.add("C"));
L10     System.out.println("Iterating contents of Hash Set one by one");
L11     for(String s:hs) System.out.println("\t"+s);
L12     System.out.println("Size of Hash Set: " +hs.size());
L13     System.out.println("null removed: " +hs.remove(null));
L14     System.out.println("Hash Set: " +hs);
L15     System.out.println("check whether Set contains C :" +hs.contains("C"));
L16     HashSet<String> hs1 = new HashSet<String>();
L17     hs1.add("D");
L18     hs1.add("B");
L19     hs1.add("E");
//subset
L20     System.out.println("hs: " +hs);
L21     System.out.println("hs1: " +hs1);
L22     System.out.println("hs1 is a subset of hs: " +hs.containsAll(hs1));
//Intersection
```

```
L23        hs.retainAll(hs1);
L24        System.out.println("Intersection of hs and hs1: " +hs);
       //Difference
L25        hs.removeAll(hs1);
L26        System.out.println("Difference of hs and hs1: " +hs);
       //Union
L27        System.out.println("Hash Set to be united with previous set: " +hs1);
L28        hs.addAll(hs1);
L29        System.out.println("Union of hs and hs1: " +hs);
       }}
```

Output

```
C:\javabook\programs\chap 10>java HashSetDemo
Hash Set: [null, D, E, A, B, C]
Re-adding C to set: false
Iterating contents of Hash Set one by one
     null
     D
     E
     A
     B
     C
Size of Hash Set: 6
null removed: true
Hash Set: [D, E, A, B, C]
check whether Set contains C :true
hs: [D, E, A, B, C]
hs1: [D, E, B]
hs1 is a subset of hs: true
Intersection of hs and hs1: [D, E, B]
Difference of hs and hs1: []
Hash Set to be united with previous set: [D, E, B]
Union of hs and hs1: [D, E, B]
```

Explanation

L1   A HashSet of string is created.

L2–7   add method is used to add String to the HashSet.

L8   Prints the HashSet (see output to check the order is not maintained).

L9   When you try to add the element which is already present in the set the method call is ignored and false is returned by the add method. (Remember: Set does not contain duplicates) (see output).

L10 and 11   Iterating the contents of the HashSet using the for-each loop.

L12   size() method is used to return the size of the HashSet, i.e., 6 as six objects have been added to the collection.

L13   remove() method is used to remove an element from HashSet and this method returns true if element is present.

L14   Prints the HashSet.

L15   To find a particular element in the set, the contains(Object o) method is used. This method returns true if element is found, else false.

L16   A new HashSet is created to show the basic operations of mathematical set: union, intersection, and difference.

L17–19   Objects of type string are added to this new HashSet.

L20 and 21   Prints both the HashSet.

L22   If a HashSet (hs) contains all the elements of another HashSet (hs1) then hs1 can be called as a subset of hs. The set provides a method containsAll(Collection<?> c) which returns true if the invoking collection contains all the element of the argument collection, else false.

L23 and 24 Intersection of two sets produces the common elements in both sets. The method provided by set is retainAll(Collection<?> c). This method removes all elements from the invoking set (hs) which are not a part of argument set (hs1) and returns true if the invoking set is changed.

L25 and 26 The elements of set A that are not contained in set B gives the difference of two set. The method removeAll(Collection<?> c) serves the same purpose for us and returns true if the invoking set is changed. The result in our case is that after this operation, hs does not contain any element because (before this operation) all elements of hs were already present in hs 1.

L27–29 L27 prints the Collection (hs1) to be united with the set (hs). addAll(Collection<?> c)is used to add all the element of the collection into the invoking set. This operation resembles the union of two sets and returns true if the invoking set is changed. L29 prints Set 'hs' (See output).

10.4.2 TreeSet Class

TreeSet offers a strict control over the order of elements in the collection. The collection is a sorted collection. But this may not offer you the best performance in terms of retrieving elements speedily (use HashSet instead of TreeSet). TreeSet does not permit null in the collection.

Example 10.8 **Demonstration of TreeSet**

```java
import java.util.*;
class TreeSetDemo
     {
     public static void main(String args[])
        {
L1      TreeSet<String> ts=new TreeSet<String>();
L2      ts.add("D");
L3      ts.add("B");
L4      ts.add("A");
L5      ts.add("C");
L6      ts.add("A");
L7      ts.add("C");
     //ts.add(null); does not accepts null values
L8      for(String s:ts)
        System.out.println(s);
L9      System.out.println("TreeSet: "+ts);
L10     System.out.println("First element of TreeSet: "+ts.first());
L11     System.out.println("Last element of TreeSet: "+ts.last());
L12     System.out.println("Size of TreeSet: "+ts.size());
      }}
```

Output

```
C:\javabook\programs\chap 10>java TreeSetDemo
A
B
C
D
TreeSet: [A, B, C, D]
```

```
First element of TreeSet: A
Last element of TreeSet: D
Size of TreeSet: 4
```

Explanation

L1 A `TreeSet` of `String` is created.
L2–7 `String` objects are added using the `add` method. The objects have been added in a random order. Duplicates as we have already discussed are ignored and add method returns false.
L8 Using `for-each` loop the contents of `TreeSet` are iterated.

L9 Prints the `TreeSet`.
L10 and 11 The first and the last elements of the `TreeSet` can be obtained using `first()` and `last()` methods of the `TreeSet` object.
L12 Prints the size of the `TreeSet`, i.e., 4.

10.5 MAPS

Map allows unique key/value pairs to be added. For searching an element from the set, you need to have an exact copy of the element to be searched from the collection but normally we do not have the exact copy. What we have is some key information about the element. We need a way to look up the element with the help of that key. A Map collection is helpful in these cases as it stores key along with their associated values. These keys in Map are unique. Map does not allow null key and values. We will discuss two of the subclasses of `Map` interface, i.e., `HashMap` and `TreeMap`.

10.5.1 HashMap Class

`HashMap`, like `HashSet` uses hashing as a technique to store key/value pairs so that the values can be searched efficiently according to the key. There order is not guaranteed by `HashMap`. The `HashMap` does not allow null key and null value pair to be stored.

Example 10.9 **Demonstration of HashMap**

```
import java.util.*;
class HashMapDemo
        {
        public static void main(String args[])
            {
L1          HashMap<String,String> hm = new HashMap<String,String>();
L2          hm.put("Emp001","Tom");
L3          hm.put("Emp002","Peter");
L4          hm.put("Emp003","Watson");
L5          //hm.add(null,null); unlike HashSet it does not accept null values
L6          System.out.println("HashMap: "+hm);
L7          System.out.println(hm.put("Emp003","David"));
L8          System.out.println("HashMap: "+hm);
L9          System.out.println("Key in Map");
L10         for(String s:hm.keySet())
L11         System.out.println(s);
L12         System.out.println("Values in Map");
```

```
L13        for(String s:hm.values())
L14        System.out.println(s);
L15        System.out.println("value associated with Emp002:" +hm.get("Emp002"));
L16        System.out.println("Size of HashMap:" +hm.size());
L17        System.out.println("remove mapping associated with Emp002:" +hm. remove("Emp002"));
L18        System.out.println("HashMap after removal:" +hm);
           }}
```

Output

```
C:\javabook\programs\chap 10>java HashMapDemo
HashMap: {Emp002=Peter, Emp003=Watson, Emp001=Tom}
Watson
HashMap: {Emp002=Peter, Emp003=David, Emp001=Tom}
Key in Map
Emp002
Emp003
Emp001
Values in Map
Peter
David
Tom
value associated with Emp002: Peter
Size of HashMap: 3
remove mapping associated with Emp002: Peter
HashMap after removal: {Emp003=David, Emp001=Tom}
```

Explanation

L1 HashMap object is created to store string key and string value. This has been specified as HashMap<String, String>.

L2–4 put (K key, V value) method is used for adding keys and values to the HashMap. This method returns null if no mapping for the key exists in the HashMap. If mapping exists the previous value associated with the key is returned.

L5 Shows null is not entertained in HashMap.

L6 Prints the HashMap (see output. All key/value pairs are shown).

L7 put method is used to overwrite the value associated with the key **Emp003** and as the mapping was already present, this method returns the previous value associated with the key, i.e., Watson (see output).

L8 Prints the HashMap. The output now reflects value associated with **Emp003** as **David**.

L9–11 Prints all the keys one by one on the standard output. The method keySet() returns a Set object of keys which is used in the for-each loop to print all the keys in the Set.

L12–14 Prints all values one by one on the standard output. The method values() returns a Collection object of all values which is used in the for-each loop to print all the values in the Collection.

L15 If you want to get the value associated with a particular key; use get method. The get method accepts the key as an argument and returns the value.

L16 size() method returns the size of the HashMap.

L17 If you want to remove ant mapping; use the remove method. This method accepts an argument, i.e., the key whose mapping is to be removed (Emp002) and returns null if key is not found or else the return the previous value associated with the key, i.e., 'Peter' (see output).

L18 Prints the resultant HashMap.

10.5.2 TreeMap Class

`TreeMap` contains sorted mapping of key/value pairs. In case we need to get sorted mapping we should use this class.

Example 10.10   **Demonstration of TreeMap**

```
import java.util.*;
class TreeMapDemo
   {
      public static void main(String args[])
      {
L1       TreeMap<String,String> tm = new TreeMap<String,String>();
L2       tm.put("Emp001","Tom");
L3       tm.put("Emp002","Peter");
L4       tm.put("Emp003","Watson");
L5       // tm.add(null,null); alike TreeSet, it does not accept null as key and value
L6       System.out.println("TreeMap: " +tm);
L7       tm.put("Emp003","David");
L8       System.out.println("TreeMap: " +tm);
L9       System.out.println("Key in Map");
L10      for(String s:tm.keySet())
            System.out.println(s);
L11      System.out.println("Values in Map");
L12      for(String s:tm.values())
            System.out.println(s);
L13      System.out.println("value associated with Emp002: " +tm.get("Emp002"));
L14      System.out.println("Size of TreeMap: " +tm.size());
      }}
```

Output

```
C:\javabook\programs\chap 10>java TreeMapDemo
TreeMap: {Emp001=Tom, Emp002=Peter, Emp003=Watson}
TreeMap: {Emp001=Tom, Emp002=Peter, Emp003=David}
Key in Map
Emp001
Emp002
Emp003
Values in Map
Tom
Peter
David
value associated with Emp002: Peter
Size of TreeMap: 3
```

Explanation

We have discussed all the methods in the previous example.

10.6 Collections CLASS

A `Collections` class contains a number of static methods that operate on `Collection` such as copy a collection, reversing the elements of a collection, replacing an element with another and so on. Let us take an example to understand better the usage of `Collections` class.

Example 10.11   Collections **Class**

```java
import java.util.*;
public class CollectionsDemo
{
     public static void main(String[] args) {
L1       List<String> l = new LinkedList<String>();
L2       l.add("Ignorance");
L3       l.add("is");
L4       l.add("a");
L5       List<String> sb = new LinkedList<String>();
L6       sb.add("Bliss");
L7       List<String> srch = new LinkedList<String>();
L8       srch.add("Bliss");
L9       System.out.println ("Elements in list : " + l);
// create a copy of defined list and print objects of copy list.
L10      Collections.copy(l,sb);
L11      System.out.println ("copy of list : " + l);
// find and display index of first occurrence of sublist in the list.
L12  System.out.println("First index of 'Bliss':" + Collections.indexOfSubList(l, srch));

// replace all objects in list by a new given object.
L13      Collections.replaceAll(l, "Bliss", "welcome");
L14      System.out.println("After replace all 'Bliss': " + l);
// list in reverse order.
L15      Collections.reverse(l);
L16      System.out.println("List in reverse order: " + l);
// swaps specified element with element at 1st(second) position
L17      Collections.swap(l, 1, l.size() - 1);
L18      System.out.println("List after swapping : " + l);
// Replace all the element with given element using fill()
L19      Collections.fill(l, "Bliss");
L20      System.out.println("After filling all 'Bliss' in list : "+ l);
// getting an enum type of specified list through enumeration().
L21      Enumeration<String> e = Collections.enumeration(l);
L22      while (e.hasMoreElements())
L23          System.out.println(e.nextElement());
}}
```

Output

```
C:\javabook\programs\chap 10>java CollectionsDemo
Elements in list : [Ignorance, is, a]
copy of list : [Bliss, is, a]
```

```
First index of 'Bliss': 0
After replace all 'Bliss': [welcome, is, a]
List in reverse order: [a, is, welcome]
List after swapping : [a, welcome, is]
After filling all 'Bliss' in list : [Bliss, Bliss, Bliss]
Bliss
Bliss
Bliss
```

Explanation

L10 All elements from list `sb` are copied to list 1 starting from the first location in the list 1. The elements in 1 will be overwritten by the elements in sb. The only requirement is that the destination list should be as long as source list to accommodate the elements otherwise an `IndexOutOfBoundsException` is generated. The signature of copy method is as follows:

```
public static <T> void copy(List<? super T>
dest, List<? extends T> src)
```

L11 Prints the list after copying (see output).

L12 Prints the first occurrence of `srch` in list 1. The method

```
index Of SubList(List<?> src, List<?>
target)
```

returns the first occurrence of target in src. (see output)

L13 and 14 All occurrences of a given object are replaced by another in a given specified list. The method `replaceAll (List<T> list, T oldval, T newval)` replaces `oldval` with `newval` in list 1. L14 prints the modified list (see output).

L15 and 16 `reverse(List<?> l)` reverses the specified list 1 and prints it.

L17 and 18 `swap` method is used to swap two elements in the list 1 at position i and j. `swap (List<?> l, int i,int j)`. L18 prints the revised list after swapping (see output).

L19 and 20 The `fill (List<? super T> l, T obj)` method is used to replace all the elements in list 1 with the object `obj`.

L21–23 A linked list works with iterators rather than an enumeration. Both interfaces are used for the same purpose, i.e., iterating through the collection elements yet they have differences which we will discuss in the next section. In case you want to obtain an enumeration of the `LinkedList`; use the `enumeration` method of the Collections class as shown in L21. This method accepts the collection (`List`) and returns an enumeration. Now you can iterate through the elements of the collection list using methods of the enumeration, as shown in L22 and 23.

> **Note** List <? super T> means that the list will hold objects of either T or any of its superclass. This is in contrast to '? extends T' which means the collection will hold objects of T or its subclasses.

10.7 LEGACY CLASSES AND INTERFACES

In this section, we will discuss one legacy class, i.e., vector, and one interface, i.e., enumeration. Also we would highlight the difference between the legacy class/interface and newer class (`ArrayList`)/interface (`Iterator`).

10.7.1 Difference Between Vector and ArrayList

`Vector` and `ArrayList` classes are both used to support the functionality of dynamic arrays. Array cannot grow/shrink in size so these classes have been provided in `java.util` package to support collection that can grow/shrink in size. Although these classes are used for the same purpose yet they have differences and based on these differences a programmer can decide which class has to be used when.

Vector is synchronized whereas ArrayList is not. That means a vector collection is thread-safe when accessed by multiple threads. On the other hand, an ArrayList offers better performance as it is not synchronized. ArrayList can be used when the collection will not be accessed by multiple threads. To iterate through the Vector collection we use a legacy interface Enumeration whereas for ArrayList, we use iterator interface.

We have already used ArrayList in the examples throughout the chapter. A Vector object can be created in a similar fashion as shown:

```
Vector<String> v = new Vector<String>();
```

The elements can be added to the vector using the add(E e) method as shown

```
v.add("One");
v.add("Two");
```

The method v.elements() returns an enumeration of object in the vector which can be iterated as shown earlier.

```
Enumeration<String> e = v.elements();
while(e.hasMoreElements())
    System.out.println(e.nextElement());
```

10.7.2 Difference Between Enumerations and Iterator

Enumeration is a legacy interface. The enumeration interface works with classes like vector. Suppose the vector contains integer objects. To iterate through the collection we obtain an enumeration by calling the elements() method of the vector object. This enumeration has two methods: hasMoreElements() that returns a boolean value to indicate that the collection has more values and nextElement() that returns the next element in the collection.

```
Enumeration<Integer> en = v.elements();
while(e.hasMoreElements())
    System.out.println(e.nextElement());
```

This enumeration is replaced by a newer interface; iterator. The iterator works with new classes such as ArrayList, LinkedList, and so on. The iterator differs from enumeration in the sense that it provides a method to delete element from the collection during the iteration. It has three methods:

- hasNext() returns boolean value to indicate that the iterator has next element in the collection.
- next() returns the next element in the collection.
- remove() method removes the last element returned by the iterator.

We have already shown you how to use iterator with ArrayList in Example 10.1.

10.8 UTILITY CLASSES: Random Class

Java provides an easy to use Random class to generate random numbers. This class is defined in the java.util package. The easiest way to create a random number generator is to instantiate the Random class using the parameter less constructor as shown below:

```
Random generator r = new Random();
```

Or use a parameterized constructor that accepts an argument, i.e., seed for the random generator. A seed is a number used to initialize a pseudorandom number generator,

```
Random generator r = new Random(long seed);
```

A random integer can be generated from a `Random` object using two methods: `nextInt()` and `nextInt(int n)`. They may return any integer: positive or negative. The overloaded method that accepts an argument can be used to generate random integers between 0 and some limit. For example, the following will generate a number between 0 and $n - 1$.

```
int randomInt = r.nextInt(n);
```

A random real number uniformly distributed between 0.0 and 1.0 can be generated using the `nextDouble` or `nextFloat()` method. Table 10.5 lists the methods of the `Random` class.

Table 10.5 Methods of Random Class

`protected int next (int bits)`	Returns the next random number as `int`.
`public boolean nextBoolean ()`	Returns the next boolean value.
`public void nextBytes (byte[] bytes)`	Generates random bytes and puts them into a byte array.
`public double nextDouble ()`	Returns the next random uniformly distributed double value between 0.0 and 1.0.
`public float nextFloat ()`	Returns the next random uniformly distributed float value between 0.0 and 1.0.
`public double nextGaussian ()`	Returns the next random Gaussian distributed double value with mean 0.0 and standard deviation 1.0.
`public int nextInt ()`	Returns the next random, uniformly distributed `int` value.
`public int nextInt (int n)`	Returns a random uniformly distributed `int` value between a range 0 (inclusive) and the user specified value (exclusive).
`public long nextLong ()`	Returns the next random uniformly distributed `long` value.
`public void setSeed (long seed)`	Sets the seed of this random number generator.

Let us take an example to show how random numbers can be generated.

Example 10.12 **Random Class**

```
L1    import java.util.Random;
L2    class RandomNumbers {
L3      public static final void main(String args[]){
        // creates a Random Object
L4        Random randomGenerator = new Random();
L5        for (int i = 1; i <= 6; ++i)
          {
          /** Generate a random integers in the range 1 and 6 for e.g. A Dice has numbers
          from one to six so when you roll the dice, any number can appear within this
          range*/
```

```
L6          int randomInt = randomGenerator.nextInt(6)+1;
L7          System.out.println(i+ ". Integer Random Number: "+randomInt);
        }
        /** Generate random double in the range 0.0 to 1.0 */
L7      double randomDouble = randomGenerator.nextDouble();
L8      System.out.println("Double Random Number: "+ randomDouble);

    /** Generate random float in the range 0.0 to 1.0 */
L9      float randomFloat = randomGenerator.nextFloat();
L10     System.out.println("Float Random Number: "+randomFloat);

    /** Generate random long */
L11     long randomLong = randomGenerator.nextLong();
L12     System.out.println("Long Random Number: "+ randomLong);
        }
    }
```

Output

```
C:\Windows\system32\cmd.exe

D:\javabook\chapter of java book\Second Edition\programs\chap 10>java RandomNumb
ers
1. Integer Random Number: 3
2. Integer Random Number: 3
3. Integer Random Number: 4
4. Integer Random Number: 6
5. Integer Random Number: 1
6. Integer Random Number: 4
Double Random Number: 0.04659591865268009
Float Random Number: 0.24931222
Long Random Number: 1627290471755325824

D:\javabook\chapter of java book\Second Edition\programs\chap 10>_
```

10.8.1 Observer and Observable

The `Observer` interface and `Observable` class is based on Observer pattern. This pattern states that a particular object (i.e., Observer) should be notified when the state of another object (i.e., Observable object) changes. In other words, the Observer observes the state of another object and wants itself to be notified about any changes in that object and the Observable object is the one in which the Observer is interested in. For example, you (Observer) are notified about the transaction updates of your bank account (Observable), as soon as the data (Observable) related to the pie chart or bar chart is updated the graphs (Observer) automatically adjust to the changes and so on.

> **Note** This pattern is also used in MVC architecture. MVC stands for **M**odel **V**iew **C**ontroller. The model object manages the behavior and data of the application, view takes care of the graphical or textual representation and the controller is used to interpret the user commands. The model responds to user requests from the controller by changing its state which is presented to the user through view. View can be treated as the observer on the model, i.e., observable object.

To illustrate the concept of observer pattern implementation, we consider a sample situation of customer and account. The account is held by a customer (account holder) of the Bank. As soon as the customer account balance is credited and debited, the customer will be updated about the information of his/her transaction. In this case customer is the observer and account possessed by the customer is the observable entity.

Example 10.13　`Observer and Observable`

```java
L1    import java.util.Observable;
L1    import java.util.Observer;
L3    class Bank
      {
          // Two References of Account
L4        Account a,a1;
          // Two customer references created
L5        Customer c,c1;
L6        public Bank()
          {
L7            c = new Customer("Rahul","C001",a=new Account(12000,"A001"));
L8            c1 = new Customer("Ram","C002",a1=new Account(12000,"A002"));
L9            a.addObserver(c);
L10           a1.addObserver(c1);
          }

L11       public static void main(String[] args)
          {
L12           Bank b = new Bank();
L13           b.demo();
          }

L14       public void demo()
          {
L15           a.credit(1000);
L16           a.debit(500);
L17           a1.debit(2000);
L18           a1.credit(6000);
          }
      }// Bank class ends here

L19   class Customer implements Observer
      {
L20       String custName;  // customer name
L21       String custId;    // customer id
L22       Account account;  // account object held by customer
L23       Customer(String custName,String custId,  Account account)
          {
L24           this.custName = custName;
L25           this.custId = custId;
L26           this.account = account;
          }
```

```java
                /** Print the fact that are notified. */
L27     public void update(Observable obs, Object x)
        {
L28         System.out.println(custName+ " Account Update" + ": " + ((Account)obs).getBal
            ance());
        }
        } // Customer class ends here

        /** The Observable entity i.e., Account maintains the data */
L29     class Account extends Observable
        {
L30         float balance;
L31         String accountNo;
L32         Account(float b, String acc)
            {
L33             balance = b;
L34             accountNo = acc;
            }
L35         Account()
            {
L36             balance = 0;
L37             accountNo = "";
            }
L38         float getBalance()
            {
L39             return balance;
            }
L40         void setBalance(float b)
            {
L41             balance = b;
            }
L42         String getAccountNo()
            {
L43             return accountNo;
            }
L44         void setAccountNo(String acc)
            {
L45             accountNo = acc;
            }
L46         public void credit(float amount)
            {
L47             balance = balance+amount;
            /* Mark the Observable object as having been changed*/
L48         setChanged();
            // Notify observers of change
            //notifyObservers(this);
L49         notifyObservers();
            }
L50         public void debit(float amount)
            {
L51             balance=balance-amount;
```

```
L52        setChanged();
           // Notify observers of change
           //notifyObservers(this);
L53        notifyObservers();
           }
        }// Account class ends here
```

Output

Explanation

L1–2 Import the `Observer` interface and `Observable` class.

L3 class `Bank` is defined.

L4–5 A `Bank` has many customers and a customer owns an account. (Although a customer can hold more than one account but for simplicity we assumed that a customer will have only one account. You can change the program to accommodate n number of customers by creating an array of customers). So for the same two customers are created with two account references which are instantiated (in L7 and 8) within the constructors of the `Bank` class.

L9–10 We wish that as soon as the account of a customer is credited or debited, the customer should be notified about it. So the customer is the observer on the account (i.e., observable entity). Customer objects (c and c1) are added as observers to the account (a and a1) objects using the `addObserver` method.

L11–13 `main` method.

L14–18 `demo` method is created. The account balance is credited and debited using the two methods of the account class, i.e., credit (L45–48) and debit (L49–52).

L19 Customer, in order to become an observer has to inherit the `Observer` interface and override the update method.

L20–26 Instance variable for the customer class are defined, which are initialized by the constructor of the customer class.

L27 `update` method is overridden. This method is invoked automatically as soon as the `Observable` entity is changed and the `Observer` is notified using `notifyObserver` method (L49 and 53). This method accepts two arguments: first one is the `Observable` object which is being watched and second one is an object passed to the `notifyObserver()` method.

L28 Prints the customer name along with the updated balance. The updated balance is obtained using the `getBalance()` method of the `Account` class.

L29 Class `Account` inherits the `Observable` class to denote that its object will be watched.

L30–31 An account will have a number and balance. Therefore, two instance fields have been defined for the same.

L32–37 Overloaded constructor for initializing the instance variables are defined.

L38–45 `getter` and `setter` methods have been defined for the returning and setting the value of the instance fields of the account class.

L46–53 Account will be either credited (added) or debited (deducted) with amount. Two methods credit and debit have been created. They accept an argument, i.e., the amount to be credited or debited.

After the credit or debit operations have been performed, i.e., the account balance either increases or decreases, the observer has to be notified about this change. So setChanged() method is used to mark this object as its state has changed and notifyObserver() method is used to notify the Observer about this change thereby calling the update (L28) method of the Observer (i.e., customer in our case).

> **Note** As getBalance() is a method of the Account class and not the observable class we need to cast it back into the account and then invoke the getBalance() method. This cast is legal because the Observable reference actually would contain an Account object and also Account is a subclass of Observable class.

10.9 Runtime CLASS

The Runtime class is used to know the information about free memory and total memory. In addition to that it is also used for executing additional processes. The current runtime instance is obtained using a static method of the Runtime class, i.e., getRuntime(). Table 10.6 shows few methods of Runtime class.

Table 10.6 Few methods of Runtime Class

Method	Description
Process exec(String command)	Executes the command in a separate process.
Process exec(String[] cmdarray)	Executes the command stored in an array in a separate process.
void exit(int status)	Terminates the currently running JVM.
long freeMemory()	Returns the amount of free memory as a long in the JVM.
void gc()	Runs the garbage collector.
static Runtime getRuntime()	Returns the runtime object associated with the current Java application.
void halt(int status)	Forcibly terminates the currently running JVM.
void load(String filename)	Loads the specified filename as a dynamic library.
void loadLibrary(String libname)	Loads the dynamic library with the specified library name.
long maxMemory()	Returns the maximum amount of memory in the JVM as a long.
void runFinalization()	Runs the finalization methods of any objects pending finalization.
long totalMemory()	Returns the total amount of memory in the JVM.
void traceInstructions(boolean on)	Enables or disables tracing of instructions.
void traceMethodCalls(boolean on)	Enables or disables tracing of method calls.

Let us take an example to see how Runtime class can be used to know the memory details and execute processes.

Example 10.14 **Runtime Class**

```
L1    import java.io.*;
L2    class RuntimeDemo
      {
L3    public static void main(String args[])
      {
```

```
L4          try{
        //
L5          Runtime r = Runtime.getRuntime();
L6          System.out.println("Free Memory"+r.freeMemory());
L7          System.out.println("Total Memory"+r.totalMemory());

        // for opening a new dos prompt
L8          Process pr1 = r.exec("cmd /c start");

        // for creating a new process opening notepad
L9          Process pr2 = r.exec("notepad RuntimeDemo.java");

        // creates a new command to be executed
L10         Process pr3 = r.exec("cmd /c dir");
L11         InputStream is = pr3.getInputStream();
L12         InputStreamReader isr = new InputStreamReader(is);
L13         BufferedReader br = new BufferedReader(isr);
L14         String line=null;
L15         while ((line = br.readLine()) != null)
L16            System.out.println(line);
        }
L17         catch(Exception e)
            {
L18            System.out.println(e);
            }
        }}
```

Output

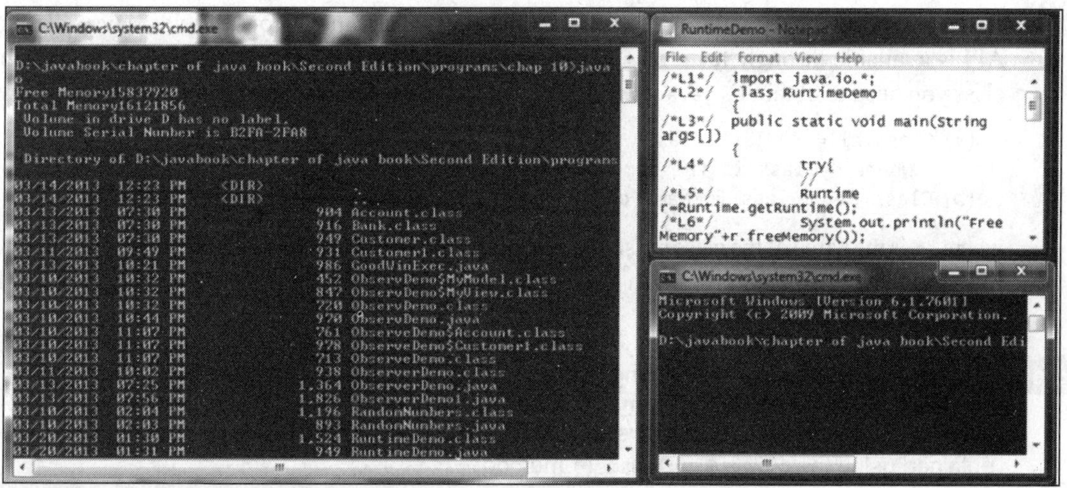

Explanation

L1 The `java.io` package is imported to use classes like `BufferedReader`, `InputStream`, `InputStreamReader`, and `IOException`.

L2 Class declaration.

L3 main method defined for the class.

L4 try block starts.

L5 A `Runtime` object, associated with the current Java application, is obtained using the static method `getRuntime()`.

L6–7 `freeMemory()` method returns the free amount of memory available in the Java virtual machine and `totalMemory()` returns the total amount of memory in the Java virtual machine.

L8–10 The exec method can be used to execute commands and create process objects. The commands that are passed as arguments to the exec method are as follows:

```
cmd /c start - for starts a new dos prompt (See Output)
notepad filename - for opening notepad with the file within it. (See Output)
cmd /c dir - for showing all directories and files within the current directory (See Output)
/c option of the cmd, executes the command specified and then terminates
```

L11–16 The `dir` command within the exec method creates a process which will return the names of file and directories present in the current directory. In order to display it to the user we will have to read the output from the `Process` object created in L10. For reading the `getInputStream` method is used (in L11) to obtain an `InputStream` object from the `Process` object. This object is converted to a character stream using the `InputStreamReader` object (L12) and then buffered by passing the `InputStreamReader` object within the constructor of `BufferedReader` (L13). Now you can use the `readLine` method (L15) of the `BufferedReader` object to read from the `Process` object (created in L10) line by line.

L17–18 For catching any exceptions that may arise.

10.10 REFLECTION API

The reflection API is used to obtain information about the class with its various characteristics like attributes, constructors, methods, packages, modifiers (public, private, etc.), interfaces, arrays, exceptions, and generic types at runtime. It can also be used to instantiate new objects, call methods, know about the setter/getter methods of a class and get or set fields. Java reflection API is available through `java.lang.reflect` package. Before you can use reflection API on a class you need to obtain its `java.lang.Class` object. A class object can be obtained in two ways:

```
(a) Class cl = MyClass.class;
        where MyClass is the name of the class
(b) Class cl = Class.forName(cn);
```

where `cn` is the name of the class passed as a string. The `forName` method causes the class represented by `cn` to be initialized and returns a `Class` object. It may throw a `ClassNotFoundException` if the class cannot be found at runtime.

> **Note** Fully qualified class name including all package names must be specified while using `Class.forName()`. This fully qualified name can be obtained using the `cl.getName()` method (This method is extensively used in our example below). If the class name is only desired, it can be obtained using the `cl.getSimpleName()` method.

Not only we can know about the name of the class but can also get details about the

(a) Superclass of a class.

(b) Constructors of a class, their arguments with their types and modifiers as well.

(c) Fields with their arguments along with their types and modifiers.

(d) Package that a class belongs.

(e) Methods of a class along with their modifiers, exceptions thrown by methods.

(f) Interface that a class inherits.

and much more. Let us take an example to show how.

Example 10.15 Reflection API

```
L1    package ref;
L2    import java.lang.reflect.*;
L3    import java.io.*;
L4    class Reflection implements Serializable
      {
L5        private int demo;
L6        public Reflection(int d, float b)
          {
L7            demo=d;
          }

L8        public final void show() throws ArithmeticException{
L9            System.out.println("Within show method of Reflection class");
          }

L10       public static void main(String args[]) throws Exception
          {
L11           Reflection r=new Reflection(10,20);
L12           System.out.println("Class Name: "+ r.getClass().getName());

       // constructors
L13           Class c=Class.forName("ref.Reflection");
L14           System.out.println("class modifier is : "+Modifier.toString(c.getModifiers()));

L15           Constructor cs[] = c.getDeclaredConstructors();

L16           System.out.println("Constructor:"+ cs[0].getName());

L17           System.out.println("Constructor Modifier:"+ Modifier.toString(cs[0].getModifiers()));

L18           System.out.println("Constructor Modifier is public: "+Modifier.isPublic(cs[0].
              getModifiers()));

       // parameter types in the constructor
L19           Class pt[] = cs[0].getParameterTypes();
L20           System.out.print("Constructor Parameter Types: ");
L21           for(int i = 0;i<pt.length;i++)
              System.out.print(pt[i] + " ");
L22           System.out.println();
```

```java
    // Methods
L23     Method m[] = c.getDeclaredMethods();
L24     for(int i = 0;i<m.length;i++)
        {
L25             System.out.println("Method: "+ m[i].getName());
L26             System.out.println("Method Modifiers is : "+Modifier.toString(m[i].
                getModifiers()));
L27             System.out.println("Method Modifiers is public: "+Modifier.
                isPublic(m[i].getModifiers()));
L28             System.out.println("Method return type: "+m[i].getReturnType());
        }
L29     m[0].invoke(r);

    // Exception declared to be thrown by methods
L30     Class et[] = m[0].getExceptionTypes();
L31     for(int i = 0;i<et.length;i++)
L32     System.out.println("Method Exception Types: "+et[i].getName());

    // Super class info
L33     Class s = c.getSuperclass();
L34     System.out.println("Super Class Name: "+s.getName());

    // Fields and their values
L35     Field f[] = c.getDeclaredFields();
L36     for(int i = 0; i<f.length;i++)
        {
L37     System.out.println("Field name: "+f[i].getName());
L38     System.out.println("Field Type: "+f[i].getType());
L39     System.out.println("Field value: "+f[i].get(r));
L40     System.out.println("Field value Modifiers is "+Modifier.toString(f[i].
        getModifiers()));
L41     f[i].set(r,56);
L42     System.out.println("New Field value: "+f[i].get(r));
        }

    // interfaces
L43     Class in[]=c.getInterfaces();
L44     System.out.println("Interfaces: "+in[0].getName());

    //packages
L45     Package cpackage=c.getPackage();
L46     System.out.println("Package of the class: "+cpackage);

    }
}
```

Output

```
D:\javabook\chapter of java book\Second Edition\programs>java ref.Reflection
Class Name: ref.Reflection
class modifier is :
Constructor:ref.Reflection
Constructor Modifier:public
Constructor Modifier is public: true
Constructor Parameter Types: int float
Method: show
Method Modifiers is : public final
Method Modifiers is public: true
Method return type: void
Method: main
Method Modifiers is : public static
Method Modifiers is public: true
Method return type: void
Within show method of Reflection class
Method Exception Types: java.lang.ArithmeticException
Super Class Name: java.lang.Object
Field name: demo
Field Type: int
Field value: 10
Field value Modifiers is : private
New Field value: 56
Interfaces: java.io.Serializable
Package of the class: package ref

D:\javabook\chapter of java book\Second Edition\programs>
```

Explanation

L1 Package `ref` is declared to hold the class `Reflection`.

L2 `java.lang.reflect` subpackage is imported to use the reflection API. Please remember the sub-packages have to be imported explicitly.

L3 `java.io` package is imported as the class implements `Serializable` interface. (The class will not be serialized in our program. This interface is inherited to demonstrate how reflection API can be used to know the interfaces inherited by a class. So we need to inherit an interface and for the same we had inherited the `Serializable` interface.)

L4 Class declaration.

L5–7 A private field: `demo`, is declared within the class which is initialized using the constructor. The constructor accepts two arguments one is used in our program to initialize the instance variable: demo and the other parameter is used for illustration purpose.

L8–9 Show method is declared and it specifies that it may throw `ArithmeticException`.

L10 main method.

L11 An object of the `Reflection` class is created.

L12 The name of the class can be obtained at runtime by invoking the method `getClass()` on the object. `getClass()` method returns an object of type `java.lang.Class` and `getName()` is invoked on this object to return the name of the class, i.e., `ref.Reflection` (see output).

L13–18 A `Class` object is created to represent the class whose details are required. The class name is passed as an argument to the `forName` static method of the `java.lang.Class` class. All constructors of a class can be accessed using the `getDeclaredConstructors()` method of the `Class` object as it returns an array of all constructors present in it (as a `java.lang.reflect.Constructor` array). The constructors name can be obtained by invoking the `getName()` method (L16) on the individual constructor object present in the array (L15). The modifiers used in the constructors can be obtained by invoking the method `getModifier()` (L17) on the individual constructor object present in the array. This method returns an `int` representing the different modifiers of Java which can be converted to string using the `Modifier.toString` method (as shown in L16). [Note 1]

L19–22 If constructors accept arguments of any type, their respective types can also be known using the getParameterTypes method on the java.lang. reflect.Constructor object. This method returns an array of type Class. The array length is determined to loop through and display the types of all the arguments within a constructor. [Note 2]

L23–28 Shows how to get details about methods of a class using reflection API at runtime. getDeclared-Methods()method is invoked on the Class object (created in L13) to extract details about methods of a class. This method returns an array of type java. lang.reflect.Method. The method name is obtained by invoking the method getName() on the individual elements of the Method array. The method modifiers can be obtained using the method getModifiers(). This method returns an int representing the modifier. To get the name of the modifier we convert the int value of the modifier into its name using the Method. toString (int modifier) method.

L29 The methods of a class can be invoked at runtime using the invoke() method of the java. lang.reflect.Method class. The method object is used to call invoke() and the object on whom to invoke this method is passed as an argument to the invoke method (In other words an instance of the class that declares the method). [Note 3]

L30–32 Shows how to get details about exceptions thrown by the methods of a class. getException() method of the Method object returns an array of type Class containing all the exceptions declared in the throws clause of a particular method. The exception name is obtained by invoking the method getName() on the individual elements of the array object.

L33–34 The getSuperClass() method of the class java.lang.Class is used to determine the superclass of a class whose object is created in L12. This method returns an object of type java.lang.Class.

L35–42 Shows how to determine the fields of a class with their respective names, types, modifiers and values. getDeclaredFields() method of the java.lang.Class returns an array of type java. lang.reflect.Field class. Each element of the Field array object represents the fields of the class. The name, type, value, and modifier of the fields can be extracted using the methods of the Field class like getName() used in L33, getType() in L34, get(r) (for extracting value of that field) and getModifiers() respectively. Not only the value can be extracted, they can also be set using the setter method as shown in Table 10.7. The first argument is the object whose fields value is to be set and the second is the value which is to be set. We have use the set method wherein the first argument is the object on which to set the value and second is the value to be set. The question that may arise at this point is

Table 10.7 Setter Methods of the java.lang.reflect.Field Class

public void set(Object obj, Object val)	Changes the field value represented by this Field object on the object obj to the new value specified in the second argument.
public void setBoolean(Object obj, boolean b)	Sets the boolean value (b) in a boolean field of the object obj.
public void setByte(Object obj, byte b)	Sets the byte value (b) in the byte field of the object obj.
public void setChar(Object obj, char c)	Sets the char value (c) in the char field of the object obj.
public void setDouble(Object obj, double d)	Sets the double value (d) in the double field of the object obj.
public void setFloat(Object obj, float f)	Sets the float value (f) in a float field of the object obj.
public void setInt(Object obj, int i)	Sets the int value (i) in a int field of the object obj.
public void setLong(Object obj, long l)	Sets the long value (l) in long field of the object obj.
public void setShort(Object obj, short s)	Sets the short value (s) in short field of the object obj.

that: The second argument in the `set` method is of type `Object` and we are passing an `int` value in our method yet still it compiles and executes. Why? The answer is because of autoboxing features of Java you are able to pass values to `Object` directly. You can also use `setInt` method for the same.

L43–44 Shows how to get the details of the interfaces inherited by the class. `getInterfaces()` method of the `java.lang.Class` class is used to return an array of interfaces inherited by the class. The name of the interface is printed using the method `getName()`. [Note 4]

L45–46 `getPackage()` is invoked through the `Class` object (created in L13) to returns the package to which this class belongs as a `Package` object.

Notes

1. You can also check these modifiers using the following methods of `java.lang.reflect.Modifier` class:

    ```
    Modifier.isAbstract(int modifiers)
    Modifier.isFinal(int modifiers)
    Modifier.isInterface(int modifiers)
    Modifier.isNative(int modifiers)
    Modifier.isPrivate(int modifiers)
    Modifier.isProtected(int modifiers)
    Modifier.isPublic(int modifiers)
    Modifier.isStatic(int modifiers)
    Modifier.isStrict(int modifiers)
    Modifier.isSynchronized(int modifiers)
    Modifier.isTransient(int modifiers)
    Modifier.isVolatile(int modifiers)
    ```

2. You can also get the types of parameters used in the methods by using the `getParameterTypes()` method explained in L19–22.

3. If the method is static, then the specified `object` argument is ignored and it may be null.

4. The interfaces specifically declared by the class will only be returned by the `getInterfaces()` method. If the superclass of the class implements an interface and this fact is not specifically stated by the class, then the interface name will not be returned. For getting a complete list of the interfaces implemented by a class you will need to look in the class as well as its super class/classes recursively.

SUMMARY

The `java.util` revolves around collections (bag of objects). To provide compile-time safety for collections, generics were introduced in Java 5. The collection can be ordered or unordered and may also contain duplicates. For example, a `Set` does not allow duplicates whereas a `LinkedList` does. This package deals with data structure concepts such as Linked list, stack, queues, trees, and hashing. The classes like `LinkedList`, `Stack`, `HashSet`, `TreeSet` encompass these concepts. For mapping keys to their values `java.util` package provides a `Map` interface.

In addition to these, the `util` package also provides utility classes such as `Date` and `Calendar` for getting date and time which we have already discussed in the earlier chapters. `StringTokenizer` class used for splitting strings has already been discussed in the earlier chapters under the topic 'String'. This package also came up with a `Scanner` class which we had touched in Chapter 9. Dynamic array functionality is provided by two classes: `ArrayList` and `Vector`. `ArrayList` methods are not synchronized but `Vector` is synchronized. Legacy interface `Enumeration` and newer `Iterator` interface are used for iterating over the collection of objects.

This chapter discusses about utility classes like the Random class for generating random values (like `int`, `double`, `float`, and `long`), the observer pattern along with `Observable` class and `Observer` interface for keeping an eye on other objects. `Runtime` class, although a part of `java.lang` is also discussed here to show its features and utilities.

Finally the reflection API is discussed in detail to show how the details of a class can be known at runtime.

EXERCISES

Objective Questions

1. What will happen if a list is created as shown below:

   ```
   List l = new LinkedList(); ?
   ```
   (a) compiles and executes
   (b) compile time error
   (c) run time error
   (d) raises an unchecked exception

2. Which collection does not contain duplicates?
   (a) Set   (b) List
   (c) Map   (d) Queue

3. Which collection contains the mapping of keys to their values?
   (a) Set   (b) List
   (c) Map   (d) Queue

4. What collection class is synchronized to hold elements?
   (a) HashMap   (b) TreeMap
   (c) Vector   (d) ArrayList

5. Which collection contains an unordered collection of elements?
   (a) TreeSet   (b) HashSet
   (c) TreeMap   (d) LinkedList

6. Which collection contains an ordered collection of elements?
   (a) TreeSet   (b) HashSet
   (c) TreeMap   (d) LinkedList

7. What are used to provide compile-time safety to your programs?
   (a) List   (b) collections
   (c) Interfaces   (d) Generics

8. What feature of Java 5 enables a collection class to hold objects as elements of same type?
   (a) Generics   (b) Annotations
   (c) Enumerations   (d) Assertions

9. In case, you do not use generics in your programs what option of `javac` is used to compile the program?
   (a) javac -d
   (b) javac -s
   (c) javac -classpath
   (d) javac -Xlint:unchecked

10. What collection class is used to hold elements (similar to dynamic arrays) and is not synchronized?
    (a) HashMap   (b) TreeMap
    (c) Vector   (d) ArrayList

Review Questions

1. What is a collection in Java? Can you identify any real life example which is similar to a collection in Java?

2. Explain the difference between:
   (a) Vector and ArrayList
   (b) Enumeration and Iterator

3. What are Generics and how are they used in Java? (Use an example in support of your answer)

4. What are bounded wildcards? How are they used?

5. Explain the union, intersection, and the difference operation of a mathematical set. How is it related to the `Set` interface in Java?

6. Explain the unique features of a `Map` interface.

7. What is reflection API used for?

8. What is observer pattern? How is it useful?

9. Explain `Runtime` class with its features.

Programming Exercises

1. Reverse the `LinkedList` and then copy all the elements of a `LinkedList` into another list.

2. Write a program to iterate a `LinkedList` using `for-each` and traditional `for` with a `ListIterator`.

3. Write a program to convert an array to a collection and back.

4. Create a `Collection` class named Queue to implement the FIFO order of queues. [Use Generics]

5. Demonstrate the `Collections` class and use the following methods in the class:
   (a) rotate
   (b) max
   (c) min
   (d) disjoint
   (e) sort
   (f) binary search

6. Create a class to simulate a dictionary of words along with their meanings. The words/meaning should be stored in such a way that retrieval of meaning is as fast as possible.

7. Rewrite the above program to display the list of words along with their meanings in the dictionary in a sorted order.

8. Write a program to generate 20 unique random integers from 1 to 100.

9. Rewrite the observer example to use *n* customers instead of just two customers as depicted in the example. You are required to get the details of the Customer from the user. Also try to figure out whether there can be more than one Observer on an Observable object?

Answers to Objective Questions

1. (b)	**2.** (a)	**3.** (c)	**4.** (c)
5. (b)	**6.** (a)	**7.** (d)	**8.** (a)
9. (d)	**10.** (d)		

Network Programming

> *Communication is a continual balancing act, juggling the conflicting needs for intimacy and independence. To survive in the world, we have to act in concert with others, but to survive as ourselves, rather than simply as cogs in a wheel, we have to act alone.*
>
> **Deborah Tannen**

After reading this chapter, the readers will be able to

- understand the programming concepts behind client and server
- learn the concepts behind sockets
- understand how threads can be used to create concurrent servers
- learn about network interface

11.1 INTRODUCTION

Computer network is an interconnected collection of computers. The nodes of a network communicate with each other using a wired/wireless medium. This communication is actually carried between two processes residing in two different machines. The process on one machine initiates the request and another responds to the requests. The initiator is the *client* and the responder is the *server*.

Network programming deals in the implementation of client/server concept. The client and server communicate via protocols. TCP/IP protocol suite is followed in all networks including the Internet. Protocols are a set of rules and regulations to be followed for the purpose of communication.

11.1.1 TCP/IP Protocol Suite

TCP/IP protocol suite contains a number of protocols. It is a four-layered model followed by the networks. Internet also follows the same model. Figure 11.1 shows the TCP/IP model.

The client and server applications created by the users reside at application layer. They interact with the transport layer using sockets API, i.e., classes in the `java.net` package. The transport layer takes data from the application layer (sender) and breaks it up into segments, attaches the port number used by application to the data, and passes it to the network layer.

Depending upon the protocol used, a connection is established (TCP) or not (UDP) at the transport layer.

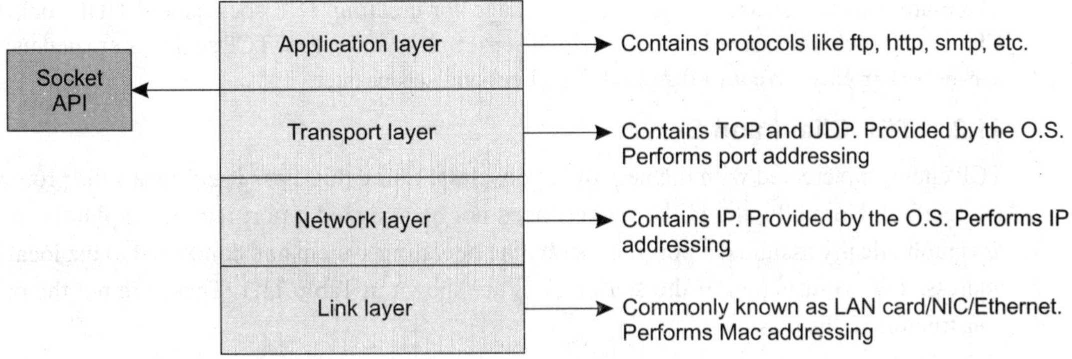

Fig. 11.1 TCP/IP Model

The two protocols used for the purpose are TCP and UDP. Both client and server use the same protocol. TCP is a connection-oriented protocol, while UDP is a connectionless protocol. Connection-oriented protocols ensured guaranteed delivery, sequence of data, and acknowledgement for the data sent. On the other hand, connectionless protocols neither guarantee delivery nor sequencing and acknowledgement. All standard applications run on standard port numbers also known as *well-known port numbers* (from 0–1023), e.g., HTTP (80), FTP (20/21), DAYTIME (13), ECHO (7), TELNET (23), SMTP (25), etc. Mostly server applications use well-known port numbers. The client applications use *ephemeral port numbers* (i.e., short-lived) starting from 1024 onwards.

The network layer creates packets by encapsulating the segments into its own header format, attaches the source and the destination IP address to it and passes it to the link layer. IP protocol is a connectionless routed protocol. The `java.net` package supports both versions of IP protocol (IPv4 and IPv6). IPv4 addresses are of 32 bits in size and IPv6 addresses are of 128 bits in size.

The link layer frames the data received from the network layer according to its own format, converts the data to bits and subsequently, signals are sent over the wire to the other side. The other side repeats the same steps, but in reverse order, decapsulating the data at each layer. Network programming is supported in the `java.net` package of Java.

11.2 SOCKETS

Network programming revolves around the concept of sockets. A *socket* is an end-point of communication. Sockets are created at both ends of communication, i.e., at the client as well as the server. A socket is defined by three things: *IP Address, port,* and the *protocol* to be used for communication. IP address is the unique address assigned to every machine on the network and port is a unique logical number on that IP address used for identifying the applications running on that particular machine. IP address exists on network layer and port numbers on the transport layer of the TCP/IP protocol suite.

Note Do not confuse the concept socket with the class `Socket` in `java.net`. Till now, we have covered the concept socket and now, we will discuss the class `Socket`.

There are separate classes in `java.net` package for creating TCP sockets and UDP sockets. Client TCP socket is created with the help of `Socket` class and server TCP socket is created using `ServerSocket` class. We will discuss UDP client and server later.

11.2.1 TCP Client and Server

TCP clients are created with the help of `Socket` class. Using this class itself means the protocol is specified. Normally, the client sockets need not be assigned a port number explicitly; they are automatically assigned a port number by the operating system and connected to the local IP address. The constructors of the `Socket` class are shown in Table 11.1. These are not the only constructors in the class.

Table 11.1 Constructors of `Socket` Class

Constructor	Description
`Socket()`	An unconnected socket is created.
`Socket (InetAddress addr, int port) throws IOException`	Creates a socket that connects to the specified InetAddress on the port number specified.
`Socket (String host, int port) throws UnknownHostException, IOException`	Creates a socket that connects to the specified host on the port number specified.
`Socket (String host, int port,InetAdddress addr, int localPort) throws IOException`	In earlier constructors, we have not specified the local addresses and local port number. If you wish to do so, use this constructor.
`Socket (InetAddress addr, int port, InetAddress localaddr, int localport) throws IOException`	The only difference here is that the remote host address is specified as an InetAddress object, not as a String as in the earlier constructor.

In the following example, the server sends its current date and time to the client as soon as a client sends a request to the server. The client receives it and prints it on to its own standard output. Let us take a look at the client first.

Example 11.1(a) **TCP Client**

```
L1    import java.net.*;
L2    import java.io.*;
L3    public class SocketDemo {
L4      public static void main(String args[]) {
L5      try{
L6          Socket s = new Socket(InetAddress.getLocalHost(),7);
L7          System.out.println("Socket created");
L8          System.out.println("Local Address: " +s.getLocalAddress());
L9          System.out.println("Local Host: " +InetAddress.getLocalHost());
L10         System.out.println("Local Port : " +s.getLocalPort());
L11         System.out.println("Inet Address: " +s.getInetAddress());
L12         InputStream in = s.getInputStream();
L13         System.out.println("Streams created");
```

```
L14    BufferedReader br = new BufferedReader(new InputStreamReader(in));
L15    String x = null;
L16    while((x = br.readLine())!= null)
L17    System.out.println(x);
L18    in.close();
L19    s.close(); }
L20    catch(Exception e)
L21    {System.out.println(e);}
     }}
```

Explanation

L1 and 2 Imports the necessary packages.

L3 and 4 Class defined with the `main` method within it.

L5 All the statements have been placed in a try/catch block to catch the necessary exceptions thrown by statements in try block.

L6 `Socket` class used to create a socket at the client side. As soon as the object of this created, a request is automatically sent to the specified server at the specified port. The first argument in the constructor is the `server name` and the second argument is the `port` on which the server application is running. If some problem occurs while creating a socket, then an `IOException` is thrown.

The local machine address is obtained using the static method `getLocalHost()` of the `InetAddress` class. The `InetAddress` represents an IP address. This class has two subclasses `Inet4Address` (for IPv4 addresses) and `Inet6Address` (for IPv6 addresses). This method throws an `UnknownHostException` if no host could be found.

L8 Prints the local address of the machine associated with the client socket (see output). The loopback address (127.0.0.1) is printed. Packets destined for loopback address are routed back to the same machine from which they are sent. The method `getLocalAddress()` returns an `InetAddress` object which is then printed. The `toString()` method of the `InetAddress` object is called before writing it on the standard output which converts the IP address to a string.

L9 Print the local host (see output). This method, like the previous one, returns an `InetAddress` object.

L10 `getlocalPort()` method prints the local port to which the socket is connected. In case you want the remote port to which the socket is connected, use `getport()` method.

L11 Prints the address with which the socket is connected. If you see the output, this line prints the same output as L9 because both the client and the server are running on the same machine. If they would have been running on different machines, this line would have given the address of the server. The method `getInetAddress()` returns an `InetAddress` object.

Reading data from server through sockets

L12 Using the `getInputStream()` method of the `Socket` class, we obtain an `InputStream` to read contents from the socket and using `getOutputStream()` method of the `Socket` class, we can obtain an `OutputStream` to write contents to the socket.

L14 `BufferedReader` object is created to read strings from the socket. The byte stream is converted to character stream using the `InputStreamReader` object.

L15 to 17 String `x` is created. A `while` loop is used to iterate and print string until the socket has no more strings to be read. We have already discussed this in Chapter 9. The only difference is that there, we were reading data from files and here, we are reading data from sockets.

L18–19 Closes the streams and the socket.

L20–21 `catch` clause.

The server program for the client in Example 11.1(a) is shown below. The server programs are meant to be up and running all the time and serve many clients at a time. But this server program (Example 11.1(b)) cannot serve multiple clients at one time. There are two types of servers: *iterative* and *concurrent*. Iterative servers process only one request at a time, so the other client requests have to wait until the first one is processed. The other type is a concurrent server which we will discuss in Section 11.4. ServerSocket class is used for creating a socket at the server side. The constructors of this class are shown in Table 11.2.

Example 11.1(b) TCP Server

```
L1      import java.net.*;
L2      import java.io.*;
L3      import java.util.*;
L4      class ServerSocketDemo {
L5        public static void main(String args[]) {
L6        try{
L7            ServerSocket ss = new ServerSocket(7);
L8            while(true){
L9            Socket client = ss.accept();
L10           System.out.println("Socket created");
L11           System.out.println("client inet address: " +client.getInetAddress());
L12           System.out.println("client port: " +client.getPort());
L13           OutputStream out = client.getOutputStream();
L14           PrintWriter pw = new PrintWriter(out, true);
L15           System.out.println("Streams created ");
L16           String x = "Hello, How are you? ";
L17           Calendar c = Calendar.getInstance();
L18           pw.println(x);
L19           pw.println("The server date and time is :" +c.getTime());
L20           System.out.println("Contents written to" +client.getInetAddress().getHostName());
L21           pw.close();
        }}
            catch(Exception e){
            System.out.println(e);
        }}}
```

Table 11.2 Constructor of ServerSocket Class

Constructors	Description
ServerSocket() throws IOException	Creates a socket that is not bound to any port.
ServerSocket(int port) throws IOException	Creates a socket that is bound to the specified port number and size of listen queue set to 50 by default.
ServerSocket (int port, int backlog) throws IOException	Creates a socket that is bound to the specified port number with the length of the listen queue (client request) specified as backlog.
ServerSocket(int port, int backlog, InetAddress addr) throws IOException	Creates a socket that is bound to the specified port number and local address with the length of the listen queue specified as backlog.

How to Run the Client and Server?

The client and server programs will execute in two different DOS shell. Open two DOS shells (using cmd/command at the run in XP/Vista/NT/2000 etc.), one for client and the other for server.

First execute the server in one DOS window and then, execute the client from the other DOS prompt.

Output

Server

```
C:\javabook\programs\chap11>java ServerSocketDemo
Socket created
client inet address: /127.0.0.1
client port: 49362
Streams created
Contents written to sachin-pc
```

Client

```
C:\javabook\programs\chap11>java SocketDemo
Socket created
Local Address: /127.0.0.1
Local Host: sachin-pc/127.0.0.1
Local Port : 49362
Inet Address: sachin-pc/127.0.0.1
Streams created
Hello, How are you?
The server date and time is: Sun Mar 29 19:06:18 IST 2009
```

Explanation (Server)

L1 to 3 Imports the necessary packages.

L6 `try` block begins.

L7 `ServerSocket` object is created to create a server socket. This application will run on Port number 7.

L8 An infinite loop is created to process client's request one by one.

L9 `accept` method of `ServerSocket` object listens for client's requests and as soon as one is received, accepts it and returns a `Socket` object connected to the client. Now this socket is responsible for handling client's requests.

L11 Prints the client's IP address using `getInetAddress()` on the socket object (see output).

L12 Prints the client's port number (remote port) using `getPort()` method on the `Socket` object (see output).

L13 `InputStream` and `OutputStream` objects can be obtained from `Socket` object returned in L9 using `getInputStream()` and `getOutputStream()`. These streams can be obtained to read and write data to the client socket. Anything written to socket at server side is eventually sent to client as a connection exists between them.

Connection between client and server

Client .... Server

L14 `PrintWriter` object is created to write the character to the `OutputStream` directly. The first argument is used to connect the `PrintWriter` object to the `Socket` output stream and second argument sets the auto-flush property to true.

L16 String declared.

L17 `Calendar` instance created.

L18 String created in L17 is written to the output stream connected to the socket.

L19 Current date and time of the server is written to the client.

L20 Prints a string on the server standard output console "contents written to" followed by the client's name.

L21 `PrintWriter` object is closed.

11.2.2 UDP Client and Server

UDP clients and servers are created with the help of `DatagramSocket` and `DatagramPacket` classes. If UDP protocol is used at transport, then the unit of data at the transport layer is called a *datagram* and not a *segment*. In UDP, no connection is established. It is the responsibility of the applications to encapsulate data in a datagram (using `DatagramPacket` class) before sending it. If TCP is used for sending data, data can be directly written to the socket (client or server) and it reaches the other side as a connection exists between them. The datagram sent by the application using UDP may or may not reach the UDP receiver. As the error ratio in LANs is less, UDP is a good choice for creating LAN-based applications, as it saves the application from the overhead of connection establishment and termination. Tables 11.3 and 11.4 show the constructors for `DatagramSocket` and `DatagramPacket`, respectively.

Table 11.3 Constructors of `DatagramSocket` Class

Methods	Description
`DatagramSocket() throws SocketException`	Constructs a datagram socket that is bound to any available port on the local machine.
`DatagramSocket(int port) throws SocketException`	Constructs a datagram socket that is bound to the specified port on the local machine.
`DatagramSocket(int port, InetAddress iadd) throws SocketException`	Creates a datagram socket, bound to the specified local address and port number.
`DatagramSocket(SocketAddress baddr) throws SocketException`	Creates a datagram socket, bound to the specified local socket address.

Table 11.4 Constructors of `DatagramPocket` Class

Methods	Description
`DatagramPacket (byte[] buf, int len)`	Creates a datagram packet for receiving packets of length len.
`DatagramPacket (byte[] buf, int len, InetAddress addr, int p)`	Creates a datagram packet for sending packets of length len to the specified port number (p) on the specified host (addr).
`DatagramPacket (byte[] buf, int off, int len)`	Creates a datagram packet for receiving packets of length len, specifying an offset (off) into the buffer (buf).
`DatagramPacket (byte[] buf, int off, int len, InetAddress add, int port)`	Creates a datagram packet for sending packets of length len with offset (off) to the specified destination port number on the specified destination host.
`DatagramPacket (byte[] buf, int off, int len, SocketAddress address) throws SocketException`	Creates a datagram packet for sending packets of length len with offset off to the specified destination socket address.
`DatagramPacket (byte[] buf, int len, SocketAddress address) throws SocketException`	Creates a datagram packet for sending packets of length len to the specified destination socket address.

Let us take an example of how UDP can be used in network programming. In the following example, the client sends a datagram to the server. The server receives the datagram and generates another datagram in response to it. The server code is shown in Example 11.2(a).

Example 11.2(a) UDP Server

```java
L1    import java.net.*;
L2    import java.io.*;
L3    public class DatagramServer {
L4    public static void main(String args[]){
L5    try{
L6        DatagramSocket ds = new DatagramSocket(8);
L7        byte[] b = new byte[50];
L8        DatagramPacket in = new DatagramPacket(b,b.length);
L8        ds.receive(in);
L10       System.out.println(new String(b));
L11       String x = "Hello client";
L12       byte buff[] = x.getBytes();
L13       DatagramPacket out = new DatagramPacket (buff, buff.length, in.getAddress(), in.getPort());
L14       ds.send(out);
          ds.close();
      } catch(Exception e) {System.out.println(e);}
      }}
```

Explanation

L6 `DatagramSocket` has been created with the UDP server running on port number 8.

L7 and 8 `DatagramPacket` object (L8) is created to hold the data received in the byte array (L7) through the datagram socket.

L9 `receive()` method of datagram socket object is used to receive data from UDP client and put it in the byte array.

L10 Byte array converted to string and is printed on the standard output.

L11 and 12 String to be sent to client is created and converted to bytes using the `getByte()` method.

L13 A new `DatagramPacket` is created for sending it to the client. The constructor arguments are

(a) `buff`–byte array to be sent to client

(b) `buff.length`–length of the array

(c) `in.getAddress()`—to get the address of the client. We have extracted it from the datagram received by the client.

(d) `in.getPort()`—to get the port address of the client. We have extracted it from the datagram received by the client.

L14 `send` method is used to send `DatagramPacket` to the client.

Example 11.2(b) UDP Client

```java
L1    import java.net.*;
L2    import java.io.*;
L3    public class DatagramClient {
L4    public static void main(String args[]){
L5    try{
L6        InetAddress ia = InetAddress.getLocalHost();
L7        DatagramSocket ds = new DatagramSocket (1024,ia);
L8        String x = "Hello Server";
L9        byte[] b = x.getBytes();
L10       DatagramPacket dp = new DatagramPacket(b, b. length, ia,8);
L11       ds.send(dp);
L12       System.out.println("sending to server: "+(new String(b)));
L13       byte[] buff = new byte[50];
L14       DatagramPacket in = new DatagramPacket(buff, buff.length);
L15       ds.receive(in);
```

```
L16        System.out.println("received from server: "+(new String(buff)));
L17        ds.close();
        } catch(SocketException se){System.out.println(se);}
        catch(IOException ie){ System.out.println(ie);}
        }}
```

Output

Server

```
C:\javabook\programs\chap11>java DatagramServer
Hello Server
```

Client

```
C:\javabook\programs\chap11>java DatagramClient
sending to server: Hello Server
received from server: Hello client
```

Explanation

L6 and 7 `DatagramSocket` object is created to create a socket for the UDP client. As both client and server are running on the same machine, we pass the local machine address using `getLocalHost()` static method of the `InetAddress` class. This method throws an `UnknownHostException` if no host could be found. It is a subclass of the `IOException` class, so if this exception is thrown, it will be caught by the catch having a reference of `IOException` class.

L8 to 16 A datagram packet (i.e., `dp`) is created and sent to server. In response to this, the server also sends a datagram which is received by client in a `DatagramPacket` object (i.e., `in`).

11.3 URL CLASS

URL stands for uniform resource locator. It is a standard way of locating resources on the Internet, e.g., www.yahoo.com. A URL has some basic parts

(a) protocol name: http/file/mailto, etc.
(b) host: www.yahoo.com
(c) port: this is an optional attribute specified after the host name, e.g., www.yahoo.com:80
(d) file: name of the file to be accessed, e.g., www.yahoo.com/index.html
(e) Reference: name of named reference within the page (i.e., cs), e.g., www.yahoo.com/index.html#cs

The constructor of the URL class used in the example is shown below:

```
public URL(String res) throws MalformedURLException
```

In the following example, we have used the URL class to refer to a resource on the local machine. The methods of the URL class are used to parse the URL and read the file. Let us take an example to understand the concept.

Example 11.3 Reading from a URL

```
L1    import java.net.*;
L2    import java.io.*;
L3    class URLExample{
```

```
L4      public static void main(String args[]){
L5      try {
L6              URL u = new URL(args[0]);
L7              System.out.println("The Protocol used is:" +u.getProtocol());
L8              System.out.println("The Host used is:" +u.getHost());
L9              System.out.println("The File used is:" +u.getFile());
L10             System.out.println("The Port used is:" +u.getPort());
L11             System.out.println("The Reference in page is:" +u.getRef());
L12             URLConnection uc = u.openConnection();
L13             InputStream in = uc.getInputStream();
L14             BufferedReader br = new BufferedReader(new InputStreamReader(in));
L15             String x = null;
L16             while((x = br.readLine())!= null)
L17             System.out.println(x);
L18             br.close();
L19     }catch(MalformedURLException e)
           {System.out.println(e);}
           catch(IOException e){System.out.println(e);}
        }}
```

Output

```
C:\javabook\programs\chap11>java URLExample file:\\localhost\jdk-6-doc\docs\ api\index.html
The Protocol used is: file
The Host used is: localhost
The File used is: /jdk-6-doc/docs/api/index.html
The Port used is: -1
The Reference in page is: null
<!DOCTYPE HTML PUBLIC "-//W3C//DTD HTML 4.01 Frameset//EN" "http://www.w3.org/TR /html4/
frameset.dtd">
<!--NewPage-->
<HTML>
<HEAD>
<!-- Generated by javadoc on Wed Nov 29 02:28:47 PST 2006-->
<TITLE>
Java Platform SE 6
</TITLE>
<SCRIPT type = "text/javascript">
targetPage = "" + window.location.search;
if (targetPage != "" &&targetPage != "undefined")
targetPage = targetPage.substring(1);
functionloadFrames() {
if (targetPage != "" &&targetPage != "undefined")
top.classFrame.location = top.targetPage;
}
</SCRIPT>
<NOSCRIPT>
</NOSCRIPT>
</HEAD>
<FRAMESET cols = "20%,80%" title = "" onLoad = "top.loadFrames()">
```

```
<FRAMESET rows = "30%,70%" title = "" onLoad = "top.loadFrames()">
<FRAME src = "overview-frame.html" name = "packageListFrame" title = "All Packages">
<FRAME src = "allclasses-frame.html" name = "packageFrame" title = "All classes and in
terfaces (except non-static nested types)">
</FRAMESET>
<FRAME src = "overview-summary.html" name ="classFrame" title ="Package, class and interface
descriptions" scrolling = "yes">
<NOFRAMES>
<H2>
Frame Alert</H2>

<P> This document is designed to be viewed using the frames feature. If you see this
message, you are using a non-frame-capable web client.
<BR> Link to <A HREF = "overview-summary.html"> Non-frame version.</A>
</NOFRAMES>
</FRAMESET>
</HTML>
```

Explanation

L6 Object of class URL is created and the URL is passed to the constructor. We have accessed the resource on the local machine. That is the reason we have used the file protocol followed by the name of the machine (i.e., `localhost`) and the path of the file, e.g.

file:\\localhost\jdk-6-doc\docs\api\index.html

L7 Prints the protocol used in the URL using the `getProtocol()` method.

L8 Prints the host used in the URL using the `getHost()` method.

L9 Prints the file to be accessed on the host used in the URL using the `getFile()` method.

L10 Prints the port used in the URL using the `getPort()` method. The output shows -1 as no port has been specified.

L11 Prints the protocol used in the URL using the `getProtocol()` method.

L12 To access the resource, we have to open a connection to the resource. The `openConnection()` method of the URL object is used to return a `URLConnection` object. This object represents a connection to the resource (remote or local).

L13 We have to read the contents of that file (`index.html`) so an `InputStream` is required for reading the contents. The connection object provides a method `getInputStream()` which returns an `InputStream` object connected to the `URLConnection`.

L14 to 18 We have used these lines for reading the file.

L19 The constructor of URL class may throw a `MalformedURLException` if the protocol specified in the URL is unknown, so it is necessary to catch it. The `IOException` needs to be caught as discussed in earlier chapters (`MalformedURLException` is a subclass of `IOException`).

11.4 MULTITHREADED SOCKETS

Concurrent client and server application can be built in Java using the concept of multithreading. Concurrent servers are those that can process many clients at a time. Clients need not wait for other clients to finish their interaction with the server. In other words, parallel execution takes place. A client's request arrives at the server, it is accepted and a thread is created for handling the client's request. The server then continues to listen to requests from other clients. Figure 11.2 illustrates the concept better.

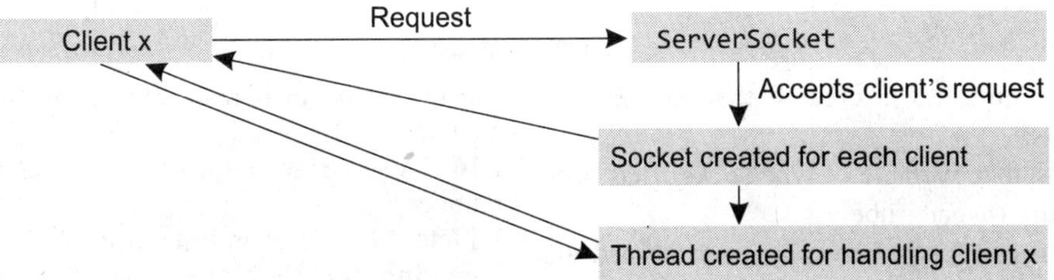

Fig. 11.2 Concurrent Server

Let us take an example to see how multithreading is helpful in client/server programming. In the following example, we will create a multithreaded server which will echo back the client's data to the appropriate client. The following code shows a concurrent server.

Example 11.4(a) **Multithreaded Server**

```java
import java.net.*;
import java.io.*;

public class ThreadedEchoServer extends Thread {
Socket client;
public ThreadedEchoServer(Socket s) {
  client = s;
  start(); }
  public void run() {
  try {
    OutputStream os = client.getOutputStream();
    InputStream in = client.getInputStream();
    PrintWriter pw = new PrintWriter(os,true);
    BufferedReader br = new BufferedReader(new InputStreamReader(in));
    while (true) {
    String n = br.readLine();
    System.out.println("From client: "+n);
    pw.println("echo from server: "+n);
    } }
    catch (IOException ex)
    {System.out.println(ex);}
    }
public static void main(String[] args) {
try{
    ServerSocket ss = new ServerSocket(7);
    while (true) {
    Socket s = ss.accept();
    ThreadedEchoServer tes = new ThreadedEchoServer(s);
  } }
  catch (IOException ex) {
  System.err.println(ex);
  }}}
```

Explanation

L1   A `Server` class is created that extends the `Thread` class.

L2   An instance variable of type `Socket` has been created in the `Thread` subclass.

L3   Constructor for the server has been defined and it accepts an instance of `Socket`.

L4   Initializes the instance `Socket` variable.

L5   The thread is started using `start` method (refer Chapter 8).

L6 to 14   `run` method has been overridden to provide the details for the thread. We have already discussed the code written in the `run` method many times. It is actually to read and write data to the socket. Whatever is read from the client is written back to client.

L16   A server socket is created which run on Port number 7.

L17 to 19   An infinite loop is defined to accept incoming client's request. As soon as a client's request is received, it is accepted (via the `accept()` method in L18) and a `Socket` instance (s) i returned (for handling client). A `Thread` is created (L19) and socket instance (created L18) is passed to the thread (as an argument in the constructor of `ThreadedEchoServer`). This `Socket` instance is assigned to the client instance variable (L4) in the constructor of `ThreadedEchoServer`.

Now we will create a client that establishes a connection with the server and writes contents to it which is echoed back to the client by the server.

Example 11.4(b)   Echo Client

```
L1      import java.net.*;
L2      import java.io.*;
L3      public class EchoClient {
L4      public static void main(String[] args) {
          try {
L5            Socket s = new Socket(InetAddress.getLocalHost(),7);
L6            OutputStream os = s.getOutputStream();
L7            InputStream in = s.getInputStream();
L8            PrintWriter pw = new PrintWriter(os,true);
L9            BufferedReader br = new BufferedReader(new InputStreamReader(System.in));
L10           BufferedReader brs = new BufferedReader(new InputStreamReader(in));
L11           while (true) {
L12               String n = br.readLine();
L13               pw.println(n);
L14               System.out.println(brs.readLine());
          }}
            catch (IOException ex) {
            System.err.println(ex);
            }}}
```

How to Run Multithreaded Server and Clients?

We will run multithreaded server in one DOS shell and start the clients in individual DOS shells. First of all the server has to be executed at DOS prompt and then `client1` needs be started on another. The first client (`client1`) types the input "Hello" which is echoed back to `client1`. Meanwhile `client2` is executed from another DOS prompt and `client2` types the input "Hi I am new Client"; which is echoed back to `client2`.

Output

Server

```
C:\javabook\programs\chap11>java ThreadedEchoServer
From client: hello
From client: Hi I am new Client
From client: hi i am the First client
From client: how are you
```

Client1

```
C:\javabook\programs\chap11>java EchoClient
hello
echo from server: hello
hi i am the first client
echo from server: hi i am the first client
```

Client2

```
C:\javabook\programs\chap11>java EchoClient
Hi I am new Client
echo from server: Hi I am new Client
how are you
echo from server: how are you
```

11.5 NETWORK INTERFACE

Java 1.4 introduced NetworkInterface class to get the details about the local network interface such as the name of the interface, the MAC address of the interface, MTU (maximum transmission unit) of the interface, list of IP addresses attached to the interface, whether the interface is up or down and whether it supports multicasting. Let us take an example to see how we can get these details.

Example 11.5 **List of Network Interfaces and its Details**

```
import java.io.*;
import java.net.*;
import java.util.*;
    public class NetInterfaceDemo{
    public static void main(String args[]) throws SocketException
    {
L1  Enumeration<NetworkInterface> nets=NetworkInterface.getNetworkInterfaces();
L2  for (NetworkInterface netint :Collections.list(nets))
    {
L3      System.out.println("Display name:" + netint.getDisplayName());
L4      System.out.println("Name:" + netint.getName());
L5      System.out.println("MTU:" + netint.getMTU());
L6      System.out.println("Interface is up:" + netint.isUp());
L7      Enumeration<InetAddress> inetAddresses = netint.getInetAddresses();
L8      for (InetAddress inetAddress :Collections.list(inetAddresses))
        {
```

```
L9                    System.out.println("InetAddress:" +inetAddress);
         }
L10    System.out.println();
       } }}
```

Output

```
C:\javabook\programs\chap11>java NetInterfaceDemo
Display name: Software Loopback Interface 1
Name: lo
MTU: -1
Interface is up: true
InetAddress: /0:0:0:0:0:0:0:1          //IPv6 Address
InetAddress: /127.0.0.1                //IPv4 Address

Display name: Intel(R) PRO/Wireless 3945ABG Network Connection
Name: net2
MTU: 1500
Interface is up: true
InetAddress: /fe80:0:0:0:8c3d:30ab:4e1b:76a%8
InetAddress: /172.16.1.98

Display name: Marvell Yukon 88E8036 PCI-E Fast Ethernet Controller
Name: eth2
MTU: 1500
Interface is up: false
InetAddress: /fe80:0:0:0:54c4:d989:7f07:b780%9

Display name: TeredoTunneling Pseudo-Interface
Name: net3
MTU: 1280
Interface is up: false
InetAddress: /fe80:0:0:0:0:100:7f:fffe%10

Display name: isatap.{3712CAC6-7755-4525-8119-37BA0015FE46}
Name: net4
MTU: 1280
Interface is up: false

Display name: Microsoft ISATAP Adapter #2
Name: net5
MTU: 1280
Interface is up: false

Display name: Microsoft ISATAP Adapter #3
Name: net6
MTU: 1280
Interface is up: true
InetAddress: /fe80:0:0:0:0:5efe:ac10:162%17
```

Note This is a sample output and not complete. Besides, the value of parameters may vary from machine to machine.

Explanation

L1 A machine having more than one network interface is called a `multi-homed` machine. For example, all routers are multi-homed as they will have at least two interfaces on for the internal network (LAN) and another for outer world (WAN). To obtain all interfaces on the machine, we use the static method `getNetworkInterfaces()` of the `NetworkInterface` class. This method returns an enumeration of objects and throws a `SocketException` if any problem occurs. Enumeration is a collection of objects which can be iterated successively one at a time. The name mentioned in the angle brackets <> specifies the class of objects that the enumeration can hold. The `getNetworkInterfaces()` method returns an enumeration which contains `<NetworkInterface>` objects only.

L2 The `Collections` class (`java.util` package) operates on the collections (like enumeration). This class provides a static method list (`Enumeration<T> n`) that takes an enumeration as an argument and returns an `ArrayList` containing elements of the enumeration. One by one the elements of the `ArrayList` are assigned to `NetworkInterface` variable 'netint' in the `for-each` loop. L3–L10 execute as long as there are objects in the `ArrayList`.

L3 and 4 Prints the display name and the name of the interfaces using simple methods (see output).

L5 MTU defines the size of the packet that can be sent over the network. The `getMTU()` method is used to return the MTU of the interface. This method was added in Java 6. It returns −1 if no MTU is associated with an interface like `loopback` interface. The `loopback` does not need to send anything on the network. All data sent to `loopback` is reverted back to client.

L6 `isUp()` method prints whether the interface is up or down.

L7 to 9 Prints the IP addresses associated with an interface. The `getInetAddresses()` method of the `NetworkInterface` class is used to return an enumeration of IP addresses. We iterate through the enumeration as we have done earlier in L2. It is possible that an interface may have an IPv6 address as well as an IPv4 address associated with it (as shown in the output).

Note IPv4 addresses are represented in dotted decimal notation. 32 bits are divided into 4 parts of 8 bits each. These 8 bits are converted to their respective decimal equivalent and then written with a dot in between them.

IPv6 addresses are represented in colon hexadecimal format. 128 bits are divided into 8 parts of 16 bits each. Then these 16 bits are grouped (4 groups of 4 bits each). Each 4 bit binary value is converted to its corresponding hexadecimal value. The hexadecimal value of all the 16 bits is written separated by a colon, for example, `fe80:0:0:0:8c3d:30ab:4e1b:76a%8`. The number mentioned after the % determines the scope of this address.

For more details on IPv6 addressing architecture, refer IPv6 addressing draft and RFC 4007.

SUMMARY

Network programs in Java (compared to C language) are short in size, easier to code, and debug. The extensive support of multithreading in the language makes it easier to implement concurrent client/server applications in Java. Java network programming has evolved since its inception and it has added a lot of features like support for newer IPv6, knowledge of your local network interfaces, URLs, multicasting, cookie handling, and so on.

-- **EXERCISES** --

Objective Questions

1. What is the value of backlog by default?
   (a) 10   (b) 20   (c) 30   (d) 50
2. A socket is comprised of 3 identifiers. What are they?
   (a) MAC Address, Port and Protocol
   (b) IP address, Port, Protocol
   (c) MAC Address, IP Address and Port Number
   (d) MAC Address, IP Address and Protocol
3. What is the size of an IPv6 address?
   (a) 32   (b) 64   (c) 128   (d) 16
4. What is the size of an IPv4 address?
   (a) 32   (b) 64   (c) 128   (d) 16
5. Which class is used for creating a TCP socket at server?
   (a) Socket   (b) ServerSocket
   (c) DatagramPacket   (d) DatagramSocket
6. Which method of the `NetworkInterface` class is used to obtain the maximum transmission unit?
   (a) `getMaximumTransmissionUnit()`
   (b) `getTU()`
   (c) `getMTU()`
   (d) `getMaxTU()`
7. What is the address of the loopback address?
   (a) 127.0.0.0   (b) 10.1.1.1
   (c) 192.168.10.1   (d) 126.255.255.255
8. Which five parameters uniquely identify a connection?
   (a) Local IP, Remote IP, Local MAC, Remote MAC and Protocol
   (b) Local IP, Local port, Remote MAC, Remote port and Protocol
   (c) Local MAC, Local port, Remote MAC, Remote port and Protocol
   (d) Local IP, Local port, Remote IP, Remote port and Protocol
9. `SocketException` is a subclass of
   (a) `IOException`
   (b) `ReadWriteException`
   (c) `FileNotFoundException`
   (d) `NullPointerException`
10. `UnknownHostException` is a subclass of
    (a) `IOException`
    (b) `ReadWriteException`
    (c) `FileNotFoundException`
    (d) `NullPointerException`

Review Questions

1. Explain the TCP/IP protocol suite.
2. Explain the difference between TCP and UDP. Use real-life situations in your explanation to describe the differences.
3. Explain what is URL with all its parts. Which methods of the URL class can be used to obtain the individual parts of a URL?
4. Explain the following terms:
   (a) MAC address   (b) IPv4
   (c) IPv6   (d) MTU
   (e) Unicasting   (f) Multicasting
   (g) Broadcasting   (h) Port address
5. Explain the role of the following classes:
   (a) Socket   (b) ServerSocket
   (c) DatagramPacket   (d) DatagramSocket
6. What is URL connection class used for and how an instance of it is obtained from the URL object? Explain.

Programming Exercises

1. Create a UDP echo client/server application, wherein whatever is written to a UDP server is written back to the client.
2. Create a sample TCP chat application where client and server can chat with each other.
3. Use multithreading in the previous example to make it a multithreaded chat application.
4. Write a Java program that implements a simple client/server application. The client sends data to a server. The server receives the data, uses it to produce a result, and then sends the result back to the client. The client displays the result on the console. For example, the data sent from the client is the radius of a circle, and the result produced by the server is the area of the circle.

5. Write a program to return the hardware address of your machine.

   [**Hint:** Use `getHardwareAddress()` method of `NetworkInterface` class introduced in Java 6]

6. Create a client/server application where the client requests for a particular file on the server. If the file exists on the server, then write the contents of the file to the client.

Answers to Objective Questions

1. (d)	2. (b)	3. (c)	4. (a)
5. (b)	6. (c)	7. (a)	8. (d)
9. (a)	10. (a)		

Applets

Ideologies, however appealing, cannot shape the whole structure of perceptions and conduct unless they are embedded in daily experiences that confirm them.

Christopher Lasch

After reading this chapter, the readers will be able to
- understand the difference between applet and application
- understand the lifecycle of an applet
- learn how applets are created and executed
- create GUI within applets

12.1 INTRODUCTION

Many of you must have come across the word 'Applet'. What is this applet? Applets are basically small Java programs which can be easily transported over the network from one computer to other. This is the reason why applets are used in Internet applications, where these applets (i.e., small Java programs), embedded in an html page, can be downloaded from the server and run on the client, so as to do a specific kind of job. These applets have the capability of displaying graphics, playing sound, creating animation, and performing other jobs that can be done by simple application programs. To execute these applets on the client, the client must have either a Java-enabled browser or a utility known as appletviewer (comes as part of JDK).

If we could develop simple Java standalone application programs, what was the need to have applets? Actually applets are not full-featured programs, as these are usually written to accomplish small tasks or part of bigger tasks. Before getting further, you must understand the difference between an applet and an application. Table 12.1 illustrates the differences between applets and applications.

In Java, applets can be dealt in two ways. One is the conventional applets, which are directly evolved from 'Applet' class. Theses applets use Abstract Window Toolkit (AWT) to get the GUI features. The other kinds of applets are those which are based on swing class, `JApplet`. We will discuss AWT-based applets in this chapter, while swing-based applets will be discussed in Chapter 15.

Table 12.1 Difference between Applet and Application

Applet	Application
The execution of the applet does not start from `main()` method, as it does not have one.	The execution of an application program starts from `main()`.
Applets cannot run on their own. They have to be embedded inside a web page to get executed.	These can run on their own. In order to get executed, they need not be embedded inside any web page.
Applets can only be executed inside a browser or appletviewer.	Applications are executed at command line.
Applets execute under strict security limitations that disallow certain operations (sandbox model security).	Applications have no inherent security restrictions.
Applets have their own life cycle `init()`→`start()`→`paint()`→`stop`→`destroy()`	Applications have their own life cycle. Their execution begins at `main()`.

12.2 APPLETS

`java.applet.Applet` is the superclass of all the applets. Thus all the applets, directly or indirectly, inherently use the methods of `Applet` belonging `java.applet` package. This class provides all the necessary methods for starting, stopping, and manipulating applets. It also has methods providing multimedia support to an applet. `Applet` class has a predefined hierarchy in Java, which shows the classes extended by `Applet` class.

Figure 12.1 simply makes it easy for you to understand that an applet, which is a subclass of `java.applet.Applet`, also inherits the methods of the other classes like `java.awt.Panel`, `java.awt.Container`, `java.awt.Component`, and `java.lang.Object`, indirectly.

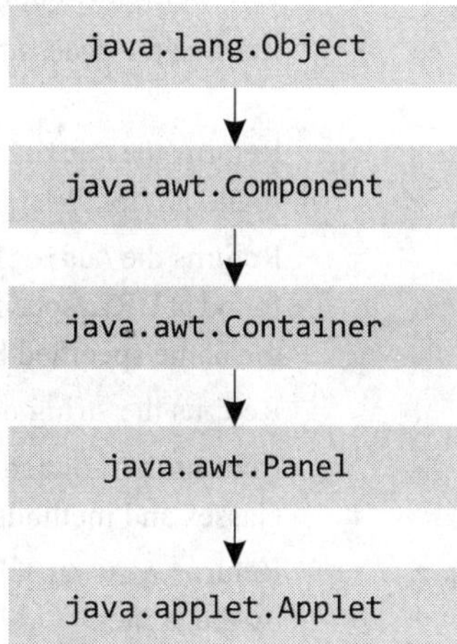

Fig. 12.1 Hierarchy of `Applet` Class

You can see that these classes are the ones which provide support for Java's window-based GUI, thus making an applet capable of supporting window-based activities. The common methods belonging to the `Applet` class are mentioned in Table 12.2.

Table 12.2 Applet Class Methods

Method	Description
void init()	First method to be called when an applet begins execution.
boolean isActive()	Returns true if the applet is running, otherwise false.
URL getDocumentBase()	Gets the URL of the document in which this applet is embedded.
URL getCodeBase()	Returns the URL of the directory where the class file of the invoking applet exists.
String getParameter (String name)	Returns the value of the parameter associated with parameter's name. Null is returned if the parameter is not specified.
AppletContext getAppletContext()	Determines this applet's context, which allows the applet to query and affect the environment in which it runs.
void resize (int width,int height)	Resizes the applet according to the parameters, *width* and *height*.
void showStatus(String msg)	Displays the string, *msg*, in the status window of the browser or appletviewer (only if they support status window).
Image getImage(URL url)	Returns an object of image, which binds the image found at the URL, specified as the argument of the method.
Image getImage(URL url, String imgName)	Returns the image object which encapsulates the image found at the specified URL and having the name specified by imgName.
static final AudioClip newAudioClip(URL url)	Returns an AudioClip object that encapsulates the audio found at the URL specified as the argument.
void start()	Starts or resumes the execution of applet.
void stop()	Stop or suspends the applet.
void destroy()	Terminates the applet.
AccessibleContext getAccessibleContext()	Returns the accessibility context for the invoking object.
AudioClip getAudioClip(URL url)	Returns the AudioClip object, which encapsulates the audio clip found at the URL, specified as the argument to the method.
AudioClip getAudioClip(URL url,String clipName)	Returns the AudioClip object, which encapsulates the audio clip found at URL, specified as the argument to the method and having the name specified by clipName.
String getAppletInfo()	Returns the string describing the applet.
Locale getLocale()	Returns the Locale object that is used by various locale sensitive classes and methods.
String[][] getParameterInfo()	Returns a string table that describes the parameter recognized by the applet.

12.3 APPLET STRUCTURE

Apart from using the services of Applet class, an applet also uses the services of Graphics class of the java.awt package. The Applet class has methods such as init(), start(), destroy(), and stop(), which are responsible for the birth and behavior of an applet. We have already mentioned in Section 12.1 that unlike an application program, Java runtime system does not call the `main()` method to start the execution of an applet, rather it just loads the methods of `applet` class which are responsible for starting, running, stopping, and manipulating an applet. The complete life cycle of the applet will be taken up in the next section.

There is a method, `paint()` in the `Container` class, which is inherited by `Applet` class (as you can make out from Fig. 12.1), carrying the signature,

```
public void paint(Graphics g)
```

This method, when called, displays the output of applet as per the code written on the applet's panel. You can see the argument of this method; it is nothing but an object of `Graphics` class. The object makes it possible for an applet to output text, graphics, sound, etc. One thing you must remember, you cannot take the services of `Graphics` class unless you import the package it belongs to, i.e., `java.awt`. The output operations for an applet requires the methods contained in the `Graphics` class, that is why its `Graphics` object is passed as argument to `paint()`. Now that you know some details about the internals of an applet, we can discuss the program structure of an applet.

When an applet is first loaded, Java runtime system creates an instance of the main class, which is `FirstApplet` in this case. Then the methods belonging to the `Applet` class are called through this object.

12.4 AN EXAMPLE APPLET PROGRAM

Let us take an example applet, which displays the statement "This is my first applet program."

Applet Program Structure

```
import java.awt.*;
//so as to make Graphics class available

import java.applet.*;
//so as to make Applet class available

.........................................

.........................................


public class NewApplet extends Applet
// new applet with the name, newApplet declared
{
        .........................................

        .........................................


        public void paint(Graphics g)
        // paint() of Applet class overridden to contain output operations
        {
            .........................................

            .........................................

        }
        .........................................

        .........................................

}
```

Example 12.1(a) First Applet Example

```
L1    import java.applet.*;
L2    import java.awt.*;
L3    public class FirstApplet extends Applet
      {
L4        public void paint(Graphics g) {
L5        g.drawString("This is my First Applet", 10, 10);
L6        }
L7    }
```

Explanation

L1 All applets are the subclasses of `Applet` class. All applets must import the `java.applet` package.
L2 The applet uses the methods of `java.awt` package; it must be imported.
L3 The `FirstApplet` class is declared public so that the program that executes the applet (a Java-enabled browser or applet viewer, which might not be local to the program) can access it. This class extends the `Applet` class of `java.applet` package, thus inheriting the features of `Applet` class.

L4 The `paint()` method defined by AWT `Container` class is overridden. Any output to be shown by an applet has to be taken care by this method only. Please note that an object of `Graphics` class is passed as parameter to this method.
L5 The object of the `Graphics` class is used to invoke `drawString()` method, which is responsible for printing the string ("This is my First Applet") at x-coordinate 10 and y-coordinate 10.

12.4.1 How to Run an Applet?

There are two ways to run an applet. We will explain these in context to the above example. These approaches are

(a) Save the file as `FirstApplet.java` and compile it by using `javac`. Now, type in the following HTML code in your editor and save the file as `FirstApplet.html` (here, the file name is not necessarily the same as the class name, as it was for the `java` file.)

```
<HTML><BODY>
<APPLET code = "FirstApplet.class" WIDTH = 200 HEIGHT =
150></APPLET>
</BODY></HTML>
```

You can execute the HTML file by giving

```
appletviewer FirstApplet.html
```

Note If you wish to run the above html file in any web browser, instead of using applet viewer, you must have Java-enabled web browser. Otherwise, you will have to install Java plug-in, which lets you run your applets as web pages under 1.2 version of JVM instead of the web browser's default virtual machine.

(b) Just as above, save the file as `FirstApplet.java` and compile it by using `javac`. In order to run the applet, you have to give the below HTML coding as a comment in `FirstApplet.java`.

```
/* <APPLET code = "FirstApplet.class" WIDTH = 200 HEIGHT = 150></APPLET> */
```

Execute the applet as,

```
appletviewer FirstApplet.java
```

In this chapter, we will be using the second approach throughout. So Example 12.1(a) should have been actually written as shown in Example 12.1(b).

Example 12.1 (b) **First Applet Example (Revised)**

```
/* <APPLET code = "FirstApplet.class" WIDTH = 200 HEIGHT = 150></APPLET>
*/ import java.applet.*;
import java.awt.*;
public class FirstApplet extends Applet {
   public void paint(Graphics g) {
      g.drawString("This is my First Applet",10,10);
}}
```

Output

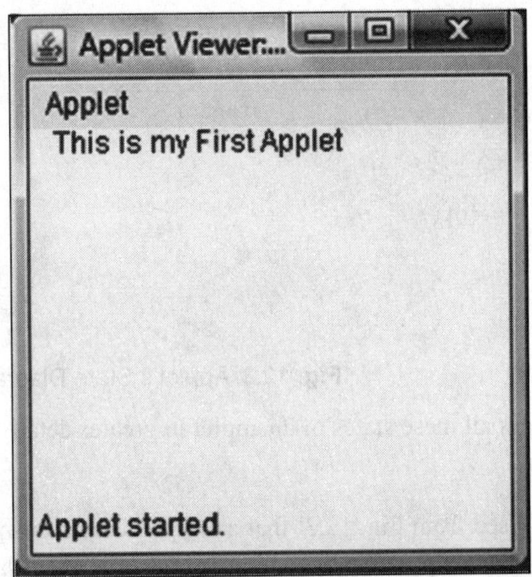

Fig. 12.2 Output Shown with the Help
of Applet Viewer

12.5 APPLET LIFE CYCLE

An applet may move from one state to another depending upon a set of default behaviors inherited in the form of methods from Applet class. These states can be summed up as,

- Born
- Running

- Idle
- Dead

Figure 12.3 shows the flow an applet takes while moving from one state to another.

As mentioned before, an applet may override some of the basic methods of class `Applet`. Note that these methods are responsible for the lifecycle of an applet. These methods are

- `init()`
- `start()`
- `stop()`
- `destroy()`

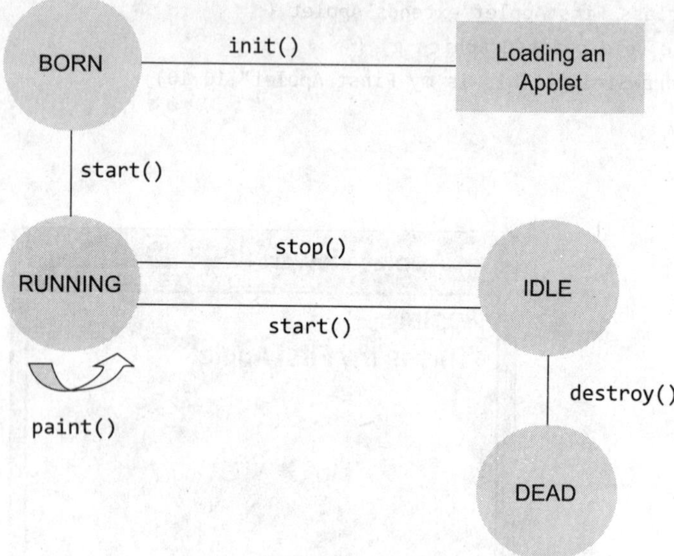

Fig. 12.3 Applet's State Diagram

Let us discuss all these states of an applet in greater detail.

Born State

You can easily see from Fig. 12.3, that an applet enters this phase as soon as it is first loaded by Java. This is made possible by calling `init()` of `Applet` class. Now, what are the things that Java runtime system does, while loading the applet, i.e., when `init()` is called? It creates the objects needed by the applet; it might set initial values, load font and images or set up colors. The method `init()` is called only once during the lifetime of an applet.

> **Note** In order to initialize an applet, we must override the `init()` method of `Applet` class.

Running State

Applet moves to the running state by calling `start()`. An applet moves to this phase automatically after the initialization state. But if the applet is stopped or it goes to idle state, `start()` must be called in order to force the applet again to the running state. Suppose you have opened a web page (having an applet) and you move temporarily to another web page (by minimizing it) the first one goes to the idle state; when you return back to the first page, start() is called to put the applet in the running state again. Unlike init(), start() can be called more than once.

> **Note** start() can be overridden to create a thread to control an applet.

You can see the paint() method in Fig. 12.3. This method is responsible for forcing the applet to an intermediary state (display state), which is actually a part of the running state itself. While running, an applet may need to perform some output and display it on the panel of the applet. The paint() method, which is a part of Container class (a superclass of Applet class), needs to be overridden for the purpose. This method is called each time to draw and redraw the output of an applet. We already know the drawing of output of an applet. Let us discuss redrawing the output of an applet with an example. An applet window may be minimized and then restored. This restoration is nothing but redrawing of applet's output and could be achieved by calling paint(). Actually when an applet in restored, start() and paint() are called in sequence. We will revisit this method in Section 12.7.1.

Idle State

An applet goes to idle state, once it is stopped from running. If we leave a web page containing an applet (i.e., minimize it), the applet automatically goes to idle state. An applet can also be forced to stop or go to idle state by calling stop().

> **Note** If a thread has been created to control an applet by overriding start(), then we must use stop() to stop the thread, by overriding the stop() method of the Applet class.

Dead State

Terminating or stopping an applet should not be confused with destroying an applet. An applet goes to dead state when it is destroyed by invoking the destroy() method of Applet class. It results in complete removal of applet from the memory. Whenever we quit the browser, destroy() is called automatically. You should free up the resources being used by applet (if any) by overriding the destroy() method. Like init(), destroy() is also called only once. stop() is always called before destroy().

12.6 COMMON METHODS USED IN DISPLAYING THE OUTPUT

There are certain methods which you should be acquainted with, as they might be used in applet programming further down the chapter. These are the methods belonging to different classes, which can handle the AWT windowed environment.

drawString()

This method is a member of Graphics class, used to output a string to an applet. It is typically called from within the paint() or update() method. Its form is

```
void drawString(String msg, int a, int b)
```

Here, the string `msg` is the string output to be displayed by the applet and `a`, `b` are the `x`, `y` coordinates respectively of the window, where the output has to be displayed.

setBackground()

This method belongs to component class. It is used to set the background color of the applet window. Its form is

```
void setBackground(Color anyColor)
```

The above method takes the color to be set as background, as argument. The `Color` class has certain predefined constants for each color, such as `Color.red`, `Color.blue`, `Color. green`, and `Color.pink`.

setForeground()

This method is similar to `setBackground` method, except that these are used to set the color of the text to be displayed on the foreground of the applet window. Its form is

```
void setForeground(Color anyColor)
```

Component class has two more methods `getBackground()` and `getForeground()`, having the following forms:

```
Color getBackground();
Color getForeground();
```

You can very well see that these methods return the current context of the `Color`, showing the background and foreground colors, respectively.

showStatus()

This method is a member of `Applet` class. It is used to display any string in the status window of the browser or `appletviewer`. Its from is

```
void showStatus(String text)
```

Here, the argument of the method is basically the string which you want to be displayed in the status window.

Before going any further, we should better take an example which uses these methods, discussed until now.

Example 12.2 **Applet Methods**

```
     /* <APPLET code = "ExampleApplet.class" WIDTH = 200 HEIGHT = 150></APPLET> */
L1     import java.applet.Applet;
L2     import java.awt.Color;
L3     import java.awt.Graphics;
L4     public class ExampleApplet extends Applet{
L5     String text;
L6     public void init() {
L7        setBackground(Color.white);
L8        setForeground(Color.red);
L9        text = "This is an example applet";
L10    System.out.println("....Initialized the applet"); }
```

```
L11    public void start() {
L12       System.out.println("....Starting of the applet");
L13    }
L14    public void stop() {
L15       System.out.println("....Stopping the applet");
L16    }
L17    public void destroy() {
L18       System.out.println("....Exiting the applet");
L19    }
L20    public void paint(Graphics g) {
L21       System.out.println("....Painting the applet");
L22       g.drawString(text, 30, 30);
L23       showStatus("This is status bar"); }}
```

Output

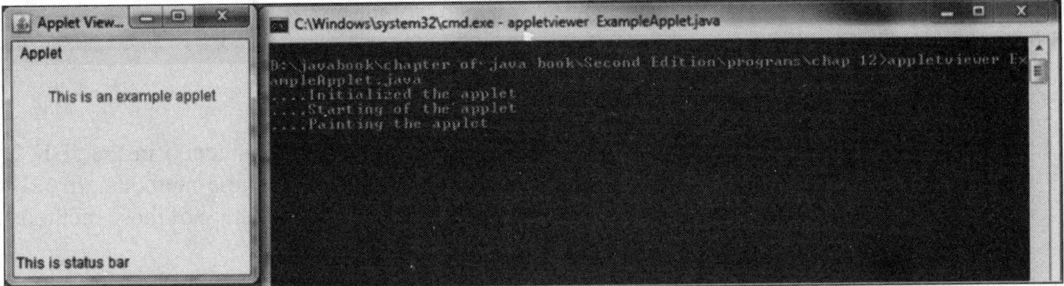

Fig. 12.4(a) Applet Initialized Using Applet Viewer

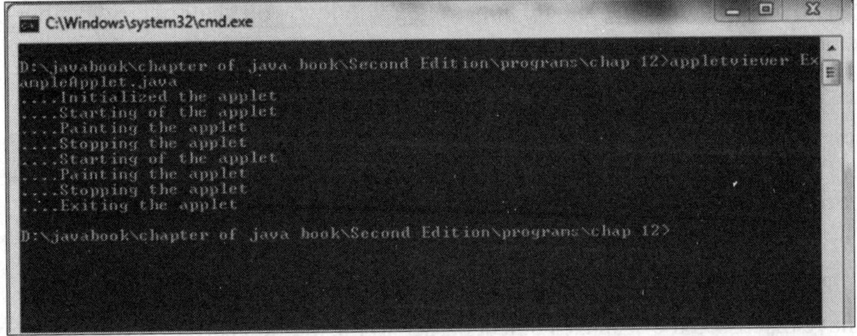

Fig. 12.4(b) Strings Printed by Various Methods of the Applet

Explanation

L1–3   All the important classes (belonging to their respective packages), whose members are to be used in the applet are imported.

L6–10   This section shows the implementation of init(), where the background and foreground of the applet is set to white and red, respectively (see L7–8). White and red are static fields of the Color class (part of java.awt package). In L9, the text is initialized by a string, This is an example applet.

L11–13   These lines account for the implementation of start(), responsible for forcing the applet in running state. L13 displays the message about the start of the applet on the screen. Note that this message will not be displayed on the applet window;

it will be displayed as seen by you in earlier chapters (by the use of `System.out.println()`).

L14–16 These lines take care of the implementation of `stop()`. L16 just displays the message about stopping an applet. As many a times you will stop the applet, this message will be displayed on the screen. You can visualize easily that even minimizing the applet window stops or forces the applet into idle state. If restored after getting minimized, it will again invoke `start()` and `paint()`.

L17–19 These lines take care of the implementation of `destroy()`. Try closing the applet window and you will see the message "……Exiting the applet" (L19). Here, this message simply means that the applet is destroyed or has moved to the dead state.

L20–23 These lines are accountable for the implementation of `paint()` method. In L22, `Graphics` object g is used to invoke its `drawString()` method, which is actually used for writing on an applet window. See the arguments passed to this method: *text*, which contains the string, "This is an example applet" and the *x, y* coordinates from where this text will start in the displayable part of the applet. `paint()` is also called when the window containing applet is covered by another window and they later uncovered. (not minimized and restored)

L22 You can see the method, `showStatus()`, having the text, which has to be shown in the status window of the applet, as argument.

12.7 `paint()`, `update()`, and `repaint()`

All components and containers (since containers are actually components) in the JDK have two methods that are called by the system to paint their surface. These methods are `paint()` and `update()`, belonging to component class (see Fig. 12.1). The signature of these methods are shown below,

```
public void paint(Graphics g);
public void update(Graphics g);
```

If you wish that a drawing should appear in a window, you shall override either or both of the methods. Let us discuss these methods in detail.

12.7.1 `paint()` Method

When a component needs to draw/redraw itself, its `paint()` method is called. The component draws itself when it first becomes visible. The component `paint()` method is also invoked when the window containing it is uncovered, if it is covered by another window.

The simplest `paint()` method looks like the following:

```
public void paint(Graphics g) {... }
```

We have discussed the `Graphics` object passed to the method earlier. It will be discussed in more detail in the next chapter.

Example 12.3 **Set the Color of the Applet and Draws a Fill Oval**

```
     /* <APPLET code = "FillOval.class" WIDTH = 200 HEIGHT = 200></APPLET> */
L1   import java.applet.Applet;
L2   import java.awt.Color;
L3   import java.awt.Graphics;
L4   public class FillOval extends Applet
     {
L5   public void paint(Graphics g)
     {
```

```
L6        g.setColor(Color.red);
L7        g.fillOval(20, 20, 60, 60);
L8    }
L9  }
```

Output

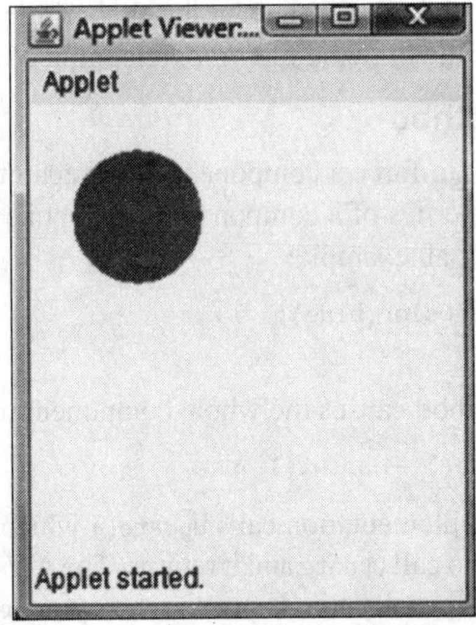

Fig. 12.5 Fill Oval with Red Color

Explanation

L5–8 These lines are accountable for the implementation of `paint()` method. The `setColor()` method of `Graphics` class is used to set the drawing color of the applet to red (L6). Another method, `fillOval()`, belonging to the `Graphics` class is invoked at L7. It fills an oval bounded by the specified rectangle with the current color. The parameters passed to the method are the x-coordinate, y-coordinate, width, and height, respectively.

12.7.2 update() Method

Another method which does the same job as `paint()` method, which is called by AWT components to paint its surface is the `update()` method.

Now let us discuss what this method does. It clears the surface of the calling component to its background color and then calls `paint()` to paint the rest of the component. It makes the job easier because one does not have to draw the whole component within a `paint()` method, as the background is already filled. Then, when one overrides `paint()`, he/she only needs to draw what should appear on the foreground.

It simply does not mean that you will never override `update()`. Let us consider a case where you would like to draw a large, red oval inside a window having yellow background. Now take the case where you do not override `update()`, the window's entire background will be drawn by the `update()` method, and then the red oval will be drawn by the `paint()` method. A large area of one color is first drawn and then the large area of the oval in another color (red in this case) is redrawn. You, as a user can see some slight flickering while displaying the result, especially if you try to draw the oval a number of times in succession.

The above problem can be overcome by overriding `update()`. You would override `update()` to call `paint()`. Then this `paint()`will first draw only the background areas surrounding the red oval and then draw the red oval. Obviously, the flickering problem found earlier is removed because of elimination of the drawing of two overlapping objects of different colors.

12.7.3 `repaint()` Method

Sometimes you may want to force a component to be repainted manually. For example, if you have changed certain properties of a component to reflect its new appearance, you can call the `repaint()` method. Here is an example:

```
text.setBackground(Color.blue);
text.repaint();
```

Calling the `repaint()` method causes the whole component to be repainted.

```
repaint() → update() → paint()
```

`repaint()` in its default implementation calls `update()` which in turn calls `paint()`. `repaint()` method requests the AWT to call `update` and it returns. The AWT combines multiple rapid `repaint` requests into one request (usually this happens when you `repaint` inside a loop). So the last repaint in the sequence actually causes `paint()`. We will discuss these topics in Chapters 13 and 14, where we will illustrate the use of `repaint()` with proper examples.

12.8 MORE ABOUT APPLET TAG

We have used the APPLET tag while writing code for applets. An applet has to be specified in an HTML file. This is done by using APPLET tag in an HTML file. Applets are executed by a Java-enabled web browser as soon as it encounters the APPLET tag inside the HTML file. If you want to view and test an applet using the utility, `appletviewer`, of JDK, you just have to include a comment containing the APPLET tag, just above the actual applet code. We have already discussed how that has to be done.

Till now, we have been using the following form of APPLET tag:

```
<APPLET CODE = filename WIDTH = pixels HEIGHT = pixels></APPLET>
```

This is the most simplified form of APPLET tag, having only the mandatory fields as attributes. Actually this particular tag has many more attributes which are optional but worth discussing. The full syntax of the APPLET tag is shown below.

```
<APPLET [CODEBASE= codebasedURL]
CODE = appletFile [ALT= alternateText] [NAME = appletInstanceName] WIDTH
= pix els HEIGHT = pixels [ALIGN = alignment] [VSPACE = pixels]
[HSPACE = pixels]>
[<PARAM NAME = attributeName VALUE = attributeValue>]
[<PARAM NAME = attributeName VALUE = attributeValue>]
...............................
</APPLET>
```

In the above syntax, the attributes which are put inside the big braces are optional ones. Let us discuss about the use of these attributes in detail.

Codebase Here, we may specify the URL of the directory where the executable class file (specified by CODE attribute) of the applet will be searched for.

Code It gives the name of the file containing the applet's compiled class file. It is a mandatory attribute, which should always be present in APPLET tag.

Alt It is an attribute, which is used to specify the alternate short text message that should be displayed in case the browser recognizes the HTML tag but cannot actually run the applet because of some reason.

Name It is possible to give a name to an applet's instance using this optional attribute. If any other applet on the same web page wants to communicate with this applet, it is referenced through its NAME only.

Width It gives the width of the applet display area in terms of pixels.

Height It gives the height of the applet display area in terms of pixels.

Align This optional attribute is used to set the alignment of an applet. The alignment can be set as LEFT, RIGHT, TOP, BOTTOM, MIDDLE, BASELINE, TEXTTOP, ABSMIDDLE, and ABSBOTTOM.

Vspace These are used to specify the space, in pixels, above and below the applet.

Hspace These are used to specify the space, in pixels, on each side of the applet.

You can use PARAM tags between the <APPLET> and </APPLET> tags to provide information about parameters, or arguments, to be used by the Java applet. The <PARAM> tag is simple—it NAMES a parameter the JAVA applet needs to run, and provides a VALUE for that parameter.

Note User-defined parameters can be supplied to an applet using <PARAM.......> tags.

This tag has two parameters: NAME and VALUE.
Name Attribute name.
Value Value of the attribute named by corresponding PARAM NAME.
The applets access their attributes using the `getParameter()` method. Its signature is as follows:

```
String getParameter(String name);
```

Let us take an example applet which uses the concept of passing parameters.

Example 12.4 **Param Tag**

```
/*<APPLET CODE = ParamPassing.class WIDTH = 300 HEIGHT = 250>
<param NAME = yourName VALUE = John>
<param NAME = yourProfession VALUE = consultant>
<param NAME = yourAge VALUE = 35>
</applet>*/

L1      import java.awt.*;
L2      import java.applet.*;
```

```java
L3      public class ParamPassing extends Applet {
L4          String name;
L5          String profession;
L6          int age;
L7          public void start() {
L8              String str;
L9              name = getParameter("yourName");
L10         if (name == null) name = "not found";
L11         str = getParameter("yourProfession");
L12         if (str != null) profession = str;
L13         else profession = "No job";
L14         str = getParameter("yourAge");
L15         try {
L16         if (str != null) age = Integer.parseInt(str);
L17         else age = 0;
L18     } catch (NumberFormatException e) {}
L19     }
L20     public void paint(Graphics g) {
L21     g.drawString("your name: "+name, 10, 10);
L22     g.drawString("your profession: "+profession, 10, 30);
L23     g.drawString("your age: " +age, 10, 50);
L24     }}
```

Output

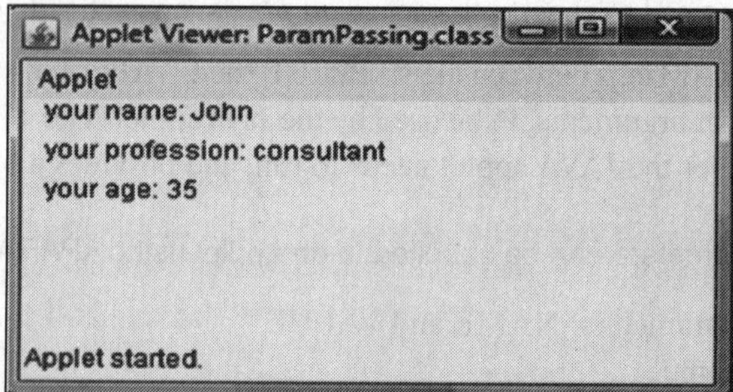

Fig. 12.6 Parameter Passing through Applets

Explanation

Let us start with the APPLET tag placed as comment before the actual code for the program starts. Three PARAM tags are between the start and close of the APPLET tag. All the three PARAM tags have NAME and its corresponding VALUE, such as *yourName* has the value *John*, *yourProfession* has the value *consultant* and *yourAge* has the value 35.

L1–2 For importing necessary classes from their respective packages.

L3 A class named as ParamPassing is declared to extend the Applet class of the java.applet package.

L4–6 References to the String class is declared as name and profession in L4 and L5, respectively. A variable, age, of integer type is declared in L6.

L7–19 Implementation of start() method is shown. At L9, getParameter() method returns the value of the parameter name, yourName, passed as argument. The returned value is stored in name, declared at L4 as string reference. Similarly, two more getParameter() methods are used at L11 and L14, returning the values for the respective parameters names passed as arguments. The use of these values returned by getParameter() methods is too simple to be explained here. Only point worth mentioning here is the use of wrapper class, Integer, at L16. The value returned by getParameter() at L14 is of Stringtype, and it needs to be converted to integer, which is done by the use of parseInt()

method of Integer class. This method throws an exception, named as NumberFormatException, which is caught at L18.

L20–24 Implementation of paint() method is shown, where values for name, profession, and age are displayed on the applet window.

The APPLET parameters stored in the PARAM tag actually have little directly to do with HTML. As you have already seen in the previous example, that it is the responsibility of the applet to check the parameter values and respond accordingly. One more interesting thing worth noting here is that you can increase the flexibility of the applet by making the applet work in multiple situations without recoding and recompiling it, by defining and redefining the parameters (as these are placed as comments, so they are not checked during compilation).

We can sum up the use of PARAM tag for passing parameters to applets in two steps:

- Place the PARAM tag with names and corresponding values between the start and end of the APPLET tag.
- Write the needed code for the applet to retrieve these parameter values, as shown in Example 12.4.

12.9 getDocumentBase() AND getCodeBase() METHODS

Suppose a directory holds the HTML file, responsible for starting the applet and you need the applet to load data (i.e., media and text) from this directory, which is known as document base. We can get the URL of this directory in the form of URL object by using the method getDocumentBase(). Similarly, there is another method, getCodeBase(), which returns the URL object of the directory from where the class file of the applet is loaded. The following example illustrates the use of these methods:

Example 12.5 getCodeBase() and getDocumentBase() Methods

```
    /*<APPLET CODE = BaseMethods.class WIDTH = 300 HEIGHT = 250></applet>*/
L1    import java.awt.*;
L2    import java.applet.*;
L3    import java.net.*;
L4    public class BaseMethods extends Applet {
L5    public void paint(Graphics g) {
L6    String str;
L7    URL url;
L8    url = getCodeBase();
L9    str = "Code Base: "+url.toString();
L10   g.drawString(str, 20, 40);
L11   url = getDocumentBase();
L12   str = "Document Base: " +url.toString();
```

```
L13    g.drawString(str, 20, 60);
L14    }}
```

Output

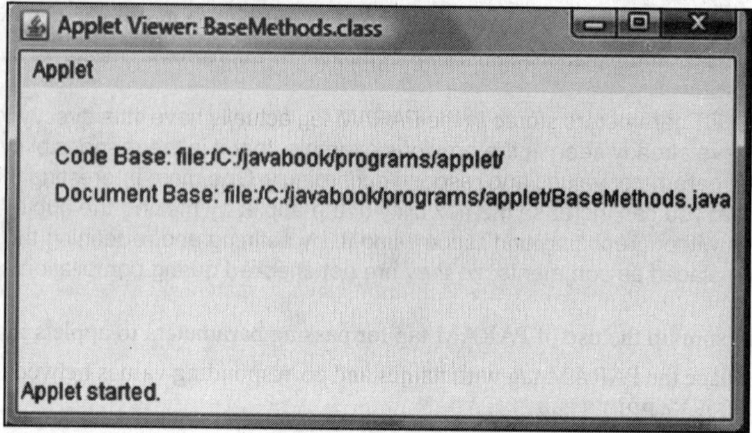

Fig. 12.7 Applet's Code Base and Document Base are Displayed

Explanation

L1–3 All the classes belonging to different packages are imported, so that they can be made available to the program. We require the URL class of `java.net` package in the program, so we are importing all the package `java.net` (L3).

L4 Public class 'BaseMethods' extending the Applet class is declared.

L5–14 `paint()` method is overridden. A reference to `String` class with the name of `str` is created at L6. Another reference of URL class of `java.net` package is created with the name of `url`. At L8, `getCodeBase()` is called, which returns the URL object of the directory where the class file of the applet is loaded. This returned object is stored in `url`. At L9, the URL object stored in `url` is converted to string by using `toString()` and stored in `str`. Similarly, you can see the use of `getDocumentBase()`, which returns the URL object of the directory that holds the HTML file, responsible for starting the applet at L11.

12.10 AppletContext INTERFACE

This interface corresponds to an applet's environment: the document containing the applet and other applets in the same document. In other words, this interface determines this applet's context, which allows the applet to query and affect the environment in which it runs. This environment of an applet represents the document that contains the applet.

The methods in this interface can be used by an applet to obtain information about its environment. The frequently used methods have been provided within the Applet class. These methods are mentioned in Table 12.3.

Table 12.3 `AppletContext` Methods in the `Applet` class

Name	Description
`Enumeration getApplets()`	Finds all the applets in the document represented by this applet context.
`Applet getApplet (String name)`	Finds and returns the applet in the document represented by this applet context with the given name.
`Image getImage(URL url)`	Returns an image object that can then be painted on the screen.
`AudioClip getAudioClip (URL url)`	Creates an audio clip.
`void showDocument(URL url);`	Replaces the Web page currently being viewed with the given URL.
`void showDocument (URL url, String target)`	Requests that the browser or applet viewer show the Web page indicated by the URL argument.
`void showStatus (String status)`	Requests that the argument string be displayed in the "status window".

12.10.1 Communication between Two Applets

There is a method defined in `AppletContext` interface, which enables your applet to transfer control to any other URL. It is `showDocument()`. The signature of this method is as follows:

```
public abstract void showDocument(URL url);
```

The `url`, where you want your applet to transfer control to, is specified as the argument of this method. You can use this method only with the object of the currently executing applet, which can be obtained by `getAppletContext()` defined in the `Applet` class.

Once you have obtained the context of the currently executing applet, your browser or `appletviewer` can show another document or web page by using `showDocument(url)`.

There is another form of `showDocument()` method, having the signature,

```
public abstract void showDocument(URL url, String target)
```

The only new thing you see here is the second argument, `target`. This argument indicates in which HTML frame the document is to be displayed. The `target` arguments can be used in following forms as shown in Table 12.4.

Table 12.4 Values of the Argument of `showDocument()` Method

Target Argument	Description
`"_self"`	Show in the window and frame that contain the applet, i.e. the current frame.
`"_parent"`	Show in the applet's parent frame. If the applet's frame has no parent frame, it acts the same as "_self".
`"_blank"`	Show in a new, unnamed top-level window.
`"_top"`	Show in the topmost frame of the applet's window. If the applet's frame is the top-level frame, it acts the same as "_self".
`Name`	You can specify a name which causes the document to be shown in a new browser window by that name.

> **Note** The file whose URL is passed as argument to the `showDocument()` method must be in same directory on the `server` as the applet.

The method can be evoked in the form:

```java
try {
    getAppletContext().showDocument(new URL(url));
    }
catch (java.net.MalformedURLException e) {
    System.out.println("URL could not be reached");
    }
```

You can see the `try...catch` block around the `showDocument()` method. It has been put because this method throws an exception named `MalformedURLException` which must be caught and handled.

12.11 HOW TO USE AN AUDIO CLIP?

You can load a clip using the method `getAudioclip()` of the `Applet` class, which returns an `AudioClip` object. The signature of this method is

```java
AudioClip getAudioClip(URL url)
```

This object actually encapsulates the audio clip found at the specified URL, passed as the argument to the method (refer to Table 12.1).

We have already told that an applet can take care of audio also. There are various methods defined in `AppletContext` interfaces that take care of manipulating the activities related to an audio clip. A few of these methods are

`play()`: plays a clip from the beginning

`stop()`: stops playing the clip

`loop()`: plays the clip in loop continuously

The above methods can be used by the audio clip object (returned by `getAudioClip()`), to either play, stop, or loop an audio clip. An example applet for loading and playing a sound file is given below.

Example 12.6 **Playing Audio Clips**

```java
L1   import java.applet.*;
L2   import java.lang.*;
L3   import java.net.URL;
L4   public class AudioDemo extends Applet {
L5   AudioClip aud_clip;
L6   public void init() {
L7     aud_clip = getAudioClip(getDocumentBase(), "magic.au");
L8   }
L9   public void start() {
L10    aud_clip.play();
L11  }}
```

Explanation

L7 The clip is loaded during init() using the getAudioClip() method, which takes the url (from getDocumentBase() method) of the audio clip and the name of the audio file. The object of the audio clip returned by the method is stored in aud_clip.

L8 The object aud_clip is used to invoke the pay() method of AppletContext interfaces.

Limitations of Audio Methods

Following are the limitations of the audio methods:

- Currently these methods only support **.au** format sound files.
- The methods are not very robust. You can only play a sound file, but you cannot pause a sound clip.
- Audio features, which can be used by applets, are very limited because of the lack of audio context methods.

Note You can use the Java media framework API for playing sound files of different formats with enhanced functionality.

12.12 IMAGES IN APPLET

The drawImage() method of the Graphics object is used to draw an image on the applet. This method requires an Image object which can be obtained using the getImage method of the Applet class. This method returns an Image object which can be painted on the applet.

Example 12.7 Displaying Images in Applets

```
L1    import java.awt.*;
L2    import java.applet.*;
L3    /*<applet code=ImageDemo.class width=700 height=700></applet>*/
L4    public class ImageDemo extends Applet
      {
L5       Image image;
L6       public void init() {
         // Obtain Image object to be pained or Loads the image
L7          image = getImage(getDocumentBase(),"bulbon.gif");
         }
L8       public void paint(Graphics g) {
         // Draw image
         //drawImage(Image img,int x,int y,int width, int height, ImageObserver observer)

L9          g.drawImage(image, 0, 0, image.getWidth(this),image.getHeight(this), this);
L10         g.drawImage(image, 0, 200, 70,90, this);
         }
      }
```

Output

Fig. 12.8

Explanation

L1–2 Import the required packages; `awt` and `applet`.

L3 The applet html tag (commented) is inserted. This html statement is commented so that it is ignored by the complier as this code does not belong to Java. This html tag is inserted for running the applet through the `appletviewer` utility. In case you run the applet through html file, this tag should be written within the body tag of the html file.

L4 All applets have to be publicly defined and they must be subclasses of the `Applet` class. So `ImageDemo` is a public class and it inherits the `Applet` class.

L5 An instance variable of type `Image` is defined outside (any of) the methods and within the `Applet` class so that it can be used within all the methods of the class.

L6–7 The image is instantiated inside the `init` method, which is called only once during the lifetime of the applet. The image object is obtained using the `getImage()` method and the path of the image file is passed as an URL argument to this method. We have used `getDocumentBase()` as the first argument to the `getImage` method for retrieving the path (upto the base directory) where the applet is stored and the second argument is the Image file name. `getDocumentBase()` will fetch the base directory of the applet as a URL object. We have fetched the base directory of the applet because the applet and the image are placed in the same directory. (Moreover you do not have to change the path every time you copy your applets to other directories or to a directory on different machines.)

L8–10 `paint` method defined to display the image on the applet. The `drawImage` method is used to draw an image on the applet. L9 shows how to draw an image with its default height and width at a particular *x–y* position (second and third arguments) and L10 shows how to change the height and width of the `Image`. The difference is evident in the output. The current applet needs to be notified about the images that is why `this` keyword is used as an argument in the `drawImage` method.

12.12.1 MediaTracker Class

The MediaTracker class is used to track the status of a number of images. If you want to be sure of the fact that images are fully loaded beforehand, you can add all the images to an instance of the MediaTracker class and then check whether the images are loaded before proceeding. You need to create an instance of MediaTracker class and call its addImage method for each image to be tracked. Let us take an example to display two images of a MediaTracker object back to back.

Example 12.8 MediaTracker class

```
L1      import java.applet.Applet;
L2      import java.awt.*;

L3      /*<applet code="MediaTrackerDemo" width=400 height=400></applet>*/

L4      public class MediaTrackerDemo extends Applet implements Runnable
        {
        // image array to hold images
L5      Image[] imageArray = null;

        // to track the images
L6      MediaTracker m = null;
L7      int current = 0;
L8      Thread t=null;

L9      public void init()
        {
        // Create a new media tracker, to track loading images
L10     m = new MediaTracker(this);

        // Create an array of three images
L11     imageArray = new Image[2];

        // Start downloading the first images into the image array
L12     imageArray[0] = getImage(getDocumentBase(), "bulboff.gif");

        // Register it with media tracker
L13     m.addImage(imageArray[0], 0);

        // second image
L14     imageArray[1] = getImage(getDocumentBase(), "bulbon.gif");
L15     m.addImage(imageArray[1], 1);

        // Start thread to begin blinking of images
L16     t = new Thread(this);
L17     t.start();
        }

L18     public void paint (Graphics g)
        {
L19     g.setColor(Color.white);
```

```
        // Sets the background with White Color
L20     g.fillRect(0,0, 400, 400);
        // Sets the Color as black, so that any text written will be black
L21     g.setColor(Color.black);

        // Check to see if images have loaded
L22     if (m.checkAll())
        {
L23         g.drawImage(imageArray[current++], 0, 0, this);
L24         if (current >= imageArray.length)
L25             current = 0;
        }
L26     else // Still loading
        {
L27         g.drawString ("Images are still loading...", 20,20);
        }
    }

L28     public void run()
        {
L29     try
        {
        // waits until all the images have finished loading
L30     m.waitForAll();
L31     for (;;)
          {
          // Repaint the images
L32       repaint();
L33       Thread.sleep(2000);
          }
        }
L34         catch (InterruptedException ie){}
        }
    }
```

Output

The applet starts with the bulb 'off' image and then switches to bulb 'on' image and it keeps on repeating.

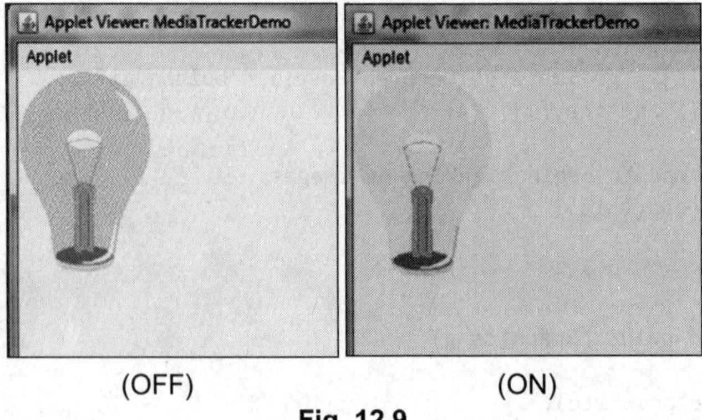

(OFF)   (ON)

Fig. 12.9

Explanation

L1–2 Imports the `awt` and the `applet` packages.

L3 Commented html APPLET tag meant to run the applet through the applet viewer utility.

L4 Public class `MediaTrackerDemo` is declared to inherit the `Applet` class.

L5–8 Instance variables are created of type Image array, `MediaTracker`, `Thread` and an `int` variable meant to change the images. Image array is defined to store images. `MediaTracker` instance will be tracking the status of images stored in the image array. A `Thread` instance is required for changing the images and it acts as a counter for deciding which image to be shown.

L9–15 `init` method is defined for the applet. So all one-time initializations will be done in this method. L10 creates a `MediaTracker` object and `this` is passed as an argument within the constructor to signify the component on which the images will be drawn. L11 creates an image array of two images. The image array is populated with two images in L12 and L14 using the `getImage` method. We have already discussed this method in the above example. These images are added to the `MediaTracker` instance using the `addImage` method in L13 and L15. The first argument is the image and the second is an integer id which is used to track the image.

L16–17 Instantiates the thread and starts it. Remember `this` (current object) is passed in the constructor of `Thread` class to signify the object (i.e., the applet in our case) whose `run` method will be invoked when this thread is started.

L18–21 `paint` method is declared. L19 set the color as white. L20 fills the rectangle (i.e., entire applet) with white `color` so it erases whatever is there on the applet in every paint attempt and then restores the black color in L21. (It is better to whitewash the applet so that there is no overlapping of images).

L22 Checks whether all images have loaded and if yes, draws the images on the applet using the `drawImage` method in L23 else displays a string mentioned in L27. We have already discussed the `drawImage` method above.

L24–25 Shows statements to change the images. We are using the current variable as an index into the image array which is incremented to change the image. The value of the current variable is checked against the length of the image array (so that all images in the image array are shown) and then reset to 0.

L28 `run` method is defined to tell what the thread is supposed to do.

L29 `try` block defined to catch the exceptions that arise in the code.

L30–33 `waitForAll()` method has been used on the tracker object to wait for all images to finish loading and then an infinite loop is executed (L31) to repaint (L32) the applet. Thread is made to sleep in L33 to introduce a delay effect.

L34 Catches the exception raised by sleep method, if any.

12.13 Graphics CLASS

You know about applets in Java now. But these applets are incomplete without their ability to draw graphics. You can write Java applets that can draw lines, figures of different shapes, images, and text in different fonts, styles, and colors. Every applet has its own area on the screen known as canvas, which is actually the display area. To create this display area, you must have the knowledge of Java coordinate system. This coordinate system has the origin (0, 0) in the upper-left corner. Positive x values are to the right and positive y values to the bottom. The values of (x, y) are in pixels.

Now let us discuss the class which makes the use of graphics possible in Java. It is the `Graphics` class belonging to the `java.awt` package, defined as

```
public abstract class Graphics extends Object
```

Note The Graphics class is the abstract base class for all graphics contexts that allows an application to draw onto components that are realized on various devices, as well as onto off-screen images.

This class has a number of methods defined in it, some of which are mentioned below in Table 12.5.

Table 12.5 Few Methods of the Graphics Class

Name	Description
`drawArc(int x, int y, int width, int height, int startAngle, int arcAngle)`	Draws the outline of a circular or elliptical arc covering the specified rectangle.
`drawLine(int x1, int y1, int x2, int y2)`	Draws a line.
`finalize()`	Disposes of this graphics context once it is not referenced.
`translate(int x, int y)`	Translates the origin of the graphics context to the point (x, y) in the current coordinate system.
`drawOval(int x, int y, int width, int height)`	Draws the oval.
`drawPolygon(int[] xPoints, int[] yPoints, int nPoints)`	Draws a polygon defined by arrays of x and y coordinates.
`drawRect(int x, int y, int width, int height)`	Draws the specified rectangle.
`getClip()`	Returns the bounding rectangle of the current clipping area.
`fillArc(int x, int y, int width, int height, int startAngle, int arcAngle)`	Fills a circular or elliptical arc covering the specified rectangle.
`fillOval(int x, int y, int width, int height)`	Fills an oval bounded by the specified rectangle with the current color.
`fillPolygon(int[] xPoints, int[] yPoints, int nPoints)`	Fills a closed polygon defined by arrays of x and y coordinates.
`fillRect(int x, int y, int width, int height)`	Fills the rectangle.
`getColor()`	Returns this graphic context's current color.
`getFont()`	Returns the current font.
`setColor(Color c)`	Sets the drawing color.
`setFont(Font font)`	Sets this graphic context's font to the specified font.
`fillRoundRect(int x, int y, int width, int height, int arcWidth, int arcHeight)`	Fills the specified rounded corner rectangle with the current color.
`drawRoundRect(int x, int y, int width, int height, int arcWidth, int arcHeight)`	Draws an outlined round-cornered rectangle using this graphic context's current color.
`drawString(String str, int x, int y)`	Draws the string on the specified coordinates.
`clearRect(int x, int y, int width, int height)`	Clears the specified rectangle by filling it with the background color of the current drawing surface.

(Contd)

(*Table 12.5 Contd*)

Name	Description
`clipRect(int x, int y, int width, int height)`	Intersects the current clip with the specified rectangle.
`copyArea(int x, int y, int width, int height, int dx, int dy)`	Copies an area of the component by a distance specified by *dx* and *dy*.
`create()`	A graphics object is created.
`create(int x, int y, int width, int height)`	Creates a new Graphics object based on this Graphics object, but with a new translation and clip area.
`dispose()`	Disposes of the current graphics context and releases any system resources used by it.
`draw3DRect(int x, int y, int width, int height, boolean raised)`	Draws a 3-D highlighted outline of the specified rectangle.
`drawArc(int x, int y, int width, int height, int startAngle, int arcAngle)`	Draws the outline of a circular or elliptical arc covering the specified rectangle.
`drawBytes(byte[] data, int offset, int length, int x, int y)`	Draws the text given by the specified byte array, using this graphic context's current font and color.
`drawChars(char[] data, int offset, int length, int x, int y)`	Draws the text given by the specified character array, using this graphic context's current font and color.
`fill3DRect(int x, int y, int width, int height, boolean raised)`	Paints a 3-D highlighted rectangle filled with the current color.
`fillArc(int x, int y, int width, int height, int startAngle, int arcAngle)`	Fills a circular or elliptical arc covering the specified rectangle.

12.13.1 An Example Applet Using Graphics Class

Herein we give an example applet, which uses graphics. The methods of the Graphics class has been called in the paint() method. Note that the object of the Graphics class is passed as argument to the paint()method and this object only helps in invoking all the member methods of the Graphics class.

The following example takes care of different shapes which can be drawn using Graphics class.

Example 12.9 Graphics Class Methods

```
/* Applet code=DrawLineRect width = 600 height = 40></Applet>*/
    import java.awt.* ;
    import java.applet.* ;
    public class DrawLineRect extends Applet {
L1      public void paint(Graphics g){
L2          g.drawRect(10,60,40,30);
L3          g.fillRect(60,10,30,80);
L4          g.fillOval(140,160,170,170);
L5          g.drawRoundRect(10,100,80,50,10,10);
L6          g.fillRoundRect(20,110,60,30,5,5);
L7          g.drawArc(280,210,250,220,30,90);
```

```
L8        g.drawLine(100,10,230,140);
L9        g.drawLine(100,140,230,10);
}}
```

Output

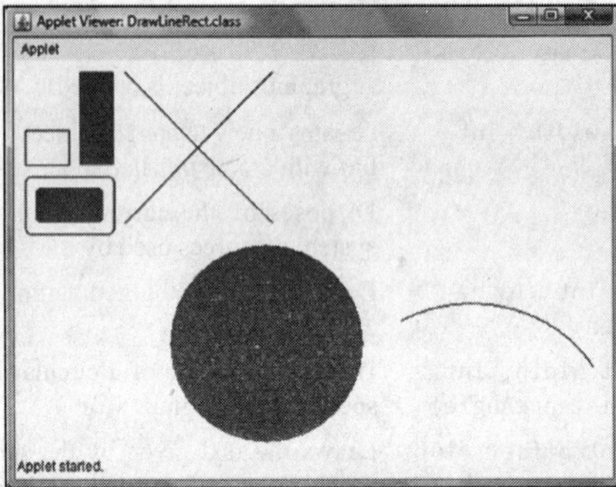

Fig. 12.10 Applet Showing Demonstration of Methods of Graphics Class

Here, we will stick to the paint() method only as all the methods of the Graphics class are used inside this method only. The description of these methods is available in Table 12.5.

Explanation

L2   The drawRect method is used to draw a rectangle. The first two arguments specify the *x* and *y* coordinates and later two specify the width and height of the rectangle.

L3   The fillRect method is used to draw a rectangle that is filled with a color. The default color is black. You can always change the color using the setColor method.

L4   The fillOval method is used to draw an oval that is filled with the default color. The first two arguments specify the *x* and *y* coordinates and the latter two specify the width and height of the oval.

L5 and 6   The drawRoundRect method is used to draw a rectangle with rounded corners. The additional arguments (last two) are the width of the arc (i.e., 10) and height of the arc (i.e., 10).

fillRoundRect is same as drawRoundRect. The only difference is that in this case the rounded rectangle is filled with a color.

L7   drawArc method is used to draw an arc (as shown in the output). The first argument is *x* coordinate of the upper left corner of the arc to be drawn. The second argument is the *y* coordinate of the upper left corner of the arc to be drawn. The third and fourth argument specifies the width of the arc and height of the arc. The fifth argument is the starting angle of the arc. The arcs begin at starting angle and extend to arc angle which is the last argument.

L8 and 9   drawLine is used to draw lines between points x1, y1 and x2, y2 (which are specified as four arguments to this method.)

12.14 Color CLASS

Color is a class which is inherited from Object class and implements Paint and Serializable interfaces. We have RGB colors as default color for monitors and TV screens. In Java, color is portable and machine independent. Using Color class, you can specify any color in Java. Apart from specifying a particular color, you can also create your own color in Java. It is an astonishing fact; you can create up to 24 million different colors in Java. Color class has various constants specifying a number of common colors. These constants are as shown below:

Color.Black	Color.DARK_GRAY	Color.GRAY
Color.LIGHT_GRAY	Color.WHITE	Color.MAGENTA
Color.RED	Color.PINK	Color.ORANGE
Color.YELLOW	Color.GREEN	Color.BLUE

Some of the constructors and methods of Color class are shown in Table 12.6

Table 12.6 Color Class

Constructor of Color Class	
Constructor	**Description**
Color(Color space cspace, float[] components, float alpha)	Creates color in a specific ColorSpace with specified color components.
Color(float r, float g, float b)	Creates a mix color of red (r), green (g), and blue (b) and the values are in the range of (0.0–1.0).
Color(float r, float g, float b, float a)	Creates a mix color of red, green, and blue and alpha (α) values in the range of (0.0–1.0).
Color(int rgbValue)	Creates a mix color of red, green, and blue and the bits for red component is 16–23, bits for green component is 8–15, and bits for blue component is 0–7.
Color(int r, int g, int b)	Specify a color of mix red, green, and blue values in the range of (0–255).
Color(int r, int g, int b, int a)	Creates a color of mix colors red, green, blue, and alpha values in the range of 0–255.
Methods of Color Class	
Methods	**Description**
brighter()	Creates a brighter version of a color.
createContext(ColorModel cm, Rectangle r, Rectangle2D r2d, AffineTransform xform, RenderingHints hints)	This method is used to create a solid color pattern.
darker()	Creates a darker, brighter version of a color.
decode(String nm)	It translates a String to an integer that returns the specific Color.
equals(Object obj)	Checks that another object is equal or not to this Color.
getAlpha()	Returns an alpha component whose range is 0–255.
getBlue()	A blue component is returned by this method in the range 0–255 in the default red, green, blue space.
getColor(String nm)	Finds a color in the system properties.

(Contd)

(Table 12.6 Contd)

Methods	Description
getColorComponents(ColorSpace cspace, float[] compArray)	A float array is returned. It contains color components specified by the escape parameter.
getColorSpace()	ColorSpace of the Color is returned by it.
getComponents(float[] compArray)	An array of float type is returned which contains the color and alpha components of the Color.
getGreen()	A green component is returned by it in the range 0–255 in the default red, green, blue space.
getRGBComponents(float[] compArray)	An array of float type is returned which contains color and alpha components of the Color which represents red, green, blue color space.
HSBtoRGB(float hue, float saturation, float brightness)	Using HSB model, it returns a packed RGB value with the help of Color(int) constructor.
RGBtoHSB(int r, int g, int b, float[] hsbvals)	The color of component is converted to HSB model specified by RGB model.
toString()	A color is represented as a string.

How to create your own color? Let us take an example constructor for creating a light 'red' color object.

We can use the fifth constructor from Table 12.6 for the purpose,

```
Color c= new Color (255, 100, 100)
```

Once a color object is created by using any of the above constructors, it can be used to set the foreground and background colors by using the setForeground() and setBackground() methods, respectively.

The constructors of color class and some of its methods are listed in Table 12.6 along with their description.

12.15 Font CLASS

Font class extends Object class and implements Serializable interface. Various fonts are represented by Font class to write text. If you have used MS office application, you must be aware of the importance of font manipulation. AWT provides this flexibility of manipulating fonts during the execution of the program itself.

Three important attributes of font are

- *Family name* It is the name of the font generally given, such as 'Times New Roman'.
- *Logical font name* It specifies the font category, such as monospaced.
- *Face name* It specifies a specific font, such as 'Courier italic'.

Various fields, constructor, and methods of Font class are shown in Table 12.7.

How would you determine the available fonts on your machine? There is a method, getAvailableFontFamilyNames(), belonging to the GraphicsEnvironment class for the purpose. This method returns an array of strings, containing the names of the available font family. One more method belonging to the same class is `getAllFonts()`, which returns an array of font objects of all the available fonts.

As mentioned above, these methods belong to `GraphicsEnvironment` class, so we would need a reference to this class for calling these methods. There is a static method in `GraphicsEnvironment` class, named `getLocalGraphicsEnvironment()`, which returns this reference. The signature of this method is follows:

```
static GraphicsEnvironment getLocalGraphicsEnvironment()
```

Example 12.10 clarifies the use of this method. The next question is, how to create and select a new font? For this, you need to construct a `Font` object, describing that font. Obviously, one of the constructors mentioned in Table 12.7 will help in constructing a `Font` object. Let us talk about the second constructor of the table, i.e.,

```
Font(String name, int style, int size)
```

Table 12.7 Font Class

Fields of Font class	
Field Name	**Description**
BOLD	A constant style bold.
CENTER_BASELINE	For various similar scripts like Chinese, Japanese, and Korean, baseline is used.
DIALOG	Verified the name of font at compile time in Font construction.
ITALIC	Italic style constant.
pointSize	The point size of a Font in float type value.
Style	Font's style is passed to a constructor.
TRUETYPE_FONT	Checks weather the font resource is of TRUETYPE or not.
ROMAN_BASELINE	In Roman scripts, it is used for writing text.
Constructors of Font class	
Constructor Name	**Description**
Font(Font font)	New Font is created from a specified font.
Font(String name, int style, int size)	New Font is created from the specific name, style, and point size.
Methods of Font class	
Method Name	**Description**
canDisplay(char c)	Checks weather this Font has a glyph for the specific character or not.
canDisplayUpTo(String str)	Mentions that this Font can display a specified String or not.
createFont(intfontFormat, File fontFile)	Using a particular font type and font file, it returns a new font.

(Contd)

(*Table 12.7 Contd*)

Method Name	Description
`createGlyphVector(FontRenderContextf rc, char[] chars)`	Creates a `GlyphVector`.
`decode(String str)`	A font is retuned.
`deriveFont(AffineTransform trans)`	A new font object is created and replaced the current font object.
`equals(Object obj)`	Comparison between a `Font` object to the specific `Object`.
`Finalize()`	Disposal of native `Font` object.
`getAttributes()`	A map of font attributes is returned.
`getAvailableAttributes()`	Keys of attributes supported by font are returned.
`getBaselineFor(char c)`	Baseline is retuned to display character.
`getFamily()`	Family name of this `Font` is returned.
`getFont(String nm)`	`Font` object is returned from the system properties list.
`getFontName()`	Font face name is returned of this `Font`.
`getItalicAngle()`	Italic angle is returned.
`getMaxCharBounds FontRenderContextfrc)`	Bounds for a character are returned.
`getMissingGlyphCode()`	glyphCode is returned.
`getName()`	Logical name of Font is returned.
`getNumGlyphs()`	Returns the number of glyphs.
`getPSName()`	Postscript name of this `Font` is returned.
`getSize()`	Returns the point size of this `Font`, rounded off to an integer.
`getStringBounds(char[] chars, intbeginIndex, int limit, FontRenderContextfrc)`	Returns the logical bounds of a particular array of characters.
`getStyle()`	Style of a font is returned.
`isBold()`	Indicates style is Bold for this `Font` object.
`isPlain()`	Indicates style is PLAIN or not of `Font` object.
`isTransformed()`	The affect of transformation 8 in its size is indicated.
`toString()`	Font object is converted to a `String` representation.

Three arguments to this constructor are

- ***name*** It specifies the name of the desired font.
- ***style*** It specifies the style of the desired font, which can be one or more of the three constants, `Font.PLAIN`, `Font.BOLD`, and `Font.ITALIC`. If you want to combine two styles, you can do it as, `Font.ITALIC !Font.BOLD`. It simply means ITALIC and BOLD styles for font.
- ***size*** It specifies the size of the font in points.

Once the font is created, `setFont()` method of component class is used to select it. The signature of this method is as follows:

```
void setFont(Font fontObject)
```

Here the argument `fontObject` is the object that contains the desired font.

If you have a font and you want to get information about that font, `getFont()` method of `Graphics` class will be helpful. It returns the current font. It has the following signature:

```
Font getFont()
```

Once you have obtained the current font, you can easily get the other related information about the font using the various methods of `Font` class, like `getName()`, `getStyle()`, `getSize()`, `getFamily()`, etc. (for more details, refer to Table 12.7). The following example shows the use of `Color` and `Font` classes.

Example 12.10   Usage of Font and Color Class

```
     /*<applet code = ColorFont.class width = 600 height = 270></applet>*/
L1   import java.awt.*;
L2   public class ColorFont extends java.applet.Applet
     {
L3   public void init() {
L4   Color color1 = new Color(230, 220, 0);
L5   setBackground(color1);
L6   }
L7   public void paint(Graphics g) {
L8   String str = " ";
L9   String FontList[];
L10  GraphicsEnvironment ge = GraphicsEnvironment.getLocalGraphicsEnvironment();
L11  FontList = ge.getAvailableFontFamilyNames();
L12  for (int i = 0; i<FontList.length; i++) {
L13  g.drawString("FONTS AVAILABLE ARE:", 5, 30);
L14  str += FontList[i] + ", ";
L15  g.drawString(str,5, 50);
L16  }
L17  Color color2 = new Color(235, 50, 50);
L18  g.setColor(color2);
L19  g.drawString("Hey Look!!!", 5, 180);
L20  Font currentFont = new Font("TimesRoman", Font.PLAIN, 20);
L21  g.setFont(currentFont);
L22  g.drawString("This is an example", 5, 220);
L23  currentFont=new Font("TimesRoman", Font.ITALIC, 40);
L24  g.setFont(currentFont);
L25  g.drawString("You must have understood.....", 5, 260);
L26  }
L27  }
```

Output

The output of the above program shows the available fonts on the machine as well as some sentences painted, using the `Font` class, on the applet window:

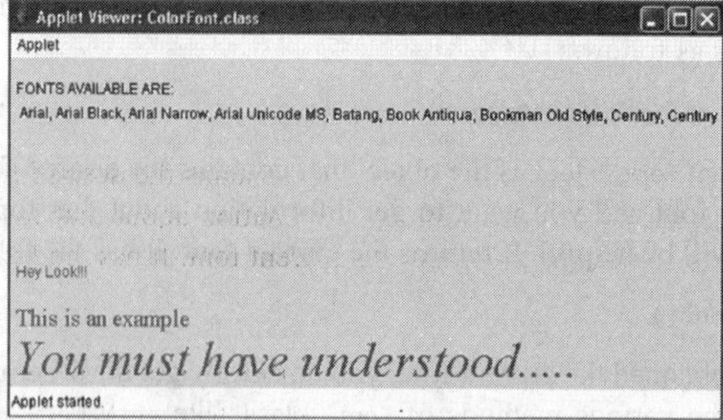

Fig. 12.11 Output Showing Available Fonts and How to Use Color Class

Explanation

L1 All the required classes of AWT package are imported.

L2 A class named as `ColorFont` extending the `Applet` class is declared.

L3–6 `init()` is declared and implemented, where a reference to the `Color` class with the name of `color1` is created in L4. The arguments passed to the constructor, `Color()`, are responsible for the output color, which you are seeing in the output window. These arguments are integer values signifying red, green, and blue, respectively (in the range of 0–255). Once the `Color` object is created in L5, it is passed to `setBackground()`, responsible for setting the background of the applet window as per the color mix.

L7 The `paint()` method, with graphics reference as argument, is declared. This method ends at L26.

L9 An array of `String` is declared as `FontList`.

L10 The `getLocalGraphicsEnvironment()` method of `GraphicsEnvironment` class returns the reference to `GraphicsEnvironment`, which is stored in ge.

L11 The `getAvailableFontFamilyNames()` method, which returns the array of fonts available on machine, is called using the reference ge. The resultant array is stored in array, `FontList`, declared at L9.

L12–16 In L12, `for` loop is used to increment the integer, i, by 1, till it reaches the maximum size of the array, i.e., the length of the array. Each element of the array `FontList` is drawn on the applet surface using `drawstring()` (L15).

L17 Another object of the `Color` class, `color2` is constructed.

L18 `Graphics` class reference is used to set the `Color` to `color2`, using `setColor()`. This color is set for the text to be displayed on the applet.

L19 `drawString()` is used to display the string, "Hey Look!!!" on the **x** and **y** coordinates specified as the second and third argument respectively of the `drawString()`.

L20 Constructor belonging to `Font` class is used to construct a `Font` object, `currentFont`, encapsulating font name as 'Times New Roman', Font style as 'Font.PLAIN' and font size as 20 (see the constructor's arguments).

L21 Reference of `Graphics` class is used to call `setFont()` of component class to set the font to 'currentFont'.

L22 `drawString()` is used to display the string `Thisisanexample` at the location specified as arguments of the method.

12.16 FontMetrics CLASS

The font metrics objects are defined by `FontMetrics` class which extends `Object` class and implements `Serializable` interface. You must be aware with the term 'metrics'. Its literal meaning is ' a system or standard of measurements'. The `java.awt.FontMetrics` class is helpful in determining the measurements associated with characters and strings (group of characters). The texts can be positioned precisely using these measurements. The following table shows a few font terminologies.

The various attributes which contribute to font metrics can be visualized in Fig. 12.12.

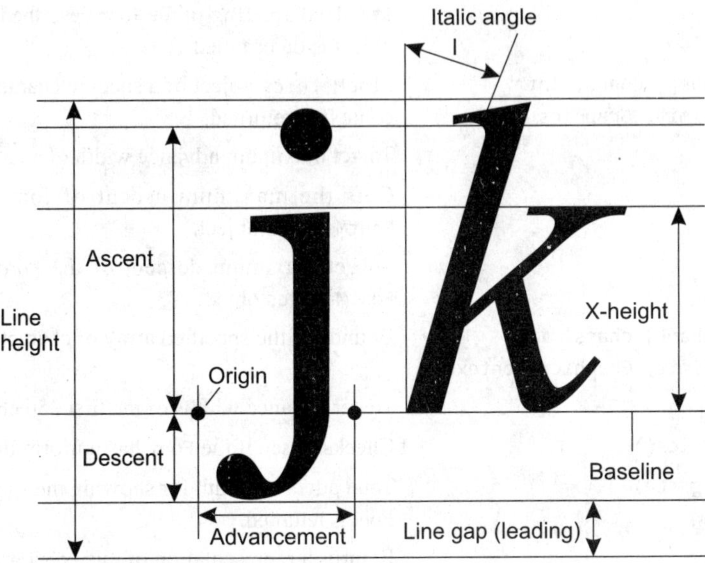

Fig. 12.12 Terminologies Used in the `FontMetrics` Class

FontMetrics Object

Font metrics are determined by the font and the graphics context. To create a `FontMetrics` object, where `g` is a `Graphics` object and `f` is a `font` object, the following constructor can be used:

```
FontMetrics fm = g.getFontMetrics(f);
```

The object `fm` is created to find out the height and width information about a specified `Font` and specific character glyphs in that `Font`.

FontMetrics Methods

Table 12.8 provides a brief description of the methods in `FontMetrics` class.

Table 12.8 Methods of `FontMetrics` Class

Method	Description
`bytesWidth(byte[] data, int off, int len)`	Width to show a specific array of bytes in this font is returned.
`charsWidth(char[] data, int off, int len)`	Width to show a specific array of character in this font is returned.
`getAscent()`	Font ascent is determined by it.
`getDescent()`	Font descent is determined by it.

(Contd)

(*Table 12.8 Contd*)

Method	Description
getFont()	Gets the Font.
getFontRenderContext()	Gets the FontRenderContext.
getHeight()	Gets the standard height of line of text.
getLeading()	Standard leading of the Font described by this FontMetrics object is determined.
getLineMetrics(char[] chars, int beginIndex, int limit, Graphics context)	LineMetrics object of a specific character array in graphics context is returned.
getMaxAdvance()	To get maximum advance width of a character in this Font.
getMaxAscent()	Gets the maximum ascent of font explained by this FontMetrics object.
getMaxDescent()	To get maximum descent of the Font described by this FontMetrics object.
getStringBounds(char[] chars, int beginIndex, int limit, Graphics context)	Bounds of the specified array of characters are returned.
getWidths()	To get advance widths of the first 256 characters in the Font.
hasUniformLineMetrics()	Checks to see if the Font has uniform line metrics.
stringWidth(String str)	Total advance width for showing the specified String in this Font is returned.
toString()	Returns a representation of this FontMetrics object's values as a String.

Example 12.11 Class Demonstrating FontMetrics Class

```
     /*<applet code = DemoFontMetrics.class width = 300 height = 300></applet>*/
L1   import java.awt.*;
L2   import java.applet.*;
L3   public class DemoFontMetrics extends Applet {
L4   public void init() {
L5   Color color1 = new Color(255, 255, 250);
L6   setBackground(color1);
L7   }
L8   public void paint(Graphics g) {
L9   int fontSize = 20;
L10  g.setFont(new Font("TimesRoman", Font.PLAIN,fontSize));
L11  FontMetrics fm = g.getFontMetrics();
L12  String s = "Its my Applet";
L13  int sw = fm.stringWidth(s);
L14  int w =300;
L15  int h = 300;
L16  int x = (w - sw) / 2;
L17  int baseline = fm.getMaxAscent() + (h - (fm.getAscent() + fm.getMaxDescent())))/2;
L18  int ascent = fm.getMaxAscent();
L19  int descent = fm.getMaxDescent();
```

```
L20    int fontHeight = fm.getMaxAscent() + fm.getMaxDescent();
L21    g.setColor(Color.pink);
L22    g.fillRect(x, baseline-ascent , sw, fontHeight);
L23    g.setColor(Color.red);
L24    g.drawLine(x, baseline+descent, x+sw, baseline+descent);
L25    g.setColor(Color.blue);
L26    g.drawLine(x, baseline-ascent, x+sw, baseline- ascent);
L27    g.setColor(Color.black);
L28    g.drawString(s, x, baseline);
L29    }
L30    }
```

Output

Fig. 12.13 Output Produced Using `FontMetrics` Class

Explanation

L1–2 The required packages are imported.

L3 A class named `DemoFontMetrics` extending the `Applet` class is declared.

L4 `init()` method is overridden.

L5 The arguments passed to the constructor, `Color()`, are responsible for the output color, which you are seeing in the output window, in Fig. 12.13. These arguments are integer values signifying red, green, and blue colors respectively (in the range of 0–255). Once the `Color` object is created, in L6, it is passed to `setBackground()` method, responsible for setting the background of the applet window as per the mixture of colors specified as numbers.

L8 `paint()` method is defined.

L9 An integer variable named `fontSize` is declared.

L10 A method named `setFont()` is used to set font and its size.

L11 A `FontMetrics` object `fm` is created.

L12 A string is declared.

L13 An integer variables `w` has been created to denote the width of string.

L14–15 Two integer variables (`w` and `h`) are declared for positioning of string. `w` and `h` actually denote the width and height of the applet.

L16 x coordinate is calculated by subtracting the string width from the width of the applet and then dividing it by 2. This will form the x coordinate of the string to be printed on the applet.

L17–20 In these lines, we have calculated baseline, ascent, fontHeight, descent, values for positioning of string using getMaxAscent(), getAscent(), and getMaxDescent() methods.

L21–22 It will fill pink color into the specified area.

L23–24 We have drawn a red line below the string using drawLine() method.

L25–26 We have drawn a blue line above the String using drawLine() method.

L27–28 drawString() method is called to draw the string and setColor() is used for setting black color.

12.17 PRACTICAL PROBLEM: DIGITAL CLOCK

We have already discussed an example of digital clock in Chapter 8. But that was not graphically impressive, so let us create an applet which displays the current date and time digitally and in a presentable manner. This applet will use threads, so you will get to know how threads can be used in applets.

Example 12.12 Digital Clock

```
L1    import java.util.*;
L2    import java.applet.*;
L3    import java.awt.*;
L4    import java.text.*;

L5    /*<applet code=DigitalClock.class width=450 height=100></applet>*/

L6    public class DigitalClock extends Applet implements Runnable
      {
L7        Thread t;
L8        Calendar c;
L9        Date d;
L10       DateFormat df;
L11       public void init()
          {
L12           t=new Thread(this,"Time Thread");
L13           t.start();
L14           df=DateFormat.getInstance();
          }
L15       public void run()
          {
L16           for(;;)
L17           {
L18               try{
L19               c=Calendar.getInstance();
L20               d=c.getTime();
L21               Thread.sleep(1000);
              }
L22           catch(Exception e){}
L23               repaint();
L24           }
          }
L25       public void paint(Graphics g)
```

```
        {
L26         g.setFont(new Font("Courier New", Font.ITALIC, 20));
L27         g.drawString(d.toString(),30,20);
L28         g.drawString("Different Format " +df.format(d),30,40);
        }
    }
```

Output

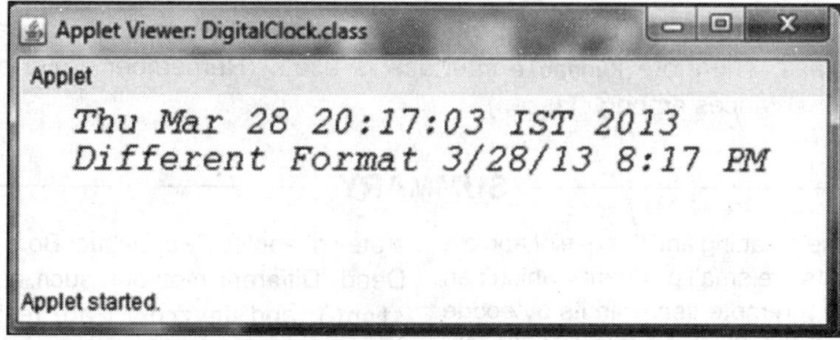

Fig. 12.14

Explanation

L1–4 Imports the required packages: `java.util`, `java.applet`, `java.awt`, and `java.text`. `Date` and `Calendar` classes belong to `java.util` package; `Applet` class belongs to `java.applet` package, `Graphics` class is of `java.awt` package and `DateFormat` belongs to `java.text` package.

L5 The applet html tag (commented) is inserted. This html statement is commented so that it is ignored by the complier, as this code does not belong to Java. This html tag is inserted for running the applet through the `appletviewer` utility.

L6 Public class `DigitalClock` is declared to inherit the `Applet` class and `Runnable` interface.

All applets have to be publicly defined and they must be subclasses of the `Applet` class. In case you wish to create threads in an applet, it must inherit the `Runnable` interface.

L7–10 Instance variables of type `Thread`, `Date`, `Calendar`, and `DateFormat` are defined within the applet. The objects of these types will be used throughout the `DigitalClock` applet.

L11–14 `init` method is defined for the applet. All one time activities for the `Digital clock` can be done here. So we have initialized the Thread and started it. We have also used the `DateFormat` class in our example to specifically show how to represent the date and time in a different format.

`DateFormat` is an abstract class so it cannot be instantiated directly. It is instantiated in L14 using the `getInstance()` static method of the `DateFormat` class which returns an instance of the `DateFormat` class.

L15–24 The `run` method for the thread is defined which specifies what the thread is supposed to do. The method is supposed to extract the current date and time and set it in the `Date` object. The current date and time is extracted using the abstract class `Calendar` whose instance is created in L19 using the static method `getInstance()` of the `Calendar` class. The `getTime()` method is used on the `Calendar` instance to obtain `Date` object. L21 uses the `sleep` method to delay the thread by one second. Even in case of an exception, the `paint()` method is invoked by invoking the `repaint()` method.

L25–28 All display functionality in an applet lies within the `paint()` method, so it is the responsibility of the `paint()` method to display date and time stored in the `Date` object. L26 uses `setFont` method on the `Graphics` object to set the font and its size. `drawString()` is used in L27 to write strings on the applet at a particular `x,y` location. The first argument to this method is the `Date` object which displays the string in its standard format (see first line of the output). L28 shows how to format the date using the `DateFormat` object created in L14. The `format()` method of the `DateFormat` class is used to format the `Date` object passed to it as an argument. This method returns a formatted time string which is passed to the `drawString` method and hence it is displayed on the applet (see second line of the output). The first line of the output display time in a 24 hr format with day of the week and month name. The second line of the output display Date and Time in a 12 hr format with AM and PM along with date, month, and year in numeric format.

> **Note** `DigitalClock` applet cannot inherit the `Thread` class because it has already inherited the `Applet` class. Therefore `Runnable` interface is used. (Remember: Java does not support multiple inheritances among classes)

SUMMARY

We have explained the meaning and the use of applets in this chapter. Applets are small programs which can be downloaded from a remote server in its bytecode form and executed on the client, to do a specific job. The differences between applets and applications have already been listed out.

In Java, applets are discussed in two different packages. One is the conventional applet, which has directly evolved from `Applet` class. These applets use Abstract Window Toolkit (AWT) to get the GUI features. Other one uses swings, which we have not taken up in this chapter. These applets can be executed on the clients, with the help of either a Java-enabled browser or a utility known as `appletviewer` (comes as a part of JDK). We have discussed many methods belonging to the `Applet` class. Applets have a proper life cycle in which an applet moves from one state to other. These states of applet life cycle are: Born, Running, Idle, and Dead. Different methods such as `init()`, `start()`, `stop()`, and `destroy()` are respectively called to force an applet to different state. We have given you an insight of how to handle images and audio files and have a basic understanding of graphics.

We have not discussed all the methods of the `Applet` class. But of course, we have dealt with many of them in great detail. By now, you must have got an insight of the applet programming and the way the methods are used in applet programming. Now that the building blocks for applets have been covered in this chapter, the very essence of applet programming will seem to be more meaningful when we talk about the GUI environment presented by 'Event Handling and AWT', in Chapter 13.

EXERCISES

Objective Questions

1. Which of the following is not a method of an applet's lifecycle?
   - (a) init
   - (b) start
   - (c) sleep
   - (d) stop

2. Which tool is used to compile an applet?
   - (a) java
   - (b) javac
   - (c) appletviewer
   - (d) appletc

3. Which tool is used to execute an applet?
   - (a) java
   - (b) javac
   - (c) appletviewer
   - (d) appletrunner

4. Which method implicitly calls paint on an applet?
   - (a) paint
   - (b) repaint
   - (c) start
   - (d) callPaint

5. Which class provides the functionality to draw different shapes?
   - (a) Line
   - (b) Graphics
   - (c) Shapes
   - (d) Graph

6. Which method is used to know the directory name from where the `Applet` class is loaded?
   - (a) `getCodeBase()`
   - (b) `getDocumentBase()`
   - (c) `getClassName()`
   - (d) `getAppletLoadClass()`

7. `setFont` method belongs to which of the following classes?
   - (a) Component
   - (b) Object
   - (c) Thread
   - (d) Font

8. Which of the following does the same job as the paint method?
   - (a) init
   - (b) update
   - (c) stop
   - (d) destroy

9. What methods are called as soon as an applet is loaded?
   - (a) init, start, paint
   - (b) init, start
   - (c) init
   - (d) start, paint, stop

10. Which method of the `AppletContext` interface enables your applet to transfer the control to any other URL?
    - (a) `showPage()`
    - (b) `showDocument()`
    - (c) `displayDocument()`
    - (d) `show()`

Review Questions

1. What are applets? Differentiate them from application.
2. State the different ways of executing an applet.
3. What is the significance of `Applet` class in creating an applet? Also explain the hierarchy of `Applet` class.
4. Describe the complete life cycle of an applet.
5. Explain the use of overriding the following methods for an applet
   - `init()`
   - `start()`
   - `stop()`
   - `destroy()`
   - `paint()`
6. Differentiate `update()` and `repaint()` methods.
7. How can a message from a HTML page be passed to an applet?
8. Explain the different parameters of APPLET tag.
9. State the names of the respective classes which the following methods belong to. Also explain the use of these methods:
   - `showStatus()`
   - `drawstring ()`
   - `getCodeBase()`
   - `getDocumentBase( )`
   - `getBackground()`
   - `getForeground()`
   - `setBackground()`
   - `setForeground()`
   - `getParameter()`

Programming Exercises

1. Write a program that shows a screen shot with an applet running inside the applet viewer. The applet should display your name.
2. Write an applet that places a rectangle, a rounded rectangle, a 3D rectangle, and a fill rectangle of random sizes and colors inside the applet's visible area.
3. Create an applet having the background color as black and the foreground color as white.
4. Write an applet to get the foreground and background colors of the above applet.
5. Write a program to display the URL of the directory containing your .class file and .html file.
6. Write an applet that reads an indefinite number of strings from PARAM tags and draws them.
7. Write an applet that draws a circle, a line, an arc, and a polygon inside the applet's visible area.

Answers to Objective Questions

1. (c)	2. (b)	3. (c)	4. (b)
5. (b)	6. (a)	7. (a)	8. (b)
9. (a)	10. (b)		

Event Handling in Java

Failure is not a single, cataclysmic event. You don't fail overnight. Instead, failure is a few errors in judgment, repeated every day.

Jim Rohn

After reading this chapter, the readers will be able to

- understand the event delegation model
- understand what are events, sources, and listeners
- know about their event classes and associated listeners
- understand how basic events are handled (in applets)
- learn three ways of event handling: listeners, adapters, and inner classes

13.1 INTRODUCTION

We have learnt about objects and classes in the previous chapters. An object resides in a particular state until it is made to transit to the other state. This transition occurs due to an *event*.

For example, we want an object to invoke a function when an action is generated, e.g., pressing a key on the keyboard, moving the mouse, clicking on a button, etc. The object which generates the event, i.e., the source of the event is known as the *event generator*. If a button is pressed for an operation, the button is the event generator. The object that is responsible for performing the task when the event occurs is called the *event handler*. There may be more than one event handlers for one single event generated; each event handler responsible for doing a unique activity on account of that particular event. Now the question is, how do these handlers know that a particular event has occurred so that they can perform their activity? For this, there is a *registration process*, undertaken by the event object, for each of its event handlers. This registration involves the event handler simply asking the event generator to inform about the occurrence of an event. By registering, the event generator is able to keep track of all the registered event handlers.

This chapter deals with the event handling mechanism of Java. Without these concepts, it is impossible to enter into the world of GUI programming.

13.2 EVENT DELEGATION MODEL

Event delegation model is an approach that has been followed since Java 1.0. We will stick to this model and won't discuss much about the earlier conventional model. In the event delegation model, a source generates events which are sent to one or more listeners. The listeners are responsible for receiving the event, which once received are processed or handled in the way required. Here the processing logic applied for handling an event is totally segregated by the logic that generates the event, i.e., the event-generating component can be designed differently than the event-processing component. Actually the event generating component delegates the responsibility of performing an event-based action to a separate event-performing component. The model has three dimensions, namely events, event sources, and event listeners.

An event is an object that describes a state change in the source. It may be generated directly because of interaction with the components of GUI environment or any other reason such as expiry of timer, completion of an operation, etc.

An eventsource is an object which generates the event. Generation of event must cause a change in the state of the source. A source can generate more than one event. Event Listeners are the objects that get notified when an event occurs on an event source.

13.3 java.awt.event PACKAGE

The java.awt.event package provides interfaces and classes for dealing with different types of events fired by AWT components. The java.awt.AWTEvent class is the root class for all AWT events. This package includes the definition of events classes, listeners interfaces, and adapters classes, which form the basics of event handling.

13.3.1 Event Classes

It is very difficult to give the details about all the event classes, which are actually responsible for defining the various events in Java. In Java, events are associated with AWT and swings. The events defined by swings are dealt in Chapter 15, while those defined by AWT are described in this chapter.

Java has a predefined hierarchy of event-related classes, at the root of which is EventObject. It is a member of java.util package. This class has constructors and methods defined as its members. One such constructor is

```
EventObject(Object src_obj)
```

where src_obj is the object, which generates the event.

EventObject has methods like getSource() and toString().

- getSource() – returns the source of the event
- toString() – returns the string equivalent of the event

One of the subclass of EventObject class is AWTEvent, which is actually a part of java.awt package. All the event-based classes in AWT, supporting the event delegation model, is directly or indirectly subclass of AWTEvent class.

Herein, we will discuss the events defined by AWT. Various possible events in Java are predefined as classes. Some of the main event classes defined in `java.awt.event` package are shown in Table 13.1.

Table 13.1 Event Classes

Event classes	Description
ActionEvent	Generated when a component-defined action occurred (on button, List, Menu).
AdjustmentEvent	When scrollbar is adjusted.
ContainerEvent	When an element is added or removed from a container.
FocusEvent	When a component gains or loses focus.
KeyEvent	When input is received from keyboard.
ComponentEvent	When a component is moved, changed size, or changed visibility (also, the root class for the other component level events).
MouseEvent	An event which indicates that a mouse action occurred in a component.
InputEvent	The root class for all component-level input events.
TextEvent	When an object's text is changed.
WindowEvent	When a window has changed its status.
MouseWheelEvent	When a wheel was rotated in a component.

ActionEvent Class

An `actionEvent` class is defined in Java as

```
public class ActionEvent extends AWTEvent
```

`ActionEvent` is an event which indicates that a component-defined action has occurred. This event is generated by a component (such as a `Button`) when the component-specific action occurs (such as a click). The event is passed to an `ActionListener` object which is registered to receive the event notification using the component's `addActionListener` method. The object that inherits the `ActionListener` interface is passed to the `ActionEvent` when an event occurs. Some of the fields, constructors, and methods associated with the `ActionEvent` class are given in Table 13.2.

Table 13.2 ActionEvent Class

Field Summary	
Field Name	**Description**
ACTION_FIRST	The first number in the range of IDs used for action events.
ACTION_LAST	The last number in the range of IDs used for action events.
ACTION_PERFORMED	This event ID indicates that a meaningful action occurred.
ALT_MASK	The alt modifier, an indicator that the alt key was held down during the event.
CTRL_MASK	The control modifier, an indicator that the control key was held down during the event.

(Contd)

(Table 13.2 Contd)

Field Name	Description
META_MASK	The meta modifier, an indicator that the meta key was held down during the event.
SHIFT_MASK	The shift modifier, an indicator that the shift key was held down during the event.
Constructor Summary	
Constructor Name	**Description**
ActionEvent (Object source, int id, String command)	Generates an ActionEvent object, where source is the object that originated the event, id is an integer that identifies the event, and command is a string that may specify a command (possibly one of several) associated with the event.
ActionEvent (Object source, int id, String command, int modifiers)	Generates an ActionEvent object. Here modifiers are the modifier keys held down during this action.
ActionEvent (Object source, int id, String command, long when, int modifiers)	Generates an ActionEvent object with the specified modifier keys and timestamp. Here when is the time the event occurred and modifiers are the modifier keys held down during this action.
Method Summary	
Method Name	**Description**
String getActionCommand()	Returns the command string associated with this action.
long getWhen()	Returns the timestamp of the event that occurred.
int getModifiers()	Returns the modifier keys held down during this action event.
String paramString()	Returns a parameter string identifying this action event.

AdjustmentEvent **Class**

AdjustmentEvent class is defined in Java as,

```
public class AdjustmentEvent extends AWTEvent
```

The adjustment events are generated by adjustable objects like scroll bar. There are some adjustment events defined by AdjustmentEvent class, identified by corresponding integer constants. These constants and their meanings are shown in Table 13.3. It also enlists the constructor and methods of AdjustmentEvent class.

Table 13.3 AdjustmentEvent Class

Field Summary	
Field Name	**Description**
ADJUSTMENT_FIRST	Marks the first integer id for the range of adjustment event ids.
ADJUSTMENT_LAST	Marks the last integer id for the range of adjustment event ids.
ADJUSTMENT_VALUE_CHANGED	The adjustment value changed event.

(Contd)

(Table 13.3 Contd)

Field Name	Description
BLOCK_DECREMENT	The block decrement adjustment type.
BLOCK_INCREMENT	The block increment adjustment type.
TRACK	The absolute tracking adjustment type.
UNIT_DECREMENT	The unit decrement adjustment type.
UNIT_INCREMENT	The unit increment adjustment type.
Method Summary	
Method Name	**Description**
Adjustable getAdjustable()	Returns the adjustable object where this event originated.
int getAdjustmentType()	Returns the type of adjustment which caused the value changed event. It will have one of the following values: UNIT_INCREMENT, UNIT_DECREMENT, BLOCK_INCREMENT, BLOCK_DECREMENT, TRACK
int getValue()	Returns the current value in the adjustment event.
boolean getValueIsAdjusting()	Returns true if this is one of multiple adjustment events.
String paramString()	Returns a string representing the state of the event.
Constructor Summary	
Constructor Name	**Description**
AdjustmentEvent(Adjustable source, int id, int type, int value)	Constructs an AdjustmentEvent object with the specified adjustable source, event type, adjustment type, and value.
AdjustmentEvent(Adjustable source, int id, int type, int value, boolean isAdjusting)	Constructs an AdjustmentEvent object with the specified adjustable source, event type, adjustment type, and value.

KeyEvent Class

This class is defined in Java as,

```
public class KeyEvent extends InputEvent
```

This low-level event is generated by a component object (such as a text field, Applet, frame) when a key is pressed, released, or typed. The event is passed to a KeyListener object which is registered to receive the event notification using the component's addKeyListener method.

KeyEvent is an event which indicates that a keystroke occurred in a component. There can be three types of key events, which are identified by integer constants. These are

- KEY_PRESSED (it is generated when any key is pressed)
- KEY_TYPED (it is generated if a valid unicode character could be generated)
- KEY_RELEASED (it is generated when any key is released)

There are some more integer constants that are defined in KeyEvent. Table 13.4 shows a few of them. All fields of this class are public static and final. It also lists the constructors and methods of the keyEvent class.

The list is very long and we are unable to incorporate the complete exhaustive list here. Apart from the constants shown in Table 13.4, we have integer constants such as, VK_0 through VK_9, VK_A through VK_Z, VK_ALT, VK_Cancel, VK_SHIFT, VK_PAGE_DOWN, VK_ENTER, VK_ESCAPE, VK_CONTROL, etc., as members of the KeyEvent class.

Table 13.4 KeyEvent Class

Field Summary	
Field Name	**Description**
char CHAR_UNDEFINED	KEY_PRESSED and KEY_RELEASED events which do not map to a valid Unicode character use this for the keyChar value.
int KEY_FIRST	Denotes the first number in the range of ids used for key events.
int KEY_LAST	Denotes the last number in the range of ids used for key events.
int KEY_LOCATION_LEFT	A constant indicating that the key pressed or released is in the left key location (there is more than one possible location for this key).
int KEY_LOCATION_NUMPAD	A constant indicating that the key event originated on the numeric keypad or with a virtual key corresponding to the numeric keypad.
int KEY_LOCATION_RIGHT	A constant indicating that the key pressed or released is in the right key location (there is more than one possible location for this key).
int KEY_LOCATION_STANDARD	A constant indicating that the key pressed or released is not distinguished as the left or right version of a key, and did not originate on the numeric keypad (or did not originate with a virtual key corresponding to the numeric keypad).
int KEY_LOCATION_UNKNOWN	A constant indicating that the keyLocation is indeterminate or not relevant.
int VK_ACCEPT	Constant for the Accept or Commit function key.
int VK_ALL_CANDIDATES	Constant for the All Candidates function key.
int VK_ALPHANUMERIC	Constant for the Alphanumeric function key.
int VK_COMMA	Constant for the comma key, ","
int VK_COMPOSE	Constant for the Compose function key.
int VK_CONTEXT_MENU	Constant for the Microsoft Windows Context Menu key.
int VK_WINDOWS	Constant for the Microsoft Windows "Windows" key.

Constructor Summary	
Constructor Name	**Description**
KeyEvent (Component source, int id, long when, int modifiers, int keyCode, char keyChar)	Constructs a KeyEvent object, where • Source—the component that originated the event. • Id—an integer identifying the type of event. • When—a long integer that specifies the time the event occurred. • Modifiers—the modifier keys down during event (shift, ctrl, alt, meta) Either extended _DOWN_MASK or old _MASK modifiers should be used, but both models should not be mixed in one event.

(Contd)

(Table 13.4 Contd)

Constructor Name	Description
	• KeyCode—the integer code for an actual key, or VK_UNDEFINED (for a key-typed event).
	• KeyChar—the Unicode character generated by this event, or CHAR_UNDEFINED (for key-pressed and key-released events which do not map to a valid unicode character).

Method Summary	
Method Name	**Description**
char getKeyChar()	Returns the character associated with the key in this event. If no valid character is available, then it returns CHAR_UNDEFINED.
int getKeyCode()	Gets the integer code associated with the key.
int getKeyLocation()	Returns the location of the key that originated this key event.
static String getKeyModifiersText(int modifiers)	Returns a string describing the modifier key(s), such as "Shift", or "Ctrl+Shift".
static String getKeyText(int keyCode)	Returns a string describing the keyCode, such as "HOME", "F1" or "A".
boolean isActionKey()	Returns whether the key in this event is an "action" key.
String paramString()	Returns a string identifying this event.
void setKeyChar(char keyChar)	Sets the keyChar value to indicate a logical character where keyChar is a char corresponding to the combination of keystrokes that make up this event.
void setKeyCode(int keyCode)	Sets the keyCode value to indicate a physical key, where keyCode is an integer corresponding to an actual key on the keyboard.

MouseEvent Class

MouseEvent class is defined in Java as,

```
public class MouseEvent extends InputEvent
```

It is an event which indicates that a mouse action occurred in a component. A mouse action occurs in a particular component if and only if the mouse cursor is over the defined part of the component's bounds when the action happens.

There are eight types of mouse events defined in the MouseEvent class. The MouseEvent class defines them as public static integer constants to identify each of these events. These are shown in Table 13.5. It also shows the constructor and methods of MouseEvent class.

Table 13.5 MouseEvent Class

Field Summary	
Field Summary	**Description**
MOUSE_MOVED	Event occurs when mouse wheel is moved.

(Contd)

(Table 13.5 Contd)

Field Summary	Description
MOUSE_PRESSED	Event occurs when a mouse button is pushed down.
MOUSE_RELEASED	Event occurs when a mouse button is released.
MOUSE_CLICKED	Event occurs when a mouse button is pressed and released.
MOUSE_DRAGGED	Event occurs when the mouse is dragged.
MOUSE_ENTERED	Event when the mouse enters a component.
MOUSE_EXITED	Event occurs when the mouse exits a component.
MOUSE_WHEEL	Event occurs when the mouse wheel is moved.
Constructor Summary	
Constructor Name	**Description**
MouseEvent(Component source, int id, long when, int modifiers, int x, int y, int clickCount,boolean popupTrigger)	Constructs a MouseEvent object with the specified source component, type, modifiers, coordinates, and click count.
MouseEvent(Component source, int id, long when, int modifiers, int x, int y, int xAbs, int yAbs, int clickCount, boolean popupTrigger, int button)	Constructs a MouseEvent object with the specified source component, type, modifiers, coordinates, absolute coordinates, and click count.
Method Summary	
Method Name	**Description**
int getButton()	Returns which, if any, of the mouse buttons has caused the event.
int getClickCount()	Gets the number of mouse clicks.
Point getLocationOnScreen()	Returns the absolute x, y position of the event.
static String getMouseModifiersText (int modifiers)	Returns a string describing the modifier keys and mouse buttons that were down during the event, such as "Shift", or "Ctrl+Shift".
Point getPoint()	Gets the x and y position of the event relative to the source component.
int getX()	Gets the horizontal position of the event relative to the source component.
int getXOnScreen()	Returns the absolute horizontal x position of the event.
int getY()	Gets the vertical position of the event relative to the source component.
int getYOnScreen()	Returns the absolute vertical y position of the event.
boolean isPopupTrigger()	Returns whether this mouse event is the popup menu trigger event or not.
String paramString()	Returns a string identifying this event.
void translatePoint (int x, int y)	Translates the event's coordinates to a new position by adding specified x (horizontal) and y (vertical) offsets.

FocusEvent Class

FocusEvent class is defined as,

```
public class FocusEvent extends ComponentEvent
```

This event is generated when a component gains or loses focus. There are two types of focus events: permanent and temporary. Permanent focus event occurs when the user explicitly changes focus from one component to other, e.g., by pressing the tab key. Temporary focus event occurs when the focus is lost due to operations like window being deactivated. In this case, when the window will again be activated, the focus will be on the same component. The fields, constructors, and methods of FocusEvent class are shown in Table 13.6. All the fields of FocusEvent class are public static integer constants.

Table 13.6 FocusEvent Class

Field Summary	
Fields Name	**Description**
FOCUS_FIRST	First to gain focus.
FOCUS_LAST	Last to gain focus.
FOCUS_GAINED	Component focus gained.
FOCUS_LOST	Component focus lost.
Constructor Summary	
Constructor Name	**Description**
FocusEvent(Component src, int id)	Creates a FocusEvent object with src specifying the source of event and id is like FOCUS_GAINED or FOCUS_LOST.
FocusEvent(Component src, int id, boolean temp)	In addition to the above constructor, temp identifies change is temporary or not.
FocusEvent(Component src, int id, boolean temp, Component opp)	In addition to the above, opp identifies the other component involved in change.
Method Summary	
Methods Name	**Description**
Component getOppositeComponent()	Return the component that either got focus or lost focus.
boolean isTemporary()	Tells whether event is temporary or permanent.
String paramString()	Returns a string identifying the event.

ItemEvent Class

ItemEvent class is defined as,

```
public class ItemEvent extends AWTEvent
```

It is an event which shows whether an item was selected or de-selected. This event is generated by an ItemSelectable object (such as a list), where the event is generated when an item of the list is either selected or de-selected. The event generated is passed to every ItemListener object which is registered to receive such events. The method addItemListener() is used for this registration process. The fields, constructors, and methods of ItemEvent class are shown in Table 13.7. All fields of this class are public static integer constants.

Table 13.7 ItemEvent Class

Field Summary	
Field Name	**Particulars**
DESELECTED	This state-change-value indicates that a selected item was de-selected.
ITEM_FIRST	The first number in the range of ids used for item events.
ITEM_LAST	The last number in the range of ids used for item events.
ITEM_STATE_CHANGED	This event id indicates that an item's state changed.
SELECTED	This state-change value indicates that an item was selected.
Constructor Summary	
ItemEvent(ItemSelectable source, int id,Object item, int stateChange)	Constructs an ItemEvent object.
Method Summary	
Method Name	**Particulars**
Object getItem()	This state-change-value indicates that a selected item was de-selected.
ItemSelectable getItemSelectable()	This first number in the range of ids used for item events.
int getStateChange()	The last number in the range of ids used for item events.
String paramString()	This event id indicates that an item's state changed.

TextEvent Class

TextEvent class is defined as,

```
public class TextEvent extends AWTEvent
```

This event indicates the change in the object's text. This event is generated by an object (such as a TextComponent) whenever its text changes. The event is passed to every TextListener object which is registered to receive such events. The method addTextListener() is used for this registration process. The fields, constructor, and methods of TextEvent class are shown in Table 13.8.

Table 13.8 TextEvent Class

Field Summary	
Field Name	**Particulars**
TEXT_FIRST	The first number in the range of ids used for text events.
TEXT_LAST	The last number in the range of ids used for text events.
TEXT_VALUE_CHANGED	This event id indicates that object's text changed.
Constructor Summary	
Constructor Name	**Particulars**
TextEvent(Object source, int id)	Constructs a TextEvent object.
Methods Summary	
Method Name	**Particulars**
String paramString ()	Returns a parameter string identifying this text event.

13.4 SOURCES OF EVENTS

Sources of events can be either components of GUI or any other class derived from a component (such as an applet), which can generate event like events from keyboard and mouse. Some of the components of GUI are given in Table 13.9.

Table 13.9 Components of GUI that Can Generate Events

Button	Choice	Menu item
Check box	List	Window
Scroll bar		Text components

The classes pertaining to these GUI components will be discussed in detail in Chapter 14 (AWT).

13.5 EVENT LISTENERS

Event listeners are created by implementing one or more interfaces defined by the `java.awt.event` package. Whenever a source generates an event, it basically invokes the appropriate method defined in the listener interface. The method has an event object passed as an argument to it. Some of the frequently used listeners are given in Table 13.10.

Table 13.10 List of Event Listeners

KeyListener	ItemListener	WindowListener
MouseListener	ActionListener	ComponentListener
MouseMotionListener	TextListener	ContainerListener
MouseWheelListener	FocusListener	AdjustmentListener

Each of these listener interfaces have certain number of methods, which are given in brief below.

KeyListener Interface

This interface has three methods defined within it:

- `void keyPressed(KeyEvent e)`
- `void keyReleased(KeyEvent e)`
- `void keyTyped(KeyEvent e)`

`keyPressed()` is invoked when a key is pressed, `keyReleased()` is invoked when a key is released, and `keyTyped()` is invoked when a character is typed.

MouseListener Interface

This interface has five methods, having the signatures as follows:

- `void mouseClicked(MouseEvent e)`
- `void mouseEntered(MouseEvent e)`
- `void mousePressed(MouseEvent e)`
- `void mouseReleased(MouseEvent e)`
- `void mouseExited(MouseEvent e)`

`mouseClicked()` is invoked when a mouse is clicked, `mouseEntered()` is invoked when mouse enters a component, `mousePresssed()` is invoked when a mouse is pressed but not released, `mouseReleased()` is invoked when a pressed mouse is released, and `mouseExited()` is invoked when the mouse leaves a component.

`MouseMotionListener` Interface

This interface has two methods having the signatures,

- `void mouseMoved(MouseEvent e)`
- `void mouseDragged(MouseEvent e)`

`mouseMoved()` is invoked when the mouse is moved from one place to another and `mouseDragged()` is used when the mouse is dragged.

`MouseWheelListener` Interface

This interface has only one method, having the signature,

- `void mouseWheelmoved(MouseEvent e)`

`mouseWheelMoved()` is invoked when the mouse wheel is moved.

`ItemListener` Interface

This interface has only one method defined as,

- `void itemStateChanged(ItemEvent e)`

`itemStateChanged()` is invoked when the state of the item changes.

`ActionListener` Interface

This interface has only one method having the signature,

- `void actionPerformed(ActionEvent e)`

The method, `actionPerformed()` is invoked when any action event is performed.

`TextListener` Interface

This interface has only one method having the signature,

- `void textChanged(TextEvent e)`

This method is invoked whenever there is a change in text field or text area.

`FocusListener` Interface

This interface has two methods,

- `void focusGained(FocusEvent e)`
- `void focusLost(FocusEvent e)`

`focusGained()` is invoked when the component obtains keyboard focus and `focusLost()` is invoked when the component loses the keyboard focus.

`WindowListener` Interface

This interface has seven methods defined in it, with the following signatures:

- `void windowActivated(WindowEvent e)`
- `void windowClosed(WindowEvent e)`

- void windowClosing(WindowEvent e)
- void windowOpened(WindowEvent e)
- void windowDeactivated(WindowEvent e)
- void windowIconified(WindowEvent e)
- void windowDeiconified(WindowEvent e)

windowActivated() is invoked when window is activated, windowDeactivated() is invoked when the window is deactivated, windowClosed() is invoked when the window is closed, windowOpened() is invoked when the window is opened, windowClosing() is invoked when the window is being closed, windowIconified() is invoked when the window is iconified (minimized), and windowDeiconified() is invoked when the state of the window changes from minimized to normal state.

ComponentListener Interface

This interface has four methods, having the signatures as follows:

- void componentResized(ComponentEvent e)
- void componentMoved(ComponentEvent e)
- void componentHidden(ComponentEvent e)
- void componentShown(ComponentEvent e)

componetResized() is invoked when the size of the component is altered, componentMoved() is invoked when the component is moved, componentHidden() is invoked when the component is hidden, and componentShown() is invoked when the component is shown.

ContainerListener Interface

This interface has two methods defined in it. They are

- void componentAdded(ContainerEvent e)
- void componentRemoved(ContainerEvent e)

Both of the above methods, componentAdded() is invoked when a component is added to the container and componentRemoved() is invoked when a component is removed from the container.

AdjustmentListener Interface

The interface has only one method, defined as

- void adjustmentValueChanged(AdjustmentEvent e)

The method is invoked when an adjustment event occurs.

13.6 HOW DOES THE MODEL WORK?

Each source, generating the events must register event listeners to itself, so that listeners get the license for receiving the events from the respective source. Now how does this registration process take place? In Java, all the possible events have been given a name. Each type of event has its own registration method, having the form,

```
public void addTypeListeners(TypeListenertl)
```

In the above method, *Type* is the type of the event and *tl* is the reference to the event listener for that particular event. Different types of event listeners available in Java can be seen in Table 13.10.

Some sources allow more than one listener to get registered to receive the event, while some allow only one listener to get registered to receive the event. Former is the case of multicasting an event while the latter is unicasting an event.

These listeners, once registered for events from a particular source, can get unregistered also. The form of method used for this unregistration process is as follows:

```
public void removeTypeListener(TypeListternertl)
```

Once the listener objects are registered, they must implement the methods to receive and process the event notifications sent by source. These methods are defined in various interfaces of `java.awt.event` package.

Steps involved in using the event delegation model:

1. Implement the appropriate event listener interface so as to receive and process the type of event desired.

2. Register event listener with event source, as the recipient for event notification using the registration methods which have the following form:

```
addTypeListner(TypeListener)
```

Note If the component generates more than one event, then each event needs to be registered separately. An object may be registered to receive several types of events, but it must also implement all the interfaces that are required to receive these events.

Let us take an example to show how listener interfaces are used for handling events. The following example shows how `MouseMotionListener` can be used to track mouse movements.

Example 13.1(a)　Use of `MouseMotionListener`

```
     /*<applet code = "MouseMotionEx.class" width = 300 height = 300></applet>*/
L1   import java.awt.*;
L2   import java.applet.*;
L3   import java.awt.event.*;
L4   public class MouseMotionEx extends Applet implements MouseMotionListener {
L5     int xcord;
L6     int ycord;
L7     public void init(){
L8       addMouseMotionListener(this);
L9     }
L10    public void paint(Graphics g){
L11      g.drawString("("+xcord+","+ycord+")",xcord,ycord);
L12    }
L13    public void mouseMoved(MouseEvent me){
L14      xcord = me.getX();
L15      ycord = me.getY();
L16      repaint();
L17    }
L18    public void mouseDragged(MouseEvent me){}
L19    }
```

Output

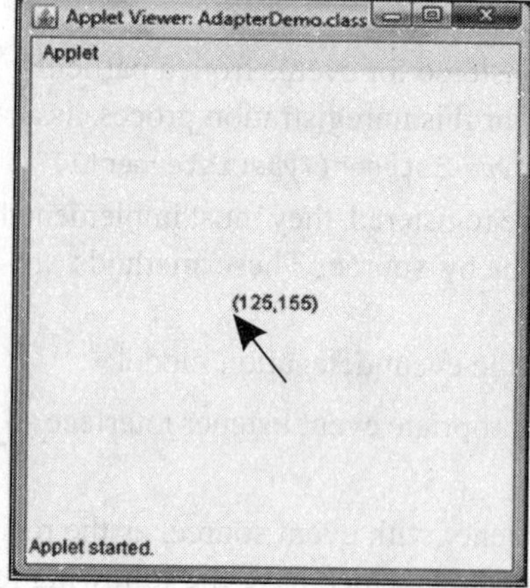

Fig. 13.1 *x* and *y* Coordinates Using `MouseMotionListener`

Explanation

L1–3 All the required packages are imported, so that their members can be used inside the program.
L4 Handler class with the name `MouseMotionEx` declared. This class extends `Applet` class and implements the `MouseMotionListener` so that it can receive the type of event desired.
L5–6 Instance variables, `xcord` and `ycord`, to store the value of *x*-coordinate and *y*-coordinate are declared to be of integer type.
L7–9 Inside `init()` method of applet, the `MouseMotionListener` is registered as the recipient of the event notification.
L8 The `MouseMotionListener` have been registered on the `Applet` itself (event source). The question arises: Why is 'this' passed as an argument to add `MouseListener` method? Because the `MouseMotionEx` has implemented `MouseMotionListener` interface and overrides the methods of the interface, the current object will tell how to handle the event once the mouse is moved or dragged. So 'this' (current object) is passed as an argument to `addMouseMotionListener` method. [We can also create another class (e.g., `Demo`) which would implement `MousemotionListener`

interface. This class would override the methods of `MouseMotionListener` interface and now this classes object will be passed in registration method: `addMouseMotionListener (new Demo())`. Note now `MouseMotionEx` will not inherit the `MouseMotionListener` interface. Example 13.1(a) shows this concept.]
L10–12 `paint()` is defined and implemented, where the `drawstring()` method of the graphics class is used to display the string at *x* and *y* coordinates. The string here is the value of *x* and *y* coordinates inside parenthesis.
L13–17 `mouseMoved()` defined in `MouseMotion-Listener` interface is implemented. This method actually takes care of the action to be performed on a mouse event (see the `MouseEvent` object being passed as argument to the method in L13). Instance variables, `xcord` and `ycord`, declared earlier as integers are used to store the values of *x*-coordinate and *y*-coordinate returned by the `getX()` and `getY()` methods of `MouseEvent`, respectively (L14 and L15). In L16, `repaint()`is called, which ultimately calls the paint method.

We can rewrite Example 13.1(a) as follows to show how another class object can be used to process the events.

Example 13.1(b) `MouseMotionListener`

```java
/* <applet code = "MouseMotionEx.class" width = 700 height = 700>
</applet> */
import java.awt.*;
import java.applet.*;
import java.awt.event.*;
public class MouseMotionEx extends Applet
{
    int  xcord;
    int ycord;
public void init()
{
    addMouseMotionListener (new Demo(this));
}
public void paint (Graphics g)
{
  g.drawString ("("+xcord +", "+ycord+")", xcord,ycord );
}
}
class Demo implements MouseMotionListener {
  MouseMotionEx m;

Demo(MouseMotionEx m)
{
this.m=m;
}
public void mouseMoved(MouseEvent me) {
        m.xcord = me.getX();
        m.ycord = me.getY();
        m.repaint();
}
public void mouseDragged(MouseEvent me){}
}
```

Explanation

One important thing to note is that while Demo's objects have been registered for event notification, the current object (i.e., `MouseMotionEx` object) has been passed to the Demo object. The reason is we need to paint the applet (i.e., `MouseMotionEx` object) based on mouse movement which are being tracked by demo's object now. The coordinates of `MouseMo-`tionEx need to be set based on mouse movements and later `MouseMotionEx` needs to be repainted. So we need a reference to `MouseMotionEx` to perform this task and that's why the object of `MouseMotionEx` (represented by this keyword) has been passed in Demo's constructor.

13.7 ADAPTER CLASSES

An interface holds only abstract methods and its implementation requires all its methods to be implemented, i.e., overridden with real methods in the implementing class. This is true for listener interfaces also; if you are implementing a particular listener interface, you have to implement all the methods defined in that interface. This can really be annoying at times, where you must also implement all those methods of the listener interface, which might not actually be used. In order to simplify things, Java came up with the concept of adapter classes.

For listener interfaces containing more than one event handling methods, JDK defines corresponding adapter classes. For example, for `MouseMotionListener` interface, there is an adapter class, `MouseMotionAdapter`. Adapter classes provide empty definitions for all the methods of their corresponding listener interface. It means that `MouseMotionAdapter` class inherently implements `MouseMotionListener` interface.

So how would the `MouseMotionListener` interface be defined by Java? As we know, this interface has two methods defined as follows:

```
public interface MouseMotionListener {
   public void mouseDragged (MouseEvent e);
public void mouseMoved (MouseEvent e);
   }
```

The corresponding adapter class, i.e., `MouseMotionAdapter` is predefined in Java as follows:

```
public class MouseMotionAdapter implements MouseMotionListener {
   public void mouseDragged (MouseEvent e) { }
   public void mouseMoved (MouseEvent e) { }
   }
```

See the empty curly braces for the above two methods, which simply show the body of the methods to be empty.

13.7.1 How to Use Adapter Classes?

If you are not using adapter classes, your event handler class needs to implement listener interface as,

```
public class HandlerClass implements MouseMotionListener
{

   ...........................................
   ...........................................
   ...........................................

}
```

And as mentioned earlier, the handler class, which is here named as `HandlerClass` has to implement all the methods inside that `MouseMotionListener` (as shown in Example 13.1 (a)).

Now if you use the adapter class, the handler class will inherit from adapter class by extending it.

```
public class HandlerClass extends MouseMotionAdapter
{
    ...........................................
    ...........................................
    ...........................................
}
```

Due to inheritance, all the methods of the `MouseMotionAdapter` class will be available inside our `HandlerClass`. As the adapter classes have already provided definitions with empty bodies, you do not have to provide implementations for all the methods again. It simply means we only need to override our methods of interest. Let us take Example 13.1(a) where we had to override all the methods of `MouseMotionListener` within the handler class. But in order to achieve the same objective as in Example 13.1(a), we now show the use of adapter classes and how its use makes things simpler in writing the code. Note that in the following adapter class example, it is not mandatory to override all the methods of `MouseMotionlistener`; only the method (here, `mouseMoved()`) is overridden.

Example 13.2 **Use of `MouseMotionAdapter`**

```
     /*<applet code = "AdapterDemo.class" width = 300 height = 300></applet>*/
L1   import java.awt.*;
L2   import java.awt.event.*;
L3   import java.applet.*;
L4   public class AdapterDemo extends Applet{
L5   int xcord, ycord;
L6   public void init(){
L7       addMouseMotionListener(new MouseDemo(this));
L8   }
L9   public void paint(Graphics g){
L10      g.drawString("("+xcord+","+ycord+")",xcord,ycord);
L11  }
L12  }
L13  class MouseDemo extends MouseMotionAdapter{
L14  AdapterDemo d;
L15  MouseDemo(AdapterDemo d){
L16  this.d = d;
L17  }
L18  public void mouseMoved(MouseEvent me){
L19      d.xcord = me.getX();
L20      d.ycord = me.getY();
L21      d.repaint();
L22  }}
```

Output

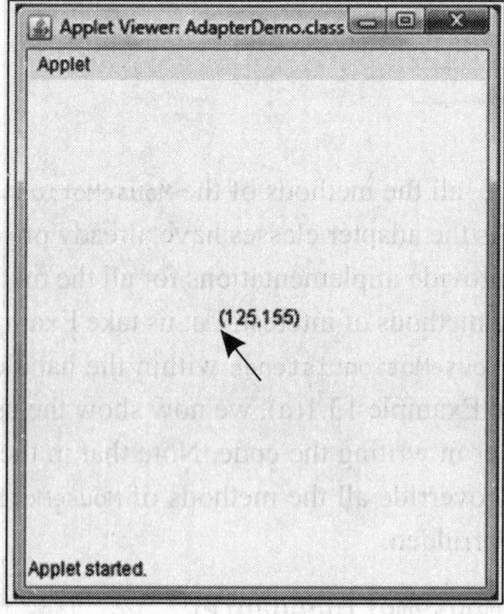

Fig. 13.2 Applet Showing Mouse Coordinates

Explanation

L6–8 Applet's `init()` method is implemented, where in `MouseMotionListener` is registered. An interesting thing which is to be noted here is the method of registration. See the argument passed through the method of registration in L7. Till the last example we passed the current class's object to this method. But here, we pass the object of the current class (`AdapterDemo`) to the constructor of the class extending the adapter class (i.e., `MouseDemo`) and ultimately the object of the class extending the adapter class is passed as an argument to the `addMouseMotionListener()` (L7), used for registering the `MouseMotionListener` as the recipient of mouse event notifications. All this is done, so that the methods of different classes can communicate with each other through their objects.

L9–11 Graphics object is used to call the `draw-String()` method inside paint method to display the values of *x*-coordinate and *y*-coordinate.

L12 The end of the class `AdapterDemo` specified by closing parenthesis.

L13 Class `MouseDemo`, extending `MouseMotion-Adapter` is declared.

L14 A reference to `AdapterDemoclass` is created.

L15–17 A constructor of `MouseDemo` is declared and object of `AdapterDemo` class is passed as an argument to this constructor (L15). The member of the object constructed by the constructor is initialized with the object of class `AdapterDemo` (L16).

L18–22 The `mouseMoved()` method with `Mou-seEvent` object as argument is defined and implemented. `MouseEvent` object is used to call the `getX()` and `getY()` methods in L19 and 20, respectively. `getX()` returns the value of *x*-coordinate and `getY()` returns the value of *y*-coordinate. In L16, `repaint()` of the `Applet` class is called using the reference of class `AdapterDemo`, which extends the `Applet` class. Calling `repaint()` will call the `paint()`method elaborated in L9 and L10.

13.7.2 Adapter Classes in Java

These adapter classes are members of `java.awt.event` package. There is an adapter class for eight listener interfaces. These are as listed in Table 13.11.

Table 13.11 Adapter Classes Belonging to `java.awt.event`

Listener	Adapter Classes	Registration Methods
ComponentListener	ComponentAdapter	addComponentListener
ContainerListener	ContainerAdapter	addContainerListener
FocusListener	FocusAdapter	addFocusListener
HierarchyBoundsListener	HierarchyBoundsAdapter	addHierarchyBoundsListener
KeyListener	KeyAdapter	addKeyListener
MouseListener	MouseAdapter	addMouseListener
MouseMotionListener	MouseMotionAdapter	addMouseMotionListener
WindowListener	WindowAdapter	addWindowListener

13.8 INNER CLASSES IN EVENT HANDLING

An inner class can be defined and instantiated all inside a class, or even within an expression.

Why are we discussing inner classes in the chapter related to event handling? Actually the event delegation model allows you to make any class into a listener for your events. We can use the concept of inner class in the event handling model by putting the listener class definition adjacent to the code for the component that uses the listener.

There can be three categories of inner classes: *member* classes, *local* classes, and *anonymous* classes.

Member Classes

These classes are included in the class definition just like fields and methods. A member class can either be static or instance.

Static Member Class A member class can be static with access only to the static members of the class to which it belongs.

Instance Member Class A member class can be instance with access to both the static and instance members of the class that contains it. Example 13.3 shows how to define an inner class inside a class.

Local Classes

A local class is defined within a code block, typically in a method. An instance of a local class exists only during the execution of the method.

We have already discussed inner classes is detail in Chapter 4.

Example 13.3 **Use of Member Inner Class**

```
/*<applet code = OuterClass.class width = 600 height = 600></applet>*/
import java.awt.*;
import java.applet.*;
import java.awt.event.*;
public class OuterClass extends Applet {
    public void init(){
```

```
L6              addKeyListener(new InnerClass());
L7          }
L8          class InnerClass extends KeyAdapter {
L9          public void keyPressed(KeyEvent ke){
L10             showStatus("key Pressed");
L11         }
L12         public void keyReleased(KeyEvent ke){
L13             showStatus("key Released");
L14         }
L15         }
L16         }
```

Explanation

L4 A class named as `OuterClass`, inherits the `Applet` class.

L5–7 Applet's `init()` method is implemented, where the `addKeyListener()` method is used for registering the `KeyListener` to get the key events. Object of the inner class `InnerClass` is passed as argument to the registration method (L6).

L8–15 Inner class with the name `InnerClass` is defined to extend the adapter class `KeyAdapter` (L8). Note that this inner class is part of the outer class itself. Inside this inner class two of the three methods, `keyPressed()` and `keyReleased()` belonging to `KeyListener` interface is implemented (L9 and L12, respectively). Using adapter classes, `KeyAdapter` eliminates the compulsion of implementing all the methods belonging to `KeyListener` interface. The `showStatus()` is used at L10 and L13 in two different methods; whatever has been passed as an argument to the `showStatus()` will be displayed in the status window of the applet. Closing parenthesis at L15 signifies the end of the inner class, '`InnerClass`'.

L16 It signifies the end of the outer class, '`OuterClass`'.

Note What is magical here is that the compiler will just separate out these inner classes and create separate class files for them. The names of these inner class files will be preceded with the outer class name. You can check it simply by finding the following class file in the directory, once you compile the above code.

```
OuterClass$1InnerClass.class
```

Anonymous Inner Classes

An anonymous inner class is one that is not assigned a name. In the example below we have declared an anonymous inner class as an argument to a method. Such classes are created on the fly i.e., they are created, instantiated, used, and garbage collected when they are done. They are automatically assigned a name as `Outerclassname$1`.

This *anonymity* helps in eliminating the unnecessary named objects. Besides, it makes the program more readable.

In the code below, an anonymous inner class is created as an argument to `addKeyListener` method for capturing key events. On press of any key, the status bar displays "Key Pressed" and on the release of that key, the status bar displays "Key Released". Example 13.4 has been rewritten to show how anonymous inner classes can be used.

Example 13.4	**Use of Anonymous Inner Class**

```
     /*<applet code ="AnonyKeyListDemo.class" width = 300 height = 300></applet>*/
L1       import java.awt.*;
L2       import java.awt.event.*;
L3       import java.applet.*;
L4       public class AnonyKeyListDemo extends Applet {
L5       public void init(){
L6       addKeyListener(new KeyAdapter(){
L7       public void keyPressed(KeyEvent ke){
L8          showStatus("Key Pressed");
L9       }
L10      public void keyReleased(KeyEvent me){
L11         showStatus("Key Released");
L12      }
L13      });
L14      }}
```

Output

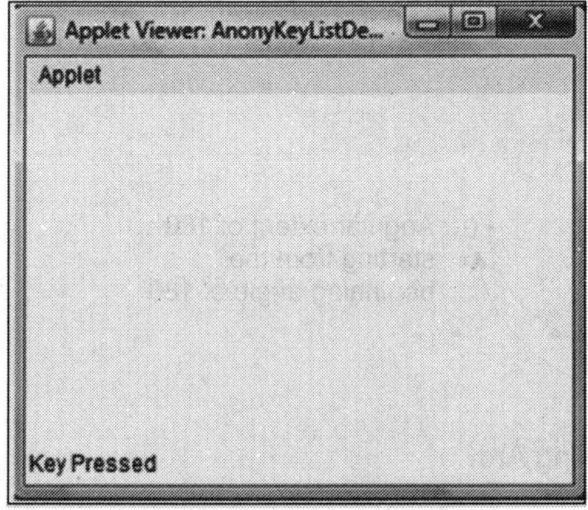

Fig. 13.3 Key Pressed Event

Fig. 13.4 Key Released Event

Explanation

The most surprising code in the program is from L6 to L13

```
addKeyListener(new KeyAdapter (){
public void keyPressed(KeyEvent ke){
   showStatus("Key Pressed");
}
public void keyReleased(KeyEvent me){
   showStatus("Key Released");
}
});
```

L6 The anonymous class is defined as an argument to the `addKeyListener` method. This anonymous class will inherit from `KeyAdapter` class and will have two methods `keyPressed` and `keyReleased` defined inside the enclosing braces. `keyPressed` method is executed when any key is pressed as shown in Fig. 13.3 and `keyReleased` method is called as shown in Fig. 13.4.

13.9 PRACTICAL PROBLEM: CARTOON APPLET

We will be creating a series of examples with revisions in all of them to enhance the functionality and then eliminate the problems in them. We will begin by creating a cartoon, one having eyes, ears, and a red nose with a black cap on his head.

13.9.1 Smiling Cartoon with Blinking Eyes (Part 1)

In the first version, if a user places the mouse pointer on the nose of the cartoon and presses the mouse button, the eyes of the cartoon turns green and the cartoon laughs with its mouth wide open. If the user presses the mouse button anywhere else, the cartoon's default smiling face (black eyes, ear, and a red nose) is shown.

The `drawArc` method of the `Graphics` class is used to create the smile on the cartoons face. This method accepts six arguments: *x* coordinate, *y* coordinate, width of the arc, height of the arc, beginning angle, and the extent of the arc relative to the beginning angle. The first four are simple to understand. Let us focus on the beginning angle and the angular extent. If a positive value for the angular extent is specified, then the arc is drawn in counter-clockwise direction from the beginning angle. If a negative value is specified, then the arc is drawn in clockwise direction from the beginning angle. If the beginning angle is specified as 180, then the arc starts from 180° as shown in Fig. 13.5. In addition to that, if you specify the angular extent as 180, then the arc is drawn in counter-clockwise direction starting from the beginning angle and goes up to additional 180° in the counter-clockwise direction.

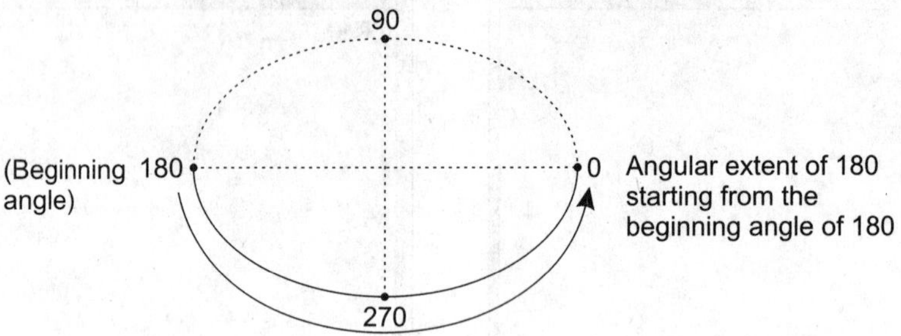

Fig. 13.5 Smiling Arc

We want to portray the cartoon as smiling, so we have specified the last arguments in the `drawArc` method as positive. If you specify the last argument as negative (−180), the arc is drawn in clockwise direction and you would get a sad cartoon as shown in Fig. 13.6.

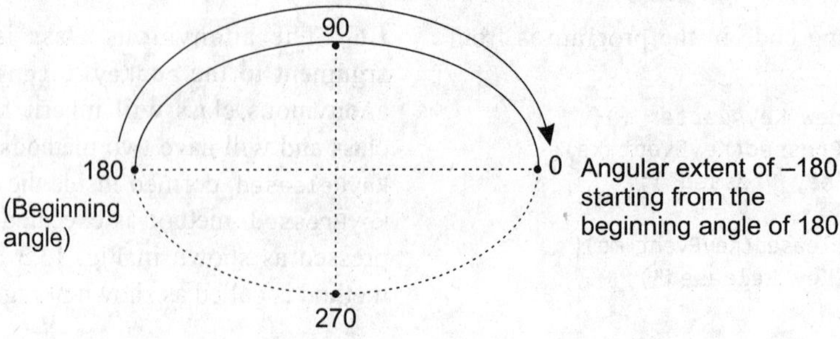

Fig. 13.6 Smiling Arc

Example 13.5　Smiling Cartoon 1

```java
L1      import java.applet.*;
L2      import java.awt.*;
        // To Use classes like MouseEvent and MouseAdapter
L3      import java.awt.event.*;

L4      /*<applet code="Cartoon.class" width=400 height=400></applet>*/
        /* A Carton Image when clicked on Nose changed the color of its eyes and smiles
        with mouth wide open */
L5      public class Cartoon extends Applet
        {
L6      boolean move;
L7      MyMouseAdapter mma;
L8      public void init()
        {
        // for capturing mouse clicks
        /* this - current object is passed so that applet context is passed to the
        Mouse Adapter class and based on the clicks the applets repaint method can be
        invoked */

L9      mma = new MyMouseAdapter(this);

        /* registers the object with the applet to handle mouse events */
L10     addMouseListener(mma);
        }

        // Draw the cartoon's Face, eyes, ears, nose and cap
L11     public void paint(Graphics g)
        {
                // creating face
L12             g.drawOval(50,40,120,150);

                // for creating hat on the head
                // Three x coordinates for the polygon
L13             int x[] = {73,115,147};
                // Three y coordinates for the polygon
L14             int y[] = {55,7,55};
L15             int n = x.length;

                /* creates a Filled Polygon with 3 points where last (x,y) and the first
                (x,y) coordinates are connected*/
L16             g.fillPolygon(x,y,n);

                // creating left eye
L17             g.drawOval(67,75,30,20);

                // creating right eye
L18             g.drawOval(120,75,30,20);
```

```
                          /* fills the eye ball with green color when clicked on nose else black
                          and mouth open else closed */
                          /* if user presses the mouse button while mouse pointer is on nose of
                          the cartoon*/

L19         if(mma.move)
            {
L20                 g.setColor(Color.green);
L21                 g.fillOval(78,81,10,10);   // green left pupil
L22                 g.fillOval(131,81,10,10);  // green right pupil
                    // open mouth with green color
L23                 g.fillArc(70,125,80,40,180,180);
L24                 mma.move=false;
            }
L25         else
            {
L26                 g.fillOval(78,81,10,10);   // black left pupil
L27                 g.fillOval(131,81,10,10);  // black right pupil

                    // smiling with mouth closed
L28                 g.drawArc(70,125,80,40,180,180);
            }

            // creating a red nose
L29         g.setColor(Color.red);
L30         g.fillOval(95,100,30,30);
L31         g.setColor(Color.black);

            // creating left ear
L32         g.drawOval(35,92,15,30);

            // creating right ear
L33         g.drawOval(170,92,15,30);

            }
            }
            // Adapter class defined for handling Mouse Events
L34         class MyMouseAdapter extends MouseAdapter
            {
            /* Applets reference is created so that its paint method can be invoked from
            this class based on mouse events*/

L35         Cartoon g;
L36         boolean move;
            /* The current object passed in L9 is stored within the constructors argument
            and assigned to the instance variable of type cartoon */

L37         MyMouseAdapter(Cartoon g)
            {
L38                 this.g = g;
L39                 move = false;
```

```
        }

        /* whenever mouse is pressed its coordinates are extracted and based on that
        the flag is set and applet is painted again*/

L40     public void mousePressed(MouseEvent me)
        {
        // extract X coordinates
L41             int x = me.getX();

        // extract y coordinates
L42             int y = me.getY();
        /* check for mouse click on nose*/
L43             if(x>85 && x<115 && y>100 && y<130)
                {
L44                     move = true;     /* set the Boolean variable*/
L45                     g.repaint();     /* call paint() of cartoon applet*/
                }
L46             else                     /*if mouse clicked anywhere else*/
        {
L47                     move = false;    /* reset the Boolean variable*/
L48                     g.repaint();     /* call paint() of cartoon applet*/
        }
        }
}
```

Output

Fig. 13.7 (a) Cartoon displayed normally or when mouse is not pointed on nose and clicked. **(b)** Cartoon is laughing with mouth wide open and green eyes when mouse is pointed on nose and clicked.

13.9.2 Smiling Cartoon with Blinking Eyes (Part 2)

In smiling cartoon (part 2), if a user places the mouse pointer on the nose of the cartoon, the eyes of the cartoon turns green and the cartoon laughs with its mouth wide open. If the user moves the mouse pointer out of the nose, the cartoon's default smiling face (black eyes, ear, and a red nose) is displayed. There is no need to click on the nose as in the previous case. So, we have used MouseMotionAdapter instead of MouseAdapter class because we need to track mouse movements, not clicks. But using MouseMotionAdapter and overriding the mouseMoved method results in some complications. Whenever the mouse is moved, the mouseMoved method is invoked and the applet is painted. The problem is that the paint method is invoked a number of times which results in flicker, prominently seen by the user. The update method is overridden to overcome the flicker. But that adds a new problem. Let us see what the problem is and what the possible solutions are.

Example 13.6 **Smiling Cartoon (Part 2)**

```
L1    import java.applet.*;
L2    import java.awt.*;
L3    import java.awt.event.*;

L4    /*<applet code = "CartoonVr2.class" width = 400 height = 400></applet>*/

      /* if you move the mouse pointer over nose of the cartoon, the color of its eyes
      should change and it should laughs with mouth wide open. If you move your mouse out
      of the nose the default cartoon with black eyes and smile should appear. */

L5    public class CartoonVr2 extends Applet
      {

      /* To track Mouse Movements we need MouseMotionListener or MouseMotionAdapter */
      /* We use adapter approach for the reasons explained in the previous program */

L6    MyMouseMotionAdapter mma;
L7    public void init()
      {
              // Instantiates the MouseMotionAdapter
L8            mma = new MyMouseMotionAdapter(this);

              // Registers the MouseMotionListener with the Applet
L9            addMouseMotionListener(mma);
      }

L10   public void paint(Graphics g)
      {

              // for creating face
L11           g.drawOval(50,40,120,150);

              // hat on the head
L12           int x[] = {73,115,147};
L13           int y[] = {55,7,55};
```

```java
L14        int n = x.length;
L15        g.fillPolygon(x,y,n);

L16        g.drawOval(67,75,30,20);            // left eye

L17        g.drawOval(120,75,30,20);           // right eye

           /* fills the eye ball with green color when mouse is over its nose else black
           and mouth open else eyes are black and mouth closed */

L18        if(mma.move)
           {
L19           g.setColor(Color.green);
L20           g.fillOval(78,81,10,10);            // green left pupil
L21           g.fillOval(131,81,10,10);           // green right pupil
L22           g.fillArc(70,125,80,40,180,180);  // mouth

           }
L23        else
           {
L24           g.fillOval(78,81,10,10);            // black left pupil
L25           g.fillOval(131,81,10,10);           // black right pupil

           /* drawArc method is used; arc is drawn with black color but it is filled with
           green color always once the mouse pointer is removed from nose. It is because
           green color is there since last paint method call, as we have used update to
           remove the flickering effect. It fills the background with the colors used and
           then only paints the changes. The background is not cleared. If we want to
           display the arc back once the mouse is moved out of the nose, we can invoke
           the paintAll method within update method or call super.update(g) from update
           method. But both methods would add flickering effect back to the cartoon, thus
           defeating the purpose of adding update method */

L26           g.drawArc(70,125,80,40,180,180); // mouth
           }

           /* create a red nose*/
L27        g.setColor(Color.red);
L28        g.fillOval(95,100,30,30);

           /*set the color as black for drawing ears*/
L29        g.setColor(Color.black);
L30        g.drawOval(35,92,15,30);  // left ear
L31        g.drawOval(170,92,15,30); // right ear
       }

/* to reduce the flickering effect when mouse is moved very quickly over the applet,
update method is overridden and paint is called from within it*/
```

```
L32    public void update(Graphics g)
       {
L33    paint(g);

       /* Using paintAll resolves the problem of green colored filled arc being displayed
       when mouse is not over nose because it paints the entire applet but adds the flicker-
       ing effect to the applet */

L34    //paintAll(g);

       /* calling update of the super class solves the problem but adds flickering effect.
       So how do we solve the problem? */

L35    // super.update(g);
       }
       }


L36    class MyMouseMotionAdapter extends MouseMotionAdapter
       {
L37        CartoonVr2 g;
L38        boolean move;

L39        MyMouseMotionAdapter(CartoonVr2 g)
           {
L40            this.g = g;
L41            move = false;
           }

       /* whenever mouse is moved its coordinates (x,y) are extracted and based on that the
       flag is set and applet is painted again*/

L42    public void mouseMoved(MouseEvent me)
       {
L43        int x = me.getX();
L44        int y = me.getY();
L45        if(x > 85 && x < 115 && y > 100 && y < 130)
           {
L46            move = true;
L47            g.repaint();
           }
L48        else
           {
L49            move = false;
L50            g.repaint();
           }
       }


       }
```

Output

(a)   (b)   (c)

Fig. 13.8 (a) The applet loads for the first time, (b) When mouse is pointed over the nose,
(c) When mouse is moved out of nose

The problems that are evident in the output are

1. The black arc is visible in (b) i.e., when the mouse is over the nose. The wide open mouth
   filled with green color should be shown but the black arc should not be displayed.

2. The mouth is still wide open in (c) with green color when the mouse pointer is removed
   from the nose. Actually it should be similar to (a).

We tried a few solutions like `paintAll()` and `super.update(g)` methods (as you can see they
are commented in L34 and L35.) but failed. How do we solve the problem?

13.9.3 Smiling Cartoon (Part 3)

Smiling cartoon (part 3) deals with the problems that arise in part 2. The code is almost entirely
similar with an exception that before repainting the applet on every mouse move event, we paint
the arc and the oval (for mouth) with white color, thus erasing what was there from the previous
paint. Let us see the code for the applet.

Example 13.7 **Smiling Cartoon (Part 3)**

```
import java.applet.*;
import java.awt.*;
import java.awt.event.*;

/*<applet code = "CartoonVr3.class" width = 400 height = 400></applet>*/

/* if you move the mouse pointer over nose of the cartoon, the color of its eyes
should change and it should laugh with mouth wide open. If you move your mouse out
of the nose the default cartoon with black eyes and smile should appear. */

public class CartoonVr3 extends Applet
{
```

```java
   MyMouseMotionAdapter mma;
   public void init()
   {
     mma = new MyMouseMotionAdapter(this);
     addMouseMotionListener(mma);
   }

   public void paint(Graphics g)
   {
     // face
     g.drawOval(50,40,120,150);

     int x[] = {73,115,147};
     int y[] = {55,7,55};
     int n = x.length;
     g.fillPolygon(x,y,n);

     g.drawOval(67,75,30,20);          // left eye

     g.drawOval(120,75,30,20);         // right eye

     if(mma.move)
     {
     /* wipes out the smile with white colored arc */
        g.setColor(Color.white);
        g.drawArc(70,125,80,40,180,180);

     /* set the color as green and draws green pupil instead of black*/
        g.setColor(Color.green);
        g.fillOval(78,81,10,10);       // green left pupil
        g.fillOval(131,81,10,10);      // green right pupil

        /* opens the mouth */
        g.fillArc(70,125,80,40,180,180);        // mouth


     }

     else
        {
        g.fillOval(78,81,10,10);       // black left pupil
        g.fillOval(131,81,10,10);      // black right pupil
```

/* To solve the problem we turn the color to white and then draw a filled arc with white color. This white arc covers the green color and then we set the color as black and draw the arc */

```java
g.setColor(Color.white);
        g.fillArc(70,125,80,40,180,180);        // mouth
        g.setColor(Color.black);
```

```java
      g.drawArc(70,125,80,40,180,180);          // mouth

    }

    // create a red nose
    g.setColor(Color.red);
    g.fillOval(95,100,30,30);

    //set the color as black for drawing ears
    g.setColor(Color.black);
    g.drawOval(35,92,15,30);                    // left ear
    g.drawOval(170,92,15,30);                   // right ear

  }

  public void update(Graphics g)
  {
    paint(g);
  }
}

class MyMouseMotionAdapter extends MouseMotionAdapter
{
  CartoonVr3 g;
  boolean move;

  MyMouseMotionAdapter(CartoonVr3 g)
  {
    this.g = g;
    move = false;
  }

  public void mouseMoved(MouseEvent me)
  {

    int x = me.getX();
    int y = me.getY();
    if(x > 85 && x < 115 && y > 100 && y < 130)
    {
      move = true;
      g.repaint();

    }
    else
    {
      move = false;
      g.repaint();
    }
  }
}
```

Output

(a) (b) (c)

Fig. 13.9 (a) The applet is loaded first, (b) When mouse pointer is put over its nose, (c) When mouse pointer is moved out of the nose.

SUMMARY

In this chapter, we have emphasized on the features that enhance the GUI capabilities of Java by using event handling. But before moving to the AWT components in Java, it was imperative to discuss about the event handling model of Java, as the knowledge about the use of applets and other GUI-based programs is incomplete without the study of this model. Actually applets are event-driven programs that use a GUI to interact with the users. The modern approach to event handling uses event delegation model where a source generates events, which are sent to one or more listeners. These listeners receive the event notifications, which are handled as required by the different methods of event classes.

EXERCISES

Objective Questions

1. Which of the following statements are true?
   - (a) All events will be processed in the order, the listeners were added
   - (b) Using the adapter approach to event handling means creating blank method bodies for all event methods
   - (c) A component may have multiple listeners associated with it
   - (d) Listeners may be removed once added

2. Which of the following are correct event handling methods?
   - (a) `mousePressed(MouseEvent e){}`
   - (b) `MousePressed(MouseClick e){}`
   - (c) `functionKey(KeyPress k){}`
   - (d) `componentAdded(ContainerEvent e){}`

3. What will happen when you attempt to compile and run the following code?

```java
import java.awt.*;
import java.awt.event.*;
public class Demo extends Applet im-
plements MouseListener{
public static void main(String argv[])
{
   Demo s = new Demo();
}
Demo() {
   this.addMouseListener(this);
}
```

```java
public void mouseClicked(MouseEvent
e){
   System.out.println(e.getWhen());
   }
}
```

(a) Compile time error
(b) Run time error
(c) Compile and at runtime the date and time of each click will be output
(d) Compile and at runtime a timestamp will be output for each click

4. Which of the following statements are true about event handling?
   (a) The 1.1 Event model is fully backwardly compatible with the 1.0 event model
   (b) Code written for the 1.0x Event handling will run on 1.1 versions of the JVM
   (c) The 1.1 Event model is particularly suited for GUI building tools
   (d) The Drag and Drop event handler was added with the 1.1 version of event handling.

5. Which of the following statements are true?
   (a) For a given component events will be processed in the order that the listeners were added
   (b) Using the Adapter approach to event handling means creating blank method bodies for all event methods
   (c) A component may have multiple listeners associated with it
   (d) Listeners may be removed once added

6. Which of the following are correct event handling methods?
   (a) `mousePressed(MouseEvent e){}`
   (b) `MousePressed(MouseClick e){}`
   (c) `functionKey(KeyPress k){}`
   (d) `componentAdded(ContainerEvent e){}`

7. What will happen when you attempt to compile and run the following code?

```java
import java.awt.*;
import java.awt.event.*;
```

```java
public class Click extends Frame
implements MouseListener{
   public static void main(String
argv[]){
      Click s = new Click();
}

Click(){
   this.addMouseListener(this);
}

public void mouseClicked(MouseEvent
e){
   System.out.println(e);
   }
}
```

(a) Compile time error
(b) Run time error
(c) Compile and at runtime prints the object
(d) Compile and at runtime a timestamp will be output for each click

8. Which of the following is the correct sequence of calling `paint()` method?
   (a) update() → repaint() → paint()
   (b) repaint() → update() → paint()
   (c) repaint() → paint() → update()
   (d) None of the above

9. Which of the following methods is used to remove the flickering effect?
   (a) `update()`
   (b) `repaint()`
   (c) `paint()`
   (d) None of the above

10. Which of the following is advantage of adapter class over `Listener` interfaces?
    (a) You need to override all the methods of `Listener` interface within the adapter class
    (b) You need to override only the methods required and not all the methods within the adapter class
    (c) All the above
    (d) None of the above

Review Questions

1. What do you mean by event delegation model in Java?

2. How do the event objects register the event `Listener` in Java?

3. Some of the constraints of using `Listener` interfaces are removed by using adapter classes. Comment.

4. How is the concept of inner classes used for event handling?

5. What is the advantage of having anonymous classes while handling events in Java?

Programming Exercises

1. Create an applet which when gains focus shows "Focus gained" in the status bar.

2. Create an applet to identify the key pressed in the window and display the character associated with the key in the status window.

3. Create an applet that inherits `MouseListener` interface and displays appropriate messages for each of the methods in the interface.

4. Use the concept of adapter class in the previous exercise.

5. Create an anonymous inner class for handling mouse entered event into an applet.

Answers to Objective Questions

1. (c) and (d)	**2.** (a) and (d)	**3.** (a)	**4.** (b) and (c)
5. (c) and (d)	**6.** (a) and (d)	**7.** (a), each method of the `Listener` interface should be overridden in the `Click` class.	
8. (b)	**9.** (a)	**10.** (b)	

Abstract Window Toolkit

Different people get different things out of the images. It doesn't matter what it's about, all that matters is how it makes you feel.

Adam Jones

After reading this chapter, the readers will be able to
- know the set of GUI components
- understand the use of event-handling model for different components
- explain the layout managers for flexible window layouts

14.1 INTRODUCTION

The Abstract Window Toolkit (AWT) provides many classes—which can even be used inside applets—for programmers to use. It is the connection between your application and the native GUI. The AWT hides the complexities of the GUI your application will be running on.

The Java foundation classes (JFC) provide two frameworks for building GUI-based application and interestingly both rely on the same event handling model:

- AWT
- Swing

AWT relies on the underlying operating system on a specific platform to represent its GUI components (i.e., components in AWT are called heavyweight), while swing implements a new set of lightweight GUI components that are written in Java and has a pluggable look and feel. These lightweight components are not dependent on the underlying window system.

In this chapter, we will put emphasis on AWT, while swings will be covered in the next chapter. AWT API can be used in any Java program by importing the `java.awt.*` package.

14.1.1 Why AWT?

Each application developed in a programming language must have a user interface, which is actually that part of the application that is responsible for directly interacting with the user. These user interfaces can either be command-line interfaces or graphical user interfaces.

At the lowest level, the operating system transmits information from the input devices to the program as input, and provides the output. The AWT was designed so that programmers need not worry about tracking the mouse movements or reading the keyboard characters or writing to the screen. The AWT is a well-designed object-oriented interface between the application and the low-level resources.

The advantage of AWT is that it preserves the native look and feel of the platform on which the AWT application is running because the components (user interfaces) in AWT are implemented using the native GUI toolkit. On the other hand, the drawback is that the applications will have different look and feel when executed on different platforms.

14.1.2 `java.awt` Package

The package `java.awt` contains all classes used for creating graphical user interfaces, painting graphics, images, colors, and fonts. A user interface element such as a button or a textbox is called a *component*. The `Component` class is the superclass of all AWT components. These components fire events when users interact with these components, e.g., when a user clicks on a button. These events are handled by event handling classes, i.e., `AWTEvent` and its subclasses.

A container is one which contains components and other containers. A container has a layout manager that determines the visual placement of components in the container. The `java.awt` package contains several classes which are used for laying out components in a container.

The package `java.awt` contains many interfaces and classes. It is very difficult to elaborate all these members of this package here. Some of the commonly used classes in the package are given in Table 14.1.

Table 14.1 Classes in AWT Class

Classes	Description
AWTEvent	The root event class for all AWT events.
BorderLayout	Lays out components in a container according to five regions: north, south, east, west, and center.
Button	Creates a button.
Canvas	Represents a blank rectangular area of the screen onto which drawing can be done or from which input events from the user can be trapped.
CardLayout	Layout manager which can contain other layouts.
Checkbox	A component that can be in one state: either "on" (true) or "off" (false) state.
CheckboxGroup	Groups together a set of checkboxes so that they work as radio buttons.
CheckboxMenu Item	This class is used for creating a checked menu item.
Choice	Opens up a pop-up menu of choices.
Color	Represents colors in the RGB or arbitrary color spaces as identified by a `ColorSpace`.
Component	A component is an object having a graphical representation that can be displayed on the user screen and the users can interact with it.
Container	Contains other AWT components.

(Contd)

(Table 14.1 Contd)

Classes	Description
`Dialog`	A top-level window with a title and a border.
`Dimension`	This object encapsulates the width and height of a component.
`FileDialog`	This class displays a dialog window from which the user can select a file.
`FlowLayout`	Displays components in a directional flow.
`Font`	This class represents fonts, which are used to render text in a visible way.
`FontMetrics`	Encapsulates information about how a particular font will be rendered on a particular screen.
`Frame`	A top-level window (container) with a title and a border, used for containing other components.
`Graphics`	The `Graphics` class is the abstract base class that allows an application to draw onto components like drawing lines, circles, etc.
`GridBag Constraints`	This class specifies constraints for components that are laid out using the `GridBagLayout` class.
`GridBagLayout`	This layout is a flexible layout manager that aligns components vertically, horizontally or along their baseline without requiring that the components be of the same size.
`GridLayout`	Lays out components in a rectangular grid.
`Image`	This abstract class represents graphical images.
`Insets`	Specifies how much space must be left at all edges of a container.
`Label`	Used for placing text in a container.
`List`	A scrollable list of string items.
`MediaTracker`	Used for tracking the status of a number of media objects.
`Menu`	A pull-down menu deployed from a menu bar.
`MenuBar`	Menus are added on a `MenuBar` attached on to a frame.
`MenuItem`	All items in a menu are `MenuItems`.
`MenuShortcut`	This class represents a keyboard shortcut for a `MenuItem`.
`MouseInfo`	Provides methods for getting information about the mouse location, etc.
`Panel`	It is a container class.
`Point`	Represents a location in (x, y) coordinate space.
`PopupMenu`	A menu which can be dynamically popped up at any specified position within a component.
`Scrollbar`	The `Scrollbar` class embodies a scroll bar either vertical or horizontal.
`ScrollPane`	A container class which implements automatic horizontal and/or vertical scrolling for a single child component.
`TextArea`	An object that allow user to enter/edit multi-line input.
`TextComponent`	Superclass of `TextField` and `TextArea`.
`TextField`	It is a text component that allows the user to enter/edit a single line of text.
`Window`	It is the parent of `Dialog` and `Frame` and represents a top-level window with no borders and no menubar.

14.2 COMPONENTS AND CONTAINERS

A graphical user interface is developed with the help of graphical elements such as buttons, scrollbars, lists, and textfields. These elements are called components. These components are generally the source of events that allow the user to interact with the program (remember, the event handling mechanism). In AWT, these components are instances of the respective `Component` classes.

Components cannot exist alone; they are found within containers. The layout of the components are contained and controlled within the containers. In fact, containers are themselves components, thus they can be placed inside other containers. In AWT, all containers are objects of class `Container` or one of its subtypes.

Components must fit completely into the container that contains them. There exists an inheritance relationship between the user interface components classes provided by the AWT. Component class defines the interface to which all components must adhere. Figure 14.1 shows the hierarchy of different AWT classes in Java.

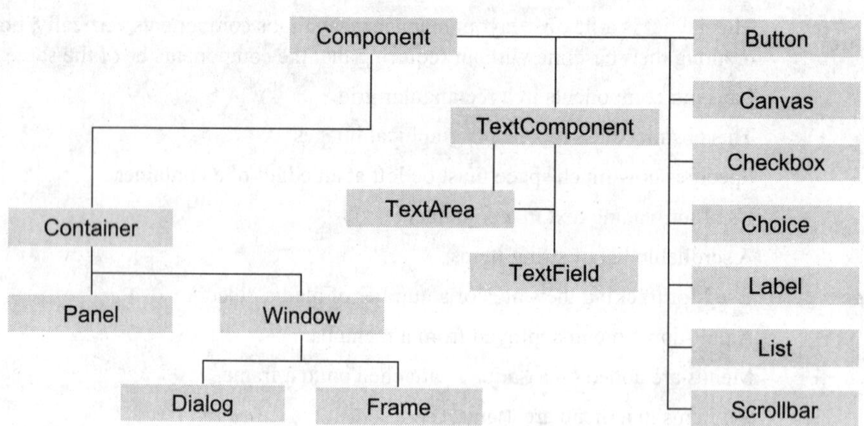

Fig. 14.1 Hierarchy of Classes in AWT

14.2.1 Component Class

Let us discuss the `Component` class, which is actually a subclass of the `Object` class and superclass of various classes such as `Button`, `Label`, `CheckBox`, `RadioButton`, `Choice`, `Canvas`, `TextComponent`, `List`, and `ScrollBar`.

You must have an idea of creating the above-mentioned components. In order to have a particular component in a window, you must add that particular component to the window. `Container` class has a method, `add()`, for the purpose.

```
Component add(Component ComObj)
```

The object of the `Component`, which is to be added, is passed as the argument to the above method. This method returns the reference to the `ComObj`. If you wish to remove a `Component` from a window, you can use `remove()` method for the same.

```
void remove(Component ComObj)
```

In the above syntax, the object of the `Component` which is to be removed is passed as the argument to the above method.

14.2.2 Components as Event Generator

All the controls, except label, can generate events. The notifications for the events generated by these controls are received by the registered listeners. This notification helps the listeners in identifying the type of control that generated event. Till the last chapter, we had been dealing with applets as the event generator. Now we will deal with other event generators, say the components. Before moving further, it is important to let you know which `Listener` interface is appropriate for receiving notification from which control and what are the methods responsible for handling a particular type of event (Table 14.2).

Table 14.2 Events Associated with Components

Components	Event	Events Type	Event Listeners	Method Name
Button	Click	ActionEvent	ActionListener	actionPerformed()
	Focus gained/ focus lost	FocusEvent	FocusListener	focusGained()and focusLost()
Checkbox	Selection/ Deselection	ItemEvent	ItemListener	itemStateChanged()
Choice	Selection/ Deselection	ItemEvent	ItemListener	itemStateChanged()
List	Selection/ Deselection	ItemEvent	ItemListener	itemStateChanged()
	Double clicking on an item	ActionEvent	ActionListener	actionPerformed()
MenuItem	Click	ActionEvent	ActionListener	actionPerformed()
TextField	Focus gained/ focus lost	FocusEvent	FocusListener	focusGained()and focusLost()
	Presses Enter key	ActionEvent	ActionListener	actionPerformed()
	Text changes	TextEvent	TextListener	textValueChanged()
TextArea	Focus gained/ focus lost	FocusEvent	FocusListener	focusGained()and focusLost()
	Text changes	TextEvent	TextListener	textValueChanged()
Scrollbar	Change the value of scrollbar by mouse/Keyboard	Adjustment Event	Adjustment Listener	adjustment ValueChanged()

(Contd)

(*Table 14.2 Contd*)

Components	Event	Events Type	Event Listeners	Method Name
	Focus	FocusEvent	FocusListener	focusGained() and focusLost()
	Key events	KeyEvent	KeyListener	keyPressed() keyReleased() keyTyped()
	Mouse events	MouseEvents	MouseListener	mouseClicked mouseEntered() mouseExited() mousePressed() mouseReleased()
Frame/ Applet	Mouse motion events	MouseEvent	MouseMotion Listener	mouseMoved() and mouseDragged()
	Window events	WindowEvent	WindowListener	windowActivated() windowClosed() windowClosing() windowDeactivated() windowIconified() windowDeiconified() windowOpened()

14.3 BUTTON

```
Button() throws HeadlessException
Button(String str)throws HeadLessException;
```

The first constructor, when called, creates a Button with no label displayed on it. The second constructor creates a Button, displaying the string 'str' on it.

Now, how is a Button actually created? See the syntax below,

```
Button buttonName = new Button(Str);
```

where buttonname is the name of the button object and str is the text which you want to set as the caption of the button. Once the object for Button is created, it needs to be added to the applet, frame or any other container. The syntax for it is as follows:

```
add(buttonname);
```

The methods like setLabel() and getLabel() are used for changing the button's label and getting the label's text respectively. The signatures of these methods are

```
void setLabel(String str)
String getLabel()
```

Table 14.3 lists other methods that belong to the class `Button`.

Table 14.3 Methods of `Button` Class

Method	Description
`void addActionListener(ActionListener al)`	Adds the specified action listener to receive action events from this button.
`void addNotify()`	Creates the peer of the button.
`AccessibleContext getAccessibleContext()`	Gets the `AccessibleContext` associated with this button.
`String getActionCommand()`	Returns the command name (caption of the button) of the action event fired by this button.
`ActionListener[] getActionListeners()`	Returns an array of all the action listeners registered on this button.
`String paramString()`	Returns a string representing the state of this button.
`void processActionEvent (ActionEvent ae)`	Processes action events occurring on this button by dispatching them to any registered `ActionListener` objects.
`void processEvent(AWTEvent awte)`	Processes events on this button.
`void removeActionListener (ActionListener al)`	Removes the specified action listener so that it no longer receives action events from this button.
`void setActionCommand (String command)`	Sets the command name for the action event fired by this button.

Example 14.1 shows an example that demonstrates how to create buttons and handle their events using the listener approach of handling events.

Example 14.1 **Button Demonstration**

```
     /*<applet code = ButtonClass.class width = 400 height = 150></applet>*/
L1       import java.applet.*;
L2       import java.awt.*;
L3       import java.awt.event.*;
L4       public class ButtonClass extends Applet implements ActionListener {
L5       Button red, white, blue;
L6       Label hit;
L7       public void init(){
L8          red = new Button("Red");
L9          white = new Button("white");
L10      blue = new Button("blue");
L11      hit = new Label("Hit a Button to change the screen color");
L12      add(red);
L13      add(white);
L14      add(blue);
L15      add(hit);
L16      red.addActionListener(this);
```

```
L17        white.addActionListener(this);
L18        blue.addActionListener(this);
L19        }
L20        public void actionPerformed(ActionEvent ae){
L21        String str = ae.getActionCommand();
L22        if (str.equals("Red")) {
L23           setBackground(Color.red);
L24        }
L25        else if (str.equals("white")) {
L26           setBackground(Color.white);
L27        }
L28        else if (str.equals("blue")){
L29           setBackground(Color.blue);
L30        }
L31        repaint();
L32        }
L33    }
```

Output

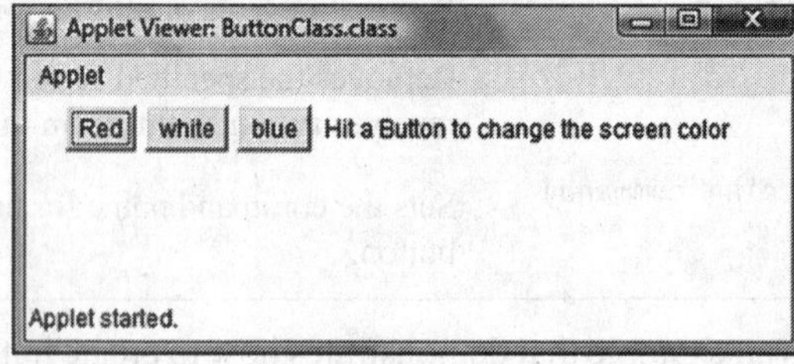

Fig. 14.2(a) Applet with White Background When it is Displayed for the First Time or When the White Button is Pressed

Fig. 14.2(b) Applet with Red Background When the Red Button is Pressed

Fig. 14.2(c) Applet with Blue Background When the Blue Button is Pressed

Explanation

L1–3 All the facilities of the applet and the AWT that Java has to offer are imported by using the * wildcard.

L4 An applet with the name of `ButtonClass`, extending the `Applet` class and implementing the `ActionListener` interface, is defined.

L7–19 The `init()` method of the applet is defined and implemented, wherein three buttons having labels, red, white, and blue, respectively, are created (see L8–10). Then the three buttons and a label (created in L11) are added to the current applet window (see L12–15). These buttons with the reference names red, white, and blue are registered by the `addActionListener()` method (L16–18). Note that all components (buttons) are registered with the `Listener` interface because we want to capture events from all buttons.

L20–31 When an action takes place, the default `handleEvent` method calls the action method of our component. If it is not a button event, we simply return. Otherwise check the button's label to determine which button was pressed. Then set the background to the appropriate color, and repaint and update the screen.

14.4 LABEL

This component is the simplest one in Java's AWT. Labels consist of a text string for display only and they never call an action method. The constructors responsible for creating labels are given in Table 14.4.

Table 14.4 Constructors of `Label` Class

Constructor Name	Description
`Label()`	Creates an empty label.
`Label(String label)`	Creates a new label with the specified string of text, left justified.
`Label(String label, int alignment)`	Constructs a new label that presents the specified string of text with the specified alignment.

Example 14.2 uses the second type of constructor mentioned in Table 14.4.

```
Label labelname = new Label("This label is for demonstration.");
```

Here, a label's object is created with the name 'labelname', with the string 'This label is for demonstration' displayed on it. A label can be justified LEFT, RIGHT, or CENTERED. The following line will create a label that is right justified:

```
Label labelname = new Label("This label is for demonstration.", Label.RIGHT);
```

We can change the text of a label by,

```
labelname.setText("This is new text.");
```

Apart from setting the text on label, we can also get the label's text using the method as shown below,

```
String labelText = labelname.getText();
```

We can change the alignment or get the alignment of a label with the methods shown as follows:

```
labelname.setAlignment(Label.CENTER);
```

or

```
int labelAlignment = labelname.getAlignment();
```

Example 14.2 shows an applet demonstrating the properties of a label.

Example 14.2 An Applet Illustrating a Simple Label

```
     /*<applet code = "LabelClass.java" width = 350 height = 100></applet>*/
L1   import java.applet.*;
L2   import java.awt.*;
L3   public class LabelClass extends Applet {
L4   public void init(){
L5   Label firstLabel = new Label("Labels exist simply ");
L6   add(firstLabel);
L7   Label secLabel = new Label("to place text on the screen");
L8   add(secLabel);
L9   Label thirdLabel = new Label("They can be aligned left, right or center.");
L10  add(thirdLabel);
L11  }}
```

Output

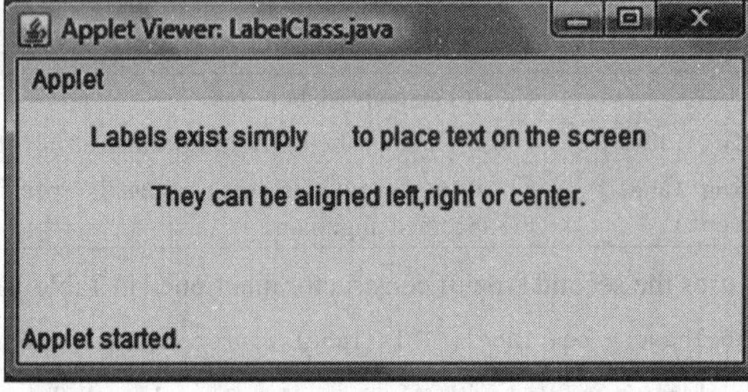

Fig. 14.3 Label Displayed in an Applet

Explanation

L1–2 We import all the facilities of the AWT and applet that Java has to offer by using the * wildcard. **L3** An applet with the name LabelClass is defined, extending the Applet class.

L5–11 Three labels are created and added to the applet window inside the init() method of applet.

14.5 CHECKBOX

Checkboxes are used as on-off or yes-no switches since every time you click on one, you toggle to the opposite selection, i.e., if you click on an unchecked checkbox, it will get checked and if you click on the checked box, it will get unchecked. You can check as many checkboxes as you wish to, as there is no constraint on selecting the number of checkboxes. Your program can be made to respond as per the state of each checkbox. An element-like button might be needed to trigger an event to check the state of the checkboxes. The checkboxes are the objects of Checkbox class, which support the following constructors:

```
Checkbox()
Checkbox(String str)
Checkbox(String str, boolean on)
Checkbox(String str, CheckBoxGroup cbg, boolean on)
```

The first form of constructor creates a checkbox whose label is blank initially and the state of the checkbox is unchecked. In the other forms of constructors, string argument accounts for the label of the checkbox, boolean argument (true/false) accounts for whether the checkbox will be created checked or unchecked, i.e., if the argument passed is true, the created checkbox will be initially checked, otherwise if the argument is false, the checkbox will be initially unchecked and the CheckBoxGroup argument is accountable for specifying the checkbox group (the group argument is used for radio buttons which are a special kind of checkboxes).

The following line will create a checkbox with Names as a label, null as a placeholder for a group argument, and false to indicate that it is not selected:

```
Checkbox names = new Checkbox("Names", null, false);
```

Once you create the Checkbox, just add it to the applet (or other container) by entering the following command:

```
add(names);
```

where names is the Checkbox name. A few of the methods belonging to the Checkbox class are given in Table 14.5.

Table 14.5 Methods of Checkbox

Method	Description
void addItemListener (ItemListener il)	Adds the specified item listener to receive item events from this Checkbox.
CheckboxGroup getCheckboxGroup()	Returns the associated checkbox's group.
ItemListener[] getItemListeners()	Returns an array of all the item listeners registered with this checkbox.
String getLabel()	Returns string in the form of Checkbox text.
Object[] getSelectedObjects()	Returns an array (length 1) containing the Checkbox label or null if the Checkbox is not selected.
boolean getState()	Returns boolean in the form of true or false, depending on whether the Checkbox is selected or unselected.
String paramString()	Returns a string representing the state of the Checkbox.
void processEvent(AWTEvent awte)	Processes events on this Checkbox.
void processItemEvent(ItemEvent ie)	Processes item events occurring on this checkbox by dispatching them to any registered ItemListener objects.

(Contd)

(*Table 14.5 Contd*)

Method	Description
`void removeItemListener (ItemListener l)`	Removes the association between item listener and `Checkbox`.
`void setCheckboxGroup (CheckboxGroup ckbg)`	Sets this checkbox's group to the specified checkbox group.
`void setLabel(String label)`	We can change the `Checkbox` label and set it to the argument, 'label'.
`void setState(boolean state)`	Changes the checkbox's state to true (for selected) or false (for unselected).

Example 14.3 illustrates how checkboxes can be created and used. The button 'SUBMIT' created in the program triggers an event in order to check which boxes are selected. A list of selected names is then painted on the applet window.

Example 14.3 **Demonstration of Checkboxes**

```
     /*<applet code = CheckboxClass.class width = 400 height = 100></applet>*/
L1        import java.applet.*;
L2        import java.awt.*;
L3        import java.awt.event.*;
L4        public class CheckboxClass extends Applet implements ActionListener {
L5        Button submit;
L6        Checkbox name1;
L7        Checkbox name2;
L8        Checkbox name3; Font f;
L9        public void init(){
L10       name1 = new Checkbox ("Ram",null,false);
L11       name2 = new Checkbox ("Ramesh",null,false);
L12       name3 = new Checkbox ("Naresh",null,false);
L13       f = new Font ("Arial",Font.ITALIC,14);
L14       submit = new Button("SUBMIT");
L15       add(name1);
L16       add(name2);
L17       add(name3);
L18       add(submit);
L19       submit.addActionListener(this);
L20       }
L21       public void actionPerformed(ActionEvent ae){
L22               String str = ae.getActionCommand();
L23               if (str.equals("SUBMIT"))
L24               repaint();
L25       }
L26       public void paint (Graphics g){
L27               g.setFont(f);
L28               g.setColor(Color.blue);
L29               if (name1.getState())
L30                     g.drawString("Ram",50,60);
```

```
L31          if (name2.getState())
L32                  g.drawString("Ramesh",50,80);
L33          if (name3.getState())
L34                  g.drawString("Naresh",50,100);
L35      }
L36  }
```

Output

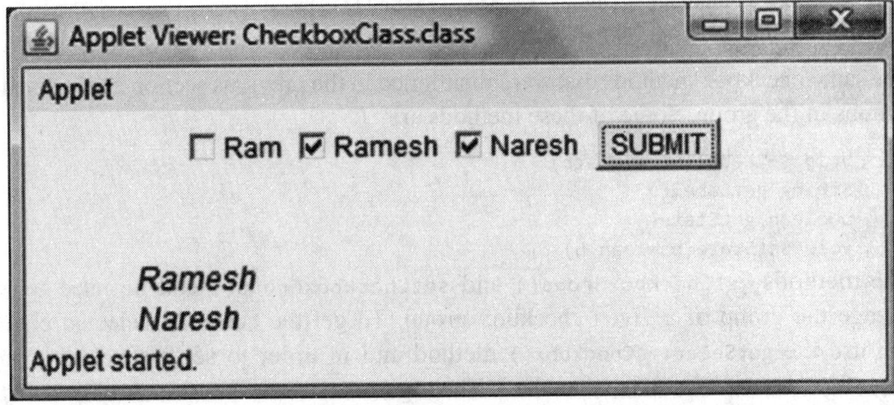

Fig. 14.4 Checkboxes Inside Applet

Explanation

L4 An applet implementing `ActionListener` with the name of `CheckboxClass` is created.

L5–8 Reference variables for `Button` checkboxes and Font are created.

L9 The `init()` method for applet has been defined.

L10–14 Checkboxes and the button are instantiated. L13 instantiates the font name as Arial, specifies the style to be italicized, and the size of the font as 14 point.

L15–18 Checkboxes and the button are added to the frame.

L19 `ActionListener` is registered with the button.

L21–24 `actionPerformed()` is overridden. If submit button is pressed, repaint the applet.

L26–35 `paint()` is defined. The font defined in L13 is set using `setFont()`. `setColor()` is used to set the color of the text to be written as blue. Depending upon which checkbox is selected, its name is written on the applet. `getState()` returns true if the checkbox is selected, else false.

14.6 RADIO BUTTONS

Radio buttons, which are also called checkbox groups, are a special kind of checkboxes, where within a particular group, only one box can be selected at a time. The `CheckboxGroup` class is used to group together a set of checkboxes and thereafter, only a single selection is allowed among them, i.e., they behave as radio buttons. Checkbox groups are objects of type `CheckboxGroup` class. There is only one constructor (the default constructor) which creates an empty group. The following line will create a checkbox group, named `fruits`:

```
CheckboxGroup fruits = new CheckboxGroup();
```

Once you create the checkbox group, add the individual checkboxes to that group. There are three arguments to be specified in the constructor. The first argument is the radio button `label`, the second argument is the `group` of which it is a part of, and the third is the state, `true` or `false`, depending on whether the button is selected or not.

```
add(new Checkbox("mango", fruits, false));
add(new Checkbox("papaya", fruits, false));
add(new Checkbox("guava", fruits, false));
add(new Checkbox("apple", fruits, true));
```

The same checkbox methods that were mentioned in the previous section can be used with radio buttons in the group. Some of these methods are

```
void setLabel(String str)
String getLabel()
boolean getState()
void setState(boolean b)
```

The methods `getCheckboxGroup()` and `setCheckboxGroup()` can be used to access and change the group of a given checkbox group. To get the currently selected checkbox, you can use the `getSelectedCheckbox()` method and in order to set a checkbox, you can use `setSelectedCheckbox(chkbox)` method. The argument 'chkbox' is the checkbox that you want to be selected.

The example below shows how radio buttons can be used to change the background color of the applet window. Remember, only one radio button can be selected at a time.

Example 14.4   **Demonstration of Radio Button**

```
/*<applet code = "RadioDemo.class" width = 300 height = 200></applet>*/
L1    import java.applet.*;
L2    import java.awt.*;
L3    import java.awt.event.*;
L4    public class RadioDemo extends Applet implements ItemListener{
L5        Checkbox red, white, green;
L6        CheckboxGroup cbg;
L7    public void init(){
L8    add(new Label("The 3 radio buttons will change the screen color."));
L9    cbg = new CheckboxGroup();
L10   red = new Checkbox("Red",cbg,false);
L11   white = new Checkbox("White",cbg,false);
L12   green = new Checkbox("Green",cbg,false);
L13   add(new Label("Notice that you can only select one radio button."));
L14   add(new Label("And selecting a radio button triggers an event"));
L15   add(new Label("that we use to change the screen color."));
L16   add(red);
L17   add(white);
L18   add(green);
L19   red.addItemListener(this);
```

```
L20        white.addItemListener(this);
L21        green.addItemListener(this);
L22        }
L23        public void itemStateChanged(ItemEvent ie){
L24        String str = (String) ie.getItem();
L25        if (str.equals("Red")){
L26            setBackground(Color.red);
L27        }
L28        else if (str.equals("White")) {
L29            setBackground(Color.white);
L30        }
L31        else if (str.equals("Green")){
L32            setBackground(Color.green);
L33        }
L34        repaint();
L35        }}
```

Output

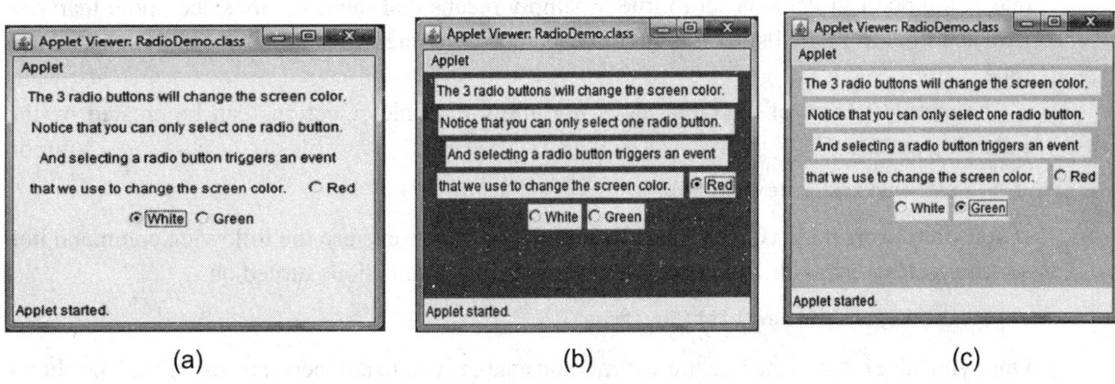

(a)   (b)   (c)

Fig. 14.5 Color of the Applet Changes Based on the Selection

Explanation

L1–3 Necessary packages are imported.

L4 `Applet` class is defined and it inherits the `ItemListener` interface for handling the events related to the checkbox.

L5 Three checkbox references are created.

L6 `CheckboxGroup` reference is created.

L7 The `init()` method is defined.

L8 A label is added to the applet.

L9–12 The `CheckboxGroup` instantiated along with three checkboxes is. The checkboxes are made part of a group (L10–12) so that they behave as a radio button and only one from the group can be selected at a time. All radio buttons are not selected by default, as the third argument passed in the constructor of checkbox is false.

L13–15 Labels are instantiated and added to the applet.

L16–21 All radio buttons are added to the applet and they are registered with their associated listener for capturing events.

L23–34 `ItemListener` interface has one method, i.e., `itemStateChanged(ItemEvent e)` which is overridden. This method checks which radio button has been checked and then changes the color of the background according to the name of the radio button. The `getItem()` method of the `ItemEvent`

class returns the caption of the checked radio button as an object of type `Object` class which is then cast to `String`. Based on this `String`, we change the color of the background using the `setBackground(Color.XXX)` method and then repaint the applet.

14.7 LIST BOXES

The `List` class provides a multiple choice, scrolling list of values that may be selected alone or together. A list can be created to show any number of choices in the visible window. `List` class has the following constructors:

```
List()
List (int no_of_rows)
List(int no_of_rows, boolean multi_select)
```

Note All the above constructors throw `HeadlessException`.

In the default constructor case, only one item can be selected at a time. In the second constructor, you can specify the number of rows in the list that you want to be always visible. In the third one, if the boolean value is set to true, it simply means that the user can select more than one item at a time from the list. If it is set to false, then only one item of the list can be selected at a time.

The simplest form of `List` that does not allow multiple selections can be created by the following syntax:

```
List anyList = new List();
```

If you want to create a list that does allow multiple selections, use the following command line which creates a list with 10 visible entries and multiple selections turned on.

```
List anyList = new List(10, true);
```

Once you have created the list, the `add` method enables you to add new entries. Table 14.6 shows the methods of `List` class.

```
anyList.add("apple"); anyList.add("mango");
anyList.add("guava");
```

To add an item at a particular location in the list, e.g., the first position, use the following line of syntax:

```
anylist.add("Coffee", 0);
```

Adding an item to (position–1) or at a higher position than the number on the list, adds it to the end of the list.

Implementation of `ActionListener` interface is necessary for handling list events. A double click on a particular list item generates an `ActionEvent` object. As used in the case of buttons, `getActionCommand()` can be used to get the name of the double clicked item. If selection or de-selection of an item takes place because of a single click, an `ItemEvent` is generated. Whether this `ItemEvent` is generated because of `selection` or `de-selection` can be determined by the use of `getStateChange()` method of `ItemEvent` class.

Let us take an example which creates two lists. One list is filled with items while the other list is empty. As you select items from the first list and click on the button with the right arrows, the selected item is deleted from the first list and added in the second list. The *clear* button will clear the second list and reset the first list to its original values. The code for the applet is listed in Table 14.6.

Table 14.6 Methods of `List` Class

Method Name	Particulars
`void add(String item)`	Adds the specified item to the end of scrolling list.
`void add(String item, int index)`	Adds the specified item to the scrolling list at the position indicated by the index.
`void addActionListener (ActionListener l)`	Adds the specified action listener to receive action events from this list.
`void addItemListener(ItemListener il)`	Adds the specified item listener to receive item events from this list.
`void deselect(int index)`	De-selects the item at the specified index.
`AccessibleContext getAccessibleContext()`	Gets the `AccessibleContext` associated with this list.
`ActionListener[] getActionListeners()`	Returns an array of all the action listeners registered on this list.
`String getItem(int index)`	Gets the item associated with the specified index.
`int getItemCount()`	Gets the number of items in the list.
`ItemListener[] getItemListeners()`	Returns an array of all the item listeners registered on this list.
`String[] getItems()`	Gets the items in the list.
`Dimension getMinimumSize()`	Determines the minimum size of this scrolling list.
`Dimension getMinimumSize(int rows)`	Gets the minimum dimensions for a list with the specified number of rows.
`Dimension getPreferredSize()`	Gets the preferred size of the scrolling list.
`Dimension getPreferredSize(int rows)`	Gets the preferred dimensions for a list with the specified number of rows.
`int getRows()`	Gets the number of visible lines in this list.
`int getSelectedIndex()`	Gets the index of the selected item on the list.
`int[] getSelectedIndexes()`	Gets the selected indexes on the list.
`String getSelectedItem()`	Gets the selected item on this scrolling list.
`String[] getSelectedItems()`	Gets the selected items on this scrolling list.
`Object[] getSelectedObjects()`	Gets the selected items on this scrolling list in an array of objects.
`int getVisibleIndex()`	Gets the index of the item that was last made visible by the method `makeVisible`.

(Contd)

(Table 14.6 Contd)

Method Name	Particulars
`boolean isIndexSelected (int index)`	Determines if the specified item in this scrolling list is selected.
`boolean isMultipleMode()`	Determines whether this list allows multiple selections.
`void makeVisible(int index)`	Makes the item at the specified index visible.
`protected void processEvent(AWTEvent e)`	Processes events on the list.
`void remove(int position)`	Removes the item at the specified position from this scrolling list.
`void remove(String item)`	Removes the first occurrence of an item from the list.
`void removeActionListener (ActionListener l)`	Removes the specified action listener so that it no longer receives action events from this list.
`void removeAll()`	Removes all items from this list.
`void removeItemListener(ItemListener l)`	Removes the specified item listener so that it no longer receives item events from this list.
`void replaceItem(String newValue, int index)`	Replaces the item at the specified index in the scrolling list with the new string.
`void select(int index)`	The item at the specified index is selected in the list.
`void setMultipleMode (boolean b)`	Sets the flag that determines whether this list allows multiple selections.

Example 14.5 Demo of List

```
     /*<applet code = ShopList.class width = 600 height = 600></applet>*/
L1   import java.applet.*;
L2   import java.awt.*;
L3   import java.awt.event.*;
L4   public class ShopList extends Applet implements ActionListener {
L5   List original; List copy;
L6   public void init(){
L7      original= new List(8,false);
L8      copy = new List(10,false);
L9      populateList();
L10     add(original);
L11     Button b1 = new Button(">>>>");
L12     add(b1);
L13     add(copy);
L14     Button b2 = new Button("Clear");
L15     add(b2);
L16     add(new Label("Select an item from the list on the left and hit >>>> to place
        it in the other list"));
L17     b1.addActionListener(this);
```

```
L18        b2.addActionListener(this);
L19        }
L20        public void populateList(){
L21        original.add("Grocery");
L22        original.add("Fruits");
L23        original.add ("Ice-cream");
L24        original.add("Shop");
L25        original.add("Vegetables");
L26        original.add("Books");
L27        original.add("AC");
L28        original.add("Garments");
L29        original.add("Baby Food");
L30        }

L31        public void actionPerformed(ActionEvent ae){
L32        String str = ae.getActionCommand();
L33        if (str.equals(">>>>") && original.getSelectedIndex() >= 0) {
L34        copy.add(original.getSelectedItem());
L35        original.remove(original.getSelectedIndex());
L36        }
L37        else if(str.equals("Clear")){
L38        original.removeAll();
L39        copy.removeAll();
L40        populateList();
L41        }
L42        repaint();
L43        }
L44        }
```

Output

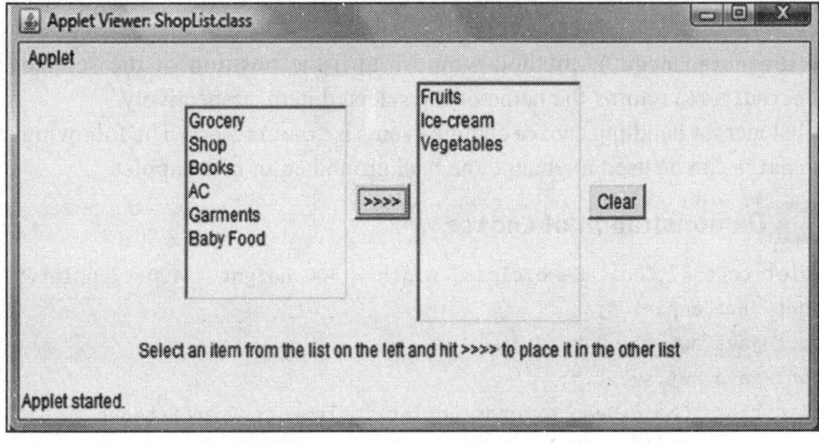

Fig. 14.6 Output Showing Two Lists

Explanation

L1–3 Packages are imported.

L4 Class declaration.

L5 Two list references have been created which are instantiated in L7 and L8. The first argument in the constructor specifies the number of items in the list to be shown and the second argument specifies whether multiple selections are allowed or not.

L9 The method `populateList()` is defined in L20–L30 for adding items into the list: original.

L10 The list `original` is added to the applet.

L11–18 Two buttons are created, added to the applet and registered with `ActionListener` for handling events of the button. Apart from this, a label is also added.

L31–43 The `actionPerformed()` method has been overridden to handle the button event. If the user has selected an item in the original list (`original.getSelectedIndex()`) and pressed the button >>>>, then the selected item is copied to list *copy* using `copy.add(original.getSelectedItem())` and removed from the list *original* using the `original.remove(original.getSelectedIndex())`. If the *clear* button is pressed, then all items in the list *copy* and *original* are removed using the `removeAll()` and the *original* list is populated again using `populateList()` method.

14.8 CHOICE BOXES

The `Choice` class is a lot like lists, but it allows you to conserve space since it provides a pop-up menu of text string choices. The current choice is displayed on top. In order to work with a choice box, an instance of the `Choice` class must be created.

```
Choice c = new Choice();
```

Once you have created the choice, the `add` method enables you to add new entries.

```
c.add("Red");
c.add("Green");
```

The currently selected item can be changed by using `select()` method. The selection can be made based on name or index. For example,

```
c.select("Red");
```

or

```
c.select(0);
```

The `getSelectedIndex()` method would return the position of the selected item and the `getSelectedItem()` returns the name of the selected item, respectively.

The listener for handling `Choice` change events is `ItemListener`. The following example shows how a `choice` can be used to change the background color of an applet.

Example 14.6 **Demonstration of Choice**

```
      /*<applet code = "ChoiceDemo.class" width = 400 height = 400></applet>*/
L1    import java.applet.*;
L2    import java.awt.*;
L3    import java.awt.event.*;
L4    public class ChoiceDemo extends Applet implements ItemListener {
L5    String currentColor = " ";
```

```
L6      Choice theOptions;
L7      Label l;
L8      public void init(){
L9         add(l = new Label("Make a choice from the choice box"));
L10        theOptions = new Choice();
L11        theOptions.add(" ");
L12        theOptions.add("Red");
L13        theOptions.add("Green");
L14        theOptions.add("Blue");
L15        theOptions.add("White");
L16        theOptions.add("Cyan");
L17        theOptions.add("Yellow");
L18        theOptions.addItemListener(this);
L19        add(theOptions);
L20     }
L21     public void itemStateChanged(ItemEvent evt){
L22        currentColor = theOptions.getSelectedItem();
L23        repaint();
L24     }
L25     public void paint(Graphics g){
L26     if (currentColor.equals("Red")) {
L27        setBackground(Color.red);
L28        l.setBackground(Color.red);
L29     }
L30   else if (currentColor.equals("Blue")){
L31        setBackground(Color.blue);
L32        l.setBackground(Color.blue);
L33   }
L34   else if (currentColor.equals("Green")){
L35        setBackground(Color.green);
L36        l.setBackground(Color.green);
L37   }
L38   else if (currentColor.equals("Cyan")){
L39        setBackground(Color.cyan);
L40        l.setBackground(Color.cyan);
L41   }
L42   else if (currentColor.equals("Yellow")){
L43        setBackground(Color.yellow);
L44        l.setBackground(Color.yellow);
L45   }
L46   else {
L47        setBackground(Color.white);
L48        l.setBackground(Color.white);}}}
```

Output

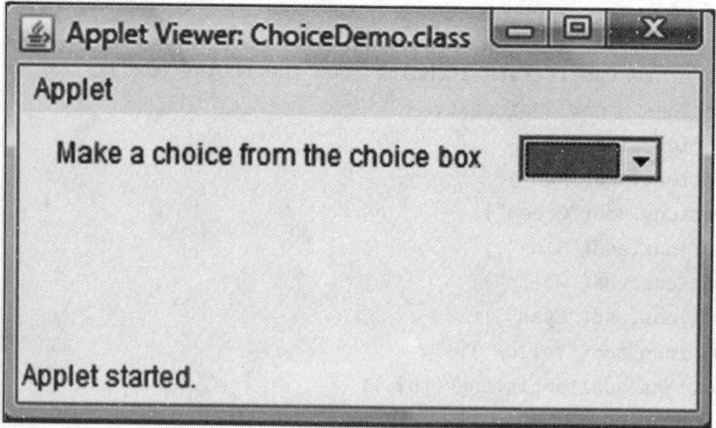

Fig. 14.7(a) Choice Demo

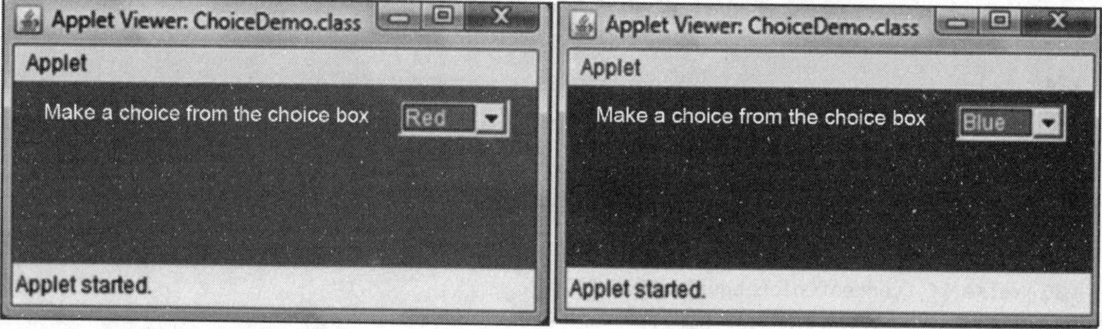

Fig. 14.7(b) Color of the Frame Changes Based on the Selection in the Choice

Explanation

L1–3 Packages are imported.

L4 `Applet` class defined to implement `ItemListener` interface for handling events of the component `Choice`.

L5–7 Label and choice reference variables are created. A string is also defined that represents the current color of the background.

L8 The `init()` method for the applet is defined.

L9 The label is instantiated and added to the applet.

L10–19 The `Choice` object is instantiated. Individual items are added to the `Choice` object using the `add()` method and later the choice object is added to the applet. The `Choice` object is registered with the `ItemListener` to receive change events when an item in the `Choice` object is selected.

L21–23 `itemStateChanged(ItemEvent e)` method of the `ItemListener` is overridden. When an item is selected by the user, the current color is set based on the selection of the items in the choice and then it is repainted using the `repaint()` method.

L24–48 Within the `paint` method, the value of `currentColor` is matched with various colors and if true, the background of the applet is set according to the color mentioned in the `currentColor` along with the background of the label.

14.9 TEXTFIELD AND TEXTAREA

The `TextField` and `TextArea` classes are two different Java classes for entering text data. The `TextField` class handles the single line of text and the `TextArea` is used for handling multiple lines of text. Example 14.7 illustrates the use of `Textfield`.

The following line will create a `TextField` with 20 columns.

```
TextField plaintext = new TextField(20);
```

The `Textfield` can also be initialized with some text when it is created.

```
TextField plaintext = new TextField("First Name Last Name");
```

Tables 14.7 and 14.8 list the constructors and methods of `TextField` and `TextArea`, respectively.

Table 14.7 `TextField` Class

Constructors of `TextField`	
Constructor	**Description**
`TextField()`	Constructs a new textfield.
`TextField(int columns)`	Constructs a empty textbox with the number of columns specified as argument.
`TextField(String text)`	Constructs a new textbox initialized with the specified string.
`TextField(String text, int columns)`	Constructs a new textbox initialized with the specified string, and specified number of columns.
Methods of `TextField`	
Method	**Description**
`void addActionListener (ActionListener l)`	Adds the specified action listener to receive action events from this textfield.
`boolean echoCharIsSet()`	Indicates whether or not this textfield has set a character for echoing.
`AccessibleContext getAccessibleContext()`	Returns the `AccessibleContext` associated with this textField.
`ActionListener[] getActionListeners()`	Returns an array of all the action listeners associated with the textfield.
`int getColumns()`	Returns the number of columns in this textfield.
`char getEchoChar()`	Returns the character that is to be used for echoing.
`Dimension getMinimumSize()`	Returns the minumum dimensions for this textfield.
`Dimension getMinimumSize (int columns)`	Returns the minumum dimensions for a textfield with the specified number of columns.
`Dimension getPreferredSize()`	Returns the preferred size of this textfield.
`Dimension getPreferredSize (int columns)`	Returns the preferred size of this textfield with the specified number of columns.
`String paramString()`	Gets a string representing the state of this textField.
`void process ActionEvent(ActionEvent e)`	Processes action events of the textfield by dispatching them to any registered `ActionListener` objects.

(*Table 14.7 Contd*)

Methods of `TextField`	
Method	**Description**
`void processEvent(AWTEvent e)`	Processes `AWTEvent` on this textfield.
`void removeActionListener (ActionListener l)`	Removes the associated action listener from this textfield.
`void setColumns(int columns)`	Sets the number of columns for the textfield.
`void setEchoChar(char c)`	Sets the echo character.
`void setText(String t)`	Sets the string within the textfield.

Table 14.8 `TextArea` Class

Constructors of `TextArea`	
Constructor	**Description**
`TextArea()`	Constructs a new textarea with the empty string.
`TextArea(int rows, int Columns)`	Constructs a textarea with the specified number of rows and columns and empty string.
`TextArea(String text)`	Constructs a textarea with the specified string.
`TextArea(String text, int Rows, int columns)`	Constructs a textarea with the specified string, and with the specified number of rows and columns.
`TextArea(String text, int rows, int columns, int scrollbars)`	Constructs a textarea with the specified string, and with the rows, columns, and scroll bar.

Methods of `TextArea`	
Method	**Description**
`void append (String str)`	Appends the given text to the textarea's current text.
`int getColumns()`	Returns the number of columns.
`Dimension getMinimumSize()`	Determines the minimum size of this textarea.
`Dimension getMinimumSize (int rows, int columns)`	Determines the minimum size of a textarea with the specified number of rows and columns.
`Dimension getPreferredSize()`	Returns the preferred size of this textarea.
`Dimension getPreferredSize (int rows, int columns)`	Returns the preferred size of a textarea with the specified number of rows and columns.
`int getRows()`	Returns the number of rows.
`void insert(String str, int pos)`	Inserts the specified text at the specified position in this textarea.
`protected String paramString()`	Returns a string representing the state of this textarea.
`void replaceRange(String str, int start, int end)`	Replaces string between the start and end positions with the specified replacement string.
`void setColumns(int columns)`	Sets the number of columns.
`void setRows(int rows)`	Sets the number of rows for this textarea.

Example 14.7 Event Handling for a `TextField`

```java
/*<applet code = "TextFieldDemo.class" width = 200 height = 100></applet>*/
import java.awt.*;
import java.awt.event.*;
import java.applet.Applet;
    public class TextFieldDemo extends Applet implements TextListener,
    FocusListener, ActionListener {
    Label l;
    Button b;
    TextField tf;
    public void init(){
        tf = new TextField("Textfield");
        l  = new Label("Make selection",Label.CENTER);
        b = new Button("Submit");
        b.addFocusListener(this);
        tf.addTextListener(this);
        tf.addFocusListener(this);
        tf.addActionListener(this);
        tf.selectAll();
        setLayout(new BorderLayout());
        add(l,BorderLayout.NORTH);
        add(tf,BorderLayout.CENTER);
        add(b,BorderLayout.SOUTH);
    }
public void focusGained(FocusEvent e)
{
        if(e.getSource() == tf)
            l.setText("Focus Gained by Text box");
        else if(e.getSource() == b)
            l.setText("Focus Gained by Button");
}
public void focusLost(FocusEvent e)
{

    l.setText("Focus not on Frame now");
}
public void actionPerformed(ActionEvent e)
{
    l.setText("action event");
}
public void textValueChanged(TextEvent e)
{
    l.setText("Trying to change text");
}
}
```

Output

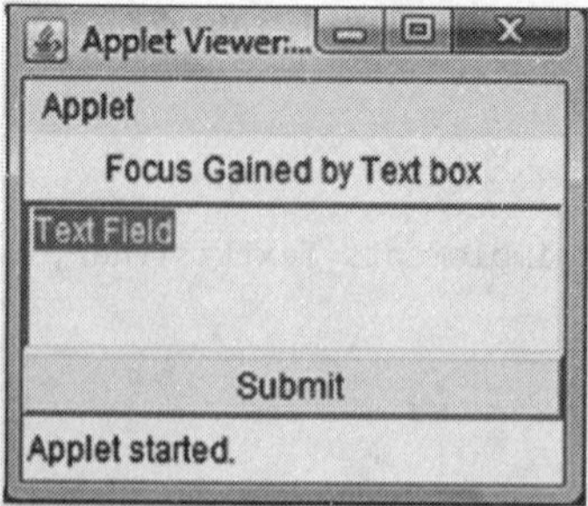

Fig. 14.8(a) Focus on `TextField` and the Contents of `TextField` Selected

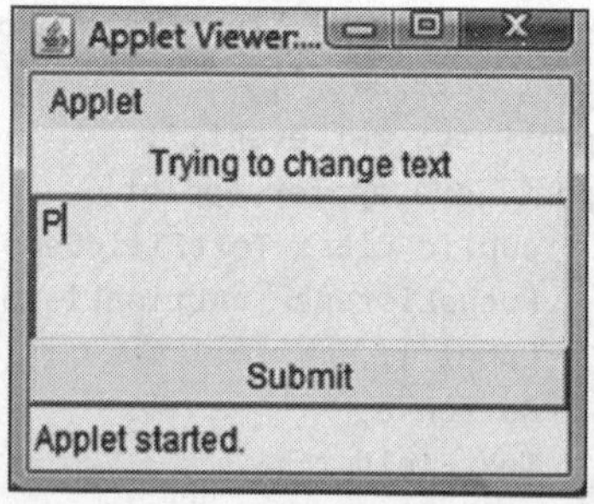

Fig. 14.8(b) Contents of the `TextField` Altered

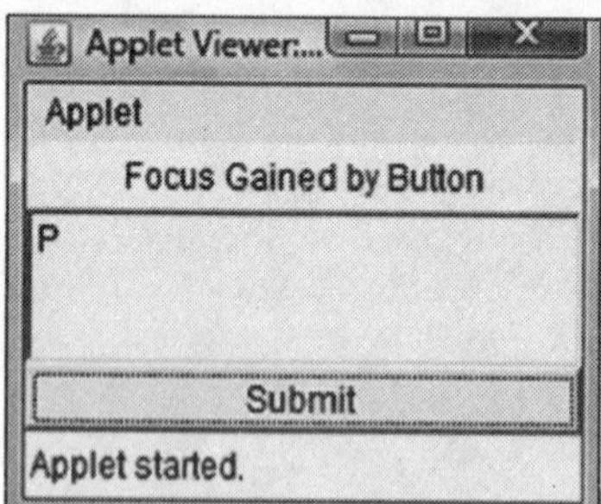

Fig. 14.8(c) Focus Gained by Button

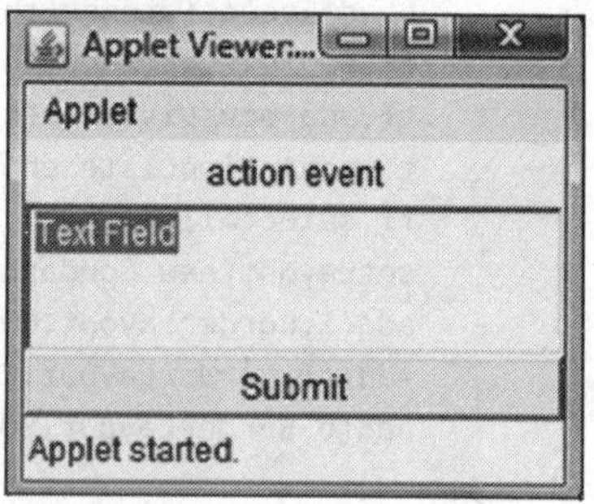

Fig. 14.8(d) Enter Pressed While Focus on `TextField` Generates an `ActionEvent`

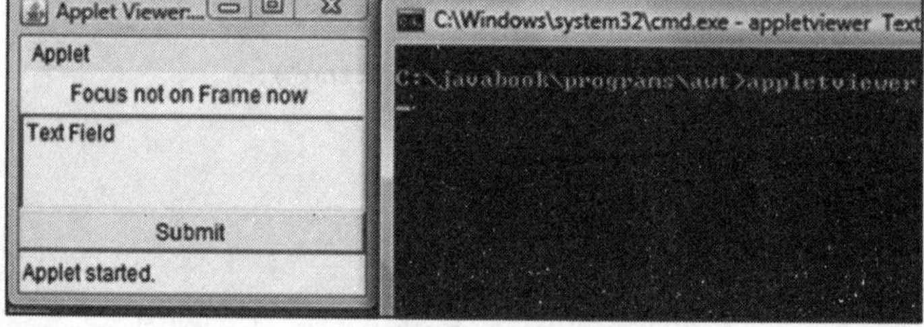

Fig. 14.8(e) Focus on the DOS Prompt Besides `appletviewer` Window

Explanation

L1 An `Applet` is created which inherits three interfaces: `TextListener` for tracking changes in `TextField`, `FocusListener` for determining which component has focus, and `ActionListener` for performing an action when the user presses enter in a `TextField`. The methods of the interfaces have been implemented later in the program.

L2–4 `Label`, `TextField`, and `Button` reference variables are created.

L5 `init()` methods defined for the applet.

L6–8 `tf, 1` and `b` are instantiated. The text passed as an argument to the `TextField` constructor will be displayed in the `TextField`. The button when displayed will have the caption 'Submit' which is passed in the constructor of the `Button` object. The label is assigned an orientation, i.e., `Label.CENTER` which displays the caption of the label in the middle.
L9 `FocusListener` is registered on button to capture focus lost and gained status.
L10–12 `TextListener`, `FocusListener`, and `ActionListener` are registered on `TextField` to capture various events.
L13 The Text in the `TextField` is already selected when it is displayed to the user. `selectAll()` is used for this purpose (see Fig. 14.8(d)).
L14 The layout of the applet is changed to `BorderLayout`.
L15–17 The label is added to NORTH, `TextField` in CENTER, and button in SOUTH.
L18–24 The methods of `FocusListener` interface are overridden, i.e., `focusGained(FocusEvent e)` and `focusLost(FocusEvent e)`. L19 checks the source of the event, i.e., which component has focus. If it is `TextField`, the label is set with the text `FocusGainedbyTextbox`, else if the focus is on `Button`, the label is set with the text 'Focus Gained by `Button`. Focus lost by the `TextField` is actually focus gained by the `Button` and when the focus is lost by the `Button`, it is gained back by the `TextField`. If the ALT+TAB key combination is pressed, the window loses focus and the other window gains focus. The `focusLost` method is called in that case (see Fig. 14.8(e)).
L25–26 If ENTER is pressed in the `TextField`, an `ActionEvent`is generated and passed to the `actionPerformed` method which sets the text of the label to the `ActionEvent`.
L27–28 If the value in the `TextField` changes, the `TextEvent` is generated and passed to `textValueChanged` method which sets the text of the label to `Trying to change Text` (see Fig. 14.8(b)).

14.10 CONTAINER CLASS

Containers allow us to organize components into manageable groups which are extremely important in order to create a good user interface. A component in the AWT can only be used if it is held within a container. A component without a container is like a door without a house. This section covers panels (applets are a subclass of panels.), frames, and dialog boxes (which are both subclasses of windows).

The AWT provides four container classes: `Panel`, `Window`, `Dialog`, and `Frame`. Note that these four classes can work as containers because of inheritance.

`Window` It is a top-level display surface. An object of `Window` class is not attached to nor embedded within another container. An instance of the `Window` does not have border, title bar or menu.

`Frame` It is a top-level window with a border and title. An instance of the `Frame` class may have a menu bar, title bar, and borders. It is otherwise like an object of the `Window` class.

`Dialog` It is a top-level display surface (a window) with a border and title. An object of the `Dialog` class cannot exist without an associated object of the `Frame` class.

`Panel` It is a generic container for holding components. An instance of the `Panel` class provides a container to which components can be added. It does not add any new method; it simply implements the container.

14.10.1 Panels

The definition of the `Panel` class is as follows:

```
public class Panel extends Container implements Accessible
```

The Panel class is a direct subclass of the Container class. We have made so many applets by now. The Panel class is a superclass of the applet that makes all the applets be drawn on the surface of the panel. Panel is a window that does not contain a title bar or a menu bar. Components (such as label and button) can be added to the panel object by using the add() method. This add() method actually belongs to the Container class, the superclass of the panel class. The constructors responsible for constructing panels are listed in Table 14.9.

Table 14.9 Constructors of Panel Class

Constructor	Description
Panel()	Creates a new panel using the default layout manager.
Panel(LayoutManager layout)	Creates a new panel with the specified layout.

How to Use Panels?

The following steps are followed while creating a panel:

- Create the panel by writing the following piece of code:

```
Panel panel = new Panel();
```

- Add components to panel by using add() method

```
panel.add(someComponent);

panel.add(someOtherComponent);
```

If you want to add to an external container, then you have to call the add() method in the following ways:

```
container.add(panel);
```

or if you want to add from within a container, then call the add() method directly,

```
add(panel);
```

14.10.2 Window

This class creates a top-level window. Top-level window means that it is not contained within any other object. It has the following signature:

```
public class Window extends Container implements Accessible
```

A Window object is a window with no borders and no menubar. The default layout for a window is BorderLayout, which we have covered later in the chapter. A window must have a frame, dialog, or another window defined as its owner when it is constructed, out of which only Frame is most often used.

14.10.3 Frame

If you are not creating an applet, then you will be most likely creating a Frame window. The constructors responsible for creating a Frame are

```
Frame()
Frame(String title)
```

The first constructor simply creates a `Frame` window without any title, while the second one creates a `Frame` with the title specified as string in the argument. Some of the methods that can be used while working with the `Frame` object are given in Table 14.10.

Table 14.10 Methods of `Frame` Object

Method	Description
`void setSize(int width, int height)`	It is used to set the dimensions of the window. The new dimension in the form of width and height is passed as argument.
`void setSize(Dimension size)`	Sets the size of the frame with dimension specified.
`Dimension getSize()`	It is used to return the current size of the window, contained within the width and height fields of `Dimension` object.
`void setVisible(boolean flag)`	It is used to make the window visible after its creation. The component is visible only if the argument passed is true.
`void setTitle(String title)`	The title in the frame window can be used to set to a new title, passed as argument.

Example 14.8 demonstrates how frames are created and used.

Example 14.8 **Demonstration of Frame Class**

```
L1    import java.awt.*;
L2    public class FrameDemo extends Frame {
L3        public FrameDemo(String title) {
L4            super(title);
L5    }
L6    public static void main(String[] args) {
L7      FrameDemo frameDemo = new FrameDemo("Demo Frame");
L8      frameDemo.setSize(200, 300);
L9      frameDemo.setVisible(true);
L10   }}
```

Output

Fig. 14.9 Frame

Creating a framed application is easy. The typical procedure for frame development is as follows:

1. Create an instance of the main frame.
2. Set the frame width and height.
3. Display the frame.

Explanation

L2 `FrameDemo` class extends the `java.awt.Frame` class.

L3–5 The constructor belonging to the `Frame` class sets the frame instance title. So, the `FrameDemo` class accepts a string as parameter for title of the frame. In L4, the `super` keyword is used to set the title by calling the constructor of the superclass. L5 signifies the end of the constructor method.

L6–10 In these lines, `main()` method is elaborated. In **L8**, the `setSize()` method is used to set the width and height of the frame to 200 and 300 pixels, respectively.

14.11 LAYOUTS

Java has the mechanism to specify the type of layout schemes, where components can be added to a `Frame` instance. This mechanism is specified by `LayoutManager`, which is used to specify how the components can be arranged inside a container, say a `Frame`. The various `LayoutManagers` available in AWT are children of this interface and explained in the sections to follows:
This `LayoutManager` is actually an interface in **java.awt**, defined as

```
public interface LayoutManager
```

The above interface is defined for classes that know how to layout `Containers`. The various methods defined in the interface are

```
void addLayoutComponent(String name, Component comp)
```

If the layout manager uses a string per component, the above method adds the component, 'comp' to the layout, associating it with the string specified by 'name'.

```
void removeLayoutComponent(Component comp)
```

The method removes the specified component, 'comp' from the layout.

```
Dimension preferredLayoutSize(Container parent)
```

The method returns the preferred size dimensions for the specified container, 'parent', given the components it contains.

```
Dimension minimumLayoutSize(Container parent)
```

Returns the minimum size dimensions for the specified container, 'parent', given the components it contains.

```
void layoutContainer(Container parent)
```

The method is responsible for laying out the specified container, 'parent'. Some of the famous layouts in Java are discussed below.

14.11.1 `FlowLayout`

There is class belonging to the package `java.awt`, named as `FlowLayout`, having the following signature:

```
public class FlowLayout extends Object implements LayoutManager, Serializable
```

`java.awt.FlowLayout` arranges components from left-to-right (items) and top-to-bottom (lines), centering components horizontally. There is five pixel gap between the components arranged in this layout. `FlowLayout` recomputes new positions for the components, subject to the constraints provided, whenever the container size is changed. Example of changing a container size is resizing a window. This is the default layout for the Applet.

A flow layout arranges components in a directional flow similar to lines of text in a paragraph. The direction of flow is determined by the container's `componentOrientation` property. The value of this property can be either of the two:

- **`ComponentOrientation.LEFT_TO_RIGHT`** Items run left to right and lines flow top to bottom, e.g., English, French, etc.

- **`ComponentOrientation.RIGHT_TO_LEFT`** Items run right to left and lines flow top to bottom, e.g., Arabic, Hebrew, etc.

More often than not, flow layouts are used to place the buttons on a panel, in a horizontal manner, until no more buttons fit in the same line. These lines of buttons can be aligned by using the align property, which can have any one of the following values:

- RIGHT
- CENTER
- LEFT
- TRAILING
- LEADING

Flow layouts are one of the simplest layouts available in Java. Here the components are arranged in a row/line, within a container. When the row is filled completely, the components begin to group in the next row. The fields, constructors, and methods belonging to the `FlowLayout` class are given in Table 14.11.

Table 14.11 `FlowLayout` Class

Fields of `FlowLayout`	
Field Name	**Particulars**
`static int CENTER`	This value shows that each row of components should be centered.
`static int LEADING`	This value shows that each row of components should be justified to the leading edge of the container's orientation, e.g., to the right in right-to-left orientations.
`static int LEFT`	This value shows that each row of components should be left-justified.
`static int RIGHT`	This value shows that each row of components should be right-justified.
`static int TRAILING`	This value shows that each row of components should be justified to the trailing edge of the container's orientation, e.g. to the left in right-to-left orientations.

(Contd)

(*Table 14.11 Contd*)

Constructors of **FlowLayout**	
Constructor Name	**Particulars**
`FlowLayout()`	Constructs a new `FlowLayout` with a centered alignment and a default 5-unit horizontal and vertical gap.
`FlowLayout(int align)`	Constructs a new `FlowLayout` with the alignment specified as argument and a default 5-unit horizontal and vertical gap.
`FlowLayout (int align,int hzgap, int vrgap)`	Constructs a new `FlowLayout` with the indicated alignment and the indicated horizontal and vertical gaps.
Methods of FlowLayout	
Method Name	**Particulars**
`void addLayoutComponent (String name, Component comp)`	Adds the component specified as the argument to the layout.
`int getAlignment()`	Returns the alignment for the layout.
`boolean getAlignOnBaseline()`	Returns true in case of vertical alignment of components along their baseline.
`int getHgap()`	Returns the horizontal gap between components and between the components and the borders of the container.
`int getVgap()`	Returns the vertical gap between components and between the components and the borders of the container.
`void layoutContainer (Container target)`	Lays out the container.
`Dimension minimumLayoutSize (Container target)`	Returns the minimum dimensions needed to layout the visible components in the target container.
`Dimension preferredLayout Size(Container target)`	Returns the preferred dimensions for this layout, given the visible components in the target container.
`void removeLayoutComponent (Component comp)`	Removes the component, specified as, 'comp' from the layout.
`void setAlignment(int align)`	Sets the alignment for this layout, as per the argument.
`void setAlignOnBaseline (boolean alignOnBaseline)`	Sets whether or not components should be vertically aligned along their baseline.
`void setHgap(int hgap)`	Sets the horizontal gap between components and also between the components and the borders of the container.
`void setVgap(int vgap)`	Sets the vertical gap between components and also between the components and the borders of the container.
`String toString()`	Returns a string representation of the `FlowLayout` object and its values.

Example 14.9 `FlowLayout`

```
     /*<applet code = FlowLayoutDemo.class width = 200 height = 200></applet>*/
L1       import java.applet.Applet;
L2       import java.awt.*;
L3       public class FlowLayoutDemo extends Applet{
L4       LayoutManager flowLayout;
L5       Button [] Buttons;
L6       public FlowLayoutDemo() {
L7       int i;
L8       flowLayout = new FlowLayout ();
L9       setLayout (flowLayout);
L10      Buttons = new Button [6];
L11      for (i = 0; i < 6; i++) {
L12          Buttons[i] = new Button ();
L13          Buttons[i].setLabel ("Button " + (i + 1));
L14          add (Buttons[i]);
L15      }
L16      }
L17      }
```

Output

The output of the program shows the six buttons arranged or added to the applet window in the `FlowLayout` fashion.

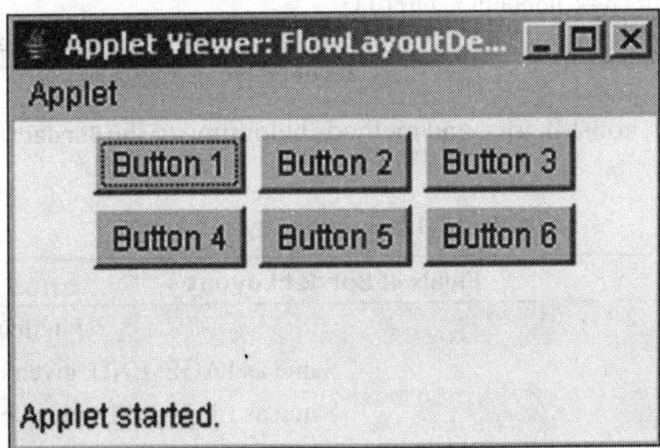

Fig. 14.10 `FlowLayout`

Explanation

L1–2 All the necessary classes belonging to the packages like `java.applet` and `java.awt` are imported.

L3 An applet with the name `FlowLayoutDemo` is declared.

L4 A reference to the `LayoutManager` class is declared as 'flowLayout'.

L5 An array of buttons of button type with the name 'Buttons' is declared.

L6–16 A constructor, `FlowLayoutDemo()`, is declared at L6. In L8, the reference declared at L4, as `flowLayout`, is created. In L9, the `setLayout()` method is used to set the layout of the window by passing the object of the `FlowLayout` class as its argument. In L10, an array of six buttons is created. In L11–15, the labels of the six buttons are set using the `setLabel()` method of the `Button` class. After the labels are set for each button, the buttons are added to the applet window. In order to avoid setting the label for each button and then adding it to the container, a `for` loop is used for simplifying the purpose.

14.11.2 BorderLayout

It is the default layout of the frame. The class belonging to `java.awt`, named as `BorderLayout`, has the following signature:

```
public class BorderLayout extends Object implements LayoutManager2, Serializable
```

The `BorderLayout` is a layout where the components can be arranged and resized to fit in five different regions: north, south, east, west, and center. There can be only one component in each region and the regions are identified as constants: `NORTH`, `SOUTH`, `EAST`, `WEST`, and `CENTER`. Any of these five constant names can be used while adding a component to a container. For example:

```
Panel pnl = new Panel();
pnl.setLayout(new BorderLayout());
pnl.add(new Button("submit"), BorderLayout.NORTH);
```

By default, if you do not mention the string specification, `BorderLayout` interprets the absence of a string specification the same as the constant `CENTER`:

```
Panel p2 = new Panel();
p2.setLayout(new BorderLayout());
p2.add(new TextArea());        // Same as p.add(new TextArea(),
                               // BorderLayout.CENTER);
```

The various fields, constructors, and methods belonging to the `BorderLayout` class are mentioned in Table 14.12.

Table 14.12 BorderLayout Class

Fields of BorderLayout	
Field Name	**Particulars**
String AFTER_LAST_LINE	Same as PAGE_END, given below.
String AFTER_LINE_ENDS	Same as LINE_END, given below.
String BEFORE_FIRST_LINE	Same as PAGE_START, given below.
String BEFORE_LINE_BEGINS	Same as LINE_START, given below.
String CENTER	Middle of container.
String EAST	The east layout constraint (right side of container).
String LINE_END	The component goes at the end of the line direction for the layout.
String LINE_START	The component goes at the beginning of the line direction for the layout.

(Table 14.12 Contd)

Fields of `BorderLayout`	
Field Name	**Particulars**
`String NORTH`	The north layout constraint (top of container).
`String PAGE_END`	The component comes after the last line of the layout's content.
`String PAGE_START`	The component comes before the first line of the layout's content.
`String SOUTH`	Bottom of container.
`String WEST`	The west layout constraint (left side of container).

Constructors of `BorderLayout`	
Constructor Name	**Particulars**
`BorderLayout()`	Constructs a new border layout with no gaps between components.
`BorderLayout(int hgap, int vgap)`	Constructs a border layout with the specified horizontal and vertical gap between components.

Methods of `BorderLayout`	
Method Name	**Particulars**
`void addLayoutComponent (Component comp, Object constraints)`	Adds the specified component to the layout, using the specified constraint object.
`Object getConstraints (Component comp)`	Gets the constraints for the specified component.
`int getHgap()`	Returns the horizontal gap between components.
`float getLayoutAlignmentX (Container parent)`	Returns the alignment along the x-axis.
`float getLayoutAlignmentY (Container parent)`	Returns the alignment along the y-axis.
`Component getLayoutComponent(Container target, Object constraints)`	Returns the component that corresponds to the given constraint location based on the target container's component orientation.
`Component getLayoutComponent (Object constraints)`	Gets the component that was added using the given constraint.
`int getVgap()`	Returns the vertical gap between components.
`void invalidateLayout (Container target)`	Invalidates the layout, indicating that if the layout manager has cached information it should be discarded.
`void layoutContainer(Container target)`	Lays out the container argument using this border layout.
`Dimension maximumLayoutSize (Container target)`	Returns the maximum size as dimension object for this layout given the components in the specified target container.
`Dimension minimumLayoutSize (Container target)`	Determines the minimum size of the target container using this layout manager.
`Dimension preferredLayout Size(Container target)`	Determines the preferred size of the target container using this layout manager, based on the components in the container.

(Contd)

(Table 14.12 Contd)

<table>
<tr><th colspan="2" align="center">Methods of <code>BorderLayout</code></th></tr>
<tr><th>Method</th><th>Particulars</th></tr>
<tr><td><code>void removeLayoutComponent (Component comp)</code></td><td>Removes the specified component from this border layout.</td></tr>
<tr><td><code>void setHgap(int hgap)</code></td><td>Sets the horizontal gap between components.</td></tr>
<tr><td><code>void setVgap(int vgap)</code></td><td>Sets the vertical gap between components.</td></tr>
<tr><td><code>String toString()</code></td><td>Returns a string representation of the state of this border layout.</td></tr>
</table>

Let us take an example for `BorderLayout`. Since the default layout manager for frames is `BorderLayout`, we do not explicitly set the layout manager.

Example 14.10 BorderLayout

```
L1      import java.awt.*;
L2      public class BLayoutDemo extends Frame {
L3      public BLayoutDemo(String title) {
L4          super(title);
L5          add(new Button("North"),BorderLayout.NORTH);
L6          add(new Button("South"),BorderLayout.SOUTH);
L7          add(new Button("East"),BorderLayout.EAST);
L8          add(new Button("West"),BorderLayout.WEST);
L9          add(new Button("Center"),BorderLayout.CENTER);
L10         setSize(400, 270);
L11         setVisible(true);
        }
L12     public static void main(String[] args) {
L13         BLayoutDemo blaypout = new BLayoutDemo("Border Layout Example");
        }}
```

Output

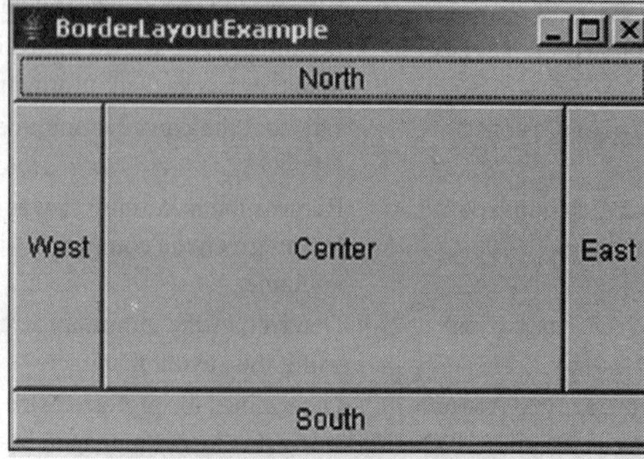

Fig. 14.11(a) `BorderLayout`

In the above frame, components placed within a region extend to fit it. For example, components in NORTH and SOUTH have stretched themselves horizontally to fit in that entire region and similarly, components in the EAST and WEST have stretched themselves vertically. The component in the CENTER stretches both horizontally and vertically to fill any leftover space.

Explanation

L2 Class BLayoutDemo declared to extend the frame.

L3–11 The constructor belonging to the Frame class sets the Frame instance title. Likewise, the BlayoutDemo class accepts a string as parameter for the title of the frame. In L4, super keyword is used to set the title by calling the constructor of the superclass. In L5–9, button objects are created and added to the frame using the add() method. The constraints for the button are specified as the second argument, i.e., BorderLayout.NORTH and so on. L9 signifies the end of the constructor method.

If no constraint is specified and add(Component c) is used for adding buttons, then by default, all buttons would be placed in center and they will occupy the entire frame. The button added in the end would be displayed on top of the frame. The remaining buttons will be beneath the top button displayed to the user. Figure 14.11(b) shows when buttons are added using add(Component c).

The code that produces the above output is shown below:

```
add(new Button("North"));
add(new Button("South"));
add(new Button("East"));
add(new Button("West"));
add(new Button("Center"));
```

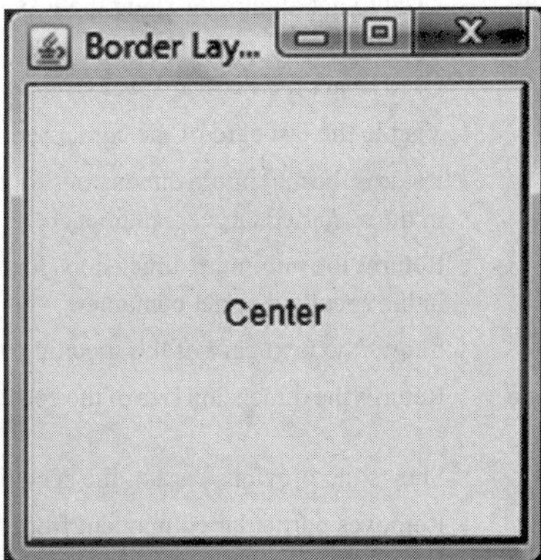

Fig. 14.11(b) BorderLayout with Default Settings

14.11.3 CardLayout

CardLayout class inherits Object class and implements LayoutManager2, serializable interfaces. Object of cardLayout acts as layout manager for a container. In a container each component is treated as a card by `cardLayout` object. Each card is kept on another like a stack and only one card can be visible at a time. When the container is displayed after adding the first component, then the first component is visible.

The ordering of cards is determined by the container's own internal ordering of its component objects. `CardLayout` defines a set of methods that allow an application to flip through these cards sequentially, or to show a specified card. The various constructors and methods belonging to the `cardLayout` class are mentioned in Table 14.13.

Table 14.13 CardLayout

Constructors of CardLayout	
Constructors Name	**Particulars**
`CardLayout()`	Creates a new default card layout with space of size zero.
`CardLayout (int h, int v)`	You can create a new card layout with the specific horizontal and vertical space.
Methods of CardLayout	
Method Name	**Particulars**
`addLayoutComponent (Component cmp, Object name)`	Adds the specific component to the internal table of card layout.
`void first(Container cont)`	Visible the first card of the container.
`int getHgap()`	Used to get the horizontal space between components.
`float getLayoutAlignmentX (Container cont)`	Used to get alignment along the x axis.
`float getLayoutAlignmentY (Container cont)`	Used to get alignment along the y axis.
`int getVgap()`	Used to get the vertical space between components.
`void last(Container cont)`	Visible the last card of the container.
`Dimension maximumLayoutSize (Container target)`	Returns the maximum dimensions for this layout given the components in the specified target container.
`Dimension minimumLayoutSize (Container target)`	Returns the minimum dimensions for this layout given the components in the specified target container.
`void next(Container cont)`	Shows the next card of the specific container.
`Dimension preferredLayout Size (Container cont)`	Returns the dimension size of the container argument using card layout.
`void Previous(Container cont)`	Shows the previous card of the specified container.
`void removeLayoutComponent (Component cmp)`	Removes particular component from the layout.
`void setHgap(int h)`	Sets the horizontal space between components.
`void setVgap(int v)`	Sets the vertical space between components.
`void show(Container cont, String name)`	Shows the components that were added to the layout with the specific name by using add layout component.
`String toString()`	Returns the state of card layout as string representation.

Example 14.11   CardLayout Demo

```
L1      import java.awt.*;
L2      import java.awt.event.*;
L3      public class CardDemo extends Frame implements ActionListener {
L4      Panel cardPanel;
L5      Panel p1, p2, p3;
L6      Panel buttonP;
L7      Button B1,B2,B3;
L8      CardLayout cLayout;
L9      public void cardDemo(){
L10         cardPanel = new Panel();
L11         cLayout = new CardLayout();
L12         cardPanel.setLayout(cLayout);
L13         p1 = new Panel();
L14         p1.setBackground(Color.red);
L15         p2 = new Panel();
L16         p2.setBackground(Color.yellow);
L17         p3 = new Panel();
L18         p3.setBackground(Color.green);
L19         B1 = new Button("Red");
L20         B1.addActionListener(this);
L21         B2 = new Button("Yellow");
L22         B2.addActionListener(this);
L23         B3 = new Button("Green");
L24         B3.addActionListener(this);
L25         buttonP = new Panel();
L26         buttonP.add(B1);
L27         buttonP.add(B2);
L28         buttonP.add(B3);
L29         cardPanel.add(p1, "B1");
L30         cardPanel.add(p2, "B2");
L31         cardPanel.add(p3, "B3");
L32             setLayout(new BorderLayout());
L33             add(buttonP, BorderLayout.SOUTH);
L34         add(cardPanel, BorderLayout.CENTER);
L35             setVisible(true);
L36             setSize(300,200);
L37             setTitle("DemoCard");
L38             addWindowListener(new WindowAdapter(){
```

```
            public void windowClosing(WindowEvent we){
            System.exit(0);
        }});
        }
L39     public void actionPerformed(ActionEvent e){
L40     if (e.getSource() == B1)
L41     cLayout.show(cardPanel, "B1");
L42     if (e.getSource() == B2)
L43         cLayout.show(cardPanel, "B2");
L44     if (e.getSource() == B3)
L45         cLayout.show(cardPanel, "B3");
        }
L46     public static void main(String a[]){
L47     CardDemo demo = new CardDemo();
L48     demo.cardDemo();
        } }
```

Output

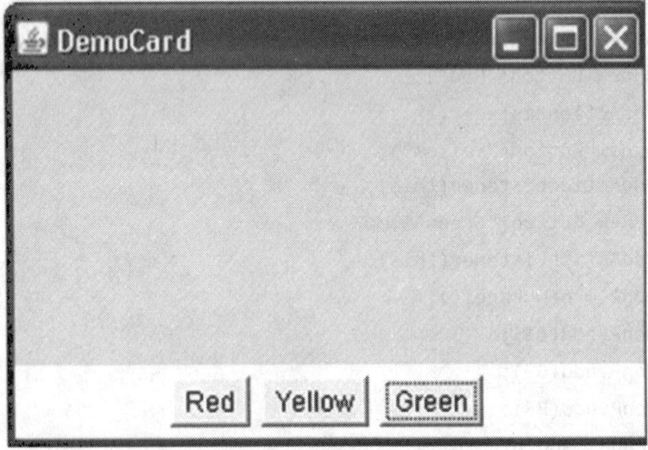

Fig. 14.12 CardLayout

Explanation

This example shows the CardLayout manager. Pressing any one of the three buttons available will show a different "card".

L4–8 In these lines, we have created reference variables for panels, buttons, and card layout. The cardPanel will hold various cards. Three panels (p1, p2, p3) will constitute different cards. A panel button is created.

L9 Method declaration.

L10 A cardPanel that will contain cards created in this program.

L11 We have created a CardLayout object named as cLayout.

L12 Sets the layout of the `cardPanel` as `CardLayout`.

L13–18 In these lines, three dummy panels are created to show the cards, and their backgrounds are set with three different colors: red, green, and yellow.

L19–24 We have created three buttons and added the `ActionListener` to it.

L25–28 A panel (`buttonP`) is created and buttons are added to this panel.

L29–31 Three panels (p1, p2, p3) are added to cardPanel. These will be flipped based on the user interaction with these three buttons.

L32 Sets the layout of the frame as `BorderLayout`.

L33–34 Both panels, button panel (`buttonP`) and card panel (`cardPannel`), are added to the frame.

L38 Closes the window when cross is clicked on the frame.

L40–45 If red button is clicked, the panel with red background is shown. Panels in card layout are switched using `show()` method.

14.11.4 `GridLayout`

The class belonging to `java.awt`, named as `GridLayout`, has the following signature:

```
public class GridLayout extends Object implements LayoutManager, Serializable
```

The `GridLayout` class is a layout manager that lays out a container's components in a rectangular grid. This is a layout manager which can be used to arrange controls in a container. `GridLayout` has a specified number of rows and columns, where the container is divided into equal-sized rectangles, and one component is placed in each rectangle.

The `GridLayout` arranges the components in rows and columns order. Each component fills up its respective grid cell. Table 14.14 describes the constructors and methods of `GridLayout`.

Table 14.14 `GridLayout` Class

Constructors of `GridLayout`	
Constructor Name	**Particulars**
`GridLayout()`	Creates a grid layout with a default of one column per component, in a single row.
`GridLayout(int row, int cols)`	Creates a grid layout with the specified number of rows and columns.
`GridLayout(int row, int cols, int hzgap, int vrgap)`	Creates a grid layout with the specified number of rows and columns with horizontal and vertical gap.
Methods of `GridLayout`	
Method Name	**Particulars**
`void addLayoutComponent (String name, Component comp)`	Adds the specified component with the specified name to the layout.
`int getColumns()`	Gets the number of columns in this layout.
`int getHgap()`	Returns the horizontal gap between components.
`int getRows()`	Gets the number of rows in this layout.
`int getVgap()`	Returns the vertical gap between components.
`void layoutContainer(Container parent)`	Lays out the specified container using this layout.

(Contd)

(*Table 14.14 Contd*)

Methods of GridLayout	
Method Name	**Particulars**
Dimension minimumLayoutSize (Container parent)	Determines the minimum size of the container argument using this grid layout.
Dimension preferredLayout Size(Container parent)	Determines the preferred size of the container argument using this grid layout.
void removeLayoutComponent (Component comp)	Removes the specified component.
void setColumns(int cols)	Sets the number of columns in this layout to the specified value.
void setHgap(int hgap)	Sets the horizontal gap between components to the specified value.
void setRows(int rows)	Sets the number of rows in this layout to the specified value.
void setVgap(int vgap)	Sets the vertical gap between components to the specified value.
String toString()	Returns a string representation of the grid layout's object.

Example 14.12 GridLayout

```
L1    import java.awt.event.*;
L2    import java.awt.*;
L3    class GridLayoutDemo extends Frame{
L4    public GridLayoutDemo() {
L5      super("Laying Out Components using GridLayout");
L6      Panel p = new Panel(new GridLayout(5,2, 20,50));
L7      p.add(new Label("Name"));
L8      p.add(new TextField(5));
L9      p.add(new Label("Roll No"));
L10     p.add(new TextField(3));
L11     p.add(new Label("Class"));
L12     p.add(new TextField(3));
L13     p.add(new Label("Total Marks"));
L14     p.add(new TextField(3));
L15     p.add(new Button("Submit"));
L16     p.add(new Button("Cancel"));
L17     add(p);
L18     setSize(400,400);
L19     setVisible(true);
L20     addWindowListener(new WindowAdapter(){
L21     public void windowClosing(WindowEvent e){
L22     System.exit(0);
L23     }
L24     });
L25     }
L26   public static void main(String[] args) {
L27     GridLayoutDemo g=new GridLayoutDemo();
      }}
```

Output

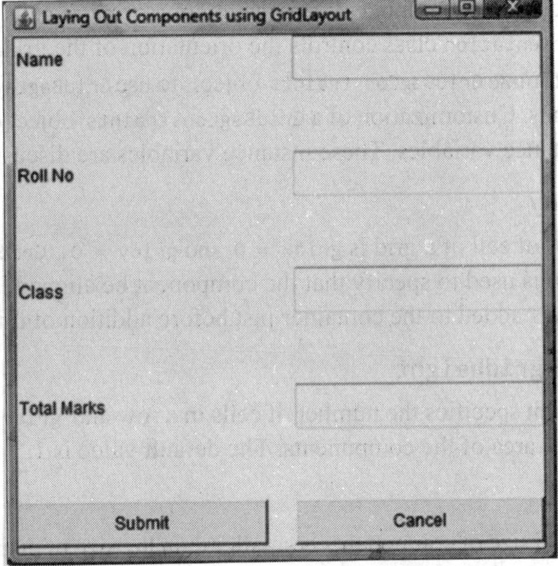

Fig. 14.13 Demo of GridLayout

Explanation

L1–2 `java.awt` and its sub-package `awt.event` are imported.

L3 A frame is created.

L4 Constructor for the class is defined.

L5 The constructor of `Frame` is called using the `super` keyword. The string passed to it is used as the title of the frame.

L6 A `Panel` object is created to hold the component. The layout for `Panel` object is specified as an argument in the constructor. The layout specified is `GridLayout` with number of rows as 5, number of columns as 2, horizontal gap between the columns is specified as 20, and vertical gap between the rows is specified as 50.

L7–17 Components are added to the panel. `Labels` and `TextFields` are added to the panel object along with two other buttons. The panel object is added to frame using `add(Component c)` method.

L18–19 The size of the frame is set and the visibility of the frame is set to `true`.

L20–25 `WindowListener` is registered with frame so that when the cross on the frame title bar is pressed, the application frame is closed.

14.11.5 `GridBagLayout`

`GridBagLayout` class extends `Object` and implements interfaces `LayoutManager2` and `Serializable`. Using `GridBagLayout` class, we can arrange components in a more controlled way in horizontal as well in vertical direction. In `GridBagLayout`, the components need not be of same size in a row. We can arrange different sizes of components by specifying their position within the cell of a grid in the same row. One more advantage is that each row can contain dissimilar number of columns. In `GridBagLayout`, the size and position of components are dependent on set of constraints linked to it.

An object called `GridBagConstraint` contains the constraint which includes the height, width of a cell, placement, and alignment of components. Each `GridBagLayout` object maintains a rectangular grid of cell. A component can occupy one or more cells and it is called its display area. `ComponentOrientation` class controls the orientation of the grid.

We need to customize `GridBagConstraints` objects to use `GridBagLayout` effectively associated with its components. Customization of a `GridBagConstraints` object can be done by setting one or more of its instance variables. These instance variables are discussed below.

gridx and gridy

The initial address of cell of a grid is `gridx = 0` and `gridy = 0`. `GridBagConstraints.RELATIVE` (the default value) is used to specify that the component be aligned immediately following the component that was added to the container just before addition of this component.

gridwidth and gridheight

`gridwidth` constraint specifies the number of cells in a row and `gridheight` specifies number of columns in display area of the components. The default value is 1.

fill

When the requested size of components is smaller than the size of display area, then we use this. We can also use it to resize the component. It is used to determine whether (and how) to resize the component. Values for this field are as follows:

- `GridBagConstraints.NONE` (default value–does not grow when the window is resized)
- `GridBagConstraints.HORIZONTAL` (this value fills all the horizontal display area of a component, but it does not change height).
- `GridBagConstraints.VERTICAL` (it changes the height of a component, but does not change its width)
- `GridBagConstraints.BOTH` (makes the component fill its display area horizontally and vertically, both).

ipadx and ipady

The `ipadx` and `ipady` fields are used for internal padding of components in given layout. If `ipadx` is specified, the width of the component will be the minimum width plus `ipadx` pixels. Similarly, `ipady` plus minimum height is the height of the component.

insets

The insets field is used for external padding of components. It is used for spacing between the component and the edges of its display area. For example,

```
GridBagConstraints c = new GridBagConstraints();
c.insets = new Insets(int top, int left, int bottom, int right)
```

anchor

The anchor field specifies the position of a component in its display area. There are three types of possible values: absolute, orientation-relative, and baseline-relative.

Absolute Values are used to place components at specific locations. These absolute values can be any of the following:

```
GridBagConstraints.NORTH
GridBagConstraints.SOUTH
GridBagConstraints.WEST
GridBagConstraints.EAST
GridBagConstraints.NORTHWEST
GridBagConstraints.NORTHEAST
GridBagConstraints.SOUTHWEST
GridBagConstraints.SOUTHEAST
GridBagConstraints.CENTER (The default)
```

Orientation-relative Values are relative to the orientation of container. These can be any of the following:

```
GridBagConstraints.PAGE_START
GridBagConstraints.PAGE_END
GridBagConstraints.LINE_START
GridBagConstraints.LINE_END
GridBagConstraints.FIRST_LINE_START
GridBagConstraints.FIRST_LINE_END
GridBagConstraints.LAST_LINE_START
GridBagConstraints.LAST_LINE_END
```

Baseline-relative Values were added by JDK 6. With the help of these values, you can place a component vertically relative to the baseline of row. Possible values are as follows:

```
GridBagConstraints.BASELINE
GridBagConstraints.BASELINE_LEADING
GridBagConstraints.BASELINE_TRAILING
GridBagConstraints.ABOVE_BASELINE
GridBagConstraints.ABOVE_BASE LINE_LEADING
GridBagConstraints.ABOVE_BASELINE_TRAILING
GridBagConstraints.BELOW_BASELINE
GridBagConstraints.BELOW_BASELINE_LEADING
GridBagConstraints.BELOW_BASELINE_TRAILING
```

weightx and weighty

These are used to distribute space (horizontal and vertical). If two weights are specified, then all the components will clump at the center of the container. The value of weight lies between 0.0 and 1.0. The weight of `GridBagLayout` object is by default zero. The following example shows how components are displayed using `GridBagLayout` when no constraints for the specified have been specified.

Example 14.13 · `GridBagLayout` without Constraints

```java
L1    import java.awt.*;
L2    public class GBLayoutDemo1 extends Frame {
L3    public GBLayoutDemo1()
        {
L4        setLayout(new GridBagLayout());
L5        setTitle("GridBagLayout Without Constraints");
L6        Label l=new Label("Name");
L7        add(l);
L8        TextField t = new TextField();
L9        add(t);
L10       Button b = new Button("Submit");
L11       add(b);
L12       Button b1 = new Button("Reset");
L13       add(b1);
L14       setSize(200,200);
L15       setVisible(true);
        }
L16   public static void main(String args[]){
L17   GBLayoutDemo1 d = new GBLayoutDemo1();
        }}
```

Output

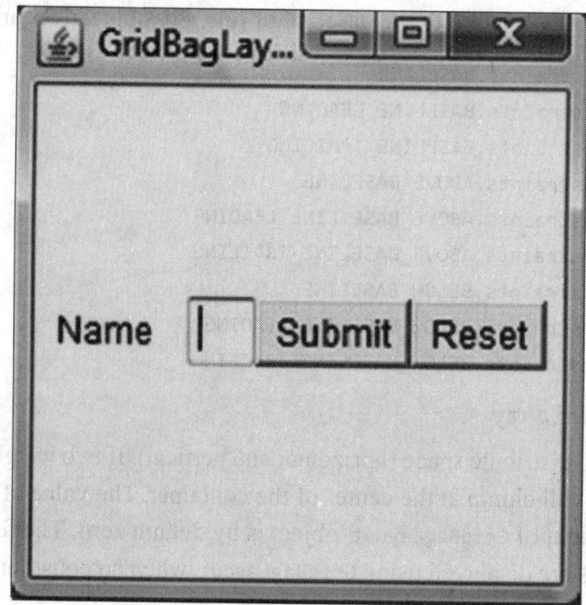

Fig. 14.14 GridBagLayout with no Constraint Specified

Explanation

L1 Imports the `java.awt` package.

L2 Class definition begins.

L3 Constructors defined.

L4 The layout is set to `GridBagLayout()` using `setLayout` method.

L5 `setTitle` method is used for setting the title of the frame.

L6–13 `Label`, `TextField`, and two `Buttons` are created and added to the frame. All the components are displayed by default in a single row and center aligned.

L14–15 Sets the size and visibility of the frame.

Example 14.13 does not place any constraint on the alignment of the components. In the next example, we would place constraint like `fill`, `gridx`, and `gridy` on the components. The `fill` attribute specifies whether components should occupy the entire available space horizontally, vertically, in both directions or not. The `gridx` and `gridy` attributes specify the row and column combination to display the components.

Example 14.14 `GridBagLayout` with `fill`, `gridx`, and `gridy` Constraints

```
L1    import java.awt.*;
L2    public class GBLayoutDemo2 extends Frame {
L3    public GBLayoutDemo2()
      {
L4        setLayout(new GridBagLayout());
L5        setTitle("GridBagLayout With fill, gridx and gridy Constraints");
L6        GridBagConstraints c = new GridBagConstraints();
L7        c.fill = GridBagConstraints.HORIZONTAL;
L8        Label l = new Label("Name");
L9        add(l,c);
L10       TextField t = new TextField();
L11       add(t,c);
L12       c.gridx = 0;
L13       c.gridy = 1;
L14       Button b = new Button("Submit");
L15       add(b,c);
L16       c.gridx = 1;
L17       c.gridy = 1;
L18       Button b1 = new Button("Reset");
L19       add(b1,c);
L20       setSize(200,200);
L21       setVisible(true);
      }
L22   public static void main(String args[])
      {
L23       GBLayoutDemo2 d = new GBLayoutDemo2();
      }
      }
```

Output

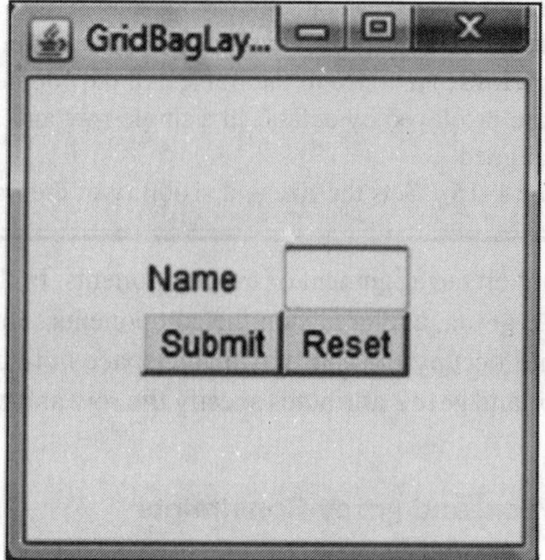

Fig. 14.15(a) `GridBagLayout` with `fill`, `gridx`, and `gridy` Constraints Specified

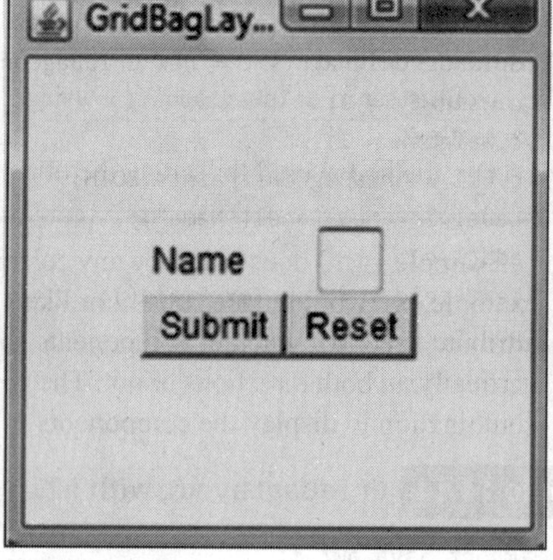

Fig. 14.15(b) Output is Displayed when the `Fill` Attribute is None (L7 is commented)

Explanation

L6 `GridBagConstraints` object is created.

L7 The `fill` attribute is set as HORIZONTAL. The `fill` attribute makes the component fill the space horizontally in its display area and aligns all the components (see Fig. 14.15(a)). If this line is commented, the output displayed is shown in Fig.14.15(b). Note the size of the `TextField`.

L8–9 Label is instantiated and added to the frame along with the constraints specified as second argument in the add method.

L10–11 `TextField` is instantiated and added to the frame along with the constraints specified as second argument in the add method.

L12–13 Specifies `gridx` and `gridy` constraints with values 0 and 1, respectively. The `gridx` constraint is assigned 0 to indicate first column and `gridy` is assigned 1 to indicate second row.

L14–15 A button is added with all the constraint mentioned above, i.e., the button will be added in second row, first column (see Fig.14.15(a)).

L16–17 Specifies `gridx` and `gridy` constraints with values 1 and 1, respectively. The `gridx` constraint is assigned 1 to indicate second column and `gridy` is assigned 1 to indicate second row.

L18–19 Another button is added with a new constraint mentioned above, i.e., the button will be displayed in second row, second column (see Fig. 14.15(a)).

In Example 14.14, we had used only `gridx`, `gridy`, and `fill` constraints. But still the components are displayed only in the center of the frame. To distribute the extra horizontal and vertical space in the rows and columns, the `weightx` and `weighty` attributes are used.

Example 14.15 `GridBagLayout with weightx, weighty, and ipady Constraints`

```
L1    import java.awt.*;
L2    public class GBLayoutDemo3 extends Frame {
```

```
L3    public GBLayoutDemo3() {
L4      setLayout(new GridBagLayout());
L5      setTitle("GridBagLayout with weightx, weighty and ipady Constraints");
L6      GridBagConstraints c = new GridBagConstraints();
L7      c.weighty = 1;
L8      c.weightx = 1;
L9      c.fill = GridBagConstraints.BOTH;
L10     Label l = new Label("Name");
L11     add(l,c);
L12     TextField t = new TextField();
L13     add(t,c);
L14     c.gridx = 0;
L15     c.gridy = 1;
L16     Button b = new Button("Submit");
L17     add(b,c);
L18     c.fill = GridBagConstraints.NONE;
L19     c.gridx = 1;
L20     c.gridy = 2;
L21     c.ipady = 30;
L22     Button b1 = new Button("Reset");
L23     add(b1,c);
L24     setSize(200,200);
L25     setVisible(true); }
L26     public static void main(String args[])
        {
L27       GBLayoutDemo3 d = new GBLayoutDemo3();
        }
      }
```

Output

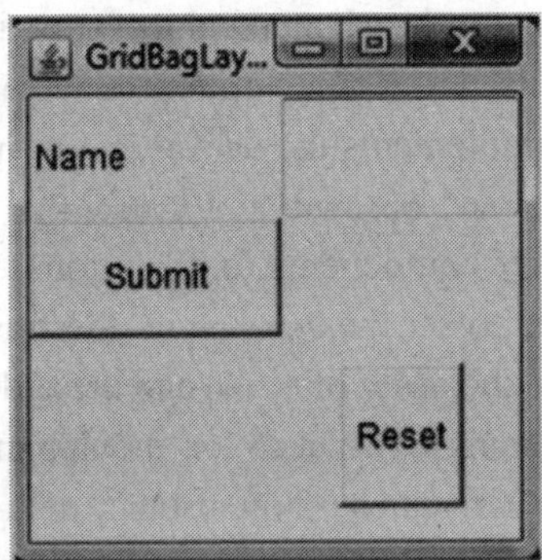

Fig. 14.16(a) GridBagLayout with Constraint of weighty specified Apart from weightx and ipady

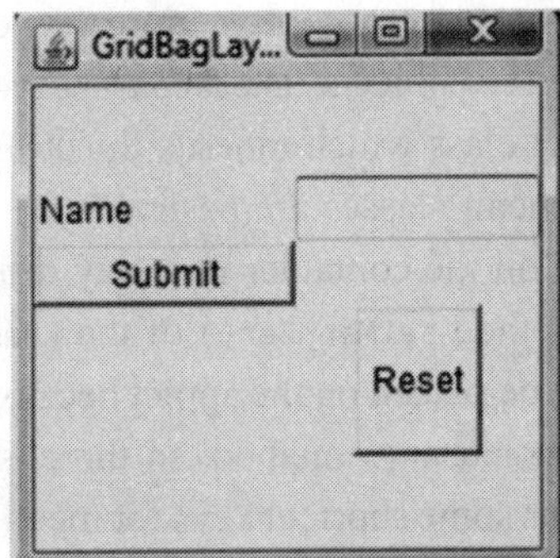

Fig. 14.16(b) GridBagLayout with weightx and ipady Constraints Specified (L7 commented)

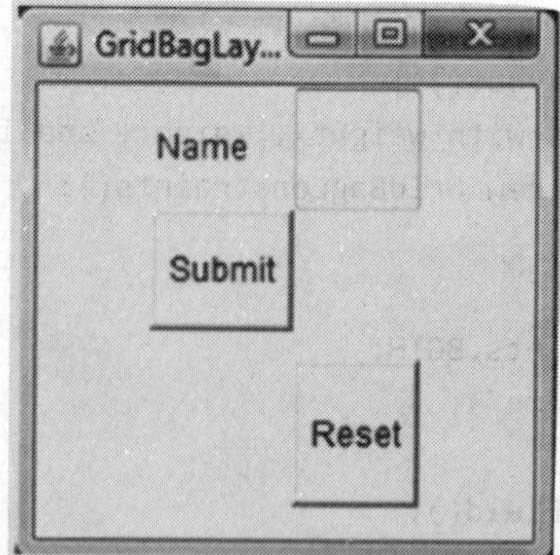

Fig. 14.16(c) GridBagLayout with weighty and ipady Constraints Specified
(L8 commented)

Explanation

L7–8   weightx and weighty are specified as 1 and the fill attribute is specified as BOTH, so the components fill up the area horizontally and vertically (see Fig. 14.16(a)). If only weightx is specified, then components occupy the area horizontally (see Fig. 14.16(b)) because the extra horizontal space is distributed among columns. If only weighty is specified, then components occupy the area vertically (see Fig. 14.16(c)) because extra vertical space is distributed among rows.

L18   The fill attribute is specified as none for the reset button.

L21   The ipady attribute is used to specify the vertical pad for the reset button. Take a note of the size of the reset button in Fig. 14.16(a).

14.12 MENU

Menu is a class which inherits MenuItem class and two interfaces: MenuContainer and Accessible. Menubar deploys a menu object which is a dropdown menu component. It shows a list of menu choices. To implement this concept, we use three classes: MenuBar, Menu, and MenuItem. The various fields, constructors, and methods belonging to the Menu class are mentioned in Table 14.15.

A menubar may contain more than one menu objects and each menu object contains a number of MenuItem objects. CheckboxMenuItem can also be used as a menu option. MenuComponent is an abstract class which inherits the Object class and implements the Serializable interface. All these menu classes are basically the subclasses of MenuComponent, not Component. So they are placed on the container in a way different from other components (e.g., buttons, labels, etc.). The method setMenuBar() of the Frame class is used to set the menubar on the frame. Menubar cannot be placed on the applet because they are not subclasses of Frame and these do not inherit the setMenuBar() method, so there is no way of placing a menubar on the applet. A menubar contains some shortcut keys for menu items. A menu item can have an instance of MenuShortcut. Menu subclass overrides the method and does not send any event to the frame until one of its subitems is selected. The setMenuBar() method is used to associate a menu bar with frame. The constructors and methods belonging to the MenuBar class are mentioned in Table 14.16.

Table 14.15 Menu Class

Constructors of Menu	
Constructors	**Description**
`Menu()`	Creates a new menu.
`Menu(String label)`	Creates a new menu with a label.
`Menu(String label, boolean tearOff)`	Creates a new menu with a label, indicating whether the menu can be torn off.
Methods of Menu	
Methods	**Description**
`add(MenuItem m)`	Adds the specified menu item to the menu.
`add(String label)`	Adds a item with the specified label to the menu.
Methods of Menu	
Methods	**Description**
`deleteShorcut(MenuShortcut s)`	Used to delete the menu shortcuts.
`getAccessibleContext()`	Gets the `AccessibleContext` associated with this menu.
`getItemCount()`	Gets the number of items in the menu.
`getItem(int index)`	Gets the item located at the given index of the menu.
`removeAll()`	Removes all items from the menu.

Table 14.16 MenuBar Class

Constructors of MenuBar	
Constructors	**Description**
`MenuBar( )`	Creates a new menubar.
Methods of MenuBar	
Methods	**Description**
`add(Menu m)`	Adds the particular menu to the menu bar.
`deleteShorcut(MenuShortcuts)`	Used to deletes the specified menu shortcut.
`getAccessibleContext()`	Gets the `AccessibleContext` associated with this `MenuBar`.
`shortcuts()`	Used to manage menu bar shortcut as an Enumeration.
`remove(int index)`	Removes the menu placed at the specified index from the Menubar.

Steps to Add Menus to a Frame

- Create a menu bar instance and set the menu bar

```
setMenuBar(mbar);
```

- Create a menu

```
Menu fmenu = new menu ("File")
```

- Create `MenuItem`'s for menu

```
MenuItem n = new MenuItem ("New")
CheckboxMenuItem o = new CheckboxMenuItem ("Abc")
```

- For handling events

```
n.addActionListence (this)
```

- Add `menuItem` to the menu

```
fmenu.add(n); fmenu.add(o);
```

- Add menu to the `menubar`

```
mbar.add(fmenu);
```

MenuItem It extends the `MenuComponent` class and implements the `Accessible` and `Serializable` interface. All items contained in a menu must belong to the class `MenuItem`, or one of its subclasses. Table 14.17 shows the constructors of `MenuItem`.

MenuShortcut It inherits the `Object` class and implements `Serializable` interface. The `MenuShortcut` class acts as a keyboard accelerator for a `MenuItem`. These are not created by characters but by some keycodes like `Ctrl-c`, `Ctrl-v`. Table 14.18 lists the constructors of `MenuShortcut`.

Table 14.17 Constructors of `MenuItem`

Constructor Name	Description
`MenuItem()`	Constructs a new `MenuItem` with an blank label and there is no keyboard shortcut.
`MenuItem(String label)`	Constructs a new `MenuItem` with the mentioned label and also there is no keyboard shortcut.
`MenuItem(String label, MenuShortcut s)`	Create a menu item with particular keyboard shortcut.

Table 14.18 Constructors of `MenuShortcut`

Constructor Name	Description
`MenuShortcut(int key)`	Constructs a menu shortcut with a keycode.
`MenuShortcut(int key, boolean useShiftModifier)`	The menu shortcut creates with a keycode and boolean value indicates that shift key be used with keycode.

Example 14.16 **Menu Demo**

```
L1    import java.awt.event.*;
L2    import java.awt.*;
L3    public class DemoMenu extends Frame implements ActionListener {
L4    public void demoMenu() {
L5    setTitle("MenuDemo");
L6    setSize(250,150);
L7    MenuBar menuBar = new MenuBar();
L8    setMenuBar(menuBar);
L9    MenuShortcut n = new MenuShortcut(KeyEvent.VK_N);
```

```java
L10      MenuShortcut o = new MenuShortcut(KeyEvent.VK_O);
L11      MenuShortcut x = new MenuShortcut(KeyEvent.VK_X);
L12      Menu fileMenu = new Menu("File");
L13      Menu editMenu = new Menu("Edit");
         // create and add simple menu item to one of the dropdown menu
L14      MenuItem newAction = new MenuItem("New",n);
L15      MenuItem openAction = new MenuItem("Open",o);
L16      MenuItem exitAction = new MenuItem("Exit",x);
L17      MenuItem cutAction = new MenuItem("Cut");
L18      MenuItem copyAction = new MenuItem("Copy");
L19      MenuItem pasteAction = new MenuItem("Paste");
L20      newAction.addActionListener(this);
L21      openAction.addActionListener(this);
L22      exitAction.addActionListener(this);
L23      fileMenu.addSeparator();
L24      fileMenu.add(newAction);
L25      fileMenu.addSeparator();
L26      fileMenu.add(openAction);
L27      fileMenu.addSeparator();
L28      fileMenu.add(exitAction);
L29      menuBar.add(fileMenu);
L30      cutAction.addActionListener(this);
L31      copyAction.addActionListener(this);
L32      pasteAction.addActionListener(this);
L33      editMenu.add(cutAction);
L34      editMenu.addSeparator();
L35      editMenu.add(copyAction);
L36      editMenu.addSeparator();
L37      editMenu.add(pasteAction);
L38      editMenu.addSeparator();
L39      menuBar.add(editMenu);
L40      setVisible(true);
L41      addWindowListener(new WindowAdapter(){
L42      public void windowClosing(WindowEvent we){
L43      System.exit(0);
         }
         });
         }
L44  public void actionPerformed(ActionEvent e) {
L45      String action = e.getActionCommand();
L46      if(action.equals("New")){
L47         System.out.println("New");
         }
L48      else if(action.equals("Open")){
L49         System.out.println("File");
         }
L50      else if(action.equals("Exit")){
```

```
L51         System.exit(0);
        }
L52     else if(action.equals("Cut")){
L53         System.out.println("Cut");
        }
L54     else if(action.equals("Copy")){
L55         System.out.println("Copy");
        }
L56     else if(action.equals("Paste")){
L57         System.out.println("Paste");
        }
    }
L58  public static void main(String[] args) {
L59      DemoMenu demo= new DemoMenu();
L60      demo.demoMenu();
    } }
```

Output

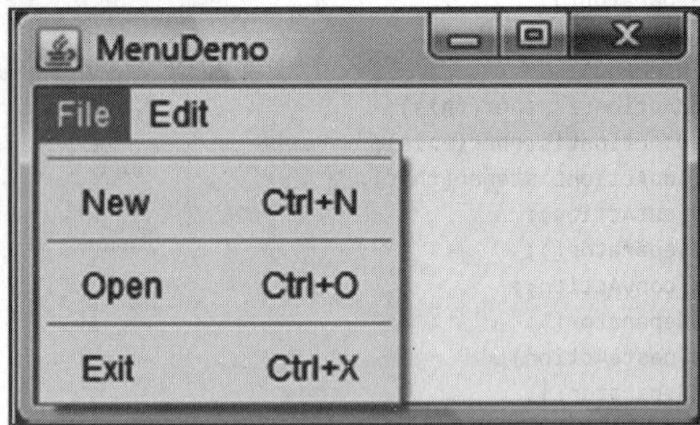

Fig. 14.17(a) A Sample Menu

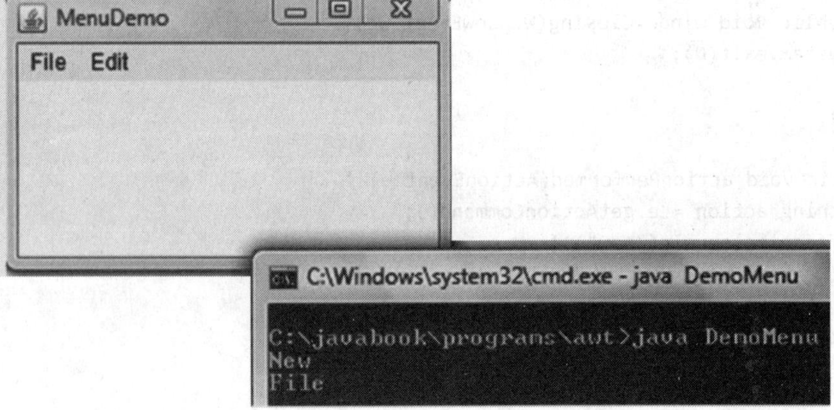

Fig. 14.17(b) A Sample of Output Displayed from Menu by Pressing Shortcut Keys

Explanation

L7–8 `MenuBar` object is created and it is set on the frame using the method `setMenuBar`.

L9–11 Three `MenuShortcuts` have been created with the keys n, o, and x. Pressing `Ctrl + n` would refer to a menu onto which it is added.

L12–13 Two menus have been created: `fileMenu` and `editMenu`.

L14–16 Three `MenuItems` have been created and shortcuts have been specified for all the three as arguments in the constructors (these will be added to file menu).

L17–19 Three other `MenuItem` have been created without any shortcuts (these will be added to edit menu).

L20–22 The menu items are registered with `ActionListener` for receiving event notifications.

L23–28 Three menu items created in L14–16 are added to the `fileMenu` using the add method. A separator (line) is added after every menu item using `addSeparator` method.

L 29 `fileMenu` is added to `MenuBar`.

L30–32 Three menu items (created in L17–19) are registered with `ActionListener` for receiving event notifications.

L33–38 Three menu items created in L17–19 are added to the `editMenu` using add method. A separator (line) is added after every menu item using `addSeparator` method.

L39 The `editMenu` is added to the menu bar.

L46–57 If *New* menu item is clicked or `ctrl+n` key is pressed, then L47 is executed and so on for the rest of cases.

14.13 SCROLLBAR

Scrollbars are used to select continuous values through a range of integer values (the range set between maximum and minimum). These scrollbars can either be set horizontally or vertically. The scrollbar's maximum and minimum values can be set along with line increments and page increments.

For creating a scrollbar, you have to create an instance of the `Scrollbar` class. This class defines the following constructors:

```
Scrollbar() throws HeadlessException
Scrollbar(int direction) throws HeadlessException
Scrollbar(int direction, int initValue, int pageSize, int min, int max) throws
HeadlessException
```

The first constructor does not have any argument; by default it creates a vertical scrollbar. In the second and third constructors, the direction as argument specifies the orientation of the scrollbar. If the directions can either be specified as `Scrollbar.VERTICAL` or `Scrollbar.HORIZONTAL`, then vertical or horizontal scrollbars respectively are created. The third constructor can have the initial value of the scrollbar passed as argument `initValue`, the number of units represented by height of the page that gets incremented or decremented when the scrollbar is clicked between the arrow and the scroll box is passed as argument `pageSize` and the minimum and maximum values for the scrollbar passed as argument 'min' and 'max'.

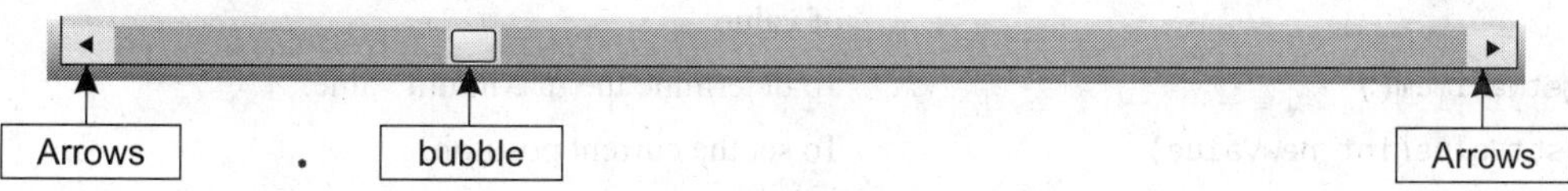

Fig. 14.18

The following line will create a horizontal scrollbar:

```
Scrollbar demoScroll1 = new Scrollbar(Scrollbar.HORIZONTAL);
```

The following line will create a vertical scrollbar with a starting position of 0, a thumb (bubble) size of 5, a minimum value of 0, and a maximum value of 255:

```
Scrollbar demoScroll2 =new Scrollbar(Scrollbar.VERTICAL, 0, 5, 0, 255);
```

There are three different parts of a scrollbar that allow you to select a value between the maximum and minimum in different ways. The arrows increment or decrement with the line updates which can be set to a small unit. By default its value is 1. If you click anywhere within the maximum and minimum range on a scrollbar, the page value will be either incremented or decremented by a value 10 (default value). The bubble in the middle allows you to traverse the scrollbar quickly from one end to the other by clicking and dragging it. The visible portion is represented by the bubble (box in scrollbar). The size of the bubble is represented by the third argument (5) as shown in the constructor. Table 14.19 lists the methods that can be used with scrollbars.

Interaction with the scrollbar generates an `AdjustmentEvent` object. The `getAdjustment()` method of the `AdjustmentEvent` class is used to obtain the type of adjustment. The types which can be returned by this method are

- BLOCK_DECREMENT: means 'page-down event been generated.
- BLOCK_DECREMENT: means 'page-event event has been generated'
- TRACK: means 'absolute tracking event has been generated'
- UNIT_DECREMENT: means 'line-down button in the scrollbar has been generated'
- UNIT_INCREMENT: means 'line-up button in the scrollbar has been generated'

Table 14.19 Methods of `Scrollbar`

Method	Description
`void setValues(int initValue, int pageSize, int min, int max)`	The parameters here mean the same as in the third constructor mentioned above. If you have used either of the first two constructors to create a scrollbar you set the values by the above method so that the values of the above parameters are set for the scrollbar.
`int getLineIncrement()`	To determine the value of the line increment.
`void setPageIncrement(int pageSize)`	To set the page increment.
`int getPageIncrement()`	To determine the value of the page increment.
`int getMinimum()`	To determine the minimum value.
`void setUnitIncrement(int newUnitInc)`	To set the unit increment by new value.
`int getValue()`	To determine the current position of the scrollbar in terms of value.
`int getMaximum()`	To determine the maximum value.
`void setValue(int newValue)`	To set the current position.
`void setBlockIncrement (int newBlockInc)`	To set the block increment for page-up and page-down by a new value.

Example 14.17   Scrollbar

```java
import java.awt.*;
import java.awt.event.*;
public class ScrollbarDemo extends Frame implements AdjustmentListener {
Scrollbar HScroll, VScroll;
Label lbl;
int X = 100,Y = 150;
public ScrollbarDemo () {
  HScroll = new Scrollbar (Scrollbar.HORIZONTAL);
  VScroll = new Scrollbar (Scrollbar.VERTICAL);
  lbl = new Label ("",Label.CENTER);
  HScroll.setMaximum (400);
  VScroll.setMaximum (400);
  setBackground (Color.cyan);
setTitle("Oval size changes with scrollbar movements");
setLayout (new BorderLayout());
add (lbl,BorderLayout.NORTH);
add (HScroll,BorderLayout.SOUTH);
add (VScroll, BorderLayout.EAST);
HScroll.addAdjustmentListener (this);
VScroll.addAdjustmentListener (this);
HScroll.setValue (X);
VScroll.setValue (Y);
lbl.setText ("HScroll = " + HScroll.getValue() + ", VScroll = " + VScroll.getValue());
setSize(500,500);
setVisible(true);
addWindowListener(new WindowAdapter()
{
public void windowClosing(WindowEvent e) {
    System.exit(0);
}
});
}
public void adjustmentValueChanged(AdjustmentEvent e){
X = HScroll.getValue();
Y = VScroll.getValue ();
lbl.setText ("HScroll =" + X + ", VScroll =" + Y);
repaint();
}
public void paint (Graphics g) {
    g.drawOval (50, 60, X, Y); }
public static void main(String args[])
{
    ScrollbarDemo d = new ScrollbarDemo();
}}
```

Output

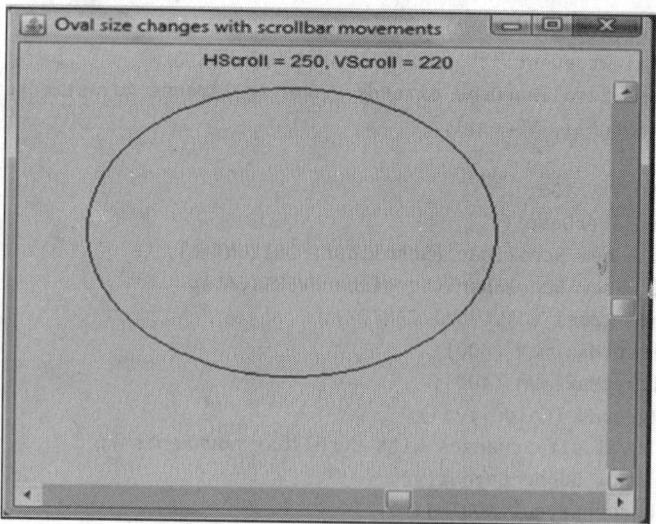

Fig. 14.19

Explanation

L1–2 Imports the necessary packages.

L3 Frame is created which inherits `AdjustmentLis-tener` for tapping scrollbar events.

L4–6 Two scrollbar references (one for horizontal and another for vertical scrollbar) have been created with one label for displaying the position of the horizontal and vertical scrollbars. Two integer variables, X and Y, are defined for specifying the exact position of the scrollbars. Also, these two variables form the width and height of our oval (see Fig. 14.19(b)).

L7 Constructor for the class has been defined.

L8–9 Horizontal and vertical scrollbars are instantiated. Their orientations have been specified as `Scrollbar.HORIZONTAL` and `Scrollbar.VERTICAL`.

L10 Label is instantiated to show the value of the scrollbar.

L11–12 The maximum range is set for both the scrollbars using the method `setMaximum(400)`. Actually if you click on the arrow in the scrollbar and scroll it till the maximum, the value that the label will show will be 390 because the size of the bubble is 10 by default. So the range is actually 0 to 390.

L13 The background color is set as cyan.

L14 The title of the frame is set using the method `setTitle()`.

L15 The layout is set to `BorderLayout`.

L16–18 The three components: horizontal scrollbar, vertical scrollbar, and label are added in the EAST, SOUTH, and NORTH directions, respectively.

L19–20 Both scrollbars are registered with `AdjustmentListener`.

L21–23 The initial value for the horizontal and vertical scrollbar is set as 100 and 150 respectively using the `setValue` method and initial scrollbar values are set as text of the label in L23.

L24–28 The size of the frame and its visibility is set. Apart from this, the frame is registered with the `WindowListener` to track window closing event.

L29–33 The method of the `AdjustmentListener` is overridden, i.e., `adjustmentValueChanged (AdjustmentEvent e)`. This method will be invoked whenever the scrollbar is adjusted. As the scrollbars are moved, the **x** and **y** values change and so the width and height of the oval. The label is set with the current values of the horizontal and vertical scrollbar and then the frame is repainted.

L34–35 `paint` method is overridden and oval is drawn using the `drawOval` method of the `Graphics` object. The first two coordinates in the oval are fixed.

The width and height are variables and they depend upon the scrollbar movements. The signature of drawOval method is shown below:

```
g.draw Oval (int x, int y, int width, int
height)
```

L36–37 In the main method, the frame is instantiated.

14.14 PRACTICAL PROBLEM: CITY MAP APPLET

CityMap applet shows map of a city (top view) with five buttons namely hospitals, shopping malls, police station, post office, and stadium. If a user presses the hospital button, all hospitals are shown on the map with a specific color and likewise for malls, police station, post office and stadium.

Example 14.18 `CityMap.java`

```java
import java.applet.*;
import java.awt.*;
import java.awt.event.*;

/*<applet code = "CityMap.class" width=650 height=600></applet>*/

public class CityMap extends Applet
 {
   Button b1,b2,b3,b4,b5;

   /* boolean Variables used as flag variables */
   boolean hospital,mall,pstation,po,stadium;

   public void init()
   {
     /* Buttons are created and added on the applet. */
     b1 = new Button("Hospital");
     add(b1);
     b2 = new Button("Shopping Malls");
     add(b2);
     b3 = new Button("Police Station");
     add(b3);
     b4 = new Button("Post office");
     add(b4);
     b5 = new Button("Stadium");
     add(b5);
```

```
/* Anonymous inner classes are defined for all buttons. If listener approach (for
event handling) is used and ActionListener is implemented by the Applet class for
handling button events, then for all five buttons, we have a single "actionPerformed"
method. In the "actionPerformed" we use the if...else..if conditional statement for
knowing which button has been pressed and then we perform the desired task within
that. So there will be five if conditions, one for each button, and these conditions
will be checked every time the button is pressed till a match is found. In our ex-
ample below, each button is registered with its own Event handler, thereby eliminat-
ing the annoying multiple if statements and saving execution time*/
```

```
/*creates an Anonymous inner class for hospital button. As soon as the hospital but-
ton is pressed, the actionPerformed of this class is invoked which sets the hospital
Boolean variable to true and repaints the applet. Explicit class name is not provid-
ed by the programmer but the compiler generates the .class file for this inner class
with the name "CityMap$1.class" */


b1.addActionListener(new ActionListener()
    {
        public void actionPerformed(ActionEvent ae)
        {
            /*sets the Boolean variable to true and repaints the applet*/
            hospital = true;
            repaint();
        }
    });


    b2.addActionListener(new ActionListener()
    {
        public void actionPerformed(ActionEvent ae)
        {
            /*sets the Boolean variable to true and repaints the applet*/
            mall = true;
            repaint();
        }
    });
    b3.addActionListener(new ActionListener()
    {
        public void actionPerformed(ActionEvent ae)
        {
            /*sets the Boolean variable to true and repaints the applet*/
            pstation = true;
            repaint();
        }
    });


    b4.addActionListener(new ActionListener()
    {
        public void actionPerformed(ActionEvent ae)
        {
            /*sets the Boolean variable to true and repaints the applet*/
            po=true;
            repaint();
        }
    });

    b5.addActionListener(new ActionListener()
    {
        public void actionPerformed(ActionEvent ae)
        {
            /*sets the Boolean variable to true and repaints the applet*/
            stadium = true;
```

```java
            repaint();
        }
    });
}

public void paint( Graphics g)
{
   /* outer black rectangle*/
   g.drawRect(5,40,630,550);

   g.drawLine(106,41,106,167);
   g.drawArc(77,150,30,30,-10,-70);
   g.drawLine(6,180,95,180);

   /*Rectangle with rounded edges is created with black color*/
   g.drawRoundRect(155,50,180,100,30,30);

   g.drawLine(400,41,400,200);
   g.drawLine(410,210,600,210);
   g.drawArc(400,191,18,20,-90,-90);
   g.drawArc(590,210,18,20,-10,90);

   g.drawLine(609,222,609,319);
   g.drawArc(590,309,18,20,0,-90);
   g.drawLine(550,400,603,327);
   g.drawArc(545,400,20,20,110,90);
   g.drawLine(545,407,545,541);
   g.drawLine(220,550,538,550);
   g.drawArc(213,550,20,20,90,90);
   g.drawArc(524,530,20,20,0,-90);
   g.drawLine(170,180,250,180);
   g.drawArc(160,180,20,20,90,90);
   g.drawArc(240,180,20,20,90,-90);
   g.drawLine(260,190,260,230);
   g.drawArc(260,220,20,20,-180,90);
   g.drawLine(270,241,320,241);
   g.drawArc(307,241,20,20,90,-90);
   g.drawLine(327,252,327,283);

   g.setColor(Color.GREEN);
/* The drawOval of fillOval method creates a circle if width and height of oval is
same. creates a circle which is filled with green color*/
   g.fillOval(305,165,60,60);

/* creates an inner circle with white color at x=310 (5 pixels ahead of the previous
circle) and y=170 (5 pixels below the previous circle)
   with width and height=50*/
   g.setColor(Color.WHITE);
   g.fillOval(310,170,50,50);

/*creates an unfilled circle with black color within the broad lined circle created above */
```

```java
g.setColor(Color.BLACK);
g.drawOval(330,190,10,10);

g.drawArc(306,273,20,20,0,-90);
g.drawLine(170,293,315,293);
g.drawLine(160,190,160,283);
g.drawArc(160,272,20,20,-180,90);
g.drawLine(400,240,546,240);
g.drawArc(532,240,20,20,0,90);
g.drawLine(552,250,552,315);
g.drawArc(531,305,20,20,0,-70);
g.drawLine(500,400,548,323);
g.drawArc(497,398,10,10,110,130);
g.drawLine(498,408,498,510);
g.drawArc(477,498,20,20,0,-90);
g.drawLine(400,519,488,519);
g.drawArc(390,498,20,20,-90,-90);
g.drawLine(390,250,390,510);
g.drawArc(390,239,20,20,90,90);
g.drawRoundRect(6,200,115,230,20,20);
g.drawLine(6,480,112,480);
g.drawArc(98,480,20,20,0,90);
g.drawLine(116,486,150,570);
g.drawLine(212,561,220,580);
g.drawOval(170,330,150,150);

/*if Hospital button is pressed*/
if(hospital)
{
g.setColor(Color.BLACK);
g.fillOval(100,100,10,10);
g.fillOval(250,250,10,10);
g.fillOval(120,500,10,10);
g.fillOval(400,200,10,10);
g.fillOval(450,400,10,10);
hospital=false;
}
/*if shopping mall button is pressed*/
if(mall)
{
g.setColor(Color.PINK);
g.fillOval(200,70,10,10);
g.fillOval(450,100,10,10);
g.fillOval(110,300,10,10);
g.fillOval(400,300,10,10);
g.fillOval(250,550,10,10);
   mall=false;
}
/*if police station button is pressed*/
if(pstation)
{
```

```
g.setColor(Color.YELLOW);
g.fillOval(220,70,10,10);
g.fillOval(300,550,10,10);
g.fillOval(110,500,10,10);
g.fillOval(420,200,10,10);
g.fillOval(500,350,10,10);
   pstation=false;
}
/*if post office button is pressed*/
if(po)
{
g.setColor(Color.BLUE);
g.fillOval(80,150,10,10);
g.fillOval(100,350,10,10);
g.fillOval(500,80,10,10);
g.fillOval(590,400,10,10);
g.fillOval(390,550,10,10);
po=false;
}
/*if stadium button is pressed*/
if(stadium)
{
/*sets the color as black and creates 10 adjacent Circles. First Circle at
(x=170,y=330), second at (x=171,y=331), third at (x=172,y=332) and soon.*/
   g.setColor(Color.BLACK);
   for(int i=0;i<10;i++)
   g.drawOval(i+170,i+330,150,150);
   stadium=false;
}
      }
   }
}
```

Output

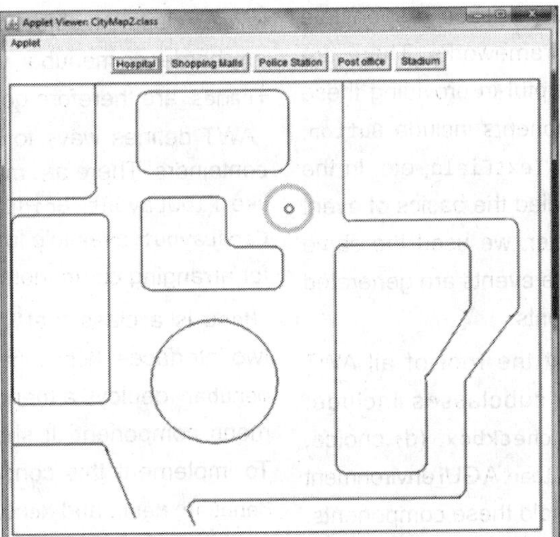

Fig. 14.20(a)

Figure 14.20(a) shows the map of a city with roads, buildings, round circles, and a stadium.

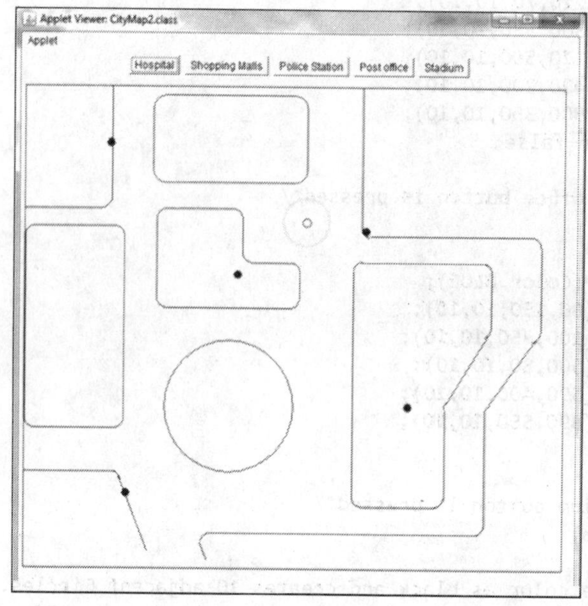

Fig. 14.20(b)

Figure 14.20(b) highlights the hospitals in the map as the hospital button is clicked.

SUMMARY

In this chapter, we have emphasized on those computing aspects of Java that use graphical user interface (GUI) for input and output. Java has a package named as `java.awt`, having various classes responsible for generating various GUI frameworks. There are various AWT components helpful in providing these GUI structures. These components include `Button`, `Scrollbar`, `Choicebox`, `List`, `TextField`, etc. In the previous chapter, we had studied the basics of event handling model. In this chapter, we used the same event delegation model, where events are generated through various GUI components.

The `Component` class is at the root of all AWT components whose direct subclasses include: (a) `button`, (b) `canvas`, (c) `checkbox`, (d) `choice`, (e) `label`, (f) `list`, and (g) `scrollbar`. A GUI environment always needs a container to hold these components.

For this purpose, AWT package has a class known as 'Container'. It may be noted that `Panel` class is a superclass of `Applet` class. `Frame` is a subclass of `Window` class. An object of `Window` class does not have any border or menubar, while a `Frame` can have these. `frames` are therefore generally used as containers.

AWT defines ways to lay the AWT components in containers. There are many layout managers in AWT like `FlowLayout`, `GridLayout`, `GridBagLayout`, and `CardLayout`, available for setting out different patterns for arranging components in containers.

`Menu` is a class that inherits `MenuItem` class and two interfaces: `MenuContainer` and `Accessible`. The menubar deploys a menu object which is a dropdown menu component. It shows a list of menu choices. To implement this concept, we use three classes: `MenuBar`, `Menu`, and `MenuItem`.

EXERCISES

Objective Questions

1. What will be the result of compiling and running the following code?
   ```java
   import java.awt.*;
   import java.applet.*;
   public class Test extends Applet {
     Label l = new Label("Hello");
     public void init() {
       setSize(200,100);
       setVisible(true);
       l.setBackground(new Col
   or(0,100,180));
       setLayout(new GridLayout(1,1));
       add(l);
       setLayout(new FlowLayout());
       l.setBounds(0,0,100,24);
     }
   }
   ```
   (a) The label will fill half the display area of the applet.
   (b) The label will be wide enough to display the text "Hello"
   (c) The label will not be visible.
   (d) The label will fill the entire display area of the applet

2. Which of the following are valid constructors for a `TextField`?
   (a) `TextField();`
   (b) `TextField(int cols);`
   (c) `TextField(int rows, int cols);`
   (d) `TextField(int cols, String txt);`

3. What is the default layout for a `Dialog`?
   (a) `FlowLayout`   (b) `GridLayout`
   (c) `CardLayout`   (d) `BorderLayout`

4. What is the default layout for `Frame`?

   (a) `FlowLayout`   (b) `GridLayout`
   (c) `CardLayout`   (d) `BorderLayout`

5. What is the default layout for `Applet`?
   (a) `FlowLayout`   (b) `GridLayout`
   (c) `CardLayout`   (d) `BorderLayout`

6. What method is used to change the layout of a container?
   (a) `setLayout`   (b) `setFlowLayout`
   (c) `setBorderLayout`   (d) `setCardlayout`

7. Using `BorderLayout`, you can place components along
   (a) NORTH   (b) CENTER
   (c) SOUTH   (d) All of the above

8. Which listener is associated with `MenuItem` class?
   (a) `ActionListner`   (b) `MouseListner`
   (c) `ItemListner`   (d) `EventListner`

9. What are the possible types of values of an anchor field in a `GridBagLayout`?
   (a) absolute
   (b) orientation-relative
   (c) baseline-relative
   (d) all the above

10. Which of the following is true about `GridBagCon-straints`?
    (a) It contains the constraint which includes the height, width of a cell, placement and alignment of components.
    (b) Each `GridBagLayout` object maintains a rectangular grid of cell.
    (c) A component can occupy one or more cells and it is called its display area.
    (d) None of the above.

Review Questions

1. What are the component and container classes?

2. Which method of the component class is used to set the position and size of a component?

3. What is the difference between the `Font` and `FontMetrics` class?

4. Explain the hierarchy of classes in the `java.awt` package.

5. What are the different types of AWT components? How are these components added to containers?

6. Explain the process of creating a frame and adding a button to it.

7. Compare the different layout managers in brief.

8. What are the methods used to set foreground and background colors?

Programming Exercises

1. Write an AWT program to create checkboxes for different courses belonging to a university such that the courses selected would be displayed.

2. Create a frame having `Menubar` and `MenuItems` attached to it as follows:

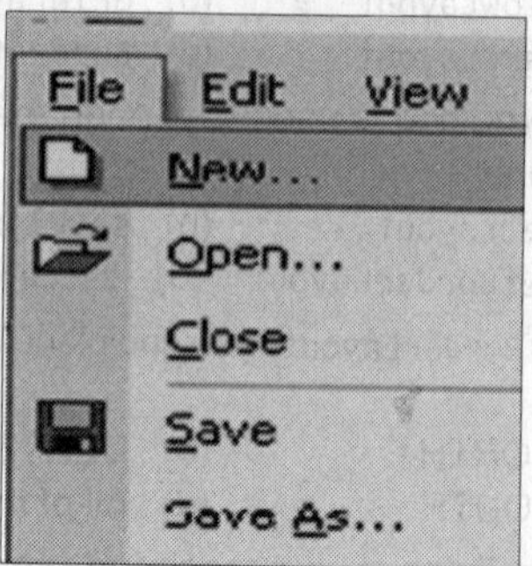

3. Create a frame and set the color of the frame to red.

4. Create a list of vegetables. If you click on one of the items of the list, the item should be displayed in a textbox.

5. Write a program using AWT to create a simple calculator. (Hint: Use proper `Layout Manager`)

6. Write a temperature conversion program that converts from Fahrenheit to Celsius. The Fahrenheit temperature should be entered from keyboard (via `Textfield`). A `Textfield` should be used to display the converted temperature. Use the following formula for the conversion:

Celsius = 5/9*(Fahrenheit–32)

7. Write an application that plays 'guess the number' as follows:

Your application chooses the number to be guessed by selecting an integer at random in the range 1–1000. The application then displays the following in a label:

I have a number between 1 and 1000. Can you guess my number?

Please enter your first guess.

A `Textfield` should be used to input the guess. As each guess is input, the background colour should change to either red or blue. A label should display either 'Too High' or 'Too Low' to help the user zero in. When the user gets the correct answer, 'Correct' should be displayed, and the `TextField` used for input should be changed to be uneditable. A button should be provided to allow the user to play the game again. When the button is clicked, a new random number should be generated and the input `TextField` changed to be `editable`.

Answers to Objective Questions

1. (b)	**2.** (a), (b)	**3.** (d)	**4.** (d)
5. (a)	**6.** (a)	**7.** (d)	**8.** (a)
9. (d)	**10.** (a), (b) (c)		

Swing

A picture is worth a thousand words   **Napoleon Bonaparte**

After reading this chapter, the readers will be able to

- understand the difference between AWT and swing
- program various swing containers and components
- play with new layouts
- use components and create GUI
- learn dialog boxes in swings
- understand the pluggable look and feel

15.1 INTRODUCTION

AWT is used for creating GUI in Java, but the components in `java.awt` are heavyweight components. AWT provides graphical user interface with certain limitations. One major limitation is the translation of various components into their corresponding, platform-specific equivalents or operating system equivalents. The look and feel of a component is not defined by Java but by the platform itself. The components of AWT use native code resource and are therefore called heavyweight components. These components look different on different platforms and even they act differently on different platforms. Heavyweight components also have a restriction that they are always rectangular. It is very difficult to work with AWT, for example, if we want to re-position a button slightly to the right or left, we have to do various modifications in our source code and recompile it again.

Swing (`javax.swing`) is the solution for the problems faced in AWT. Swing is the set of GUI-related classes supplied with JDK1.2 and later. Swing components use *modelview-controller* architecture for all its components, thus providing greater flexibility. All swing components have a model, view, and a controller. *Model* manages the state and the behavior of the component. *View* manages the display of the component depending upon the state, and *controller* governs the interaction of the user with the model. *Controller* basically determines when and how the state of the model will change.

Swing GUI components are event-driven. Swing provides a very good programming approach to build a GUI application using OOP concepts. It is included in Java as a part of JFC (Java foundation classes). It contains all the features of AWT but swing components are called lightweight because they are developed using Java and hence they are platform independent. In other words, they do not depend on native counterparts (peers) to handle their functionality. In total, swings have 18 packages but generally, most programmers use the following packages:

- `javax.swing`
- `javax.swing.event`

15.1.1 Features of Swing

Some of the common features of swing are

- Swing components are lightweight. They are not built on native window-system.
- It has a number of built-in controls: trees, tabbed panes, sliders, toolbars, tables, etc.
- We can customize our GUI application, e.g., we can change the border, text alignment, or add an image to almost any control, and also we can separate internal representation from visual appearance.
- A very attractive feature of swing is its pluggable look and feel. You can change the look and feel of a swing GUI.
- Internationalization allows developers to build applications that can be used across the world in different languages.
- All components are named as `Jxx`, e.g., `JApplet`, `JFrame`, `JButton`, `JLabel`, etc.
- After Java 5, components can be added using `add (Component c)` method. Earlier they were added to containers via the method `getContentPane().add()`.
- All drawing is done in `paintComponent` rather than `paint`.
- Swing is not thread safe. When creating a swing GUI, you need to take extra care if multiple threads are accessing it.

15.1.2 Differences between Swing and AWT

Table 15.1 lists the differences between swing and AWT. Table 15.2 shows some of the classes of AWT and their counterparts in swing. Apart from the classes shown in the table, some other classes have been added in `javax.swing` such as `JRadioButton`, `ButtonGroup`, `JToggleButton`, `JSplitPane`, `JTabbedPane`, `JTree`, `JTable`, `JFileChooser`, `JColorChooser`, `JInternalFrame`, `JDesktopPane`, `JEditorPane`, `JOptionPane`, `JPopUpMenu`, and `Look` and `Feel` classes. We will discuss all these classes in this chapter. We will discuss two new layouts later in the chapter that have been added in the swing package, namely `BoxLayout` and `SpringLayout`.

Table 15.1 Differences between AWT and Swing

AWT	Swing
Heavyweight	Lightweight.
Look and feel is OS based	Look and feel is OS independent.
Not pure Java-based	Pure Java-based.
Platform specific limitation for some components	Fewer platform limitations for components.

(Contd)

(Table 15.1 Contd)

AWT	Swing
Faster	Slower.
Applet portability: mostly web browser supports for applet	Applet portability: A plug-in is required.
Does not support features like icons and tool-tips	Supports features like icons and tool-tips.
The default layout manager for applet: `FlowLayout` and `Frame` is `BorderLayout`	The default layout manager for content pane is `BorderLayout`.

Table 15.2 Classes of AWT and their Counterparts in Swing

Classes in AWT	Corresponding classes in swings	Classes in AWT	Corresponding classes in swings
`Frame`	`JFrame`	`List`	`JList`
`Applet`	`JApplet`	`Menu`	`JMenu`
`Panel`	`JPanel`	`MenuBar`	`JMenuBar`
`Label`	`JLabel`	`MenuItem`	`JMenuItem`
`Button`	`JButton`	`Choice`	`JComboBox`
`TextField`	`JTextField`	`TextArea`	`JTextArea`
`Checkbox`	`JCheckBox`		

Note You can use either swing or AWT for your Java program development, but avoid mixing the two.

15.2 `JFrame`

Swing provides a top-level container to which components are added, e.g., `JFrame`, `JApplet`, etc. `JFrame` is a subclass of `java.awt.Frame` and therefore, it inherits all the features of an AWT frame. Whenever you create a top-level container, an intermediate container of the top-level container named root pane (`JRootPane`) is automatically created. This root pane has four sub-level containers (layers) as shown in Fig. 15.1.

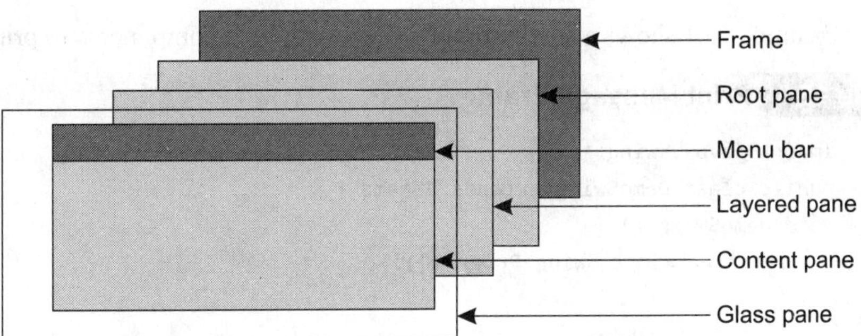

Fig. 15.1 Panes in `JFrame`

- Layered pane (`JLayeredPane`)
- Content pane ()
- Menu bar (optional) (`JMenuBar`)
- Glass pane (`JGlass`)

Every root pane will always have a layered pane, content pane, and a glass pane. The menu bar is optional. A layered pane is a container that positions components into three-dimensions. Actually it adds depth to the container and components can be placed one over the other. The layered pane is responsible for managing the content pane and the menu bar. The glass pane is transparent. It is basically used for intercepting events so that they cannot reach the content pane. The menu bar is used to set the menu on the root pane.

All components are added to a content pane which is an intermediate container. There are two ways of getting a content pane:

- Every container has a content pane. The content pane is obtained using getContentPane()and it returns a Container object (recommended). Prior to JDK 5, the content pane has to be obtained explicitly by using getContentPane() and then add() is used on it, e.g., getContentPane(). add(Component). But now there is no need to obtain the content pane explicitly. You can directly use add() method as shown in Example 15.1.

- Build your own content pane. It is common to create a new panel for the content pane and tell the window to use this new panel as its content pane. For example,

```
class Demo extends JFrame{
...
// JPanel is a also container with FlowLayout as default layout
// so we can use it as our own content pane and add contents to it.
JPanel panel = new JPanel( );
panel.add(...);
panel.add(...);
...
panel.setOpaque(true);
setContentPane(panel);    // set JPanel as the content pane for the JFrame
...
}
```

Example 15.1 shows a small program that uses swing components to print a message.

Example 15.1 **Print Message Frame**

```
L1    import javax.swing.*;
L2    public class DemoSwing extends JFrame {
L3    void demoSwing () {
L4       setTitle("First Swing Program");

         // size of window
L5       setSize(300,200);
L6       setDefaultCloseOperation(EXIT_ON_CLOSE);

         //Add "My first Swing program" label
L7       JLabel label = new JLabel("My first Swing program");
```

```
L8          add(label);

            // Auto fit the component in container
L9          // pack();
            // Display the window.
L10         setVisible(true);
        }

        public static void main(String[] args) {
L11         DemoSwing demo = new DemoSwing();
L12         demo.demoSwing();
        } }
```

Output

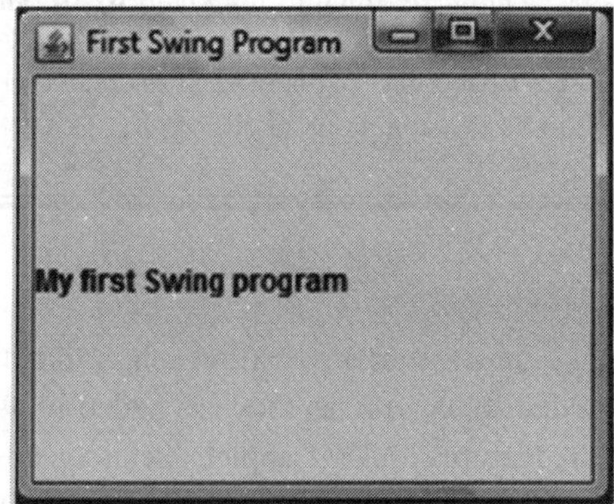

Fig. 15.2(a) Output if the Pack Method is Commented and `SetSize` is Used

Fig. 15.2(b) Output if the Pack Method (L9) is executed

Explanation

L1 For creating a GUI using swing, we have to import the package `javax.swing.*`

L2 The class inherits from `JFrame`. A class needs to be a subclass of `JFrame` for creating frames using swings. (Note that `JFrame` is one of the four heavyweight classes present in the `javax.swing` package. The others being `JApplet`, `JDialog`, and `JWindow`.)

L3 Method `demoSwing` has been defined.

L4 `setTitle` "{First Swing Program}" sets the title of the frame as `FirstSwingProgram` shown in Fig. 15.2(a).

L5 The method `setSize (300,200)` sets the size of the frame. 300 is an integer specifying width in pixels. 200 is an integer specifying height in pixels.

L6 `setDefaultCloseOperation (int operation)` is a method that specifies the operation to be performed when the user closes the frame. The following values can be passed as an argument in this method. All parameters have been defined by `WindowConstants` interface to control the window closing operations.

- `DO_NOTHING_ON_CLOSE` does nothing. It requires you to handle the event using traditional `windowClosing` method.

- `HIDE_ON_CLOSE` hides the frame after invoking any registered `WindowListener` objects.

- H `DISPOSE_ON_CLOSE` hides and disposes the frame after invoking any registered `WindowListener` objects.

- EXIT_ON_CLOSE (This has been defined in the class JFrame). It exits the application using the System exit method. In the previous chapter, we have seen the same effect when the following code was written:

```
add Window Listener (new Window
Adapter()
{
    public void windowClosing()
    {
        System.exit(0);
    }
});
```

L7   JLabel is a component to display information like text or icon. The text to be displayed is passed to the constructor.

L8   All top-level containers have a contentpane to which components are added. add(label) method is used to add labels to our frame. The add() method is inherited by JFrame from Container class of AWT. By default, content pane of JFrame uses BorderLayout.

L9   It is commented. When you try to run this example with this line uncommented, the output will be as shown in Fig. 15.2(b). The pack() method cases a Window to fit according to the preferred size and layouts of its subcomponents. Using the pack() method, we need not specify the size of window.

L10   setVisible (true) sets the visibility of frame to true. If this method is not used, the frame will not be visible. By default, the visibility of window is false.

L11–12   An object of DemoSwing is created and the method demoSwing is invoked.

15.3 JApplet

JApplet is used for creating applets using swings. JApplet is a Container class like JFrame, so it possesses all the panes. Components are added to JApplet as they are added in JFrame. JApplet extends Applet class, so it contains all the features of AWT applet. A class needs to be a subclass of JApplet for creating applets in swings. We have already seen how applets can be created using the Applet class in Chapter 12. The lifecycle of a JApplet is same as the life cycle of an applet. You can override any of the life cycle methods whichever is required by your swing applet. In swings, painting is avoided in paint() method.

The example below shows a JApplet with an init() which places three buttons within the applet (Fig. 15.3).

Example 15.2   **JApplet**

```
L1      import java.awt.*;
L2      import javax.swing.*;
        /* <applet code = "JAppletDemo.class" width = "300" height = "100"></applet>*/
L3      public class JAppletDemo extends JApplet {
L4      public void init(){
L5          setLayout(new FlowLayout());
L6          add(new JButton("Button 1"));
L7          add(new JButton("Button 2"));
L8          add(new JButton("Button 3"));
        }}
```

Output

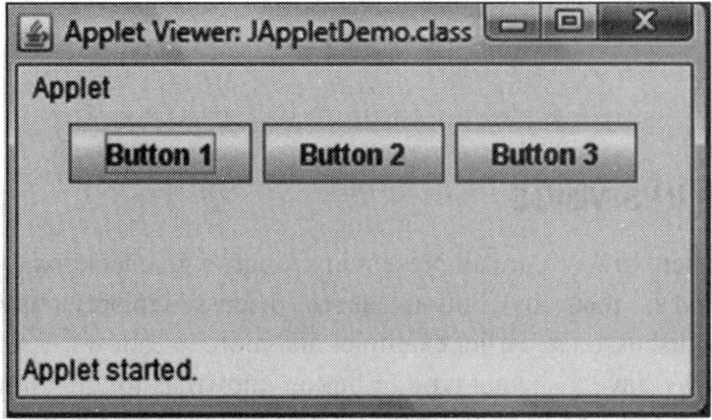

Fig. 15.3 JApplet

The HTML code to run a JApplet is as follows:

```
<html><body>
<applet code ="JAppletDemo.class" width="300" height="100"></applet></body></html>
```

Explanation

L1–2 Packages java.awt (for FlowLayout class) and javax.swing are imported.

L5 The JApplet layout is changed to FlowLayout. By default, the JApplet has BorderLayout.

L6–8 Within init(), three buttons have been added. The class for button in swing is JButton. It has been instantiated and string argument is passed in the constructor which forms the caption of the button.

15.4 JPanel

JPanel is a lightweight container used for holding components which include JButton, JLabel, JList, JToggleButton, etc. If you want to put a component to JPanel, then simply add it using add(Component c) method, then add the JPanel to its top-level container like JFrame. However, JPanel can also act as a replacement for Canvas class, as there is no JCanvas class in the swing package. If JPanel is used in place of canvas, you need to follow two additional steps. Firstly, set the preferred size via the method setPreferredSize (the preferred size of a canvas is its current size, whereas a JPanel (or panel) determines its preferred size from the components they contain). Secondly, you should use paintComponent method for drawing, not paint. In addition to that, you should first clear the screen by super.paintComponent.

```
JPanel j = new JPanel();              //assumes double buffer and flowlayout
j.add(new JLabel("Name"));            //adds Jlabel to JPanel
j.add(new JTextField(" ",15));        // adds JTextField to JPanel
j.add(new JButton());                 // adds JButton to jpanel
add(j);
    .
    .
    .
```

```
        public void paintComponent(Graphics g) {
           super.paintComponent(g);
              .
              .
              .
        }
```

15.5 COMPONENTS IN SWINGS

Components present in AWT are all present in swings, e.g., checkbox (JCheckBox), radio button (JRadioButton and ButtonGroup), button (JButton discussed in previous example), label (JLabel, we have already discussed in earlier examples and more to follow), TextField (JTextField), etc. Apart from this we have a special type of button known as toggle button which when clicked upon remains selected (see Fig. 15.4(a)) and state of the toggle button becomes deselected on clicking again (see Fig. 15.4(b)).

Fig. 15.4(a) JToggleButton Selected Upon Clicking

Fig. 15.4(b) JToggleButton Deselected Upon Clicking Again

Example 15.3 shows three components: checkbox, radio button, and toggle button, and how event handling is done for JToggleButton (Fig. 15.5).

Example 15.3 JCheckBox, JRadioButton, **and** JToggleButton

```
      import java.awt.*;
      import java.awt.event.*;
      import javax.swing.*;
      public class ComponentDemo extends JFrame implements ItemListener
      {
L1        JRadioButton m,f;
L2    JCheckBox c1,c2;
L3    JToggleButton tb;
L4    Container content;
L5    JLabel lbl;
L6    void componentDemo() {
L7    setTitle ("Demo for Checkbox RadioButton & ToggleButton");
L8    content = getContentPane();
L9    setSize(300,150);
L10   setDefaultCloseOperation(EXIT_ON_CLOSE);
L11   setLayout(new FlowLayout());
L12   c1 = new JCheckBox("Music");
L13   c2 = new JCheckBox("Dancing");
```

```
L14    c1.addItemListener(this);
L15    c2.addItemListener(this);
L16    add(c1);
L17    add(c2);
L18    m = new JRadioButton("Male");
L19    f = new JRadioButton("Female");
L20        ButtonGroup bg = new ButtonGroup();
L21        bg.add(m);
L22        bg.add(f);
L23        m.addItemListener(this);
L24        f.addItemListener(this);
L25        add(m);
L26        add(f);
L27        tb = new JToggleButton("Change Color");
L28        lbl = new JLabel();
L29        add(lbl);
L30        tb.addItemListener(this);
L31        add(tb);
L32        setVisible(true);
       }


L33    public void itemStateChanged(ItemEvent ae)
       {
L34    if(ae.getItem() == tb && ae.getStateChange() == ItemEvent.SELECTED)
L35        content.setBackground(Color.blue);
L36    if(ae.getItem() == tb && ae.getStateChange() == ItemEvent.DESELECTED)
L37        content.setBackground(Color.red);
L38    if(ae.getItem() == c1 && ae.getStateChange() == ItemEvent.SELECTED)
L39        lbl.setText("Music");
L40    if(ae.getItem() == c2 && ae.getStateChange() == ItemEvent.SELECTED)
L41        lbl.setText("Dancing");
L42    if(ae.getItem() == m && ae.getStateChange() == ItemEvent.SELECTED)
L43        lbl.setText("Male");
L44    if(ae.getItem() == f && ae.getStateChange() == ItemEvent.SELECTED)
L45        lbl.setText("Female");
       }


       public static void main(String[] args) {
L46        ComponentDemo demo = new ComponentDemo();
L47        demo.componentDemo();
       }}
```

Output

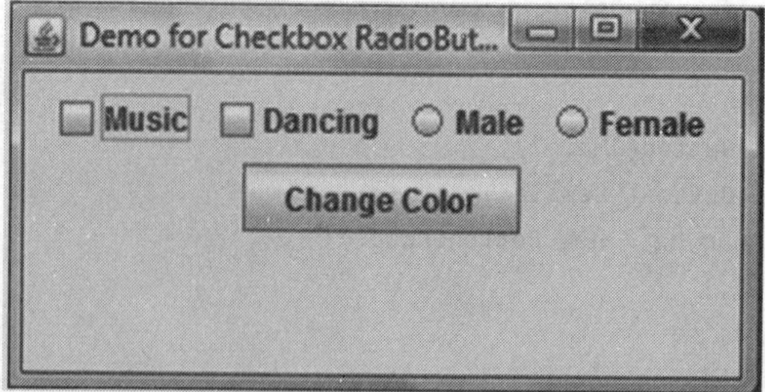

Fig. 15.5(a) Frame Showing Check Boxes, Radio Buttons, and Toggle Button

Fig. 15.5(b) On Selection of Toggle Button, the Color of the Frame Turns Blue

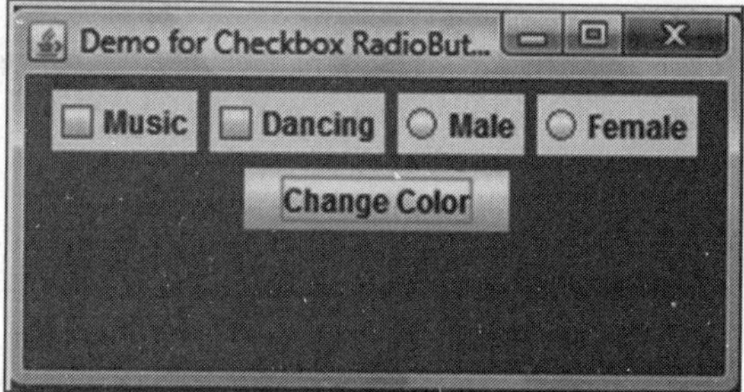

Fig. 15.5(c) On De-selection of Toggle Button, the Color of the Frame Turns Red

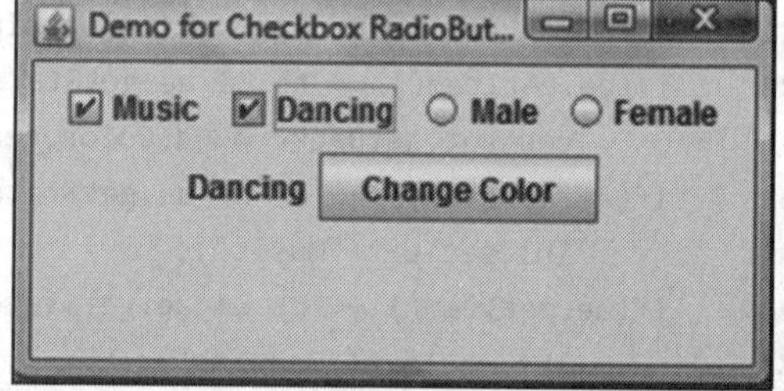

Fig. 15.5(d) On Selection of Checkbox, the Label is Set with the Text

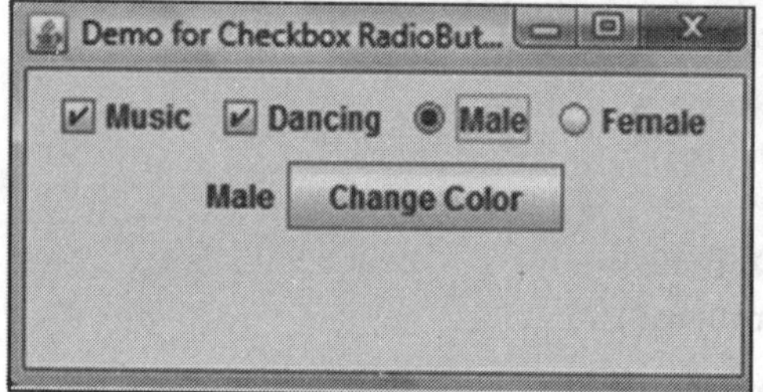

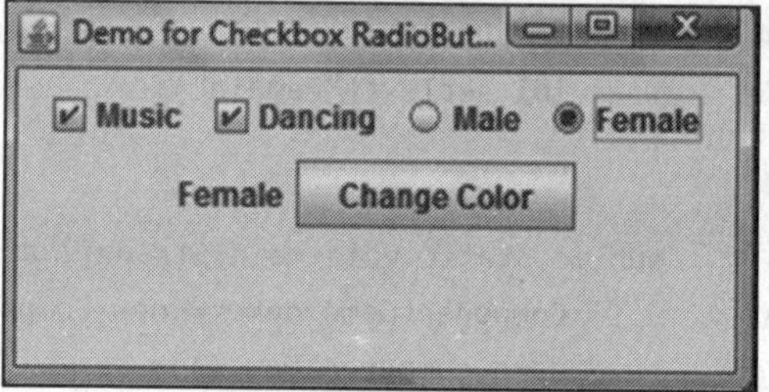

Fig. 15.5(e) On Selection of Radio Button, the Label is Set with the Text

Explanation

L1–5 The reference variables for various components are created like `JRadioButton`, `JCheckBox`, `JToggleButton`, and `JLabel`. A reference variable for container is also created for content pane. These variables have been declared outside the method because the instances will be required in other methods as well.

L12–13 Two checkboxes have been created with the captions passed as arguments to the constructors as string. The constructors for `JCheckBox` are shown in Table 15.3.

L14–15 Both checkboxes are registered with `ItemListener` to handle events using the method `addItemListener(this)`.

L16–17 Both checkboxes are added to the frame.

L18–19 Two radio buttons are created and their captions are passed as argument to the constructor. The constructors for `JRadioButton` are shown in Table 15.4.

L20 An instance of `ButtonGroup` is created. This class is used to group components into a group so that only one may be selected out of them. Typically it is used for `JRadioButton` and `ToggleButton`. We are using it for `JRadioButton` in this example.

L21–22 Both radio buttons are added to a button group. Now only one can be selected.

L23–24 Both radio buttons register themselves with `ItemListener` using `addItemListener` method for listening event.

L25–26 The radio buttons are added to the `JFrame`.

L27 Toggle button is created with caption passed as an argument to the constructor of `JToggleButton`. The constructors of this class are shown in Table 15.5.

L28–29 A new `JLabel` is instantiated and added to the frame.

L30 The `ItemListener` is registered with `JToggleButton`. Whenever you select or de-select the toggle button, the state of toggle button changes generating an `ItemEvent` which is passed to the method `itemStateChanged(ItemEvent e)`.

L31 Adds the toggle button to `JFrame`.

L33 Method `itemStateChanged(ItemEvent e)` is overridden. As soon as a checkbox is checked or radio button selected or a toggle button selected/deselected, an `ItemEvent` is generated and this method is invoked.

L34–45 Checks who generated the event using `getItem()` and what is the state of the component: SELECTED or DESELECTED. The state can be obtained using the method `getStateChange()`. Different event handing code is written for different components depending upon which component generated the event, e.g., if toggle button is selected, we have changed the color of content pane to blue and when it is de-selected, we have changed the color of content pane to red. For check box and radio button, the label is set with a string whenever a checkbox or a radio button is checked.

Table 15.3 Constructors of `JCheckBox`

Constructor	Description
`JCheckBox (String txt)`	Creates an unselected checkbox with txt.
`JCheckBox (String txt, boolean selected)`	Creates a selected checkbox if selected is set as true.
`JCheckBox (String txt, Icon i, boolean selected)`	The checkbox will have an icon image too, apart from text and boolean selection.

Table 15.4 Constructors of `JRadioButton`

Constructor	Description
`JRadioButton(String txt)`	Creates an unselected radio button with txt.
`JRadioButton (String txt, boolean selected)`	Creates a selected radio button if selected is set as true.
`JRadioButton(String txt, Icon i, boolean selected)`	The radio button will have an icon image too, apart from text and boolean selection.

Table 15.5 Constructors of `JToggleButton`

Constructor	Description
`JToggleButton(String txt)`	Creates an unselected toggle button with txt.
`JToggleButton (String txt, boolean selected)`	Creates a selected toggle button if selected is set as true.
`JToggleButton(String txt, Iconi, boolean selected)`	The toggle button will have an icon image too, apart from text and boolean selection.

15.6 LAYOUT MANAGERS

Apart from the layouts introduced in AWT (Chapter 14), a few new layouts have been introduced in swing package as well. For example,

- `BoxLayout`
- `SpringLayout`

15.6.1 SpringLayout

The `SpringLayout` is a very flexible layout in the sense that it does not place components on its own but according to the constraints specified by the `putConstraint` method. The constraints specify the distance between two edges of component or distance between the edges of a component and its container. The edges can be in any direction: north, south, east, or west. Let us take an example to illustrate this concept (Fig. 15.6).

Example 15.4 `Springlayout`

```
L1    import java.awt.*;
L2    import javax.swing.*;
L3    public class SpringDemo extends JFrame {
L4    void springDemo() {
L5    setDefaultCloseOperation(EXIT_ON_CLOSE);
L6        setTitle("Spring Layout");
L7        Container contentPane = getContentPane();
L8        SpringLayout layout = new SpringLayout();
```

```
L9        contentPane.setLayout(layout);
L10       setSize(250,100);

          //Create and add the components.
L11       JLabel label = new JLabel("Name: ");
L12       JTextField textField = new JTextField("", 15);
L13       add(label);
L14       add(textField);
L15       JButton b1= new JButton("Submit");
L16       add(b1);
L17       layout.putConstraint(SpringLayout.WEST, label,5,SpringLayout.WEST, contentPane);
L18       layout.putConstraint(SpringLayout.NORTH,label,5,SpringLayout.NORTH,contentPane);
L19       layout.putConstraint(SpringLayout.WEST, textField,5,SpringLayout.EAST,label);
L20       layout.putConstraint(SpringLayout.NORTH, textField,5,SpringLayout.
             NORTH,contentPane);
L21       layout.putConstraint(SpringLayout.HORIZONTAL_CENTER,b1,0,SpringLayout.HORIZON
             TAL_CENTER,contentPane);
L22       layout.putConstraint(SpringLayout.SOUTH,b1,-5,SpringLayout.SOUTH,content
             Pane);

          //Display the window.
L23       setVisible(true);
          }
          public static void main(String[] args){
          SpringDemo demo=new SpringDemo();
          demo.springDemo();
}}
```

Output

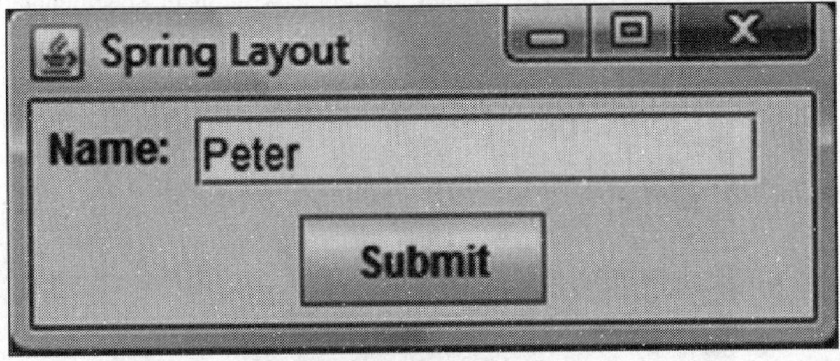

Fig. 15.6 SpringLayout

Explanation

L1–2 Packages `java.awt` (because `getContent-Pane()` returns an object of type `java.awt.Container`) and `javax.swing` are imported.

L8 `SpringLayout` object is created.

L9 `setLayout` method is used to set `SpringLayout` to the content pane.

L11 Label is created with the caption as *Name*.

L12 `JTextField` object is created with two arguments. First is a default string to be displayed in the text field and second is the number of columns that determines the width of the field. If it is made 0 and the program is executed, the frame is displayed as shown in Fig. 15.7. In the frame below, notice the width of the text field. Table 15.6 shows the constructors for `JTextField`.

L13–14 Label and text field are added to the content pane.

L15–16 A button is created with a caption *Submit* and added to the content pane.

L17 `putConstraint` method is used to specify the location of a component in the `JFrame`. The signature of `putConstraint` method is as follows:

```
public void putConstraint(String e, Component c,
int p, String e1, Component c1)
```

It specifies the distance between edges e and e1 of components c and c1, respectively as p, where

e is the edge of the dependent component

c is the dependent component

p is the distance between edge e of c and edge e1 of c1

e1 is the edge of the anchor component

c1 is the anchor component

The possible set of values for edges can be

```
SpringLayout.EAST
SpringLayout.WEST
SpringLayout.NORTH
SpringLayout.SOUTH
SpringLayout.VERTICAL_CENTER
SpringLayout.HORIZONTAL_CENTER SpringLay-
out.BASELINE
```

In this line, we set the constraints for component label and that the distance between west edge of label and west edge of content pane is just 5 pixels.

L18 The north edge of the label is just 5 pixels away from the north edge of the content pane.

L19 The west edge of the text field is 5 pixels away from the east edge of the label.

L20 The north edge of the text field is just 5 pixels away from the north edge of the content pane.

Table 15.6 Constructor of `JTextField`

Constructor	Description
`JTextField()`	Creates a text field with the number of columns as 0.
`JTextField(String txt)`	Creates a text field with String txt specified in it.
`JTextField (String txt, int column)`	Creates a text field with String specified and number of column as specified by column.

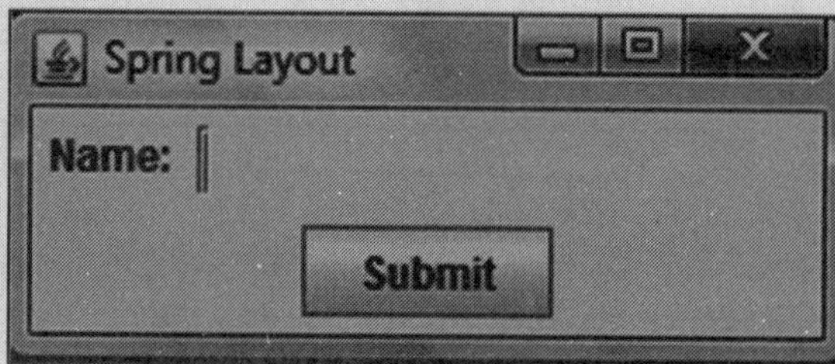

Fig. 15.7 `JTextField` width is Set to Zero

L21–22 L21 places the button in the horizontal center of the content pane. An integer value of 0 is specified so that it remains in the center. L22 specifies the distance between the south edge of the button and south edge of the content pane as –5. Specifying a negative value moves the component upwards from southern edge of the content pane and specifying a positive value moves it towards the southern edge of the content pane.

15.6.2 `BoxLayout`

The `BoxLayout` places all the components in a single row or column. Without making it complex, we can put more than one panel in horizontal and vertical directions, similar to `GridBagLayout`.

The `BoxLayout` manager is designed with an axis parameter that specifies the type of layout. This can be done in four ways:

X_AXIS—Components are placed horizontally from left to right.

Y_AXIS—Components are placed vertically from top to bottom.

LINE_AXIS—Components are placed in a line, based on the container's ComponentOrientation property.

PAGE_AXIS—Components are placed the way text lines are written on a page, based on the `ComponentOrientation` property of container.

Tables 15.7 and 15.8 list the `ComponentOrientation` property of `Page_Axis` and `Line_Axis`.

Table 15.7 `Page_Axis`

Component Orientation	Components Layout
`Horizontal`	Horizontally, else vertically placed.
`Horizontal;left to right`	Placed left to right, otherwise else right to left.
`Vertical orientations`	Laid from top to bottom

Table 15.8 `Line_Axis`

Component Orientation	Components Layout
`Horizontal`	Components are kept vertically, otherwise they are kept horizontally.
`Horizontal;left to right`	Placed left to right else right to left.
`Vertical orientations`	Laid from top to bottom.

Example 15.5 `BoxLayout`

```
L1      import java.awt.*;
L2      import javax.swing.*;
        public class BoxDemo extends JFrame {
        void boxDemo(){
        setTitle ("BoxLayout");
        Container content = getContentPane();
        setSize(200,150);
        setDefaultCloseOperation(EXIT_ON_CLOSE);
```

```
L3    BoxLayout b = new BoxLayout(content,BoxLayout.X_AXIS);
L4    setLayout(b);
L5    add(new JButton("Button 1"));
L6    add(new JButton("Button 2"));
L7    add(new JButton("Button 3"));
      setVisible(true);
      }
      public static void main (String[] args){
          BoxDemo demo = new BoxDemo();
          demo.boxDemo();
      }}
```

Output

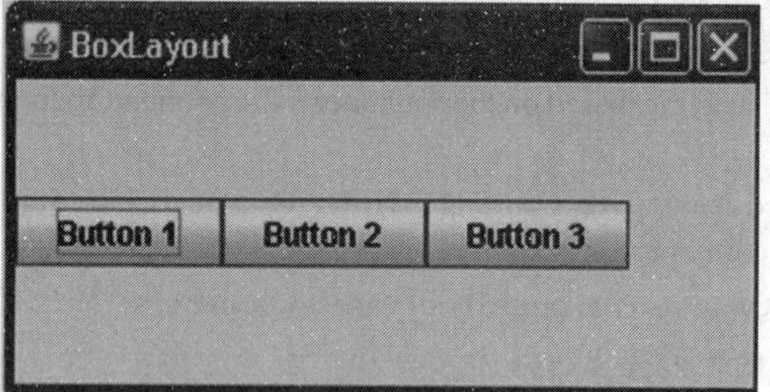

Fig. 15.8 X_AXIS Direction

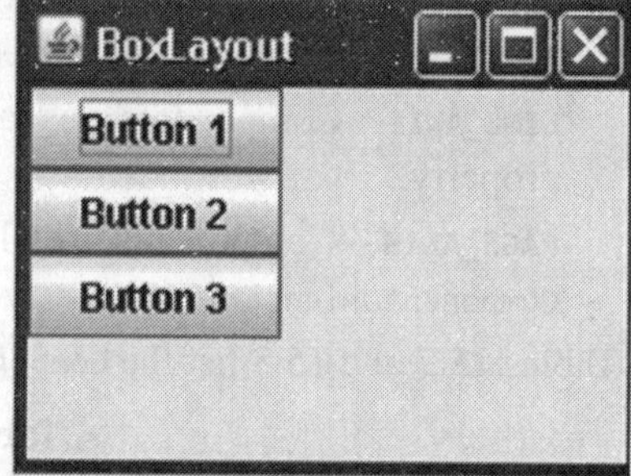

Fig. 15.9 Y_AXIS Direction

Explanation

L3 `BoxLayout` object is created. The constructor has two arguments:

```
public BoxLayout (Container target, int axis)
```

L4 `setLayout` method sets the layout of the content pane.

L5–7 Three buttons are added to the content pane. They are displayed according to their axis (see Figs 15.8 and 15.9).

15.7 `JList` AND `JScrollPane`

`JList` is a component that displays a group of items to the user and allows him/her to select one or more items from the list. A `ListModel` (interface) is used for maintaining contents of the list. A class `DefaultListModel` (inherits `ListModel`) is normally used for maintaining a list. This class provides methods to add, remove all elements or a specific element, find the index of an element, and so on. The `setModel(ListModel l)` method sets a model for the list. The selection changes on a `JList` (results in `ListSelectionEvent`) are managed by another interface `ListSelectionModel` and traced by `ListSelectionListener` (part of `javax.swing.event` sub-package). The `ListSelectionListener` has only one method, i.e.,

```
public void valueChanged(ListSelectionEvent l)
```

This method is overridden by the class that inherits the `ListSelectionListener` and wants to capture the `ListSelectionEvent`. This method is executed whenever the items in the list are selected.

The `JList` supports single selection, multiple selections, as well as multiple interval selection. The `setSelectionMode(int sm)` method is used to set the selection mode.

The integer *sm* can take any one of the three possible values as shown in Table 15.9. Example 15.6 illustrates the usage of `JLabel`. Selection is done on `JList`, the selected item is displayed in a `JLabel` (Fig. 15.10).

Table 15.9 Fields of `ListSelectionModel`

`ListSelectionModel.SINGLE_SELECTION`	Used for selecting only one item at a time.
`ListSelectionModel.SINGLE_INTERVAL_SELECTION`	Used for selecting a single contiguous range of items at a time.
`ListSelectionModel.MULTIPLE_INTERVAL_SELECTION`	Used for selecting any number of contiguous ranges of items at a time.

Example 15.6 `JList`

```
L1   import java.awt.*;
L2   import javax.swing.*;
L3   import javax.swing.event.*;
L4   public class JListDemo extends JFrame implements ListSelectionListener {
L5   JList list; JLabel l;
L6   DefaultListModel model;
L7   public JListDemo(){
L8       setTitle("JList Demo");
L9       setDefaultCloseOperation(EXIT_ON_CLOSE);
L10  l = new JLabel();
L11  setSize(260, 200);
L12  model = new DefaultListModel();
L13  list = new JList(model);
L14  JScrollPane pane = new JScrollPane(list);
L15  for (int i = 0; i < 10; i++)
L16      model.addElement("List Item:" + i);
L17      list.addListSelectionListener(this);
L18      add(pane, BorderLayout.NORTH);
L19      add(l,BorderLayout.SOUTH);
L20      setVisible(true);
     }
L21  public void valueChanged(ListSelectionEvent e)
     {
L22  l.setText((String)list.getSelectedValue());
     }
     public static void main(String s[]){
        new JListDemo();
     }}
```

Output

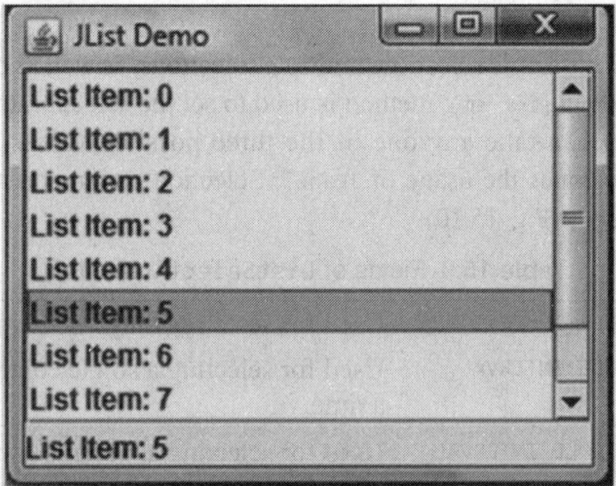

Fig. 15.10 `JList` with a `JLabel` to Display the Selected Items in the List

Explanation

L1–3 Packages `java.awt` (for `BorderLayout` class), `javax.swing`, and `javax.swing.event` are imported.

L4 Class defined to inherit `JFrame` and `ListSelectionListener`. On selection of an item in the `JList`, `ListSelectionEvent` is generated which is captured by `ListSelectionListener`.

L5–6 Three instance variables have been defined of type `JList`, `Jlabel`, and `DefaultListModel` so that they can be accessible from any method in the class.

L12–13 The `DefaultListModel` is instantiated and applied to the `JList`. The constructor of `JList` accepts a `ListModel`.

L14 A `JScrollPane` consists of a scroll bar (`JScrollBar`) as well as a view port (`JViewport`). The view port is used to manage the view of data which is scrollable. A `JScrollPane` is required when the size of data model or source exceeds the size of the frame. The component that needs a scroll pane is passed as an argument to the `JScrollPane` constructor. In this case, the horizontal and vertical scroll bars appear automatically whenever required, i.e., the data model exceeds the frame size area.

```
JScrollPane j = new JScrollPane(Component c)
```

```
// for more constructor see JDK 6 Docs
```

L15–16 The list model is populated and items are added to the list. The `addElement` method of `DefaultListModel` is used to add individual items to the list.

```
public void add Element (Object o)
```

L17 List is registered with its associated listener, i.e., `ListSelectionListener` to listen for `ListSelectionEvent` generated on change in the selection on `JList`.

L18–19 The scroll pane is added to the top, i.e., NORTH and the label is added to the bottom, i.e., SOUTH.

L20 Visibility is set to true.

L21–22 The `valueChanged` method is overridden to capture the `ListSelectionEvent`. This method extracts the selected value from the list using a method `getSelectedValue()`. This method returns an object of type `Object` class which is then cast to string type and then set as the caption for the label using `setText` method of the `JLabel`. This `setText` method accepts a string, so cast of object to string had to be performed.

15.8 SPLIT PANE

The split pane is a container that graphically separates the components, either horizontally (JSplitPane.HORIZONTAL_SPLIT) or vertically (JSplitPane.VERTICAL_SPLIT). It can display two components at a time and the display areas can be adjusted by the user. Let us take an example of it to see how JSplitPane is used (Fig. 15.11).

Example 15.7 `JSplitPane`

```
import javax.swing.*;
public class DemoSplitPane extends JFrame {
public void demoSplitPane() {
  setTitle("Split Pane");
  setSize(250, 250);
  setDefaultCloseOperation(JFrame.EXIT_ON_CLOSE);
L1    JPanel jpane1 = new JPanel();
L2    JPanel jpane2 = new JPanel();
L3    JLabel jlb1 = new JLabel("First Area 1");
L4    JLabel jlb2 = new JLabel("Second Area 2");
L5    jpane1.add(jlb1);
L6    jpane2.add(jlb2);
L7    JSplitPane splitPane = new JSplitPane(JSplitPane.VERTICAL_SPLIT,true,
      jpane1,jpane2);
L8    splitPane.setOneTouchExpandable(true);
L9    add(splitPane);
L10   setVisible(true);
  }
  public static void main(String[] args){
      DemoSplitPane demo = new DemoSplitPane();
      demo.demoSplitPane();
}}
```

Output

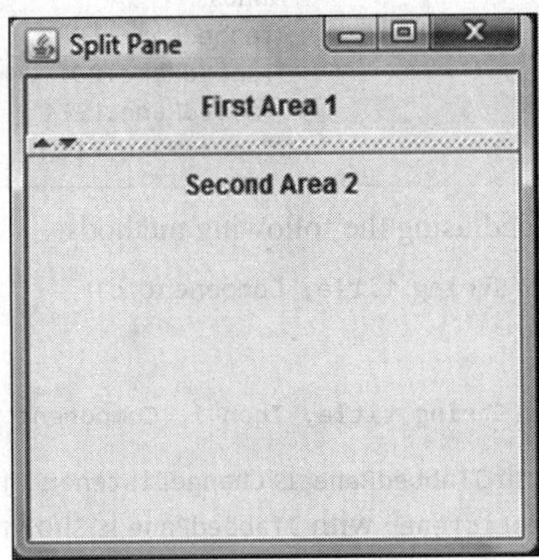

Fig. 15.11 Vertically Split `JSplitPane` Showing two `JPanel`

Explanation

L1–2   Two instances of `JPanel` are created for each portion that will be split by `JSplitPane`.

L3–4   Two labels are created, one for each panel with caption 'First Area 1' and 'Second Area 2'.

L5–6   `JLabel` are added to `JPanel`.

L7   `JSplitPane` object is created. The constructor used in the example is shown below:

`JSplitPane (int orientation, boolean newContinuouslayout, Component c1, Component c2)` where `orientation` can take two values: `JSplitPane.HORIZONTAL_SPLIT` and `JSplitPane.VERTICAL SPLIT`. `HORIZONTAL_SPLIT` will divide the entire horizontal area into parts. `VERTICAL_SPLIT` will divide the entire vertical area into parts (see Fig. 15.11).

`newContinuouslayout` is a boolean value indicating whether components will be redrawn or not when the divider is moved.

`c1` denotes that the component will be displayed in the top portion (in case of VERTICAL_SPLIT) and left portion (in case of HORIZONTAL_SPLIT).

`c2` denotes that the component will be displayed in the bottom portion (in case of VERTICAL_SPLIT) and right portion (in case of HORIZONTAL_SPLIT).

L8   `setOneTouchExpandable (true)` method of `JSplitPane` is used to provide up/down arrow on the divider. Clicking on the arrows expands/contracts the split pane.

15.9 JTabbedPane

`JTabbedPane` allows a user to switch between different tabs containing components or a group of components (see Fig. 15.12(a) and (b)). The individual tabs will have a title and may contain icons as well. Table 15.10 shows the constructors for `JTabbedPane`.

Table 15.10 Constructors of `JTabbedPane`

Constructor	Description
`JTabbedPane()`	Creates a tabbed pane with a default tab placement, i.e. `JTabbedPane.TOP`.

`JTabbedPane(int tabPlacement)`	Creates a tabbed pane with tab placement specified. The tab placement can take any one of the following values:
	`JTabbedPane.TOP`
	`JTabbedPane.BOTTOM`
	`JTabbedPane.LEFT`
	`JTabbedPane.RIGHT`

Individual tabs can be added using the following methods:

```
public void addTab(String title, Component c)
```

or

```
public void addTab(String title, Icon i, Component c)
```

The listener associated with `JTabbedPane` is `ChangeListener` (`javax.swing.event`). The method used for registering `ChangeListener` with `JTabbedPane` is shown below:

```
public void addChangeListener(ChangeListener 1)
```

This `ChangeListener` interface has a method, `publicvoidstateChanged` (`ChangeEvente`), to process the `ChangeEvent` that occurred when tabs are selected.

Let us take an example to understand `JTabbedPane` and how `ChangeListener` is used on it. In the following program, two tabs are created. Both tabs contain `JPanel`. The `JPanel` in tab1 contains a label, whereas the other `JPanel` contains a toggle button. A third label is added to the `JFrame` whose value is set when the tabs are selected.

Example 15.8 `JTabbedPane`

```
       import java.awt.*;
       import javax.swing.*;
       import javax.swing.event.*;
       public class JTabbedPaneDemo extends JFrame {
L1     JLabel lbl,txt;
L2     JToggleButton jb;
L3     JTabbedPane jt;
L4     JTabbedPaneDemo(){
L5     setTitle("JTabbedPane");
L6     setDefaultCloseOperation(EXIT_ON_CLOSE);
L7         lbl = new JLabel("Label in Tab1");
L8         JPanel panel1 = new JPanel();
L9         panel1.add(lbl);
L10        JPanel panel2 = new JPanel();
L11        jb = new JToggleButton("Change Color");
L12        panel2.add(jb);
L13        jt = new JTabbedPane();
L14        jt.addTab("Tab 1", panel1);
L15        jt.addTab("Tab 2", panel2);
L16        jt.setToolTipTextAt(0,"Tab 1");
L17        jt.setToolTipTextAt(1,"Tab 2");
L18        add(jt,BorderLayout.NORTH);
L19        txt = new JLabel();
L20        add(txt,BorderLayout.CENTER);
L21        setSize(300,200);
L22        setVisible(true);
L23        jt.addChangeListener(new ChangeListener(){
L24    public void stateChanged(ChangeEvent e){
L25        txt.setText("Tab selected: " + jt.getSelectedIndex());
       }
       });
       }
       public static void main(String args[]){
       new JTabbedPaneDemo();
       }}
```

Output

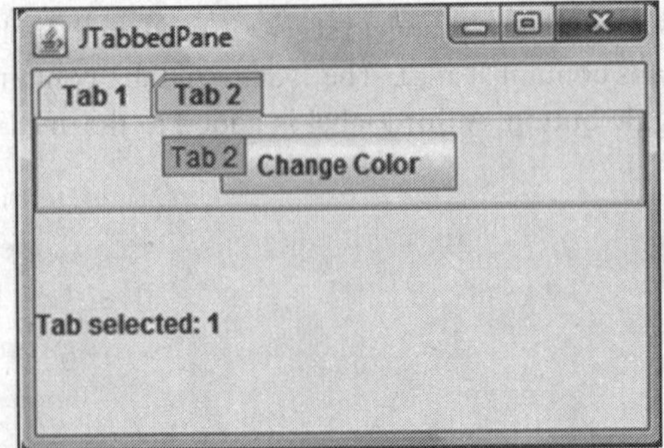

Fig. 15.12(a) `JTabbedPane` Showing `ToolTipText` and Index When Tab2 is Selected along with the Toggle Button in Tab2

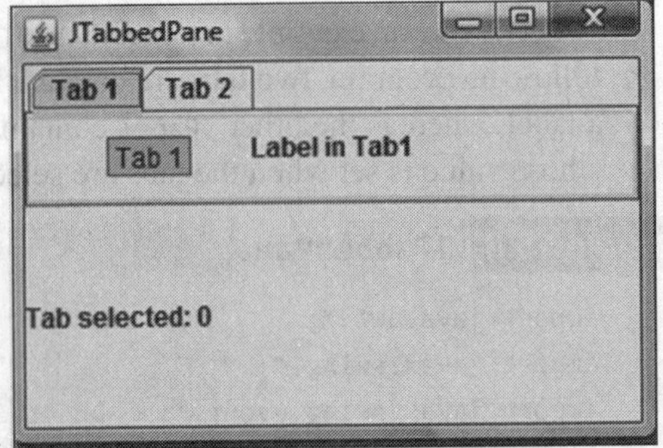

Fig. 15.12(b) `JTabbedPane` Showing `ToolTip-Text` and Index When Tab1 is Selected along with the `JLabel` in Tab1

Explanation

L7–9 `JLabel` is created with text `Label in Tab1` and added to `JPanel`.

L10–12 `JToggleButton` is created with the caption `ChangeColor` and added to another `JPanel`. We have not registered the Toggle button for event handling, so nothing will happen once you click on Toggle button.

L13 `JTabbedPane` instance is created with default placement.

L14–15 Individual tabs are added to the tabbed pane using `addTab` method. This method also specifies what the individual tabs will contain. For example, `Tab1` contains `panel1` and `Tab2` contains `panel2`.

L16–17 Tooltip can be set/get for the tabs using the following methods:

```
void setToolTipTextAt(int index, String tooltip)
```

```
String getToolTipTextAt(int index)
```
When you place your mouse over the tab, you will see the tooltip text appears as shown in Figs 15.12(a) and (b).

L18–20 The `JTabbedPane` and `JLabel` are added to the content pane.

L23–25 An anonymous inner class is defined here to handle the `ChangeEvent` generated when the user clicks on a tab. `JTabbedPane` registers itself with `ChangeListener` using `addChangeListener` method. The anonymous inner class will inherit the interface `ChangeListener` and the method `stateChanged` `(ChangeEvent e)` (L 24) will be a part of that class. This method sets the value of the `JLabel(txt)`with a string concatenated with the selected index of the tab. The selected index of the tab is obtained by `getSelectedIndex()` method of `JTabbedPane`.

15.10 JTree

The `JTree` class is used to display hierarchical data. A `JTree` object provides a view of the data. The tree obtains its data by querying its data model. The snapshot of a `JTree` is shown in Fig. 15.13

`JTree` displays the data vertically. Each row contains exactly one *node*. There are three types of nodes in a `JTree`: *root node, branch node,* and *leaf node.* All nodes will have a common *root* node at the top of the tree. A node can either have children or cannot have children. Nodes that have children are called *branch* nodes and nodes that do not have children are called *leaf*

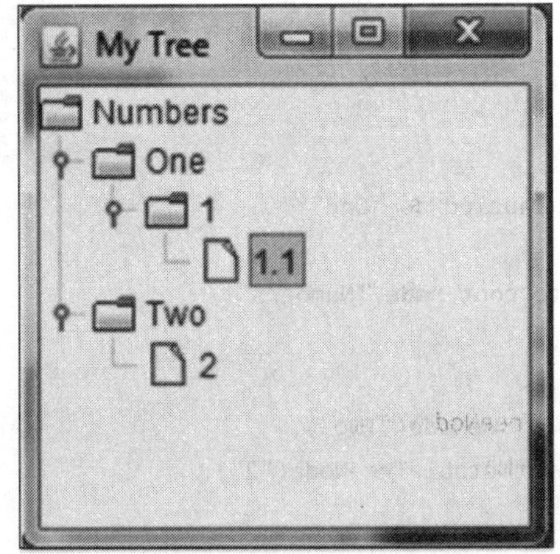

Fig. 15.13 JTree

nodes. In Fig. 15.13, nodes labeled as 1.1 and 2 are leaf nodes and rest are branch nodes except *Numbers* which is root node. We have expanded all branch nodes by clicking on them in Fig 15.13 to show the difference between three types of nodes.

The structure of a Tree is created using DefaultTreeModel class. All nodes within this model are created using DefaultMutableTreeNode class. All these nodes are first added to the model and then the model is added to the JTree. If a user wants to monitor for node expansion or collapsing events, TreeExpansionListener is used. A specific node is in expanded state when user double clicks on that node thereby displaying its child nodes. If the node is in expanded state, you can collapse it by double clicking on that node. When a node is in collapse state, all its child nodes are in hidden state. Any node can be identified by a TreePath object which encapsulates the node along with all its ancestors. Let us take an example to create a JTree and also check for user selection of nodes (Fig. 15.14).

Example 15.9 `JTreeDemo.java`

```
L1    import javax.swing.*;
L2    import javax.swing.tree.*;
L3    import javax.swing.event.*;
L4      public class JTreeDemo extends JFrame
        {
L5          JTree jt;
L6        DefaultTreeModel dtm;
L7        DefaultMutableTreeNode dtm1;
L8        JTreeDemo(String title)
          {
L9          setTitle(title);
            /* Root node creation. DefaultMutableTreeNode creates a node with no parent
            and no child but allows children.*/
L10         dtm1 = new DefaultMutableTreeNode("Numbers");

            /*Branch Node Creation */
L11         DefaultMutableTreeNode one=new DefaultMutableTreeNode ("One");

            /* Another hierarchy of branch node has to be added within the branch node one */
L12         DefaultMutableTreeNode oneInNumber=new
            DefaultMutableTreeNode("1");

            /* Leaf node created for node Labeled "1". The second argument to the con
            structor specifies that this node will not have children*/
```

```
L13        DefaultMutableTreeNode oneInNumber2=new
           DefaultMutableTreeNode("1.1", false);
           /* Leaf Node labeled "1.1" added to node "1" */
L14        oneInNumber.add(oneInNumber2);
           /*Branch node labeled 1 is added to node labeled as "One"*/
L15        one.add(oneInNumber);
           /*Branch node labeled as "One" is added to root node "Numbers"*/
L16        dtm1.add(one);

L17     DefaultMutableTreeNode two=new DefaultMutableTreeNode("Two");
L18     DefaultMutableTreeNode twoInNumber=new DefaultMutableTreeNode("2");
L19     two.add(twoInNumber);
L20     dtm1.add(two);
L21     dtm = new DefaultTreeModel (dtm1,true);
L22     jt = new JTree(dtm1);

L23     jt.addTreeExpansionListener(new TreeExpansionListener()
        {
            public void treeCollapsed(TreeExpansionEvent te)
            {
                    System.out.println("Collapsed");
            }
            public void treeExpanded(TreeExpansionEvent te)
            {
                    System.out.println(jt.getLeadSelectionPath());
                    System.out.println(
                    jt.getLastSelectedPathComponent());
            }
    });
L24     setDefaultCloseOperation(JFrame.EXIT_ON_CLOSE);

L25     add(jt);
L26     setSize(200,200);
L27     setVisible(true);
    }
L28 public static void main(String args[])
    {
L29     new JTreeDemo("My Tree");
    }
    }
```

Output

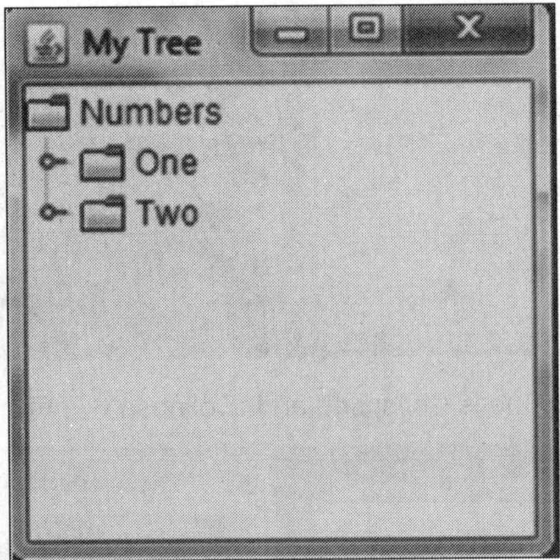

Fig. 15.14(a) `JTree` is Displayed

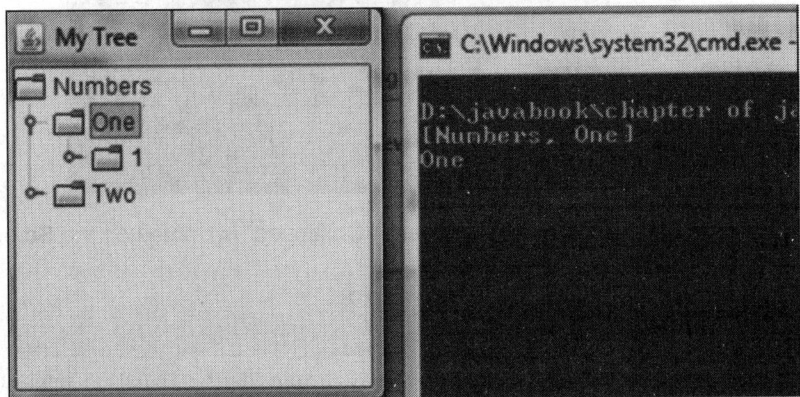

Fig. 15.14(b) Node One is Expanded and Nodes `TreePath` (i.e., [Numbers, One]) and Name is Displayed on Command Prompt

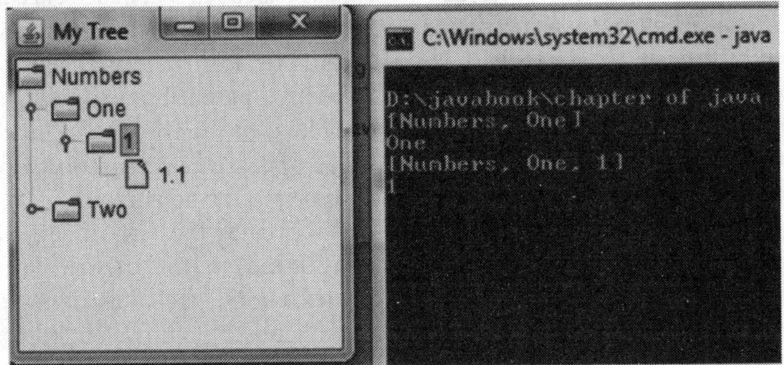

Fig. 15.14(c) Sub Node 1 is Expanded and Node's `TreePath` and Name is Displayed on Command Prompt

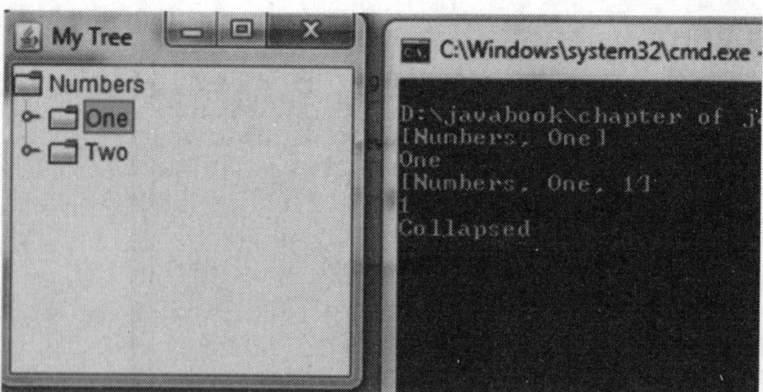

Fig. 15.14(d) Node One is Collapsed and "Collapsed" is Printed on the Screen

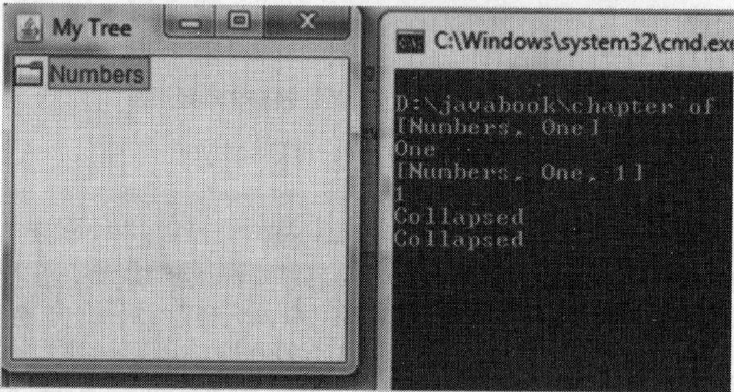

Fig. 15.14(e) Root node is Collapsed and "Collapsed" is Printed on the Screen

Explanation

L1–3 Import the required packages. The `javax.swing.tree` sub package is imported because we want to use `DefaultTreeModel` and `DefaultMutableTreeNode` class in our program.

L4 Class declaration.

L5–7 Reference variables of `JTree`, `DefaultTreeModel` and `DefaultMutableTreeNode` are created.

L8 Constructor declaration.

L9 Sets the title of the frame.

We want to create our own tree structure so we need to create a `TreeModel`. The constructor of `JTree` accepts a `TreeModel` object. `TreeModel` is an interface in the `java.swing.tree` package, so we use `DefaultTreeModel` class which inherits the `TreeModel` interface. We have passed the `DefaultTreeModel` object within `JTree` constructor. A `TreeModel` will have nodes. The constructor of `DefaultTreeModel` accepts an object of type `TreeNode` which is an interface in `java.swing.tree` package. For creating nodes of `JTree`, we use `DefaultMutableTreeNode` (which inherits the `TreeNode` interface) class. The caption for the node is passed within the constructor of the `DefaultMutableTreeNode`.

First of all a root node (dtm1) is created using `DefaultMutableTreeNode` class. The branch nodes and their child branch nodes are also created using `DefaultMutableTreeNode` class and are added to their respective parent branch nodes. The branch nodes are added to the root node. Lastly the root node is added to the `DefaultTreeModel` object (dtm), which is passed in the constructor of `JTree` object.

L10 Creates the first node (root node, i.e., dtm) using `DefaultMutableTreeNode` class. The statement creates a node labeled as "Numbers" with no parent and no child but allows children.

L11 Creates a branch node (i.e., one) using `DefaultMutableTreeNode` class. The statement creates a node labeled as "One" with no parent and no child but allows children. This is a branch node within the root node so it will be added to root node in L16.

L12 Creates another branch node to be added within the branch node labeled "One".

```
DefaultMutableTreeNode oneInNumber=new
DefaultMutableTreeNode("1");
```

L13 Creates a leaf node labeled as "1.1" to be added within branch node labeled as "1". The second argument (false) to the constructor specifies that this node will not have children.

```
DefaultMutableTreeNode oneInNumber2=new De-
faultMutableTreeNode("1.1", false);
```

L14 Shows how to add leaf node labeled "1.1" to node "1".

```
oneInNumber.add(oneInNumber2);
```

L15 Branch node labeled "1" is added to node labeled as "One".

```
one.add(oneInNumber);
```

L16 Branch node labeled as "One" is added to root node "Numbers".

```
dtm1.add(one);
```

L17–20 Creates another hierarchy of branch node within the root node. The node labeled "2" is added to node labeled "Two" of the root node.

L21 Creates a `DefaultTreeModel` object and `DefaultMutableTreeNode` (root node) object is passed within the constructor of `DefaultTreeModel`. The boolean argument in the constructor of `DefaultTreeModel` specifies that any node can have children including the last nodes. If we omit this statement and add `dtm1` (root node object) directly to the `JTree`, then the last branch nodes like 2, as in our case, are not considered for `TreeExpansionListener` event. (Try to see the difference in output by adding dtmto `JTree` and later by adding dtm1to `JTree`.)

L22 Adds the `DefaultTreeModel` to the `JTree` object.

L23 Uses an anonymous inner class for handling tree events. `TreeExpansionListener` is used for handing `TreeExpansionEvent`. This event is raised as soon as the Tree is expanded or collapsed. `TreeExpansionListener` has two methods: `treeCollapsed` and `treeExpanded`. These two methods are overridden in the anonymous inner class with a print statement within them. As the node is double clicked, `treeExpanded` method is invoked. This method prints the `TreePath` of the node on which the user has double clicked. The `TreePath` is obtained using the `getLeadSelectionPath` method of `JTree` class. `TreePath` is path of the node starting from the root node up to the node on which the user has clicked (see output). The node label can also be obtained using the `getLastSelectedPathComponent()` of the `JTree` class.

L24–29 These have already been discussed in various examples.

15.11 `JTable`

The `JTable` class lets you display tables of data. Figure 15.15 shows a simple table:

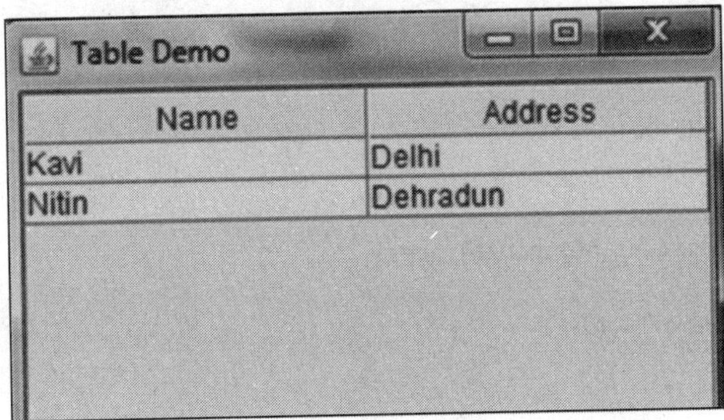

Fig. 15.15 `JTable` with Two Columns and Rows

Let us create a `JTable` for Fig. 15.15 and monitor it for cell selections. As soon as a user selects a cell, its value is displayed to the user (Fig. 15.16).

Example 15.10 `JTable` Demo

```
L1      import javax.swing.*;
L2      import java.awt.event.*;
L3      class TableDemo extends JFrame
        {
L4      JTable jt;
L5      JScrollPane jsp;
L6      TableDemo(String title)
        {
L7        setTitle(title);
L8        Object row[][]={{"Kavi","Delhi"},{"Nitin","Dehradun"}};
L9        Object col[]={"Name","Address"};
L10       jt = new JTable(row,col);

L11       setDefaultCloseOperation(JFrame.EXIT_ON_CLOSE);

/* if this value is set, a column can be selected otherwise the entire row is high
lighted.*/
L12       jt.setCellSelectionEnabled(true);

L13       jt.addMouseListener(new MouseAdapter()
          {
          public void mouseClicked(MouseEvent me)
          {
          String string = (String)jt.getValueAt (jt.getSelectedRow() ,jt.getSelectedColumn());

          // Display the selected item
          System.out.println( "Value selected = " + string );
          }
        });
L14       jsp=new JScrollPane(jt);
L15       add(jsp);
L16       setSize(300,400);
L17       setVisible(true);
        }
L18     public static void main(String[] args)
        {
L19       new TableDemo("Table Demo");
        }
        }
```

Output

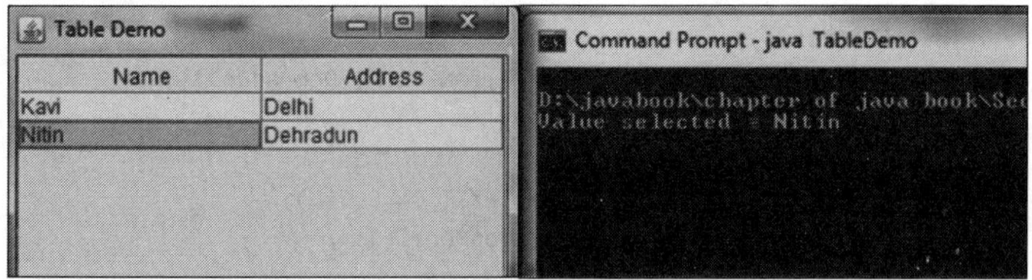

Fig. 15.16 `JTable` with Cell Selection Being Monitored

Explanation

L1–2 Imports the required packages.

L3 Class declaration.

L4–5 A reference variable of `JTable` and `JScrollPane` is created.

L6–7 Constructor is declared to accept a string which is used for setting the title of the `JFrame`.

L8–10 Table is a collection of row and columns. Therefore, two arrays have been created in L9 and L10, a two-dimensional array for populating the rows and one-dimensional array for column names. These are added to the `JTable` by passing in its constructor in L11.

L11 Exits the application as soon as a user clicks on the **X** button on the upperleft corner of the `JFrame`.

L12 By default, complete row are selected on user clicks. We want to select a particular cell in any row. So, we have to enable cell selections as shown in this statement.

L13 `MouseListener` is registered with `JTable` to track mouse click events on individual cell elements of the `JTable`. Anonymous inner class is created for handling mouse events. We wanted to track mouse click only, so we have overridden the `mouseClicked` `(MouseEventme)` method only. As soon as the mouse is clicked on a cell, this method extracts the value of that cell and prints it on the console. The `getValueAt` method of `JTable` is used to extract the value of particular cell. We want to get the value of the selected cell, so we have passed the index of the selected row (`getSelectedRow()`) and the selected column (`getSelectedColumn()`) in the `getValueAt` method.

```
String string = (String)jt.getValueAt
(jt.getSelectedRow(),
jt.getSelectedColumn());
```

L14–15 `JTable` is added to `JScrollPane`, which is added to the frame.

L16–19 All these lines have already been explained.

In the previous example, we have monitored for only cell selections. In the following example we will be monitoring selection of a complete row and even multiple rows. Let us create another `JTable` and monitor it for row selections (Fig. 15.17).

Example 15.11 **JTable Demo 2**

```
L1      import javax.swing.*;
L2      import java.awt.event.*;
L3      class TableDemo2 extends JFrame
        {
L4      JTable jt;
L5      JScrollPane jsp;
L6      //ListSelectionModel selectionModel;
```

```
L7      TableDemo2(String title)
        {
L8          setTitle(title);
L9          Object row[][]={{"Kavi","Delhi"},{"Nitin","Dehradun"}};
L10         Object col[]={"Name","Address"};
L11         jt=new JTable(row,col);
L12         setDefaultCloseOperation(JFrame.EXIT_ON_CLOSE);
L13         /*selectionModel = jt.getSelectionModel();*/

L14 /*selectionModel.setSelectionMode(ListSelectionModel.SINGLE_SELECTION);*/
L15         jt.addMouseListener(new MouseAdapter(){

            public void mouseClicked(MouseEvent me)
            {
                    int rowcount=jt.getSelectedRowCount();
                    int colcount=jt.getColumnCount();
                    String string=null;
                    /*get an index of all the selected rows*/
                    int[] sel=jt.getSelectedRows();
                    /*Determine and print the selected item */
                    for(int i=0;i<rowcount;i++)
                    for(int j=0;j<colcount;j++)
                    {
                    string = (String) jt.getValueAt (sel[i],j);

                    // Display the selected item
                    System.out.println("Value selected = " + rowcount +" ,
                    "+colcount+ ":"+ string );
                    }

            }
            });

L17         jsp=new JScrollPane(jt);
L18         add(jsp);
L19         setSize(300,400);
L20         setVisible(true);

        }
L21     public static void main(String[] args)
        {
L22        new TableDemo2("Table Demo2");
        }
        }
```

Output

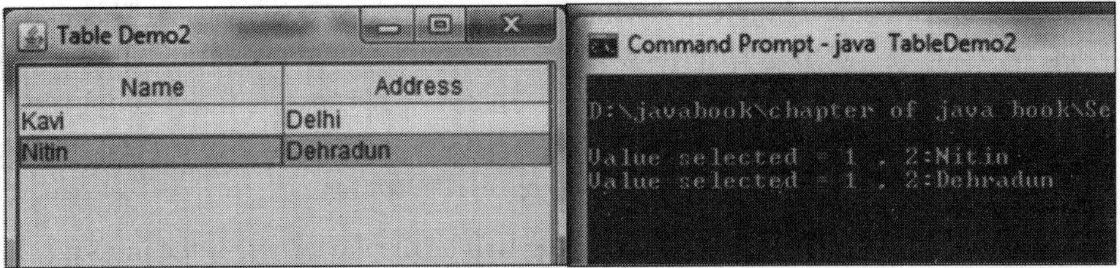

Fig. 15.17(a) Single Row Selection of the `JTable`

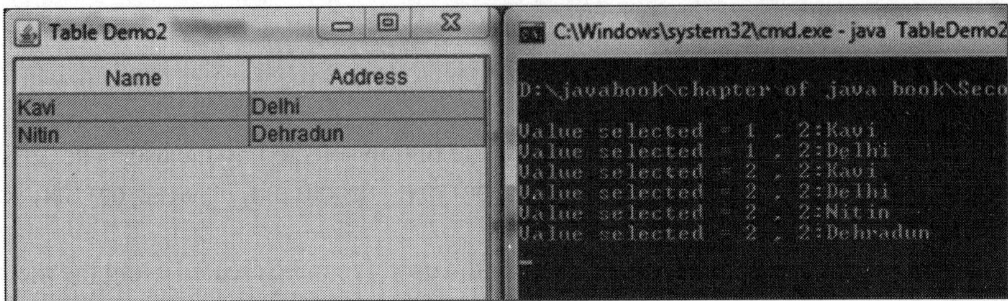

Fig. 15.17(b) Multiple Row Selection of the `JTable`

Explanation

L6, 13–14 Are commented. They are specifically commented and shown in this example for a purpose. We have allowed multiple row selections. In case you wish to allow for a single row selection, these commented statements must be uncommented. As explained earlier, `ListSelectionModel` interface provides the user with an option to set different selection modes. These modes are provided as static fields of `ListSelectionModel` interface and these modes are used to set the `selectionMode` field of `JTable` class. These modes have already been discussed in Table 15.9.

L15 A user can select any number of rows and we need to print all the selected rows. So first of all, we need to determine the number of rows that have been selected by the user. This information can be obtained using the `getSelectedRowCount()` method. Subsequently we extract the number of columns in that table using the `getColumnCount()` method. Thereafter we use the `getSelectedRows()` method to obtain the index of all the selected rows. This method returns an integer array (i.e., `sel[]`). To iterate and print the selected rows a nested `for` loop is created. The outer loop is used to iterate through the selected rows and inner `for` loop is used to print all the column values of a selected row. The `getValueAt()` method is used to obtain cell values of selected rows as in the previous example. All the selected row indexes are stored in an integer array `sel`, which is passed as first argument in the `getValueAt` method.

15.12 DIALOG BOX

There are four types of dialog boxes available in Java swings:

1. *Confirm dialog*: It seeks the user's response, e.g., YES/NO/CANCEL.
2. *Message dialog*: Informs the user about something.

3. *Input dialog*: Asks the user to enter a value.

4. *Option dialog*: Asks the user to choose a value from a given set of values.

These dialog boxes can be created with the help of a class: `JOptionPane`. This class provides static methods for creating all these dialogs, like for creating a confirm dialog, the following method is used:

```
public static int showConfirmDialog(Component parent, Object msg, String
title, int optiontype) throws HeadlessException
```

where `parent` is the frame in which the dialog will be displayed. `msg` is the message that will be displayed in the dialog. `title` sets the title of the dialog. `optiontype` may be one of the following:

- `JOptionPane.DEFAULT_OPTION`
- `JOptionPane.YES_NO_OPTION`
- `JOptionPane.YES_NO_CANCEL_OPTION`
- `JOptionPane.OK_CANCEL_OPTION`

This method returns an `int` value indicating the option selected by the user. The possible return values could be one of the following: `YES_OPTION`, `NO_OPTION`, `CANCEL_OPTION`, `OK_OPTION`, `CLOSED_OPTION`.

The message dialog displays a message to the user. It can be created using the method shown below:

```
public static void showMessageDialog(Component parent, Object msg) throws
HeadlessException          // creates an information message dialog
```

or

```
public static void showMessageDialog(Component parent, Object msg, String
title, int messagetype) throws HeadlessException
```

where `messagetype` may be one of the following:

- `JOptionPane.ERROR_MESSAGE`
- `JOptionPane.INFORMATION_MESSAGE`
- `JOptionPane.WARNING_MESSAGE`
- `JOptionPane.QUESTION_MESSAGE`
- `JOptionPane.PLAIN_MESSAGE`

The input dialog is used to get input from the user and it can be created using the methods shown below:

```
public static String showInputDialog(Component parent, Object msg) throws
HeadlessException
```

It seeks input from the user and returns it as a string.

or

```
public static String showInputDialog(Component parent, Object msg, String
title, int messagetype) throws HeadlessException
```

It seeks input from the user and returns it as a string. The option dialog displays a list of options to the user and prompts him to choose one. The following method shows how it can be created and used:

```
public static int showOptionDialog(Component parent, Object msg, String
title, int optiontype, int messagetype, Icon i, Object[] option, Object
initialValue) throws HeadlessException
```

It requires the user to select an option from the available set of options specified by the `Object[]` option. `i` specifies an image icon for the dialog. `initialValue` specifies the default value. All methods throw a `HeadLessException` which occurs when this code is invoked in an environment which does not support mouse or keyboard.

Example 15.12 Dialog Boxes using `JOptionPane` in Swing

```java
import javax.swing.*;
import java.awt.event.*;
import java.awt.*;
  public class DialogBoxDemo extends JFrame{
     JFrame frame; JLabel l;
     public DialogBoxDemo(){
          JButton b1 = new JButton("Message Dialog");
          JButton b2 = new JButton("Confirm Dialog");
          JButton b3 = new JButton("Input Dialog");
          JButton b4 = new JButton("Option Dialog");
          getContentPane().setLayout(new FlowLayout());
L1    b1.addActionListener(new MyAction());
L2    b2.addActionListener(new MyAction());
L3    b3.addActionListener(new MyAction());
L4    b4.addActionListener(new MyAction());
L5    l = new JLabel();
L6    add(b1);
L7    add(b2); add(b3); add(b4); add(l);
          setSize(350, 200);
          setVisible(true);
          setDefaultCloseOperation(JFrame.EXIT_ON_CLOSE);
L8    frame = new JFrame("Message Dialog Frame");
     }

     // Inner class to handle ActionEvent for buttons
L9    class MyAction implements ActionListener {
L10   public void actionPerformed(ActionEvent e)
     {
L11   if(e.getActionCommand().equals("Message Dialog"))
L12       JOptionPane.showMessageDialog(frame,"DialogBox");
L13   else if(e.getActionCommand().equals("Input Dialog"))
L14       l.setText(JOptionPane.showInputDialog(frame,"Enter a value"));
L15   else if(e.getActionCommand().equals("Confirm Dialog")){
L16       int i = JOptionPane.showConfirmDialog(frame,"Choose","Choose
          One",JOptionPane. YES_NO_OPTION);
L17   if(i== JOptionPane.YES_OPTION)
          l.setText("YES");
L18   else if(i== JOptionPane.NO_OPTION)
```

```
            l.setText("NO"); }
L19    else if(e.getActionCommand().equals("Option Dialog"))
       {
L20        String values[] = { "Car", "Bike", "Bus" };
L21        l.setText((String)JOptionPane.showInputDialog(frame,"Select one", "Enter
           Your Choice",JOptionPane.INFORMATION_MESSAGE, null,values,values[0]));
       }
       }
       } // inner class ends here

       public static void main(String[] args){
       DialogBoxDemo db = new DialogBoxDemo();
       } }
```

Output

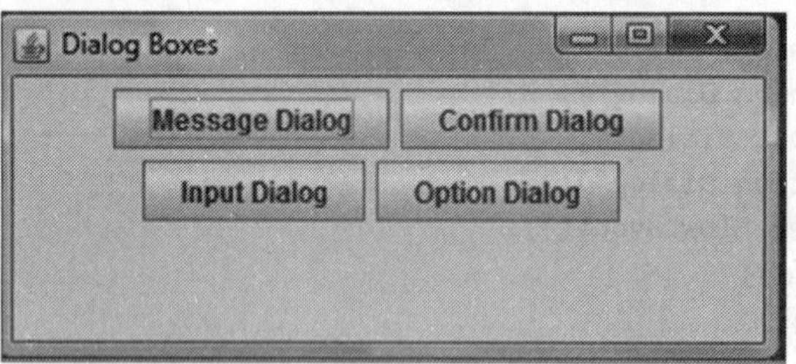

Fig. 15.18(a) JFrame with Four JButtons

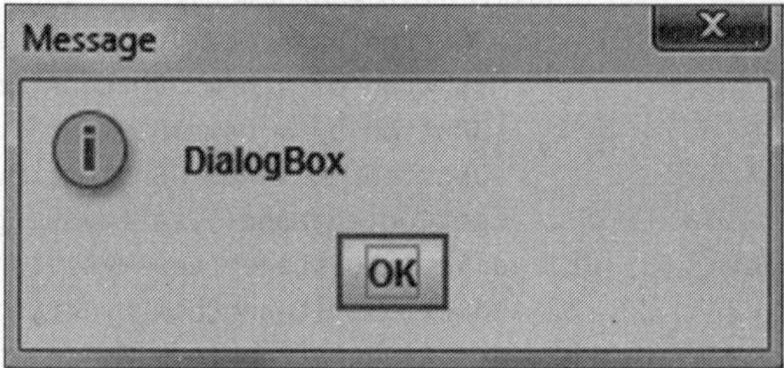

Fig. 15.18(b) Message Dialog

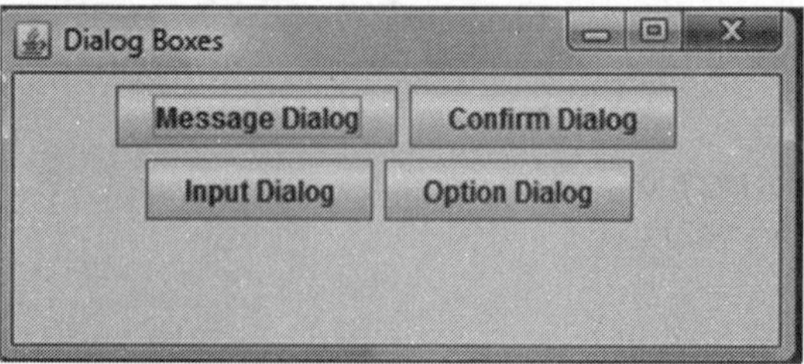

Fig. 15.18(c) Confirm Dialog

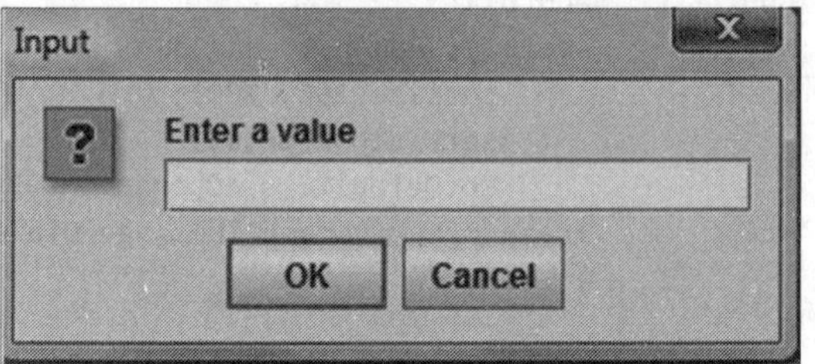

Fig. 15.18(d) Input Dialog

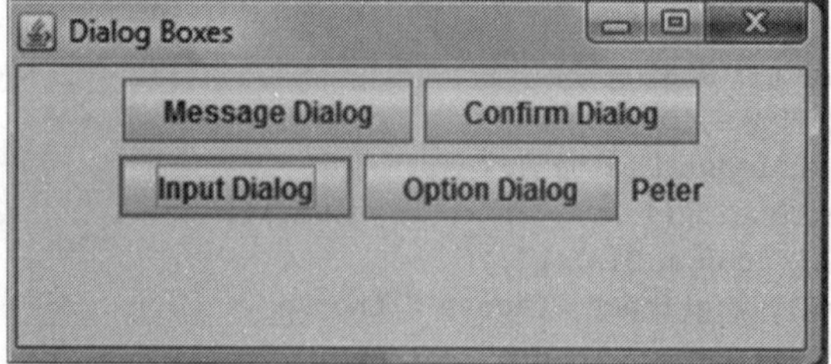

Fig. 15.18(e) JLabel Showing the Value Typed
in Input Dialog

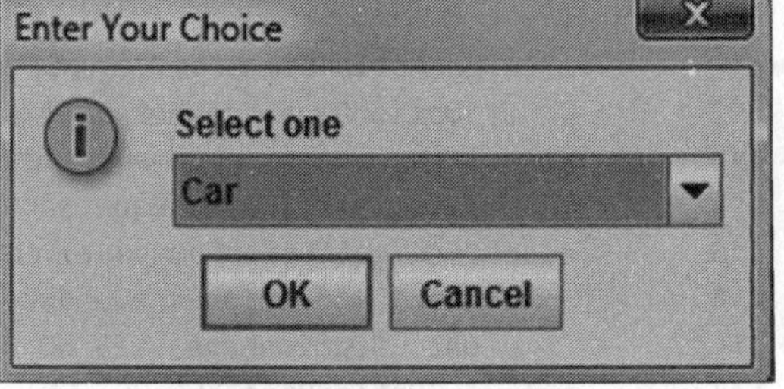

Fig. 15.18(f) Option Dialog

Explanation

L1–7 Four buttons are created and `ActionListener` is registered with all of them. The `JButton` along with a label are added to the frame.

L8 A new `JFrame` is constructed for holding dialog boxes (frame).

L9–20 An inner class has been defined for capturing `JButton` events.

L9 When a button will be clicked, `ActionEvent` will be handled by `MyAction` object.

L10 Method `actionPerformed` overridden.

L11–12 Uses `if` statement to confirm which button has been clicked upon. If it is a message dialog button, the user is shown a message in a message dialog box. The `getActionCommand` method returns the caption of the button as a string. The method used to create a message dialog is `showMessageDialog` which we have already discussed.

L13–14 If the user clicked on input dialog button, an input dialog is shown to the user. He/she can enter the value desired which is returned as a string. The returned value is set as text for the string.

L15–18 If the user clicked on confirm dialog button, a confirm dialog is displayed. Method `showConfirmDialog` is used to create a confirm dialog. The title of the dialog is `ChooseOne` and the message inside the dialog is `Choose`. The user clicks on either yes or no. To check what is the response of the user, we have used `if` statement and matched the return value with `JOptionPane.YES_OPTION` (if yes is clicked) and `JOptionPane.NO_OPTION` (if no is clicked). The label is set accordingly.

L19–21 If the user clicks an option dialog button, an option dialog is displayed. A list of options is displayed in a lookalike combo box control and the user makes a single selection in this control. The default value can also be specified. L20 shows a list of all values that will be inserted in an option dialog. L21 creates an option dialog using the method `showOptionDialog` as discussed. The selection is returned as an object of type `Object` which is then cast to a string and set as the caption for the label (Fig. 15.18).

15.13 JFileChooser

`JFileChooser` class provides a file open dialog where a user can choose to open or save files. `JFileChooser` class navigates the file system to choose a file or directory. Figure 15.19 shows the `JFileChooser` used to open a file. Note the title of file chooser is "Open" and the two buttons towards the end are Open and Cancel.

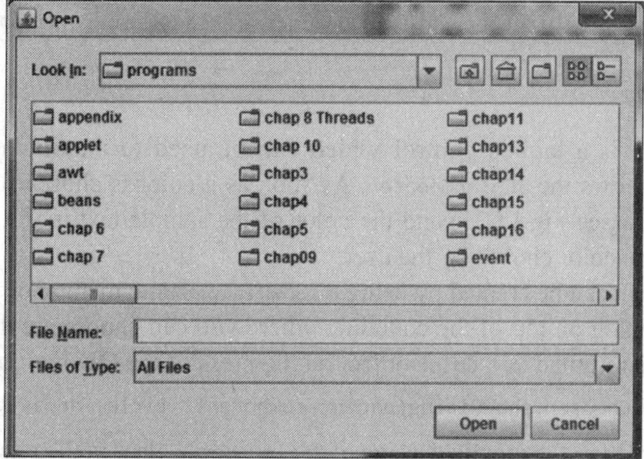

Fig. 15.19 `JFileChooser` Open Dialog

Figure 15.20 shows the `JFileChooser` save dialog. Please note the title at the top is "Save" and the two buttons towards the bottom are "Save" and "Cancel".

The file chooser class is instantiated and the `showOpenDialog` method is used to show the Open file dialog and `showSaveDialog` method is used to show the Save file dialog. Some of the constructors of `JFileChooser` class are shown below in Table 15.11. We will be depicting the practical usage of `JFileChooser` class in the practical problem (Section 15.17).

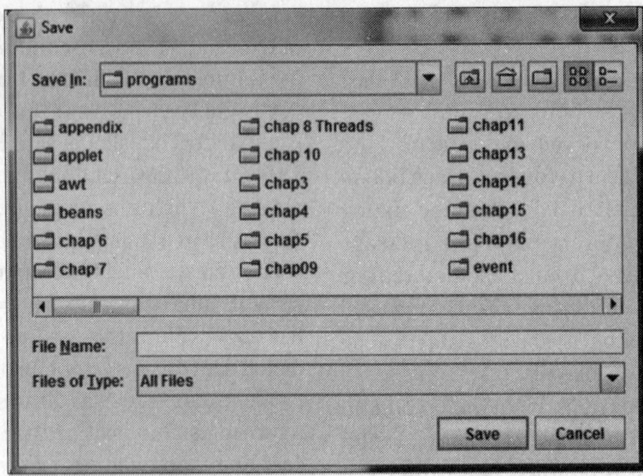

Fig. 15.20 `JFileChooser` Save Dialog

Table 15.11 Few Constructor of `JFileChooser` Class

`JFileChooser()`	Constructs a file chooser which points to the user's default directory.
`JFileChooser(File currentDirectory)`	Constructs a file chooser which points to the directory referred by the `File` object. If `File` object does not refer to any directory (i.e., null), then the user default directory is shown in the `File` chooser.
`JFileChooser(String currentDirectoryPath)`	Constructs a `File` chooser which points to the given path.

15.14 JColorChooser

`JColorChooser` is a tabbed control which can be used to manipulate and select a color. Figure 15.21 shows the `JColorChooser`. As soon as a color is chosen it is added in the list of **Recent:** Colors (see Fig.15.21) and the color of the sample text in the preview pane changes according to the color chosen by the user.

`JColorChooser` can be created by using a `showDialog` static method of this class. This method displays the dialog on top of the container where you can choose a color of your choice. The chosen color is returned as a `Color` object on the press of the **OK** button.

```
JColorChooser.showDialog(parent component, title, default color)
```

We will be depicting the practical usage of `JFileChooser` class in the practical problem (Section 15.17).

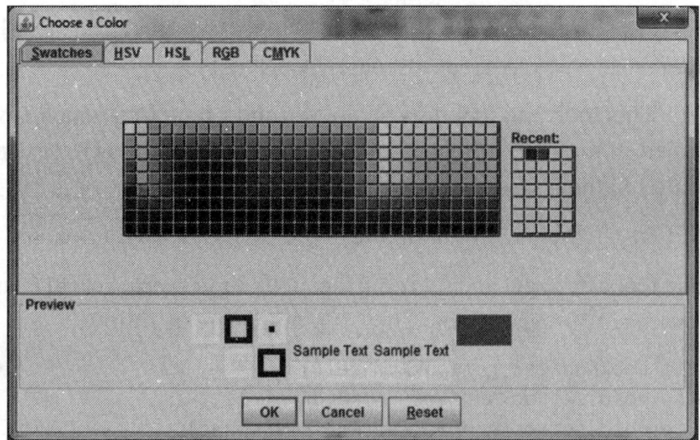

Fig. 15.21 `JColorChooser`

15.15 PLUGGABLE LOOK AND FEEL

Java provides pluggable look and feel. You can change the look and feel of the GUI displayed to the user. The look and feel is provided by the following packages and their sub-packages:

```
javax.swing.plaf
javax.swing.plaf.basic
javax.swing.plaf.metal
javax.swing.plaf.multi
javax.swing.plaf.synth
javax.swing.plaf.nimbus (introduced in Java 6 update 10)
```

Although not part of Java API, the following `Look and Feel` packages are shipped along with Java SDK.

```
com.sun.java.swing.plaf.gtk.GTKLookAndFeel (for Solaris/Linux)
com.sun.java.swing.plaf.motif.MotifLookAndFeel (runs on any platform)
com.sun.java.swing.plaf.windows.WindowsLookAndFeel (only Windows)
```

Java provides the following look and feel:

- *A cross-platform look and feel* (*also known as Metal*) is the default look and feel in Java. The beauty of this look and feel is that it looks uniform on all platforms.

  (`javax.swing.plaf.metal.MetalLookAndFeel`).

- *A system-defined* (*native*) *look and feel* shows the GUI according to the look and feel of the native system.

- *Synth* Using this, you can create your own look and feel

  (`javax.swing.plaf.synth.SynthLookAndFeel`).

- *Multiplexing* Delegates to different look and feel at same time

  (`javax.swing.plaf.multi.MultiLookAndFeel`).

- *Nimbus* A new cross-platform look and feel introduced Java 6 update 10

  `(javax.swing.plaf.nimbus.NimbusLookAndFeel)`.

- *GTK*+ This look and feel runs on Solaris and Linux O.S which have GTK+ 2.2 or later installed in them. The Solaris and Linux O.S without GTK or earlier version of GTK installed in them will have Motif Look and Feel.

- IBM Unix, HP Unix, and Macintosh provide their own Look and Feel.

The look and feel can be get and set using the methods `getLookAndFeel()` and `setLookAndFeel()` of the `javax.swing.UIManager` class. Their signatures are as follows:

```
static LookAndFeel getLookAndFeel()
static void setLookAndFeel(LookAndFeel l)
static void setLookAndFeel(String className)
```

`LookAndFeel` class is the parent of all the look and feel classes in Java. It has two subclasses, `BasicLookAndFeel` and `MultiLookAndFeel`. The `BasicLookAndFeel` is inherited by `MetalLookAndFeel` and `SynthLookAndFeel`. The `NimbusLookAndFeel` class inherits the `SynthLookAndFeel` class.

The metal look and feel has themes associated with it. The default theme is `OceanTheme`. Prior to JDK5 the default theme was `DefaultMetalTheme` (also known as steel). These themes can be get/set using `MetalLookAndFeel` class methods:

```
public static void setCurrentTheme(MetalTheme m)
public static MetalTheme getCurrentTheme()
```

Let us take an example to see how look and feel can change according to an event. There are five buttons in the frame; one for each `Look And Feel`. The look and feel of the frame changes as soon as these buttons are pressed.

Example 15.13(a) Java Look and Feel

```
      import javax.swing.*;
      import java.awt.*;
      import java.awt.event.*;
L1    import javax.swing.plaf.synth.*;
      public class LookAndFeel extends JFrame implements ActionListener
      {
      JButton b1;
      JButton b2;
      JButton b3;
      JButton b4;
      JButton b5;

Container c;
LookAndFeel()
{
      setTitle("LookAndFeel");
      setDefaultCloseOperation(JFrame.EXIT_ON_CLOSE);
      b1 = new JButton("Metal");
```

```java
        b2 = new JButton("Motif");
        b3 = new JButton("System");
        b4=new JButton("Nimbus");
        b5=new JButton("Synth");

        c=getContentPane();
        c.setLayout(new FlowLayout());

        b1.addActionListener(this);
        b2.addActionListener(this);
        b3.addActionListener(this);
        b4.addActionListener(this);
        b5.addActionListener(this);

        add(b1);
        add(b2);
        add(b3);
        add(b4);
        add(b5);

        setVisible(true);
        pack();

    }
    public static void main(String args[]) throws Exception
    {
        SwingUtilities.invokeLater(new Runnable() {
            public void run() {
                    new LookAndFeel();

            }
        });

    }
    public void actionPerformed(ActionEvent ae)
    {
        try{
        String str=ae.getActionCommand();
        if(str.equals("Metal"))
        {
        UIManager.setLookAndFeel(UIManager.getCrossPlatformLookAndFeelClassName());
        //UIManager.setLookAndFeel(javax.swing.plaf.metal.MetalLookAndFeel);
        }
        if(str.equals("Motif"))
            UIManager.setLookAndFeel("com.sun.java.swing.plaf.motif.MotifLookAndFeel");
```

```
L7          if(str.equals("System"))
L8          UIManager.setLookAndFeel("com.sun.java.swing.plaf.windows.WindowsLookAndFeel");
L9          //UIManager.setLookAndFeel(UIManager.getSystemLookAndFeelClassName())


L10         if(str.equals("Nimbus"))
                UIManager.setLookAndFeel("javax.swing.plaf.nimbus.NimbusLookAndFeel");


L11         if(str.equals("Synth"))
    {
L12         SynthLookAndFeel slaf = new SynthLookAndFeel();
L13         slaf.load(LookAndFeel.class.getResourceAsStream("rules.xml"),LookAndFeel.
            class);
L14         UIManager.setLookAndFeel(slaf);
            }
            }catch(Exception e){}
L15         SwingUtilities.updateComponentTreeUI(c);
            }
    }
```

Example 15.13(b) `rules.xml`

```xml
<synth>
<style id="buttonStyle">
    <insets top="5" left="5" right="5" bottom="5"/>
    <font name="Courier New" size="20"/>
    <state>
        <imagePainter method="buttonBackground" path="/images/button.png"
        sourceInsets="10 10 10 10" />
    </state>
</style>
<bind style="buttonStyle" type="region" key="button"/>
</synth>
```

Output

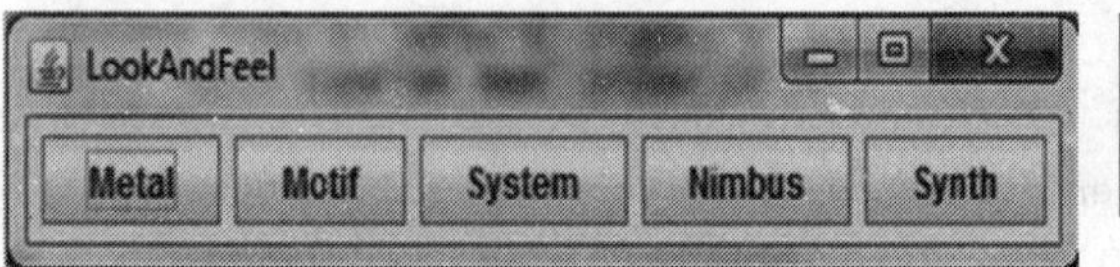

Fig. 15.22(a) Java Metal Look and Feel (Default)

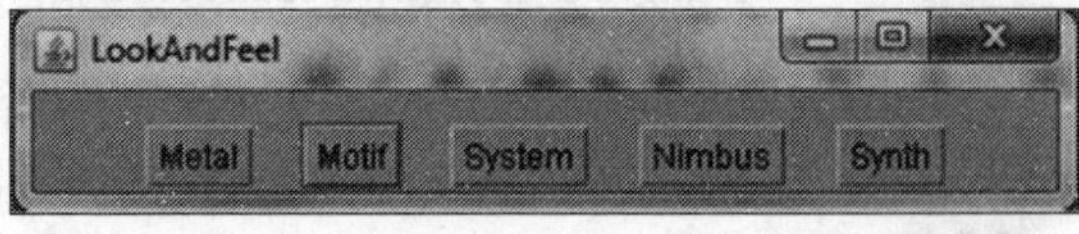

Fig. 15.22(b) The Motif Look and Feel

Fig. 15.22(c) The System-defined Look and Feel (on Windows 7)

Fig. 15.22(d) The Nimbus Look and Feel

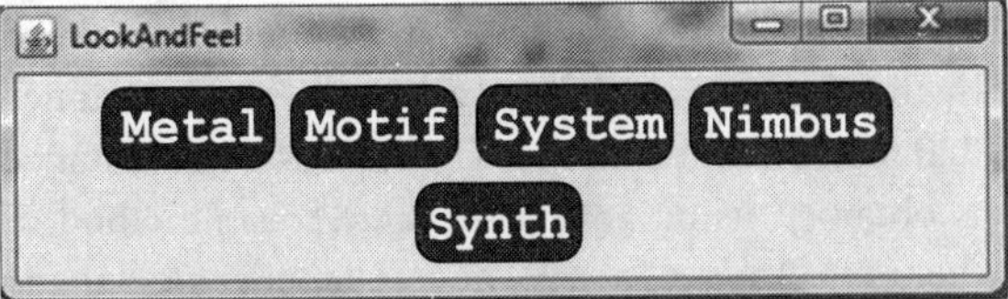

Fig. 15.22(e) The Synth Look and Feel

Fig. 15.22(f) `button.png`

Explanation

L1 Imports the `synth` package. The other classes have been referred by their complete names.

L2 As already told, the swing framework is not thread safe. A swing programmer has to take care in programming GUI so that his GUI is always responsive. Swing provides three types of threads, namely `initial`, `eventdispatching`, and `workerthreads`. The job of initial threads is to schedule a task for execution of event dispatching thread. The task is scheduled using two methods `invokeAndWait` and `invokeLater`. These methods are provided by the class, `SwingUtilities`. The responsibility of an initial thread is to create a runnable object which would initialize the GUI and then schedule the object on an event dispatching thread. Worker threads are used for executing long running task, normally background task. The difference between `invokeLater` and `invokeAndWait` is that, `invokeLater` schedules a job and returns, whereas `invokeAndWait` schedules a job and then waits for it to complete.

```
public static void invokeLater(Runnable r)
public static void invokeAndWait(Runnable r)
```

(**Note:** It should be used in all examples above)

L3–4 If Metal button is clicked, the cross-platform look and feel is set using the method `UIManager. getCrossPlatformLookAndFeelClassName()`. This method returns the `LookAndFeel` subclass name (i.e., `MetalLookAndFeel`)that has cross-platform look and feel. This class name is passed to `setLookAndFeel` method. The class name can also be directly mentioned as shown in comments below L5.

L6 If Motif button is clicked, the motif look and feel is set using method `UIManager.setLookAndFeel()`. The class name has been directly mentioned `"com. sun.java.swing.plaf.motif.MotifLookAndFeel"`.

L7–8 If System button is clicked, the native look and feel is set using the method `UIManager. setLookAndFeel()`. The class name has been directly mentioned `"com.sun.java.swing.plaf. windows.WindowsLookAndFeel"`. The class name can automatically be retrieved using the method

`UIManager.getSystemLookAndFeelClassName()`

as shown in commented line below L9.

L10 If Nimbus button is clicked, the native look and feel is set using the method `UIManager. setLookAndFeel()`. The class name has been directly mentioned `"com.sun.java.swing.plaf.nimbus. NimbusLookAndFeel"`.

L11–14 If Synth button is pressed, all components on the frame should be shown according to the `Synth Look And Feel`.

`Synth Look and Feel` is highly customizable. You can specify style rules for each `Synth` component such as button, label, and text field. Each component has defined region associated with it. Region is a way of identifying all or part of the component. Normally a component has a single region associated with it but some components can have more than one region associated with themselves like split pane, tabbed pane, and scrollbar . Regions for various components are defined as constant in the `javax.swing.plaf.synth.Region` class. Some of the common regions are shown in Table 15.12. The style rules are specified using `SynthStyle`. Using `SynthStyle`, you can specify style rules that affect the size, layout, font, color, etc. Even you can specify background images for components. The most important part of `SynthStyle` is that different styles can be specified for different components. These styles are obtained through a `SynthStyleFactory`. All components contact the `SynthStyleFactory` to obtain synth styles for all its regions. The `SynthStyleFactory` can be defined either by creating an XML file or by creating a class. We will be using the first approach of creating an XML file which will contain all the styles rules. The benefit of putting style rules in an XML file is that if you want to change the look and feel of any or all the components, you just need to change the rules in XML file and the look and feel of your GUI will change automatically. As well as, there is no need to compile the program again and again. The style rules (.xml file) are separate from your program. This XML file is loaded in the program using the `load` method of the `SynthLookAndFeel` class. The `load` method (L13) accepts an object of type `InputStream` (which refers to the XML file) along with the resource base (which is the class itself in our case). XML files have to read by the class hence we need an `InputStream` instance that refers to the .xml file. The `InputStream` instance is obtained using `getResourceAsStream` method of the `java.lang.Class`. The `getResourceAsStream` method is used to refer to external resources like XML configuration files and property files, etc. and return an `InputStream` instance. You can refer to files using absolute and relative pathnames. An absolute path is preceded by a slash (e.g. `/chap 15/rules.xml`) whereas relative path is not preceded by a slash and name is relative to the location from where the method is invoked (e.g., `rules.xml`) (Fig. 15.22).

L15 Whenever the look and feel is changed, all the swing components have to be updated to reflect the look and feel changes. The method used for this purpose is shown below:

```
SwingUtilities.updateComponentTreeUI(c);
```

Table 15.12 Some of the Constant Defined in the Region Class

`BUTTON`	Button region
`CHECK_BOX`	CheckBox region
`CHECK_BOX_MENU_ITEM`	CheckBoxMenuItem region
`COLOR_CHOOSER`	ColorChooser region
`COMBO_BOX`	ComboBox region
`DESKTOP_PANE`	DesktopPane region
`EDITOR_PANE`	EditorPane region
`FILE_CHOOSER`	FileChooser region
`LABEL`	Label region
`LIST`	List region
`MENU`	Menu region
`MENU_BAR`	MenuBar region
`MENU_ITEM`	MenuItem region
`RADIO_BUTTON`	RadioButton region.

(Contd)

(*Table 15.12 Contd*)

RADIO_BUTTON_MENU_ITEM	RegionButtonMenuItem region.
SCROLL_BAR	ScrollBar region.
SCROLL_BAR_THUMB	Thumb of the ScrollBar.
SCROLL_BAR_TRACK	Track of the ScrollBar.
SCROLL_PANE	ScrollPane region.
SPLIT_PANE	SplitPane region.
SPLIT_PANE_DIVIDER	Divider of the SplitPane.
TABBED_PANE	TabbedPane region.
TABBED_PANE_CONTENT	Region of a TabbedPane containing the content.
TABBED_PANE_TAB	Region of a TabbedPane for one tab.
TABBED_PANE_TAB_AREA	Region of a TabbedPane containing the tabs.
TABLE	Table region.
TABLE_HEADER	TableHeader region.
TEXT_AREA	TextArea region.
TEXT_FIELD	TextField region.
TEXT_PANE	TextPane region.
TOGGLE_BUTTON	ToggleButton region.
TREE	Tree region.
TREE_CELL	Region of the Tree for one cell.

The argument passed is the content pane so that all components in the content pane reflect the new look and feel.

Overview of XML

To understand the XML file, we first need to understand XML along with its structure and its rules of creation. So let us take an overview of XML.

XML stands for extensible markup language. XML file have an extension .xml and they can be written in any editor like notepad. XML is a case sensitive language. Unlike HTML, XML provides a clear cut separation of contents from presentation and is hierarchical in nature. An XML files contains user defined tags. These tags conform to some rules specified in a DTD (document type definition) file like

   (a) Name of the root tag.

   (b) Which tags will have attributes?

   (c) What will be name of the attributes?

   (d) What is the possible value of these attributes?

   (e) Which tags will have text or sub tags or a combination of both etc.?

We will be following a predefined DTD structure so the tags that we are going to use in our xml file are already defined. There are certain rules that we should know before creating an XML file.

(a) Every XML document has a root tag.

(b) Every opening tag has a closing tag (e.g. <synth> is an opening tag and </synth> is a closing tag).

(c) All attribute values are in double quotes.

(d) XML is case sensitive so opening and closing tags must match case by case.

(e) Empty tags are those that do not have a closing tag. In other words opening and closing tags are combined and they cannot have sub tags. (e.g. <font name="Courier New" size="20" />

If any rule mentioned above is violated while creating xml then the style rules will not be applied.

Explanation of `rules.xml`

L1 Specifies the root tag. <synth> is the root tag of this xml file.

L2 <style> is a sub tag of <synth> tag. We can specify styles within this tag and apply these styles to components. To identify the styles, an identifier is associated with these styling rules. The identifier is specified in the id attribute of the <style id=""> tag. Different types of styles can be created in different style tags with different ids.

L3 Shows an empty tag. The <insets> tag is used to specify the spaces that should be left on top, bottom, right, and left side after the component has acquired its natural space. (The natural space required by the component would be the space required by the caption of the component). To specify this it uses four attributes as shown: <insets top="5" left="5" right="5" bottom="5"/>. Note the slash before last angle bracket.

L4 Shows another empty tag. The font tag is used to specify the font of the caption or text of the component. The name and size of the font are specified in the attribute of the <font> tag. Note that all attribute are specified in double quotes.

L5 The state tag is used to specify the state of the component. There are seven possible values of the state tag. These values are

  (a) ENABLED

  (b) MOUSE_OVER

  (c) PRESSED

  (d) DISABLED

  (e) FOCUSED

  (f) SELECTED

  (g) DEFAULT

If no value is applied, the rules apply to all the states. A component can be in various states, either it will be pressed or focused or disabled etc. In our example the rules mentioned within state tag will be applicable for all states of the component as we have not mentioned any of the seven values. If we wish to apply the rules (mentioned in this tag) only when mouse is put over the component, the state tag should be as follows:

  <state value="MOUSE_OVER">

  ....

  </state>

L6 In case you wish to specify a background image for your component, then you can use the <imagePainter> tag. The <imagePainter> tag has three attributes: method, path, and `sourceInsets`.

- *Method attribute* It is required to specify which method of `SynthPainter` class is to be invoked for painting. In our case we wish to set a background image for our component, i.e., button. The method that would be used to achieve it is `paintButtonBackground` (....). So the value in this attribute will be "buttonBackground". To determine this value, the paint word in the beginning of method name has been removed and first alphabet of the subsequent words, i.e., B (for button) is converted to lower case and the rest of the word remains as it is.

- *Path attribute* specifies the path of the image to be used as background for your component. We have kept the `button.png` file in images folder which is created in the same directory as that of the program.

- *SourceInsets* **attribute** is used to specify width and height of the corner areas of an image. The significance of this attribute is that image should not be stretched at corners beyond these values. The four values passed as in this attribute correspond to top, left, bottom and right corners of the image.

L7   Closes the state tag.

L8   Closes the style tag.

L9   Shows an empty tag <bind>. This tag is used to bind the style rules mentioned in the above lines to a component. The identifier of the style tag is passed in the style attribute of the bind tag. You will have more than one bind statement to bind styles to different components. In case you wish to apply rules to all the components used in the GUI, the bind tag will be as shown below

```
<bind style=" StyleId " type="region" key=".*"/>
```

We want to specify rules for buttons. The type attribute of the bind tag is used to specify a "region" and key will be "button". The rules apply to all the buttons on the frame. In case you wish to apply separate rules for separate buttons, the bind tags should be used in the following way:

```
<bind style="StyleId" type="name" key="name
of the button" />
```

For example, if the button name is Nimbus and style id is nimbusStyle, then bind tag will be as follows:

```
<bind style="nimbusStyle" type="name"
key="Nimbus" />
```

L10   Closes the root tag <synth>.

15.16 INNER FRAMES

Inner frame is a frame within a frame. Inner frames are created using `javax.swing.JInternalFrame` class. It is a lightweight object that provides many features of a `JFrame`, like dragging, closing, becoming an icon, resizing, title display, and support for a menu bar. The `JInternalFrame` is added to a `JDesktopPane` which is a subclass of `JLayeredPane`. You can also add components to content pane of `JInternalFrame` using the add method. Let us create internal frames within a frame.

Example 15.14 **Inner Frames**

```
L1      import java.awt.event.*;
L2      import java.awt.*;
L3      import javax.swing.*;
L4      import javax.swing.event.*; /* for InternalFrameListener */
L5      public class DemoInternalFrame extends JFrame implements ActionListener
        {
        /* Subclass of Layered Pane */
L6      JDesktopPane dp;
L7      JInternalFrame jif;
L8      JMenuBar jmb;
L9      JMenu File;
L10     static int count=0;
L11     DemoInternalFrame()
        {
L12         super("Inner Frame Example");

L13         dp=new JDesktopPane();
        /* set the Desktop Pane as the content pane */
```

```
L14            setContentPane(dp);

               /* public void setBounds(int x,int y,int width,int height) */

L15            setBounds(100,100,600,600);
L16            setVisible(true);
L17            setDefaultCloseOperation(JFrame.EXIT_ON_CLOSE);

               /* Creates a Menu bar */
L18            jmb=new JMenuBar();
L19            setJMenuBar(jmb);

L20            File=new JMenu("File");
L21            File.setMnemonic(KeyEvent.VK_F);
L22            jmb.add(File);

L23            JMenuItem newItem = new JMenuItem("New");
L24            newItem.setMnemonic(KeyEvent.VK_N);
L25            File.add(newItem);

L26            newItem.addActionListener(this);

               }
L27            public void actionPerformed(ActionEvent ae)
               {
               /* (title, resizable,closable,maximizable,iconifiable) */
L28            jif=new JInternalFrame("Internal Frame"+count++,
                       false,true,true,true);
L29            jif.add(new JLabel("This an Internal Frame"));
L30            jif.setSize(300,200);

L31            jif.setLocation(20*count,20*count);
L32            jif.setDefaultCloseOperation(DISPOSE_ON_CLOSE);
L33            jif.setCursor(new Cursor(Cursor.HAND_CURSOR));

L34            jif.addInternalFrameListener(new InternalFrameAdapter() {

L35            public void internalFrameActivated(InternalFrameEvent i)
               {
L36                    System.out.println(" Internal Frame Activated");

               }
L37            public void internalFrameOpened(InternalFrameEvent i)
               {
L38                    System.out.println("New Internal Frame Opened");

               }
```

```
L39         public void internalFrameIconified(InternalFrameEvent i)
            {
L40                 System.out.println(" Internal Frame Minimized ");
            }
L41         public void internalFrameDeiconified(InternalFrameEvent i)
            {
L42                 System.out.println(" Internal Frame Maximized");
            }
L43         public void internalFrameDeactivated(InternalFrameEvent i)
            {
L44                 System.out.println(" Internal Frame Deactivated");
            }
L45         public void internalFrameClosing(InternalFrameEvent i)
            {
L46                 System.out.println(" Internal Frame Closing");
            }
L47         public void internalFrameClosed(InternalFrameEvent i)
            {
L48                 System.out.println(" Internal Frame Closed");
            }
        });

L49         jif.setVisible(true);

            /* adds inner frame to desktop pane */
L50         dp.add(jif);
            /* if this line is moved after the jif.selected(true), the new inner frame
            are displayed beneath the older frames because setSelected method selects the
            window if the window is displayed */

L51         try{
L52                 jif.setSelected(true);
L53         }catch(java.beans.PropertyVetoException p){}
L54         /*dp.add(jif);*/
        }
L55    public static void main(String args[])
       {
L56                 SwingUtilities.invokeLater(new Runnable()
                    {
                    public void run()
                    {
                            new DemoInternalFrame();
                    }
        });
    }
    }
```

Output

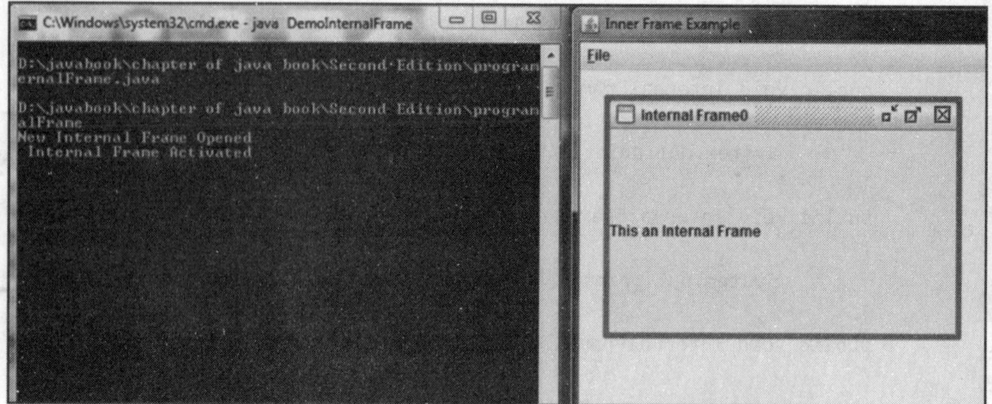

Fig. 15.23(a) A New Internal Frame is Created and Activated

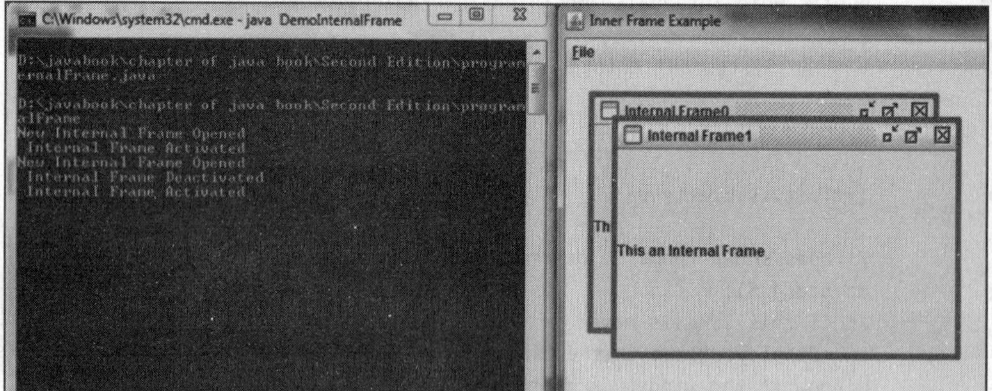

Fig. 15.23(b) Another Internal Frame is Created. The Previous Frame (Frame 0) is Deactivated and New Frame is Opened and Activated

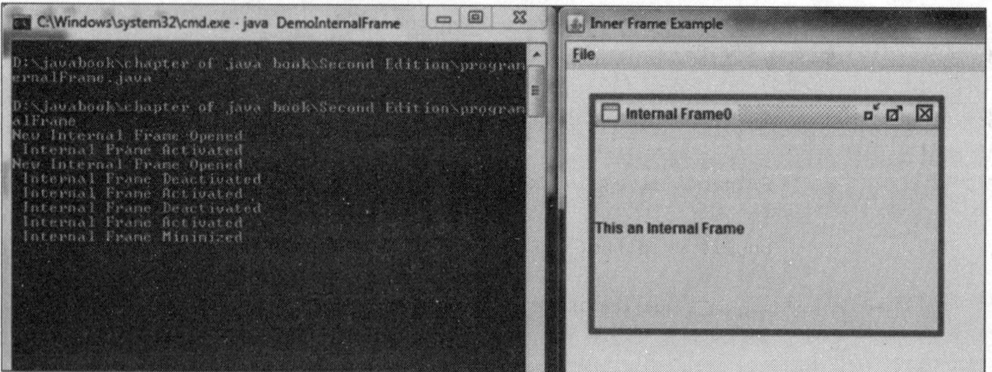

Fig. 15.23(c) Internal Frame 1 is Iconified. So it becomes Deactivated. The Frame Beneath it Becomes Activated and the Internal Frame 1 is Minimized

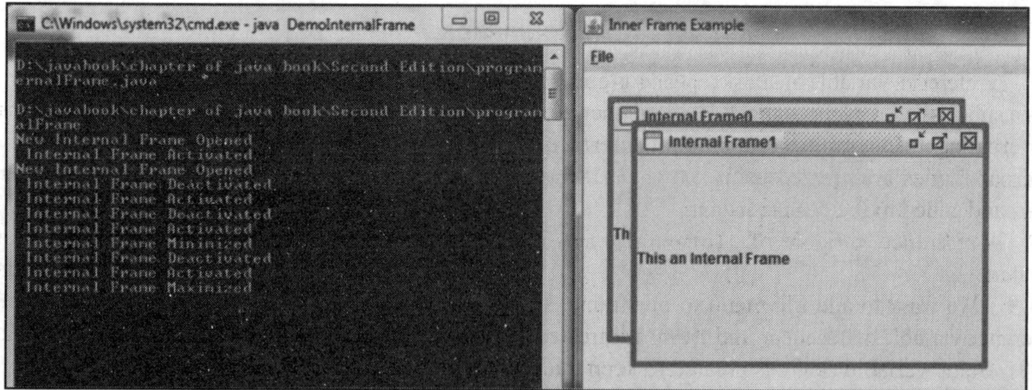

Fig. 15.23(d) Internal Frame 1 is Deiconified. Internal Frame 0 becomes Deactivated. The Frame 1 is Activated and Maximized

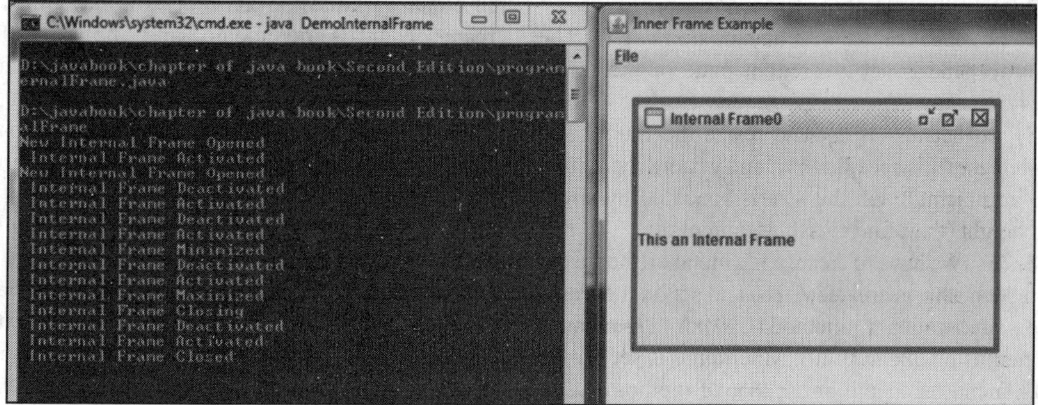

Fig. 15.23(e) Internal Frame 1 is Closed. The Closing Method is Called and Frame is Deactivated. The Frame Beneath it becomes Activated and the Internal Frame 1 is Closed

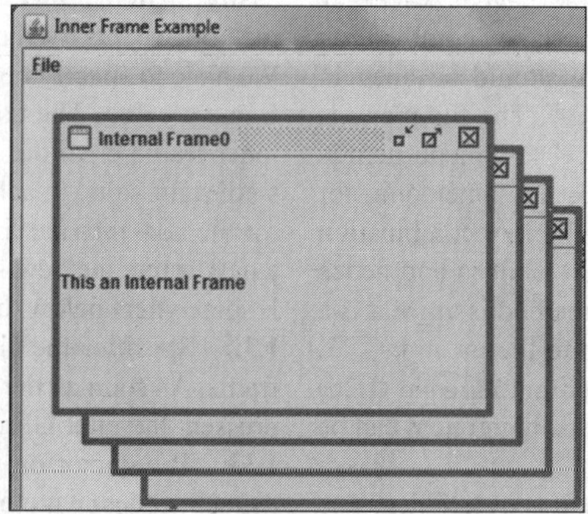

Fig. 15.23(f) If L50 is Commented and L54 is Uncommented

Explanation

L6 A reference variable of JDesktopPane is created. It is a subclass of JLayeredPane. It is a container used for creating MDI (multiple-document interface). Internal frames are created using JInternalFrame class and added to the JDesktopPane.

L7 A reference variable of JInternalFrame is created.

L8–9 We want to add file menu to our frame, so reference variable of JMenuBar and JMenu are created.

L10 Static variable count is created to keep track of the number of internal frames created.

L11 Constructor for the class is declared. L11–26 show the constructor of the class.

L12 Sets the title of the frame.

L13–14 JDesktopPane is instantiated in L13. The desktop pane is set as content pane of the frame (L14).

L15 setBounds is used to resize the frame. The top-left corner is specified by x and y coordinates (first two arguments), and the size is specified by width and height (third and fourth arguments).

L18–26 We have to create a file menu on the frame. So a JMenuBar is created (L18) and set on the frame using setJMenuBar() method (L19). A File menu is created using JMenu (L20). Mnemonic is set for the File menu using the setMnemonic method (L21). Mnemonic is a key which if used in combination with alt key activates the menu / menu item on which it has been set. Mnemonics are specified as static integer constants in java.awt.event.KeyEvent class. We have specified that when key combination alt+f is pressed, the file menu should be opened. So the argument passed is VK_F. The file menu is added to the menu bar in L22. A New menu item is created in L23 using JMenuItem. A mnemonic for New menuitem is set in L24. The key combination used to activate this menu item is alt+n and hence the argument to setMnemonic method is VK_N. it is a part of file menu so it is added to file menu in L25. Lastly, it is registered with ActionListener (L26) so that the click event on this New menu item can be monitored and handled.

L27 actionPerformed method is overridden. The ActionEvent is passed to this method as soon as the user clicks on the new menu item or the mnemonic combination is pressed on the file menu.

L28–54 Execute on every New menu item click.

L28 An internal frame is created using the JInternalFrame class. Five arguments are passed within the constructor of JInternalFrame class. The first one specifies the title of the internal frame, second argument specifies whether the internal frame can be resized or not, third argument specifies whether the internal frame can be closed or not, forth argument specifies whether the internal frame can be maximized or not, and final argument specifies whether the internal frame can be iconified (i.e., minimized) or not. The title of the frame includes the count variables so as soon as a new frame is created, count is incremented and title is set. The internal frame cannot be resized as second argument is specified as false.

L29 To show how components can be added to the internal frames, we have added a label on the internal frame using the add method.

L30 The size of the internal frame is set using the setSize method.

L31 Location for the internal frame has been specified using the setLocation method. If the location is not specified, new internal frames will appear on top of older internal frames once they are created. In other words they will fully cover the older inner frames. So location is set to show the user that internal frames are created and user can easily switch between frames. The setLocation method accepts two arguments: x and y coordinates. We have to specify new coordinates for every inner frame created. The count value increases on every inner frame creation. This value is multiplied with a constant value to achieve new x and y coordinates for the new internal frame. So whenever you create a new frame the new location for the internal frame is somewhere below the older frame (see Fig. 15.23).

L32 Specifies the close operation for the internal frame. As soon as the cross on the internal frame is pressed, the internal frame is disposed.

L33 The cursor on the internal frame is changed using setCursor method. The cursor class has static constants to change the visual display of the cursor. The following values can be specified:

```
Cursor.HAND_CURSOR
Cursor.CROSSHAIR_CURSOR
Cursor.MOVE_CURSOR
```

(For more details see cursor class in Java documentation)

L34–48 InternalFrameListener is registered with every internal frame that is created. An anonymous inner class is created which inherits the InternalFrameAdapter class. InternalFrameAdapter is an adapter class which inherits the InternalFrameListener interface. Although not required but we have overridden all the methods of the interface to show you the calling sequence of these methods. When a new internal frame is created, the internalFrameOpened (InternalFrameEvent i) is called and then this new frame is selected so internalFrameActivated (InternalFrameEvent i) is called (see Fig. 15.23(a)). If another frame is created; firstly the new frame is opened, the previous frame is deactivated and this new frame is activated (see Fig. 15.23(b)). When this activated internal frame (Frame 1) is minimized, firstly it is deactivated, the previous inner frame (Frame 0) is

activated and theinternalFrameIconified(InternalFrameEvent i) on the frame 1 is invoked (see Fig. 15.23(c)). If the minimized frame (i.e., Frame 1) is de-iconified (maximized), then firstly the frame 0 is deactivated, frame 1 is activated and then it is maximized by calling its internalFrameDeiconified (InternalFrameEvent i). If the activated Frame 1 cross button is pressed, firstly the closing method (internalFrameClosing(InternalFrameEvent i)) on this frame is invoked, this frame is deactivated, the frame beneath it (if any) is activated and lastly the internal frame is closed (see Fig. 15.23(e)).

L49 The internal frame visibility is set to true.

L50 The internal frame is added to Desktop pane.

L51–54 The newly created internal frame will be selected by this statement. As we have added the internal frame first and then selected them, the newly added frames will appear on top of each other. If we reverse the order, that is if you select it first and then add the frames, the new frames will be added but will appear beneath the older frame. If you put L50 in comment and uncomment L54. The output will be as shown in Fig. 15.23(f).

15.17 PRACTICAL PROBLEM: MINI EDITOR

The following program shows a menu-based editor with minimal functionality. The functionality provided by our editor is as follows:

(a) Creating a new file
(b) Opening an existing file,
(c) Saving a file,
(d) Editing a file–change the contents of the file and then save it
(e) Perform cut, copy and paste operation on the file.
(f) Change the color of the text in the editor.
(g) Exit the editor

Note Note that we have created a very basic editor. We have purposely not created the entire editor for you because we want you to create it on your own. Many students find it difficult to start with a project. So, we have provided a beginning to you. While making enhancements to this editor, you might change the structure of the program or may create more classes to support your editor.

Example 15.15 `Editor.java`

```java
import javax.swing.*;
import java.awt.*;
import java.awt.event.*;
import java.io.*;
import java.net.*;

public class Editor extends JFrame implements ActionListener
{
    JEditorPane j;
    Container c;
    JPopupMenu pum;
    String selText;
    Editor()
    {
        super("Editor");
        c=getContentPane();
        j=new JEditorPane();
        JMenuBar mb=new JMenuBar();
        JMenu mn=new JMenu("File");
        JMenuItem n=new JMenuItem("New");
        JMenuItem op=new JMenuItem("Open");
        JMenuItem saveas=new JMenuItem("Save As");
        saveas.addActionListener(this);
        JMenuItem exit=new JMenuItem("Exit");
        n.addActionListener(this);
        op.addActionListener(this);
        exit.addActionListener(new ActionListener()
        {
        public void actionPerformed(ActionEvent ae)
        {
            System.exit(0);
        }
        });

        mn.add(n);
        mn.add(op);
        mn.add(saveas);
        mn.add(exit);
        mb.add(mn);

        JMenu ed=new JMenu("Edit");
        JMenuItem copy=new JMenuItem("Copy");
        JMenuItem cut=new JMenuItem("Cut");
        JMenuItem paste=new JMenuItem("Paste");

        copy.addActionListener(this);
        cut.addActionListener(this);
        paste.addActionListener(this);
```

```java
        ed.add(copy);
        ed.add(cut);
        ed.add(paste);
        mb.add(ed);

        /*Pop up Menu created which will be displayed once a user right clicks on the editor*/
        pum=new JPopupMenu();

        /*The pop up menu will have the following options: copy,cut,paste, change
        color of the text*/

        JMenuItem pumcopy=new JMenuItem("Copy");
        JMenuItem pumcut=new JMenuItem("Cut");
        JMenuItem pumpaste=new JMenuItem("Paste");
        JMenuItem changecolor=new JMenuItem("Change Color");
        /*add the menu items to the pop up menu*/
        pum.add(pumcopy);
        pum.add(pumcut);
        pum.add(pumpaste);
        pum.add(changecolor);

        /*registers pop up menu items with action listener so that something happens
        when user clicks on those Pop up menu items*/
        pumcopy.addActionListener(this);
        pumcut.addActionListener(this);
        pumpaste.addActionListener(this);
        changecolor.addActionListener(this);
        /*adds pop up menu to the editor*/
        j.add(pum);

        /* On mouse click we want to show the Pop up Menu, so we obtain the (x,y)
        position of the mouse click using me.getX() and me.getY() methods and show
        the pop up menu on those coordinates using the show() method of pop up menu.
        The pop up menu has to be shown on the JEditor so the first argument is the
        JEditor object.*/

        j.addMouseListener(new MouseAdapter()
        {
                public void mousePressed(MouseEvent me)
                {

                if(me.isPopupTrigger())
                {
                        int x=me.getX();
                        int y=me.getY();
                        pum.show(j,x,y);
                }
        }

public void mouseReleased(MouseEvent me)
{
```

```java
                    if(me.isPopupTrigger())
                    {
                            int x=me.getX();
                            int y=me.getY();
                            pum.show(j,x,y);
                    }
            }
        });

    setJMenuBar(mb);
    c.add(new JScrollPane(j),BorderLayout.CENTER);
    setSize(300,500);
    setVisible(true);
    setDefaultCloseOperation(JFrame.EXIT_ON_CLOSE);
}

public void actionPerformed(ActionEvent ae)
{

    if(ae.getActionCommand().equals("Open"))
    {

    /* To Open an existing File, a JFileChooser Dialog object is created. The default
    directory is set using the setCurrentDirectory method and the content of this di-
    rectory are shown to the user within the File Chooser Dialog. The dialog is shown
    to the user on the editor (parent component) using showOpenDialog method of the
    JFileChooser object. This method returns an int value corresponding to the state of
    the JFileChooser object like JFileChooser.CANCEL_OPTION, JFileChooser.APPROVE_OPTION
    and JFileChooser.ERROR_OPTION. If the user has not pressed the cancel button (int
    value is not equal to the CANCEL_OPTION), then get the selected file (getSelected-
    File() method) and display the file on the JEditorPane. */

    JFileChooser choose = new JFileChooser();
    choose.setCurrentDirectory(new File ("d: /javabook/ programs"));

    if(choose.showOpenDialog(this)!=JFileChooser.CANCEL_OPTION)
      {
        try
        {
    /* The toURL of the file class is deprecated so to convert it into URL we first have
    to convert it to URI and then the URI object to URL */

        URL u=choose.getSelectedFile().toURI().toURL();
        j.setPage(u);
        }catch(MalformedURLException e){}
        catch(IOException e){}
      }
    }
    else if(ae.getActionCommand().equals("New"))
      j.setText("");
```

```java
    else if(ae.getActionCommand().equals("Save As"))
    {
      JFileChooser choose=new JFileChooser();
      choose.setCurrentDirectory(new File ("d:/ javabook /programs"));
      choose.showSaveDialog(this);

      try{
          FileWriter fw=new FileWriter (choose. getSelectedFile());
          fw.write(j.getText());
          fw.close();
          }catch(IOException ie){}

    }
    else if(ae.getActionCommand().equals("Copy"))
    {
      j.copy();
      System.out.println(j.getCaretPosition());
    }
    else if(ae.getActionCommand().equals("Paste"))
    {
      j.paste();
    }
    else if(ae.getActionCommand().equals("Cut"))
    {
      j.cut();
    }

      else if(ae.getActionCommand().equals("Change Color"))
    {

    /* show a dialog on top of the editor where you can choose a color of your choice.
    The chosen color is returned as a color object.*/
    /* JColorChooser.showDialog(parent component, title,default color) */

    Color col=JColorChooser.showDialog(j,"Choose a Color",Color.red);

    /* set the caret color as the color chosen by the user*/
        j.setCaretColor(col);

    /* change the color of the text in the editor as the color chosen by the user.*/
        j.setForeground(col);
      }

  }
  public static void main(String args[])
  {
    SwingUtilities.invokeLater(new Runnable() {
      public void run() {
        new Editor();
      }});
  }
}
```

Output

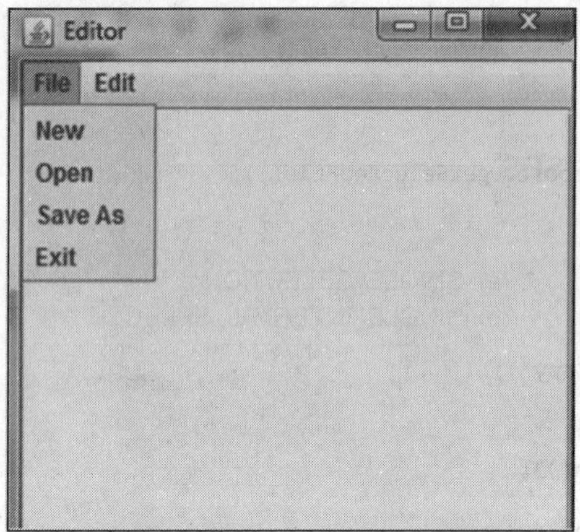

Fig. 15.24(a) File Menu of the Editor is Displayed When Mouse Click Occurs on File Menu

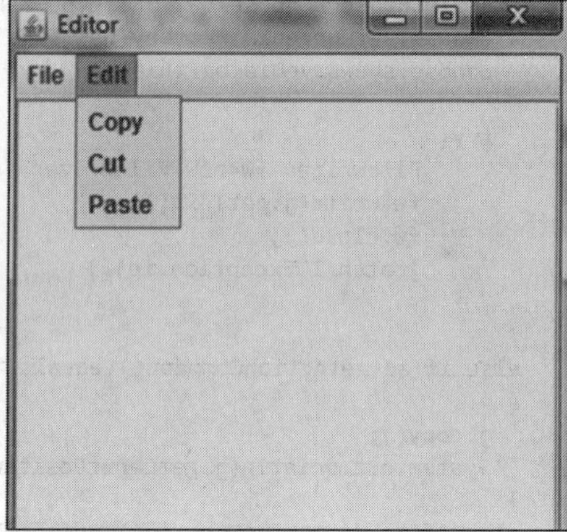

Fig. 15.24(b) Edit Menu of the Editor is Displayed When Mouse Click Occurs on Edit Menu

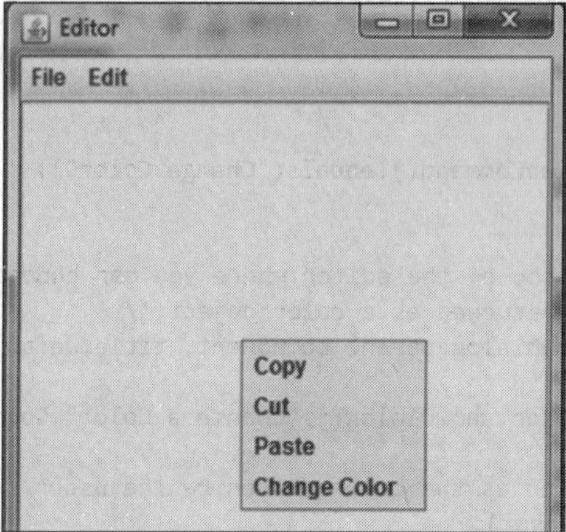

Fig. 15.24(c) Pop Up Menu on the Editor is Displayed When Right Mouse Click Occurs on Editor

SUMMARY

Swing is a very powerful API provided by Java for creating graphical user interfaces. The most important feature of swing components is that they are lightweight, swing components are written in Java, so they are portable and the GUI has a pluggable look and feel. All component names follow Jxxx format, e.g., JButton, JPanel, JLabel, JTextField, etc.

Many new components have been added in swings which help in creating more interactive GUIs. JSplitPane splits the display area into parts. JTabbedPane groups together a number of components and displays them as a unit. JScrollPane has all the functionality of a scrollbar as well as view pane. Dialog boxes (provided by other GUI software tools) are also provided by swing package.

Four types of dialog boxes have been provided, namely confirm dialog, input dialog, option dialog, and message dialog. New layouts have been added in swings like `BoxLayout` and `SpringLayout`. The pluggable look and feel feature gives Java an upper edge over other languages. The cross-platform look and feel gives Java GUI a standard look and feel which is uniform on all platforms. Apart from this, the native look and feel is also supported.

EXERCISES

Objective Questions

1. Why are swing components termed as lightweight?
   - (a) they depend on native platform
   - (b) they do not depend on native platform
   - (c) they depend on native application
   - (d) they do not depend on native application

2. Which method is used to close a swing frame?
   - (a) `setTitle()`
   - (b) `setDefaultCloseOperation()`
   - (c) `setVisible()`
   - (d) `pack()`

3. Which pane is used for placing components on a `JFrame`?
   - (a) content pane
   - (b) root pane
   - (c) layered pane
   - (d) glass pane

4. The default layout of a content pane is
   - (a) `FlowLayout`
   - (b) `BoxLayout`
   - (c) `SpringLayout`
   - (d) `BorderLayout`

5. Which method is used to set the selection mode for the `JList`?
   - (a) `setSelectionMode()`
   - (b) `setSelection()`
   - (c) `setMode()`
   - (d) `setSelectedMode()`

6. Which mode is used for setting 'multiple interval selection' mode for a `JList`?
   - (a) SINGLE_SELECTION
   - (b) SINGLE_INTERVAL_SELECTION
   - (c) MULTIPLE_INTERVAL_SELECTION
   - (d) MULTI_INTERVAL_SELECTION

7. Which method is used to make a split pane expand or contract when you click on the divider?
   - (a) setOneTouchExpandable
   - (b) setExpandable
   - (c) setExpandContract
   - (d) setDivider

8. Which method is used to add tabs to a `JTabbedPane`?
   - (a) addTabbed
   - (b) addTab
   - (c) setTabAt
   - (d) setTabbedPane

9. The class used to create input dialog box in Java is
   - (a) JInputDialog
   - (b) JDialogBox
   - (c) JOptionPane
   - (d) JConfirmDialog

10. The method used to create a confirm dialog in swing is
    - (a) showInputDialog
    - (b) showMessageDialog
    - (c) showOptionDialog
    - (d) showConfirmDialog

Review Questions

1. Explain the difference between swing and AWT.
2. Explain the difference between `invokeLater` and `invokeAndWait` methods.
3. Explain the pluggable look and feel feature of swings along with the look and feels available in Java.
4. What is the difference between `JButton` and `JToggleButton`?
5. What are the various dialog boxes available in swing and how are they created?
6. What are inner frames? What classes are used to create them?
7. Explain the role of `JFileChooser` class.
8. How are trees created in a Java GUI?
9. How can you create a table having multiple rows and columns in a Java frame?

Programming Exercises

1. Create a login form which contains a user id, password field, and two buttons, submit and reset. If the user id or password field is left blank, then on click of submit button, show a message to the user to fill in the fields. On click of reset button, clear the fields.

2. Create two lists using `JList` class with a button. On click of that button, all selected items in one list are copied to the other list.

3. Create a split pane which divides the frame into two parts. The first part possesses a list and on selecting an item in a list, the item should be displayed in the other portion.

4. Create a tabbed pane and place the login form (Exercise 1) on first tab and the list (Exercise 2) on second tab.

Answers to Objective Questions

1. (b)	**2.** (b)	**3.** (a)	**4.** (d)
5. (a)	**6.** (c)	**7.** (a)	**8.** (b)
9. (c)	**10.** (d)		

Introduction to Advanced Java

Time has been transformed, and we have changed; it has advanced and set us in motion; it has unveiled its face, inspiring us with bewilderment and exhilaration.

Kahlil Gibran

After reading this chapter, the readers will be able to

- handle databases
- do server side programming with servlets
- understand how to create and use JSP pages
- create and use Java beans
- create remote application using RMI
- understand the concept about EJB

16.1 INTRODUCTION TO J2EE

J2EE architecture is a multi-tier architecture with four tiers: client tier, web tier, enterprise tier, and information system tier. The client tier basically consists of presentation logic. Web tier consists of components that respond to clients' request over the Internet, i.e., accepting HTTP request and generating responses for them. Enterprise tier consists of business logic like the EJB, and information system tier consists of databases. J2EE consists of the following technologies: Java server pages (JSP), servlets, Java beans, Java database connectivity (JDBC), Java naming and directory interface (JNDI), enterprise Java beans (EJB), remote method invocation (RMI), Java mail API, Java messaging service, Java transaction API, and Java IDL/CORBA. We will discuss few of the technologies in this chapter.

16.2 DATABASE HANDLING USING JDBC

JDBC stands for Java database connectivity. It is a standard API for all Java programs to connect to any databases. The JDBC API is available in two packages:

- Core API `java.sql`.
- Standard extension to JDBC API `javax.sql` (supports connection pooling, transactions, etc.).

JDBC defines a few steps to connect to a database and retrieve/insert/update databases. The steps are as follows:

- Load the driver
- Establish connection
- Create statements
- Execute query and obtain result
- Iterate through the results

16.2.1 Load the Driver

If your program needs a database connection, then the first step is to load the driver. JDBC version 4.0 (works only with Java 6 and above) onwards the manual loading of database driver was done away with. It is now done automatically, but for learning purpose, we will show you all the steps involved. The driver is loaded with the help of a static method,

```
Class.forName(drivername)
```

Every database has its own driver. Table 16.1 shows the driver names for a few databases.

Table 16.1 Driver Names

Database name	Driver Name
MS Access	sun.jdbc.odbc.JdbcOdbcDriver
Oracle	oracle.jdbc.driver.OracleDriver
Microsoft SQL Server 2000 (Microsoft Driver)	com.microsoft.sqlserver.jdbc.SQLServerDriver
MySQL (MM.MySQL Driver)	org.gjt.mm.mysql.Driver

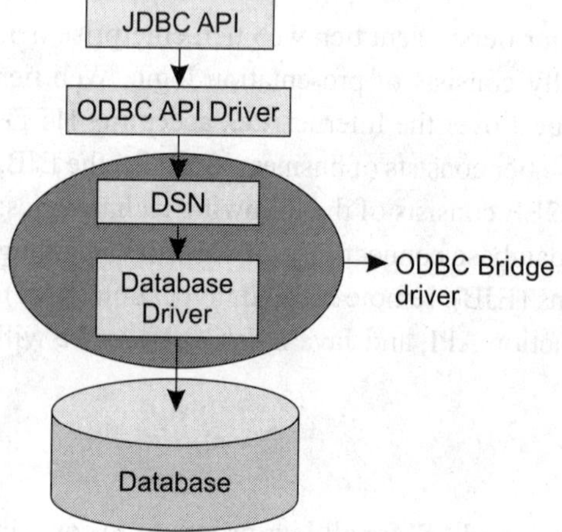

Fig. 16.1 Type 1 Driver

All the JDBC drivers have been classified into four categories:

- Type 1: JDBC ODBC bridge driver
- Type 2: Native-API/partly Java driver
- Type 3: Net-protocol driver
- Type 4: Pure Java driver

Type 1: JDBC ODBC Bridge Driver

This driver is shipped with the JDK and used only for learning/experimental purpose. This driver translates all JDBC call to ODBC and sends it to the ODBC drivers. ODBC is a standard way for accessing databases and is independent of operating system, programming languages, and databases. ODBC API is available in the administrative tools of the control panel, present in all Microsoft operating systems. Figure 16.1 illustrates the concept.

Data source name (DSN) is created by the programmer through ODBC API. DSN keeps a record of which database needs to be accessed, the location of the database, and the driver needed to access the database. Optional attributes like user id and password are also maintained with DSN. There are three types of DSN:

- User DSN—for a specific user.
- System DSN—for all users on the machine.
- File DSN—for all users who have same drivers installed and the users can be on different machines.

Anyone of these three can be created using ODBC API depending upon the requirement. The advantage of using this type of driver is that it is readily available. However, it has the following disadvantages:

- Performance is much low as JDBC calls ODBC and ODBC driver access database and then the result is retrieved.
- Not platform independent.
- Not suitable for web applications.

Type 2: Native-API/Partly Java Driver

In Type 2 driver, JDBC calls the native API driver which calls the database native API to connect to the database. This is shown in Fig. 16.2.

The advantage is that it offers better performance than Type 1 driver, but on the other side, it has the following disadvantages:

- Libraries (API) need to be installed on the client machine.
- Not suitable for web applications.

Type 3: Net-protocol Driver

Type 3 drivers are written purely in Java and used in a networked environment (3-tier architecture). The requests are routed to a middle tier which converts JDBC calls to database-specific calls. This is illustrated in Fig. 16.3.

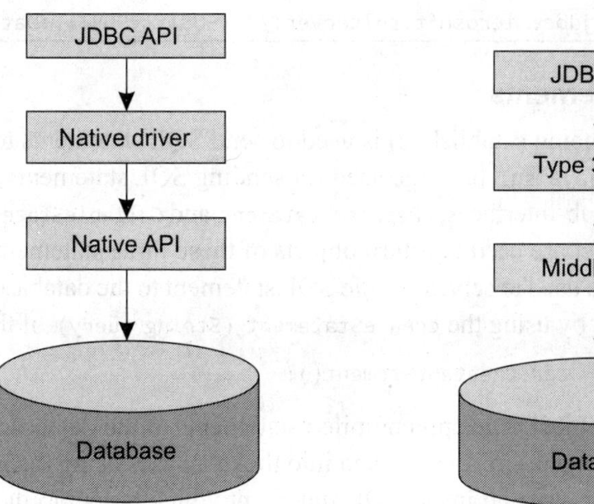

Fig. 16.2 Type 2 Driver   **Fig. 16.3** Type 3 Driver

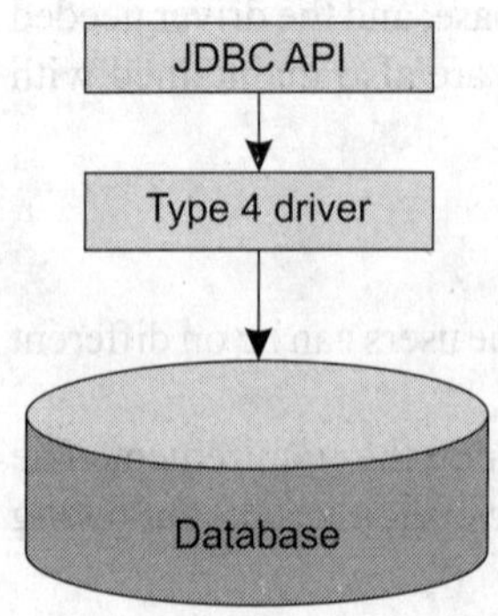

Fig. 16.4 Type 4 Driver

The advantages of this approach are

- Clients are insulated from the database specific libraries.
- It can be used in web applications.

The disadvantage of this driver is that the database-specific code has to be embedded into the middle tier.

Type 4: Pure Java Driver

Type 4 driver is a pure Java driver (similar to Type 3) that is used to connect to the database directly. Figure 16.4 illustrates this concept.

Following are the advantages of using a Type 4 driver:

- It is platform independent.
- Though its performance is very good, it requires a different driver for every database.

16.2.2 Establish Connection

A connection to the database is established using the static method `getConnection (databaseUrl)` of the `DriverManager` class. It is the class for managing JDBC drivers. The database URL takes the following shape: `jdbc:subprotocol:subname`. If any problem occurs during accessing the database, an `SQLException` is generated, else a `Connection` object is returned which refers to a connection to a database. `Connection` is actually an interface in `java.sql` package.

```
Connection con = DriverManager.getConnection(databaseUrl);
```

Table 16.2 shows the various database URLs for connecting to various databases.

Table 16.2 Few Database URLs

Database	Database URL
MS Access	`jdbc:odbc:<DSN>`
Oracle thin driver	`jdbc:oracle:thin:@<HOST>:<PORT>:<SID>`
Microsoft SQL Server 2000	`jdbc:microsoft:sqlserver:// <HOST>:<PORT>[;DatabaseName = <DB>]`

16.2.3 Create Statements

The connection (after being established) is used to send SQL statements to the database. There are three interfaces in `java.sql` package used for sending SQL statements to databases, namely `Statement` and its two sub-interfaces, `PreparedStatement` and `CallableStatement`. Three methods of the `Connection` object are used to return objects of these three statements.

A `Statement` object is used to send a simple SQL statement to the database with no parameters. Its objects are returned by using the `createStatement (String query)` of the connection object.

```
Statement stmt = con.createStatement();
```

A `PreparedStatement` object sends precompiled statements to the databases with or without IN parameters. Normally, we insert rows of data into the databases using the insert SQL statement. For every insertion, we write an insert SQL statement which is sent to the database. If n rows need to be inserted, then the same statement gets compiled n number of times. It consumes a lot of time. So to increase efficiency, we use precompiled `PreparedStatement`. In this case, only the values that have to be inserted are sent to the database again and again.

```
PreparedStatement ps = con.prepareStatement(String query);
```

A `CallableStatement` object is used to call stored procedures. It is created using the `preparecall` method.

```
CallableStatement cs = con.prepareCall(String query);
```

16.2.4 Execute Query

The SQL statements are executed with the help of three methods provided by the `Statement` interface:

```
ResultSet executeQuery(String sqlQuery) throws SQLException
int executeUpdate(String sqlQuery) throws SQLException
boolean execute(String sqlQuery) throws SQLException
```

The method `executeQuery` is used for executing SQL statements that return a single `ResultSet`, e.g., a select statement. The rows fetched from database are returned as a single `ResultSet` object. For example,

```
ResultSet rs = stmt.executeQuery("select * from emp");
```

The method `executeUpdate` is used for DDL and DML SQL statements like insert, update, delete, and create. This method returns an integer value for DML to indicate the number of rows affected/inserted (also known as update counts) and 0 for DDL statements which do not return anything. For example,

```
PreparedStatement ps = con.prepareStatement("update emp set salary = ?
where empid = ?");
```

The statement is sent to database and is prepared for execution, only the value of the IN (?) parameters need to be sent.

```
ps.setInt(1,100000);
ps.setString(2,"Emp001");
ps.executeUpdate();
```

The `PreparedStatement` has certain methods that are used to set value for the IN parameters as shown in the lines of code above. In `setInt(1,100000)`, the first argument is the ordinal position of the IN parameters. This method will set `salary = 100000` and the method `setString (2, "Emp001")` sets the second IN parameter in the query, i.e., where `empid = 'Emp001'`.

The `execute` method is used for callable statement when the statement may return more than one `ResultSet` or `update counts` or a combination of both. This happens when stored procedures are executed.

16.2.5 Iterate ResultSet

The `ResultSet` is iterated with the help of a method *next* which returns a boolean value to indicate that the `ResultSet` has more rows to be iterated. The *next* method moves the cursor to the next row. The individual column data is obtained by using accessor (i.e., getX) methods. For example, if the first column is a string, the method to fetch its value is `getString(1)`. Similar methods are available for other data types:

For int, the method is `int getInt(int columnIndex)`
For long, the method is `long getLong(int columnIndex)`
For float, the method is `float getFloat(int columnIndex)`
For short, the method is `shortgetShort(int columnIndex)`
For Boolean, the method is `boolean getBoolean(int columnIndex)`
For byte, the method is `byte getByte(int columnIndex)`
For Date, the method is `Date getDate(int columnIndex)`

The code shown below is used for iterating the `ResultSet`:

```java
while (rs.next())
    {
        System.out.println(rs.getString(1));
        System.out.println(rs.getInt(2));

        ......

    }
```

Column indexing in the `ResultSet` starts from 1, not 0. Now, how do we know what is the type of data in the first/second columns so that the appropriate methods can be used, and how many columns are returned in the `ResultSet`? All these details can be obtained using a `ResultSetMetaData` object. This object is used to obtain metadata about the `ResultSet` that include number of columns, types of columns, etc. The method `getMetaData()`is used to return the `ResultSetMetaData` object. The method `getColumnCount()` returns the number of columns in the `ResultSet`. The method `getColumnTypeName(int columnIndex)` returns the type of data the column holds.

```java
ResultSetMetaData rsmd = rs.getMetaData();
System.out.println("Column in ResultSet:" +rsmd.getColumnCount());
for(int i = 1; i < = rsmd.getColumnCount(); i++)
{
    System.out.println("Column Name :" +rsmd.getColumnName(i));
    System.out.println("Column Type :" +rsmd.getColumnTypeName (i));
}
```

> **Note** A `ResultSet` object is automatically closed when the `Statement` object (from which `ResultSet` was obtained) is closed, or re-executed.

Example 16.1 shows a program to demonstrate how the data is stored and retrieved from a database. Assuming that an emp table is already created in MS-Access with three attributes: EmpId, Name, and Salary. To access the database of dsn by the name 'sac' is also created.

Example 16.1   Storing and Retrieving Data from Database

```java
import java.sql.*;
class DatabaseConnection
{
    public static void main(String args[]) throws Exception
    {
        Class.forName("sun.jdbc.odbc.JdbcOdbcDriver");
        Connection con = DriverManager.getConnection("jdbc:odbc:sac");
        PreparedStatement ps = con.prepareStatement("insert into emp values (?,?,?)");
        ps.setString(1, "Emp001");
        ps.setString(2, "Peter");
```

```
ps.setInt(3,10000);
System.out.println("Row inserted : " +ps.execute Update());
Statement stmt = con.createStatement();
ResultSet rs = stmt.executeQuery("select * from emp");
// obtaining meta data of the result set
ResultSetMetaData rsmd = rs.getMetaData();
int cc = rsmd.getColumnCount();
System.out.println("Number of columns in result set:" +cc);
for(int i = 1;i < = cc;i++)
   System.out.print(rsmd.getColumnName(i)+ "\t");
   System.out.println();
   while(rs.next())
   {
   System.out.print(rs.getString(1)+ "\t");
   System.out.print(rs.getString(2)+ "\t");
   System.out.print(rs.getString(3)+ "\n");
   }
}
}
```

Output

```
C:\javabook\programs\chap 15>java DatabaseConnection
Row inserted : 1
Number of columns in result set: 3
EmpId      Name       Salary
Emp001     Peter      10000
```

16.2.6 Scrollable ResultSet

The `ResultSet`, before JDBC 2.1, could be scrolled in the forward direction only. JDBC 2.1 introduced the concept of moving the cursor in the backward direction also. You can even position the cursor of a `ResultSet` object on a specific row. The methods that were introduced are shown in Table 16.3.

But in order to use these methods, the scrollable `ResultSet` must be obtained. This is specified at the statement creation time by passing the following (as in Table 16.4) `ResultSet` types in the `createStatement` method.

Table 16.3 Few Methods of `ResultSet` Interface Used for Scrolling through it

`first()`	Moves the cursor to the first row of the `ResultSet`.
`last()`	Moves the cursor to the last row of the `ResultSet`.
`previous()`	Moves the cursor to the previous row of the `ResultSet`.
`absolute(int row)`	Moves the cursor to the specified row number.
`relative(int row)`	Moves the cursor relative to the current row of the `ResultSet`. A negative value can be specified to move backwards and positive value to move forward.
`getRow()`	Returns the current row number.

Table 16.4 ResultSet Types

ResultSet.TYPE_FORWARD_ONLY	Cursor can move forward only. This is the default type.
ResultSet.TYPE_SCROLL_INSENSITIVE	Cursor moves in both directions and ResultSet is insensitive to the changes made to the tables.
ResultSet.TYPE_SCROLL_SENSITIVE	Cursor moves in both directions and ResultSet is sensitive to the changes made to the tables.

The createStatement()method accepts two arguments as shown below:

```
Statement createStatement(int resultSetType, int resultSetConcurrency) throws
SQLException
```

This other argument specifies the ResultSet concurrency mode. There are two modes for specifying the concurrency of a ResultSet (Table 16.5).

Table 16.5 ResultSet Concurrency Types

ResultSet.CONCUR_READ_ONLY	ResultSet may not be updated concurrently
ResultSet.CONCUR_UPDATABLE	ResultSet may be updated concurrently

For example, the Statement object for a scrollable result set having concurrent read only mode can be created as shown below:

```
Statement stmt = con.createStatement(ResultSet.TYPE_SCROLL_INSENSITIVE, Result Set.
CONCUR_READ_ONLY);
    DatabaseMetaData dbm=con.getMetaData();
    System.out.println(dbm.supportsResultType(ResultSet.TYPE_FORWARD_ONLY));
    System.out.println(dbm.supportsResultType(ResultSet.TYPE_SCROLL_INSENSITIVE));
    System.out.println(dbm.supportsResultType(ResultSet.TYPE_ SCROLL_SENSITIVE));
    System.out.println(dbm.supportsResultTypeConcurrency(ResultSet.TYPE_ SCROLL_
    SENSITIVE,));
```

Note This feature may not be supported by all JDBC driver. The database meta data can be obtained from the connection object and queried to know whether a driver supports scrollable result sets or not as shown below. The supportsResultType method returns boolean values to tell whether a ResultSet type is supported or not. The method supportsResultTypeConcurrency also returns boolean to inform whether a type along with concurrency type are supported together or not.

16.2.7 Transactions

A transaction is a set of statements that if executed should complete it entirety. If any of the statement fails to execute in a transaction, the entire transaction should be rolled back. To enforce this and execute SQL statements in a transaction, the auto commit feature should be turned off. Auto commit feature commits the changes made by SQL statements to the database and is by default set to true. It can be set using the following method of the connection object:

```
con.setAutoCommit(false);
```

If any problem occurs during a transaction, it can be rolled back by using the rollback method on the connection object.

```
con.rollback();
```

The following code snippet will show you how a short transaction can be created and in case of a problem exception occurs and the changes are roll backed.

```
try {
        con.setAutoCommit(false);
        Statement stmt1=con.createStatement();
        Statement stmt2=con.createStatement();
        stmt1.executeUpdate("Query 1");
        stmt1.executeUpdate("Query 2");
        con.commit();            /* commit the changes to the database and make them
                                    permanent. */
        ...

} catch(SQLException se)
{
        try{
        con.rollback(); // roll back the changes made to the database.
        }
        catch(SQLException){}
}
```

Another way of carrying out a transaction is using batch updates. In this case, a batch of statements is created and then the batch is executed as a single transaction. If any of the batch statement fails to execute, the entire batch is rolled back. The following code snippet shows how a batch of statements can be created and used.

```
try {
        con.setAutoCommit(false);
        Statement stmt1 = con.createStatement();
        stmt1.addBatch("Query1");
        stmt1.addBatch("Query2");
        int[] i = stmt1.executeBatch();
        con.commit();            /* commit the changes to the database and make them
                                    permanent. */
        ...

} catch(BatchUpdateException be)
{
        try{
                stmt1.clearBatch(); // you can clear the batch by using this method
        }catch(SQLException){}
}
```

The `executeBatch` method returns an integer array of update counts. The update count refers to the number of rows that are affected on successful execution of every SQL statement. If a statement fails to execute, `BatchUpdateException` occurs.

Sometimes it is desired to allow a transaction to be committed even if one or two last steps of a transaction fail. For example, if you make a transaction like paying a bill, or purchasing an item, you get a notification in the end through an SMS/email that the transaction has occurred.

The transaction should not be rolled back just because the SMS/ email alert could not be sent at the time of the transaction. In such a case, `Savepoint` is used to roll back a transaction to a set point in a transaction. It is actually an interface in the `java.sql` package and was introduced in JDBC 3.0 API. All changes made up to the save point are committed and after the `savepoint` are rolled back. The code below shows you how to rollback upto `sp1`. It means rollback all changes made after `sql` and commit all changes before `sp1`.

```
try {
        con.setAutoCommit(false); //
        Statement stmt1 = con.createStatement();
        Statement stmt2 = con.createStatement();
        stmt1.executeUpdate("Query 1");
        Savepoint sp1 = con.setSavepoint("SavePoint1");
        stmt1.executeUpdate("Query 2");
        con.commit();           /* commit the changes to the database and make them
                                permanent. */
        ...

} catch(SQLException se)
{
        try{
        con.rollback(sp1); // roll back the changes up to the savepoint
        }catch(SQLException){}
}
```

16.3 SERVLETS

Servlets are Java server-side programs that accept client's request (usually http request), process them and generate (usually http response) responses. The requests originate from client's web browser and are routed to a servlet located inside an appropriate webserver. Servlets execute within a servlet container which resides in a webserver like Apache Tomcat. The newer release of Tomcat has a JSP (Java server pages) container also in it. Normally, HTTP (hypertext transfer protocol) is used between web client and servlets, but other protocols like FTP (file transfer protocol) can also be used.

16.3.1 Lifecycle of Servlets

Servlets have their own execution lifecycle. The lifecycle includes three methods as shown in Fig. 16.5.

Whenever a client request is received by the servlet container (part of a webserver), it

- locates the servlet responsible for handling the request and loads it.
- instantiates it.
- initializes the servlet by calling `init()` method, followed by `service` and `destroy`.

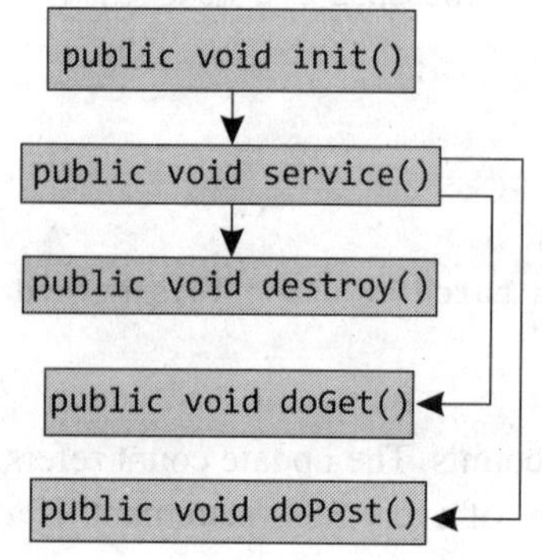

Fig. 16.5 Lifecycle of Servlets

The `init()` method is called only once during the lifetime of an applet. One time initializations are done in this method.

The `service` method is used for processing the client's request and generating responses. The request may be forwarded by `service` method to `doGet()` or `doPost()` depending upon the http request. If it is a get request, the `doGet()`method will be called and if it is a post request, the `doPost()` method will be called. The get and post are two methods of http protocol used for transmitting data to the server-side programs like servlets. The `service` method is capable of handling both types of requests (get and post). In that case, you need to override the service method in your servlet. The signature of `service` method (see Example 16.2) shows two arguments: `ServletRequest` object (to handle client's requests) and `ServletResponse` object (to write responses to the client) which are passed to it by the servlet container. The `destroy` method is called by the servlet container before the servlet is unloaded. So clean-up activities like closing the database connections can be done in this method.

16.3.2 First Servlet

Let us create a simple servlet that outputs the contents to the client.

Example 16.2 **First Servlet**

```
L1   import javax.servlet.*;
L2   import javax.servlet.http.*;
L3   import java.io.*;
L4   public class FirstServlet extends HttpServlet
     {
L5   public void service(ServletRequest req, ServletResponse res) throws
     ServletException,IOException
     {
L6       res.setContentType("text/plain");
L7       PrintWriter pw = res.getWriter();
L8       pw.println("My First Servlet is running");
     }}
```

Explanation

L1–3 The packages `javax.servlet.*`, `javax.servlet.http.*`, and `java.io.*` have to be imported to create an `HttpServlet`.

L4 The class `FirstServlet` must be a public class and it must inherit `HttpServlet`, as http protocol is used for communication between client and server. So to handle http request from client and generate http response for client, we have to create an `HttpServlet`.

L5 The `service` method is overridden. It accepts two arguments `ServletRequest` and `ServletResponse`. The entire client's request is encapsulated in `ServletRequest` object (like http, ftp) and passed to the service method by the servlet container along with `ServletResponse` object. This `ServletResponse` object is used to send responses (usually html responses) to the client. This method may throw `ServletException` and `IOException`.

L6 Before sending any data to client, the type of data to be sent to the client has to specified with the help of a method `res.setContentType ("text/plain")`. In other words, the MIME type (stands for multipurpose Internet mail extension) has to set. Nowadays, web pages contain text, images, and multimedia. A servlet informs the browser about the type of data it will be sending to browser. The servlet in our example is transmitting plain text, so the MIME type is *text/plain*. If html (webpage) is to be sent to the client, the MIME type is *text/html*.

L7–8 Using the `getWriter()` method of the *res* object, we get a `PrintWriter` object. This method may throw an `IOException` that is why we have mentioned it in the throws clause of the service method definition. The `println` method of the `PrintWriter` object is used to write the contents to the client. The string argument to the `println` method is written to the client as it is.

How to Run the Servlet?

For running the servlet, we need to follow certain steps:

1. **The first step is to compile the servlet** For compiling the servlet classes, we need to include the `servlet-api.jar` file in the `classpath` (at command prompt) as shown below.

   ```
   set classpath = %classpath%; C:\Apache\Tomcat 7.0\lib\servlet-api.jar;
   ```

   Or edit the environment variable `classpath` and append the above path in it.

2. **Steps to install Tomcat 7.0 and execute the servlets and JSP** The server used by us for running servlets and JSP is Tomcat 7.0.40. You can download the webserver installer from Apache Tomcat website (e.g., apache-tomcat-7.0.40). The webserver is very easy to install. You just need to double click on the installer and the installation starts. You need to specify the path where you want to install the webserver (if you do not specify the path it will be installed in program files of your machine). This server gets installed as a service in your machine. You can manually start/stop this service by opening the Control Panel of your machine and clicking on Administrative Tools (see Fig. 16.6). You can also set up two environment variables as shown below. It is a good practise and will help you later.

   ```
   JAVA_HOME = c:\program files\java\jdk1.6.0_01 (base directory of JDK)

   CATALINA_HOME = c:\Apache\Tomcat 5.0 (base directory of Tomcat)
   ```

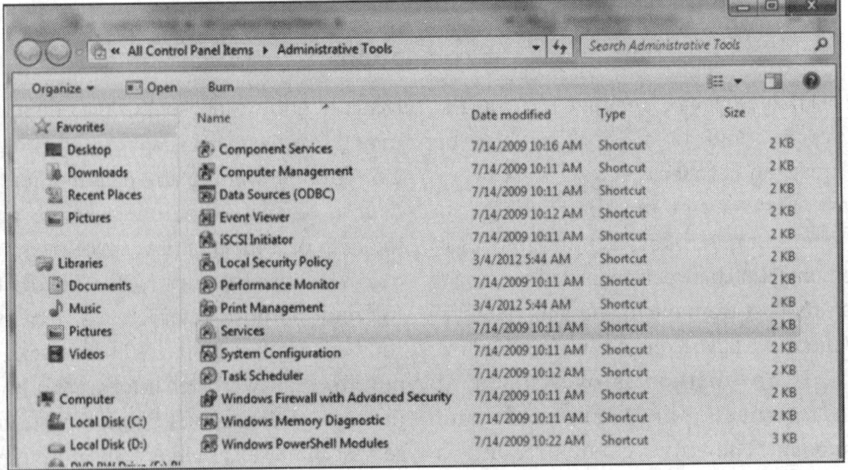

Fig. 16.6 Administrative Tools in the Control Panel

Double click on `Services` and click on the Apache Tomcat 7 entry in the Services window as shown in Fig. 16.7. The service is already running so you are shown two options, i.e., to Stop and Restart service. If the service is stopped, then only Start service option will be displayed.

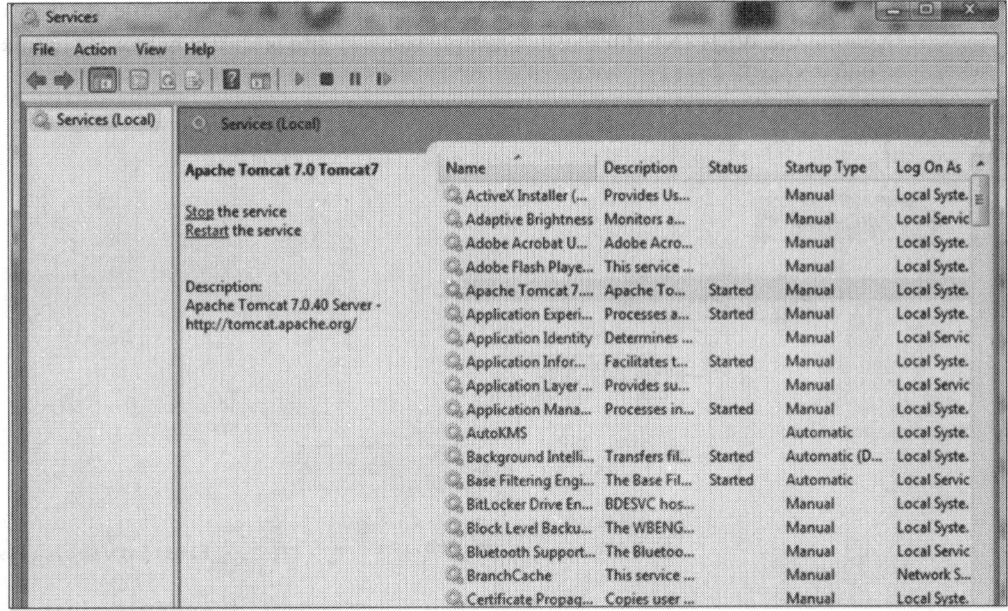

Fig. 16.7 Services within the System

To test the server and see if it is actually running, open a browser and type `http://localhost:8080` in the address bar of the browser (see the snapshot in Fig. 16.8).

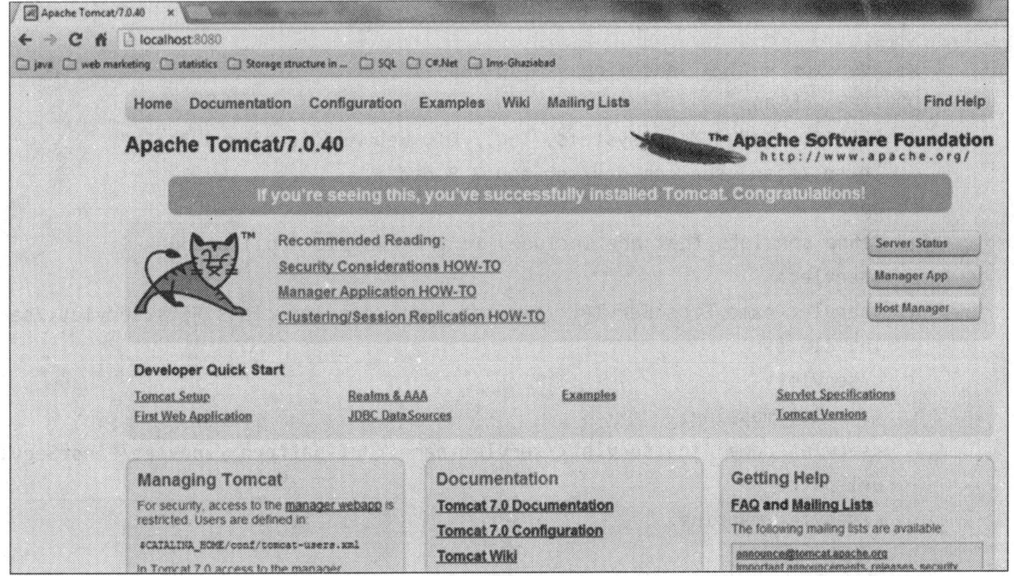

Fig. 16.8 Apache Tomcat 7 Webserver is Running

3. **The third step is to place the compiled servlet class into an appropriate directory in the Tomcat** We have created our own directory named `myproj` within `webapps` directory for placing our created servlets. Figure 16.9 shows the directory structure of Tomcat.

All the servlets class files are placed in the `classes` directory. The file `web.xml` exists within the WEB-INF directory. A sample `web.xml` file is shown below for running the `FirstServlet.class`.

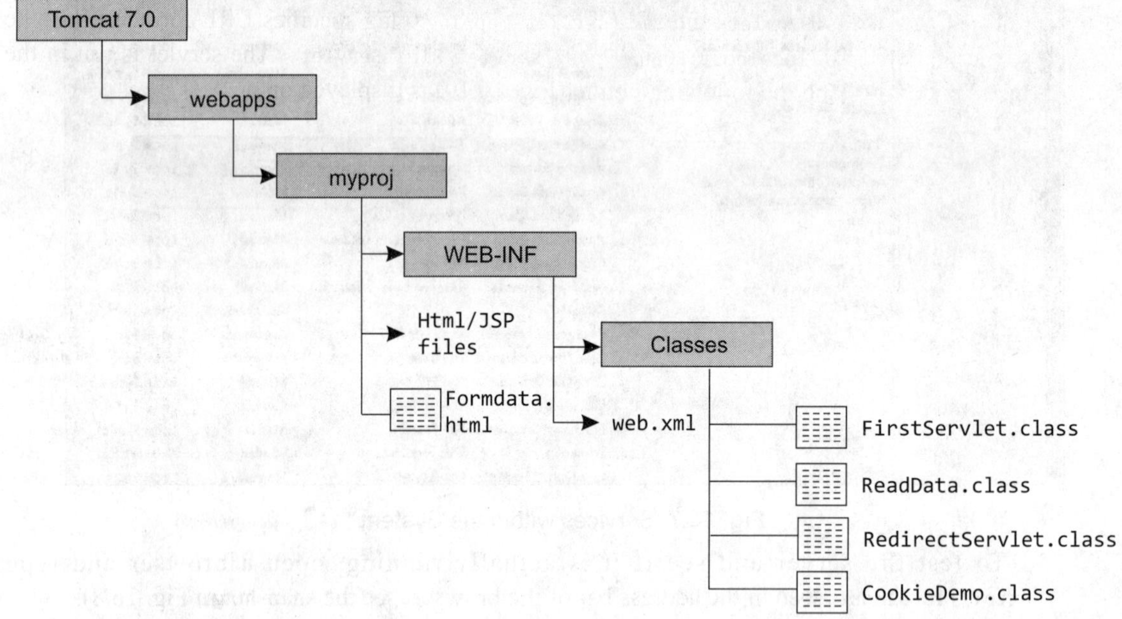

Fig. 16.9 Tomcat Home Page

```xml
<?xml version = "1.0" encoding = "ISO-8859-1"?>
<!DOCTYPE web-app
    PUBLIC "-//Sun Microsystems, Inc.//DTD Web Application 2.3//EN"
    "http://java.sun.com/dtd/web-app_2_3.dtd">
<web-app>
<!-- Define servlets that are included in the example application -->
    <servlet>
    <servlet-name>FirstServlet</servlet-name><servlet-class>FirstServlet</serv-
    let-class>
    </servlet>
    <servlet-mapping>
    <servlet-name>FirstServlet</servlet-name><url-pattern>/servlet/FirstServlet</
    url-pattern>
    </servlet-mapping>
    </web-app>
```

The `web.xml` file acts as a deployment descriptor for the servlets. This file specifies the name of the servlet and the URL mapping for the servlet. The `web.xml` file

- associates servlet class file with a name
- defines a URL mapping for the servlet.

This file has to be edited every time you add a new servlet class in the classes directory. The two tags `<servlet>` and `<servlet-mapping>` along with their sub-tags must be added for every servlet in the classes directory specifying the `name` and `URL` used to call the servlet.

For example, the `<servlet>` tag specifies that the servlet class `FirstServlet.class` will be referred to as `FirstServlet` and the `<servlet-mapping>` tag specifies URL for accessing the servlet, e.g. `http://localhost:8080/myproj/servlet/FirstServlet`. The servlet is run in the Internet explorer and the following output (Fig. 16.10) is displayed on it.

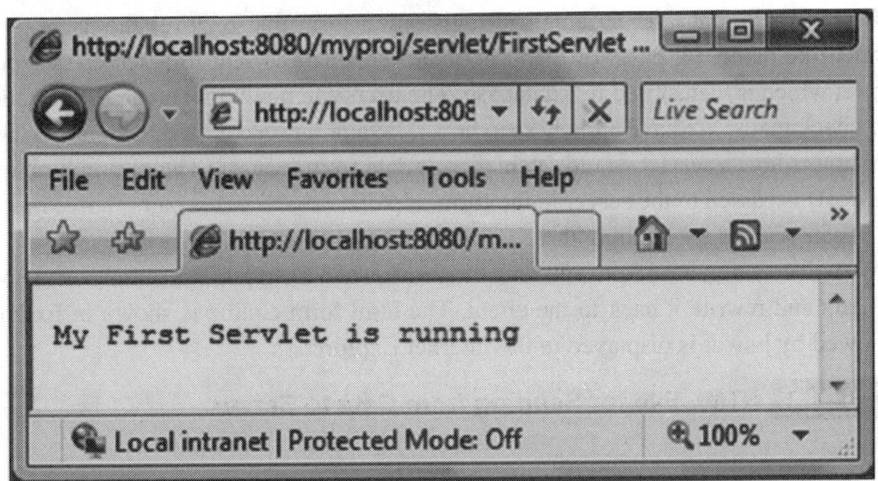

Fig. 16.10 Servlet Output Displayed on the Internet Explorer

16.3.3 Reading Client Data

The client's data is sent to the server from the client's browser via two methods of http protocols: *get* and *post*. These two methods differ in their approach of sending data from client to server. The get method appends data to the URL (of the servlet handling the request) and passes it to the server. The drawbacks of this approach are:

- The URLs are of fixed size and it puts a restriction on the amount of data that can be transmitted to the server.
- Moreover, whatever data is sent to the server is visible in clear text.

On the other hand, post method overcomes these limitations by sending data to the server as a part of http header format instead of appending it to the URL. This overcomes both the limitations of the get method.

Table 16.6 Methods Used to Fetch Values from Client's Request

Methods	Description
`String getParameter(String n)`	This method is used to return the value corresponding to a given name. The name is specified as an argument (`String n`). 'name' is the name of the control in html. To use this method we should know the name.

(Contd)

(Table 16.6 Contd)

Methods	Description
`Enumeration getParameterNames()`	We do not always know all the names in a request. This method returns all the names associated with the requests as an enumeration.
`String[] getParameterValues (String n)`	This method returns all the values associated with a single name as a string array, e.g. hobbies.

For example, consider an email id registration form that requires the users to fill in their details like name, id, password, and hobbies. This data is sent to a server-side program like servlet which is then stored in a database. The users can now login using their id and password and check mails. We have already seen how a Java program can store data into a database. The question is how a servlet would fetch client's data from request? The data in both requests (get and post) is passed to the server in the form of pairs: `name = value` pairs. Three methods (Table 16.6) can be used for fetching these names and values from the request.

We will create an html form and send the form data to a servlet. The sample servlet will retrieve the data and rewrite it back to the client. The html form coding is shown in Example 16.3(a) followed by how it is displayed in the Internet Explorer.

Example 16.3 (a)   HTML File for Sending from Data to Server

```html
<html>
<head><title> form data </title></head>
<body>
<center>
<h1><U> Registration Form </u></h1>
<form method = get action = "servlet/ReadData">
Name <input type = text name = fname><br>
Address <input type = text name = add><br>
User id <input type = text name = uid><br>
Password <input type = password name = pass><br>
Gender:
        male<input type = radio name = gender value = male>
        female<input type = radio name = gender value = female><br>
Hobbies:
        Dancing <input type = checkbox name = hobbies value = dance>
        Music <input type = checkbox name = hobbies value = music>
        Travel <input type = checkbox name = hobbies value = travel>
<br>
<input type = submit>
<input type = reset>
</center>
</body>
</html>
```

We have created a webpage using html which contains a form. The form tag has two attributes: `method` and `action`. The `method` attribute is used to specify the method used to send data to server like `get` and `post`. The `action` attribute is used to specify the URL of the servlet responsible for handling the request. The form contains textfields (e.g. name, address, and UID), password field, radio button, and checkboxes. These fields are created with the help of input tag. The input tag has attributes, `type` and `name`. The `type` specifies the type of input field. Table 16.7 shows a list of possible types. The `name` attribute is used to give a name to the control. This name will be used as an argument in the `getParameter(String n)` method to fetch its value at the servlet.

Table 16.7 A few Values for the Type Attribute of Input Tag

Values of type attribute	Description
`type = text`	Creates a text field.
`type = submit`	Creates a submit button which on click, sends the data in the form to servlet specified in the action attribute of the form tag. The mode of sending is specified by method attribute.
`type = reset`	Creates a reset button. It resets all the fields in the form.
`type = password`	Creates a password field. The characters in this field are echoed as dots.
`type = button`	Creates a normal button. If you click on this button, nothing happens (use Java script for event handling).
`type = radio`	Creates a radio button (single selection).
`type = checkbox`	Creates a checkbox (multiple selection).

The reset button resets the form by clearing all the fields and selections. The submit button sends all the input data and selections to the servlet specified in the action attribute of the form tag. On clicking submit, the URL will look like the following:

```
http://localhost:8080/myproj/ReadServlet?fname = peter&add = London&uid = pet_
007&pass = jennifer&gender = male&hobbies = music&hobbies = dancing
```

The '?' operator separates data from the address. The '&' operator separates one name/value pair from another. The form is shown below (Fig. 16.11) as it appears in Internet Explorer.

The servlet used for handling client's request and generating response is shown in Example 16.3(b) . As a response, our servlet echoes all the data back to the client.

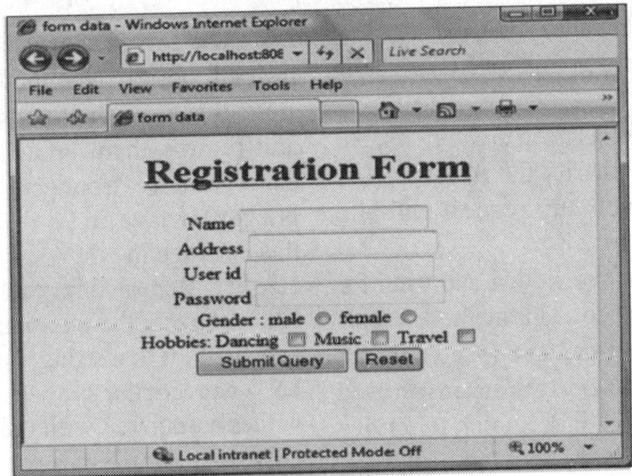

Fig. 16.11 HTML form

Example 16.3 (b) Extracting Data from Client's Request

```java
import javax.servlet.*;
import javax.servlet.http.*;
import java.io.*;
L1      import java.util.*;
L2      public class ReadData extends HttpServlet
        {
L3      public void doGet(HttpServletRequest req, HttpServletResponse res) throws
        ServletException, IOException
        {
L4      res.setContentType("text/html");
L5      PrintWriter out = res.getWriter();
L6      Enumeration e = req.getParameterNames();
L7      while(e.hasMoreElements())
        {
L8      String name = (String)e.nextElement();
L9      String[] values = req.getParameterValues(name);
L10     for(int i = 0; i < values.length; i++)
        {
L11        out.println("<html><head><title> client data</title></head>");
L12        out.println("<body><B>");
L13        out.println(name + " : <i>" +values [i] + "</i><br>");
           out.println("</body></html>");
        }
        }
        }
L14     public void doPost(HttpServletRequest req, HttpServletResponse res) throws
        ServletException, IOException
        {
L15        doGet(req,res);
        }
        }
```

Explanation

L1 Apart from other packages, `java.util` has been imported. The reason for this will be clear in the explanation below.

L2 A public servlet class has been created, named `ReadServlet`. This class inherits the `HttpServlet` class, as we are dealing with http request and http responses.

L3 The `doGet` method is overridden and used for handling get requests from client. This method accepts two arguments: `HttpServletRequest` (used only for http client request) and `HttpServletResponse` (used for sending http response to client). Similar to service method, this method also throws `ServletException` and `IOException`.

L6 The `getParameterNames()` is invoked through the `req` object. This method extracts all the names from the names/value pairs in the request object and returns them as an `Enumeration` of names. `Enumeration` is a collection interfaces. This interface is a part of `java.util` that is why we have imported this package in L1.

L7–13 Repeated for each name in the `Enumeration`.

L8 Extracts the next name from the `Enumeration` and stores it in a string variable `name`.

L9 `req.getParameterValues(name)` returns all values associated with the name as a `String` array.

L10–13 `for` loop is used to iterate through all the values of the array. HTML tags are written within the quotes in the `println` method to send html to client's browser. The names are specified in bold `<b>` and values have been specified in bold and italicized `<i>` as shown in Fig. 16.11.

L14–15 `doPost` method has been overridden. It is almost entirely similar to `doGet` method. From within `doPost`, we call `doGet` method. The reasons for overriding `doPost` and calling `doGet` from within is that the servlet is capable of handling get as well as post request. There is no need to worry about the request, whether it is a get request or a post request.

The response sent by the servlet to the client's browser will appear as shown in Fig. 16.12.

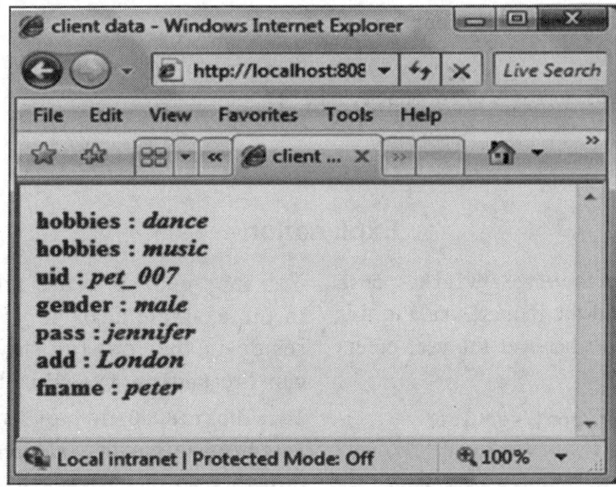

Fig. 16.12 Data Read from Client and Written Back to it

Make sure the servlet name and mapping is present in the web.xml file before running the example. The following tags must be a part of the web.xml file of the myproj web application.

```
<servlet>
<servlet-name>
ReadData</servlet-name>
<servlet-class>
ReadData
</servlet-class></servlet>
<servlet-mapping>
<servlet-name>
ReadData</servlet-name>
<url-pattern>
/servlet/ReadData
</url-pattern>
</servlet-mapping>
```

16.3.4 HTTP Redirects

Http redirect is a way of redirecting a user to another location on the Internet. Say, for example, your website has got a new domain name but the entire user base is not informed about it. So they will keep coming to the older URL. Http redirect is a way of telling the client's browser about the new URL. All the requests that arrive on the old URL are redirected to the new URL.

Example 16.4 Http Redirect

```
L1    import javax.servlet.*;
L2    import javax.servlet.http.*;
L3    import java.io.*;
L4    public class RedirectServlet extends HttpServlet
      {
L5        public void doGet(HttpServletRequest req, HttpServletResponse res) throws
          ServletException, IOException
          {
L6            res.sendRedirect ("../Formdata.html");
          }
      }
```

Explanation

L6 The redirect method of the `HttpServletResponse` object is used to redirect all the request made to this servlet to `Formdata.html`. Whenever the user enters the URL:

`http://localhost:8080/myproj/servlet/RedirectServlet,`

the user is automatically redirected and displayed the following page: http://localhost:8080/myproj/Formdata.html.

You may choose to use relative URL as shown in the example also. As you know all html files reside in the root (i.e. myproj) directory. You can fire `RedirectServlet` by invoking the path: localhost:8080/myproj/servlet/RedirectServlet and from this path you need to move to myproj/ directory so that `Formdata.html` can be accessed. So we need to move up one level and hence the two dots are specified../ followed by filename.

16.3.5 Cookies

Cookies are basically small pieces of information stored on the client's machine by the browser. A cookie contains information like user browsing preferences, user id and password combinations, session id, and the number of times a user has visited a page. This information is stored in pairs, i.e., name-value pairs. This information wrapped in a cookie object is sent to the client browser by a servlet, which stores it somewhere in its temporary Internet files. Whenever a request is sent to that particular server (from where the cookie was downloaded), all the cookies (stored in the client's machine from that very server) are attached to the http request and sent to the server. The server can then fetch the cookies from the request and then act accordingly.

Example 16.5 keeps a track of how many times a user has visited the page. For this purpose, the servlet creates a cookie and stores it in the client's machine with the number of counts in it. Every time the user requests a page, the value from the cookie is fetched, incremented by one, and stored back again on the client's machine. The common misconception is that cookies are a risk. But in reality, cookies are not interpreted or executed in any way. Moreover, 20 cookies per site are allowed and not more than 300 cookies can be stored by the browser. The size of a cookie is limited to 4kb (Fig. 16.13).

Example 16.5 Cookie Example

```java
import javax.servlet.*;
import javax.servlet.http.*;
import java.io.*;
public class CookieDemo extends HttpServlet
{
  public void doGet(HttpServletRequest req, HttpServletResponse res) throws
  ServletException,IOException
  {
L1      res.setContentType("text/html");
L2      PrintWriter out = res.getWriter();
L3      Cookie c[] = req.getCookies();
L4      if(c == null)
        {
L5      Cookie counts = new Cookie("Counts","1");
L6      out.println("<html><head><title> client data</title></head>");
L7      out.println("<body><B>");
L8      out.println("Welcome <br>");
L9      out.println("This is the first time you have visited this page");
L10         out.println("</body></html>");
L11         res.addCookie(counts);
        }
L12     else {
L13     for(int i = 0;i < c.length;i++)
        {
L14     String name = c[i].getName();
L15     String val = c[i].getValue();
L16     int accessCount = (Integer.parseInt(val) +1);
L17     out.println("<html><head><title> client data </title></head>");
L18     out.println("<body><B>");
L19     out.println("Welcome back<br>");
L20     out.println("Number of times you have visited this page: "+accessCount);
L21     out.println("</body></html>");
L22     Cookie counts = new Cookie(name,new Integer(accessCount).toString());
L23     res.addCookie(counts);
}}}
  public void doPost(HttpServletRequest req,HttpServletResponse res)
  throws ServletException,IOException
  {
      doGet(req,res);
}}
```

Output

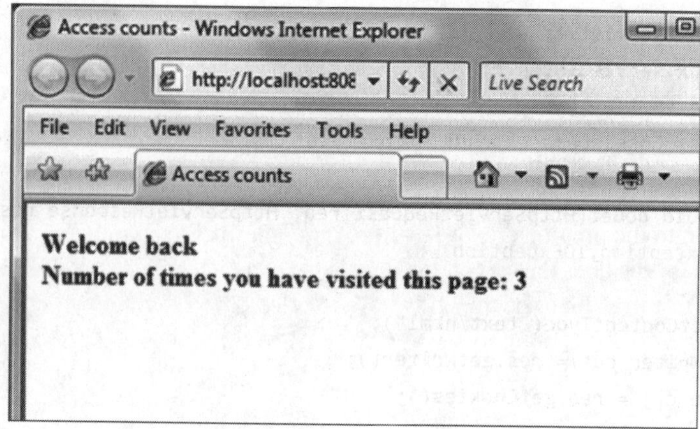

Fig. 16.13 Using Cookie to Get Access Counts

Explanation

L3–11 The servlet first checks whether any cookie did arrive with the request or not using the `req.getCookies()` method of the `HttpServletRequest` object. If none of the cookie arrived with the request (i.e. this is the first visit of the user on this page), a cookie object (counts) is created with name (as counts) and value (as 1). The message is written to the client "`Welcome this is the first time you have visited this page.`" The cookie object created in L5 is added to the client's response by using `res.addCookie (counts)` method.

L12–23 If cookies arrive with the request then obviously `c` will not be equal to null. In that case, L12–23 will be executed. All cookies arrive in the cookie array, i.e., `c[]`. A `for` loop is used to iterate the cookie array. We had only stored one cookie, so only one would be retrieved. The name of the cookie is fetched using the method `c[i].getName()` and the value is fetched using `c [i].getValue()`. This value has to be incremented by one, but the return type of `getValue` method is string, so this string has to be converted to an integer using `Integer.parseInt(val)` method and then incremented by one (incremented value is stored in integer variable `accessCount` on L16). The client is shown a message "`Welcome back Number of times you have visited this page: `"`+ accessCount`. A new cookie object is created with the new `accessCount` value and added to the response using `res.addCookie (counts)`.

16.3.6 Session Management

A session is used to track the user between successive requests from the same client to the same server. It is a kind of conversation between the server and a client. A conversation is a series of continuous requests and responses.

When the communication takes places on the Internet there are three partners in it: web client, webserver, and the protocol used for communication. Web client is the browser, webserver is where we put our servlet classes, JSP pages, and html which generates responses for the clients request or handles the request, and the protocol is normally http. There can be other as well like FTP. (But generally it is http, so we will stick to it). A browser sends an http request to a webserver for a page; the page is located by webserver and send back in response. Further if the same browser sends again an http request to the same webserver for same page (or any other) it is treated as a new http request. Http is an application layer protocol and it uses TCP at transport layer. So whenever an http request is sent from the application layer, a new TCP connection is created at transport layer. That is why, it's a new request every time an HTTP request is sent, even from the same client to the same server for the same resource.

Let us take a scenario to understand the session and its importance. When you login to Gmail server or Yahoo mail server to view your emails, Firstly you enter your user id and password to sign in. The request along with the user id and password goes to the webserver where your input values are authenticated. You are shown your mailbox with options to view mails or compose a message, etc. When you click on inbox to view your email, it is a new http request (which has no correlation to the previous request) although it goes from the same server to the same client. The question is how does the server decide, whose inbox is to be shown on this request? The user id and password that the user typed in came in the earlier request and not this one. One would think of sending the user id and password combination every time with any request and get it authenticated from the database, and generate appropriate responses. That is very impractical, tedious, time consuming, and risky option.

The real problem is to maintain the state of the client across various requests. We need to maintain the state of the client (session information) across request. Maintaining a client state will make him identifiable across requests and the server can then easily generate appropriate responses for valid clients, i.e., once you login you will be shown your emails only and not somebody else's email. The client's state is maintained till the time a client logs out. Now the question that arises is who is going to maintain the state of the client? The http protocol is stateless so it does not maintain client information; for it, every request is a new request (had it been a stateful protocol no problems would have occurred). Obviously you are left with two choices: client and server to maintain the client state. Depending on which method is chosen for session maintenance, either the client or the server will maintain the sessions.

The solution is that the client be provided with a unique identifier whenever it makes a request. This identifier will be used in all subsequent requests to identify a particular client requests from other. As soon as a user logs in, a unique session id, associated with that user is created. This id can be maintained across subsequent request using the following ways: (a) hidden fields, (b) URL rewriting, (c) cookies, or (d) HttpSession API.

Hidden Fields

Hidden fields are html fields not visible to the users. The state of the client is maintained (at the client side) in these hidden fields and embedded in the responses generated by the servlet. They are sent back to the server with the http request and extracted by the servlet. Hidden fields are inserted in html as shown below:

```
<form method ="" action="URL">
. . .
<INPUT TYPE="hidden" NAME="Id" VALUE="Unique Identifier">
<INPUT TYPE="hidden" NAME="Customer Name" VALUE="Tom">
<INPUT TYPE="hidden" NAME="Item_1" VALUE="Plastic Bottles" >
<INPUT TYPE="hidden" NAME="Item_1_Qty" VALUE="20" >
<INPUT TYPE=Submit> . . .
</form>
```

Normally there will be no hidden fields when a page is displayed for the user for the first time. Subsequent requests by the user will force a servlet to add hidden fields to maintain the history/state of the client. As soon as the submit button is pressed, all data including hidden fields are sent to the servlet mentioned in the action attribute. The information can be used by the server for session tracking. Each time the servlet is activated; it creates and sends an html form on the client browser in addition to other things. This form will have new items to gather user input (if required) along with the older items (like items checked by the user on the last page).

Earlier this solution was useful in implementing shopping carts where information of users along with their item selections have to be maintained and finally according to their selection, bills are generated. This information can be maintained using hidden fields along with a unique session id. Every time the user requests for a new page, all fields (including hidden fields) are sent to the server. These fields are extracted by the servlet and set in a new html form, as hidden fields, to be sent back to the client as part of the response. This method does not need any special configuration either from the browser or the server and is available for session tracking. However, the disadvantage is that they will only be sent to the server once the form is submitted and not when a user clicks on a hyperlink and moves on the next page. They can be used when the amount of information to be hidden is less. Hidden fields are hidden (not visible) from the users but by selecting the "View Source"option in the browser, the entire form, including the hidden fields can be viewed by the user. Hence, hidden fields cannot be used for security purposes.

URL Rewriting

Another way of achieving session management (at the client side) is using URL rewriting. URL rewriting is a technique in which history/session information/state of the client is appended to the URL before sending the page back to the client. This URL has to be rewritten in the action attribute of the form tag or the anchor tags whatever has been used in the page. For example,

If the original URL is `http://server:port/servlet/ServletName`

The rewritten URL will be

```
http://server:port/servlet/ServletName?sessionid=123456 & userid=sac123 &...
```

This technique does not need any special support from the browser but it is a tedious approach. All data associated with a user can be fetched according to the user id from the databases. (A session id can also be a combination of user id and a unique number. The user id can be extracted from the session id and then user specific data can be extracted from the database.). In this approach you need to take precaution in maintaining and appending the parameters every time while rewriting URL's until the session completes. Moreover, you cannot have static pages; each page will be dynamically generated if this approach is used.

Cookies

A cookie is a small amount of information stored on the client's machine within the browser's files. Cookie can be used to store state/session information on the client side. It is a key value pair sent by the server to the client. This pair is automatically attached with every request to the server from where it was downloaded and then sent to the server. We have already shown how cookies can be used. The advantage of using this technique of maintaining sessions is that it is a simple and easy approach. The disadvantage is that if the users disable cookies, the browser will not be able to save the cookie at client computer and session tracking fails.

Session API

Session tracking API is built on top of the methods discussed above. All servers support cookies for session tracking and if any how it cannot be done through cookies, servers switch to URL rewriting. It reduces the developer overhead as the servlet container manages the session (either way automatically by cookies or URL rewriting) and the user need not do it explicitly.

The `HttpSession` API is used for creating and maintaining sessions among clients and servers. It is within the `javax.servlet.http` package. `HttpSession` is an interface within this package and it maintains all the sessions. All incoming requests carrying session identifiers are automatically associated with their respective session objects. In other words, every client is mapped with a session object.

A session is created using a `getSession` method of the `request` object. It returns an `HttpSession` object. This method is overloaded; one that does not accept any argument and other that accepts a boolean value. If true is passed as a boolean value in this method, it returns the current `HttpSession` object associated with this request or, if none exists then it creates and returns a new session. If false is passed in the `getSession` method and the request does not contain any `HttpSession` object, this method will return null. If no value is passed in the `getSession` method, it behaves in the same way as `getSession(true)`.

A session object can be used to hold values which can be retrieved whenever required. But you can only store and retrieve objects from a session. The method `setAttribute()` and `getAttribute()` respectively are used to store and retrieve objects from the session object. The attributes will be set in key-value pairs. So in case you wish to store primitive type such as `int` and `float`, you will have to use their respective wrapper classes such as `Integer` and `Float`. The following statement shows how to get and set an attribute `name` to and from the session object with the value `Tom`:

```
session.setAttribute("name","Tom");
String n=(String) session.getAttribute(name);
```

A session can be destroyed by using the `invalidate()` function on the session object. All information corresponding to session will be lost at the server.

16.4 PRACTICAL PROBLEM: LOGIN APPLICATION

Let us create a login example to illustrate how session API can be used. The user is first displayed an html page (`Login.html`) which has two input fields (one for user id and other for password) with a submit and a reset button. The user has to enter a valid user id and password combination to login. As soon as the user submits the details in this html page, the http request is sent to an `Authenticate.java` servlet which invalidates the older sessions (if any present), establishes a connection to the database for validating the user, and if successful, creates a new session and redirects the user to `showAuthenticationDetails.java` servlet. This servlet generates a dynamic html for the user which shows certain user specific details along with two hyperlinks one to sign out and other to show messages. If the user clicks on sign out hyperlink he is redirected to `SignOut.java` servlet which invalidates and redirects the user to `Login.html` page. But if a user clicks on Show message hyperlink, his request is forwarded to `ShowMessage.java` servlet which identifies the session associated with a user and display user with some dynamic generated text along with a hyperlink to Sign out. If the user clicks on Sign Out hyperlink, the Sign Out servlet invalidates the user session and redirects the user to `Login.html`.

If the user, at any point of time, clicks on the back button of the browser, the contents of the previous page are displayed even after the user has signed out, as the html generated by the server is cached by the browser. To force the browser not to cache the pages, we create a `NoCacheFilter.java` class which is actually a `Filter` class. It forces the browser not to cache the pages but ask for a fresh copy of the pages from the server every time a URL is accessed. Along with the `NoCacheFilter` class we also have an `AlreadyLoginFilter.java` class which checks whether a user is logged in or not and if not, all requests are redirected to the `Login.html` page. This is basically created for blocking mischievous user requests who try to play tricks and put the URL of servlets like `showAuthenticate` and `showMessage` directly in the address bar without logging. The Tomcat directory structure of the application is shown in Fig. 16.14.

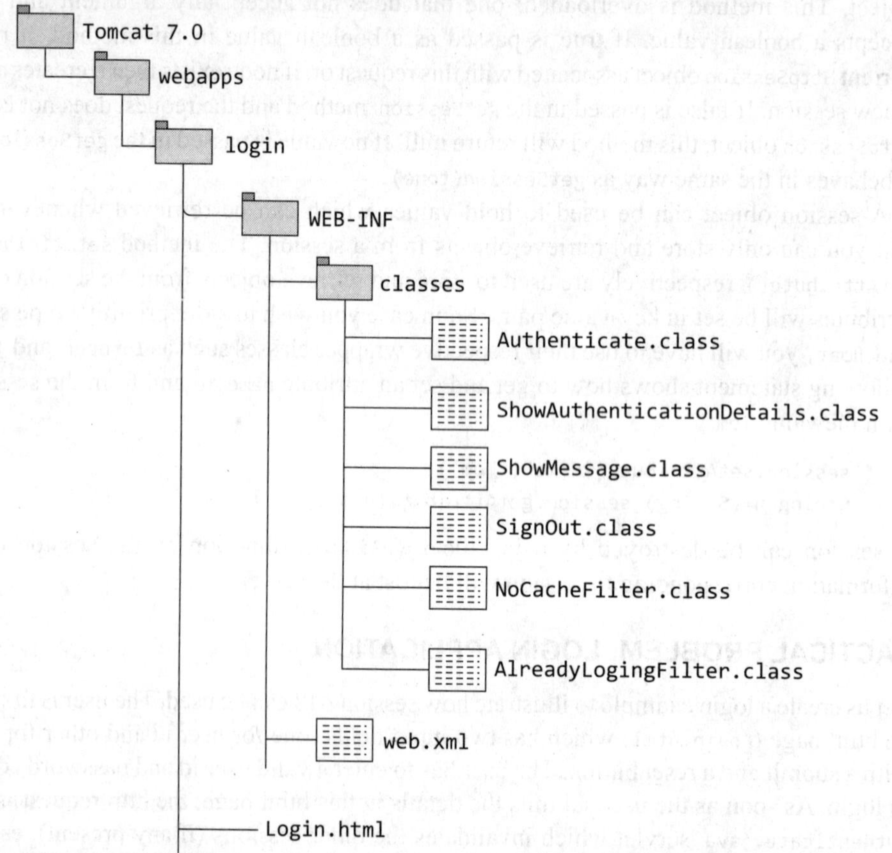

Fig. 16.14 Tomcat 7.0 Directory Structure for Login Application

Example 16.6(a) `Login.html`

```
<html><head><title> Login Page </title></head>
<body>
<form method ="post" action="auth/authenticate">
```

```
User id          <input
type="text" name="id"><br>
Password      <input type="password"
name="pass"><br>
<input type="submit" name="Submit">
<input type="reset" name="Reset">
</form></body></html>
```

Output

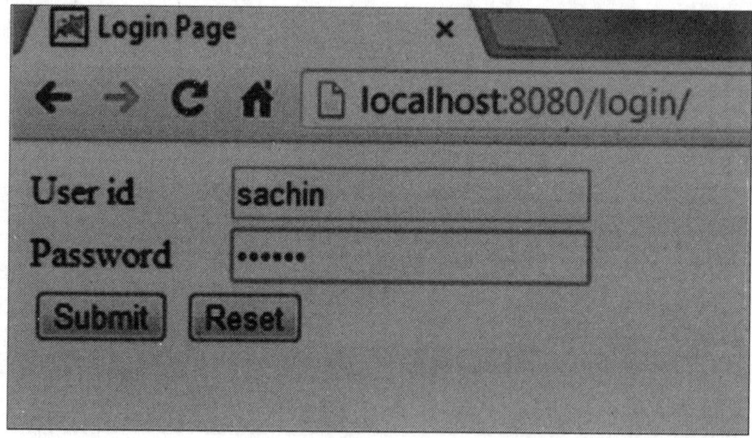

Fig. 16.15 `Login.html` webpage

Explanation

The page is invoked using the URL: `localhost:8080/login` (after starting the webserver) as shown in Fig.16.13. `/login` is the name of the directory (i.e., context root within the `webapps` directory) that holds the webpage. The point to note is that we have not mentioned the name of the file while invoking the html page (i.e., `Login.html`) but still as soon as the above mentioned URL is typed in the browser, `Login.html` file is displayed. This is because we have mentioned the `welcome-file` name in the `web.xml` file on the webserver. So as soon as the context root (`/login`) is invoked, the welcome file for that context root is displayed. See `web.xml` file in Example 16.6(h).

The title tag sets the title of the page. You can see the title (login page) on the top blue bar of the browser. The form tag is to create a form within the body tag. This form has two input fields with two special buttons submit and reset created using input tags. One input field is used for entering user id (`type=text`) and other is used for entering password (`type=password`). Submit (`type=submit`) and reset (`type=reset`) buttons are also created using input tag. On clicking submit button, the data in the form is sent to the servlet class mentioned in the action attribute of the form tag using the method specified in the method attribute of the form tag. As you already know post method instead of appending the data with the URL mentioned in the action attribute, sends data as part of header. Please note that in the action attribute you have to specify the `url-pattern` mentioned in the `servlet-mapping` tag specified in the `web.xml` file for sending the request to the appropriate servlet without the preceding slash.

Example 16.6(b) `Authenticate.java (Servlet Class)`

```java
L1    import java.io.*;
L2    import javax.servlet.*;
L3    import javax.servlet.http.*;
L4    import java.sql.*;
L5    public class Authenticate extends HttpServlet
      {
L6    public void doPost(HttpServletRequest request,HttpServletResponse response) throws
      ServletException, IOException
      {
L7    PrintWriter out = response.getWriter();
L8    String id = request.getParameter("id");
L9    String pass = request.getParameter("pass");
L10       String query="select * from Login where UserID='"+id +"' and
          Password='"+pass+"'";
          // to invalidate older sessions
L11       HttpSession session=request.getSession(false);
L12       if(session!=null)
L13              session.invalidate();

L14        try
           {
L15              Class.forName("sun.jdbc.odbc.JdbcOdbcDriver");
L16              Connection con=DriverManager.getConnection("jdbc:odbc:auth");
L17              Statement stmt=con.createStatement();
L18              ResultSet rs=stmt.executeQuery(query);
L19              if(!rs.next())
                {
L20                    response.sendRedirect("/login");
                }
L21              else
                {
L22                    session=request.getSession(true);
L23                    session.setAttribute("LOGIN_DONE",true);
L24                    session.setAttribute("User-Id",id);
L25                    response.sendRedirect("showAuthenticate");
                }

L26        } catch(Exception e){out.println(e);}
      }
  }
```

Explanation

L1–4 Imports the required packages.

L5 Shows Servlet class declaration. The Servlet class has to be a public class.

L6 As the request that arrives is a post request, the doPost method is overridden.

L7 Shows creation of a PrintWriter object so that responses can be sent to client. The getWriter method of the response object is used to obtain a PrintWriter object.

L8–9 Extract the id and password from the request object using the getParameter method and store them in the separate strings. This id and password combination will be matched from the database. These two fields are submitted by the user in the Login.html page and send to this servlet along with the http request.

L10 Shows creation of a SQL query. This query is stored in a String variable and will be executed once the database connection is established. Note that the id and password extracted from request are added to this query to authenticate the user. The table name is Login which contains two fields: UserID and Password.

L11–13 Used for invalidating any older session (if any) present. The getSession method with a false argument extracts the session from the request (if any present) and does not create a new session if none is found. The session, if found, on a user login attempt in these statements is considered by our application as an old session and is invalidated in if statement on L15 using the invalidate method.

L14 try block starts.

L15–18 Statements show how to connect to the database. We have used MS-Access 2010 for this example. L15 loads the driver, L16 establishes the connection, L17 creates the Statement and L18 executes the Statement (query) and obtains a ResultSet object. Note that in jdbc:odbc:auth, auth is the data source name. Remember this DSN is created in the Data Sources (ODBC) within the Administrative Tools of the Control Panel (see Figs 16.16 and 16.17).

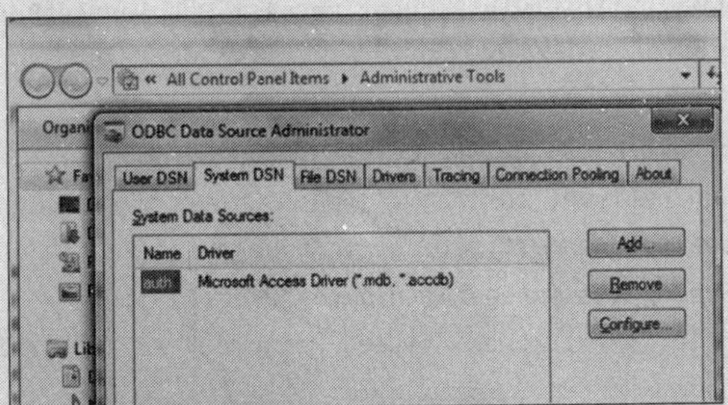

Fig. 16.16 DSN Name

Fig. 16.17 DSN Along with the Database it Refers to

L19–25 On execution of the Query if the result set contains a row it clearly specifies that the user has entered a valid user id and password and `rs.next()` will return true otherwise false. If false, the user is redirected back to the context root (`/login`) on L20 otherwise a new session is created for the valid user on L22. L23 shows an attribute is set into the new session object by the name LOGIN_DONE and value is set as true. We will illustrate its purpose later. L24 sets the user-id into the session object and the user is redirected to showAuthenticate (i.e., ShowAuthenticationDetails.class) servlet on L25. showAuthenticate name is specified as the url-pattern for servlet-class `ShowAuthenticationDetails` in the `web.xml` file. So to invoke `ShowAuthenticationDetails`, we are using the name `showAuthenticate`. But you would raise one question after having a look at the `web.xml` file in Example 16.6(h) i.e., the `url-pattern` for the said servlet is `/auth/showAuthenticate` and we have just mentioned `showAuthenticate` in L24. The reason is because the user is already in the `auth` context when the user invoked/`auth`/`authenticate`.

L26 Catches the exception raised from the `try` block, if any.

Example 16.6(c) **ShowAuthenticationDetails.java**

```
L1     import java.io.*;
L2     import javax.servlet.*;
L3     import javax.servlet.http.*;
L4     public class ShowAuthenticationDetails extends HttpServlet
       {
L5       public void doGet(HttpServletRequest request,HttpServletResponse response) throws
           ServletException, IOException
       {
L6       PrintWriter out=response.getWriter();
L7       response.setContentType("text/html");
L8       HttpSession session=request.getSession(true);
L9       String id= (String)session.getAttribute("User-Id");
L10          out.println("<Html><head><title> Welcome " +id + "</title></head>");

L11          out.println("<body><H1> Login Successful </H1>");
L12          out.println("<a href=signout> Sign Out </a><br>");
L13          out.println("<a href=showmessage> show Messages </a>");
L14          out.println("<H1> Session Details: </H1>");
L15          out.println("Session Id: "+session.getId()+"<br>");
L16          out.println("User id: "+id +"<br>");
L17          out.println("<H1>Requested URI: "+ request.getRequestURI() +"</H1><br>");
L18          out.println("</body></Html>");
       }
     }
```

Output

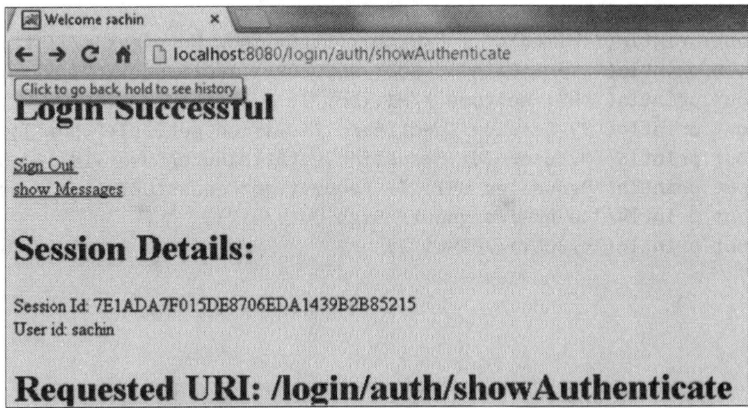

Fig. 16.18 Response Generated by `ShowAuthenticationDetails` Servlet

Explanation

L1–3 Imports the required packages.

L4 `Servlet` class declaration.

L5 `doGet` method is overridden as this request (i.e., a get request) comes through a hyperlinked URL.

L6 `PrintWriter` object is created as it is this servlet which will show the user something after it is authenticated.

L7 `contentType` is set as text/html.

L8 The session details are acquired from the request object. The same session created by the Authenticate Servlet is retrieved here.

L9 The user id is extracted and stored in a `String` variable.

L10 An html is generated for the client and sent using the `println` method of the `PrintWriter` object.

As you can see in this line, the title of page is set as "`Welcome`" along with the id of the user (see output).

L11 An `h1` heading "`Login Successful`" is sent to client.

L12–13 Two hyperlinks are sent to the client: `SignOut` and `ShowMessage`. Respective servlets are invoked on clicking either of the hyperlinks.

L14 An `h1` heading "`Session Details`" is sent to client.

L15–16 `Session Id` and `User Id` is sent to the client to be displayed.

L17 The requested URI is obtained and sent to the client.

L18 `html` file is closed.

We demonstrated in this particular servlet how to determine that this request belongs to a particular session and send some details and options back the client.

Example 16.6(d) `ShowMessage.java` (Servlet Class)

```
L1    import java.io.*;
L2    import javax.servlet.*;
L3    import javax.servlet.http.*;
L4    public class ShowMessage extends HttpServlet
         {
L5    public void doGet(HttpServletRequest request,HttpServletResponse response) throws
      ServletException, IOException
         {
```

```
L6      HttpSession session=request.getSession(true);
L7      response.setContentType("text/html");
L8      PrintWriter out = response.getWriter();
L9          out.println("<HTML>\n" + "<HEAD><TITLE> Show Messages </TITLE>");
L10         out.println(" </HEAD>\n"+"<BODY BGCOLOR=\"#FDF5E6\">\n");
L11         out.println("<H1> Welcome </H1><br>");
L12         out.println("My Session Identifier: "+session.getId()+"<br>");
L13         out.println("My User Id: "+session.getAttribute("User-Id")+"<br>");
L14         out.println("Requested URI: "+ request.getRequestURI () + "<br>");
L15         out.println("<a href=signout> Sign Out</a>");
L16         out.println("</BODY></HTML>");
        }
    }
```

Output

Fig. 16.19 Html generated by ShowMessage Servlet

Explanation

All similar lines have been explained in the previous example. The important point to note is that the session id is same in both the ShowMessage and showAuthenticationDetails servlets. The user id put in the session object is extracted again here and displayed to the user.

Example 16.6(e) **SignOut.java (Servlet Class)**

```
L1      import java.io.*;
L2      import javax.servlet.*;
L3      import javax.servlet.http.*;
L4      public class SignOut extends HttpServlet
        {
L5          public void doGet(HttpServletRequest request, HttpServletResponse response)
                throws ServletException, IOException
            {
L6          HttpSession session=request.getSession(false);
L7          session.invalidate();      //logout
L8          response.sendRedirect("/login");
            }
        }
```

Explanation

All similar lines have been explained in the previous example. The important point to note is that the session is invalidated and user is redirected to the `Login.html` page.

Example 16.6(f) `NoCacheFilter.java` **(Filter Class)**

```
L1    import java.io.*;
L2    import javax.servlet.*;
L3    import javax.servlet.http.*;
L4    public class NoCacheFilter implements Filter
      {
L5    public void doFilter(ServletRequest req, ServletResponse res, FilterChain chain)
         throws IOException, ServletException
      {
L6    HttpServletResponse hsr = (HttpServletResponse) res;

        /*Forces caches to obtain a new copy of the page from the server*/
L7      hsr.setHeader("Cache-Control", "no-cache, no-store, must-revalidate"); // HTTP 1.1.

      //HTTP 1.0 backward compatibility
L8    hsr.setHeader("Pragma", "no-cache");

      //Causes the proxy cache to see the page as "stale"
L9    hsr.setDateHeader("Expires", 0);
L10      chain.doFilter(req, res);
      }
L11   public void destroy(){}
L12   public void init(FilterConfig f){}
    }
```

Explanation

This is a filter class and is used for filtering tasks on either request or response to and from a resource or in both conditions. In other words, a filter's functionality is either performed before or after the functionality of a servlet or a JSP. For example, if a request is made for a servlet on which a filter has been applied to allow only authorized user to access the servlet, the filter may pass or block the users request on to that servlet depending on which request is legal and which one is illegal. As is evident from Fig. 16.20, that the request for a resource goes through the filter. The role of this filter class is to prevent the browser cache from storing previous pages but obtain fresh copy of the pages from the server every time a resource is accessed. This filter is applied to all the servlets and is specified in the following fashion in `web.xml` file. Note the `<url-pattern>/*</url-pattern>` specifies that it applies to all.

```
<filter>
   <filter-name>noCacheFilter</filter-name>
   <filter-class>NoCacheFilter</filter-class>
</filter>
<filter-mapping>
   <filter-name>noCacheFilter</filter-name>
   <url-pattern>/*</url-pattern>
</filter-mapping>
```

Filter, introduced in Servlet 2.3 specification is actually an interface in the `javax.servlet` package. This interface has three methods as you can see in L5, 11, 12. The filtering task is performed in the `doFilter` method. The `doFilter` method is called by the container every time a client request for a filtered resource which resides at the end of the chain. It may be possible that a filter may invoke another filter to process a request/response pair. The `FilterChain` object keeps a track of it. The `FilterChain` object allows the request and response to be passed on to the next filter in the chain, if there are more filters to be processed for a request/response pair and if it is the last filter in the chain the requested resource is invoked.

L6   As doFilter method accepts ServletRequest and ServletResponse types as its arguments, they need to be cast into HttpServletRequest and HttpServletResponse objects before their respective methods can be used on them.

L7   Sets an http header "Cache-Control" through the response object. The values are self-explanatory which specify not to cache, not to store the page and ask for a validated copy of the page from the originating server every time. This header is part of HTTP version 1.1 but some browser and caches supporting older version of http protocol ignore it so pragma and Expires header should also be set to avoid caching in any circumstance.

L8   Pragma header is part of HTTP/1.0 version. It serves the same purpose of not letting the client cache the server responses. This header is basically set for backward compatibility.

L9   The Expires header specifies the date/time after which the response is considered stale (old or expired). An entry marked as stale will not be returned normally by a cache unless it is validated with the originating server.

L10   Shows the FilterChain object calling the doFilter method. This FilterChain object represents a chain of filters which have to be invoked one after the other to fulfil a request for a resource. It causes the next filter within the chain of filter to be invoked and if the calling filter is the last filter in this chain, the resource is invoked.

L12   When the servlet filter is loaded for the first time, its init() method is invoked.

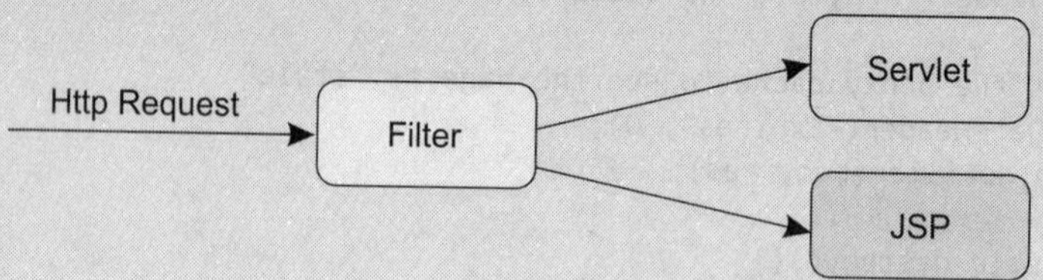

Fig. 16.20 Shows How a Request is Processed through a Filter

Example 16.6(g)   **AlreadyLogingFilter.java (Filter Class)**

```java
L1    import java.io.*;
L2    import javax.servlet.*;
L3    import javax.servlet.http.*;
L4    public class AlreadyLogingFilter implements Filter
      {
L5    public void doFilter(ServletRequest request, ServletResponse response, FilterChain
      chain) throws IOException, ServletException
      {
L6        HttpSession session=((HttpServletRequest)request).getSession(true);

L7      if(null == session.getAttribute("LOGIN_DONE"))
          {
L8      ((HttpServletResponse)response).sendRedirect("/login");
          }
L9      chain.doFilter(request, response);
      }
L10    public void destroy(){}
L11    public void init(FilterConfig f){}
      }
```

Explanation

The purpose of creating this filter is to allow only authorized session holders to view the messages and the authentication detail pages. Unlike the previous filter, this filter is applied to only to the `showmessage` and `showAuthenticate` servlets. This is specified in `web.xml` file as shown below (see `url-pattern` tag below). So, if a user, instead of accessing the login page, tries to access the `showmessage` servlet directly by typing the following URLin the browser address bar: `localhost:8080/login/auth/showmessage`, the user is automatically redirected to the login page. The request is filtered by this filter class and appropriate action is taken. The same happens in case of `showAuthenticate` servlet if user tries to access it directly (`localhost:8080/login/auth/showAuthenticate`) without logging. The following tags have to be inserted in web.xml file.

```
<filter>
  <filter-name>checkLoginFilter</filter-
  name>
  <filter-class>AlreadyLogingFilter</filter-
  class>
</filter>

<filter-mapping>
  <filter-name>checkLoginFilter</filter-
  name>
  <url-pattern>/auth/showmessage</url-pat
  tern>
  <url-pattern>/auth/showAuthenticate</
  url- pattern>
</filter-mapping>
```

L6 The session is obtained from the request object.

L7–8 Remember we had inserted an attribute in the session object "LOGIN_DONE" with the value true, as soon as user was authenticated and a new session was created. The purpose was to check for already logged in user holding valid sessions. If the LOGIN_DONE session attribute is not null, it means the user is authenticated and holds a valid session. So the requested resource is invoked. But if it is null, it means the user is not authenticated and the user is redirected to welcome page (`/login`).

Example 16.6(h) `web.xml`

```xml
<?xml version="1.0" encoding="ISO-8859-1"?>


<web-app xmlns="http://java.sun.com/xml/ns/javaee"
     xmlns:xsi="http://www.w3.org/2001/XMLSchema-instance"
     xsi:schemaLocation="http://java.sun.com/xml/ns/javaee
                    http://java.sun.com/xml/ns/javaee/web-app_3_0.xsd"
     version="3.0"
     metadata-complete="true">

    <welcome-file-list>
    <welcome-file>Login.html</welcome-file>
    </welcome-file-list>


    <!-- Define example filters -->
    <!-- Define servlets that are included in the example application -->


    <servlet>
        <servlet-name>authenticate</servlet-name>
```

```xml
        <servlet-class>Authenticate</servlet-class>
    </servlet>

    <servlet-mapping>
        <servlet-name>authenticate</servlet-name>
        <url-pattern>/auth/authenticate</url-pattern>
    </servlet-mapping>

    <servlet>
        <servlet-name>showAuthenticationDetails</servlet-name>
        <servlet-class>ShowAuthenticationDetails</servlet-class>
    </servlet>
    <servlet-mapping>
        <servlet-name>showAuthenticationDetails</servlet-name>
        <url-pattern>/auth/showAuthenticate</url-pattern>
    </servlet-mapping>

    <servlet>
        <servlet-name>showmessage</servlet-name>
        <servlet-class>ShowMessage</servlet-class>
    </servlet>

    <servlet-mapping>
        <servlet-name>showmessage</servlet-name>
        <url-pattern>/auth/showmessage</url-pattern>
    </servlet-mapping>

    <servlet>
        <servlet-name>signout</servlet-name>
        <servlet-class>SignOut</servlet-class>
    </servlet>

    <servlet-mapping>
        <servlet-name>signout</servlet-name>
        <url-pattern>/auth/signout</url-pattern>
    </servlet-mapping>

<filter>
  <filter-name>noCacheFilter</filter-name>
  <filter-class>NoCacheFilter</filter-class>
</filter>

<filter-mapping>
  <filter-name>noCacheFilter</filter-name>
  <url-pattern>/*</url-pattern>
</filter-mapping>
```

```
<filter>
  <filter-name>checkLoginFilter</filter-name>
  <filter-class>AlreadyLogingFilter</filter-class>
</filter>

<filter-mapping>
  <filter-name>checkLoginFilter</filter-name>
  <url-pattern>/auth/showmessage</url-pattern>
  <url-pattern>/auth/showAuthenticate</url-pattern>

</filter-mapping>
</web-app>
```

16.5 INTRODUCTION TO JAVA SERVER PAGES

Java server pages (JSP), in contrast to servlets, is basically a page that contains Java code embedded within html tags. Servlet is a Java program where html tags are embedded in Java code or html responses are generated through Java. JSP files have an extension .jsp and they execute within a JSP container present in the webserver. This container translates the .jsp into an equivalent servlet. In other words, JSP is a servlet in the background. The basic purpose of using JSP is also same as that of servlet, i.e., to process the request and generate dynamic web content for the client. The obvious question that arises is why is JSP required? Does it offer an advantage over a servlet?

JSP offers a significant advantage over a servlet. JSP is embedded in html with some special delimiters which look like tags. So it is easy to learn. To work with a servlet you need to learn Java and its programming styles which is not the case in JSP. Moreover, JSP pages are automatically recompiled when required, which is not the case with servlets. Servlets have to be recompiled in case they are changed. So as soon as you refresh your JSP page, changes made to it are reflected. The URL mapping required in web.xml file for servlets is not required in the case of JSP.

16.5.1 JSP Life Cycle

JSP life cycle has three methods: jspInit(),_jspService(), and jspDestroy() similar to a servlet lifecycle. These methods are automatically called when a JSP page is requested and it terminates normally.

jspInit() method is similar to the init() method of a servlet or an applet. It is called only once during the entire lifecycle and is used to initialize variables and objects that can be used throughout the JSP.

_jspService() method is automatically called and is used to generate response for the request. This method delegates request to doGet() or doPost() method of a generated servlet.

jspDestroy() method is automatically called when the JSP page terminates normally. It is used for cleaning the resources held by the JSP.

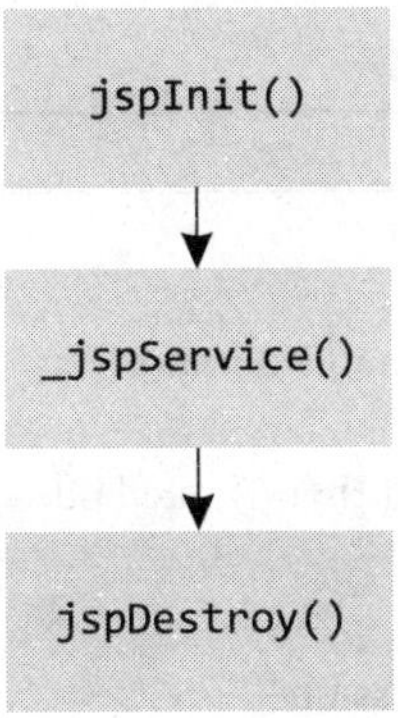

Fig. 16.21 JSP Life Cycle

16.5.2 Steps in JSP Page Execution

The following steps are followed during execution of a JSP page:

- User sends request for a JSP page to the webserver through a web browser.
- Webserver accepts the request and passes it to the JSP container.
- If the JSP file has been called for the first time then the JSP container parses the page, converts it into a servlet, and compiles the servlet.
- The container loads the `Servlet` class by instantiating it and calling the `jspInit()` and `_jspService()` methods of the JSP life cycle.
- If JSP page is called for second or *n*th time, the container checks whether the JSP page is newer than its class and if yes, the translation of JSP to servlet takes place and again it is compiled, instantiated, and loaded again; otherwise the most updated instance is already running.
- The generated HTML is displayed on the user's web browser.

16.5.3 JSP Elements

JSP has three types of components namely

- Directives
- Expression, scriptlets, and declarations
- Actions

Directives

Directives are specific instructions to the container informing it how to process the JSP page. There are three types of directives in JSP: `page`, `include`, and `taglib`. The syntax for adding directive to a JSP page is

```
<@ directive-name attribute-name="value" …. >
```

(a) page, as the name suggests, is used to specify attributes for the page, for example, what classes to be imported for the servlet or what will be the content type for the generated responses by the servlet and so on. Some of the attributes is provided in Table 16.8.

Table 16.8 Attributes of the Page Directive

Attribute	Description
`contentType`	Specifies the character encoding scheme.
`Extends`	Specifies a superclass for the generated servlet.
`Import`	Specifies the packages or classes to be imported similar to the Java import statement.
`Info`	Specifies a string that can be extracted using the `getServletInfo()` method.
`isThreadSafe`	Specifies the thread model for the generated servlet.
`Language`	Defines the programming language to be used in the JSP page.
`Session`	Specifies whether or not the JSP page is participating in a session.
`isELIgnored`	Specifies whether expression language within the JSP page will be ignored or not.
`isScriptingEnabled`	Specifies whether scripting elements are allowed or not.

If you want to use `Date` class in your JSP page you will have to import the `java.util` package in your JSP page as shown below:

```
<%@ page import="java.util.*" %>
```

or its xml equivalent tag can also be used as shown below:

```
<jsp:directive.page import ="java.util.*" />
```

(b) `include` directive is used to add the contents of another file into a JSP page. It is used as shown below:

```
<%@ include file="includedirective.html" %>
```

or its xml equivalent tag can also be used as shown below:

```
<jsp:directive.include file="includedirective.html" />
```

(c) `taglib` directive is used while creating user defined tags. It can be used as:

```
<%@ taglib uri=" " prefix="" >
```

or its xml equivalent can also be used as shown below:

```
xmlns:prefix="tag library url"
```

Expressions

To execute Java expressions like (a+b*c), we make use of JSP expression syntax. The result of expression is directly embedded in the html page. Expressions are enclosed within `<%= … %>`. Note that expressions are not terminated with a semicolon. For example,

The result of 2+22 is `<%= (2+2-2) %>`. The expression in `<% %>` is evaluated and answer is added to the html.

`<% ="Introduction to JSP" %>`. The string "Introduction to JSP" is added to the html sent to the client. It is similar to the `out.prinln()` statement.

> **Note** XML equivalent for the expression can also be used like: `<jsp:expression> … </jsp:expression>`

Scriptlets

If a number of statements have to be executed, scriptlets is the right place. Note that scriptlets are enclosed within `<% %>` delimiters and semicolons are used to terminate statements. For example,

```
<%
    out.println("This following text is visible through a Scriptlet <br>");
    d=new Date();
    out.println("<br> The Current Date is: "+d+"<br>");
    out.println("<br><b> A Sample for Loop</b><br> ");
    for (int i=0;i<5;i++)
    out.println("Iteration No :" +i+"<br>");
%>
```

The above code uses out object which is a predefined object in JSP. println and print are methods of this out object which are responsible for sending strings to the client. In other words the strings passed as parameter values in print methods are added to the generated html. Table 16.9 lists all implicit objects.

Table 16.9 Implicit Objects in JSP

Object name	Description
request	The request received by the server normally a ServletRequest or HttpServletRequest.
response	The response generated by the server normally a ServletResponseor or HttpServletResponse.
application	Provides information on server version, application level initialization parameters; can be used for logging; common for all session objects; contains all servlets, JSP, html, and other resources used in the application.
session	Unique object associated with a particular user.
pageContext	Object is used to either forward request to other resources or include output of other resources. Apart from that it is used to maintain attributes at four levels: page level, request level, session level, and application level.
exception	An instance of java.lang.Throwable class; valid only of is ErrorPage attribute of the page directive is set to true.
page	Object is used to refer to the current servlet (similar to this keyword).
config	Object is used to access the initialization parameters of the servlet mapping besides the servlet context and servlet name.
out	Object is used to write the contents back to the client.

Note XML equivalent for the scriptlet can also be used like: `<jsp:scriptlet>` … `</jsp:scriptlet>`.

Declarations

If you wish to declare any item it should be done here. Note that declarations are enclosed within <%! %>. A variable can be declared in scriptlet as well. The difference between declaring a variable in scriptlet and through declarations is that all the scriptlet code goes into the service method of the JSP page (when it is converted to servlets) and all declarations reside on top of the service method within the class. Semicolons are allowed while declaring a variable or object in a JSP page. For example,

```
<%! Date d;%>
```

Note JSP container creates a servlet automatically for every JSP page. The expression, scriptlets, and html found in the JSP page are used by JSP container to create Java code for the automatically generated _jspService() method of the servlet. This method is analogous to service() method of the servlets.

Actions

Actions are JSP elements that use, create or modify other objects and they follow strict XML syntax. Table 16.10 lists the JSP actions.

Table 16.10 Actions in JSP

`<jsp:useBean>`	To use beans in JSP pages.
`<jsp:include>`	Similar to include directive.
`<jsp:forward>`	To forward the request to some other JSP page or servlet.
`<jsp:getProperty>`	To get properties of a bean.
`<jsp:setProperty>`	To set properties of a bean.

Note We will discuss some actions later when we discuss Java beans.

16.5.4 Placing your JSP in the Webserver

The only thing that you need to do is to place your JSP according to the directory structure shown in Fig. 16.22. As is evident from the figure, all html and jsp files are placed parallel to the WEB-INF directory within the root directory of the web application (i.e., login in our case).

After placing your JSP in the appropriate directory structure as shown in Fig. 16.23, type the following in the address bar to see the output as in Fig. 16.23.

```
http://localhost:8080/login/JspElements.jsp
```

Let us put all that we have discussed into practice and create a simple JSP page. We will call it `JspElements.jsp`. We will be creating a html table to display directives, expressions, scriptlets, declarations, actions, and important implicit objects in a single JSP page, and try to show how most of them can be used in a JSP page.

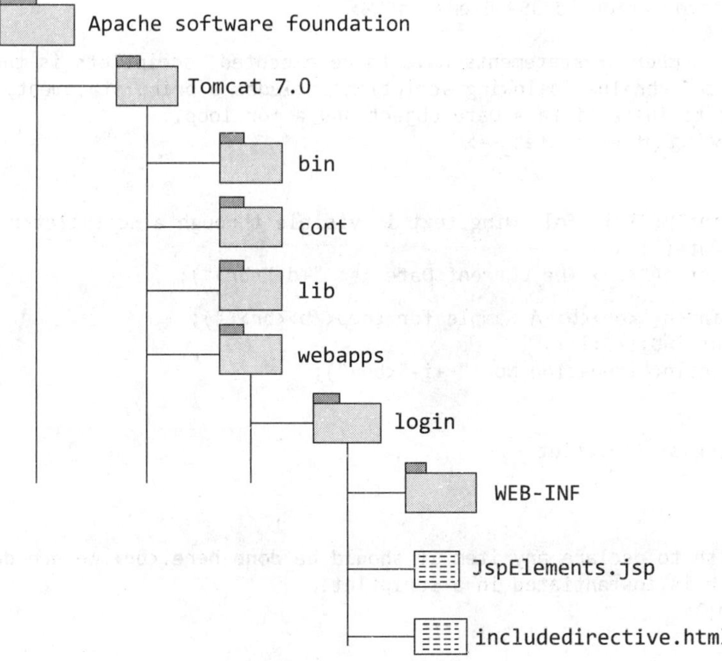

Fig. 16.22 Directory Structure for `JspElements.jsp`

Example 16.7 `JspElements.jsp`

```
<Html>
<Head>
<title> Introduction to JSP </title>
</Head>
<body><h2> Three Components of JSP </h2>
<ol>
   <li> Directives</li>
   <li> Expression, scriptlets and declarations</li>
   <li> Actions</li>
</ol>
Apart from this JSP contains implicit objects.

<table border=1><tr><td><h3> Directives </h3></td>
<td><h3> Expressions </h3></td>
<td><h3> Scriptlets </h3></td>
<td><h3> Declarations </h3>

</td>
<td><h3> Actions </h3></td>
<td><h3> Some Important Implicit Objects </h3></td></tr>
<tr>
<td>There are three types of directives:<br><em>page, include and taglib.</
em><br>The following text is generated using a include directive. <br>
<em><%@ include file="includedirective.html" %></em>
<%@ page import="java.util.*" %>
</td>
<td> The result of 2+2-2 is : <%= (2+2-2) %><br>
   <%= "Introduction to JSP Elements" %>
</td>
<td> if a number of statements have to be executed, scriptlets is the
right place. <br>The following scriptlet includes a print statement,
statement to instantiate a Date object and a for loop.
<!-- Starting of scriptlet -->

<%
   out.println("This following text is visible through a Scriptlet<br>");
   d=new Date();
   out.println("<br> The Current Date is: "+d+"<br>");

   out.println("<br><b> A Sample for Loop</b><br> ");
   for (int i=0;i<5;i++)
   out.println("Iteration No :" +i+"<br>");

%>
<!-- Ending of Scriptlet -->
</td>
<td>

If you wish to declare any item it should be done here.<br> we are declaring a Date
here which is instantiated in a scriptlet.
<%!Date d;%>
</td>
<td>
<jsp:useBean>;<br>
```

```
&lt;jsp:include&gt;<br>
&lt;jsp:forward&gt;<br>
&lt;jsp:getProperty&gt; <br>
&lt;jsp:setProperty&gt;<br>
</td>
<td>
request<br>
response<br>
session<br>
application<br>
out<br>
</td>
</tr>
</table>
<h5> NOTE: </h5>
<em>
JSP container creates a servlet automatically for everyJSP page. The expression,
scriptlets and html found in the JSPpage is used by JSP container to create the
Java code for the automatically generated _jspService() method of the servlet. This
method is analogous to service() method of the servlets
</em>
</body>
</Html>
```

Output

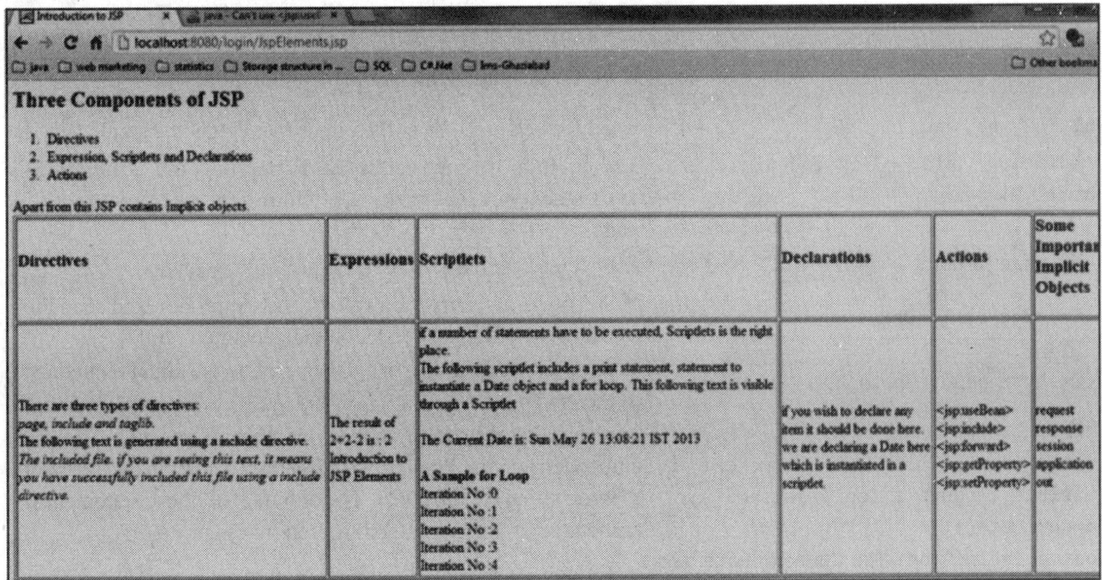

Fig. 16.23 Snapshot of the Browser Showing the `JspElements.jsp` Page

Explanation

The above example clearly shows Java code being embedded in html file. Note that the extension of file is not html. The meaning of all tags used in the example is shown in Table 16.11.

Table 16.11 Html and JSP Tags

Html and JSP tags used in examples	Description
`Html`	Root tag of html file.
`Head`	Header of the html file.
`title`	Used for specifying title of the page. It is used within the head tag
`body`	Displayable portion of the html.
`ol`	Used for creating ordered (i.e., numbered) list (see output).
`li`	Used for creating list items of the ordered (ol) or unordered list (ul) (see code).
`table`	Used for depicting data in a tabular format. A table has rows and columns.
`tr`	Row creation of a table is done using this tag.
`td`	Column creation of a table is done using this tag.
`br`	Used for line breaks.
`em`	Similar to italics.
`<`	Used for displaying less than sign in html (i.e., <).
`>`	Used for displaying greater than sign in html (i.e., >).
`h1, h2, h3, h4, h5, h6`	Used for headings. h1 is the biggest and h6 is the smallest.
`<%@include file = "includedirective.html" %>`	JSP include directive is used to include the contents of `includedirective.html` file within the `JspElements.jsp` page.
`<%@ page import = "java.util.*" %>`	JSP page directive is used to import `util` package.
`<%= (2+2-2) %> `	JSP expression is used to evaluate the expression and send the result to the client embedded in the generated html.
`<%= "Introduction to JSP Elements" %>`	JSP expression is used to send the string to the client embedded in the generated html.
`<% out.println("This following text is visible through a Scriptlet "); d=new Date(); out.println("  The Current Date is: "+d+" "); out.println(" <b> A Sample for Loop</b>  "); for (int i=0;i<5;i++) out.println("Iteration No :" +i+" "); %>`	JSP scriptlet is used to depict a number of statement can be embedded in html. Predefined object `out` is used in this scriptlet to write strings to the client. The output of all these statement is embedded in the generated html sent to client.

16.6 JAVA BEANS

Java Beans provides a standard format for writing Java classes. Java Bean is a reusable software component. Once it is designed and created, it can be used over and over again in many different applications as per their requirements. Java Beans can be used by IDE and other Java API's to create new applications. The information of these beans is automatically discovered and then manipulated without explicitly coding them again. A Java Bean may be as simple as an ordinary Java class which follows certain guidelines like:

- A bean class must have a no-argument constructor.
- A bean class should have no public properties.
- Properties should be modified and accessed through setter (setXXX) and getter (getXXX) methods, respectively.
- Supporting introspection which allows a builder tool to analyze how a bean works.
- Supporting customization thus allowing users to alter the appearance and behavior of a bean.
- Supporting events which allow beans to fire events and inform application builder tools about the events they can fire and handle.
- Supporting persistence thus allowing beans to be customized in an application builder tool to have their state saved and later restored.

16.6.1 Properties of a Bean

The properties of a bean are discussed in the following sections:

Basic Properties

A basic or simple property is one which accepts a single value. The value may be any of the primitive types or object references. These properties can be accessed using getter methods and modified using setter methods. Suppose the bean contains a property (variable or attribute) named length, the getter and setter for this property will be

```java
public int getLength()              // getter for length
{
    return length;
}
public void setLength(int l)        // setter for length
{
    length=l;
}
```

A special case is for boolean properties whose type is boolean. In such case the getter/accessor method makes use of is instead of get.

```java
public boolean isAcceptable()
{
    return acceptable;
}
```

Indexed Properties

An indexed property is one which accepts an array of values. Suppose the bean contains an integer array to hold the marks scored named marks, the getter and setter methods for this property will be

```
    public int[] getMarks()              // getter for marks
    {
      return marks;
    }

    public void setMarks(int[] m)        // setter for marks
    {
      marks=m;
    }
```

Beans must also provide methods to get and set specific elements of the array. For example,

```
    public int getMarks(int index)     // gets specific element at index
    {
      return marks[index];
    }

    public void setMarks(int index, int m)      // sets specific elements at index
    {
      marks[index]=m;
    }
```

Bound Properties

A bound property is one which is bound to the listener and this listener is notified whenever the value of this field changes. `PropertyChangeListener` and `PropertyChangeEvent` of the `java.beans` package are used for this purpose. The bean must add the methods `addPropertyChangeListener()` and `removePropertyChangeListener()` for managing the bean's listeners. As soon as the bound property is changed, the bean sends a `PropertyChangeEvent` to its registered listeners. `java.beans` package includes a utility class `PropertyChangeSupport` to keeps track of property listeners. It also includes a method that fires `PropertyChangeEvent` to all registered listeners. An instance of this class is declared as a member field of the bean and all such task are delegated to it. Let us see how this is done.

Example 16.8 **Property Change Listener for a Bound Property**

```
import java.beans.*;
public class DemoBean
{
  private int length = 10;

/*An instance of PropertyChangeSupport is created. The bean object is passed as the
source of event within the constructor. */

private PropertyChangeSupport pcs = new PropertyChangeSupport(this);

public int getLength()
{
  return length;
}

public void setLength(int l)
```

```java
{
  int oldLength = length;

  /*Change the length*/
  length = 1;

  /* And fire a property change event to the registered listener. If the old and new
  value is same, no event is fired.
  public void firePropertyChange(String propertyName,boolean oldValue,
  boolean newValue) */

    pcs.firePropertyChange("length",oldLength,l);
}

/* PropertyChangeListener is added to the listener list for all properties. */

public void addPropertyChangeListener(PropertyChangeListener listener)
{
  pcs.addPropertyChangeListener(listener);
}

/* Remove a PropertyChangeListener from the listener list. */
public void removePropertyChangeListener(PropertyChangeListener listener)
{
  pcs.removePropertyChangeListener(listener);
}
}
```

Constrained Properties

A *constrained property* is a special kind of bound property. In this case, the listeners are consulted
prior to changing the constrained property and if there is no objection from any of the listeners,
changes are made. But if any one of the associated listeners veto's the change, the property remains
unchanged. `VetoableChangeListener` and `VetoableChangeSupport` of the `java.beans` package
are used for this purpose. Let us take the previous example and add `VetoableChangeSupport` and
`VetoableChangeListener` to it.

```java
import java.beans.*;
public class DemoBean {
    private int length = 10;
    private PropertyChangeSupport pcs = new PropertyChangeSupport(this);

    /*An instance of VetoableChangeSupport is created. The bean instance is passed
    within the constructor as the source of events. */

    private VetoableChangeSupport vcs = new VetoableChangeSupport(this);

    public int getLength()
    {
```

```java
    return length;
}

public void setLength(int l) throws throws PropertyVetoException
{
int oldLength = length;

/*public void fireVetoableChange(String propertyName, Object oldValue,
        Object newValue) throws PropertyVetoException

   This method apprises the listeners about the change in the property's value.
   Any of the registered listeners can throw a PropertyVetoException to veto the
   update. In such a case the method passes an "undo" PropertyChangeEvent. This
   will revert back the old value to all listeners that confirmed this update and
   re-throws the PropertyVetoException. If the old and new values are same and
   non-null, No event is fired */
vcs.fireVetoableChange("length", oldLength, l);
length = l;

   /* fire a property change event */
   /* public void firePropertyChange(String propertyName, boolean oldValue, bool
   ean newValue)   */

   pcs.firePropertyChange("length",oldLength, l);
}
public void addPropertyChangeListener(PropertyChangeListener listener)
{
   pcs.addPropertyChangeListener(listener);
}

public void removePropertyChangeListener(PropertyChangeListener listener)
{
   pcs.removePropertyChangeListener(listener);
}

/* VetoableChangeListener is added to the listener list. It is registered for
all properties */
public void addVetoableChangeListener(VetoableChangeListener listener)
{
   vcs.addVetoableChangeListener(listener);
}

/* Remove a VetoableChangeListener from the listener list. */
public void removeVetoableChangeListener(VetoableChangeListener listener)
{
   vcs.removeVetoableChangeListener(listener);
}
}
```

16.6.2 Using Beans through JSP

`jsp:useBean` action is used to load a bean in the JSP page. The simplest syntax for using this tag is

```
<jsp:useBean id="name" class="package.Class" />
```

This action instantiates an object of the class specified in the class attribute and bind it with the name specified in the `id` attribute. So, for example, if we want to use a bean created by the name `CalculateBean.java` residing in the beans directory, the following JSP action can be used:

```
<jsp:useBean id="calc" class="beans.CalculateBean" >
```

The name `calc` specified in the `id` attribute is bound with this bean. It will be used further to access the bean class. It can be considered as equivalent to the following scriptlet code:

```
<% beans.CalculateBean calc = new beans.CalculateBean; %>
```

Note All classes should be part of a package in order to be accessible in other classes. Classes within the default package are invisible to classes of the same package. So whenever you create bean classes, make sure it is part of some package.

```
package beans;
public class CalculateBean {
 // ...
}
```

After placing the bean class (rather all classes) in a package, recompile it and place it in

```
/WEB-INF/classes/beans/CalculateBean.class
```

Then you can reference it as follows:

```
<jsp:useBean id="calc" class="beans.CalculateBean" />
```

Accessing Bean Properties in JSP

The properties of a bean can be accessed using the `jsp:getProperty` tag which takes two attributes: a `name` and `property` attribute. The value of the `name` attribute should be similar to the `id` attribute of the `jsp:useBean` and value of the `property` attribute should match with the instance variables specified in the bean class. For example, the `CalculateBean` class has a string property called `name`. An instance called `calc` is created using the `jsp:useBean` as shown above. The value of the `name` property can be accessed in either of the following ways:

```
<jsp:getProperty name="calc" property="name" />
```

or its equivalent

```
<%= calc.getName() %>
```

Setting Bean Properties through JSP

The properties of a bean can be modified using the tag which takes three attributes name (should be an exact match with the `id` specified in `jsp:useBean`), property (the name of the property to be changed), and value (the new value for the property). For example, if you wish to change the value of the `name` attribute it can be done in any of the following ways:

```
<jsp:setProperty name="calc" property="name" value="Peter" />
```

or

```
<% calc.setName("Peter"); %>        // scriptlet code
```

The property "name", is of type String whereas there may be other attributes in a bean that may be numeric in nature. But, the value that is passed will always be a String, (value = "") so conversion from string to other types will be required. This will prove to be a tedious approach while converting from one type to other. JSP provides a simple solution of letting the container automatically handle all conversions. You just need to specify

```
<jsp:useBean id = "calc" class = "beans.CalculateBean" />
<jsp:setProperty name = "calc" property = "*"/>
```

Note Moreover, the above setting is also used to synchronize html form elements (input fields) with Java Bean. In other words, it is used for form synchronization. Suppose we have an HTML form which accepts some data from the user (e.g., user id and password) and we want to pass this data to JSP. Apart from JSP, we also have a Java Bean that performs the reading and writing to and from the database based on the data which user has entered. Our JSP code will first read the HTML form data from the request object and then set all the parameters in the Java bean using the `jsp:setProperty` tag. This is perfectly right but certainly repetitive. Form synchronization lets JSP synchronize HTML forms element data directly with a Java bean thus alleviating much of this repetitive coding. Each Html form element will synchronize with a property of a Java Bean that has the exactly the same name (case-sensitive) as that of form element. Their values will be directly passed to the bean without worrying about the type conversions.

Let us take an example to practice what we have learnt so far.

16.6.3 CalculateBean Example

The following example shows how to use Java beans in JSP. We will be creating a JSP page and a Java bean class. The bean class will have three attributes: two integer variables and a String variable. The two numeric variables are added together by sum() method of bean class. These attributes are accessed and changed using set and get property tags of the JSP. The values of these attributes are passed through JSP tags to the bean classes. String which is automatically converted to their respective types wherever required (as `property = " * "` is already set in the JSP:setproperty tag). The method sum () is invoked from the JSP page. Let us first see the `JavaBeans.jsp` page.

Example 16.9(a)   JavaBeans.jsp

```
<Html>
<Head>
<title> Using Java Beans in JSP </title>
</Head>
<body>
```

```
Hello <br>
<jsp:useBean id="calc" class="beans.CalculateBean" >
After Instantiating Bean <br>
<jsp:setProperty name="calc" property="*" />
<jsp:setProperty name="calc" property="name" value="sachin" />
After Setting property: name <br>
<jsp:setProperty name="calc" property="var1" value="10" />
After Setting property: variable 1 <br>
<jsp:setProperty name="calc" property="var2" value="10" />
After Setting property: variable 2 <br>
Name: <jsp:getProperty name="calc" property="name" /><br>
Variable 1: <jsp:getProperty name="calc" property="var1" /><br>
Variable 2: <jsp:getProperty name="calc" property="var2" /><br>
<%= "Result: "+ calc.sum() %>
</jsp:useBean>
</body>
</Html>
```

Example 16.9(b)   CalculateBean.java

```java
package beans;
import java.io.*;
public class CalculateBean implements Serializable
{
    /*Attributes*/
    private int var1;
    private int var2;
    private String name=new String();

    /*getter methods*/
    public int getVar1()
    {
        return var1;
    }
public int getVar2()
{
        return var2;
}
public String getName()
{
        return name;
}

    /*setter methods*/
```

```java
public void setName(String x)
{
    name=x;
}

public void setVar1(int x)
{
    var1=x;
}
public void setVar2(int y)
{
    var2=y;
}

/*Method for calculating sum*/
public int sum()
{
    return var1+var2;
}
}
```

Output

Fig. 16.24 Output for Example 16.8

Directory Structure for the Example

We are using the same `login` directory for the accessing beans in a JSP page. The `login` directory contains `WEB-INF` which contains `classes` and the `lib` directory. The `classes` directory within the `WEB-INF` will contain the `beans` directory. All JSP pages reside in our `login` directory. Directory structure for `JavaBeans.jsp` example is given in Fig. 16.25.

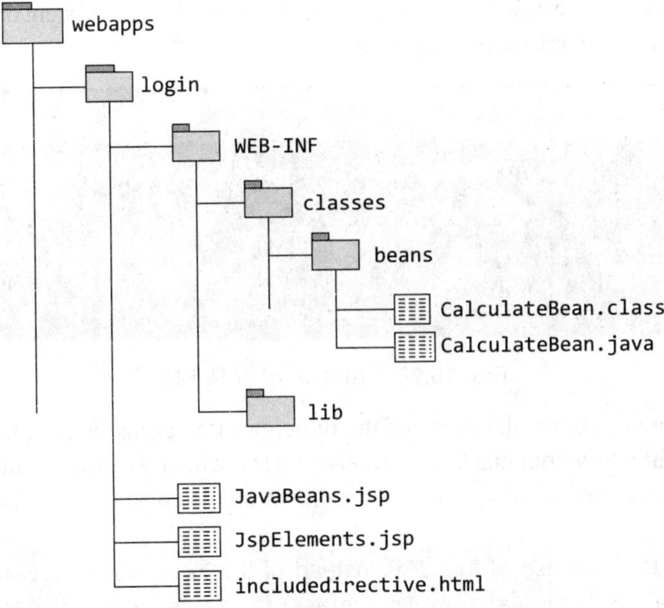

Fig. 16.25 Tomcat Directory Structure for `JavaBeans.jsp` Example

16.7 JAR FILES

JAR stands for Java archive. It is similar to a ZIP file. A Jar tool is provided with Java development kit (JDK) to perform basic tasks with Jar files. Let us see how Jar files can be created and used.

16.7.1 Creating a JAR File

The basic command for creating a Jar file is as follows:

```
jar -cvmf jar-file-name manifest-file-name input-file-names
```

The options and arguments used in this command are

- *c* option stands for *creating* a Jar file.
- *v* stands for *verbose* output on standard output. All files included in Jar will be shown on the console.
- *f* option stands for *file* to indicate that the output will go into a *file* rather than to the standard output.
- *m* stands for specifying *manifest* file to be added to the Jar. If the option is not specified, Jar utility will create a default manifest file.
- *Jar-file-name* is the names that you want the resulting Jar file to have. Jar files have a `.jar` extension.
- File names to be a part of Jar file can be specified separated by single white spaces. If a directory is specified the contents of that directories are added to the Jar archive recursively.

This command will create a compressed Jar file and place it in the current directory. For example, Fig. 16.26 shows the creation of `Calculator.jar`.

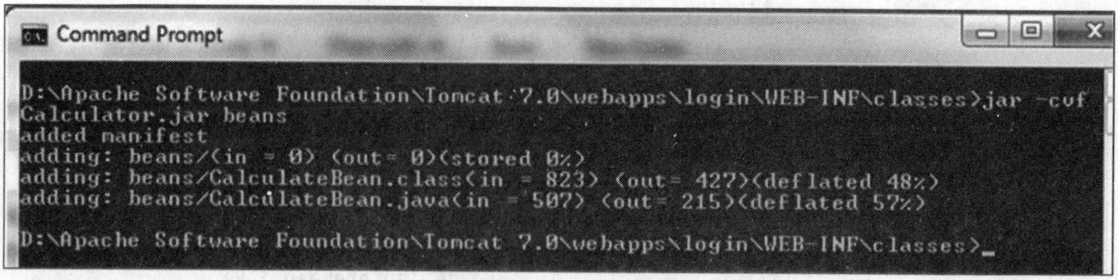

Fig. 16.26 Creation of JAR File

As you can see above, the name of the directory, i.e., `beans` is mentioned after the Jar file name. This directory contains `CalculateBean.class` which we want to include in the Jar. The verbose mode is "on" so all operations are shown on the console.

Note	If you want to make use of this JAR instead of the `beans/CalculateBean.class` (placed in `/WEB-INF/classes/beans/CalculateBean.class`) in the `JavaBeans.jsp` page example, place the `Calculator.jar` in the following folder: `webapps/login/WEB-INF/lib/Calculator.jar` and remove the beans folder from the `/WEB-INF/classes` directory. Now you can use the same `JavaBeans.jsp` page as it is.

16.7.2 Viewing the Contents of a JAR File

The command for viewing the contents of a JAR file is

```
jar -tf jar-file
```

- *t* option indicates that you want to view the contents of the Jar file.
- *f* option signifies that the Jar file whose contents are to be viewed is specified.

Figure 16.27 shows both creation and viewing of the Jar files together.

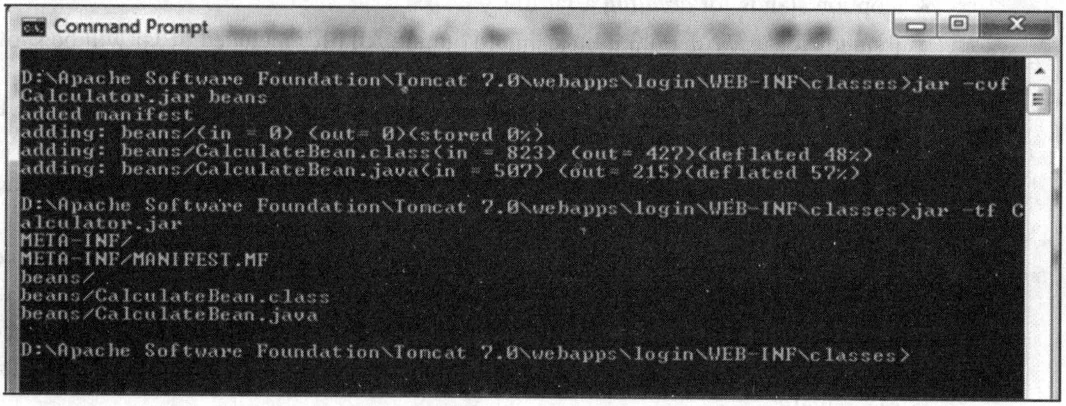

Fig. 16.27 Creation and Viewing of JAR File

16.7.3 Extracting the Contents of JAR

The -xf command is used to extract the contents of the archive. The contents of the JAR will be extracted in the current directory.

```
jar -xf jar-file-name
```

- *x* option stands for extracting the contents.
- *f* options signifies that the JAR-file whose contents need to be extracted is specified.

16.7.4 Manifest Files

Manifest file (.mf) is a special file that can contain information about the files contained in a Jar file. A manifest file could be used to tell which classes in the JAR are bean classes, or which is the main class (starting point) in the JAR, etc. A manifest file is automatically created (if not provided) when a JAR is created and there will be only one manifest file in a JAR as shown.

```
META-INF/MANIFEST.MF
```

The default manifest file will contain the following:

```
Manifest-Version: 1.0
Created-By: 1.7.0_09 (Oracle Corporation)
```

The manifest's entries are in "header : value" pairs. The first line indicates that manifest file conforms to version 1.0 of the manifest specification and is created by the 1.7.0_09 version of the JDK.

Modifying a Manifest File

The m command-line option is used to add custom information to the manifest during creation of a Jar file. In order to modify the manifest, you will have to create a text file first containing the information that you wish to add to the manifest. The general syntax for the command is as follows:

```
jar cfm jar-file manifest-file input-file(s)
```

Note Make sure you add a carriage return or new line at the end of manifest file otherwise the last statement will not be passed. As well as, the order of m and f options and their arguments must match exactly. If options are -fm then the JAR-file-name must appear before the manifest file and if —mf options are specified, the situations will be reverse. For example,

The correct statements

```
jar -cvfm Calculator.jar manifest.txt beans
jar -cvmf manifest.txt Calculator.jar beans
```

The wrong statement

```
jar -cvfm manifest.txt Calculator.jar beans
```

For example, Fig. 16.28 shows how to add manifest file to the jar. Also note the order of options and the arguments. Figure. 16.29 shows a sample manifest.txt file.

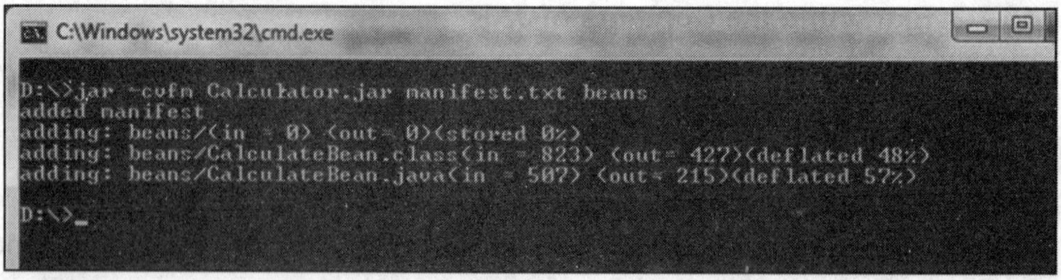

Fig. 16.28 Adding Manifest to Jar

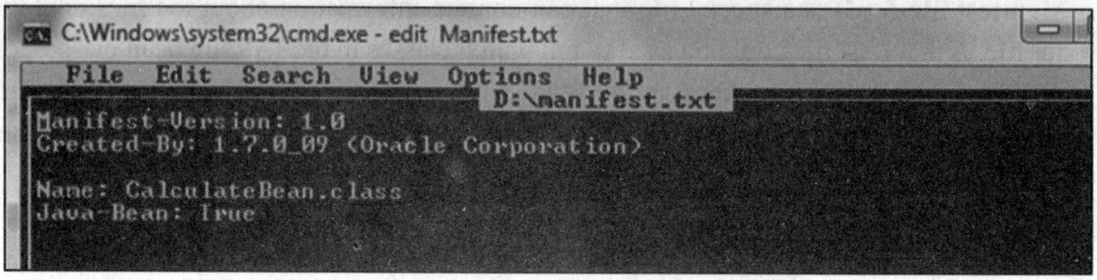

Fig. 16.29 A sample `manifest.txt` File

Application Bundled in JAR

If an application is bundled in a Jar, then there should be some way to indicate which class within the JAR file is the main class from where your application will start. This information is provided in the manifest file by adding the following header in it:

```
Main-Class: classname
```

`classname` is the name of the class which contains the main method (`public static void main(Stringargs[])`) as the execution of any Java applications begin from main method. Once this manifest is added to the JAR, the application bundled in JAR can be executed as

```
java -jar JAR-name
```

> **Note** The 'e' option (e stands for entry point) can also be used to create or override the manifest's `Main-Class` header. It is used to specify the applications starting point without editing or creating the manifest file. For example, this command creates `x.jar` where the `Main-Class` attribute value in the manifest is set to `MyMain`:
>
> ```
> jar cfe x.jar MyMain MyMain.class
> ```
>
> If the starting point or main class is in a package, the following command may be invoked. For example, `App` is the package which contains `MyMain.class`.
>
> ```
> jar cfe x.jar App.MyMain App/MyMain.class
> ```

16.8 REMOTE METHOD INVOCATION

Distributed computing allows parts of the system to be residing in separate machines located in different places. It allows business logic and data to be accessed from remote locations anytime anywhere by any one. RMI helps in accomplishing this by allowing objects running on one machine to be accessed by the clients running in different machines.

Remote method invocation (RMI) is Java's implementation of remote procedure call (RPC) for distributed computing. It is based on client/server concept. RPC is, as the name suggests, a client invoking a procedure on the remote server by passing arguments and expecting some return. RMI is a Java client (running in one JVM) invoking a procedure on a remote Java server (running in same/different JVM). RMI is not language-independent, whereas CORBA (common object request broker architecture) is language-independent. Language independency means a Java program can communicate with a program written in any language like C or C++. The low level details of communication are hidden from the programmer. Actually, a protocol named JRMP (Java Remote Method Protocol) that works over TCP/IP takes care of the communication between client and server. Sockets are also used for communication, as they are used for transferring and receiving data, whereas RMI transfers control by invoking procedure on the server.

16.8.1 RMI Networking Model

RMI client/server applications are used over TCP/IP networking model. In TCP/IP, it is the application layer's responsibility to deal with presentation as well as session layer issues. So the RMI provides the functionality for these layers, as shown in Fig. 16.30. The presentation layer's functionality at client and server is handled by *stub* and *skeleton*, respectively. Remote reference layer (RRL) handles the session layer functionality by managing the session among client and server.

Stub and Skeleton

Stub is a client-side proxy class, whereas skeleton is a server-side proxy class generated by the special compiler, *rmic* (*rmicompiler*). Both these classes are generated from the server (`.class`) class after it has been compiled by the *rmic*. (The newer version of JRMP protocol has made skeleton class obsolete and now it is not generated by the *rmic*. The functionality of skeleton is handled by it automatically. For learning purpose, we should know the functions performed by both Stub and Skeleton.)

Actually the term *proxy* has been used because the client talks to stub, assuming it to be the server, whilst its purpose is to pass the client's request to the server and the server's response to the client (vice versa for skeleton). Apart from this, the other functionalities performed by stubs are

- Marshalling arguments and unmarshalling return values.
- Informs the RRL that a call should be invoked on the server.
- Informs the RRL that the call is complete.

The functions performed by skeleton are

- Marshalling return values and unmarshalling arguments.
- Invoking the actual remote object implementation.

Parameter marshalling and unmarshalling deals with how parameters are sent to the server and responses are returned to the client. Actually networks are heterogeneous in nature. By heterogeneous, we mean machines of different make, different architecture, and different protocols are used in a network. For example, a machine 'A' which stores integers in one's compliment form and character in ASCII code wants to communicate with a machine 'B' which uses 2's compliment for integers and EBCDIC code for characters. If communication is allowed to proceed without any conversion in between, then whatever A transmits can have some other meaning when it is interpreted by B. For the communication to be unambiguous, the stubs at the client marshal the parameters, i.e., convert the parameters into a network byte order (standard conversion order used on networks) and at the server, the skeletons unmarshal the parameters, i.e., convert the network byte order into host-specific order (which is the interpretation used on the server).

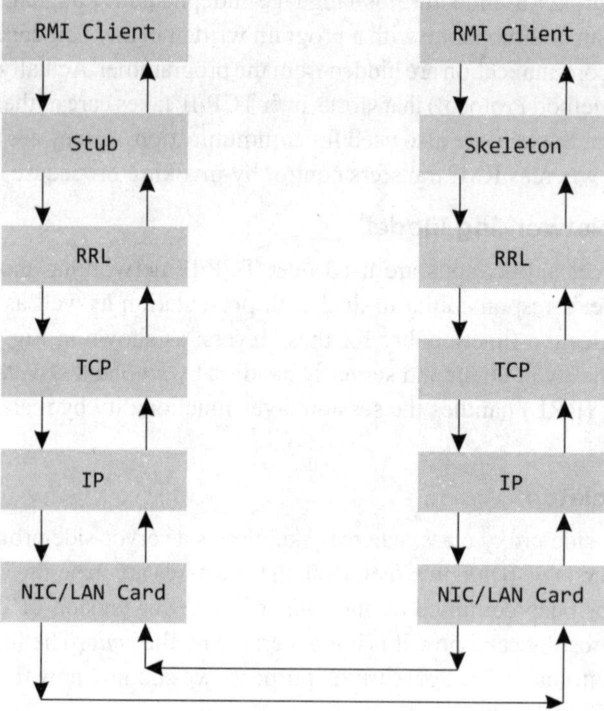

Fig. 16.30 RMI Over TCP/IP

16.8.2 Creating an RMI Application

The following steps will show how to create an RMI client/server application:

- An interface needs to be created which would contain the definition of the methods that can be invoked remotely.
- Create a `Server` class that provides the implementation of the methods in the interface.
- Generate Stubs using *rmic*.
- A client to invoke the remote methods.
- Run RMI registry.
- Run server and client.

Creating an Interface Example 16.10 shows an interface which contains the definitions of the methods that can be invoked from client remotely. The clients are provided with these interfaces to let them know about the names of the methods, their return types, and their parameters.

Example 16.10 | **Interface Declaration**

```java
import java.rmi.*;
public interface Calculation extends Remote
{
   public double remainder(double a, double b) throws RemoteException;
   public double cube(double a) throws RemoteException;
}
```

The mandatory requirement for such interfaces is that the interface should be a sub-interface of `Remote` interface. `Remote` interface is a part of *java.rmi* package, so it has to be imported. This interface is empty and is used to denote that the methods of this interface can be invoked remotely. Also note that all the methods in the interface should specify an exception to be thrown, i.e., `RemoteException` as shown above. The interface has to be `public`.

Server Class

The `Server` class should implement the `Calculation` interface defined above. The `Server` class is shown in Example 16.11.

Example 16.11 | **RMI Server**

```java
L1    import java.rmi.*;
L2    import java.rmi.server.*;
L3    public class Server extends UnicastRemoteObject implements Calculation {
L4    public Server() throws RemoteException
         {
L5          super();
         }
L6     public double remainder(double a, double b) throws RemoteException
         {
L7          return a % b;
         }
L8    public double cube(double a) throws RemoteException
         {
L9          return a * a * a;
         }
L10   public static void main(String args[]) throws Exception
          {
L11   try {
L12          Server s = new Server();
L13          System.out.println("Object created");
```

```
L14        Naming.rebind("rmi://localhost/Calculator",s);
L15        System.out.println("Object Registered");
       }
catch(Exception e)
{
    System.out.println(e);
}
}}
```

Explanation

L2 For creating server, the package `java.rmi.server` has to be imported.

L3 The `Server` class should inherit the `UnicastRemoteObject` class to create itself an RMI server. This `Server` class also inherits the `Calculation` interface and provides the implementation of the methods (remotely available) in the interface.

L4–5 Constructor for the class has been defined and the superclass constructor has been called. The superclass constructor throws `RemoteException`, so the constructor of `Server` class throws a `RemoteException`.

L6–7 Method has been overridden; `remainder (double a, double b)`. This methods turns the remainder of a/b.

L8–9 Method has been overridden; `cube(double a)`. This methods returns `a * a * a`.

L10 `main()` method defined.

L11 `try` block defined within `main()`.

L12 Object of `Server` class is created.

L14 A static method `rebind` of the `Naming` class is used to bind the server object to the registry services with a name. The first argument is the URL and the second argument is the `server` object to be bound. The URL has the following syntax:

```
protocol://host machine:[optional port no]/name of the service.
Protocol is rmi
Hostname mentions the name of the machine where registry is running i.e. localhost
By default it runs on port 1099
Name is the name by which server objects are registered.
```

This method may throw a `RemoteException` as well as a `MalformedURLException`. Apart from this, the `Naming` class provides two other methods: *bind* and *unbind*.

The `static void bind(String name, Remote obj)` method binds the server object with a name into the registry. If the name is already bound, then it throws an `AlreadyBoundException`. This is different from `rebind` method which overwrites the association of name into the registry.

The `static voidunbind(String name)` removes the association of name in the registry service.

RMI Registry RMI registry helps to locate a remote object whose methods it wishes to invoke. RMI registry is a name service which keeps an association of simple names to their corresponding remote objects. It runs on the same machine as that of RMI server.

Every object that wishes to publicize its methods must register itself by a name on the registry service. Clients look up the registered name in the registry service and get a reference to the remote object in return. Then use that reference to invoke the remote methods of the server.

Stub The `stub` class is generated by a special `rmicompiler` (`rmic`). The `Server` class is first compiled and then, the *rmic* is used on the compiled `Server` class. Do not mention `server. class` while using `rmic` for generating `stub` class. The `stub` class generated has the following name: `Server_Stub.class`. In general, its name is `<name of the Server Class>_Stub.class`. This class has to be provided to the client. As we have kept the client in a directory 'rmiclient', this stub has to be copied into the client's directory.

Client The client is created in a directory 'rmiclient'. The interface as well as the stub generated from the `Server` class must be included in this directory.

Example 16.12 **RMI Client**

```java
import java.rmi.*;
public class Client{
public static void main(String args[]) throws Exception
{
    Calculation c = (Calculation)Naming.lookup("rmi://localhost/Calculator");
    System.out.println("Remainder of 3.2 % 3.2: " +c.remainder(3.2,3.2));
    System.out. println("Cube of 3.2: " +c.cube(3.2));
}}
```

The method `Naming.lookup (String name)` is used to lookup the named service. This method returns a Remote object. If the named service could not be found, then it throws `NotBoundException`. If Registry could not be contacted, a `RemoteException` occurs. If the URL argument is not properly formatted, a `MalformedURLException` results.

Executing RMI Server and Client

Registry, server, and client are run in three separate DOS shells. The outputs at the client and server DOS shells are shown below:

```
C:\javabook\programs\CHAP15~1\rmiserver>java Server
Object created
Object Registered

C:\javabook\programs\chap 15\rmiclient>java Client
Remainder of 3.2 % 3.2: 0.0
Cube of 3.2: 32.76800000000001
```

16.9 INTRODUCTION TO EJB

EJB is a server side distributed component of the J2EE architecture that primarily provides business logic besides interacting with other server side components. EJB developers need to focus only on coding business logic leaving the system level services to be handled by EJB server such as multiple threading, object pool, security, instance management, connection pooling, and transactions. EJB is based on the concept that in a distributed computing environment, database-related logic should be independent of the business logic that relies on the data. Figure 16.31 would give a clear understanding of where EJB fits in the entire scenario and how servlets and JSP would interact with EJB resources. The servlets and JSP use Java naming and directory interface to look up EJB.

16.9.1 Types of EJB

There are three types of EJB: entity beans, session beans, and message driven beans as shown in Fig. 16.32.

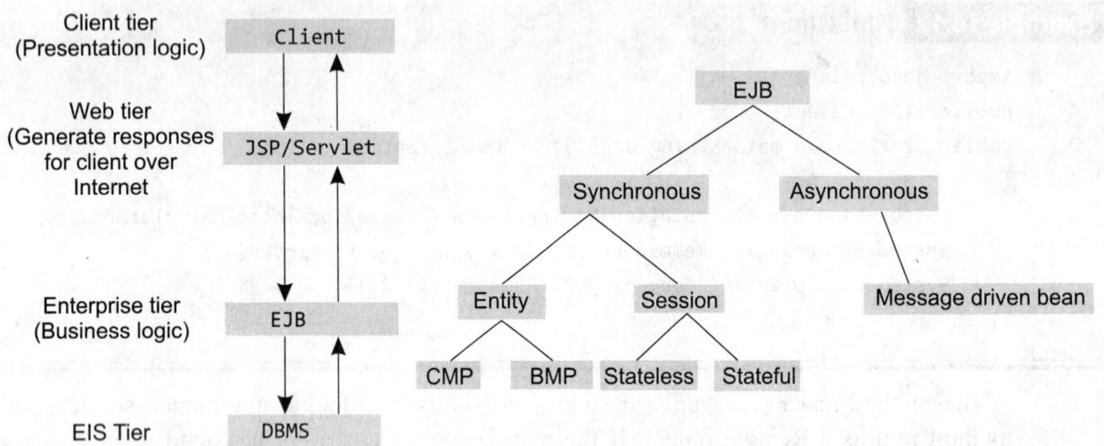

Fig. 16.31 J2EE Multitier Architecture

Fig. 16.32 Types of EJB

Entity Bean

An entity bean models real world objects/entities. These entities represent business concepts that include a customer or a product. Entity bean is used to manage a collection of data (also known as persistent data) which is retrieved from a database. An entity bean may insert, update or delete data from the database. This persistent data may be managed in two ways resulting in two types of entity beans: BMP (Bean Managed Persistence) and CMP (Container Managed Persistence). An entity bean must implement the `javax.ejb.EntityBean` interface. Entity beans, like session beans, are also transactional in nature and they can be shared among different clients.

In container-managed persistence entity beans, persistence is automatically managed by the EJB container. The bean developer instead of coding the persistence logic relies on the deployment descriptor to specify attributes whose persistence needs to be managed by the container. The container synchronizes the state of the bean with the database. In other words, it maps the attributes of the bean to the database thus performing the insert, update, and delete operations automatically.

In the bean-managed persistence entity beans, the developer codes the logic to manipulate the database. All interactions with the database take place according to the directions given by the EJB container. The EJB container informs the entity bean when to perform an operation: when to insert, update, or delete its data from the database.

Session Beans

Session beans contain business logic and are used for managing processes or tasks. A session bean provides service to the client and it exists for the entire client server session. Unlike entity beans which represent an entity into the database, a session bean does not represent anything into the database. However, it can access the database. An entity bean has persistent state whereas a session bean does not have a persistent state as it is used for modeling interactions between clients and server. Session beans are aware about transactions. Instances of session beans are not shared among clients. Unlike entity beans, session beans have a client-dependent identity. A session beans has to implement the `javax.ejb.SessionBean` interface.

Session beans, however, can be either stateful or stateless. A stateful session bean maintains or retains state across interactions between client and server. A stateful bean is able to retain state between successive calls from a client to a session bean. Therefore, a call can access data from the previous method call. This state is not written to a database, so they are not persistent but the session beans can communicate with the databases.

Stateless session beans are those that do not maintain any state between client and the session bean. A bean can be specified as stateful or stateless in the bean's deployment descriptor.

Message-driven Beans

Message-driven beans can be considered as a special kind of stateless session bean which can receive messages from Java messaging service (JMS) and perform actions. They implement business logic in response to JMS messages. MDB was introduced in EJB 2.0 specifications and can be called only implicitly by sending messages to it. Every message-driven bean will have to inherit the `javax.ejb.MessageDrivenBean` interface. Unlike the session and entity beans, message-driven beans are asynchronous in nature. The clients in session and entity beans are blocked (i.e., synchronous nature) until the container completes the execution of the bean methods. During this execution, the (session/entity) bean is unable to accept any messages from any messaging service. And hence EJB introduced the message-driven bean. A client needs to use a messaging service like JMS in order to send messages to the MDB. The MDB are registered against JMS destinations. When the messaging service receives the message for a destination, the EJB container invokes MDB associated with that destination. Hence, it is a local object and does not require home or remote interfaces.

16.9.2 EJB Architecture

Every human behaves differently at different places. For example, the way you behave/interact/roam/sit in your home will be different from the way you behave or interact in your office. So simply you have two interfaces one for your home and other for outsider (Remote). EJB architecture also specifies two kinds of interfaces for session and entity beans: `Home` interface (`javax.ejb.EJBHome`) and `Remote` interface (`javax.ejb.EJBObject`). The `Home` interface contains methods for creating, finding, and destroying remote objects. The `Remote` interface contains business methods that are exposed to the clients. The EJB container manages interaction between the EJB and other components using the `Home` and the `Remote` interface. The local clients residing on the same JVM as that of EJB use the `Home` interface for interacting with the EJB. Remote clients use the `Remote` interface to interact with the EJB through an application which is RMI and IIOP complaint. EJB 2.0 specifications added `local` (`javax.ejb.EJBLocalObject`) and `Localhome` (`javax.ejb.EJBLocalHome`)interfaces in addition to `Remote` and `Home` interface. So according to EJB 2.0, `Local` and `LocalHome` interface is used by local client, i.e., clients on the same JVM and `Remote` interface for clients outside the JVM. What `Home` interface does for a remote client, `LocalHome` does the same for a local client and likewise for local and remote interfaces.

16.10 HELLO WORLD—EJB EXAMPLE

We will be creating a stateless session bean to demonstrate how EJB can be created and used. To create this beans we will be using Eclipse Juno for Java Enterprise Edition and JBoss version 5 application server. As stated by EJB 2.0 specifications a session or entity bean will have remote, home, local, and local home interfaces. Apart from this there will be a bean class and a client to invoke the bean. The bean is deployed using deployment descriptors. All other activities are taken care of by the EJB container. We will demonstrate the example with the snapshots of Eclipse to show the creation of this bean and its associated interfaces.

EJB Container is used for managing the EJB objects and EJB homes for the beans. It also helps in managing their resources and provides services to bean instances at run time. We are using Jboss-5.1.0.GA-jdk6 application server which contains an EJB container. It can be unzipped in a folder and used with Eclipse as shown in Fig. 16.33. (We have already added this server in our eclipse that is why you are able to see `JBossv5.0` at `localhost [Stopped]` in the `Server`tab done. It has to be started before we run our EJB.)

To add a server in Eclipse, click on the `Server` tab and right click in that tab. Go to the `New` option, and you will be displayed an option: `Server`. Click on it to add a new server as shown in Fig. 16.33(a).

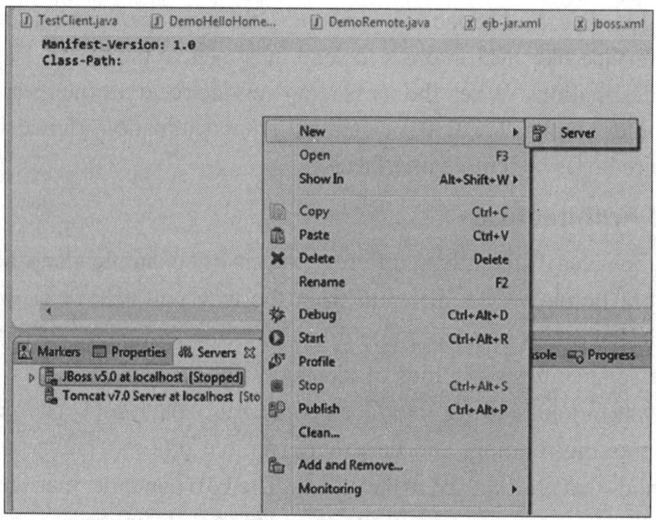

Fig. 16.33(a) Adding a Server

As you can see in Fig. 16.33(b), different versions of JBoss are displayed. You can choose a version and proceed further. If the Demo EJB bean is created then it may also ask you to deploy that bean after this step or else it can be done later as well.

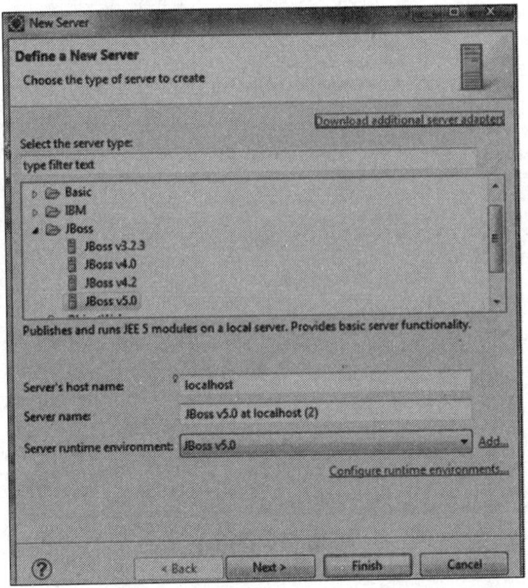

Fig. 16.33(b) Adding a Server

First of all, create an EJB Project in the project explorer window like DemoHello shown in Fig. 16.34. (Do not forget to specify the EJB module version while creating EJB Project. We are using version 2.0). Before writing our interfaces and bean classes we have to add libraries to our EJB project. Right click on the DemoHello EJB project and click on BuildPath → Configure Build Path. In the Libraries Tab, click on Add Library, choose server runtime and add the server (i.e., JBoss in our case) you had earlier added to Eclipse.

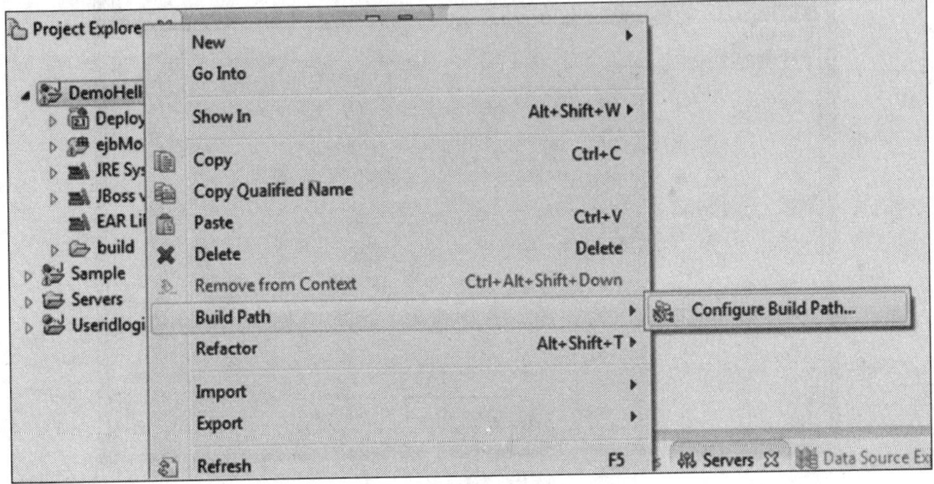

Fig. 16.34(a)

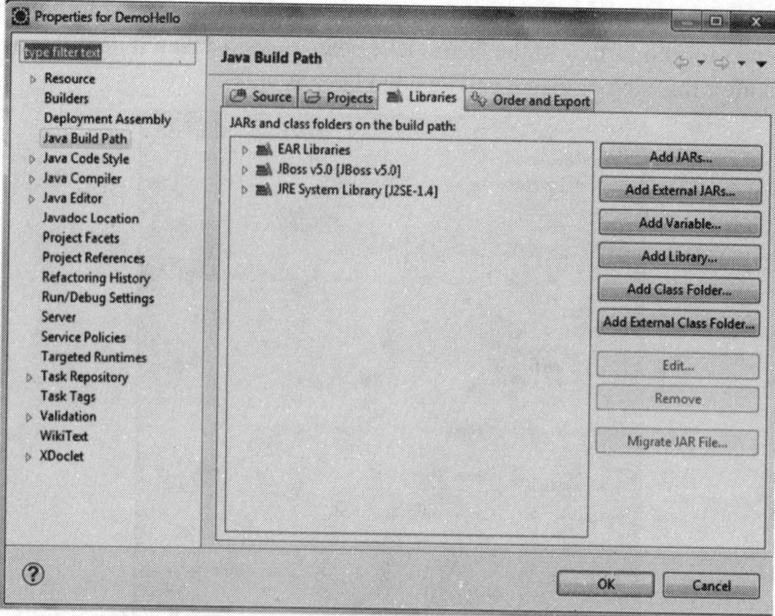

Fig. 16.34(b)

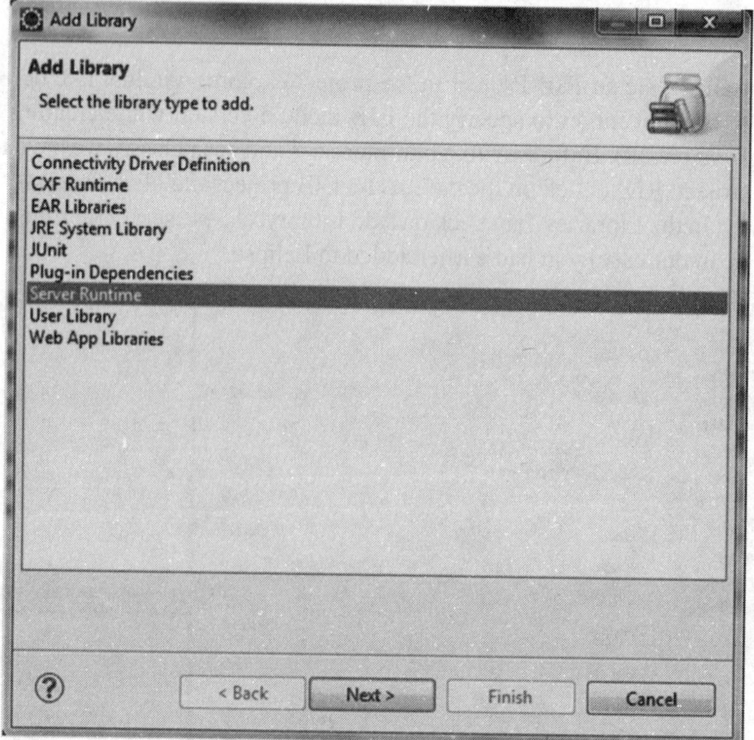

Fig. 16.34(c)

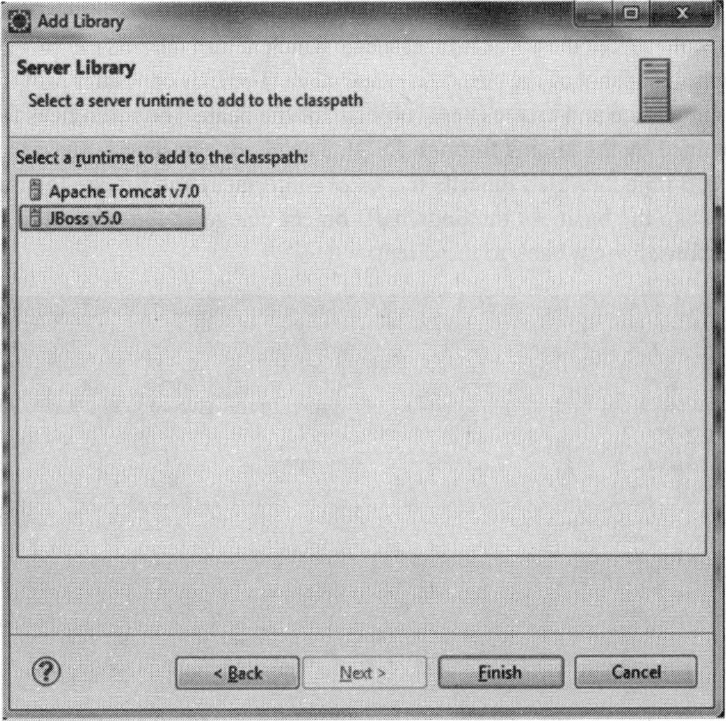

Fig. 16.34(d)

Now we will create the `Remote` interface for our first EJB to it. Right click on `ejbModule` package that was created in the `DemoHello` folder in Project Explorer window, Go to New and click on Interface. This interface will define the business methods that clients can access. As you can see, we are creating a Hello Enterprise bean. The method that client can call is defined here, i.e., `sayHello()`. This interface should inherit the `javax.ejb.EJBObject`, which in turn inherits the `java.rmi.Remote`. Figure 16.35 shows the snapshot of `DemoRemote.java` interface.

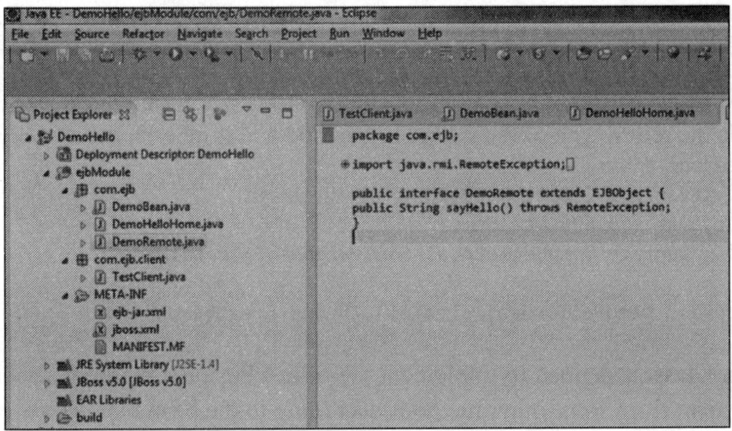

Fig. 16.35 Remote Interface for the Bean

Let us create the Home interface. This interface is responsible for defining the create method. This interface should inherit the javax.ejb.EJBHome, which in turn inherits the java.rmi.Remote. Figure 16.36 shows a snapshot of the DemoHelloHome.java. The EJB container provides implementation of the Home interface and creates Home objects for the bean. The references to these Home objects can be obtained by the clients through JNDI. The client can send request to the home object to create an EJB object (which inherits the Remote interface) and invoke the business methods. In order to invoke the business methods, EJB object delegates the request to the enterprise bean and the response is sent back to the client.

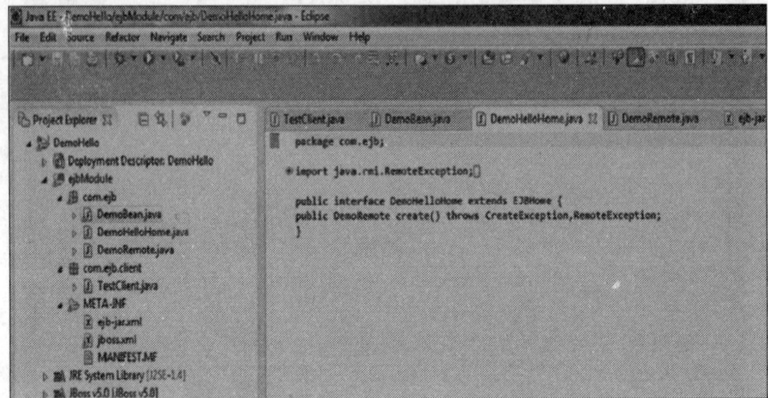

Fig. 16.36 Home Interface for the Bean

As we will be accessing the bean remotely only, we do not require the local and localhome interface but for your reference we have provided the code for these interfaces.

Local interface for the EJB is defined (similar to the DemoRemote interface). It inherits the EJBLocalObject interface.

```
package com.ejb;
import javax.ejb.EJBLocalObject;
public interface DemoHelloLocal extends EJBLocalObject
{
    public String sayHello();
}
```

LocalHome interface for the EJB (similar to the DemoHelloHome interface). The only thing that changes is the return type of the sayHello method and it inherits the EJBLocalHome interface.

```
package com.ejb;
import javax.ejb.CreateException;
import javax.ejb.EJBLocalHome;
public interface DemoHelloLocalHome extends EJBLocalHome
{
        public DemoHelloLocal create() throws CreateException;
}
```

The **Bean Class** is defined to implement the bean's business methods specified in the remote interface apart from some other methods according to the bean that we are creating, i.e., either session or entity bean. As we are creating a session bean, this class should inherit the javax.ejb.SessionBean interface. The following snapshot shows the DemoBean.java. The methods that have been overridden are: `ejbCreate()`, `ejbActivate()`, `ejbPassivate()`, `ejbRemove()`, and `setSessionContext()`. Apart from these, the `sayHello()` method defined in the `DemoRemote` interface is also overridden and implemented here. When the client calls the `sayHello()`, it is this method that is executed and the contents are returned to the client. The following snapshot in Fig. 16.37 shows the `DemoBean.java` class. A short description of the session bean method is shown in Table 16.12.


```java
package com.ejb;
import java.rmi.RemoteException;
import javax.ejb.EJBException;
import javax.ejb.SessionBean;
import javax.ejb.SessionContext;

public class DemoBean implements SessionBean {
    public void ejbCreate() {
        // TODO Auto-generated method stub
    }

    public void ejbActivate() throws EJBException, RemoteException {
        // TODO Auto-generated method stub
    }

    public void ejbPassivate() throws EJBException, RemoteException {
        // TODO Auto-generated method stub
    }

    public void ejbRemove() throws EJBException, RemoteException {
        // TODO Auto-generated method stub
    }

    public void setSessionContext(SessionContext arg0) throws EJBException,
            RemoteException {
        // TODO Auto-generated method stub
    }
    public String sayHello()
    {
        return "My First EJB";
    }
}
```

Fig. 16.37 Bean Class

In order to invoke EJB, we need a Remote client. This Remote client uses the JNDI, locate the beans on the net. It provides a uniform API for performing naming and directory services. The following snapshot in Fig. 16.38 shows the `TestClient.java`. Note that it has been created in a separate directory. This client makes use of `javax.naming.InitialContext` class (inherits the context interface) and it serves as a starting point for resolving names. This class is used by the client for looking up the enterprise bean. The constructor of this class accepts `Hashtable` of environmental properties. So a `Hashtable` object is instantiated and properties are put in it using the put method. `javax.naming.Context` is an interface which represent naming context. Three properties are set as shown in Table 16.13.

Table 16.12 Session Bean Method

• `ejbCreate`	Used for initializing your session.
• `ejbPassivate`	Called when the bean is swapped to disk.
• `ejbActivate`	Called when the bean is swapped back from disk.
• `ejbRemove`	Called before a bean is removed from memory.
• `setSessionContext`	A session context is associated with a bean which it can use to query about its state.

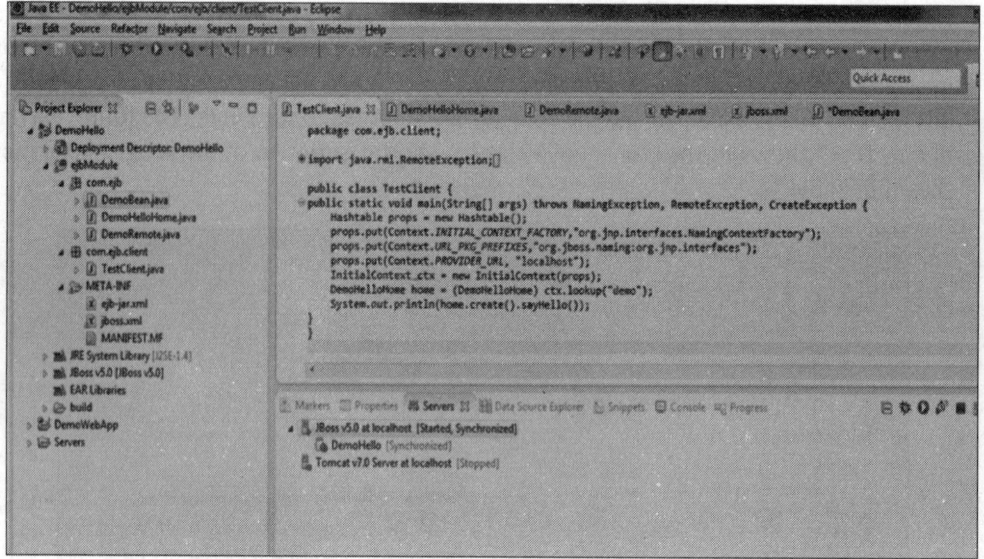

Fig. 16.38 Remote Client

Table 16.13 Properties of `javax.naming.context`

`Context.INITIAL_CONTEXT_FACTORY`	• Specifies the initial context factory (directory services provider) to be used for the bean. For example, `org.jnp.interfaces.naming-ContextFactory`. Note that it has to be a fully qualified name.
`Context.URL_PKG_PREFIXES`	• Specifies the list of packages to use while loading context factories. For example, `org.jboss.naming:org.jnp.interfaces`.
`Context.PROVIDER_URL`	• Specifies the URL of the directory services, i.e., `localhost` in our case.

Deployment Descriptors specify information about how beans will be managed at runtime. These descriptors are specified in an `xml` file. The following xml file (as shown in Fig. 16.39) shows `ejb-jar.xml` files which specify the name, remote, home interface, and the enterprise bean class. The session bean as well as the transaction type is also specified.

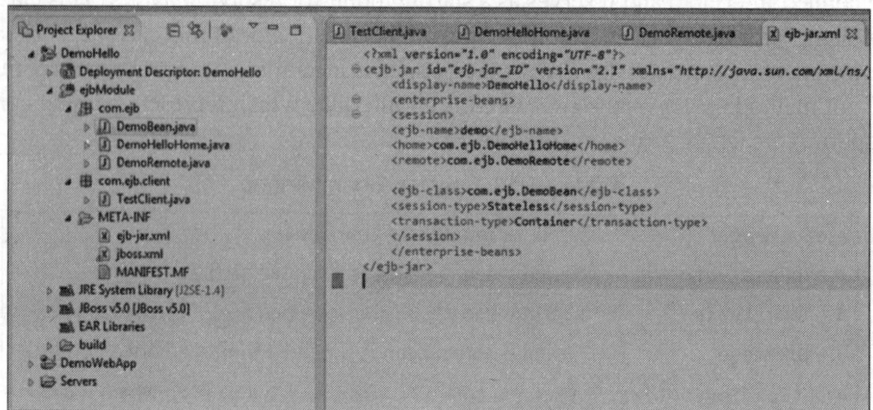

Fig. 16.39 `ejb-jar.xml` Deployment Descriptor File

Figure 16.40 shows another descriptor file, i.e., `Jboss.xml` which is specific to the container. Please note that the `ejb-name` in the `ejb-jar.xml` and `jboss.xml` must match.

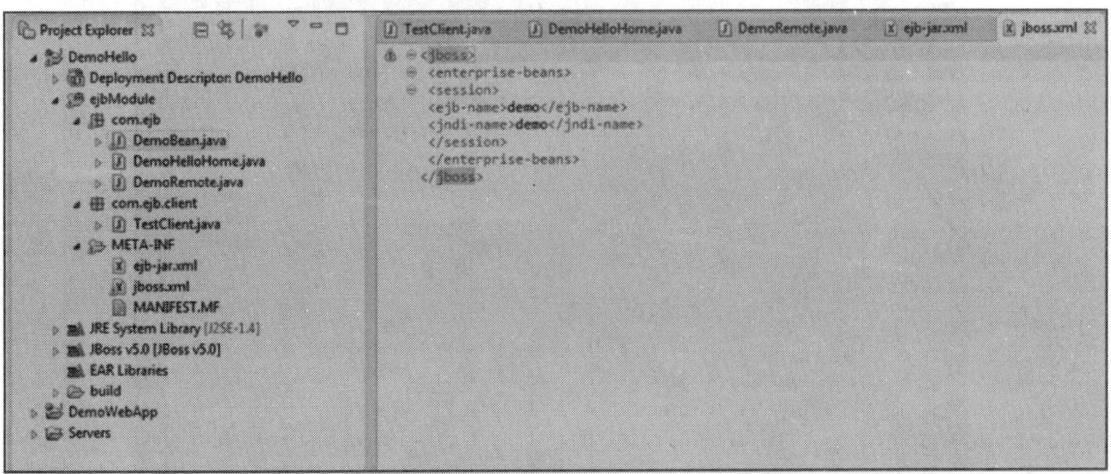

Fig. 16.40 `jboss.xml` Deployment Descriptor for the Container

You are all set to run the EJB. Start your server and deploy the `DemoHello` to it as shown in Figs 16.41 to 16.44.

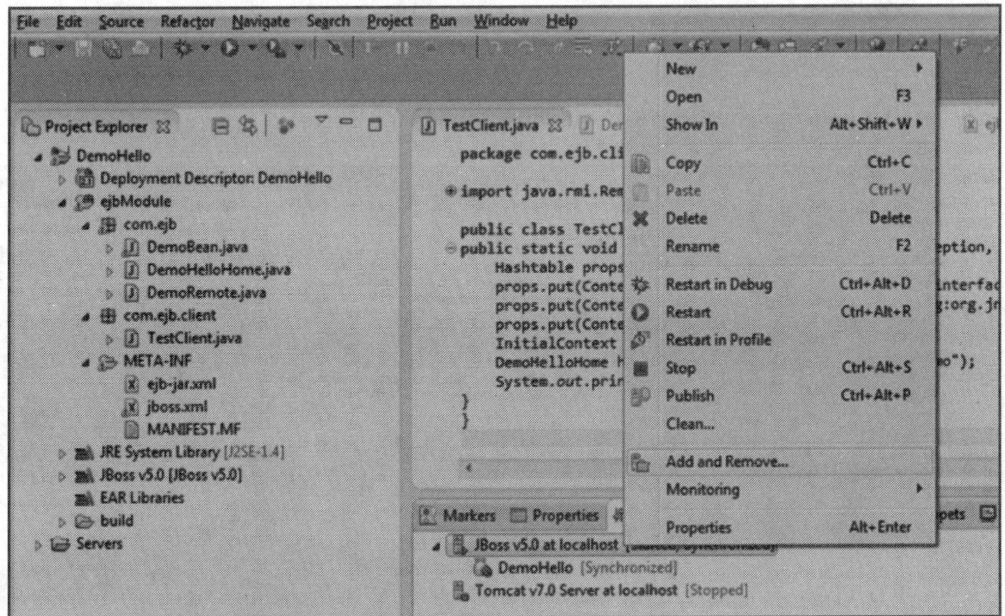

Fig. 16.41 Deploy the Bean

Go to `TestClient.java` and right click on it and select Run As → Java application. Go to Console tab besides the Server tab, to see the output (see Figs 16.43 and 16.44).

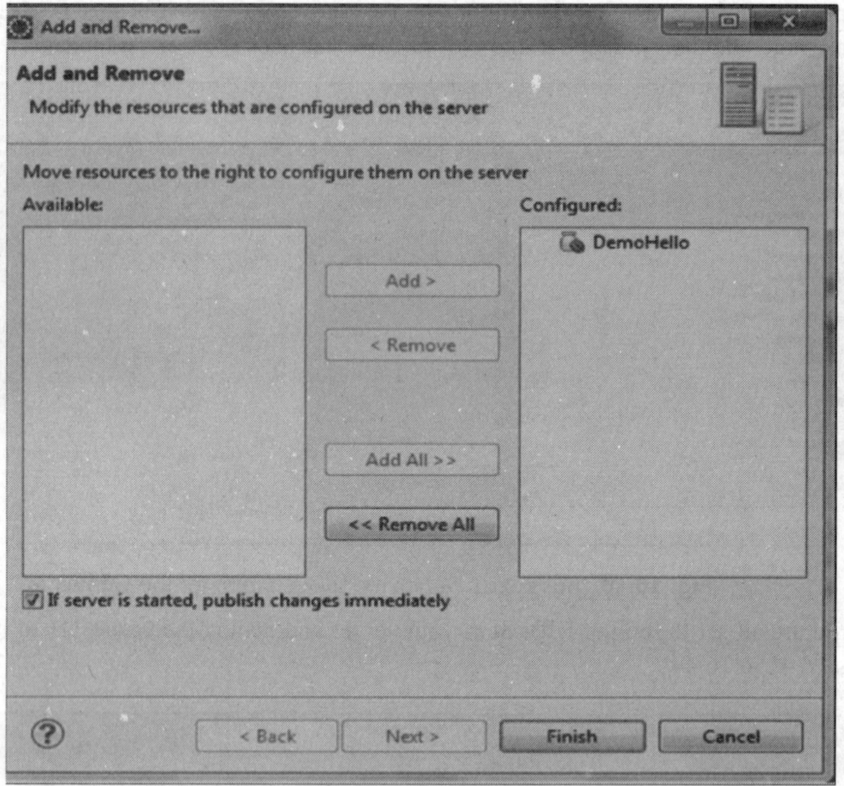

Fig. 16.42 Add the Bean to the Server

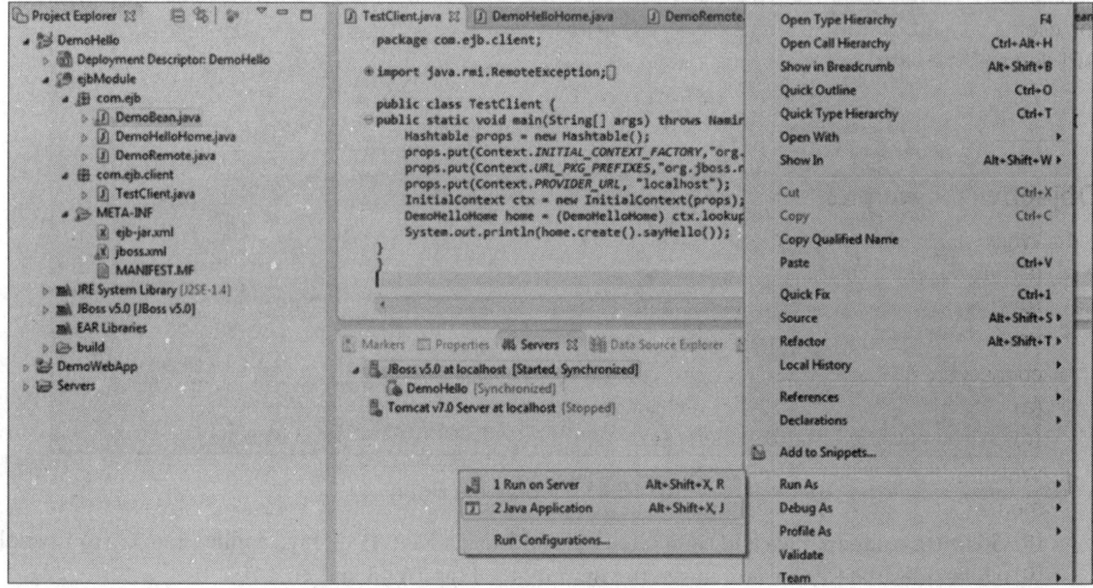

Fig. 16.43 Run the Bean

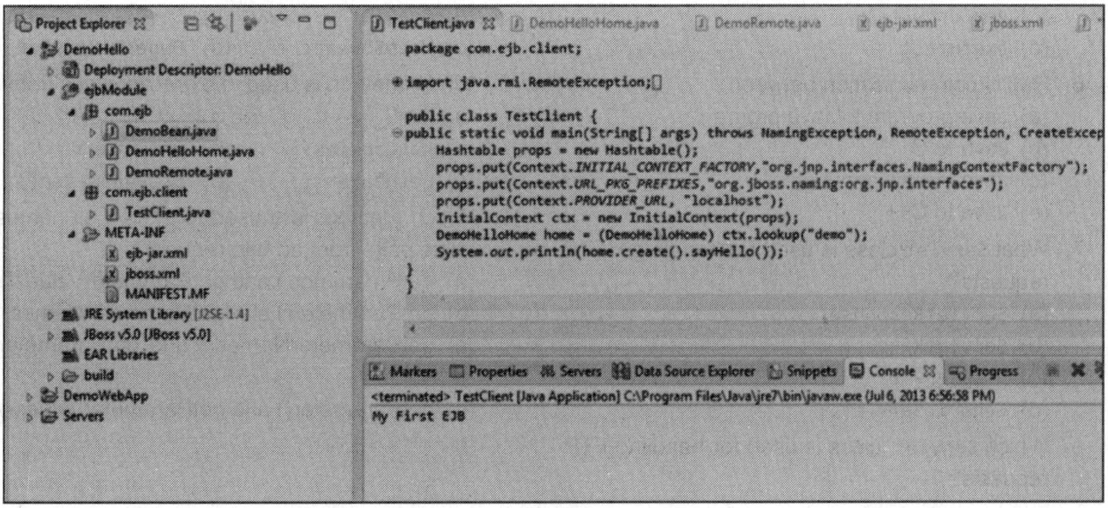

Fig. 16.44 Output

SUMMARY

Core Java deals with basic programming constructs and the classes needed for creating a standalone application. Advanced Java deals with classes that are used for creating Internet-based server-side applications. In this chapter, we have learnt about some of the concepts of advanced Java such as servlets, JSP, JDBC, RMI, Java beans, and enterprise Java beans. Servlets are used for generating responses for clients, based on the requests received. JDBC API deals with a variety of databases for storing and manipulating data within them. Java RMI is the solution for RPC, where a Java program on a remote machine can be called from a Java client program. Basically, RMI helps in distributed computing. A Java server page is an easy solution to generate dynamic contents for the client. Java beans helps in creation of reusable software components which can be used by server side technologies. EJB is a server side distributed component architecture which is used for creating enterprise wide server side applications.

EXERCISES

Objective Questions

1. Which packages contain the JDBC API?
   - (a) `java.jdbc`
   - (b) `java.sql`
   - (c) `javax.jdbc`
   - (d) `javax.sql`

2. Which class is used to establish a database connection?
   - (a) `Class`
   - (b) `DriverManager`
   - (c) `Statement`
   - (d) `ResultSet`

3. Which of the following is a precompiled statement?
   - (a) `Statement`
   - (b) `PreparedStatement`
   - (c) `CallableStatement`
   - (d) `Connection`

4. Which of the following is used for calling stored procedures?
   - (a) `Statement`
   - (b) `PreparedStatement`
   - (c) `CallableStatement`
   - (d) `Connection`

5. Which of the following methods return a connection object?
   - (a) `getConnection()`
   - (b) `getConnection(String databaseURL)`

(c) `getConnect()`
(d) `execute()`

6. RMI is communication between
   (a) Java program to Java program
   (b) Java to C
   (c) Java to any language
   (d) Java to C++

7. What `Servlet` class is used for handling HTTP requests?
   (a) `ServletResponse`
   (b) `ServletRequest`
   (c) `HttpServlet`
   (d) `GenericServlet`

8. Which `Servlet` class is used for handling FTP requests?

   (a) `ServletResponse` (b) `ServletRequest`
   (c) `HttpServlet`   (d) `GenericServlet`

9. Which method is used to extract cookies from a request?
   (a) `getCookies()`   (b) `getData()`
   (c) `getHeaders()`   (d) `getParameter()`

10. Which methods are used to extract all names/value pairs from an http request?
    (a) getParameter() and getParameterValues()
    (b) getParameter() and getParameterNames()
    (c) getParameterNames() and getParameter-Values()
    (d) getParameter() and getParameterValues()

Review Questions

1. What is the difference between `Statement`, `PreparedStatement`, and `CallableStatement`?
2. Explain the different types of JDBC drivers.
3. Explain the lifecycle of a servlet.
4. Differentiate `get` and `post` requests.
5. Explain the role of registry services in RMI.
6. Explain the following:
   (a) Http redirects
   (b) Cookie
   (c) Stubs and skeletons
   (d) `ResultSet`
   (e) `ResultSet metadata`

7. Explain all the steps used for establishing a connection to a database.
8. Explain how JSP is similar or different from servlets.
9. What is Jar file? How are they created?
10. What is a Java Bean? Explain the various properties of a bean.
11. Explain the role of EJB with its different types.
12. Explain the role of manifest file in a jar file.
13. What are the JDBC transaction? Explain what are the different ways of creating transactions in JDBC.
14. What are scrollable `ResultSets`?

Programming Exercises

1. Write a program to connect to a database and retrieve all the data. The database type (Access or Oracle), driver name, database name, DSN, etc. have to be fed by the user.
2. Write a servlet program that fetches all the data from client and stores it in a database successfully.
3. Write a remote calculator program that adds, subtracts, multiplies, divides, and gives the remainder as well. These operations should be invoked remotely by a client method.

4. Write a servlet that automatically redirects the client to another page.
5. Write a servlet that ensures authenticated users have access to important pages. The user name and password should be stored in a database and whenever a user tries to access the servlet, first he/she is authenticated.
6. Write a servlet to store the user's browsing preferences like color in a cookie and should be displayed in that color.
7. Rewrite the Programming Exercise 5 by using JSP instead of servlets.

8. Create a jar file which will store beans. This bean should be able to read all form elements of HTML page. (e.g. personal details of a user) and store them into a database, through JSP.

9. Create a GreatUser EJB which will greet the uses based on time 'for example', Good Morning John, Good AfterNoon John or Good Evening John, etc.

Appendix A: Lab Manual—Java Lab Exercises

To compile a program: `javac filename.java`
To run a program: `java classname`

1. Introduction, Compiling, and Executing a Java Program

```java
class GreetUser
{
  public static void main(String args[])
  {
  System.out.println("Hello, " +args[0] + " How are you today?");
  }
}
```

Output

```
C:\javabook\LabSyllabi> java GreetUser John
Hello, John How are you today?
```

2. Program with Data Types and Variables

```java
class Test
{
  public static void main(String[] args)
  {
    byte b1=2,b2=3;
    /* byte b3 = b1 + b2; Will not compile*/
    int b3 = b1 + b2;          /* Will compile*/
    System.out.println("Addition of two byte variables is an int, Result= "+b3);
    int c = 66;
    System.out.println("Character at Ascii value: "+c+ " is " +(char)c);
    float f = 4.28f;
    System.out.println("suffix F or f for a float variable "+f);
    double d = 1e308;
    System.out.println("double variable: "+ d);
  }
}
```

Output

```
C:\javabook\programs\LabSyllabi > java Test
Addition of two byte variables is an int, Result= 5
Character at Ascii value: 66 is B
suffix F or f for a float variable 4.28
double variable: 1.0E308
```

3. Program with Decision Control Structures: `if`, `nested-if`, etc

```java
class Distinct
{
```

```java
    public static void main(String args[])
    {
    int a=1,b=1,c=3;
    if((a == b) && (a == c))
    {
        System.out.println("No of distinct value = 0");
    }
    else if(((a == b) && (a != c))||((a == c) && (a != b)) || (b==c))
    {
        System.out.println("No of distinct value = 2");
    }
    else
        System.out.println("No of distinct value = 3");
    }
}
```

Output

```
C:\javabook\programs\LabSyllabi > java Distinct
No of distinct value = 2
```

4. Program with Loop Control Structures: `do, while, for, etc`

```java
class Pattern
{
    public static void main(String args[])
    {
      int k,l;
      for(int i=0;i<7;i++)
      {
        /* A for loop for printing blank spaces. First time 7 blank
        spaces will be printed and henceforth the number of spaces
        will reduce by 1 in every iteration */

        for(int j=7;j>i;j--)
            System.out.print(" ");
        /* ASCII value of A is taken and based value of i the loop
        is executed to print the alphabets. First time the only A will
        be printed as the value of i is 0. Second time AB will
        be printed by this loop and soon. */

        for(k=65;k<=65+i;k++)
            System.out.print((char)(k));

        /*This loop prints the alphabets in reverse order*/
        for(l=k-1;l>65;l--)
            System.out.print((char)(l-1));

        System.out.println();
      }
    }
}
```

Output

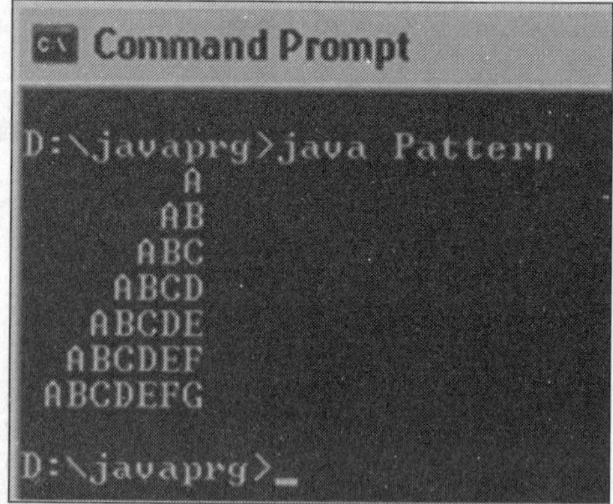

If the last `for` loop is removed then the following output is displayed:

5. Program on Usage of `switch-case` and `if` Conditional Statements

```java
class Zodiac
{
  public static void main(String args[])
  {
  int a,b;
  a = Integer.parseInt(args[0]);
  b = Integer.parseInt(args[1]);
  int z = 15;
  String
  z1[] = {"Capricorn","Aquarius","Pisces","Aries","Taurus","Gemini",
  "Cancer","Leo","Virgo", "Libra","Scorpio","Sagittarius"};
  switch(a)
  {
case 1:
    if((b < 20))
      {z = 0;}
    else if(b > 19 && b <= 31)
      {z = 1;}
    break;
case 2:
    if(b < 18)
```

```
           {z = 1;}
       else if(b > 17 && b < 30)
          {z = 2;}
       break;

case 3:
       if(b < 20)
          {z = 2;}
       else if(b > 19 && b < 31)
          {z = 3;}
       break;

case 4:
       if(b < 20)
          {z = 3;}
       else if(b > 19 && b < 30)
          {z = 4;}
       break;

case 5:
       if(b < 21)
          {z = 4;}
       else if(b > 20 && b < 31)
          {z = 5;}
       break;

case 6:
       if(b < 21)
          {z = 5;}
       else if(b > 20 && b < 30)
          {z = 6;}
       break;

case 7:
       if(b < 23)
          {z = 6;}
       else if(b > 22 && b < 31)
          {z = 7;}
       break;

case 8:
       if(b < 23)
          {z = 7;}
       else if(b > 22 && b < 31)
          {z = 8;}
       break;

case 9:
       if(b < 23)
          {z = 8;}
       else if(b > 22 && b < 30)
          {z = 9;}
       break;

case 10:
       if(b < 23)
          {z = 9;}
       else if(b > 22 && b < 31)
          {z = 10;}
       break;
```

```
        case 11:
            if(b < 22)
               {z = 10;}
            else if(b > 21 && b < 30)
               {z = 11;}
            break;

        case 12:
            if(b < 22)
               {z = 11;}
            else if(b > 21 && b < 31)
               {z = 0;}
            break;

        default :
        System.out.println("Month is not valid");
        }
    if((z >= 0) && (z <= 11))
        System.out.println("Zodiac sign is: " + z1[z]);
    else
        System.out.println("Date is not valid");
        }
    }
```

Output

```
        C:\LABSYL~1 > java Zodiac 6 7
        Zodiac sign is: Gemini

        C:\LABSYL~1 > java Zodiac 12 23
        Zodiac sign is: Capricorn

        C:\LABSYL~1 > java Zodiac 30 35
        Month is not valid
        Date is not valid
```

6. Program with Classes and Objects

```
    class Rectangle
    {
        float Length, Width;
        Rectangle()
        {
            Length = 1.0f;
            Width = 1.0f;
        }
        void setLength(float a)
            {
                if((Length > 0) && (Length <= 20))
                Length = a;
            }
        void setWidth(float a)
            {
                if((Width > 0) && (Width <= 20))
                Width = a;
            }
        float getLength()
```

```java
            {
                return Length;
            }
        float getWidth()
        {
            return Width;
        }
    float perimeter()
    {
        float p;
        p = 2*(getLength() + getWidth());
        return p;
    }

    float area()
    {
        float p;
        p = getLength() * getWidth();
        return p;
    }
}


    class Cal
    {
        public static void main(String args[])
        {
            Rectangle rr = new Rectangle();
            rr.setLength(15);
            rr.setWidth(15);
            System.out.println("Perimeter is:" + rr.perimeter());
            System.out.println("Area is:" + rr.area());
        }
    }
```

Output

```
C:\LabSyllabi > java RectangleTest
Perimeter is:60.0
Area is:225.0
```

7. Copy Constructor and Constructor Overloading

```java
class CopyConDemo {
    int m;
    String n;

    public CopyConDemo (int m, String n) {
    this.m = m;
    this.n = n;
    }


    /*Copy constructor*/
    public CopyConDemo(CopyConDemo c) {
        this(c.getM(), c.getN());
    }
```

```java
        int getM() {
        return m;
        }

        void setM(int m){
        this.m = m;
        }
        void setN(String n){
        this.n = n;
        }

        String getN() {
        return n;
        }

        public static void main (String args[]){
        CopyConDemo c1 = new CopyConDemo(12, "Original");
        CopyConDemo c2 = new CopyConDemo(c1);
        c2.setN("First Copy");
        System.out.println("Original Object m = " + c1.getM() + "n = " + c1.getN());
        System.out.println("First Copy m = " + c2.getM() + "n = " + c2.getN());
        }
    }
```

Output

```
C:\javabook\programs\LabSyllabi > java CopyConDemo
Original Object m = 12  n = Original
First Copy m = 12        n = First Copy
```

8. A Program on Function Overloading

```java
class MOverload{

public void add(int a, int b)
    {
    int addition = a + b;
    System.out.println("addition of two numbers = " + addition);
    }

void add(int a,int b,float c) {
float addition = a + b + c;
System.out.println("addition of three numbers = " + addition);
}

public static void main(String args[]) {
MOverload o = new MOverload();
double result;
o.add(5,6);
o.add(5,6,7.5f);
}
}
```

Output

```
C:\javabook\programs\LabSyllabi > java MOverload
addition of two numbers = 11
addition of three numbers = 18.5
```

9. Implementing Inheritance

(a) Single inheritance

```java
class MotorVehicle
{
String modelName;
int modelNumber;
float modelPrice;
MotorVehicle(String mname, int mnumber, float mprice)
{
    modelName = mname;
    modelNumber = mnumber;
    modelPrice = mprice;
}

void display()
{
    System.out.println("Model Name is : " + modelName);
    System.out.println("Model Number is : " + modelNumber);
    System.out.println("Model Price is : " + modelPrice);
}
}
class Car extends MotorVehicle
{
int discountRate;
Car(String mname, int mnumber, float mprice, int dr)
{
    super(mname,mnumber,mprice);
    discountRate = dr;
}
//implementing Polymorphism: Method Overriding
void display()
{
    super.display();
    System.out.println("The discount rate is :" + discountRate);
}
void discount()
{
float discount = modelPrice * discountRate/100;
float priceAfterDiscount = modelPrice - discount;
System.out.println("The discount is : " + discount);
System.out.println("The Price after discount rate is : " + priceAfterDiscount);
}
public static void main(String args[])
{
    Car c = new Car("Mercedes E series",2000, 3200000f, 10);
    c.display();
    c.discount();
}
}
```

Output

```
C:\javabook\programs\LabSyllabi > java Car
Model Name is : Mercedes E series
Model Number is : 2000
Model Price is : 32000  00.0
The discount rate is : 10
The discount is : 320000.0
The Price after discount rate is : 2880000.0
```

(b) Multiple inheritance

Multiple inheritance is implemented in Java using interfaces.

(c) Multilevel inheritance

```
    class A
{

        int n;
        A(int n)
    {
        this.n = n;
        }
    void show()
    {
        System.out.println("class A variable n = " + n);
    }
}

class B extends A
{
    B(int n)
    {
        super(n);
    }
    void show()
    {
        super.show();
        System.out.println("class B is a subclass of A");
    }
}
class C extends B
{
    C(int n)
    {
        super(n);
    }
    void show()
    {
        super.show();
        System.out.println("class C is a subclass of B");
    }

}

final class D extends C
{
    D(int n)
    {
```

```
            super(n);
        }
    void show()
    {
            super.show();
            System.out.println("final class D is a subclass of C");
    }

}
class MultiLevelInheritanceTest
{
    public static void main(String args[])
    {
            D d1 = new D(12);
            d1.show();
    }
}
```

Output

```
        C:\javabook\programs\LabSyllabi > java MultiLevelInheritanceTest
        class A variable n = 12
        class B is a subclass of A
        class C is a subclass of B
        final class D is a subclass of C
```

(d) Use of Abstract Classes

```
    abstract class Shape
    {
            abstract void numberOfSides();
    }

    class Trapezoid extends Shape
    {
            void numberOfSides()
            {
            System.out.println("The number of sides in a Trapezoid is four");
            }
    }
    class Triangle extends Shape
    {
            void numberOfSides()
            {
            System.out.println("The number of sides in a Traingle is three");
            }
    }
    class Hexagon extends Shape
    {
            void numberOfSides()
            {
            System.out.println("The number of sides in a Hexagon is six");
            }
    }
    class ShapeDemo
    {
            public static void main(String args[])
            {
```

```
                Trapezoid tp = new Trapezoid();
                tp.numberOfSides();
                Traingle tr = new Traingle();
                tr.numberOfSides();
                Hexagon h = new Hexagon();
                h.numberOfSides();
        }
    }
```

Output

```
C:\javabook\programs\LabSyllabi > java ShapeDemo
The number of sides in a Trapezoid is four
The number of sides in a Traingle is three
The number of sides in a Hexagon is six
```

10. Implementing Interfaces

(a) Developing user-defined interfaces and implementation

```
interface Calculator
{
    public int add(int x,int y);
    public int sub(int x,int y);
    public int multiply(int x,int y);
    public int divide(int x,int y);
    public int remainder(int x,int y);
}
class CalculatorDemo implements Calculator
    {
        public int add(int x,int y)
        {
            return(x + y);
        }
        public int sub(int x,int y)
        {
            return(x-y);
        }
        public int multiply(int x,int y)
        {
            return(x * y);
        }
        public int divide(int x,int y)
        {
            return(x / y);
        }

        public int remainder(int x,int y)
        {
            return(x % y);
        }
        public static void main(String args[])
    {

        CalculatorDemo cd = new CalculatorDemo();
        System.out.println("ADD of two no is: " + cd.add(10,10));
        System.out.println("SUB of two no is: " + cd.sub(1,10));
```

```java
            System.out.println("MULTIPLICATION of two no is: " + cd.multiply(5,3));
            System.out.println("Divide of two no is: " + cd.divide(50,10));
            System.out.println("REMAINDER of two no is: " + cd.remainder(50,7));
      }
}
```

Output

```
C:\javabook\programs\LabSyllabi > java CalculatorDemo
ADD of two no is: 20
SUB of two no is: -9
MULTIPLICATION of two no is: 15
Divide of two no is: 5
REMAINDER of two no is: 1
```

(a) Use of predefined interfaces

```java
class ComparableTest implements Comparable < ComparableTest >
{
      int no;
      ComparableTest(int n)
      {
      no = n;
      }
      public int compareTo(ComparableTest t)
      {
          return this.no-t.no;
      }
      public String toString()
      {
          return "Object: " + no;
      }
}

class Test
{
      public static void main(String args[])
      {
          ComparableTest t1 = new ComparableTest(12);
          ComparableTest t2 = new ComparableTest(10);
          System.out.println("First object: " + t1);
          System.out.println("Second object: " + t2);
          if((t1.compareTo(t2)) > 0)
              System.out.println("First object is greater than second object");
          else if((t1.compareTo(t2)) < 0)
              System.out.println("second object is greater than first object");
          else
              System.out.println("both are equal");
      }
}
```

Output

```
C:\javabook\programs\LabSyllabi > java Test
First object: Object: 12
Second object: Object: 10
First object is greater than second object
```

11. Handling Strings

```
class StringDemo
{
    public static void main(String args[])
    {
    String s1 = "Java Programming";
    System.out.println("The String is : " + s1.toLowerCase());
    System.out.println("The String is : " + s1.toUpperCase());
    System.out.println("The length of String is : " + s1.length());
    System.out.println("The String starts with j:" + s1.startsWith("j"));

    System.out.println("The String ends with G: " + s1.endsWith("G"));
    System.out.println("The SubString starting from index 3 is:" + s1.substring(3));
    System.out.println("The SubString starting from index 3 till index 6 is: " +
    s1.substring(3,6));

    // converting boolean to String
    boolean b = true;
    String s2 = String.valueOf(b);
    System.out.println("The converted String is : " + s2);

    // converting char to String
    char c = 'a';
    s2 = String.valueOf(c);
    System.out.println("The converted String is : " + s2);

    // converting double to String
    double d = 2.4d;
    s2 = String.valueOf(d);
    System.out.println("The converted String is : " + s2);

    // converting int to String
    int i = 24;
    s2 = String.valueOf(i);
    System.out.println("The converted String is : " + s2);
    }
}
```

Output

```
C:\javabook\programs\LabSyllabi > java StringDemo
The String is : java programming
The String is : JAVA PROGRAMMING
The length of String is : 16
The String starts with j: false
The String ends with G: false
The SubString starting from index 3 is: a Programming
The SubString starting from index 3 till index 6 is: a P
The converted String is : true
The converted String is : a
The converted String is : 2.4
The converted String is : 24
```

12. Implementing Packages

```
package mypack;
class Trignometry
    {
        static float sine(double degrees)
```

```java
    {
        double s;
        s = (Math.sin(Math.toRadians(degrees)));
        return (float)s;
    }

    static float cos(double degrees)
    {
        double s;
        s = (Math.cos(Math.toRadians(degrees)));
        return (float)s;
    }
    static float tan(double degrees)
    {
        double s;
        s = (Math.tan(Math.toRadians(degrees)));
        return (float)s;
    }

    static double cosec(double degrees)
    {
        double s;
        s = (Math.sin(Math.toRadians(degrees)));
        s = 1/s;
        return s;
    }

    static double sec(double degrees)
    {
        double s;
        s = (Math.cos(Math.toRadians(degrees)));
        s = 1/s;
        return s;
    }
    static double cot(double degrees)
    {
        double s;
        s = (Math.tan(Math.toRadians(degrees)));
        s = 1/s;
        return s;
    }

public static void main(String args[])
    {
    Trignometry an = new Trignometry();
    System.out.println("Sin value of given angle in degree is:" + an.sine(30));
    System.out.println("Cos value of given angle in degree is:" + an.cos(30));
    System.out.println("Tan value of given angle in degree is:" + an.tan(30));
    System.out.println("Cosec value of given angle in degree is:" + an.cosec(30));
    System.out.println("Sec value of given angle in degree is:" + an.sec(30));
    System.out.println("Cot value of given angle in degree is:" + an.cot(30));
    }
}
```

Output

```
C:\LabSyllabi > java mypack.Trignometry
Sin value of given angle in degree is:0.5
Cos value of given angle in degree is:0.8660254
Tan value of given angle in degree is:0.57735026
Cosec value of given angle in degree is:2.0000000000000004
Sec value of given angle in degree is:1.1547005383792515
Cot value of given angle in degree is:1.7320508075688774
```

13. Implementing Wrapper Classes

```java
class WrapperDemo
{
    public static void main(String args[])
    {
    // converting String to int
    int a = Integer.parseInt(args[0]);
    int b = Integer.parseInt(args[1]);
    System.out.println("Addition: " + (a + b));
    System.out.println("Concatenation: " + args[0] + args[1]);

    // converting int back to String
    String s1 = Integer.toString(a);
    String s2 = Integer.toString(b);
    System.out.println("Addition of String: " + s1 + s2);

    // converting int to Integer objects
    Integer i = Integer.valueOf(a);
    System.out.println("Integer Object: " + i);

    // converting Integer objects to int
    int value = i.intValue();
    System.out.println("Int value in Integer object i is : " + value);

    // some other methods of Integer Wrapper class
    System.out.println("long value in Integer object i is : " + i.doubleValue());

    System.out.println("double value in Integer object i is : " + i.longValue());

    System.out.println("float value in Integer object i is : " + i.floatValue());

    System.out.println("byte value in Integer object i is : " + i.byteValue());

    System.out.println("short value in Integer object i is : " + i.shortValue());
    }
}
```

Output

```
C:\javabook\programs\LabSyllabi > java WrapperDemo 20 10
Addition: 30
Concatenation: 2010
Addition of String: 2010
Integer Object: 20
Int value in Integer object i is : 20
long value in Integer object i is : 20.0
```

```
double value in Integer object i is : 20
float value in Integer object i is : 20.0
byte value in Integer object i is : 20
short value in Integer object i is : 20
```

14. Exception Handling Mechanism in Java

(a) Handling predefined exceptions

```java
class PredefinedExceptionDemo
{
    void show()
    {
        System.out.println("In Show");
    }
    public static void main(String args[])
    {
        try
        {
        // object not created and trying to call an instance method
            PredefinedExceptionDemo d = null;
            d.show();
        }
        catch(NullPointerException n)
        {
            System.out.println(n);
        }
    }
}
```

Output

```
C:\LabSyllabi > java PredefinedExceptionDemo
java.lang.NullPointerException
```

(b) Handling user-defined exceptions

```java
package finance;
class Money
{
    int paisa,rupees;
    Money(int c,int d)
    {
    if(d > 0 && d <= 99)
        {
        paisa = d;
        }
    else
        {
        System.out.println("Paisa values cannot be greater than 100");
            System.exit(0);
        }
        rupees = c;
    }
    public String toString()
```

```java
{
    return ("Rupees = " + rupees + " Paisa = " + paisa);
}
void addition(Money a2) throws MoneyOverflowException
{
    int r = 0;
    int p = paisa + a2.paisa;
    if(p >= 100)
    {
        p = p -100;
        r + = 1;
    }
        r + = rupees + a2.rupees;
        if(r > 100000)
    {
        throw new MoneyOverflowException("From Addition Method");
    }
    System.out.println("After Addition ::");
    System.out.println("Rupees = " + r + " \t" + "Paisa = " + p);
}


// Money Cannot be negative
void subtract(Money a2)
{
    int p = 0,r = 0;
    if(rupees <= a2.rupees)
    {
        System.out.println("Money cannot be negative");
    }
    else
    {
        if(paisa > a2.paisa)
        {
                p = paisa-a2.paisa;
                r = rupees-a2.rupees;
                System.out.println("After Subtraction ::");
                System.out.println("Rupees = " + r + " \t" + " Paisa = " + p);
        }
        else
        {
                p = paisa + 100 - a2.paisa;
                r = rupees - 1 - a2.rupees;
                System.out.println("After Subtraction ::");
                System.out.println("Rupees = " + r + " \t" + " Paisa = " + p);
        }
    }
}


float getRupees()
{
    return rupees;
}
float getPaisa()
{
    return paisa;
}
```

```java
    public static void main(String args[])
        {
            int n1 = Integer.parseInt(args[0]);
            int n2 = Integer.parseInt(args[1]);
            int n3 = Integer.parseInt(args[2]);
            int n4 = Integer.parseInt(args[3]);

            Money m1 = new Money(n1,n2);
            Money m2 = new Money(n3,n4);

            System.out.println(m1);
            System.out.println("Rupees = " + m1.getRupees());
            System.out.println("Paisa = " + m1.getPaisa());

            System.out.println(m2);
            System.out.println("Rupees = " + m2.getRupees());
            System.out.println("Paisa = " + m2.getPaisa());
            System.out.println();

            try{
            m1.addition(m2);
            }catch(MoneyOverflowException e){System.out.println(e);}
            m1.subtract(m2);
        }
}

class MoneyOverflowException extends Exception
{
    String desc;
    MoneyOverflowException(String n)
    {
        desc = n;
    }
    public String toString()
    {
        return "MoneyOverflowException generated: " + desc;
    }
}
```

Output

```
D:\>java finance.Money 24 23 20 45
Rupees = 24 Paisa = 23
Rupees = 24.0
Paisa = 23.0
Rupees = 20 Paisa = 45
Rupees = 20.0
Paisa = 45.0

After Addition ::
Rupees = 44 Paisa = 68
After Subtraction ::
Rupees = 3 Paisa = 78

D:\>java finance.Money 28 23 24 23
Rupees = 28 Paisa = 23
Rupees = 28.0
Paisa = 23.0
Rupees = 24 Paisa = 23
```

```
Rupees = 24.0
Paisa = 23.0

After Addition ::
Rupees = 52      Paisa = 46
After Subtraction ::
Rupees = 4       Paisa = 0
```

15. Concept of Threading

(a) Creation of thread in Java applications

```java
class RunThread implements Runnable
{
    Thread t;
    RunThread()
    {
        t = new Thread(this,"DemoThread");
        t.start();
        t.setPriority(3);
    }
    public void run()
    {
        for(int i = 0;i < 5;i++ )
        {
            try {
            System.out.println("Child Thread : " + Thread.currentThread().getName() + " Priority: "
            + t.getPriority());
            Thread.sleep(1000);
            }
            catch(InterruptedException e)
            {
                System.out.println(e);
            }
        }
    }
}
class TestPriority
{
public static void main(String args[])
{
new RunThread();
for(int i = 0;i < 5;i++ )
System.out.println("Parent Thread: " + Thread.currentThread().getName() + "Priority:"
+ Thread.currentThread().getPriority());
    }
}
```

Output

```
Parent Thread: mainPriority:5
Parent Thread: mainPriority:5
Parent Thread: mainPriority:5
Parent Thread: mainPriority:5
Parent Thread: mainPriority:5
Child Thread : DemoThreadPriority: 3
Child Thread : DemoThreadPriority: 3
Child Thread : DemoThreadPriority: 3
Child Thread : DemoThreadPriority: 3
Child Thread : DemoThreadPriority: 3
```

(b) Multithreading

```java
/* A simple withdraw and deposit threaded program*/
class Deposit
{
    int money = 0;
    synchronized void submit()
    {
        try{
            Thread.sleep(1000);
        }catch(Exception e) {}
        money = money+100000;
        System.out.println("Amount Has been deposited. . ."+money);
        flag=0;
        notifyAll();
    }
    synchronized int withdraw(int a)
    {
        try{
            System.out.println("wait for amount to be withdrawn");
            wait(1000);
            money = money-a;
            }
        catch(Exception e) {}
        notifyAll();
        return money;
    }
}
class Thread1 extends Thread
{
Deposit s;
Thread1(Deposit s,String str)
{
    super(str);
    this.s = s;
    start();
}
public void run()
{
    int amount = s.withdraw(3000);
    System.out.println("Amount has been submitted and can be withdrawn: " + amount);
}
}

class Thread2 extends Thread
{
Deposit s;
Thread2(Deposit s,String str)
{
    super(str);
    this.s = s;
    start();
}
public void run()
{
    s.submit();
}
}
```

```java
class TestDeposit
{
public static void main(String s[])
{
    Deposit st = new Deposit();
    Thread1 withdrawThread1 = new Thread1(st,"One");
    Thread2 submitThread1 = new Thread2(st,"Two");
    Thread1 withdrawThread2 = new Thread1(st,"Three");
    Thread2 submitThread2 = new Thread2(st,"Four");
}
}
```

Output

```
D:\javabook\appendixa>java TestDeposit
wait for amount to be withdrawn
Amount Has been deposited. . .100000
wait for amount to be withdrawn
Amount has been submitted and can be withdrawn: 97000
Amount Has been deposited. . .197000
Amount has been submitted and can be withdrawn: 194000
```

16. Working with Files

```java
import java.io.*;
class Copy
{
    public static void main(String args[])
    {
        Console cn = System.console();
        String file1,file2;
        System.out.println("Enter the file name to be copied:");
        file1 = cn.readLine();
        System.out.println("Enter the new file name:");
        file2 = cn.readLine();
    try{
        FileInputStream fis = new FileInputStream(file1);
        int n = fis.available();
        FileOutputStream fos = new FileOutputStream(file2,true);
        for(int i = 0;i < n;i++ )
        {
            fos.write(fis.read());
        }
        fis.close();
        fos.close();
        }
        catch(FileNotFoundException e)
        {
            System.out.println("FILE not found:" + file1);
        }
        catch(IOException e)
        {
            System.out.println("I/O error:" + e);
        }
    }
}
```

Output

```
C:\javabook\programs\LABSYL~1 > java Copy
Enter the file name to be copied:
```

```
TestDeposit.java
Enter the new file name:
Test2.java
```

17. Implementing Generics

```java
import java.util.*;
class A
{
    public String toString(){return "Class A Object";}
}
class B
{   public String toString(){return "Class B object";}
}
class DemoGeneric
{
    public static void main(String args[])
    {
        List < A > v = new ArrayList < A > ();
        List < B > v1 = new ArrayList < B > ();
        v.add(new A());
        v.add(new A());
        // The below statement would raise an error
        // v.add(new B());

        v1.add(new B());
        v1.add(new B());
        // The below statement would raise an error
        //v1.add(new A());

        Iterator en = v.iterator();
        while(en.hasNext())
        {
            Object o = en.next();
            System.out.println(o);
        }
        en = v1.iterator();
        while(en.hasNext())
        {
            Object o = en.next();
            System.out.println(o);
        }
    }
}
```

Output

```
C:\javabook\programs\LABSYL~1 > java DemoGeneric
Class A Object
Class A Object
Class B object
Class B object
```

APPENDIX B: Interview Questions

1. **What is the difference between an interface and an abstract class?**

   An abstract class can have concrete methods (that depict default behaviour) as well as abstract (no implementation) instance methods. An interface can only declare constants and methods, but cannot provide implementation of the methods. In other words, all the methods in the interface are implicitly abstract. In an interface, all members are public with no implementation. Refer Table 6.1 for all differences.

2. **What is the purpose of garbage collection in Java?**

   Garbage collection is used to identify and discard objects that are no longer needed by a program. The resources (e.g., memory) allocated to an object can be reclaimed when all references to it are null.

3. **What are pass by reference and pass by value?**

   In pass by reference, the addresses of the variables are passed rather than their value. Pass by value means a copy of the value is passed whereas in pass by reference no copy is created. The actual variable is referenced.

4. **Describe thread synchronization.**

   Thread synchronization is used to maintain consistency of data by preventing concurrent access of shared resources by multiple threads. A thread can modify a shared resource (variable or data structure) while another thread is using or modifying the same shared structure.

5. **What are the different ways of creating threads in Java?**

   Inherit the runnable interface or thread class.

6. **What is cloning?**

   Cloning is basically making a copy of an existing object.

7. **What is the difference between a `vector` and an `ArrayList`?**

   Vector class is synchronized, whereas `ArrayList` class is not synchronized.

8. **What is the difference between a constructor and a method?**

   A constructor is a special member function of a class that is used to initialize the objects. It has the same name as that of the class, without any return type, and is invoked using the new operator. For example,

   ```
   class Demo
   {
       Demo(){}      // constructor
   }
   ```

   A method is an ordinary member function of a class. It has a name (although not recommended but can be same as that of the class), a return type (which may be void) and are invoked using the dot operator. For example,

   ```
   public void add(int a, int b)
   ```

   It is invoked as shown below:

   ```
   objectName.add(4,5) // for instance method
   Classname.add(4,5) // for static methods
   ```

9. **Explain the keyword 'static' in Java.**

   Static members can accessed without creating an instance of a class. Static cannot be overridden because they are attached to a class, not an object. However, a static method can be shadowed by another static method in a subclass.

10. **Explain the keyword 'final' in Java.**

    The keyword 'final' can be used at three levels: class, method, and variable. A final class cannot be inherited, i.e., they cannot be sub classed. Final method cannot be overridden and you cannot change the value of a final variable (it is a constant).

11. **What are the different types of cloning objects?**

    The different types of cloning objects are deep and shallow copying.

12. **What will happen if the static modifier is removed from the main method?**

    This method becomes a normal method of the class and not the main method which is desired by the JVM to execute the method. So the program compiles, but shows a runtime error.

13. **What is observer and observable in Java?**

The observer interface and observable class is based on the observer pattern. This pattern states that a particular object (i.e., observer) should be notified when the state of another object (i.e., observable object) changes. In other words, the observer observes the state of another object and wants itself to be notified about any changes in that object and the observable object is the one in which the observer is interested in. For example, you (observer) are notified about the transaction updates of your bank account (observable), as soon as the data (observable) related to the pie chart or bar chart is updated the graphs (observer) automatically adjust to the changes and so on.

14. **What is automatic resource management?**

The applications use many resources during their lifetime by creating their objects, for example, creating a data base connection for accessing/updating databases, or creating file objects for working with files, or creating sockets for transmission/receiving of data, etc. A common mistake committed by programmers is that they often do not close/release the resources occupied by the programs, after their task is complete. This leads to many orphaned instances, inefficient memory allocation and garbage collection. Hence, the need for automatic resource management arises.

15. **How is automatic resource management done in Java?**

Using try with resources statement

```
try (resources to be used and automati-
cally released)
{
    // statements within the block
}
```

For example,

```
try (abc a = new abc(); pqr p = new pqr())
{
    // statements within the block
}
```

16. **Is it possible for an application to have multiple classes with main method?**

Yes, it is possible.

17. **Is it possible to have multiple main methods in the same class?**

Yes, but with different signatures (i.e., method overloading).

18. What is MVC?

MVC stands for Model View Controller. The model object manages the behavior and data of the application, view takes care of the graphical or textual representation and controller is used to interpret the user commands. The model responds to user requests from the controller by changing its state which is presented to the user through view.

19. **What is early binding?**

Binding is the process of connecting a method call to its body. When binding is performed before a program is executed, it is called early binding.

20. **What is overriding?**

The term overriding means having the same method name, same signature, one in superclass and other in subclass.

21. **Can we define a top level class as private or protected?**

No, a top level class cannot be private or protected, only public or default access is allowed.

22. **What is runtime class used for?**

The runtime class is used to know the information about free memory and total memory and is also used for executing additional processes.

23. **What is reflection API?**

The reflection API is used to obtain information about the class with its various characteristics like attributes, constructors, methods, packages, modifiers (public, private, etc.), interfaces, arrays, exceptions, and generic types at runtime. It can also be used to instantiate new objects, call methods, know about the setter/getter methods of a class and get or set fields. Java reflection API is available through `java.lang.reflect` package.

24. **How are objects passed in Java—by value or by reference?**

Java only supports pass by value. So when objects are passed as arguments in a method, the object references are assigned to the formal parameters.

25. **What is serialization and deserializaton?**

Serialization is a mechanism by which you can convert the state of an object into byte stream and deserialization is the reverse of this process.

26. **What is a socket?**

Sockets are created at both ends of communication, i.e., at the client as well as the server. Socket is defined by three things: IP Address, port, and the protocol to be used for communication. IP address is the unique address assigned to every machine on the network and port is a unique logical number on that IP address used for identifying the applications running on that particular machine. IP address exists on network layer and port numbers on the transport layer of the TCP/IP protocol suite. TCP clients are created with the help of `java.net.Socket` class and server with the help of `java.net.ServerSocket` class. UDP socket are created using `java.net.DatagramSocket` class.

27. What are wrapper classes?

Java provides special classes in the `java.lang` package which encapsulate the primitive data types. These are called wrapper classes. They are as follows: `Byte`, `Short`, `Integer`, `Long`, `Double`, `Float`, `Character`, and `Boolean`.

28. What is the difference between an error and an exception?

An error is an irrecoverable condition which occurs at runtime, for example, `OutOfMemory` error. While exceptions are conditions that occur because of programming mistakes or bad input, for example, `FileNotFoundException` will be thrown if the specified file does not exist or a `NullPointerException` will take place if you try to use a null reference. In most of the cases it is possible to recover from an exception.

29. Is it necessary that each `try` block must be followed by a catch block?

No, it is not necessary. `try` block can be followed by either a `catch` block or a `finally` block.

30. Overloaded methods follow early binding. Explain.

When multiple methods with the same name exist within a class (i.e., case of method overloading) which method will be executed depends upon the argument (number, type or order of arguments) passed to the method. So, this binding can be resolved by the compiler (at compile time) and hence overloaded methods follow early binding.

31. What is a URL?

URL stands for uniform resource locator. It is a standard way of locating resources on the Internet, for example, www.yahoo.com. A URL has some basic parts:

(a) Protocol name: http / file / mailto, etc.

(b) Host: www.yahoo.com.

(c) Port: this is an optional attribute specified after the host name, for example, www.yahoo.com:80.

(d) File: name of the file to be accessed, e.g., www.yahoo.com/index.html.

(e) Reference: name of named reference within the page (i.e., `cs`), for example, www.yahoo.com/index.html#cs.

32. What are anonymous classes?

An anonymous inner class is a local class that has no name. They are extensively used in event handling.

33. What is shadowing?

Shadowing of fields occurs when variable names are same. It may occur when local variables and instance variable names collide within a class or variable names in a superclass and subclass are same. In case of methods, instance methods are overridden whereas static methods are shadowed. The difference between the two is important because shadowed methods are bound early whereas instance methods are dynamically (late) binded.

34. What is dynamic binding?

Objects exist at runtime, and hence late binding is done by the JVM at runtime for resolving which method will be executed. It is also known as dynamic binding or runtime binding.

35. What are nested classes?

Nested class is a class with a class. Nested classes are of the following types:

- Non-static inner classes
- Static nested classes
- Local classes
- Anonymous classes

36. What is a non-static inner class?

A non-static inner class is a member of the outer class declared outside the functions within a class. The non-static inner class is bound to the instance of the enclosing class and has access to all the members of the enclosing class even the parent's `this` reference and `private`.

37. What are binary literals?

Binary literals are a combination of 0's and 1's. Java 7 onwards, you can assign binary literals to variables. Binary literals must be prefixed with 0b or 0B (zerob or zeroB). For example,

```
char bin1 = 0b1010000;   // value in
bin1 will be P
```

38. What is transient variable?

Transient variables are those variables which are not serialized.

39. Overridden methods follow late binding. Explain.

When a method with the same name and signature exists in superclass as well as sub class (i.e., a case of method overriding) which method will be executed (superclass version or subclass version) will be determined by the type of object from which it has been called and so it cannot be done by the compiler. Hence, it is done at runtime and that is why these methods are late bound by the runtime environment.

40. What is a static nested class?

A static nested class is a static member of a class just like normal static members of any class. They have access to all static methods of the enclosing parent class. The static nested classes cannot directly refer to instance variables and method of the outer class, similar to static parts of any class. They can only do it through an object of the outer class. Unlike the inner classes, the static nested classes can have static members.

41. Which method is used to get and set the label displayed on a button object?

    setLabel(String txt) –for setting label
and
    getLabel() – for getting the label

42. What is the difference between `Scrollbar` and `ScrollPane`?

`ScrollPane` is a container whereas `Scrollbar` is a component.

43. What is the difference between `String` and `StringBuffer`?

`String` is immutable whereas `StringBuffer` is mutable.

44. Which operators are known as short-circuit operators?

&& and || are known as short-circuit operators.

45. Which abstract class is the superclass of all classes used for writing characters?

`Writer` class is the superclass of all classes used for writing characters.

46. What is the name of the exception thrown by the read method defined in `InputStream` class?

`IOException`.

47. What is the name of the class that allows reading of Java primitives from an input byte stream?

`DataInputStream`.

48. Name the parent of all the classes in Java.

`Object` class.

49. Which abstract class is the superclass of all classes used for reading bytes?

`InputStream` is the superclass of all classes used for reading bytes.

50. What is the name of the collection interface that is used to maintain unique elements?

Set.

51. What is scrollable result set?

The `ResultSet`, before JDBC 2.1, could be scrolled in forward direction only. JDBC 2.1 introduced the concept of moving the cursor in backward direction also. You can even position the cursor of a `ResultSet` object on a specific row.

52. What is a transaction?

A transaction is a set of statements that if executed should complete in entirety. If any of the statement fails to execute in a transaction, the entire transaction should be rolled back.

53. What is auto commit?

Auto commit feature commits the changes made by SQL statements to the database and is by default set to true. It can be set using the following method of the connection object.

`con.setAutoCommit(false);`

54. What is a servlet?

Servlets are Java server-side programs that accept client's request (usually http request), process them and generate (usually http response) responses. The requests originate from the client's web browser and are routed to a servlet located inside an appropriate web server. Servlets execute within a servlet container which resides in a web server like Apache Tomcat.

55. What is lifecycle of a servlet?

The `init()` method is called only once during the lifetime of an applet. One time initializations are done in this method.

The `service` method is used for processing the client's request and generating responses. The request may be forwarded by `service` method to `doGet()` or `doPost()` depending upon the http request. If it is a get request, `doGet()` will be called and if it is a post request, `doPost()` will be called. The service method is capable of handling both types of requests (get and post).

The `destroy` method is called by the servlet container before the servlet is unloaded. So clean-up activities like closing the database connections can be done in this method.

56. What common http methods are used to send data from http client to a web server?

The client's data is sent to the server from the client's browser via two methods of http protocols: get and post.

57. What are the drawbacks of using get method for sending data to the server?

The get method appends data to the URL (of the servlet handling the request) and passes it to the server. The drawbacks of this approach are:

- The URLs are of fixed size and it puts a restriction on the amount of data that can be transmitted to the server.
- Moreover, whatever data is sent to the server is visible in clear text.

58. What is a cookie?

Cookies are basically small pieces of information stored on the client's machine by the browser. A cookie contains information like user browsing preferences, user id and password combinations, session id, and number of times a user has visited a page. This information is stored in pairs, i.e., name-value pairs. This information wrapped in a cookie object is sent to the client browser by a servlet, which stores it somewhere in its temporary Internet files. Whenever a request is sent to that particular server (from where cookie was downloaded), all the cookies (stored in the client's machine from that very server) are attached to the http request and sent to the server. The server can then fetch the cookies from the request and then act accordingly.

59. What is a session?

A session is used to track the user between successive requests from the same client to same server. A session is a kind of conversation between the server and a client. A conversation is a series of continuous requests and responses.

60. What is JSP?

JSP stands for Java server pages. JSP, in contrast to servlets, is basically a page that contains Java code embedded within html tags. Servlet is a Java program where html tags are embedded in Java code or html responses are generated through Java. JSP files have an extension `.jsp` and they execute within a JSP container present in the web server. This container actually translates the `.jsp` into an equivalent servlet. In other words, JSP is a servlet in the background.

61. What is the difference between a JSP and a servlet?

JSP offers a significant advantage over servlet. JSP is embedded in html with some special delimiters which look like tags. So it is easy to learn. To work with a servlet you need to learn Java and its programming styles which is not the case in JSP. Moreover, JSP pages are automatically recompiled when required, which is not the case with servlets. Servlet have to be recompiled in case they are changed. So as soon as you refresh your JSP page, changes made to it are reflected.

62. What is JavaBeans?

JavaBeans provides a standard format for writing Java classes. Java bean is reusable software component. Once it is designed and created, it can be used over and over again in many different applications as per their requirements. Java beans can be used by IDE and other Java API's to create new applications.

63. What is a Jar file?

JAR stands for Java archive. It is similar to a ZIP file. A JAR tool is provided with Java development kit (JDK) to perform basic tasks with JAR files.

64. What is a manifest file?

Manifest file (`.mf`) is a special file that can contain information about the files contained in a JAR file. A manifest file could be used to tell which classes in the JAR are bean classes, or which is the main class (starting point) in the JAR, etc.

65. What is EJB?

EJB is a server side distributed component of the J2EE architecture that primarily provides business logic besides interacting with other server side components. EJB developers need to focus only on coding business logic leaving the system level services to be handled by EJB server which include multiple threading, object pool, security, instance management, connection pooling, transactions, etc. EJB is based on the concept that in a distributed computing environment, database-related logic should be independent of the business logic that relies on the data.

66. What are the different types of EJB?

As per EJB 2.0 specification: session, entity, and message-driven bean.

67. What is autoboxing and unboxing?

Java 5.0 introduced a new feature for converting back and forth between a wrapper and its corresponding primitive. The conversion from primitives to wrappers objects is known as boxing, while the reverse is known as unboxing.

68. **What is `Enum` type?**

An enumerated type (enum type) is a kind of class definition, wherein we define the type along with the possible set of enum values which are listed in the curly braces, separated by commas. All enum types are the subclasses of the `java.lang.Enumclass`. Each value in an enum is an identifier.

69. **What is an assertion?**

Assertions were added in Java 1.4 to create reliable programs that are correct and robust. Assertions are boolean expressions that are used to test/validate the code. They are basically used during testing and development phases. Assertions are used by the programmers to be doubly sure about a particular condition, which they feel to be true. If you expect a number to be positive, negative, array/reference is not null, etc. then you can check these conditions by asserting them. Assertions in Java are declared with the help of assert keyword as shown below:

```
assert expression1; // assert x
    > 0;
```

70. **What is a monitor?**

Monitor is an object that is used as a mutually exclusive lock on the resource to be accessed. A monitor can be owned by only one thread at a time. A thread enters the monitor as soon as it acquires the lock. All the other threads cannot enter the locked monitor, unless it is unlocked or the first thread exits the monitor. During this period, other threads are waiting for the lock on the monitor. If a thread exits the monitor, it can again enter the same monitor at some later stage.

71. **Which class was introduced in Java 6 for reading user input?**

`java.io.Console`.

72. **Java 7 onwards, what values can be passed in a switch in a `switch…case` statement?**

`int`, `byte`, `short`, `char`, enum type, `String` or (one of the four) wrapper classes. It can also be an expression that returns an `int`, `byte`, `short`, `char` or `String`.

73. **Name the heavyweight classes in `javax.swing` package.**

`JFrame`, `JApplet`, `JDialog`, and `JWindow`.

74. **What are the differences between AWT and swing?**

AWT	SWING
Heavyweight	Lightweight
Look and feel is OS based	Look and feel is OS independent
Not pure Java-based	Pure Java-based
Platform specific limitation for some components	Fewer platform limitation for components
Faster	Slower
Applet portability: mostly web browser supports for applet	Applet portability: A plug-in is required
Does not support features like icons and tool-tips	Supports features like icons and tool-tips

75. **What is pluggable look and feel?**

Java provides pluggable look and feel. You can change the look and feel of the GUI displayed to the user. The look and feel is provided by the following packages and their sub-packages:

```
javax.swing.plaf
javax.swing.plaf.basic
javax.swing.plaf.metal
javax.swing.plaf.multi
javax.swing.plaf.synth
javax.swing.plaf.nimbus (intro
duced in Java 6 update 10)
```

76. **Is there a join in Java?**

`join()` method exists for threads in Java. The purpose of a join method is to wait for a thread (on which it has been invoked) to finish.

77. **Is it necessary to apply public privileges on a method that is overridden from an interface?**

Yes, because the methods in an interface are implicitly public.

78. **What is basic purpose of `throw` keyword?**

`throw` keyword is used to throw an exception. For example,

```
throw new MyException();
```

79. **What is the basic purpose of the keyword `throws`?**

`throw` is added to the method signature to let the caller know about what exceptions the called method can throw. It is the responsibility of the caller to either handle the exception (using `try…catch` mechanism) or it can also pass the exception (by specifying throws clause in its method declaration). If all the methods in a program pass the exception to their callers (including `main()`), then ultimately the exception passes to the default exception handler.

80. **What is platform independence?**

    Platform independence means that a Java compiled code can run on any platform provided the Java runtime environment exits on that platform.

81. **What is an applet?**

    Applet is the Java program meant to be embedded in a webpage.

82. **What is the purpose of `repaint` method?**

    `repaint()` method is used to paint the applet again. In other word, it invokes a call to the paint method of the applet on an event.

83. **What is a class?**

    Class is a collection of object with similar attributes and behavior. It is also defined as a new or user defined data type.

84. **What is an object?**

    Objects are instances of a class.

85. **What is abstraction?**

    In programming, we manage complexity by concentrating only on the essential characteristics and suppressing implementation details. Abstraction focuses on the essential characteristics rather than the details.

86. **What is encapsulation?**

    The process of binding the data procedures into objects to hide them from the outside world is called as encapsulation. It provides us the power to restrict anyone from directly altering our data. Encapsulation is also known as data hiding.

87. **What is the basic purpose of `finalize` method?**

    Before an object gets garbage collected, the garbage collector gives the object an opportunity to clean up itself through a call to the object's `finalize()` method. This process is known as finalization. All occupied resources (sockets, files, etc.) can be freed in this method. The `finalize()` method is a member function of the predefined `java.lang.Object` class. A class must override this method to perform any clean up if required by the object.

88. **What is polymorphism?**

    Poly means many and morph means forms. So basically it means more than one implementations. One name many implementations is the key idea behind polymorphism.

89. **What are the various ways of achieving polymorphism in Java?**

    Method overloading, method overriding, and constructor overloading are the various ways of achieving polymorphism in Java.

90. **What are checked and unchecked exceptions?**

    Checked exceptions are monitored by the compiler whether you have handled them in your program or not. Unchecked exceptions (or runtime exceptions) are not checked by the compiler.

91. **What is a thread?**

    Threads are parts of a process running concurrently. Threads are used for achieving multitasking.

92. **What are generics used for?**

    This feature was added in Java 5 with an aim to provide strict type checking at compile time. Generic feature also allows same class to be used by many different collections of objects such as string, and integer. It would be much better to check at compile-time what goes into a collection so that no exception occurs at run time. If we could ensure only objects of a particular type should go into the collection then most runtime problem can be solved and that is where generics help.

93. **What is an iterator interface used for?**

    Iterator interface is used for iterating through the elements of a collection.

94. **Can constructors specify the throws clause?**

    Yes.

95. **Can `switch…case` statement accept string?**

    Yes, Java 7 onwards.

96. **What is aggregation?**

    It is a part-of relationship among objects. When a particular object is a part of another object then we say that it is aggregation. For example, car is an aggregation of many objects: engine, door, etc.

97. **Can an interface inherit another interface?**

    Yes

98. **What to declare a class if it does not override all methods of an interface?**

    `abstract`

99. **Which class is the superclass of all errors and exceptions in Java?**

    `Throwable` class is the superclass of all errors and exceptions in Java.

100. **What is RMI?**

    RMI stands for remote method invocation. RMI is one of the ways by which distributed computing can be achieved. The concept of RMI is to invoke an object that resides in one JVM by another object residing in another JVM.

Index

About the Authors

Sachin Malhotra is currently Associate Professor in the IT department of IMS Ghaziabad. He has more than a decade long experience in mentoring students on developing Java applications as well as training practising professionals in the field of Java. He has also designed and conducted various corporate trainings in Java and networking.

Saurabh Choudhary is currently a practising IT consultant and corporate trainer. He has more than 12 years of experience in industry, academia, and consultancy. He has worked on positions of eminence at IMS Ghaziabad as Head of IT department and Dean Academics (University Campus). His areas of expertise include Java, Database Management System, and Information Systems.

Related Titles

Software Engineering: Principles and Practice
[9780195694840 | 520 Pages | Paperback]

- Lays emphasis on automated processes for development and testing of software.
- Discusses various software development process models of latest industrial practices including a section on capability maturity model (CMM).
- Provides exhaustive coverage of software project cost estimation models like cost constructive model (COCOMO) and Delphi model.
- Incorporates several case studies to bring out the practical implications of software engineering.

Contents: 1. Software and Software Engineering; 2. Software Engineering Process and Models; 3. Software Requirements Engineering; 4. Principles of Modelling; 5. Quantifying Software with Metrics; 6. Software Project Planning and Management; 7. Software Design and Implementation; 8. Software Testing; 9. Software Delivery and Maintenance; 10. Software Retirement

Web Technologies

[9780198066224 | 776 Pages |Paperback]

- Provides thorough understanding of the working of each technology through extensive examples along with the program codes and screenshots.
- Demonstrates where and how to use web technologies effectively.
- Provides relevant software installation and configuration information wherever necessary.
- Covers advanced concepts such as MVC and Struts and emerging topics such as XQuery.

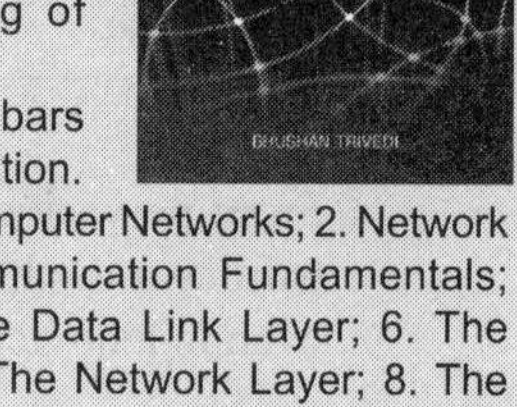

Contents: Part I—Web Fundamentals; 1. Introduction to the Web; 2. HyperText Transfer Protocol (HTTP); 3. Java Network Programming; 4. HyperText Markup Language (HTML); 5. Cascading Style Sheet (CCS); Part II—XML Technologies; 6. eXtensible Markup Language (XML); 7. XML DTD; 8. W3C XML Schema; 9. Parsing XML; 10. XPath; 11. XML Transformation; 12. Other XML Technologies; Part III—Client-side Programming; 13. JavaScript; 14. JavaScript and HTML DOM; 15. Advanced JavaScript and HTML Forms; 16. JavaScript Regular Expression; 17. AJAX; 18. Applets; Part IV—

Server-side Programming; 19. Common Gateway Interface (CGI); 20. Servlet; 21. Java Server Pages (JSP); 22. Introduction to J2EE

Computer Networks
[9780198066774 | 700 Pages | Paperback]

- Incorporates the layered approach with emphasis on TCP/IP model, Internet, and Ethernet technologies.
- Explains several new topics like Bluetooth, IPv6, QoS provided by WiMax, and the use of scalable OFDM in 802.16.
- Includes ample exercise questions to test the understanding of students.
- Provides eye-catching sidebars that supply ancillary information.

Contents: 1. Introduction to Computer Networks; 2. Network Fundamentals; 3. Data Communication Fundamentals; 4. The Physical Layer; 5. The Data Link Layer; 6. The Medium Access Sublayer; 7. The Network Layer; 8. The Transport Layer; 9. The Application Layer; 10. Cryptography and Security

Mobile Computing 2/e
[9780198068914 | 640 Pages | Paperback]

- Provides an up-to-date coverage of Wireless LAN, DECT, HSPA, WCDMA, WiMax, LTE, mobile ad-hoc and wireless sensor networks
- New sections on emerging technologies such as IPsec, i-mode, WAP, UWB, NFC, VoIP, and ZigBee
- Plenty of examples on modulation techniques, CDMA, spread spectrum, OFDM, and other communication protocols

Contents: 1. Mobile Communications: An Overview; 2. Mobile Devices and Systems; 3. GSM and Other 2G Architectures; 4. Wireless Medium Access Control, CDMA, 3G and 4G Communication; 5. Mobile IP Network Layer; 6. Mobile Transport Layer; 7. Databases and Mobile Computing; 8. Data Dissemination and Systems for Broadcasting; 9. Data Synchronization in Mobile Computing Systems; 10. Mobile Devices: Application Servers and Management; 11. Mobile Ad-Hoc and Wireless Sensor Networks; 12. Mobile Wireless Short-Range Networks and Mobile Internet; 13. Mobile Application Languages—Xml and Java; 14. Mobile Application Development Platforms